Blood in the City

Blood in the City

VIOLENCE AND REVELATION IN PARIS, 1789–1945

Richard D. E. Burton

CORNELL UNIVERSITY PRESS

ITHACA AND LONDON

First published 2001 by Cornell University Press

Printed in the United States of America

Library of Congress Cataloging-in-Publication Data

Burton, Richard D.E., 1946–
  Blood in the city : violence and revelation in Paris, 1789–1945 /
Richard D. E. Burton.
      p. cm.
  Includes bibliographical references and index.
  ISBN 0-8014-3868-3 (cloth: alk. paper)
    1. Paris (France)—History—1789–1900.   2. Paris
(France)—History—20th century.   3. Historic sites—France—Paris.   4.
Violence—France—Paris—History.   I. Title.
  DC723 .B87 2001
  944'.36—dc21   2001001239

Cornell University Press strives to use environmentally responsible suppliers and
materials to the fullest extent possible in the publishing of its books. Such materials
include vegetable-based, low-VOC inks and acid-free papers that are recycled,
totally chlorine-free, or partly composed of nonwood fibers. Books that bear the
logo of the FSC (Forest Stewardship Council) use paper taken from forests that
have been inspected and certified as meeting the highest standards for environ-
mental and social responsibility. For further information, visit our website at
www.cornellpress.cornell.edu.

Cloth printing   10 9 8 7 6 5 4 3 2 1

OEDIPUS: What is the rite of purification? How shall it be done?
CREON: By banishing a man, or expiation of blood by blood ...

Sophocles, *Oedipus the King*

Contents

Illustrations

Preface

Blood in the City is the product of a threefold obsession; the word is not, I think, too strong. I have visited and revisited Paris for over thirty years, relentlessly crisscrossing it on foot until it seems—a total illusion, of course—that there is not a street or alley in the twenty arrondissements that I have not walked. Always impatient to arrive, I walk too quickly to be considered an authentic Baudelairean *flâneur*, but I hope that I have seen something in the course of my comings and goings. Over the years I have published a number of Paris-related books and articles, principally on the subject of the greatest Parisian poet of them all, Charles Baudelaire, and I have read widely in the immense descriptive literature on the city. With the help of the great nineteenth- and twentieth-century writers on Paris (Honoré de Balzac, Victor Hugo, Emile Zola, Joris-Karl Huysmans, André Breton, Louis Aragon, as well as Baudelaire himself), I hope I have acquired the basic elements of urban literacy necessary to decode, at least in part, the immense historical cryptogram made up by the sites, streets, and buildings of this most hermeneutically inexhaustible of cities. "Tout pour moi devient allégorie" (everything becomes an allegory for me), with the emphasis equally on the "everything" and the "me," wrote Baudelaire in his greatest single Paris poem, "Le Cygne" (The Swan), whose title punningly invokes "Le Signe" (The Sign), the possibility of infinite interpretability. If nothing else, I hope that *Blood in the City* will help the interested reader share the pleasure I have found in learning how to read Paris as a historically meaningful text.

The second source of *Blood in the City* did not become an obsession until much later. Like everyone with even a casual, let alone a professional, interest in France, I was aware that periods of its history have been marked by violence of an intensity and extent unlike anything to be encountered in the history of England, if not of Britain: the Terror of 1793–94; the repression of the Paris Commune, the all too aptly named *Semaine sanglante,* or Bloody Week, of May 1871; the so-called Franco-French war, which pitted collaborators against resisters during the final months of German occupation in 1944; the Algerian War of Liberation, the violence of which was by no means confined to North Africa. As I started to read more deeply in the history of France since 1789, I began to realize that such explosions of violence, while plainly exceptional in their death toll, were by no means isolated outbursts standing out against an otherwise basically peaceful historical continuum. I became conscious of the sheer repetitiousness of politically inspired violence in postrevolutionary French history, beginning on 14 July 1789, the very day that is commonly, if with some exaggeration, held to inaugurate the first and greatest of the country's many revolutions, and continuing up to the *épuration*, or purge, that was intended to settle the political accounts of the German occupation. Time after time, with particular concentrations at certain historical conjunctures (1793–94, 1830–34, 1849–51, 1870–71, 1891–99, 1934–37, 1940–44), the same basic scenario was acted out, despite variations of setting, circumstance, and dramatis personae. One person or more, sometimes a whole human category, would be singled out from the community, scapegoated, and expelled from its midst, by imprisonment or exile if the victims were lucky, but more usually by violence, either inflicted spontaneously by the crowd or, with greater or lesser concern for legality, by the state in the form of its army, its police force, or its judiciary.

As I worked on this book, I compiled an inventory, reproduced at the end of the text, of some seventy separate incidents of politically inspired violence, official and unofficial, committed in Paris between 1789 and 1945. They ranged from the violent death of a single victim to mass killings involving scores, hundreds, thousands, and, in the case of the *Semaine sanglante*, tens of thousands of casualties. Broadening my frame of reference, I added politically inspired suicides, of which there have been a significant number in French history, most recently that of the former French socialist prime minister Pierre Bérégovoy (1993, on 1 May, no less), and funerals of such political and literary-intellectual personalities as Jean-Paul Marat (1793), Victor Hugo (1885), and Jean-Paul Sartre (1980), which have been occasions for remarkable expressions of political sentiment in France. Even without including instances of violence in the provinces that were linked to political conflicts centered on Paris (most notably the extraordinarily violent uprising in the Vendée, in the west of France, in 1793–94, which produced a total death toll conservatively estimated to exceed 300,000), I reached the conclusion that recourse to political violence was the norm, not the exception, in France during the period under consideration. Surprisingly, no existing work appears to have essayed an explanation.

The third obsession is more difficult to talk about, since it involves my own personal beliefs, or rather beliefs that I once held but from which I have now distanced myself to some considerable degree. That degree is not, however, so considerable that I feel no compulsion to go back, as here, and examine them again. *Blood in the City* is greatly concerned with the subject of Catholicism in postrevolutionary France, and particularly with that exacerbated form of Roman Catholicism known as Ultramontanism—so called because of its reverence for the absolute authority of the Supreme Pontiff "over the mountains"—which, emerging during and after the Revolution, came to dominate the French church after 1870. That *année terrible* saw in quick succession France's catastrophic defeat in the Franco-Prussian War, the declaration of papal infallibility at the First Vatican Council, and the loss of the papal territories to the new Italian state. The principal manifestations of the Ultramontane sensibility in France were the cult of the Sacred Heart of Jesus, culminating in the construction of the Basilica of Sacré-Cœur in Montmartre in penance for the sins that had brought disaster upon the nation in 1870–71; a succession of apparitions of the Virgin Mary, beginning in Paris in 1830 and culminating in Bernadette Soubirous's repeated visions at Lourdes in 1858; and the doctrine of reversibility or vicarious suffering, according to which the sufferings of the innocent, willingly assumed or actively sought, ransom or expiate the sins of the guilty. That doctrine led to what many people, Catholics and non-Catholics alike, now see as a masochistic cult of physical and moral pain, expressed most graphically in the works of Joris-Karl Huysmans (1848–1907) and Léon Bloy (1846–1917), two of the leading figures of the Catholic revival—less charitably but more accurately known as the reactionary revolution—of the late nineteenth century.

The first chapter of *Blood in the City* addresses the question of religious belief and practice in nineteenth-century Paris, and subsequent chapters are concerned with religious buildings (Notre-Dame, Sacré-Cœur) and events (Catherine Labouré's vision of the Virgin Mary in 1830, the conversions of Huysmans and Paul Claudel [1868–1955]). Even when the theme is not directly religious, a concern with the Ultramontane sensibility or *mentalité* pervades the whole book.

One of the book's principal claims is that, despite much justified comment on the dechristianization of Paris (as of huge swaths of France as a whole), Catholicism continued to inform most people's perceptions and conceptions of violence, which they habitually interpreted in the sacrificial terms made current by the Church. Both Catholic right and anti-Catholic left adopted the Crucifixion as their paradigm for subsequent acts of violence (particularly any involving the guillotine, that mechanized cross of the secular age), seeing each violent death inflicted on one of their own as a repetition or renewal of the foundational sacrifice enacted on Calvary.

Paris, political violence, Catholicism in its extreme Ultramontane form: these, then, are the three obsessions that *Blood in the City* seeks to bring together and, by treating them concurrently, to show how they feed into one another to create the distinctive tonality of French history from Revolution to Liberation. I have used literary as well as historical materials to bring out what I see as the enduring preoccupation with violence, and I have chosen a formal structure that I think accords both with the book's concern with the question of place and with the prominence it gives to Catholic themes. The structure is not chronological but topological: an overview of nineteenth-century Paris is followed by detailed discussions of what, for my purpose, are the leading Parisian *lieux de mémoire,* linked one to the other as in a somewhat abridged version of the ritual of the stations of the cross, which became so popular among French Catholics from the early nineteenth century onward. By using a nonchronological form (even though the events associated with my various "stations" do give a broadly chronological account of French history from 1789 to 1945), I hope to show the intertwining of certain significant images and themes as well as to highlight what I can only call the Via Dolorosa aspect of postrevolutionary French history. An extended conclusion attempts to explain all the blood that has been spilled in the preceding chapters.

Blood in the City is complete in itself, but it is conceived as the first part of a larger study of the connections between religion, politics, and culture in post-revolutionary France. The second part will concern itself with women and the sacred, and the third will further tackle the themes of pain, suffering, and sacrifice but in their personal rather than their collective and political dimension.

My principal intellectual debts will become clear as my argument advances, and the notes refer to the works that have been of particular value and relevance. My thinking on the question of violence has been greatly influenced by the work of René Girard, though this is not in any way a Girardian interpretation of postrevolutionary France. My preoccupation with place has been reinforced and informed by the magnificent series of studies collected under Pierre Nora's enterprising editorship in the multivolume *Les Lieux de la mémoire,* which has proved to be an inexhaustible source of information and ideas.

As I am virtually the last in my profession to write everything by hand, I owe a particular debt to Claire Gascoigne, Florence Grant, and

Suzanne Gammon, who between them processed my manuscript, and to the School of African and Asian Studies at Sussex University, which met the not inconsiderable cost of my technoplegia. Margaret Ralph performed wonders in coordinating the final manuscript. At Cornell University Press, Peter Agree responded positively to the original proposal, and Roger Haydon saw the whole project through to its conclusion.

The prefaces of many academic works contain pages of acknowledgments to colleagues who have had the time, interest, and kindness to read this chapter or that, or even whole drafts and redrafts of the manuscript: we plainly inhabit different worlds. Yet it is a pleasure to thank Frank Paul Bowman, formerly of the University of Pennsylvania, who read the manuscript for Cornell, and Beynon John, my former colleague at Sussex University, for the unfailing courtesy and unerring accuracy with which he has answered my many telephone calls on questions of both substance and detail: may all our retirements be as early, as long, and as happy.

RICHARD D. E. BURTON

Lewes, East Sussex

Blood in the City

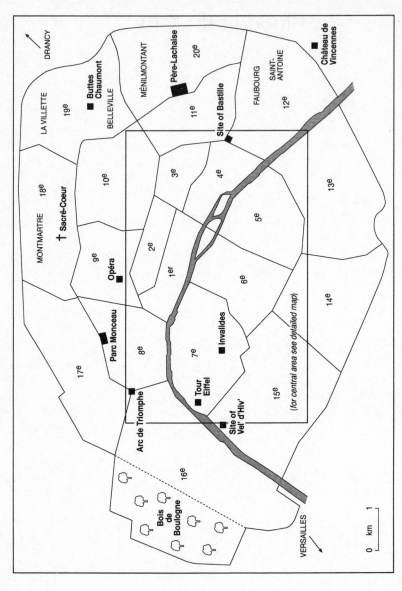

Principal sites of Paris. The boundaries of the arrondissements are those established after 1860. (Cartographic Unit, University of Sussex.)

I

PARIS À VOL D'OISEAU
(1789–1914)

In early nineteenth-century Paris it was still just possible—if one stood, for example, on the Butte Montmartre or, better yet, looked out from the supreme vantage point afforded by the towers of Notre-Dame—to embrace the whole city in a single synoptic vision. To do so was, as Théophile Gautier recorded in his poem "Notre-Dame" of 1831, to experience a rare and almost godlike sensation of power:

> Oh! le cœur en bat: dominer de ce faîte,
> Soi, chétif et petit, une ville ainsi faite;
> Pouvoir d'un seul regard embrasser ce grand tout;
> Debout, là-haut, plus près du ciel que de la terre,
> Comme l'aigle planant, voir du sein du cratère,
> Loin, bien loin, la fumée et la lave qui bout.[1]

> [Oh! how your heart pounds: to dominate from this height, / You, tiny, paltry you, a city like this; / To be able with one look to embrace this great whole; / Standing, up there, closer to heaven than to earth, / Like the eagle hovering, to see from the crater's heart, / Far, far away, the smoke and seething lava.]

But such exaltation rarely lasted. As his initial enthusiasm abated, the observer was not uncommonly seized with disquiet before the vast and incommensurable spectacle that unfolded beneath him. When later he tried to record that disquiet, images of monstrous animal growths, of volcanic eruptions, furnaces, and seething oceans flowed spontaneously from his pen. Thus Gautier in another poem of the 1830s, "Le Sommet de la tour":

> Vous débouchez enfin sur une plate-forme,
> Et vous apercevez, ainsi qu'un monstre énorme,

La Cité grommelante, accroupie alentour.
Comme un requin, ouvrant ses immenses mâchoires,
Elle mord l'horizon de ses mille dents noires,
Dont chacune est un dôme, un clocher, une tour.[2]

[You emerge at last on a platform, / And you see, like an enormous monster, / the rumbling City sprawled out around you. / Like a shark, opening its immense jaws, / It gnaws the horizon with its myriad black teeth, / Each of which is a dome, a steeple, a tower.]

Still greater anxiety intrudes into the confused panorama deployed in Alfred de Vigny's "Paris," also of 1831:

Je vois un cercle noir, si large et si profond
Que je n'en aperçois ni le bout ni le fond.
Je vois fumer, brûler, éclater des flambeaux,
Brillant sur cet abîme où l'air pénètre à peine,
Comme des diamants incrustés dans l'ébène.
Des ombres de palais, de dômes et d'aiguilles,
De tours et de donjons, de clochers, de bastilles,
De châteaux forts, de kiosks et d'aigus minarets;
Des formes de remparts, de jardins, de forêts,
De spirales, d'arceaux, de parcs, de colonnades,
D'obélisques, de ponts, de portes et d'arcades,
Tout fourmille et grandit, se cramponne et montant,
Se courbe, se replie, ou se creuse ou s'étend.
Le vertige m'enivre, et sur mes yeux il pèse.
Vois-je une Roue ardente, ou bien une Fournaise?[3]

[I see a black circle, so broad and deep / That I can discern neither its bottom not its outer limit. / I see smoking, burning, flares flashing forth, / Blazing against that airless abyss / Like diamonds encrusted in ebony. / Shadows of palaces, domes, spires, / Towers and donjons, steeples, fortresses, / Castles, kiosks, and slender minarets; / Outlines of ramparts, gardens, forests, / Spirals, arches, parks, colonnades, / Obelisks, bridges, gates, and arcades, / And all this seethes and swells, claws its way upward, / Bows down, curls up, or burrows or stretches. / A drunken giddiness seizes me and weighs down on my eyes. / Is it a fiery wheel that I see or rather a furnace?]

By the late 1830s such visions of incoherence had become commonplace. Writing in 1848, the utopian socialist Victor Considerant registered his horror at the "spectacle of disorder" to be seen from the towers of Notre-Dame, a "frightful architectural melee" in which walls of every height and roofs of every angle met in mere oppugnancy, the confused and conflictual expression of a society devoid of harmony, order, or intelligibility.[4] The city, it seemed to almost all who viewed it from above, had lost all coherence, all semblance of organic unity; it sprawled amorphously, a magma of undifferentiated buildings without pattern or purpose, uncontrolled and uncontrollable, every whit the "architectural chaos" contemptuously described by Considerant. To Lecouturier, writing in his significantly titled *Paris incompatible avec la République* of 1848, it seemed almost inconceivable that this "congestion of houses piled up at every point of a vast horizon" could be the capital of the most powerful nation in Europe.[5]

It is against such visions of urban disintegration that one can best read Victor Hugo's majestic panorama of fifteenth-century Paris in the chapter of *Notre-Dame de Paris* (1831) titled "Paris à vol d'oiseau." In many respects the medieval city imagined by Hugo is the antithesis of the city in which he lived; it confronts contemporary chaos with an image of organic unity in diversity. Viewed from the towers of Notre-Dame, Hugo claims, fifteenth-century Paris would at first appear to be no more than "a tangle of streets inextricably and bizarrely interknit," except in size not essentially different from the Paris of the early nineteenth century. But on closer inspection an underlying structure would emerge from this proliferation, a structure consisting, says Hugo, of "three completely distinct and separate cities, each having its peculiar physiognomy, specialty, mores, customs, privileges, and history: the City, the University, the Town." At the center—the spiritual center no less than the physical—was the Ile de la Cité, its cradle form aptly symbolizing its "maternal" relationship to the two other "cities" that later grew out from it. Here were located, once more with rich symbolism, the most sacred of the city's edifices: the Palais de Justice, the Hôtel-Dieu, and Notre-Dame. On the Left Bank stood the university, which for all its variety constituted, says Hugo, "a homogeneous and compact whole." When viewed from above, its "thousand closely packed, uneven, but cohesive roofs" offered "the look of a crystallization of a single substance." On the Right Bank, less unified but still far removed from the senseless profusion of the nineteenth century, was the Town (*la Ville*), the focus of political and economic activity, with the Louvre, the Hôtel de Ville, and the Halles functioning as secular counterparts to the sacred buildings on the Ile de la Cité.

Each of these "cities" possessed its distinct personality, function, and institutional order, but each was "too special to be complete." Thus the

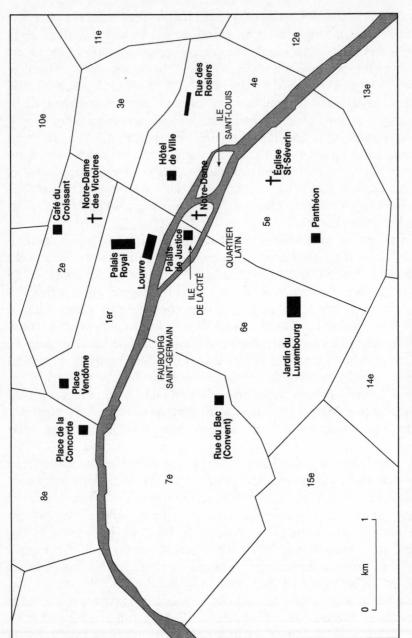

Central arrondissements of Paris. (Cartographic Unit, University of Sussex.)

three cities existed in a state of interdependence, united in a kind of trinitarian relationship, distinct yet complementary "persons" of a single organic being.

Furthermore, says Hugo, fifteenth-century Paris was stylistically "a homogeneous city, an architectural and historical product of the Middle Ages, a chronicle of stone." Both as a whole and in each of its constituent units the city was replete with meaning, and being composed almost exclusively of Romanesque and Gothic elements, it was free from the profusion of styles and architectural anachronisms that contributed, as we shall see, to the "illegibility" of nineteenth-century Paris. Hugo's medieval Paris is thus a retrospective and organic version of the planned ideal cities of the future imagined in the 1830s and 1840s by urban visionaries such as Charles Fourier, Etienne Cabet, and Victor Considerant. Circular in form, radiating out from a religious center, socially, architecturally, and ideologically integrated, it embodies both in its parts and as a whole the holistic worldview of medieval Christianity. It translates into urban terms the principles of unity in diversity already incarnated in the "vast symphony of stone" that is its center and epitome: the cathedral of Notre-Dame.[6]

Much of the impact of Hugo's re-creation of medieval Paris derived from the fact that it embodied a viewpoint that could only with difficulty—if at all—be applied to the city of the 1830s and 1840s. In both literature and painting, panoramic visions of the city depicted *sub specie aeternitatis* became increasingly rare and disappeared almost entirely after 1850; the characteristic images of Second Empire and early Third Republic Paris—Baudelaire's *Tableaux parisiens* (1861) and *Petits poèmes en prose* (1868), Zola's novels and the paintings of the Impressionists—are presented from street level, *sub specie modernitatis,* and embody not the godlike objectivity of a transcendent seer but the time- and space-bound subjectivity of an all-too-human consciousness.[7]

After 1850 it became almost impossible to perceive Paris synoptically as a totality. Technological advances, in the form first of the aerial photographs taken from balloon by Nadar from 1858 onward and then, more significantly, of the Eiffel Tower, partly restored the possibility of stereoscopic vision destroyed by the unprecedented growth of the city in the 1840s and 1850s. But Nadar's photographs were limited and fragmentary, and by the time the Eiffel Tower was constructed (1889), the city had long since spilled over the natural boundaries constituted by the surrounding hills and extended far beyond the range of even the most keen-eyed observer. Thus, although on the map and to some extent at street level Haussmann's city was undoubtedly more *organized* than *le vieux Paris,* it had even less *organic* unity, when viewed from above, than the city on which it had been superimposed. Looking out from Sacré-Cœur toward the end of the century, the priest-hero of Zola's novel *Paris* (1898) perceives the city as an "immense sea," "a chaos of stone."[8] By 1900, as Daniel Halévy stressed in his *Pays parisiens* (1932), the significant view from the Butte Montmartre was less the conventional one to the south than that across the unknown, "historyless" suburbs that had sprung up to the north from the 1880s onward. Paris had long since defied the panoramic look; the growth of the outlying areas ensured that—Eiffel Tower and airplane notwithstanding—it would never again be perceived as an organic whole. The age of the megalopolis had arrived.

Hugo concludes his breathtaking overview of medieval Paris by inviting the reader, if he or she "wants to get an impression of the old city that the modern one is no longer capable of giving," to ascend one Easter or Whitsunday morning to some lofty vantage point commanding the whole capital and there await "the awakening of the bells." At first there are but "scattered tinklings going from church to church," but soon the bells enter into dialogue with each other, and, gathering momentum and volume, merge and mingle "in one magnificent concert," a single "mass of sonorous vibrations, incessantly sent forth from the innumerable steeples, which floats, undulates, leaps, and eddies over the city, and extends far beyond the horizon the deafening circle of its oscillations." But, Hugo stresses, "this sea of harmony is by no means a chaos." Rather the *concordia discors* emitted by the city's churches and cathedral, each adding its distinctive chime to the campanological medley, becomes an aural equivalent of the now vanished unity in diversity of medieval Paris: nothing in the world, says Hugo, "is richer, more joyous, more golden, more dazzling than this tumult of bells and chimes, this furnace of music, this city that is now a single orchestra, this symphony that makes the noise of a storm."[9]

It is a magnificent finale to one of the masterpieces of nineteenth-century urban writing, but in its sheer virtuosity it elides or suppresses one crucial difference between the Paris of 1482 and that of 1831: that by 1831 the bells, holy signifiers increasingly detached from any sacred referent, were no longer drawing all or even a majority of the city's inhabitants to celebrate with any regularity or fervor the rituals, mysteries, and feast days of the Church. To be sure, to speak of "dechristianization" in 1831 would be premature: the small but significant minorities of Jews and Protestants apart, the overwhelming majority of Parisians, whether born in the city or migrants from the provinces, would describe themselves as Catholics, and would continue to do so until the turn of the century and beyond. Almost all would have been baptized, though by 1860 only 52 percent of baptisms in the working-class suburb of Belleville took place within three days of birth, as canon law required, an indication of declining belief in the efficacy and necessity of the sacrament.[10] Most would have made their First Communion, though for a growing minority their First Communion would also be their last; in many families, the First Communion was fast becoming what essentially it is today, a secular ritual of self-celebration rather than a sacred rite of passage granting access to the Church's holiest mysteries. The crucial "Easter barometer" of religious practice—that is, the proportion of the nominally faithful who communicated at least once a year—still yielded a positive reading, but regular Sunday Communion was becoming a predominantly female practice. By 1831 religious life as a whole was increasingly characterized by what one modern historian of the Church has called an all too visible "sexual dimorphism,"[11] and as the acerbic narrator of François Mauriac's *Le Nœud de vipères* (1932) would later remark, it was already becoming the custom for middle-class men, in Paris as elsewhere in France, to "accompany" their wives and children to mass rather than actively to participate themselves;[12] needless to say, working-class men absented themselves entirely. The situation was so serious that as early as 1826 the papal nuncio Macchi estimated that only one-eighth of Parisians could be regarded as practicing Catholics. Still more significant, only 10,000 men out of a total male population of around 350,000 were, he said, active members of the Church.[13]

The position regarding the Church's other great rites of passage was even more alarming. Marriages were still overwhelmingly celebrated in church, but a growing proportion of working-class unions—at least one in ten and, according to some estimates, as many as one in three—were not validated by either religious or civil ceremony; at any time between 1815 and 1848, something like 100,000 men and women were living in concubinage, and as many as 38 percent of births in the department of the Seine between 1841 and 1850 were illegitimate, compared to about 8 percent for France as a whole.[14] Finally, and perhaps most significant of all, a small but growing proportion of Parisians received civil rather than religious burials, especially, once again, in the "classic" working-class suburb of Belleville, where the percentage of civil burials rose from 20 in 1860 to 35 in 1871 before reaching a staggering 45 in 1879.[15] Clearly the lives of more and more Parisians—particularly, but by no means exclusively, those of the working class and of men rather than women—began, unfolded, and ended effectively outside the orbit and jurisdiction of the Church. In the very year that Hugo's *Notre-Dame de Paris* first appeared, one observer had already famously declared, in the wake of the first uprising of the silkworkers of Lyon, that "the Barbarians who threaten society are not in the Caucasus or in the steppes of Tartary; they are in the suburbs of our industrial towns";[16] and by the 1890s, when those suburbs were declared officially to be *pays de mission*—on a par, in other words, with France's "pagan" colonies in Africa and Asia—alarmed clerics spoke routinely of the "immense China" surrounding the central core of Paris and of the "denizens of unexplored countries" who were by now entirely beyond the Church's outreach.[17] In 1905 the archbishop of Paris, Monseigneur Bœglin, judged the "gap" between the Church and the city's working classes to be absolute.[18]

The origins of this gap are much debated. Already on the eve of the Revolution Louis-Sébastien Mercier had noted in his encyclopedic *Tableau de Paris* (1781–88) that "more than a hundred thousand men" in Paris regarded the Church "with pity." The sacraments had become an option not widely chosen, and on any religious occasion women made up three-quarters of the congregation; otherwise Parisians, if they entered churches at all, treated them like any other public space, not exactly irreverently but not reverently either, walking with heads erect, with none of the "respect due to a temple in which the creature worships the Creator."[19] When the Estates General met in May 1789, inaugurating the whole process of revolution, lower-ranking churchmen were at first among the most fervent advocates of social and political change, and soon conservatives were complaining bitterly of "those f-ing priests who caused the Revolution,"[20] and there was certainly no contradiction when, at the requiem mass held at the Eglise Saint-Jacques for the victims of the Bastille, the abbé Fauchet declared before the congregation, "Brothers, in this vessel consecrated to the Eternal, let us swear, let us swear that we shall be happy."

But soon the Church was divested both of its lands and of its principal source of income, the tithe, and on 12 July 1790 the National Assembly took the fatal step of, in effect, nationalizing the Church by ordering all clergymen, from the loftiest cardinal down to the humblest village curate, to swear allegiance to the revolutionary constitution, which henceforth would have primacy over their loyalty to Rome. When, in the spring of 1791, Pope Pius VI condemned the decree and ordered priests to refuse the revolutionary oath of allegiance, Church and Revolution were already well set on a collision course.

As it turned out, there were fewer so-called *prêtres réfractaires* or nonjuring priests in Paris than in many other part of France, perhaps a sign that it was not just the city's laity that was subject to an emerging secular worldview. Nonetheless, the Church was now publicly marked out as a potential force of counterrevolution, and its priests, as well as its monks and nuns, stood labeled as suitable targets for radical revenge in times of crisis. In the autumn of 1792 one such crisis produced the appalling bloodbath known to history as the September massacres, in which at least 220 mainly nonjuring priests were gratuitously slaughtered by revolutionary death squads, first in the garden adjoining the Eglise Saint-Germain-des-Prés, then in the Couvent des Carmes (where 114, including the archbishop of Arles and the bishops of Saintes and Beauvais, were hacked to death), and finally at the prison of Saint-Firmin, where a further 75 were savagely dispatched as part of what one revolutionary leader called "the first holocaust offered to liberty."[21] Although over a thousand wholly innocent lay men and women also perished in Parisian prisons in September, including the princesse de Lamballe, Marie-Antoinette's friend and alleged lesbian lover, whose head and, according to some accounts, mutilated genitalia were ritually displayed, it was the "martyrs of the faith" whom the Church and posterity would remember. The theme of blood sacrifice—so potent and widespread, as we shall see, in nineteenth-century French Catholicism—had found its first exemplars, shortly to be followed by thousands more during the institutionalized Terror of 1793–94, launched by the execution of the king himself on 21 January 1793.

By the time of the king's death, Church, monarchy, and aristocracy were, in the eyes of the most radical revolutionaries, one and the same thing, and from October 1793 to April 1794 the Revolution embarked on a systematic campaign of dechristianization in all areas of public life. The radicals signaled their anti-Christian intentions by promulgating a new calendar that explicitly abolished the Christian era and declared 1792, the year of the founding of the Republic, to be the new year 1. "Everything must be new in France," proclaimed the Jacobin Bertrand de Barère, "and we wish to date solely from today." The new revolutionary months—Nivôse, Pluviôse, Germinal, Thermidor, and so on—were entirely without Christian or any other nonworldly referents, and in substituting the ten-day *décade* for the traditional seven-day week, the new calendar not only disrupted the whole structure of the ecclesiastical year and provoked a short-lived war between *le dimanche* and *le décadi* (the new revolutionary day of rest) but attempted to supplant all of the Church's feast days with an annual cycle of *fêtes révolutionnaires* devoted to this or that republican virtue or hero.[22]

As part of this joint project of desacralizing the Church and sacralizing the Revolution, the cult of the assassinated revolutionary martyr

Marat took on an explicitly christological coloring; Jacques-Louis David's icon to the immolated "Friend of the People" was planned as the Pietà of the new counterreligion, and Montmartre was briefly renamed Montmarat in honor of the revolutionary messiah.[23] Notre-Dame was secularized and used to celebrate a decidedly anti-Christian "Feast of Reason" in November 1793. Bells were removed from the bell towers where they had hung for centuries and melted down to make cannon. Church steeples were torn down as architectural affronts to the principle of equality, priests were subjected to the humiliation of the *asinade* (being forced to ride back to front on a donkey wearing a bishop's miter), and statues of prophets and saints were guillotined even as Louis XVI and Marie-Antoinette were in the course of 1793.[24]

In general, the Revolution in its most radical phase sought to effect what one modern historian has called a "transfer of sacredness" from the supernatural to the natural, from the other world to this world, in practice from the Church to the rituals, values, and institutions of the Republic.[25] Dechristianization was not an accidental or contingent part of the revolutionary project; it lay at its very core. Nor was it just a question of symbolism. Between 1790 and 1797, when the anti-Christian campaign came effectively to its close, 30,000 priests had fled or been forced into exile, and somewhere between 1,000 and 3,000 had lost their lives, either "legally" during the Terror (in which priests, representing 1 percent of the population, made up 6 percent of those guillotined) or in random, unlicensed murders and massacres. Neither did nuns escape the vindictiveness of revolutionary zealots, most notably the sixteen Carmelites of Compiègne guillotined on the Place du Trône Renversé in July 1794, whose martyrdom Georges Bernanos (1888–1948) would celebrate in his posthumously published *Dialogues des Carmélites* (1949), from which, in his turn, Francis Poulenc (1899–1963) would draw his intensely moving opera of the same name.

The anti-Christian campaign did not last long (though it certainly continued beyond the fall of the Jacobins in July 1794), but it was enough to introduce serious discontinuities into a religion founded on continuities of belief, practice, institutions, and personnel. The rhythm of confession and at least annual Communion was lost to many erstwhile practicing Catholics, and many others found their local parish church given over to secular uses, vandalized, or at the very least bereft of its full complement of priests. Now the Church—many of whose clergy, not all of them low-ranking, had at first regarded the Revolution with some sympathy—viewed it in the most negative terms possible; when the ultrareactionary Catholic theorist Joseph de Maistre (1753–1820) declared in his widely read *Considérations sur la France* (1797) that "there is in the French Revolution a satanic character that distinguishes it from everything seen hitherto and perhaps from everything to be seen henceforth," he was speaking neither metaphorically nor as an isolated extremist.[26]

The gap between Church and state was papered over rather than closed when, on Easter day 1802, two years before Napoleon crowned himself emperor, he formally entered into a concordat with the Holy See that recognized the Roman Catholic Church not, as is sometimes wrongly supposed, as the state religion of France, but simply as the religion of "the great majority" (*la grande majorité,* according to the French text; *longe maxima pars,* according to the Vatican's version) of the French people, and effectively transformed the Church, along with the Protestant temple and the synagogue, into arms of the state. Henceforth the naming of bishops was controlled by the newly created Ministère des Cultes, and priests, pastors, and rabbis became in effect salaried employees of the state. The arrangement would last until the formal separation of Church and state in 1905, though many churchmen high and low, along with many members of their flock, paid only lip service to the state, reserving their allegiance for the ultimate authority "over the mountains" in Italy; whence the term "Ultramontane" to designate the most tradition-minded, Vatican-oriented (and, in political terms, usually ultrareactionary) forms of Catholicism in France.

After the fall of Napoleon in 1815 and the restoration of the Bourbons in the persons of the executed king's younger brother, Louis XVIII,[27] Church and monarchy entered into an alliance closer and certainly far more repressive than the one that had obtained under the ancien régime. Expelled from France in 1762, the Jesuits accompanied the restored king back from exile, and for the next fifteen years, Church, monarchy, and aristocracy did all in their power to suppress every trace and flicker of the Revolution, to expunge it in effect from history and return France to the status quo ante 1789. The coronation of Charles X in Reims cathedral—the cathedral of Clovis—in 1825 was a systematic if ultimately farcical attempt to resacralize the monarchy in the eyes of the French people. Clad in a flowing purple robe, Charles was anointed with the traditional nine oils that formally consecrated him to God and nation. Having been installed as commander of the chivalric orders of the Holy Spirit and Saint Michael, he proceeded to "touch" a selection of the sick and crippled of Reims in accordance with the archaic belief in the monarch's thaumaturgical powers.[28] "The king touches you, may God heal you," he declared as he laid hands on the scrofulous wretches brought before him, five of whom were later reported to have been healed. This unimpressive success rate merely confirmed the majority of French people in their view of the monarchy as at best a social and political rather than a sacred or charismatic institution and of the king himself as all too human beneath his increasingly incongruous vestments and crown.

The Bourbon monarchy and with it the political power of the old aristocracy collapsed during the "three glorious days" of July 1830, when for the first time since the 1790s the "people of Paris," that mixture of political fantasy and social fact, erupted onto the city's streets and, in alliance with the middle classes, drove Charles X into exile and installed in his place Louis-Philippe, a scion of the lesser, Orléanist branch of the French royal family, who would reign as king of an oxymoronic and self-contradictory "bourgeois monarchy" until he too was toppled by the revolution of February 1848. Wearing somber clothing and top hat and carrying an umbrella like any upper-middle-class Parisian, the "citizen king," as he was known, had been crowned king of the French rather than king of France, a semantic change of enormous significance, for it stripped the monarchy of whatever sacredness it retained and explicitly located the source of royal power in the contractual will of the people rather than in the transcendent will of God.

The Ultramontane clergy joined the legitimist aristocracy in fleeing into what was known as "internal exile," a physical or, failing that, a psychological and spiritual withdrawal from which they viewed the political and social conflicts of the Bourgeois Monarchy with something like contempt. In the early years of the new regime those conflicts were acute, and the years 1830–34—the "time of riots," as they came to be known—may plausibly be regarded as the matrix of modern French politics, for they witnessed the emergence of a largely autonomous working-class movement which, especially in Paris and Lyon, aimed less at effecting political change for its own sake than at securing political power in the form of a republic in order to bring about fundamental changes in the social and economic structure of France.

This new phase of the sociopolitical struggle found its emblematic martyrs in the working-class republicans and their families who were slaughtered by police, many while still in their beds, in the boardinghouse at 12 Rue Transnonain (on the site, more or less, of the present Centre Georges Pompidou) on 13 April 1834, an event raised to mythic proportions by Honoré Daumier's iconic lithograph *Le Massacre de la Rue Transnonain*. By the mid-1830s, both right and left could lay claim to an impressive list of sacrificial victims: Louis XVI and Marie-Antoinette on the right, supported by other casualties of revolutionary terror, from the martyr-priests

Massacre of the Rue Transnonain, 15 April 1834. This celebrated lithograph by Henri Daumier depicts the killing by government troops of eleven republicans in their lodgings at 12 rue Transnonain, not far from the present-day Centre Georges Pompidou. Published in July 1834 in *L'Association mensuelle* and also publicly exhibited at the Galerie Aubert in the Passage Véro-Dodat, the image attracted so much attention that the Bourgeois Monarchy strengthened censorship laws shortly afterward. (Reproduced by permission of the British Museum, London.)

of September 1792 to the multitudinous victims, both clerical and lay, of the peasant uprising of 1793–94 in the Vendée; and, on the left, Marat, Le Peletier de Saint-Fargeau (assassinated by a royalist zealot on the eve of the king's execution and, like Marat, the subject of a [never completed] revolutionary icon by David),[29] the boy heroes Joseph Bara and Agricol Viala,[30] the "Four Sergeants of La Rochelle" guillotined in 1822 for conspiring against the Restoration Monarchy, republican countervictims to the legitimists' duc de Berry, assassinated by a Bonapartist fanatic as he left the Opéra in 1820. Increasingly, blood sacrifice came to be one of the defining themes of French political conflict.

The new radical republicanism of the 1830s and 1840s was not viscerally anti-Christian, as its predecessor of the 1790s had been. Partly as a result of the writings and example of the renegade priest Félicité de Lamennais (1782–1854), whose *Paroles d'un croyant* (1834) was one of the most widely read works of the Bourgeois Monarchy; partly as a result of the charitable work of middle-class laypersons such as Frédéric

Ozanam (1813–53), founder of the Society of Saint Vincent de Paul; and partly because of the writings and organizational efforts of such working-class Catholics as Philippe Buchez (1796–1865) and Anthime Corbon (1808–91), founder of *L'Atelier* (1840–50), the first wholly working-class publication in France, the gap that had opened between Christianity and the lower classes began to close somewhat, though the distance between the latter and the Church remained as great as ever. Clearly distinguishing between the Christianity of Christ and the Christianity of the Church, working-class radicals developed an early form of liberation theology that would briefly surface during the first heady weeks of the Second Republic (1848–51) before succumbing in the wake of the suppression of the working-class insurrection of June 1848 and the Bonapartist coup d'état of December 1851. To such men as Buchez and Corbon, to non-Christian socialists such as Louis Blanc (1811–82) and Etienne Cabet (1788–1856), and to their hundreds of working-class supporters, Christ and the Republic were no longer set against each other; rather Christ was seen as the first and greatest of republicans, even, in the eyes of those farther to the left, as the first and greatest of socialists. For a few fragile weeks (and for much longer in the provinces), the cross reached out to the liberty tree, Catholic Mary and republican Marianne embraced, and the republican trinity of *Liberté, Egalité, Fraternité* and the Christian Trinity of Father, Son, and Holy Spirit were seen as fully congruent, even at times as identical. In Paris and elsewhere, republican "eucharists" were celebrated, often in the presence of priests, beneath liberty trees bedecked in the red, white, and blue of the Republic; "Communion" was taken under the species of red wine—red wine meant red politics in 1848–51[31]—and bread and sausage to the accompaniment of republican-socialist hymns such as "Jésus républicain" (1848), by a worker-poet from the Rue Mouffetard, in which Jesus himself becomes the supreme sacrificial victim of the democratic republic:

Au Golgotha, sanglante gémonie,
Martyr, il dit, attaché la croix:
Frères, pour vous ma suprême agonie
Va pour toujours éterniser vos droits.[32]

[On Golgotha, that bloody calvary, / He said, a martyr nailed to the cross: / Brethren, for you my final agony / Will forever eternalize your rights.]

It could not last, and it did not, at least not in Paris, where the blood-bath of June 1848 precipitated working-class radicalism directed now against Christianity, no longer merely against the Church. The tragic death of the archbishop of Paris, Monseigneur Affre, killed by an isolated insurgent as he attempted to mediate between the contending forces at the Place de la Bastille on 25 June, was blamed by the right on the republican left as a whole, and yet another martyr to the Revolution was created, to be followed shortly by General Bréa, tricked into exposing himself and promptly killed by the insurgents. The left, for its part, found a new stock of sacrificial victims in the 1,500 insurgents who perished on the barricades in June 1848, not to mention the thousands more who were imprisoned or driven into exile. The Church moved farther and farther to the right, and, with ecclesiastical control over primary education reaffirmed and strengthened by the Loi Falloux of 1850, few churchmen, whatever their rank, were moved to oppose Louis Napoleon's coup d'état of December 1851 and his subsequent installation as Emperor Napoleon III.

Few working-class radicals were prepared to defend the bourgeois republic that had betrayed and repressed them in June 1848, and resistance to the coup was limited to middle-class republicans, among them Victor Baudin, killed on the Place de la Bastille on the morning of 3 December and instantly transformed into yet another martyr of the Republic. In his defining image of 1851–52 Daumier showed the Christ-Republic being offered by Pontius Pilate to the people of Jerusalem-Paris, who shout back, "We want Barabbas!" (in other words, "We want Louis Napoleon!"), while in "Le Reniement de Saint-Pierre" Baudelaire (1821–67)—a radical republican in 1848–51, before his precipitous swerve to the right after the coup—commended Saint Peter for repudiating the all too peaceful and nonviolent Christ: "Peter rejected Jesus ... he was justified! [Saint Pierre a renié Jésus ... il a bien fait!]."[33]

With no notable exceptions the Church rallied to the Second Empire (1852–70) and, correspondingly, many previously tepid or even anticlerical members of the middle classes returned to active membership of a church that so effectively bolstered and gave supernatural sanction to their social, economic, and political interests; only the emperor's ill-advised intervention in Italian and consequently papal politics in 1859–60 led to a serious but ultimately noncritical breach between Church and state. Given the closeness of the fit between the ideology and practice of the Church and the interests of the bourgeoisie, it was hardly surprising, declared the parish priest of Saint-Eloi in the working-class faubourg Saint-Antoine in 1868, that "hatreds against us increase day by day. We are denounced to the opinion of the laboring masses as the last and only enemies who must be struck down in order to bring better times."[34]

Sure enough, when, following the Empire's collapse in the wake of the cataclysmic defeat at Sedan (September 1870) at the opening of the Franco-Prussian War, a new republic—the third since 1792—was declared, the left was now explicitly and often violently opposed not merely to the Church and to Catholicism but to Christianity, and indeed to any religious belief. For the first time, militant atheism, even militant antitheism, as opposed to militant anticlericalism, became the dominant ideology of the republican-socialist left. When, briefly, the Parisian left achieved power during the Paris Commune of March–May 1871, its draft constitution decreed the formal separation of Church and state, expropriated the property of the city's religious foundations, and formally abolished the budget for religion; unlike the typical Forty-eighter, the typical Communard was undoubtedly a dechristianizer. In a celebrated courtroom confrontation, the Commune's ultraleftist security chief, Raoul Rigault, asked an accused priest to state the name of his employer. "God," came the innocent reply. "Address?" riposted Rigault. "Everywhere," replied the priest, gesturing sweepingly about him, whereupon Rigault ordered the clerk of the court to register the accused's employer as "one called God, a vagrant."[35] Given this hostility, it is hardly surprising that priests should have been routinely harassed both within and without their churches (many of which were, as in the 1790s, converted to secular uses), that services should have been forcibly interrupted, or that, in a by no means isolated incident, forty or fifty Communards led by "a foreigner named Kobosko" should have broken into the Eglise Saint-Leu in April 1871, donned ecclesiastical garments, and sung obscene songs while their ringleader "distributed Communion to his worthy acolytes making the most grotesque of gestures; he had replaced the Host with bits of brioche."[36]

When the Commune was crushed during the all too accurately named Bloody Week of May 1871, each side duly collected a new crop of sacrificial victims, though the numerical disparity between the two was immense. If the right could virtually canonize the archbishop of Paris, Monseigneur Darboy, shot along with other clerical hostages during the death throes of the Commune, the left suffered no fewer than 20,000 victims during the repression, among them the hundreds of Communards put up against the southeast wall of the Père-Lachaise Cemetery and summarily mown down by right-wing firing squads. The appalling photograph of their stunted, twisted corpses crammed into makeshift coffins is the most memorable of all the icons of political violence in nineteenth-century France.

Corpses of the executed Communards in their makeshift coffins. Disderi's celebrated photograph was taken at the end of the *Semaine sanglante* in May 1871. (Musée Carnavalet, Paris, © Photothèque des Musées de la Ville de Paris.)

In the wake of military defeat and sociopolitical convulsion, the old aristocracy returned briefly to power, and the alliance between the Church and the most reactionary elements in French society was never closer than during the years 1871–77, known at the time and to posterity as the years of moral order. It was during this period that pilgrimages to La Salette, Lourdes, and Pontmain, the sites of Marian apparitions in 1846, 1858, and 1871, respectively, became truly national events. When the cult of the Sacred Heart of Jesus, centered on Paray-le-Monial, to the northwest of Lyon, spread throughout France, the right was prompted to support the construction of the Basilique du Sacré-Cœur on the Butte de Montmartre, as a sign of national penance for the hedonism of the Empire, for the military humiliation of the Franco–Prussian War, and for the atheistic experiment of the Paris Commune, whose epicenter had been Montmartre. Two slogans sum up the center-left's response to the phenomenon of moral order, both of them destined to pass into the legend of political-religious conflict in France: the declaration in an anonymous article published in the *Journal des Débats* on 20 October 1872, "God has become a political figure; he sits on the right";[37] and Léon Gambetta's war cry during the critical elections of May 1877: "Clericalism? There is the enemy."[38]

The slogan worked. Returned to power, the Republic embarked on a thirty-year program of progressive secularization, most notably in the domain of education. Its critical landmarks were the formal separation of Church and state in 1905 and the institution in 1880 of 14 July as a national holiday. Until the First World War, huge open-air beanfeasts in the working-class districts continued the great republican tradition of eating and drinking together in public that began at the Fête de la Fédération on the first anniversary of the storming of the Bastille and flowered briefly in the republican eucharists of 1848.[39] Finally, the Eiffel Tower, its construction completed in 1889 to mark the centenary of the Declaration of the Rights of Man, would henceforth confront Sacré-Cœur on the Butte Montmartre as an emblem in iron of modernity and rationality triumphing over obscurantism and guilt.

By 1905 it seemed that, in the words of the great Socialist leader Jean Jaurès (1859–1914), the Republic had finally achieved its historic goal of "establishing humanity without God and without king."[40] In defending the martyred Jewish officer Captain Alfred Dreyfus (1859–1935) against the antisemitic witch-hunt of the right, the Republic had, it seemed, established for all time the hegemony not only of liberty, fraternity, and equality but of the new republican trinity of reason, science, and justice. And, as the Republic's gift of Frédéric-Auguste Bartholdi's Statue of Liberty to the United States in 1886 so graphically symbolized, Marianne, like Mary before her, now stood for humanity as a whole; the Republic may have been French in its origins but it was universal in its destiny and scope. It would take a virtually worldwide descent into violence and unreason—marked, in France, by the assassination of Jaurès, the most potently symbolic of all the sacrificial victims of the left–right political struggle, gunned down by a nationalist fanatic literally on the eve of the outbreak of war (31 July 1914)—to reveal the fragility and superficiality of the internationalist dream.

We need not, at this point, take the story of Church-state relations in France much beyond the critical watershed of May 1877, when the threat of a royalist restoration—and with it the Church's assumption of a more or less institutionalized role in the imposition of moral order—was finally laid to rest. It should be stressed, however, that by 1914, even without the enlistment of the Church on the side of political reaction, the gulf between it and "the people" would have been beyond bridging or healing. Moreover, dechristianization affected not only the lower classes but middle- and upper-middle-class Parisians (especially men) as well, often those who, for social and political reasons, were most committed to an active role for the Church in the life of the nation. Already under the Restoration Paul-Louis Courier (1772–1825) had noted that the "friends of the altar"—the legitimist aristocracy—"hardly approach it," while in 1849 Ozanam tartly remarked on the same phenomenon among upper-middle-class men. In the wake of the sociopolitical upheavals of 1848, such men were beginning to see virtues in the very church they had previously sought to keep well to the margins of public life: "Today there is no Voltairean burdened with a few thousand livres of private income per year who does not wish to send everyone to mass, so long as he doesn't have to set foot there himself."[41]

Partly the problem was one of infrastructure, for as report after report made clear, the Church in Paris had singularly failed to keep pace with the quite massive growth in the city's population, which rose from 546,000 in 1801 to 1,174,000 in 1856 and again to 2,714,000 in 1901, almost entirely as a result of immigration from the provinces. Despite increases in the number of parishes (116 in 1802, 149 in 1906) and of priests (375 in 1802, 866 in 1906), the average number of inhabitants per Parisian parish rose from 3,430 to 14,580 between 1802 and 1861 and, still more alarming, to 25,829 by 1906. The number of inhabitants per priest had risen over the same period from 1,600 in 1802 to 2,956 in 1861 and to a quite impossible 4,444 in 1906.[42] But these figures conceal even greater disparities between parishes, particularly between those in the bourgeois districts to the west, where a more or less viable priest-parishioner ratio prevailed, and those that theoretically served the "immense China" encircling the east of the city, where ecclesiastical infrastructures were often in practice totally wanting. Monseigneur Bœglin of Paris lamented in 1905 that "the people have not failed the Church; it is the parish that has failed the people."[43] Moreover, styles of preaching, singing, and celebrating mass were, one anonymous Paris priest wrote to his archbishop in 1849, almost calculated to deter even committed believers from active participation in the Church. Congregations were, he said, condemned just to look and listen as "faithless and amoral actors," hired by parishes in the absence of sufficient numbers of regular clergy, performed ancillary roles in the celebration of the mass, while paid singers and musicians, together with lavish church decorations, transformed the holy mysteries into little more than an "operatic spectacle" that actively discouraged prayer and meditation and isolated the spectators from one another. Whereas a parish should be a "family fraternity," it was in practice just an aggregate of individuals, like postrevolutionary society as a whole.[44] The anomie and commercialization of urban life were reaching into the heart of the very institution that should have been the best equipped to counter them.

All these things were true, but they can hardly account in themselves for the massive move away from the Church that took place, particularly among men, between 1800 and 1850, a distancing that was, to repeat, scarcely less marked at the upper and middle points of the Parisian class spectrum than at the lower. The well-known indifference or outright hostility to the Church among teachers, doctors, and lawyers opened up a gap between husbands and wives in better-off households, and the Church, according to anticlerical propaganda, was swift to exploit it. The theme of priestly (especially Jesuit) influence over women of the bourgeoisie became a stock in trade of antichurch diatribe, particularly after the publication of Jules Michelet's *Du prêtre, de la femme, de la famille* in 1845, and would plumb ever more lurid depths during the high noon of anticlerical sniping, between 1870 and 1900. But even in middle-class families that remained formally Catholic, religious observances came more and more to be diverted from their stated sacred referents to become a form of collective self-celebration. As already stated, First Communion became more a family affair than a religious rite of passage, and the celebration of Christmas—complete with Christmas trees and Santa Claus, which, brought to Paris by refugees from Alsace, became generalized among middle-class households after 1870—so threatened to subvert orthodox meanings that the Church tried, wholly without success, to counter Père Noël with Petit Jésus in an effort to restore Christmas to its properly Christian significance.[45] Family portraits and later photographs began to hang side by side with religious images and then often to displace them, and the great "religious" occasion of the middle-class year became the annual visit to the family vault on All Saints' Day, 1 November; again it was the family and not God that was the real object of worship. On a more intimate level, more middle-class families began to practice some form of birth control, usually coitus interruptus, brutally referred to as "dry copulation" by laymen and, more ornately, as "the detestable sin of Onan" by men of the Church. Men and particularly women who resorted to such methods feared to go to confession (or concealed their sin from the priest) and, having failed to obtain absolution, were consequently not in the state of grace necessary to take even their once-a-year Easter Communion.

Although formal unbelief remained rare until the 1860s, when the publication of Ernest Renan's *Vie de Jésus* (1863) rocked the faith of many believers, theism evolved into deism and then effectively into non-belief. Perhaps the self-made man needed no creator other than himself, except, of course, when his person or property was threatened. After the convulsions of 1848–51 and 1870–71, many nominal middle-class Catholics did indeed return to a more active religious commitment, but it was more the desire to escape the straitjacket of mid-nineteenth-century positivism that precipitated the succession of spectacular "conversions" by intellectuals and artists in the decades after *l'année terrible* of 1870–71: Léon Bloy (1846–1917), Joris-Karl Huysmans (1848–1907), Paul Claudel (1868–1955), Charles Péguy (1873–1914), the philosopher Jacques Maritain (1882–1973), the literary critic Jaques Rivière (1886–1925), the poet Francis Jammes (1868–1938), and the soldier-novelist Ernest Psichari (1883–1914). For all these intellectuals, as well as for thousands of other Catholics, the figure of Jeanne d'Arc was scarcely less vital to their recovered belief than were Jesus and Mary, and for all of them the masterpieces of French Gothic—Notre-Dame, Rouen, Amiens, Reims, and Chartres—stood as incarnations in stone of an age of faith whose widely reported demise they refused to accept. For those who lived to witness it, the First World War, and especially the ordeal of Verdun, was a purgatorial, sanctifying experience from which both they and France would emerge renewed and restored. Those who were killed—Péguy, Alain-Fournier, Psichari—were readily cast, as they had willing cast themselves, as sacrificial offerings to both France and the Church.

Many of the factors that caused middle-class Parisians to distance themselves from the Church also applied to the lower classes. In their case, recourse to "dry copulation" and other methods of birth control was complicated by the fact that many lower-class couples were not married in the first place. But two further deterrents to active Church membership (and, in the long run, to belief itself) bore with particular weight upon the lower classes: the Church's condemnation of Sunday work and its antagonism to cabarets and to dancing of all kinds. Partly as a result of the disruptions caused by the revolutionary calendar, Sunday work—"that French sin," as one archbishop called it[46]—had become widespread by the early 1800s. Thousands of working-class Parisians, particularly servants and waiters, self-employed laborers such as coal and water carriers, and home-based seamstresses, milliners, and glovemakers, routinely worked on Sundays by choice or through necessity, to the noisy consternation of the Church. Significantly, one of the Virgin's main admonitions to the shepherd children to whom she appeared at La Salette in the French Alps in 1846 was that Sunday be kept holy ("I granted six days for work, I kept the seventh for myself, and people refuse to grant it to me; that is what so weighs down the arms of my son"). At a later and lesser apparition at Saint-Bauzille-de-la-Sylve in the Hérault in 1873 she delivered the same stern message, this time in patois: "Cal pas trabalhar lo Dimenge!"[47]

Those lower-class Parisians who did not spend their Sundays working devoted them to drinking and dancing, commonly at the cabarets and open-air cafés that had sprung up outside the customs barriers on the city's periphery, where drink was cheaper. Their counterparts in the provinces did likewise, provoking still more anguished jeremiads from Church moralists. For Jean-Marie Vianney (1786–1859), the saintly curé of the village of Ars, near Lyon, dancing was "the rope with which the devil drags the majority of souls into hell," and he promptly banned it throughout his parish. A priest from Brest complained in 1821 that "Women who waltz are driving me out of my mind, they no longer make their Easter Communion, and on the pretext that they will be refused absolution, no longer even present themselves at the Tribunal of Penitence."[48] Cabarets were even worse than dance halls, for there not only was red wine consumed in abundance, but the politics of the Red Republic were discussed, disseminated, and, when the time was right, put into action. Renan would later write that the cabaret was for the gospel of socialism what the catacombs had been for the Gospel.[49]

More and more church and cabaret confronted each other as foci of wholly impermeable cultures, and there must have been hundreds of priests in both Paris and the provinces for whom Sunday was the kind of purgatorial ordeal described by one such in the mid-1870s:

> I arrive at mass, and find there about thirty women, two or three men: what to say to them? I feel more like weeping than speaking. At vespers, nobody. All day long, I close myself off in my presbytery, but I can't close and bury myself there deeply enough not to hear the singing of men drinking like brutes at the cabaret, and the violin of the dances that carry off women and girls.[50]

More often than not, priest and parish were mirror images of each other, each stricken with what the eponymous hero of Bernanos' *Journal d'un curé de campagne* (1936) calls "a stillborn despair, a torpid form of despair that is doubtless like the fermentation of a decomposed Christianity."[51]

Clearly, then, even without the Church's contribution to the politics of reaction, the gulf between it and lay society, both popular and bourgeois, would have been immense; with it, it was effectively insuperable.

The fundamental problem, as the pioneering Christian socialist Anthime Corbon wrote to Archbishop Dupanloup of Orléans (the probable originator of the loaded term "déchristianization") in 1876, was that "modern society"—its upper, middle, and lower sections alike—"does not postpone Redemption until the Day of Judgment; it does its utmost to achieve it without delay and also without conditions."[52] Writing just over thirty years later, in 1909, Charles Péguy saw things in altogether more radical and despairing terms: the problem was not that his contemporaries had lost their Christian faith or abandoned their Christian practice but that they had never been Christians in the first place.[53]

To be sure, there were at regular intervals, usually at times of social or political crisis, recrudescences of religiosity if not of religion among the rich, the middling, and the poor alike. The cholera epidemic of 1832 led to a revival in the popular cult of Saint Roch, and the cult of Sainte Philomène, promoted by the Lyonnaise laywoman Pauline Jaricot (1799–1862), likewise reached far beyond formally practicing Catholics.[54] In the early twentieth century, the cult of the Little Flower, Sainte Thérèse de l'Enfant Jésus et de la Sainte Face (1873–1897), would have such enormous popular appeal, particularly among soldiers in the First World War, that she was canonized in almost record time in 1925. Finally, the first of the apparitions of the Virgin to the novice Catherine Labouré (1806–76), which took place between April and December 1830 at the house of the Sisters of Charity on the Rue du Bac in Paris, opened the way for the later and still more influential apparitions at La Salette, Lourdes, and Pontmain. The fact that 8 million copies of the miraculous medal struck to commemorate the novice's vision were in circulation by 1838 and an incredible 100 million by 1842 gives some idea of the potential market for religious experience of a direct charismatic and therapeutic kind that Lourdes in particular would later meet in abundance.[55]

It may be significant—it is certainly striking—that almost all of these forms of popular Catholicism were mediated through women and children, and that, four years after the promulgation of the doctrine of the Immaculate Conception of the Virgin Mary (1854), a barely literate shepherdess in the Bigorre could speak directly and repeatedly with the Virgin herself. If, in the year after Pius IX's proclamation of papal infallibility (1870), the Virgin revealed herself directly to four children in Normandy, where did this place the Church's claim to be sole mediator between the human and the divine?

By the early 1830s, then, it is possible to discern in outline the major themes that would dominate the culture and politics of French

Catholicism up to the outbreak of war in 1914. The alliance of throne and altar between 1815 and 1830 had led many middle-class men to distance themselves from the Church, and a mixture of deism and anti-clericalism, if not yet actual unbelief, was already widespread. "Are you asking me if the Parisian bourgeois is religious?" wrote the perceptive Anaïs de Raucon in her *Epoque sans nom* of 1833. "A pointless question. He got married in church; he had his children baptized. He even finds it highly desirable that his wife should go to mass on Sunday. It's a good example, and, if you press him, he will tell you that religion is necessary for the people."[56]

Signs of ambivalence can be seen among lower-class Parisians as well. On the one hand, hostility to the Church as a social and political institution was made manifest when disgruntled workers (supported by disaffected republicans, mainly ex-soldiers and students) sacked the Archepiscopal Palace of Paris in February 1831 after legitimists celebrated an anniversary mass at the Church of Saint-Germain l'Auxerrois in honor of the martyred duc de Berry. On the other hand, we have seen the beginnings of the briefly influential primitive liberation theology in the early months of the Second Republic. This movement of certain sections of *le peuple* toward a radical version of Christianity was paralleled by a reciprocal movement of a small number of middle-class Catholics toward *le peuple*: Lamennais's increasingly vocal option for the poor led to his excommunication by papal fiat in February 1834, and by the 1840s significant numbers of young middle-class Catholics were prepared to follow Frédéric Ozanam's exhortation to "go over to the barbarians" and follow Pope Pius IX, who at that time was still viewed as a spokesman and standard-bearer for the impoverished masses.[57]

By the mid-1830s both left and right had their emblematic martyr figures or holocaustal victims: on the right, the victims of the September massacres, Louis XVI and Marie-Antoinette, their son (still alive and suffering the torments of exile and rejection, according to the most ultra of the ultraroyalists), and, most recently, the assassinated duc du Berry, while the left could point to Marat, the Four Sergeants of La Rochelle, and the victims of the massacre of the Rue Transnonain in April 1834. Later clashes would yield all too many candidates for beatification. Both left and right would come to view Christ's agony on the cross as a model and symbol of their own real and imaginary sufferings, and, right across the political-religious spectrum, blood would become the symbolic substance par excellence. The right had the Precious Blood of Christ himself; that of his martyred representatives on earth; and the uncanny blood that issued from the wounds of stigmatics, such as the German

Catherine Emmerich (1774–1824) and the Belgian Louise Lateau (1850–83), both of whom would greatly exercise the minds and imagination of French Catholics.[58] The left pointed to the all too real blood of the victims of the Lyon silkworkers' uprisings of 1831 and 1834, of the June insurrection of 1848, and of the Bloody Week of May 1871.

The theme of sacrifice was inseparable, on both left and right, from the obsession with conspiracy. If the right had been, from the time of the Revolution onward, haunted by the idea of a Masonic conspiracy against the old regime of Church, king, and aristocracy—an idea first formulated in the abbé Barruel's *Mémoire pour servir à l'histoire du jacobinisme* of 1797—the left was just as convinced that the Church, and particularly its clandestine shock troops, the Jesuits, were engaged in a massive secret war against the emerging secular order of France.[59] Both conspiracy theories would reach their apogee in the 1880s and 1890s, at the time of the head-on collision between the Church and the Republic over the linked questions of control over education and of the place and power of religious orders in France. More sinister still, both left and right—initially the former, but then increasingly the latter—became preoccupied with the alleged influence of Jews in contemporary France, and the publication of *Les Juifs, rois de l'époque: Histoire de la féodalité financière* by the utopian socialist Alphonse Toussenel in 1845 marked the first appearance in print of a theme that would poison French politics and society in the 1890s, when Captain Alfred Dreyfus became one more martyr figure in the mythology of the left, and, with far more tragic results, in July 1942, when over 13,000 Parisian Jews were rounded up by French police and dispatched to the east, from which only a handful would return.

These and similar themes will guide our pilgrimage around the holy and unholy places of nineteenth- and early twentieth-century Paris. But now we must abandon the panoramic viewpoint hitherto adopted and study from street level certain crucial Parisian *lieux de mémoire,* beginning with the place on and around which the history of modern France began with a series of acts of exemplary violence on 14 July 1789.

2

VIOLENT ORIGINS
The Taking of the Bastille
(July 1789)

There was one monument of the ancien régime—the most famous or rather infamous of all—that the city scanner of the 1830s or 1840s could not see, not because of the smog that now shrouded the city more or less permanently but for the simple reason that it had disappeared entirely. This was, of course, the Bastille, the huge eight-towered fortress built between 1356 and 1382 at the eastern entrance of the city. From the 1460s until its capture and destruction in 1789 by the quasi-mythical "people of Paris" it was a prison, and because it was directly under the king's control, its significance lay more in its symbolism than in the actual number of prisoners it contained. In sharp contrast to the fortress's mythical image, its prisoners always lived in conditions of relative latitude and comfort.[1] Among its more celebrated residents were—allegedly—the "man in the iron mask," supposedly an illegitimate brother or other rival of Louis XIV imprisoned there from 1698 until his death in 1703; Voltaire, detained for eleven months in 1717–18 for hinting at incestuous goings-on between the regent and his daughter, the duchesse de Berry, and again for twelve days in 1726 after an all too public quarrel with the chevalier de Rohan-Chabot; Mirabeau, the aristocratic bankrupt, pornographer, and future spokesman of the Third Estate, imprisoned from 1777 to 1781 for the alleged abduction of a minor, Sophie de Monnier; and the marquis de Sade, interned in 1784 at the behest of his family on account of his bizarre sexual tastes and transferred from the Bastille to the lunatic asylum of Charenton just days before the prodigious events of 14 July 1789. But it was two minor detainees, Henri Masers de Latude (intermittently held from 1749 to 1784) and Simon-Nicholas-Henri Linguet (imprisoned 1780–82), who, through their writings and sedulous courting of publicity, were most responsible for the myth of the Bastille, not merely as the familiar "symbol of absolutism" but as a complex of psychological and anthropological meanings whose power to fascinate and obsess we can, thanks to a number of outstanding modern studies, begin to understand.

In text after text concerning the Bastille, two themes—that of eating and that of secrecy—combine to form a nexus of fears and phobias whose hold over the eighteenth-century Parisian mind is not to be doubted. Time after time the Bastille is figured mythopoeically as a devouring monster, a whale, a Leviathan, into whose maw prisoners, guilty and innocent alike, were sucked, never to appear again; an invisible, unknowable world, given over to darkness and mystery: the very antithesis, in short, of the sunlit, public world that the monarchy officially inhabited. The salience of the theme of eating and being eaten transforms the fortress into an anti-image of the conventional figure of the king. The Bastille embodies not the benevolent king who feeds his people but his ogreish counterpart, who not only withholds food from his people but cannibalizes and bleeds them dry through taxes. To this extent, the myth of the Bastille links up with two of the most contagious "moral panics" of the eighteenth century: the rumor that children were being abducted—swallowed up, as it were—by the state that had produced the Parisian riots of May 1750 and the ritual killing of the commander of the watch Labbé[2] and, more generally, the rumored famine plot that had at regular intervals—1725–26, 1738–41, 1747, 1751–52, 1765–70, 1771–75—precipitated riots throughout France directed against that sinister bogeyman of the popular imagination, the *accapareur*, the stealer and hoarder of food supplies.[3] If the "hoarder" is the obsession of conspiracy made flesh, the Bastille is, so to speak, "plotomania" (*complomanie*) made iron and stone. The imagined labyrinth of its interior represents, like the castles of the contemporaneous Gothic novels it so much resembles, the political unconscious of the age, haunted by figures of tyrants, torturers, traitors, and spies: in what Linguet, the most famous of the fortress's mythographers, called the "universal abstraction," the nothingness and darkness of his cell, the prisoner is a total victim, an object utterly at the mercy of a power whose absoluteness lies in its invisibility, the impenetrable mystery in which it cloaks itself. In the most general sense, the Bastille embodies a paranoid perception of politics, society, the economy, and the state. More specifically, it incarnates the power of the father—be he king, lord, or tyrannical paterfamilias—in its most negative and arbitrary form, a power to which the lettres de cachet responsible for most imprisonments in the fortress gave tangible expression.[4]

By the summer of 1788, the situation of France's king-provider was so grave that he was constrained, in effect, to entreat his children to succor him in his desperation. His treasury exhausted by the recent war that France had fought against Britain alongside the nascent United States, Louis XVI announced on 8 August 1788 that the Estates General—a consultative body comprising the three estates or orders of the kingdom, which had not met since 1614—would convene at Versailles at the beginning of May the following year. With elections scheduled for March 1789, an extraordinary sounding of public opinion was undertaken, as communities and corporations throughout France were invited to submit their complaints and grievances against the status quo. Over 60,000 were submitted, most of them targeting inequitable taxes and denouncing the arbitrary privileges and exemptions of the First and Second Estates (the Church and aristocracy). The sun that sustained the traditional cosmos, the king himself, was left largely unscathed, but not his ministerial satellites and still less his consort-moon, the Austrian Marie-Antoinette.

On 5 May 1789 the deputies—291 representing the Church, 270 the aristocracy, and 578 the Third Estate, representing at least 95 percent of the population—processed in ceremony before the king, those of the Third Estate bringing up the rear and dressed entirely in black to symbolize their subordinate status. From the outset, the objective of the leaders of the Third Estate—Mirabeau, Sieyès, Barnave—was to ensure that the traditional practice of voting by order, thanks to which Church and nobility could always combine to defeat the commoners, was replaced by the democratic principle of voting by head, whereby the Third Estate (whose quota of deputies had already been doubled as a concession to representativeness) could normally expect to outvote their two rivals, especially if they took some votes from churchmen and nobles sympathetic to their cause. After long but fruitless negotiations, the deputies of the Third Estate declared themselves a "National Assembly" on 17 June 1789; in other words, a part of the nation—an overwhelmingly large part, to be sure—claimed the right to speak for the nation as a whole, from which it implicitly excluded the two other estates. On 20 June, finding themselves locked out of the hall in which they normally conducted their debates, the self-styled national deputies repaired to the royal tennis court nearby, and there, under the presidency of the astronomer Bailly, they passed, by 577 votes to 1, the celebrated Tennis-Court Oath, committing themselves not to separate until a democratic constitution had formally been established. For the first time, the sons, united together as brothers against their father's will, declared themselves to constitute an autonomous and self-sufficient source of power.

On 23 June, when Louis XVI still insisted that he had convoked them as "the common father of all my subjects,"[5] the deputies retorted through their president that "the assembled Nation does not have to take orders," and Mirabeau added for good measure that "we are here through the will of the people and we will leave our places only if forced to do so by bayonets." On 9 July the deputies took the next logical step and declared themselves to be a "Constituent National Assembly." The program announced by Sieyès in his celebrated pamphlet of January 1789, *Qu'est-ce que le tiers état?* already made up the new political agenda: "What is the Third Estate?—EVERYTHING. What has it been up to now in the political order?—NOTHING. What does it demand?—TO BECOME SOMETHING."[6]

Such was the general political context in which the assault on the Bastille took place three weeks or so after the father-centered universe of what was already being called feudalism came under concerted ideological attack from the sons forgathered fifteen miles away at Versailles. The immediate cause of the eruption was the king's decision, on 11 July, to dismiss his popular chief minister, Necker, and to ensure the submission of Paris by surrounding the city with troops—*foreign* troops, for the loyalty of French troops could no longer be automatically assumed. Since the end of 1788, Paris, in common with much of the rest of France, had been awash with fear, resentment, and distress caused principally by the summer's disastrous harvest and the glacial winter that followed. From March until May, Picardy and Provence were convulsed by agrarian disorder, a harbinger of the generalized rural panic that would erupt in July and August.[7] In late April the crisis spread to Paris when some ill-advised comments by a wealthy wallpaper manufacturer named Réveillon led to widespread rioting in the faubourg Saint-Antoine and adjacent working-class districts. Réveillon's factory—he employed 350 workers, a huge figure for the time—and house were ransacked by the crowd, prompting the editor of the *Mercure de France*, Mallet Du Pan, to write, in remarkable anticipation of Saint-Marc Girardin's better-known declaration of 1831, that "the Huns, the Herules, the Vandals, and the Goths will not come from the north or from the Black Sea, they are already among us." For two or three days cries of "Death to the rich! Death to all aristocrats! Death to hoarders! Drown the f-ing priests! [*A l'eau les foutus prêtres!*]" rang through the streets of the east and southeast of the city, as violence, fanned by the widespread belief in the existence of an "aristocratic plot," claimed up to 300 victims, far more than would die on both sides during the storming of the Bastille; at least three rioters were hanged for their part in the disturbances.[8] Conspiracy theories and scapegoating—those two traditional components of the Parisian bread riot—were already taking on an explicitly political coloration.

When news of Necker's dismissal reached Paris, there was rioting in the Tuileries and at the Palais-Royal, where Camille Desmoulins (1760–94), his demagogic skills already well honed, spoke wildly of an impending "Saint Bartholomew's massacre of patriots [*une Saint-Barthélémy des patriotes*]." On 12 and 13 July forty of the fifty-four customs posts surrounding Paris were attacked in the hope of bringing down the price of bread and alcohol, a foretaste of the red wine/red politics connection so widely made in the century to come. A number of prisons, including the Conciergerie, were taken by storm and their inmates released. In another paradigmatic act that would be repeated in every subsequent revolutionary conjuncture, the Hôtel de Ville was occupied by members of the capital's Electoral Assembly, who promptly constituted themselves as a de facto municipal council under the presidency of Jacques de Flesselles, the *prévôt des marchands* (the old regime equivalent of mayor). As we shall see, de Flesselles was shortly to become one of the earliest of the fledgling revolution's emblematic victims. But the insurgents—even those who belonged to the Parisian national guard that had been formally set up on 11 July—had few weapons at their disposal, and on the afternoon of 13 July, when they stormed the military barracks of the Invalides, in the southwest of the city, they found that although there were guns and bullets aplenty, the indispensable third element—gunpowder—had been secretly transported some days before to the Bastille, on the other side of Paris.

There were now practical as well as psychological or mythical reasons for an assault on the symbol par excellence of royal despotism, and by nine o'clock on the morning of 14 July a substantial crowd had already assembled at the entrance to the fortress, most of them members of the National Guard resident in the faubourg Saint-Antoine, including the famous revolutionary brewer Santerre, who would be present at Louis XVI's execution less than four years later. A delegation from the Hôtel de Ville was admitted to negotiate the release of the prison's gunpowder and, as an afterthought, of its detainees. There turned out to be but seven of them: four counterfeiters; a young aristocratic hothead, the comte de Solage, held there on the instructions of his parents; and two lunatics, one of them an Irishman named White who believed himself alternately (or simultaneously) Jesus, Julius Caesar, and Saint Louis.

The governor of the Bastille, the vicomte de Launay, invited the delegates to breakfast with him. For more than an hour nothing was seen or heard of them, and the steadily growing crowd outside began to fear that, like so many before them, they had been swallowed up in the maw of the immense Leviathan. With no apparent leaders or coordinating strategy, the crowd stormed the fortress entrance, which was guarded only by a force of veterans and Swiss mercenaries, who nonetheless succeeded in exacting a final sacrificial tribute in the form of ninety-eight assailants—as against one defender—who were killed in the attack. The threshold between past and future had been crossed, and by five o'clock in the afternoon the insurgents, steadily reinforced by new arrivals, were masters of the building that more than any other represented what within a few days observers would already be calling the ancien régime.[9]

How the children—or, more precisely, the sons—of Paris captured this icon of the bad father is less important in the present context than what they did once the prison-fortress was in their hands; in particular, the ghoulish fate they inflicted on its governor, the vicomte de Launay, and various other royal officials, none of them directly connected with the Bastille, in the aftermath of the capture. No less crucial is the language in which the events of 14 July were almost instantly mythologized by memorialists such as Jean Dusaulx, himself a participant in the stirring narrative he told in *L'Œuvre des sept jours*—the self-consciously biblical title is a manifesto in itself—published in 1790, along with the speech he made in honor of the so-called victors of the Bastille before the National Assembly in February that year. All the quotations that follow come, unless otherwise stated, from these two works.[10]

Not surprisingly, the instinctive urge of the heroes of July and the vast crowd that thronged into the Bastille in their wake was to scour "all the ins and outs of that gruesome lair" from its "chilly catacombs" to its battlements, smashing as they went the double and triple doors they met, stoning to smithereens "a sundial whose supports represented two slaves bowed beneath the weight of their chains," heaving into the courtyard or moat "enormous stones whose noise, as they fell, reverberated in every Frenchman's heart, communicating, by echo, from one to the next and sounding from afar the signal of victory." Dusaulx suggests that this was not mere vandalism but a symbolic taking possession of an (imagined) locus of power. Significantly, the metaphors he deploys evoke not expulsion but ingestion:[11] "Like vultures, [the conquerors] fell upon the entrails of their recent prey," as though impelled to devour the monster that so recently had threatened to devour them, as it supposedly had devoured tens of thousands of prisoners in the past. What the invaders were most eager to seize and make their own were symbols of power and strength, such as lances and helmets or "those ancient, heavy suits of armor that our fathers, much more robust than we, wore into battle." It was trophies such as these that—along with, as we shall see, the severed head of the prison governor—the crowd would carry through the city streets to offer as it were in homage to the Paris electors, "like the corpse of a poisonous monster that one has had the good fortune to defeat," as Dusaulx so tellingly puts it. According to another witness, Pitra, like Dusaulx an elector of Paris, one of the insurgents bore skewered on his bayonet "a huge register said to be the Bastille's regulations"; another brought the fortress's standard, others still the governor's silverware, which they proceeded to present to the electors along with, according to Dusaulx, a bloodstained lock of de Launay's hair. More sinisterly, says Pitra, another victor "showed the people the keys of the Bastille, which he dangled for a time over the head of M. de Flesselles, as though it were the thunderbolt that was shortly to strike him down."[12]

The political, psychological, and anthropological significance of these almost ritualistic actions can readily be discerned. The sons of the people have slain the monster, the bad father, and have made his power their own. By killing and as it were devouring the monster, they have crossed the threshold from adolescence to authentic manhood. They have wrested the phallus from the bad father and now they offer it to their elected representatives, though first they must slay the hapless *prévôt des marchands,* who, we shall shortly see, is just as much an agent and image of the bad father as was de Launay. That done, the Paris electors become authentic fathers of the city, and at the Te Deum celebrated at Notre-Dame the following day, Bailly, the new mayor (and president of the National Assembly), was greeted by "a multitude of young children, kneeling, hands clasped," with the cry of "Our father! O our father!" They were orphans whom the state had taken under its wing, and "forgetting both ceremony and his new function, our worthy leader rushes toward these creatures who had been abandoned at birth, clutches them to his heart, and drenches them with his freely flowing tears; he promises them tenderness, help, and protection in the name of the Supreme Being; he showers on them not the gold of the nation [*la patrie*] but the little gold that he owed to his native gifts, his talents." Nothing could be clearer: although the nominal father of the people remains the king, the true father is now the self-made, democratically elected individual. The power of the father has not so much been done to death as transferred to the "eldest" of his sons, who now exercises it on behalf and in the name of his brothers.

Let us now return to 14 July and follow the last hours of the vicomte de Launay and Jacques de Flesselles, who would shortly share his fate of death and dismemberment at the hands of the revolutionary crowd. Everything marked out de Launay as potential scapegoat and victim. Not only was he the governor of the Bastille but, the son of a governor, he had actually been born there: the identification of man and monster was virtually complete. He was known to be in contact with Besenval, the commander of the royal troops ringing Paris, and he was believed— wrongly, in fact—to have lured the Bastille's assailants into the inner courtyard in order to mow them down; the fact that only one defender had died during the attack probably sealed his fate. As Simon Schama has written:

> The imbalance was enough for the crowd to demand some sort of punitive sacrifice, and de Launay duly provided it. All the hatred which to a large degree had been spared the garrison was concentrated on him. His attributes of command—a sword and baton—were wrenched away from him and he was marched towards the Hôtel de Ville through enormous crowds, all of whom were convinced he had been foiled in a diabolical plot to massacre the people.[13]

With cries of "Cut off his head," "Hang him," and "Tie him to a horse's tail" ringing about him, de Launay lashed out in desperation, kicking an unemployed pastry cook named Desnot in what Jacques Godechot decorously calls his "parts." Desnot went down, presumably clutching said parts and wailing, "I'm done for, I'm wounded," whereupon, in Schama's words again, de Launay was "instantaneously covered with darting knives, swords and bayonets, rolled to the gutter and finished off with a barrage of pistol shots."[14] The honor of decapitating the corpse went to Desnot ("Here, since you've been wounded, cut off his head"), who, unable to handle the saber handed him by someone in the crowd, finally performed the act with the kitchen knife he opportunely had about him. The severed head was mounted on a pike, and the crowd as one bore it through the street of Paris to the Hôtel de Ville, leaving the trunk of the "scum" (galeux) and "monster" they had killed to bleed in the gutter. "The Nation demands his head to display it to the public": by slaying the monster in whom is concentrated all the negative power of the bad father, the sons attain to authentic manhood, with Desnot's phallic kitchen knife more than avenging any rough treatment visited on his own parts. The nation is born in the blood of the scapegoat, whose remains are transported through the streets like some grotesque parody of the Blessed Sacrament on the feast

LA JOURNÉE MÉMORABLE *Du Mardi 14 Juillet 1789*

Tous les Citoyens réunis aux Braves Grenadiers et Soldats du Regiment des Gardes Francaises après avoir conquis la Bastille en 4 heures de tems Couperent la tête à M. De Launay Gouverneur de cette Citadelle effroyable, ainsi que celle de M. De Flesselles Prevot des Marchands de Paris, Les promenerent en triomphe, de la Greve au Palais Royal et les remirent à la Morne ou ils furent exposés à la vue du Publique pendant plusieurs jours, et jettés ensuite dans la Riviere.

C'est ainsi que tôt ou tard la justice Divine punit les Traitres.

The memorable day of Tuesday, 14 July 1789. This anonymous print shows the ritual display of the severed heads of the vicomte Charles de Launay and Jacques de Flesselles on the Place de Grève. "Thus it is that divine justice sooner or later punishes traitors." (Musée Carnavalet, Paris, © Photothèque des Musées de la Ville de Paris.)

of Corpus Christi. The newborn brothers communicate and attain to self-consciousness in and through the victim's mutilated remnants.

A few hours later it would be the turn of de Flesselles (b. 1721), whose "long and cruel agony" was directly witnessed by both Dusaulx and Pitra. Ever since his appointment as *prévôt des marchands* in April 1789, de Flesselles's relations with the emerging political forces in Paris had been tense and equivocal. On 27 May the electors of Paris had asked to participate in the running of the city by attending meetings at the Hôtel de Ville. A man of the government, de Flesselles had refused, but when the demand was renewed on 25 June, he grudgingly admitted twelve electors to the meetings. On 13 July the electors effectively invaded the Hôtel de Ville to constitute themselves as a city assembly, of which de Flesselles, as we have seen, was duly elected president. Forced to accept the creation of a civilian militia and faced with an immediate demand for weapons, de Flesselles stalled as best he could, uttering the fateful and, in the context of the present argument, highly significant words: "My friends, I am your father, and you will be satisfied." De Flesselles promised that 12,000 guns would shortly arrive from Charleville. Some crates marked "Artillerie" did indeed reach the Hôtel de Ville that evening, but they were found to contain nothing more than old rags and bits of wood. It seemed to many present that de Flesselles— already rumored to be part of an inevitable famine plot—was also engaged in a plot to hoodwink the people and hand them over to their enemies: "the *prévôt des marchands* was bitterly reproached for having, for whatever reason, deceived honest people [*braves gens*], who were unable to forgive him for it." Already by the 13th, de Flesselles had been marked out as a suitable case for treatment.

Two things sealed de Flesselles's fate the following day: his failure to back the assault on the Bastille with either arms or words and, crucially, the discovery, real or rumored, on de Launay's body of a letter from de Flesselles urging him to resist to the last. As the day advanced, in Michelet's words, "all the fury of the people was concentrated on the *prévôt des marchands*,"[15] and, thanks to the accounts of Dusaulx and Pitra, we can follow hour by hour de Flesselles's "trances"—the word is Dusaulx's—as his awful fate became clear to him.

At first, says Dusaulx, "he tried to show, and did indeed show, a kind of assurance, opening packets and listening to everyone with such keenness and affability that he would have got out of it if the decision to have done with him had not been taken irrevocably." But terror steadily seized hold of him and "all his faculties were suspended to such an extent that I saw him chew his last mouthful of bread for a whole hour, without being able to swallow it." When the crowd from the Bastille stormed into the Hôtel de Ville, pandemonium broke loose, and it seemed to Dusaulx—he used an expression whose full significance will become clear when we survey all these instances of collective violence together—that "the total decomposition of society" was upon them, as the tempest, tumult, drunkenness, fermentation, and mayhem grew into a state of undifferentiated violence, with the crowd clamoring not just for de Flesselles's blood but for that of anyone else—Dusaulx included— whose support for the uprising was in any way suspect.

Amid mounting chaos, de Flesselles seems to have decided of his own free will to leave the Hôtel de Ville and face his accusers outside, slipping out inconspicuously with the alleged parting words: "Because I am suspect to my fellow citizens, it is indispensable that I withdraw." No sooner was he outside than he was killed "by someone unknown, with a pistol shot, on the corner of the quai Pelletier." His head was severed forthwith, mounted on a pike, and paraded along with de Launay's through the streets. Did de Flesselles offer himself up as a sacrificial victim to save the lives of his fellow electors? Or was it rather the electors who, as has been recently suggested, sent de Flesselles out to his fate as "a kind of 'sacrificial offering' to the People, an 'offering' which not only helped ensure their own safety but also facilitated the subsequent pardon of the less personally responsible Bastille defenders"?[16] Further research is needed to supplement Dusaulx's cagey and inconclusive account.

Whatever the truth about de Flesselles's final minutes, the meaning of his sacrifice is not in doubt. Unlike de Launay, de Flesselles had a foot in both camps as royal official and elected president of the new city assembly. He was neither wholly innocent nor wholly guilty of the charges made against him, and rightly or wrongly he was believed to be actively engaged in all manner of plots—a military plot, a famine plot—against the very people whose supposed representative he was. Unlike de Launay, who is an agent pure and simple of the bad father, de Flesselles is the false father who promises and then denies his children the lethal playthings they crave; "he could never satisfy them" is Dusaulx's dry comment. If metaphors of ingestion preside over the storming of the Bastille and the killing of de Launay, the expulsion motif dominates that of de Flesselles: it is less a question of absorbing his power than of expelling a waverer and traitor from the newly constituted polis.[17] By displaying and parading the mutilated remnants of the bodies, the killers—the *sacrificateurs,* in the term of Henri Hubert and Marcel Mauss's classic study of sacrifice[18]—involve the onlookers as *sacrifiants* in a collective act of creative murder: all are now parties to the deed, innocent and guilty together.

Tragically, however, this bloody eucharist needed to be regularly renewed if it was to preserve its efficacy as the sacrament of the new revolutionary community, and less than ten days after the killing of de Launay and de Flesselles, on 22 July, two further sacrificial victims, Foulon, a prospective government minister, and his son-in-law, Bertier de Sauvigny, the intendant of Paris, were torn to pieces by the crowds and their severed heads mounted on pikes and paraded in the now ritualized fashion through the streets of Paris. Once more the motif of eating, ghoulishly parodied in the hay, grass, and other ordure stuffed into the victims' mouths, forms an essential part of the sacrificial paradigm. By coincidence, the killers and their retinue passed beneath the windows of the boardinghouse where the young Chateaubriand, recently arrived

Messieurs Delaunay Flesselles Berthier Foulon et les deux Gardes du Corps qui ont été Decolés par le Peuple, voudraient passer jusqu'aux Champs Elisées en depit de Caron qui ne reçoit dans sa barque que le Sr Remy François Boulanger Victime innocente de la Fureur Aristocratique. l'infortuné Calas & autres viennent le recevoir a l'autre bord.

Anonymous print of 1789. The decapitated corpses of de Launay, de Flesselles, Bertier, and Foulon, along with other victims of popular vengeance in July 1789, try to cross the river Styx to the Elysian Fields. They are refused passage by Charon, who welcomes into his bark only an "innocent victim of aristocratic fury," one Rémy François Boulanger, whose severed head wears the Phrygian cap. On the opposite shore, earlier victims of the ancien régime's injustice, notably Jean Calas (executed in 1762), prepare to welcome the revolutionary martyr. (Musée Carnavalet, Paris, © Photothèque des Musées de la Ville de Paris.)

in Paris from his ancestral home in Combourg in Brittany, was staying; it was the sight of an eye wrenched out of its socket and of a pike thrust into an open mouth in such a way that "the teeth were biting the iron" that, along with other "cannibalistic feasts" he claimed to have witnessed shortly afterward, persuaded the young aristocrat that there was no place for him henceforth in his native land.[19] Others, though, far from being repelled, positively rejoiced in the bloodletting. Justifying the mutilation of Bertier's body, the revolutionary journalist Loustalot wrote that whoever was responsible for "tearing his heart from his palpitating viscera" was doing no more than "avenging himself on a monster, the monster who had *killed* his father":[20] once more the slaying of the alleged monster (in fact both Bertier and Foulon were innocuous minor officials) becomes a supposedly liberating act whereby the killer arrogates the power of the father and attains to full adult humanity. Violent in its origins, the Revolution could not be other than violent in its development, with each sacrificial murder justifying and indeed necessitating further killings of a similar "liberating" or "purifying" kind. "Was the blood that was shed all that pure?" asked the revolutionary Barnave in justification of the murder of Foulon and Bertier, thus unwittingly preparing and justifying his own death on the guillotine a few years later at the height of the Terror.

Scarcely had the Bastille been captured than work on its demolition began under the canny entrepreneurial eye of a prosperous building contractor named Pierre-François Palloy (1755–1835). Patriot Palloy, as he quickly styled himself, successfully marketed the massive stone blocks of which the fortress was built as "ex votos" or "pledges of freedom": he had some of them chiseled into miniatures of the Bastille or inscribed with the text of the Declaration of the Rights of Man, distributed them free of charge to the new departments, and sent out "apostles of freedom"—in effect teams of traveling salesmen—to sell them to municipal councils and private individuals the length and breadth of France.[21] It was, once again, a parody, this time in stone rather than in flesh and blood, of the fraction and distribution of the Communion Host, a secular eucharist in which the power, if not the love, of the father was transmitted to the people as a whole, in which each department, each district, and indeed, theoretically, each individual communicated in the body of the reconstituted nation.

The eucharistic dimension is still more apparent in the Fête de la Fédération, held on 14 July 1790 to commemorate the taking of the Bastille and to renew—though this, of course, was never stated in so many words—the sacramental bond first celebrated in the bodies and blood of de Launay, de Flesselles, Bertier, and Foulon. From all over France columns of citizens converged on Paris as though, the nineteenth-century republican historian Edgar Quinet would say, it were a holy city, and headed for the Champ de Mars, where a mass collective meal involving thousands of "communicants" was held in the open air, its every detail timed to coincide precisely with similar patriotic repasts in the provinces. Thus the Oath of Loyalty was taken simultaneously throughout the land, whereafter, seated at what one delegate called the "great national table," the whole of France—supposedly—raised its glasses and broke bread as a single entity, affirming its unity in the deep-red wine of revolutionary fraternity.[22]

Although this national agape was in no way antireligious—mass was duly celebrated by a clutch of bishops—there can be no doubt, as Michelet was quick to discern, that its object was man, not God, Christ, or king, and that, just as the Revolution rejected the feudal principle of the transmission of status and merit by blood, so it rejected the key Christian principle of the blood transmission of sin: the Fête, like the Revolution itself, was a revolt against original sin in the name of the "natural goodness" of man.[23] Nor was the Fête de la Fédération explicitly antiroyal, though illustrations of the event show the king reduced to the role of spectator, at times barely visible; in the new revolutionary sacrament the nation stood at the center, while the king—no longer needed as the nation's visible incarnation—was relegated to the periphery. Watching the nation constitute itself outside and implicitly against him, Louis XVI was already, two and a half years before his actual death, a condemned man on a stay of execution.

How, finally, to replace the Bastille? An initial project by Palloy to construct a Colonne de la Liberté on the site of the fortress (now inevitably named the Place de la Liberté) had to be shelved because of France's worsening external situation, and in July 1793 a fifteen-meter-high plaster statue of Isis was erected temporarily in its stead. Water gushed from the ample breasts of this so-called fountain of regeneration, the idea being that every 14 July "patriots" would forgather there to drink the revivifying milk of fraternity that the destruction of the old fortress had allowed to flow. Just as full-breasted Marianne had replaced the king as the embodiment of the French nation, so a benevolent maternal image displaced that of the bad father.[24]

When Napoleon came to power, the idea of a column was revived, but modified fundamentally in location and significance: not a Colonne de la Liberté but a victory column celebrating Napoleon's military triumphs, erected in 1806 on the Place Vendôme, in the west-central part of the city, where it would stand until a later revolutionary regime—the Paris Commune of 1871—would send it toppling amid great ceremony and rejoicing as a symbol of (patriarchal) tyranny in all its forms. On the site of the Bastille, Napoleon envisaged a colossal statue of an elephant—presumably chosen as a thoroughly depoliticized symbol of anything and nothing—to be made from the bronze of cannon captured in Spain; it was to serve as a fountain and reservoir, and water would flow from the elephant's trunk. A twenty-four-meter-high, plaster-and-wood maquette of the statue was constructed in 1810 and would remain on the site until 1847, a "wretched old mastodon," wrote Victor Hugo, whose archetypal Parisian gamin Gavroche makes it his home in Les Misérables

(1862), "invaded by vermin and oblivion, covered with warts, streaks of mould and ulcers, tottering, worm-eaten, abandoned, condemned, a kind of colossal beggar beseeching in vain a charitable look."[25]

Meanwhile, in 1833, the Bourgeois Monarchy of Louis-Philippe began the construction of a liberty column to commemorate the "Three Glorious Days" of July 1830 that had brought it to power. Completed in 1840, the column contains at its base the remains of the 504 victims of the July revolution (which may in the meantime have become mixed up with the decomposing debris of mummies brought back from Egypt by Napoleon),[26] to which were added, in March 1848, the remains of the 196 victims of the recent February revolution.[27] To Hugo the Colonne de Juillet, that "botched monument of an aborted revolution," epitomized the essential hollowness and insignificance of the regime it supposedly celebrated. Many radicals thought likewise, and in 1871 an attempt was made to blow it up in the manner of the Colonne Vendôme. To no avail, however: the column was more robust than the regime it commemorates, and it still stands, melodramatic and incongruous at the center of the Place de la Bastille, its hyposignificance rivaled only by the adjacent Opéra-Bastille constructed by another supposedly radical government—that of the latter-day Louis-Philippe, François Mitterrand—to honor the bicentenary of 1789. Where once the working people of the faubourg Saint-Antoine risked their lives to destroy a detested symbol of tyranny and so found in blood—their own and that of their emblematic scapegoat-victims—the history of modern France, the *fine fleur* of the Parisian bourgeosie, the principal beneficiary of that history, now comes to enjoy superlavish productions of *Tristan und Isolde, Madame Butterfly,* and *Pelléas et Mélisande.* Thus is history dehistoricized by its very commemoration and mythologization, a process also illustrated, though in a somewhat different way, at the Place de la Concorde, in the center of Paris, to which we now head.

3

KILLING THE KING
Place de la Révolution/Concorde
(21 January 1793)

On the morning of 21 January 1793, after an ordinary supper and three hours' sleep, Louis Capet, otherwise Louis XVI or Louis the Last, was awakened at five o'clock by his aide-de-camp, Cléry. He attended mass and took Communion at 6 A.M., spent a further hour and a half with his confessor, the abbé Edgeworth de Firmont, and at 8 A.M., having distributed various valuables and keepsakes to his family and retainers, walked out to the green carriage that awaited him in the courtyard of the Temple, the semi-abandoned tower in the northeast of Paris where, hemmed in on all sides by the typically hodgepodge working-class population of the district, he and his family had been held prisoner since the final collapse of the monarchy on 10 August 1792. A request that he be given a pair of scissors to have his hair cut having been refused, Louis and his confessor entered the coach, where they sat side by side with two gendarmes on the seats opposite, and the coach moved slowly off on its journey to the Place de la Révolution—the former Place Louis XV and now the Place de la Concorde—in the center of the city. The streets were virtually deserted and, according to *Les Révolutions de Paris,* "the most profound silence reigned on all sides";[1] there was nothing to distract Louis from his reading of the Psalms and the prayers of the dying.

The journey to the Place de la Révolution was a continuation and direct consequence of an equally fateful carriage journey undertaken eighteen months earlier, on 20 June 1791, when, in a desperate bid to break with and break the Revolution, Louis and his family had fled Paris for the eastern frontier, where antirevolutionary forces consisting of Austrian, Prussian, and French royalist troops were gathered. Spotted and identified at Sainte-Ménehould by the local postmaster, Drouet, they were arrested at Varennes, the next village on their route to the frontier, and, accompanied by a huge and hostile escort, forced to return to Paris. It was, wrote Michelet, this four-day journey back to the capital, constantly jeered and spat upon by his erstwhile subjects, that constituted the real trial and execution of the king. Back in Paris, the royal family was greeted not by angry crowds but—Michelet's expression again—by an "excommunication of silence" as the carriage drove in total solitude back to the Tuileries; it was a case of a "general union of France and one single family excluded."[2]

Henceforth Louis was, in Sébastien Mercier's words, no more than a king of fools (un roi de la basoche) awaiting ritual immolation.[3] No longer the provider or boulanger of "his" people, the king was represented in revolutionary cartoons as a glutton stuffing his rotund frame with food and drink even as "the nation" came to arrest him. As it happened, Sainte-Ménehould was renowned for its pied de porc (pig's feet), and, as if by some psychohistorical necessity, the prosecutor of Varennes responsible for the arrest was none other than a Citoyen Sauce. But, after his forced return to the royal "sty," Louis became food, or potential food, himself, and was routinely caricatured as a pig being driven to the slaughterhouse by a representative sans-culotte or consigned already to the cooking pot. A famous cartoon captioned "Les deux ne font qu'un" (The two are only one) shows Louis and Marie-Antoinette as, respectively, a pig and a hyena joined together as a single bicephalous hybrid, openly inviting ritual separation and slaughter.[4]

As the external situation of France deteriorated, demands for the king's deposition and for the monarchy to be abolished became ever more pressing, and on 20 June 1792 a crowd of revolutionaries stormed the Tuileries and forced Louis to don the Phrygian cap—the symbol par excellence of liberty and equality—and to drink to the health of the nation, even as a butcher named Legendre, addressing him as Monsieur rather than Sire, upbraided him as a traitor (un perfide) who had never ceased to deceive them and was deceiving them still. Humiliated and threatened in both his royal and his human body, Louis nonetheless had the strength to reply that he was still their king and would do what the law and the constitution required of him.[5] A satirical image published shortly afterward shows the cap perched limply on the royal head like some detumescent phallus or "drooping signifier," adding to and confirming the reputation of sexual impotence that had dogged Louis—a sufferer from phimosis, or nonretractability of the foreskin, whose hobby was unpicking locks—since the beginning of his reign.[6] After 20 June, the king's impotence was systemic rather than local, and his castration by caricature preceded and made possible the amputation of his executive power and eventual decapitation. A further invasion of the Tuileries on 10 August led to the formal abolition of the monarchy and declaration of the Republic on 21 September 1792.

When Louis was brought to trial on the inevitable charge of treason, there was never any doubt that he would be convicted; the only real issue was whether he would be punished by exile (as the "moderate" Girondins and their allies preferred) or by death (the penalty argued for with unwavering revolutionary logic by their Jacobin rivals). Although the final vote in favor of death was as close as it possibly could be—361 votes for, 360 against—the Jacobin case, particularly as presented by Saint-Just and Robespierre, possessed a rectitude and consistency that overrode all counterarguments, both political and humanitarian. For Saint-Just it was axiomatic that the king must be not so much judged as combated as an enemy, it being impossible "to reign innocently." Since it was also impossible for the king to live and not to reign (*cet homme doit mourir ou régner*), it followed that Louis must be punished—and punished with death—"or the French republic is an illusion [*une chimère*]." With even greater revolutionary rigor, Robespierre argued that "Louis must die because the Republic must live." Not only that, but it was necessary "to cement freedom and public tranquility through death of the tyrant."

The most telling formula was that of the revolutionary priest Henri Grégoire, for whom "kings are to the moral order what monsters are to the physical order." The analogy was repeated by speaker after speaker during the trial: Louis was a "monster made out of blood and mud" (Lakanal), a "monster covered with all species of crime" (Jean-Louis Carra), "a carnivorous monster" (Bouquier), a "monster dripping with the blood of the French" (Jean-Bon Saint-André), and so on.

The premises of the trial ultimately permitted one verdict and one punishment only: not only did "the salvation of the people" lie "in cutting off the head of a monster so as to paralyze his whole race with fear" (Bertucat), but it was only through the act of killing the monster that people would become truly The People, the "one and indivisible nation" that the constitution proclaimed them to be. The "spontaneous" foundational killings of July 1789 were to be corroborated and authenticated by a fully legal, rational, and deliberate sacrificial act, a sacrifice that would both inaugurate a new cosmos in and through violence and abolish the need for violence in the future; in short, a sacrifice to end all sacrifices, the republican equivalent of the full and final sacrifice of Christ. The revolutionaries, including Robespierre himself, intended, in the words of one of their number, that Louis's head should be the last to fall and that "the death penalty be abolished as soon as the tyrant has been struck down" (Robert): by doing violence to the cause of violence as they saw it (the monarchical principle embodied in the dethroned king), by putting death to the source of death, it was as though the revolutionaries sought nothing less than the death of death itself.[7]

Louis's carriage reached the Place de la Révolution around ten past ten on the morning of 21 January, having taken close to two hours to cross the city. Alighting, Louis was placed forthwith in the hands of the chief executioner, Charles-Henri Sanson, the latest in a family lineage of executioners that stretched back to 1688 and that was linked by marriage—executioners being a virtually endogamous caste—to the executioners of Etampes, Meaux, Rennes, Orléans, Reims, Soissons, Tours, Blois, Melun, and many others: in short, a parodic replica of the Bourbon dynasty, just as the headsman himself was both mirror image and antithesis of the king, his person, attributes, and possessions charged with a negative mana that matched and inverted the positive sacrality with which the monarch was invested.[8]

Removing his coat and collar uninvited or under duress (depending on which of the many accounts of the execution one follows), Louis strenuously objected to having his hair cropped in public (whence his earlier unsuccessful request for a pair of scissors), and still more to having his hands bound behind his back. He was pacified only when the abbé Edgeworth, according to *his* account, told the king that "this new outrage" was just "a final point of similarity [*un dernier trait de ressemblance*] between your majesty and the God who is going to be his recompense."

At those words Louis, for whom trial, condemnation, and now execution were likewise an *imitatio Christi* from beginning to end, turned toward his executioners and, an *alter Christus* down to the last utterance, declared: "Do what you will, I shall drink of the cup unto the lees [*je boirai le calice jusqu'à la lie*]." Ascending the scaffold, the king then delivered, "his face bright red" according to almost all accounts, his final would-be Christlike words to the assembled throng—usually reported as "I die innocent of all the crimes imputed to me. I forgive the authors of my death, and I pray to God that the blood you are about to shed will never fall back on France"[9]—before being cut off by a thunderous drum roll probably ordered by the brewer Santerre, a leading "conqueror of the Bastille" and one of his tormentors at the Tuileries on 20 June 1792. At this point Louis was seized by his executioners, and, in Sébastien Mercier's eyewitness account, "was undressed by force and

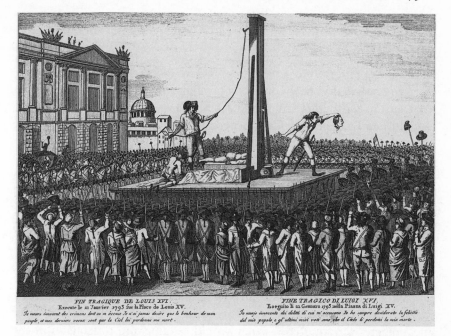

FIN TRAGIQUE DE LOUIS XVI.
Execute le 21 Janvier 1793 sur la Place de Louis XV.
Je meurs innocent des crimens dont on m'accuse Je n'ai jamais desire que le bonheur de mon
peuple, et mes derniers voeux sont que le Ciel lui pardonne ma mort.

FINE TRAGICO DI LUIGI XVI.
Eseguito li 21 Gennaro 1793 nella Piazza di Luigi XV.
Io muojo innocente dei delitti di' cui m'accusano Io ho sempre desiderato la felicità
del mio popolo, e gl' ultimi miei voti sono, che il Cielo li' perdoni la mia morte.

The tragic end of Louis XVI, executed on the Place Louis XV on 21 January 1793. This anonymous royalist print bears the king's alleged final words: "I die innocent of the crimes of which I am accused. I have ever desired only the happiness of my people, and my final wish is that Heaven forgive them for my death." (Musée Carnavalet, Paris, © Photothèque des Musées de la Ville de Paris.)

tethered, still struggling, to a plank," with the result that he received the guillotine's blade "so badly that he had not his neck but the back of his head [*occiput*] and jaw horribly severed." Details apart, and with some differing interpretations of the mood of those present and involved, all accounts agree with Mercier's concerning what happened next:

> His blood flows; the joyful cries of eighty thousand people rise to the heavens and strike my ears; they are repeated all along the quais; I see schoolboys from the Quatre-Nations throwing their caps in the air. His blood flows; people struggle to dip in it their fingertips, a pen, a piece of paper. Someone tastes it and says: it's damn salty [*bougrement salé*]! Standing on the scaffold's edge, one executioner sells and distributes little packets of his hair; the cord that held them is bought; everyone carries off a little fragment of his clothes or some other bloody vestige of this tragic scene. I saw the whole people file past arm in arm,

laughing, chatting familiarly, as when one returns from some
festivity [*une fête*].[10]

Soldiers are reported to have dipped sabers or pikes in the royal blood,
"claiming that this new form of talisman would make them triumph
over all the aristocrats and tyrants of the earth"; according to the same
account, an English onlooker steeped his handkerchief in the blood, and
a few days later said handkerchief was to be seen "flying like a flag" on
the Tower of London.[11]
One need not believe every last detail of each account to grasp the
sacrificial logic of what was going on. One citizen reportedly clambered
onto the guillotine, plunged his bare arm into the copious pool of blood,
and "three times sprinkled it over the throng of those present, who
pressed around the foot of the scaffold to receive each one a drop on the
brow," all the time crying, "Republicans, a king's blood brings happiness to all [*Républicains, le sang d'un roi porte bonheur*]."[12]
Almost immediately the Christological comparison was made by
writer after writer in the Catholic-royalist camp, and the key words of
the Vulgate were quoted, as they would be time and time again in the
decades to come: *Scinderunt vestimenta sua* (They shared out my
clothing among them: John 19:24).[13] A royalist engraving of 1793 titled
Le Nouveau Calvaire shows Louis being crucified between his two
brothers while the Princesse de Polignac clutches the foot of the cross
like Mary Magdalene and Robespierre extends to him a wine-soaked
sponge; a Phrygian cap surmounts the cross.[14]
But the Christological, even the eucharistic, dimension of the king's
death was present also in republican discourse, if only in disguised or inverted terms. Just as Palloy had distributed blocks of the Bastille to each
of the new departments, so Legendre—who, after all, was in the meat
trade—seriously proposed that Louis's corpse "be cut into eighty-four
portions, one to be sent to each department," there to be incinerated before a liberty tree. Curiously echoing the ritual circumambulation of
parish boundaries on Rogation Sunday, he also suggested that the head
be ceremonially paraded on a pike around the nation's frontiers "to
frighten the despots who would dare to soil the name of liberty."[15]
The parallel between 21 January 1793 and the first Good Friday was
also recognized, and partially endorsed, by nineteenth-century republican historians, such as Lamartine and Michelet. Michelet drew a further
analogy between the decapitation of Louis and the burning at the stake
of Joan of Arc at Rouen in 1431, which later right-wing writers would
exploit and elaborate with a vengeance.[16] To the many Joan/Louis parallels they would make it might be added that nothing of the body of ei-

The new Calvary. This anonymous royalist print shows "the Passion of Louis XVI," flanked by his two brothers, "bound by the decrees of the rebels [*factieux*]." Mounted on the centaur-like constitution, Robespierre presents the king with "a sponge drenched in bile [*fiel*]" on the end of his lance. To the right of her husband, Marie-Antoinette points to the victims and "demands immediate vengeance," while, in the traditional posture of Mary Magdalene, the duchesse de Polignac embraces the foot of the cross, which is made to resemble the fasces of the Republic. On the far right, the prince de Condé draws his sword from its scabbard to avenge the king. (Musée Carnavalet, Paris, © Photothèque des Musées de la Ville de Paris.)

ther remained, Joan's ashes having been cast into the Seine, while Louis's headless corpse had been promptly dissolved in quicklime lest it survive as a relic for votaries of the royalist cause. Willingly or unwillingly, republicans had to acknowledge the potency of Louis as an *alter Christus*. That was why, for Michelet and others, his execution was such a catastrophe for the Revolution.

But it was, of course, in Catholic-royalist writing that the king's "passion" stirred the most powerful Christological imaginings, and it is to the remarkable Joseph de Maistre (1755–1827) and his scarcely less gifted epigone Pierre-Simon Ballanche (1776–1847) that we must turn in order to grasp the full import of this crucial nineteenth-century French Catholic theme. De Maistre, writing in his *Considérations sur la France* of 1797, had no doubt that 21 January was, as he said, a "catastrophe," but precisely for that reason, it, like its prototype, the first Good Friday, contained within it the potential for resurrection and redemption; like the willed self-sacrifice of Christ, the deaths of Louis and other members of his family bore witness to "an acceptance, capable of saving France." The whole French nation participated in the act of regicide—"never did a greater crime have more accomplices," he writes—and, far from bringing to a close the violence of history as its instigators had intended, "every drop of Louis XVI's will cost torrents of French blood; four million French people, perhaps, will pay with their heads for the great national crime of antireligious and antisocial insurrection, crowned by regicide." Yet the shedding of this blood, like the shedding of the king's blood that precipitated it, will ultimately have a salvific effect. By chastising and killing its king, the French nation has brought retribution and death upon itself, but such are the inscrutable operations of Providence that France and the French monarchy will ultimately emerge purified and renewed from the holocaust to which the regicides condemned it. "The crimes of the tyrants of France became the instruments of Providence"; if Providence "employs the most ignoble instruments, it is because it punishes in order to regenerate," it being the mainspring of de Maistre's soteriological system that "there is no punishment that does not purify." Thus "the horrible effusion of human blood" is "a means as much as a punishment." While "the effusion of blood is never suspended in the universe" and while there is everywhere on view "the wearisome spectacle of the innocent perishing with the guilty," none of this bloodletting is ultimately without beneficial purpose and effect. Invoking, as he and other Catholic or Catholic-influenced writers—Baudelaire and Blanc de Saint-Bonnet, Barbey d'Aurevilly, Léon Bloy, Huysmans, Bernanos—will so often in the cen-

tury and a half to come, the crucial Catholic doctrine of "the reversibility of the sufferings of the innocent to the advantage of the guilty," de
Maistre is able to present the whole of French history since 1789 as a
drama of sacrificial atonement from which ultimately—that word
again—France and its monarchy will be reborn, purged and pruned of
its impurities and excesses.[17]

Like the shameful and wondrous cross, so its modern analogue, the
guillotine; and just as Christ's killers (whom, like his age, de Maistre
identified with the Jews) are, by a truly miraculous reversal, the agents
of mankind's salvation, so Louis's executioner—whose name some writers spelled "Samson" and whom not a few held to be a Jew—will, by a
similar reversal, become the redeemer of both monarchy and nation. By
extension, every capital execution becomes a recapitulation of 21 January, which in its turn reenacted the paradigmatic sacrifice on Calvary; it
further follows that the executioner is a properly sacred figure, *fascinans
et tremendus,* as vital to the proper functioning of the polis as the king
of whom he is both mirror image and antithesis, bringing salvation to
the criminal even as he inflicts suffering and death. In short, the whole
unfolding of revolutionary and postrevolutionary history becomes an illustration of that cosmic principle of redemption through pain, suffering, and death that de Maistre will later sum up in the final terrifying
words of his *Eclaircissements sur les sacrifices* of 1821, which would
echo down the century to come: "LE SALUT PAR LE SANG [salvation
through blood]."[18]

The sacrificial interpretation of the king's execution is pushed still
further in Ballanche's remarkable *L'Homme sans nom,* first published
in a limited edition of a hundred copies in 1820 and reissued in February 1830, a few months before the ritual scapegoating and expulsion of
Louis XVI's successor, Charles X. *L'Homme sans nom* relates the narrator's encounter in 1814 with an anonymous regicide of 1793 who has
withdrawn into an Alpine retreat where, "branded [*flétri*] with the seal
of hatred and horror," he lives cut off from the rest of humanity like "a
plague victim [*un pestiféré*] of the social world, a sort of leper condemned to solitude and opprobrium." "I have become the son of my
crime," he says, "the child of reprobation," and he goes on to describe
how he is treated by local people: as "a sacred being, in the ancients'
sense of the word, namely a being visibly pursued by heavenly wrath."
The execution of the king, to which the "nameless man" was a willing
party, is presented as a reenactment of the atoning death of Christ in
which "the victim, already dressed in the winding cloths of sacrifice
[*toute couverte déjà des bandelettes du sacrifice*]," offers himself up for

the salvation of his people: "Thus the divine Representative of human nature, after having been subjected to the most ignoble treatment, appeared before the people with a crown of thorns and reed in his right hand [*un sceptre de roseau dans la main*]." But in condemning and killing the king, the Convention spread "fateful and delirious contagion." The whole of the French people are party to "this odious confraternity of parricide," for which the nameless regicide holds himself responsible:

> That terrible burden of celestial vengeance, which weighed so long
> on my unhappy homeland, it is I who attracted it. God had to
> punish the nation that became through me the regicidal nation.
> And it is I, great heavens, who am the author of so many ills. It is
> I who created for our beautiful and noble France the appalling
> solidarity of my parricide.

Having participated in the shedding of the king's blood, regicide and nation must now atone for their sin: "People of France, no doubt you had too much to expiate for innocent blood not to be shed for you and in your name!" The execution was nothing less than "the immolation of the father of the nation [*la patrie*]," for which regicides and people are themselves "immolated," either physically of morally. Many die, but "the man of 21 January," the anonymous king murderer, is mysteriously spared in order that he may himself undergo an atoning sacrifice in his Alpine Gethsamene and Calvary; the executioner of yesterday becomes the victim of today.

He is visited by two priests, who tell him that—the principle of reversibility at work again—"Louis XVI, in heaven, has not ceased to be the minister of God's forgiveness," and that, while some regicides were "odious executioners" and others "somber fanatics," others still

> were, without knowing it, kinds of priests or sacrificers for the
> immolation of the expiatory victim. From the height of his un-
> changing throne and above all mutability, God had perhaps con-
> demned the just man for the salvation of the France he loves. Did
> not this god wish that his Son should pay humanity's debt? The
> king ransomed [*a racheté*] France as Jesus Christ ransomed the
> human race.

The priests explain to the nameless man the sense of "the doctrine of solidarity," whereby "the king had to pay the debt of France, and

France, in its turn, had to expiate the judicial murder of its king, who was felled by the same blow that overthrew the ancient institutions." For their part, the two priests must sacrifice themselves in order to lead the regicide to self-sacrificial atonement with God: "[they] dared to descend to the very bottom of the pit [*l'abyme*] into which the regicide had fallen, in order to lose and save themselves with him. They became his accomplice, even as the divine Repairer of human nature made himself sin [*s'était fait péché*]."

They evidently succeeded in their redemptive mission, for the regicide dies within the Church, having continued to live alone, but "like an anchorite, and not like a leper or one excommunicated." In some notes discovered after his death, he speaks of the king's execution as a "holocaust" or "ransom" (*rançon*), and of the king himself as "the mystical victim of a social transformation." His sin, thanks to the mysterious operations of Providence, has become his salvation, as it has become, *in potentia*, the salvation of the entire French nation: "that scaffold which I caused my king to ascend has become the expiatory altar of a new social religion."[19]

While the Christological interpretation of 21 January became a commonplace of nineteenth-century Catholic-royalist writing,[20] permitting hope to be drawn from even the direst of circumstances, the republican version of the sacrificial myth encountered an impassable obstacle, since manifestly the act of violence to end all violence that the execution was projected to be had failed utterly to stanch the flow of French blood both within and without the nation's frontiers. On the contrary, as the most intelligent republican commentators clearly perceived, it was precisely the king's execution that had precipitated the headlong recourse to violence; for, in the words of Edgar Quinet, writing in 1869,

> so long as Louis XVI was alive, the different factions [of the Revolution] concentrated their hatred against him; they at least united to fear and accuse him. When he had disappeared, these same factions could no longer agree on anything; there was no longer a single moment of truce between them, all that remained was for them to destroy each other.[21]

Thus it was that, in the telling image of the Girondin Vergniaud, himself shortly to perish at the hands of the Jacobins, the Revolution began, like Saturn, to devour its own children,[22] or, in de Maistre's less heroic but brutally accurate summation, successive groups of *scélérats* (rogues) killed off the other groups of *scélérats* before being killed off themselves.[23] Having killed the father, the brothers now engaged in fratricidal strife, today's executioners becoming tomorrow's victims, and so inexorably on until, finally, a father substitute from outside the nation proper, the Corsican Napoleon Bonaparte, arrived like some deus ex machina to reimpose order and create his own series of victims before himself suffering victimization, scapegoating, and double expulsion and death. The Republic was, in short, undone by the sacrificial killing that founded it. If Louis's blood did not, as de Maistre and Ballanche would claim, redeem the French nation, it certainly doomed the Republic, as the Girondins said it would, and as the neo-Girondin Lamartine eloquently recognized in 1847:

> Louis XVI's blood was in the treaties that the European powers agreed among themselves to incriminate and stifle the Republic; Louis XVI's blood was in the oil that consecrated Napoleon so little time after the oaths to liberty; Louis XVI's blood was in the monarchical enthusiasm that greeted the return of the Bourbons to France at the Restoration; it was even present in 1830 in the repulsion toward the word "republic," which cast the hesitant nation into the arms of another dynasty. It is republicans who must most lament this blood, for it is on their cause that it has constantly fallen, and it is this blood that cost them the Republic![24]

Here, then, is the principal paradox regarding the botched would-be sacrificial killing of 21 January 1793. If legitimists could hardly commend the execution of the king (but where save in Christ's death is the Christian's salvation?), they could, thanks to the twin doctrines of expiation and reversibility, derive a positive meaning from it. The act that killed the king and founded the Republic had paradoxically renewed and strengthened the monarchy—or at least it seemed to have done so until the Three Glorious Days put an end to the legitimists' aspirations pending their brief and illusory revival in the wake of the bloodbath of May 1871. For republicans, though, there was no such possibility of negating the negation and drawing a positive value from the sacrifice of 21 January. That sacrifice had rebounded disastrously on the sacrificers themselves, whence, in part, the determination of nineteenth-century liberals and republicans to abolish the death penalty for political offenses, an objective achieved within two days of the overthrow of the Bourgeois Monarchy in February 1848: if the first republic constituted itself through the guillotine, the second did so by abolishing it, an act confirmed (and extended to civil as well as political offenses) under the Commune by the public "execution"—by "dismemberment" and burning at the foot of Voltaire's statue on the Rue de la Roquette—of the guillotine itself on 6 April 1871.[25]

If every guillotining conducted in 1793–94 was in some way a re-enactment of the Republic's foundational *mise à mort* of 21 January, then the Jacobin Amar's exhortation to his fellow members of the Convention to "go to the foot of the great altar to see the red mass celebrated" needs to be treated less as a tasteless joke than as a political-anthropological insight of considerable acumen: the scaffold was indeed an altar at which, in a violent and sacrilegious parody of the mass, the revolutionaries "communicated" with each other through the gushing blood of their victim. Likewise the blasphemous litanies *sacrae sanctae Guillotinae*—"Sainte Guillotine, protectress of patriots, pray for us! Sainte Guillotine, scourge of aristocrats, protect us!"—underline the properly cultic significance of the public execution, a ritual of retribution to which the victims, from their very different but nonetheless related ideological position, willingly contributed in their often entirely conscious holocaustal offering of themselves. Many victims, particularly priests and nuns (Abbé Turpin du Cormier, Chanoine Gigot, Sœur Gertrude d'Alausier, among others), actually embraced the guillotine as though it were the True Cross. Marie-Louise Agricourt knelt before the guillotine "to offer herself as a holocaust to God," and more than one priest sang the *Introïbo ad altare Dei* as he walked to the scaffold.[26]

Amid all the talk of hecatombs, holocausts, and Tarpeian rocks (a rhetorical figure favored by Saint-Just in particular),[27] the sacrificial character of the executions themselves is hardly to be doubted. What still astounds is the intensity of what was literally a head count, particularly in the last month of the Terror. Time after time—twenty-six times a day on average during Messidor Year II[28]—a victim was displayed publicly to the fury of the crowd; and while the actual instant of decapitation may have been concealed from the onlookers, the ritual brandishing of the severed head provided a cynosure for their anger and aggression, a momentary focus around which the broken unity of the nation might be vicariously reconstituted. "Blood is needed to cement the Revolution," declared the Girondine Madame Roland (1754–93), little realizing, one assumes, where the logic of her words would lead her.[29] But each execution, far from driving out "bad" violence with "good" and so "cementing the Revolution," merely precipitated further conflicts requiring resolution by bloodshed, leading, by the remorseless logic of sacrifice, to the situation represented in a post-Thermidorean print titled "Robespierre guillotining the executioner after having had everyone in France

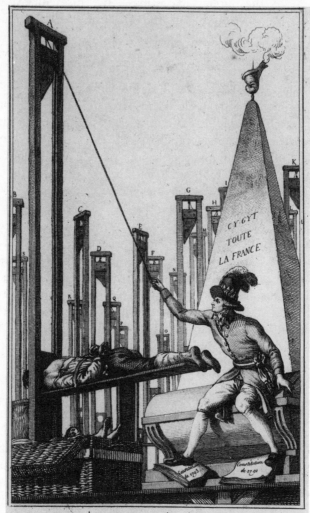

ROBESPIERRE, guillotinant le boureau après avoir fait guillot: tous les Francais

A le Bourreau, B le comité de Salut Public, C le comité de Sureté générale, D le Tribunal Révolution.^{re}
E les Jacobins, F les Cordeliers, G les Brissotins, H Girondins, I Phlipotins, K Chabotins, L Hébertistes,
M les Nobles et les Prêtres, N les Gens à talens, O les Vieillards, Femmes et Enfants, P les Soldats et
les Généraux, Q les Autorités Constituées, R la Convention Nationale, S les Sociétés Populaires.

Robespierre guillotining the executioner after having had the entire French nation guillotined. Each of the guillotines indicates a particular category of victims, among them the Brissotins (B), the Girondins (H), nobles and priests (M), old people, women, and children (O), and popular societies (S). The funerary pyramid bears the words "Here lies the whole of France." Holocaustal smoke emanates from the inverted Phrygian cap at its tip. (Musée Carnavalet, Paris, © Photothèque des Musées de la Ville de Paris.)

guillotined." It is reproduced and described in Simon Schama's *Citizens:* amidst a "monstrous forest" of guillotines, each bearing a letter that designates a particular category of victims, Robespierre is shown about to release the blade onto the executioner's neck, while behind him on top of an obelisk bearing the legend "Cy-gyt toute la France" (Here lies the whole of France) "an inverted liberty bonnet has been spiked through and turned into a chimney of cremation."[30] All that remains is for Robespierre, somewhat in the manner of the officer in Franz Kafka's *In the Penal Colony,* to mount the guillotine in his turn and bring down the blade upon himself, which, in a sense, is what he did, for his conduct during the final months of the Terror suggests a man obsessed with martyrdom and unconsciously willing—and perhaps even consciously collaborating in—his own imminent undoing. Thus at the Fête de l'Être Suprême held on 20 Prairial Year II (8 June 1794), just six weeks before his fall from power and death, Robespierre stood apart from the other members of the Convention, dressed, remarkably, in yellow trousers and blue jacket, exactly the blue-and-yellow "suicide costume" of Goethe's Werther, who so obsessed the late eighteenth century. One historian concluded that Robespierre's "presentation of his public persona attired in his widely understood sign of impending sacrifice carried the message that the Terrorist was to be known as his own victim."[31]

When the end duly came, it was sordid and ignoble in the extreme. Accused, absurdly, of plotting to be king, Robespierre became the monster he had always held his enemies to be and was instantly threatened with the Tarpeian rock to which he and Saint-Just had so often consigned their foes.[32] If a kind of mythical logic commanded that Louis should be arrested by a Citoyen Sauce, one can only wonder at the onomastic appropriateness of Robespierre's captor being none other than a Citoyen Méda or Merda. Excreted, as it were, from the body politic and with his jaw held together by a paper bandage after a botched attempt to blow his brains out, Robespierre was taken along with twenty-one of his fellow monsters to the Place de la Révolution on the morning of 10 Thermidor (28 July 1794), it having been decided that it was here, on the site of Louis's execution—and not at the Place du Trône Renversé, on the eastern periphery of the city, whither executions had recently been transferred—that the would-be king and his courtiers should atone for their sin against the People. Inevitably, it was Sanson who clamped him on the plank and, snatching off the paper bandage lest it prevent the "national razor" from doing its work, activated the mechanism. A common grave on the Monceau plain was the final destiny of the corpses. Equally inevitably, the mythologization, both positive and negative, that was well under way during Robespierre's lifetime gathered momentum after his death. A "new Catiline" to his enemies, Robespierre was to his nineteenth-century neo-Jacobin successors a figure to be set beside "the Galilean" and Rousseau, "three names which march inseparably together and which are deduced logically from one another, like three terms in the same theorem; a holy and sublime trinity which contains the principle of equality and fraternity."[33] Once launched, the Christological paradigm was susceptible of being indefinitely multiplied and transposed.

Of the major emblematic victims of the Terror—Charlotte Corday (executed 17 July 1793, "superb in her long red chemise that the rain caused to cling to her body" as, unconstrained, she placed her neck in the lunette of the guillotine "with that seemly and voluptuous abandonment of self that transcends beauty");[34] Marie-Antoinette (16 October); the early feminist and Girondine Olympe de Gouges, author of a searing *Déclaration des droits de la femme et de la citoyenne* (1791), dedicated to Marie-Antoinette (executed 3 November 1793); Madame Roland (8 November); Barnave (29 November); Jacques-René Hébert (24 March 1794); Georges-Jacques Danton and Camille Desmoulins (5 April); Mesdames Hébert and Desmoulins (both executed essentially for being the widows of proscribed "monsters," on 10 and 13 April respectively)—only Marie-Antoinette requires close attention here in her characteristically double aspect as monster and martyr.[35] Much of the most interesting recent writing on Marie-Antoinette has focused less on the queen herself than on the way in which, virtually from the moment she arrived in France in 1770 as the bride of the future Louis XVI, she was almost systematically constructed as "other" by French public opinion: first in the gutter press and pornographic literature of the 1770s and 1780s and then, after the outbreak of revolution, in newspaper articles, political pamphlets, caricatures, and speeches in the National Assembly, the whole scabrous campaign culminating in the speeches made against her at her trial in October 1793.[36]

Not only was Marie-Antoinette other in her nationality, she was also held to be radically other in her sexual tastes. After having been deflowered, it was claimed, by her brother, the future Joseph II, she had, after marriage, rendered the dauphin impotent through the exorbitance of her sexual demands; engaged in threesomes with her brother-in-law, the duc d'Artois, and the princesse de Polignac; had a passionate lesbian relationship with the princesse de Lamballe; enjoyed sex with practically every footman and chambermaid at Versailles, not to mention an assortment of animals at Trianon; and initiated her son, whose possible survival would so exercise nineteenth-century French legitimists, into the more recherché techniques of autoeroticism. What was being denigrated, marginalized, and eventually suppressed through the scapegoating and finally the execution of Marie-Antoinette was, it is now commonly argued, not just the monarchy or the ancien régime but the female sex and female sexuality, a more than plausible case given the close correlation between the execution of Marie-Antoinette, the executions of Madame Roland and Olympe de Gouges, and the wholesale suppression of women's political clubs and other organizations, all of which took place in October–November 1793.[37]

In the eyes of her enemies, then, Marie-Antoinette was quite simply a monster whom it was necessary to cast out of the polis in order that it be ritually cleansed and the Republic installed in all its purity. Yet the logic of sacrificial violence is such that, a monster in the eyes of the monarch's enemies, Marie-Antoinette necessarily and automatically became a martyr in the eyes of its friends and, in royalist discourse, passed overnight from the status of scapegoat to that of secular saint. Her late husband was already, of course, undergoing similar beatification, but the would-be cult of the new "Saint Louis" had its limits, so egregiously bereft was he of true martyrological charisma, and as the nineteenth century advanced it was more and more his doomed wife, Marie-Antoinette, who took his place as the sacrificial victim par excellence. Thus we find legitimist works such as Henri Monier de la Sizeranne's "poème historique" *Marie-Antoinette* of 1860 talking routinely of the queen's "Calvary," [38] and the abbé Mourot's three-act drama *Marie-Antoinette, ou Les Sourires et les tristesses d'une reine* of 1889 stressing that king and queen alike have been "mysteriously chosen for the holocaust."[39] The theme of Marie-Antoinette as exemplary martyr was still alive and well in 1955 when the great French orientalist Louis Massignon (1883–1962) published his *Un vœu et un destin: Marie-Antoinette, reine de France,* in which he speaks of her death, remarkably, as "a heroic and self-conscious appropriation of the sacred, expiating the crisis of the collectivity [*une prise de conscience héroïque du sacré, expiatrice de la crise collective*]."[40] A recent browse among the right-wing Catholic pamphlets on sale in and around the Eglise Saint-Nicolas-du-Chardonnet on the Boulevard Saint-Germain after full Tridentine Latin mass on Sundays suggests that this well-worn Catholic-royalist topos, like the parallel campaign for the canonization of Louis XVI, enjoys continued vitality among a not inconsiderable ultrarightist constituency.

Few of the works that advance the myth of Marie-Antoinette as exemplary victim can be said to possess anything more than circumstantial interest, and their literary quality is, with one exception, negligible. That exception was Léon Bloy's remarkable essay "La Chevalière de la Mort," written in 1877, the year the legitimist cause finally collapsed in France, but not published until 1891 in a suitably obscure Belgian review. It was Bloy's first literary effort, and it sets the tone for the whole of his subsequent output: utterly wrongheaded and excessive, irredeemably over the top in everything it advances, interspersing passages of extraordinary poetic beauty with page upon page of apoplectic calumny and polemic. Bloy was some kind of royalist, but he was a Catholic before all else, having nothing but contempt for "the Bourbons through whom great Catholic France was killed,"[41] and especially for Louis XVI, whom he memorably (if untranslatably) describes as "the pneumatic automatic royal Nothing, a killer of swallows, and locksmith; capable at best of thrashing small dogs with his cane and of laughing at this prank, inexhaustibly; an excellent subject for the guillotine and an invaluable treasure for the diptychs of the martyrology of the imbeciles."[42] It was in part this contempt for Louis XVI that led Bloy to apotheosize Marie-Antoinette and, still more improbably, to follow the ultraroyalist lunatic fringe in elevating Charles Naundorff, the purported Louis XVII, to the status of exemplary victim whom "it had pleased God to crush in a mortar in expiation of the crimes of his race," a "monster of misfortune" who, having spent his life fleeing from country to country like some "Cain vomited forth by each and every people," eventually died—poisoned by his enemies, Bloy believed—in Holland in 1845, "when he had finished carrying the penitence of sixty kings." For Bloy, and for a whole school of ultraroyalist thought, Naundorff was nothing less than a prefiguration of the Second Coming of Christ.[43]

Bloy denies any such sacral significance to Marie-Antoinette—she was, he says, not "a saint and her sufferings bear no mark of the supernatural"[44]—but he presents the whole of her life, from her birth on the Day of the Dead 1755 until her death by guillotine on 16 October 1793, as one of virtually uninterrupted suffering. Her woes make her the "archduchess of the Holy Empire of the Seven Sorrows," virtually on a par with Saint Veronica and Mary Magdalene, even with the Mater Dolorosa herself. For Bloy, Marie-Antoinette is the victim of victims, singled out by the Revolution in the person of its Caiphas, Antoine-Quentin Fouquier-Tinville, that "retiary of innocence," not just for death but for ritual humiliation and debasement. What appalls and fascinates Bloy is the "savage hostility of a whole people against a dying woman." At both her trial and her execution, she is exposed, "a solitary soul, abandoned, perhaps as never soul was before," exposed "in full sunlight and before an entire people that demands to be fortified with the spectacle of this expiatory ritual [*cette fête expiatoire*]. Expedit UNAM mori pro populo." The Christological reference—presaged in the parallel between Marie-Antoinette's "I am thirsty" at her trial and Jesus' "I thirst" on the cross—is obvious, intended, and, like so much else in the text, teetering on the brink of blasphemy.

All this leads up to, and culminates in, Marie-Antoinette's transfiguration on the scaffold. Unlike her husband, who, says Bloy, needed his confessor to tell him of his victim's role, the queen knew instinctively "that she is the royal scapegoat [*la Reine émissaire*] for all the sins of the Race of Saint Louis and that on the shameful moving plank [*bascule*] of the guillotine, she is bringing to the glory of Paradise [*elle enfante à la gloire du Paradis*] all the ancestors of her spouse." Finally, the identification of queen and Saviour is total and explicit:

> But when perfect ignominy is added to supreme suffering; when universal contempt, in its most fearful form, comes to dishonor punishment, the human sublime is transfigured and raised to a new empyrean. The Poetry of blood and tears is then revealed, stripped of its rhetoric and veils, bereft of its terrible blindfold. It is the supernatural poetry of the Saviour's Passion.

Even the queen's enemies felt that she was transfigured by her death. She may have been a pig, wrote one semiliterate provincial revolutionary to his local committee, but she died "as beautifully as one of Godille's pigs, our local pork butcher [*charcutier*], she went to The sca fold [*Le cha fau*] with incredible courage. She crossed almost the whole of Paris, looking down on people with contempt and Disdain. The bitch [*la coquine*] had guts right up to The Sca Fold [*Le Cha Fau*] without Flinching."[45]

Thanks to the more or less continuous performances of the "red theater" on the Place de la Révolution and elsewhere in 1793–94, the severed head rapidly became the supreme iconic image of the Revolution and continued to haunt the French imagination for well over a century; perhaps it still does. A rich body of folklore and *bons mots* swiftly accrued—the cheeks of Charlotte Corday's severed head reputedly blushed when slapped by an irate supporter of Marat, and Danton, having been prevented by Sanson from embracing Hérault de Séchelles at the scaffold, told the executioner that their heads would nonetheless kiss in the basket [*tu n'empêcheras pas nos têtes de se baiser dans le panier*] and that he should show his severed head to the public "because it was well worth it" [*tu montreras ma tête au peuple; elle en vaut la peine*].[46]

Sick humor flourished in fashionable and unfashionable circles as never before. There were miniature guillotines for slicing bread and fruit at the dinner table, and dolls resembling one's enemies could be decapitated over dessert, disgorging a red liquid into which ladies present would dip handkerchiefs. At so-called victims' balls, attended by close relatives of those who had undergone "national shortening" (*raccourcissement national*), both men and women wore their hair cropped or tied up *à la victime,* with thin red ribbons or threads around their necks to simulate the mark of the blade.[47] A voluminous medical and philosophical literature lasting well into the next century debated whether the severed head felt pain,[48] and from 1789 onward the severed head was a favorite motif of cartoonists and fine artists alike. At the very outbreak of revolution, Anne-Louis Girodet made a memorable sketch of the heads of Bertier de Sauvigny and Foulon, the latter complete with tufts of straw sticking out of his mouth, and there is no more riveting revolutionary icon than Villeneuve's 1793 engraving of Louis's severed head being held by the hair as "food for thought for crowned charlatans" *(matière à réflection pour les jongleurs couronnées)* to digest. Shortly after the fall of Napoleon, Théodore Géricault—who would remain haunted by the public hangings he saw and sketched in London—painted a series of severed heads and other limbs that "shockingly [combine] the cool, clinical observation of the dissecting table with the paroxysm of romantic melodrama,"[49] while Hugo's remarkable graphic work includes many guillotines and guillotinings, not least the stunning *Iustitia* of 1857, in which a screaming severed head has literally been launched into space by the force of the blow that has been dealt to it.

All of these images owe something to the traditional motif of the Medusa's head, and, like that motif, all no doubt relate to fears of castration[50]—not for nothing was the guillotine known as "la Veuve" (the Widow)—but all likewise gain resonance from their obvious historical contexts. Perhaps, indeed, the head of Edouard Manet's Olympia owes something of its power to haunt to the black ribbon that neatly divides it from her body; and the fin-de-siècle obsession with the linked figures of Judith and Holofernes, Samson and Delilah, and Salome and Jokanaan (variously treated by Gustave Flaubert, Stéphane Mallarmé, Joris-Karl Huysmans, Jules Laforgue, and Gustave Moreau, as well as by Oscar Wilde and Richard Strauss), while it plainly articulates a whole mass of male obsessions in the face of a rampant or revengeful femininity, also reactivates the motif of ritual decapitation that inaugurates the modern

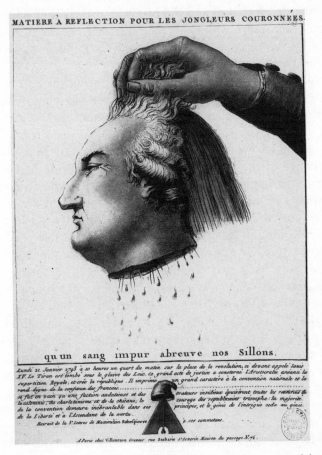

Something for crowned charlatans to think about. In Villeneuve's celebrated engraving the severed head of Louis XVI is held up for the derision of "the people." Citing the "Marseillaise," the engraving depicts the king's "impure blood" fertilizing the nation's fields, while at the bottom the Phrygian cap sits atop the square base (*équerre*) of republican equality. (Musée Carnavalet, Paris, © Photothèque des Musées de la Ville de Paris.)

history of France.[51] And finally, as Alain Brossat has argued in *Les Tondues* (1992), the ritual cropping and shaving in 1944–45 of the heads of French women held to have German lovers was a kind of "burlesque parody" of the *guillotinade*, a "gentle decapitation" (*décapitation douce*) in which the fallen hair becomes a metonymy for the severed head, and the whole "ugly carnival" (*carnival moche*) of revenge "a pseudo-Terror that paraphrases the spectacle of the scaffold, but minus the descent of the blade."[52] Framed at one end by the ritual beheadings of de Launay, de Flesselles, and the rest and at the other by the mock guillotining of the shorn women, French history from the Revolution to the Liberation is indeed a headless history, its emblem the Medusa's head, its muse an acephalous Clio.

The eponymously renamed Place de la Révolution had originally been called the Place Louis XV when it had been inaugurated in 1763 with the unveiling of Bouchardon's bronze equestrian statue of that king, and almost from the outset its history had been tragic. On 30 May 1770 a huge fireworks display held on the square to celebrate the recent marriage of the dauphin and his Austrian bride had caused a fire, which in turn unleashed a panic among the crowd and resulted in no fewer than 133 deaths. Hugo seemed to recall this disaster, as well as the later double execution of the royal pair, in a poem of April 1839, "En passant dans la place Louis XV un jour de fête publique."[53] The statue of Louis XV was removed and melted down in August 1792 (when the square itself was renamed), its replacement being Lemot's massive plaster-and-masonry statue of Liberty, to which Madame Roland reputedly addressed her celebrated dying apostophe in November 1793: "Liberty, Liberty, what crimes are committed in thy name!" By the following year, Lemot's statue was as warped and cracked as the cause of liberty itself, and was temporarily replaced by a fasces of eighty-three rods (one per department) with a massive Tricolor flying at its center, which survived five years before giving way to another statue of Liberty, this time with a globe containing a nestful of live turtledoves in her hand. This was too much for Napoleon; in 1800 he ordered its removal, proposing in its stead a "national column" that failed to materialize, then a statue of Charlemagne (1806, also abandoned), and finally the ultimate uncontroversial standby, a fountain (1811). Clearly it was no easy matter to decorate the largest square in central Paris and at the same time conceal its significance as the site where God's representative on earth had been decapitated by his former subjects.

Returning to Paris in 1800 after ten years of almost continuous exile in America and Britain, that connoisseur of severed heads, Chateaubriand, had cause to cross what had by then been renamed the Place de la Concorde and was amazed to find it lined on its western edge by a group of open-air dance halls (bastringues), where couples were dancing to the music of violins, clarinets, horns, and drums. "As for the Place Louis XV," he continues, still giving the square its original name, as well a convinced royalist might do, it was bare; it had the dilapidation, the melancholic, abandoned aspect of an old amphitheater; people passed by quickly; I was staggered not to hear cries of woe [*des plaintes*]; I was afraid of putting my foot in blood of which not the slightest trace remained; my eyes could not detach themselves from the part of the sky where the instrument of death had risen up; I had the feeling of seeing my brother and my sister-in-law, clad in their shirts, bound close to the bloody machine; it was there that the head of Louis XVI had fallen. Despite the joys of the street, the church towers were silent; I felt I had returned on the day of the greatest of sorrows, on Good Friday itself.[54]

On *his* return from exile in 1814, the restored Louis XVIII decided provocatively to rename the square the Place Louis XVI and planned to commemorate his executed brother by repaving part of it in black marble and constructing an "expiatory chapel," complete with weeping willows, at its center. Nothing came of this plan,[55] and in 1826 his successor, Charles X, laid the first pedestal stone of a projected statue of Louis XVI, which likewise failed to materialize. In 1828, presumably in an attempt to assuage liberal hostility, the name reverted to Place Louis XV. In 1830, on his accession to the throne, Louis-Philippe, anxious to avoid controversy at all costs (and to conceal the origins of his own power in revolutionary violence), resorted to the fail-safe, catch-all name of Place de la Concorde as a sign of the new regime's desire to placate, blur, and defuse all the competing ideological strands in the country.

The disjunction of form and content that was everywhere present in *juste-milieu* architecture in general was nowhere more evident than in the "embellishment" of the Place de la Concorde carried out under the Bourgeois Monarchy. Writing in 1838, Gérard de Nerval denounced the way in which "le Louis-Philippe" had been crudely superimposed on "le Louis XV" without the two stylistic layers being in any way harmonized; the statues that were supposedly to symbolize the various cities of France were, to all intents and purposes, interchangeable in their neoclassical sameness, while the columns surrounding the square appeared to have been designed to serve indifferently as boundary marks, candelabra, fountains, triumphal pillars, or rostra: "that which has so many uses," Nerval commented acidly, "is normally of no use whatsoever."

It was the erection, in 1836, of the obelisk of Luxor, dating from the reign of Rameses II (thirteenth century B.C.) and donated by Mehemet Ali to Louis-Philippe in 1831, on the still unoccupied pedestal of the statue of Louis XVI, that epitomized for many observers the internal contradictions, timid eclecticism, and ideological hollowness of the Bourgeois Monarchy. Perhaps for the first time in history a public monument was deliberately selected for its very meaninglessness, because, Louis-Philippe told his prefect of Paris, "it will recall no political event and because it is sure to remain there whereas you might one day see there an expiatory monument or statue of Liberty."[56] For Pierre-Joseph Proudhon, writing in 1865, the obelisk, together with the Pantheon and the Madeleine, symbolized a whole culture in which signs had become detached from what they signified, in which grandiose surfaces concealed an underlying void. The art and architecture of modern Paris was simply so much bric-a-brac, now "meaning" one thing, now another: "Taken as a whole, our monuments denote a people whose conscience is empty and whose sense of nationality is dead. We have nothing in our minds, neither law, morality, philosophy, nor economic sense, only sham, pure arbitrariness, error, disguise, mendacity, and the cult of pleasure."[57]

It is this sense of hollowness, futility, and ideological obfuscation that Edgar Degas brilliantly captures in his painting La Place de la Concorde of 1875, long thought to have been lost or destroyed but now resurfaced in Russia. A well-dressed, top-hatted, bearded gentleman, cane under arm and cigar jutting aggressively from his lips, crosses an empty, hyposignificant space in the company of two little girls and a dog; all are looking in separate directions out of the painting into yet further vacant space, while on the left-hand margin, his body sliced through by the frame, another well-dressed gentleman, almost identical to the first, looks past rather than at the principal group toward the center of the canvas. The full title of the painting tells us that the main adult figure is Ludovic Lepic and that the girls are his daughters; he transpires to be none other than the vicomte Ludovic-Napoléon Lepic, son of an aide-de-camp of the first Napoleon, who, in a fit of misplaced Bonapartist fervor, bestowed the name of Eylau, a celebrated Napoleonic victory of 1807, on one of his daughters. In his superb analysis of the painting, Albert Boime has shown how Lepic's top hat screens out the female statue representing Strasbourg in the top left-hand corner of the painting; it is a significant "eclipse," for in 1875 the statue in question was still veiled in crêpe in mourning for the surrender of Alsace-Lorraine to the Prussians in 1871.[58] The Lepics are a (motherless?) family of Bonapartists, defeated, disoriented, and adrift in a quasi-republic that is still in its birth throes, divided between a resurgent monarchist right and an uncertain moderate center-left. The far left (who had celebrated the declaration of the Commune with a huge *fête nocturne* on the Place de la Concorde and had built a massive barricade there to defend it) are dead, imprisoned, or exiled, their memory repressed, and even the official injunction regarding the loss of Alsace-Lorraine—"never speak of it, always think of it"—seems to have been floated by the Bonapartist relics before us. The painting evokes less a sense of impending chaos (as Boime argues) than indirection, aimlessness, amnesia, entropy: the death of the king has been forgotten along with everything else, the very center of the pseudo-republic has no center, and those who momentarily converge there only to diverge immediately thereafter are not active citizens but merely inhabitants of the city, effectively anonymous even when they sport such egregious forenames as Ludovic-Napoléon and, absurdly, Eylau.

Only once in the subsequent history of the Third Republic did the Place de la Concorde belie its name and explode into violence, on the evening of 6 February 1934, and then in a manner that, briefly and very incompletely, called into question the very survival of the regime. The crisis was crystallized—as the political crises of the Third Republic so often were—in an emblematic scapegoat figure, in this instance Alexandre Stavisky, a racketeer and naturalized French citizen of Jewish Ukrainian origin whose death—allegedly by his own hand—on 8 January 1934 in a chalet near Chamonix acted as a focus for all the antirepublican hatreds that had been mounting in certain sections of French opinion, most notably among disaffected war veterans, since the Wall Street crash of 1929, and whose roots go back to the 1880s and 1890s in the form of Boulangism, anti-Dreyfusism, and the ultraroyalism of Action Française.[59] As a Jew with links to prominent republican politicians (often Freemasons) who time and again had kept him out of prison, Stavisky was a symbol par excellence of *la gueuse* (the slut) that Marianne had become in the eyes of the ultraright. He also had links to the right-wing prefect of police, Jean Chiappe, and it was the latter's dismissal by the centrist government of Edouard Daladier that precipitated the crisis that briefly challenged the existence of the Republic.

On the evening of 6 February, as a result of semicoordinated action that stopped well short of a concerted plot and far from an attempted coup d'état, right-wing militants of the Action Française, the Croix-du-feu, the Jeunesses Patriotes, Solidarité Française, and the Francistes gathered on and around the Place de la Concorde, planning to cross the Seine by the Pont de la Concorde and put direct physical pressure on the deputies assembled in the Palais Bourbon, on the Left Bank opposite. Confronted by a combined force of gendarmes, *gardes républicains,* and firemen, the rioters set fire to vehicles, used razors to slash the legs of the horses of mounted police, or strewed marbles and ball bearings in their path. An assortment of cudgels, knives, razors, improvised spears, and firearms came into action, prompting the forces of order to retaliate with gunfire. Fourteen civilians, only seven of them actual members of ultraright groupings, were killed as against one paramilitary, and almost 1,500 participants on both sides were treated for wounds. It was the gravest instance of civil disorder in central Paris since the Commune, and though the crossing to the Palais Bourbon was never effected, Daladier resigned on the morning of 7 February, the first prime minister of the Third Republic to do so as a direct result of actual or threatened street violence.

On the 12th, the left responded by calling a widely observed general strike, and in the massive demonstrations that day Socialists and Communists marched together for the first time since they split at the Congrès de Tours in 1920, creating the initial entente that would evolve into the formation of the Popular Front in 1935 and, beyond that, into the united left electoral victory of May 1936 as a counter to the threat of fascism both at home and abroad.[60]

The importance of 6 February for our purpose is not just that a number of French Catholics were involved in it either as active participants or as passionate spectators on one side or the other (such as the group of intellectuals associated with the journal *Esprit,* founded by Emmanuel Mounier [1905–50], who, though appalled by the "established disorder" of existing society, nonetheless opposed the solutions put forward by the far right),[61] but rather that the riots contributed their stock of martyrs, this time on the right, to the increasingly potent holocaustal interpretation of political conflict in France. In his *Notre Avant-guerre* of 1941 the fascist intellectual Robert Brasillach (1909–45) wrote that, for him and his comrades, 6 February was an "instinctive and magnificent revolt," "a night of sacrifice" that "remains in our memories with its smell, its cold wind, its pale running figures, its human groups along the pavements, its invincible hope of a national Revolution, the exact birth of the national socialism of our country," and, as such, worthy of the most solemn commemoration: "Every year we take violets to the Place de la Concorde, before that fountain that has become a cenotaph (an ever more empty cenotaph), in memory of the twenty-two [*sic*] dead."[62]

Still more remarkable is the reaction of the eponymous hero of the autobiographical novel *Gilles* (1939), by the best known of all French fascist writers, Pierre Drieu La Rochelle (1893–1945). Though never quite so involved in events as he would have liked (or claims) to be,

Gilles feels "transfigured" by the cathartic experience of 6 February, during which it seems that he is pressed in on all sides by the "divine couple, back at last, of Fear and Courage, the couple that presides over war." It is as though he were back at the front, at Verdun, as he sprints over to the obelisk and beyond: "He was alone. A woman astray on the asphalt called to him as though she were his mistress, took several steps toward him, stopped, stepped back, abandoned him." Alone now in a world of men, Gilles sees the government forces deployed on the Pont de la Concorde, sees the burning vehicles, the phalanges of veterans all waving their flags. He is swept up in a "whirlwind, now tight, now loose, spurting forth, drawing back, alternately heaped up and lost," until finally, exhausted, he finds a spot on the pavement "not occupied by a fallen body" on which to sit down and rest. And that is all, though it does not stop him from telling his friend and mentor Clérences the next day that it was the first time he had felt alive in twenty years. "You lost your head," retorts Clérences, at which Gilles explodes: "Too true, I lost it. And I'm proud of it. At last I lost my head, I offer it up to be cut off [*je la donne à couper*]. That's what I was dying of for twenty years: not knowing where and what to stick my head out for [*ne savoir où donner de la tête*]."[63]

And indeed, beginning in February 1934 on the site of the king's decapitation, Drieu did "offer up his head" for the cause of fascism in France, "coming out" with the publication of *Socialisme fasciste* that year, joining Jacques Doriot's Parti Populaire Français as principal theorist in 1936 and advocating out-and-out collaboration with Nazi Germany while editor of the *Nouvelle Revue française* from 1940 to 1943. When, after several characteristically botched attempts, he finally managed to commit suicide on 15 March 1945, there were those on the left, not least Sartre, who admired the "authenticity" of his "commitment" and "sacrificial" death: "He made a mistake, but he was sincere, he has proved it."[64]

Similarly, Brasillach's open espousal of the fascist cause took him before the firing squad in 1945, and the Catholic deputy Philippe Henriot graduated from orchestrating the parliamentary outrage at the Stavisky affair to joining the Milice in the last months of the war, being shot by the resistance on 28 June 1944 for his part in the killing of the former (Jewish) minister of the Popular Front, Jean Zay, his death being in its turn avenged by the killing, a few days later, of another Socialist ex-minister, also Jewish, Georges Mandel.[65] In a very real sense, both the outer reaches of collaboration and the expiatory settling of accounts before and after the Liberation were an exfoliation of the sacrificial logic contained *in nuce* in the events of 6 February 1934, themselves a distant consequence of the primal sacrifice performed on the same site on 21 January 1793.

It is not known whether Georges Bataille (1897–1962) was present on or around the Place de la Concorde on the evening of 6 February, not as a participant (though with him, as with so many French intellectuals between the wars—Drieu, André Malraux, Louis-Ferdinand Céline, Georges Bernanos—the distance between ultraleft and ultraright often seems thin in the extreme) but as a seeker after expressions of the sacred in contemporary life, be it in eroticism, bullfighting, or the violence of crowds. A former Catholic, Bataille had abandoned thoughts of a monastic vocation in the early 1920s, published a pornographic novel of extraordinary violence titled *Histoire de l'œil* in 1928 (the novel recounts the torture and murder of a Spanish priest on the altar of his church and culminates in the narrator's female accomplice removing one of his eyes and inserting it in the lips of her vulva), collaborated on the dissident Surrealist review *Documents* in the late 1920s and on the Trotskyist *Critique sociale* and *Contre-Attaque* in the early 1930s, all the time leading a respectable professional existence as a specialist in numismatics at the Bibliothèque Nationale.

Ever since witnessing the goring to death of the torero Manuelo Granero while in Spain in 1922, Bataille had been obsessed with the theme of violent death, to which he had already been exposed on a day-to-day basis as a youth through the appalling sufferings of his blind, syphilitic, and intermittently deranged father, Joseph-Aristide Bataille, who would eventually die, alone and abandoned by his family, in the bomb-stricken Reims of November 1915. This obsession was given a still sharper focus by Bataille's discovery, in 1925, of a photograph of a young Chinese man undergoing the so-called death of a hundred cuts (in effect human vivisection), hoisted and tethered on a stake, with a look of ecstasy, combining and transcending the extremes of agony and pleasure, as in some ultimate mystical orgasm, transfiguring his face. "That photo played a decisive role in my life," Bataille later said; he always kept it with him, and the whole of his subsequent life may be interpreted as a quest, even a craving, for that state of sacred ecstasy, beyond good and evil, beyond life and death, that he saw imprinted on the face of the martyred Fou-Tchou-Li. [66]

In April–May 1936 Bataille and the Surrealist painter André Masson jointly founded the review *Acéphale,* which was to serve as a (semi)respectable front for a secret society of the same name that enjoyed a shadowy and erratic existence almost up until the outbreak of war in

September 1939. The society included, at one time or another, the anthropologist Roger Caillois (1913–78), author of the seminal *Le Mythe et l'homme* (1938) and *L'Homme et le sacré* (1939); the Hegelian and later Christian philosopher Jean Wahl (1888–1974); the novelist and essayist Pierre Klossowski (born 1905), author of the well-known study *Sade, mon prochain* (1947); the English Surrealist artist Patrick Waldberg (and possibly his wife, Isabelle); Bataille's companion, Colette Peignot (1903–38), better know as Laure; and the Martinique-born philosopher and sociologist Jules Monnerot, whose intellectual and political trajectory would take him from Marxism, Surrealism, and anti-imperialism in the 1930s to militant anticommunism in the 1950s and 1960s and finally to membership in Jean Le Pen's Front National in the 1980s, where he remained, a man of color, as philosopher in residence until he apparently split with Le Pen in the mid-1990s.

According to Caillois's later testimony, Bataille actually wanted to perform a human sacrifice in order to bring this disparate band of rebels together as a kind of godless monastic order dedicated to what, in a famous article published in the review's last number (June 1939), he called "the practice of joy in the presence of death" (*la pratique de la joie devant la mort*), and there are reports of unspecified "rites," presumably stopping short of any actual killing, around a lightning-blasted tree in the forest of Saint-Nom-la-Bretèche in the vicinity of Saint-Germain-en-Laye, to the west of Paris, where Bataille and Laure were living at the time.[67] Bataille later said that he felt called upon, "at least in a paradoxical form," to found a new religion, a religion without God, dedicated to the ecstatic experience, beyond all considerations of good and evil, life and death, of the "sacred" or the "impossible," which was more likely to be experienced in such famous brothels as the One-Two-Two on the Rue de Provence and the Sphinx on the Boulevard Edgar-Quinet in Montparnasse than in the church or temple of any recognized religion. "I am GOD," proclaims Madame Edwarda in the novel of that name (1941) as she opens her labia (which Bataille archly calls her *guenilles*, her "rags") to the ecstatic horror of the narrator.[68] For Bataille, Eros and Thanatos are not so much opposed as inseparable.

It was, of course, no accident that Bataille's sacrificial obsessions came to crystallize around the Place de la Concorde, site of the passion of the divinely consecrated king of France—not for nothing did Bataille hail from Reims, the *ville du sacre*—and of his queen, who, as it happened (not that for the author of *Ma mère* [1954–55] anything ever merely "happened"), bore the same name as his own mother, Marie-Antoinette Bataille. The *Acéphale* group reputedly commemorated

Louis's beheading by forgathering, each 21 January in the late 1930s, on the Place de la Concorde—not, as some legitimist groupuscule might have done, to deplore but to applaud it, it being a key element of Bataille's anticredo that "the head, conscious authority [or the authority of consciousness] or God, represents one of the *servile functions* that constitutes itself as an end in itself [*qui se donne et se prend elle-même pour une fin*], and must consequently be the object of the liveliest aversion."[69] Only when God, king, and man have all alike been "decephalized" will man be able to realize to the full his sacred, superhuman potential; whence André Masson's dramatic logo for the review and the godless *Bruderbund* it fronted: a headless man with a skull for a phallus, holding what seems to be a flaming Sacred Heart in his extended right hand and a sacrificial dagger in his left.[70]

It is this desire to out-Nietzsche Nietzsche (and, correlatively, to outfascism fascism) that emerges from Bataille's article "L'Obélisque," published in *Mesures* in April 1938. For Bataille, the Place de la Concorde might better be named the Place de la Mort de Dieu, for it was here that the negative sacrament of killing the divinely appointed king was first accomplished,[71] and here, in consequence, that the prophecy of Nietzsche's madman was first symbolically fulfilled. Yet paradoxically the site of the killing of the divine father substitute is marked by an obelisk, which, says Bataille, is traditionally "the purest image of the head [or leader, chief] and of heaven"; in ancient Egypt it "was to the armed sovereignty of the Pharaoh what the pyramid was to his desiccated remains. It was the surest and most durable obstacle to the agitated passing away of everything." But, wrenched from the contexts of power and belief that first sustained it, transported and remounted in the center of a far-off city with wholly different foundational beliefs, the obelisk of Luxor merely underlines through its very incongruity the eclipse of the transcendent in the modern European world: "the very stone that had once tried to fix the limits of the storms is only the marker [*jalon*] indicating the immensity of a catastrophe that nothing can sustain any longer. A sense of an explosion to come, a vertiginous feeling of lightness well up before an imperious, heavy obelisk." Erected in the 1830s by a fearful regime committed to the golden mean, the obelisk has for a hundred years been the "measured navel of the land of measure" (*le nombril mesuré du pays de la mesure*), concealing and repressing the sacred depths, above all the sacred blood, beneath, its function being precisely to deny the violence of history it once affirmed: "Rarely was an operation of this kind more successful: the apparently meaningless image imposed its calm grandeur and pacifying power upon the very places where memory threatened to recall the worst.[72]

But, as the 1930s draw toward their close, and particularly, perhaps, since the night of 6 February 1934, there are signs, as the war clouds gather, that the obelisk is failing in its repressive task, and that the sacred depths are once more about to be revealed. The sheer absurdity of the obelisk, a symbol and agent of desacralization, betrays the need to resacralize reality and, above all, to resacralize man by freeing him from his head, as Louis XVI was freed of his on 21 January 1793, so that his repressed divinity may be released. As the outline of the scaffold looms up behind the obelisk, it is not difficult to see where Bataille's thought is heading: "The time of ecstasy [le temps extatique] can be found only in the vision of things that puerile chance abruptly brings about: corpses, naked bodies, explosions, the shedding of blood, abysses, bursts of sunlight and of thunder."[73]

Scarcely two years after the publication of "L'Obélisque," France would learn all too pertinently what Acéphale's brand of fascism might involve,[74] but by then Masson had fled, via Martinique, to the United States, Caillois had left for Latin America, and Bataille, exempted from military service on health grounds, withdrew in 1943 to Vézelay, where he appears to have played no significant part, either in deed or in word, in the mounting opposition to the occupiers and their Vichyist allies.[75] Many of the latter dated the crisis of authority in France (as they saw it) from what happened on the Place de la Révolution on the morning of 21 January 1793. Perhaps some of them also appreciated the symmetry, if not the irony, of history in the fact that it was in a hotel, the Majestic, overlooking the same square (since hopefully renamed Concorde in order to obscure the ideological cleavages that had rent France ever after), that in 1940 the victorious Germans established the headquarters from which they extended their grip over the nation for four years.

4

VENDÔME/INVALIDES
The Paris of the Bonapartes
(1802–1871)

On 18 April 1802—Easter Sunday—a solemn Te Deum was celebrated at Notre-Dame to mark the signing of the concordat that officially closed the rift between the French nation and the Holy See. The conflict, which had sprung from the Civil Constitution of the Clergy in 1791, had been exacerbated during the systematic dechristianization campaign of 1793–94 before subsiding somewhat in the second half of the 1790s with the installation of first the Directorate and then, after Napoleon's coup d'état of 18 Brumaire Year VIII (9 November 1799), of the Consulate. The Te Deum marked the final restoration of the cathedral—secularized in 1793 and partially returned to religious uses after 1799—to full Church control, in honor of which the complete text of Louis XIII's self-consecration of 1638 to Our Lady (the so-called *Vœu de Louis XIII*) was returned to its former place before the high altar; the royal statues that had been removed and sometimes ritually "guillotined" in 1793, however, remained conspicuous by their absence.

Into the cathedral filed the dignitaries of the Consulate—the three consuls (with Napoleon as first consul clearly at their head), members of the Council of State, Senate, court, and legislature, plus, of course, the generals—to be *followed* by the archbishops and bishops of the nation, who in due course clasped hands with the first consul in solemn token of their allegiance to the state. Nothing could demonstrate more clearly the primacy that the state, in the person of Napoleon, would henceforth enjoy over the Church. As we have seen, the Concordat declared Roman Catholicism to be the religion of "the majority of the French people" (and not, as the papal negotiator, Consalvi, had sought, to be the national religion) and effectively subordinated Church affairs in their entirety to state control. Henceforth Napoleon would speak interchangeably of "my prefects, my bishops, my police force."[1]

The new arrangement, sanctioned under duress by Pope Pius VII and subsequently modified to the state's further advantage, was rejected by certain sections of the Church, which split off to form the so-called Petite Eglise, a virtually underground organization. It survived for many years, principally in the Vendée and Poitou, feeding into various heterodox political-religious movements such as Eugène Vintras's Œuvre de la Miséricorde, which we will encounter later in connection with the highly unusual circumstances of Joris-Karl Huysmans' conversion to Catholicism in the 1890s.

For the anticlerical republican remnant in France, too, the Concordat was a source of disgust rather than celebration: "A fine load of religious buffoonery [belle capucinade]," General Delmas is said to have muttered as he emerged from the service. "All that was missing were the hundred thousand men who got killed trying to suppress all that."[2] It was noted, however, that Napoleon himself did not take Communion, and much laughing and chattering among the "congregation" effectively drowned out the archbishop of Tours's homily. Some of those present distinguished themselves by munching bread or chocolate throughout the ceremony.

"Do you know what the Concordat I've just signed really is?" Napoleon asked the atheist philosopher Pierre Cabanis shortly afterward. "It's a way of vaccinating against religion [c'est la vaccine de la religion]; in fifty years' time it will have disappeared from France." To show who or what was the real object of worship in the new France, Napoleon had an illuminated star nine meters in diameter hoisted from the towers of Notre-Dame on the eve of his birthday and declared the following day—15 August, the feast of the Assumption of the Blessed Virgin Mary, no less—to be a national holiday. For the rest of the Consulate and Empire, a docile, even enthusiastic church would celebrate the 15th as la Saint-Napoléon.[3]

The signing of the Concordat marked a crucial stage both in Napoleon's process of self-legitimation and in his long-term project of halting (rather than reversing or undoing) the march of revolution in France. Always conscious, as he would tell Metternich in 1813, of being a "parvenu soldier"[4] or even, in the eyes of some of his enemies, of being simply "not French" by dint of his Corsican birthplace,[5] Napoleon proceeded cautiously before imposing himself as de jure rather than simply de facto absolute ruler of France. A plot by diehard republicans to stab the first consul to death in his box at the Opéra was unmasked in October 1800, and in December of that year another group of conspirators planted a bomb to blow him up on his way, once more, to the Opéra. The would-be assassins were guillotined, clad—and this is symptomatic of the growing monarchization or sacralization of the first consul's person—in the red shirts that parricides customarily wore when they went to their death.[6] In January 1804 yet another assassination attempt was foiled by the police, and twelve of the conspirators, led by the veteran *chouan* Cadoudal, went to the guillotine; another, the equally celebrated Pichegru, supposedly strangled himself in prison before he could be executed.

In a state of mounting paranoia, Napoleon had the young duc d'Enghien, a direct descendant of the great prince de Condé and supposed pivot of all the recent royalist conspiracies, kidnapped in Germany in March. Brought secretly to Paris, he was tried by a hastily convened court-martial at the Château de Vincennes, taken outside, and shot at night in the castle ditch (21 March 1804); the whole process from capture to murder was over in less than a week.

For royalist opinion, Chateaubriand at its head, the killing of Enghien was yet another "holocaust" or "holy immolation" to be set alongside the execution of Louis XVI. The "ancient glory" of France had perished "under the eyes of the great Condé, in a ditch at Vincennes; perhaps at the very place where Louis IX, to whom his subjects went as to a saint, sat beneath an oak tree" dispensing justice to his people. Again the Christological parallel lurks just beneath the surface; at thirty-one years and seven months, Enghien was close to the traditional age of the crucified Christ, and, in common with the emerging archetypal pattern, his martyred body was reduced to "the broken fragments of a soldier's carcass"; like Christ, he died utterly alone, without priestly solace, unable to send any token of his love to his wife. Yet, like Christ and the king, the young duke was transfigured in and by death; the glory of heaven was added to the pardon of heaven, and "religion makes everlasting the pomp of unhappiness when, after the catastrophe is accomplished, the cross rises up on the abandoned spot."[7] The sacrificial death of the duc d'Enghien would long be a topos in royalist discourse, not least in the poetry of Lamartine and Hugo during their royalist phases under the Restoration.[8]

By 1804, however, it was Napoleon himself who was subject to more and more explicit Christologization at the level of both elite and masses, as official propaganda combined with popular mythmaking to transform the military hero into a potent blend of liberator, lawgiver, healer, and redeemer not just of France but of all Europe. The image of the messianic Napoleon was constructed through speeches and sermons, popular songs and cartoons, works of pseudo-religious speculation and scholarship, and, not least, through the mighty canvases of David,

Ingres, and Antoine-Jean Gros, in the most telling and typical of which—Gros's *Bonaparte visitant les pestiférés de Jaffa le 11 mars 1799* (1804) and *Napoléon visitant le champ de bataille d'Eylau le 9 février 1807* (1808)—Napoleon appears as a blend of Christlike miracle worker and *roi thaumaturge* who characteristically visits scenes of slaughter and suffering like some deus ex machina, as though he were not in large measure responsible for the wounds and diseases he heals.[9] Writers, speakers, and image makers of all kinds drew parallel after parallel between the vertiginously successful career of the general-cum-statesman and the somewhat less triumphant worldly life of Jesus of Nazareth, one favorite topos being that deployed by the obsequious archbishop of Savone: "It is out of Egypt that Jesus Christ went into Palestine to make public his Gospel and to establish his religion. And it is from that same country that God protected the passage of the Great Napoleon, in order that religion itself should regain its former luster."[10]

The Christological comparison would be developed still further after Napoleon's "passion" at Waterloo—commonly likened to Christ's at Golgotha—and his exile and death on Saint Helena, and there is no reason to view as atypical or aberrant the peasant described in Alfred de Vigny's *Servitude et grandeur militaires* (1835) who shows his local curé a picture of Napoleon and declares, "Look here, Vicar, this for me is the Eternal Father!"[11]

Napoleonic messianism peaked in the 1830s and 1840s, as much outside France as within; subsided with the coming to power of his nephew Louis Napoleon—"Napoléon le Petit," in Hugo's withering dismissal—in 1851; plummeted after the latter's defeat, fall, and exile in 1870; and revived in the late 1880s and 1890s at the time of the Boulangist crisis and the Dreyfus affair. It reached a belated and improbable apotheosis in Léon Bloy's *L'Ame de Napoléon* of 1912, in which Napoleon is seen as a prophetic figure in the "immense liturgical Text" that is History, as the "Precursor of HIM who must come," "the Face of God in the darkness," whose martyrdom, like that of Marie-Antoinette and the pretender Naundorff before him, is the necessary precondition of the ultimate redemption of France. Had not Napoleon himself said that "if Christ had not died on the cross, he would not be God"?[12]

The systematic promotion of Napoleon as national savior and healer culminated in the Constitution of 28 Floréal Year XII (18 May 1804), which transformed the first consul into "emperor of the French," the title and powers to pass after his death to his "direct, natural, legitimate, and adoptive descendants" and, failing that, to the offspring of his brothers Joseph and Louis. Upon ratification of his new status by a huge majority in a national plebiscite (3,572,329 votes to 2,569), Napoleon proceeded next to arrange his own coronation and that of his French creole consort, Joséphine—the happy possessor, in her husband-lover's words, of "the prettiest little bum you could ever imagine"—to take place in the presence of Pius VII, but *not,* emphatically, at his hands, it having been arranged in advance that Napoleon would crown first himself and then the empress. The coronation itself has rightly been described as a "horrible cocktail" of symbols, a *bricolage* of pseudo-imperial bits and pieces—a fake medieval scepter, a mock-up of Charlemagne's crown, a would-be Augustan tunic and gold laurel coronet—put together in haste to create "a hugely overdetermined figuration of legitimacy" that contrived somehow to place Napoleon in the lineage of at once Clovis, Saint Louis, Louis XIV, and the Committee of Public Safety.[13]

The meaning of all this semiological overkill was apparent to all: Napoleon was supreme not just in France but in Europe, indeed on earth, for, from the moment of Pius VII's enforced arrival in Paris, the unfortunate pontiff had been forced to walk and sit on Napoleon's left, and in David's curiously one-dimensional painting of the ceremony he looks on with a vacant, melancholy gaze, as though uninvolved in the whole wretched business, while, as a final deliberate touch, the imperial eagle that surmounts a staff held by a guard almost entirely obscures the crucifix nestling on the ample paunch of another of the prelates. In the cathedral the letter *N* almost drowned out any religious imagery, and the ceremony proper was conducted in a kind of neo-Greek temple erected in the central nave; it was as though the medieval Gothic of Catholicism was almost completely screened out by the neoclassicism of empire. One way and another, the sacralization of Napoleon marks a crucial stage in the desacralization of the world; it was, beneath its pseudo-religious trappings, an entirely secular ritual held almost provocatively in what, after Reims, was the holiest cathedral in France. The one cross in David's paintings hangs stranded as if in a void, an index of the disconnection of heaven and earth that anticipates the suspended cross of Gustave Courbet's great *Enterrement à Ornans* of 1849–50. The ceremony disgusted religious and nonreligious alike, and caused former admirers of Napoleon—most famously Beethoven—radically to revise their opinion of the erstwhile hero and liberator.[14]

His constitutional position ensured, Napoleon, believing, as he put it to General Chasseloup-Laubat in 1804, that "men are great only by virtue of the monuments they leave,"[15] moved beyond self-legitimization into systematic self-glorification. He embarked on a series of architectural projects designed to "Romanize" his capital and, in doing so, not only to perpetuate the memory of himself and his armies but to create the conditions for the continuation beyond his death of the dynasty he believed he had founded. In 1808 the Arc de Triomphe du Carrousel, modeled on the Septimus Severus arch in Rome, was inaugurated on the esplanade separating the palaces of the Louvre and the Tuileries, and work was already proceeding on the much grander Arc de Triomphe de l'Etoile; it was still uncompleted at the time of his fall and, after desultory work under the Restoration (Louis XVIII wanted it to be rededicated to the royalist army that had fought *against* Napoleon under the duc d'Angoulême in the Peninsular War), was not finally inaugurated until 1836, under Louis-Philippe.

A far more personal monument was the Colonne Vendôme, which, when first proposed in 1803, was to be surmounted by the statue of Charlemagne taken at the capture of Aix-la-Chapelle in 1794 and transported to Paris. By 1806, however, the statue had been returned to its city of origin, and the decision was made to rededicate the column (on which work had not yet begun) to the glory of the Grande Armée and its victories at Austerlitz and Ulm and to surmount it with a statue of the emperor himself. Modeled on Trajan's column in Rome, the Colonne Vendôme was inaugurated amid a spasm of nationalistic-imperial fervor on 15 August—*la Sainte Napoléon* once more—1810. Forty-four meters high, it was erected on the pedestal of an earlier equestrian statue of Louis XIV that had been removed and melted down on 12 August 1792, a hundred years to the day after it had been cast. A massive sequence—over 200 meters in length—of bronze bas-reliefs celebrating the military triumphs of 1805, made of metal obtained by melting down 1,250 enemy cannon, coiled around the column. On top of the column, clad in Roman tunic and coronet of laurels and holding a globe in his hand, stood Chaudet's statue of the emperor. It was this personalization of the monument that would make it, unlike the two Arcs de Triomphe, an object of such obsessive concern for Bonapartists and anti-Bonapartists alike in the decades to come: "The Arc de Triomphe is France, the Colonne de Vendôme is Bonaparte," said the aristocratic Communard Henri de Rochefort in 1871[16] at the climax of more than fifty years of controversy concerning the column's function and form, as the efforts of each incoming regime to define itself vis-à-vis the Napoleonic legend and legacy precipitated structural changes and compromises similar to those that occurred on the site of the Bastille and the Place de la Concorde.

For the Restoration Monarchy, of course, the solution was simple. No sooner had Paris been restored to Bourbon control than on 8 April

1814—by the logic of myth it was Good Friday that year—the statue of Napoleon was hauled down and, its bronze cheeks having been ritualistically slapped, replaced by the white fleur-de-lys of the monarchy, which, but for the interlude of the Hundred Days, would continue to fly over the column until July 1830. But already the decapitated column had become a symbol of France's international impotence for patriots of every political hue, and in his "Ode à la Colonne de la Place Vendôme" of February 1827 Victor Hugo had created a sensation when he celebrated its "glory and nothingness" and called for a return of France to its former geopolitical and military standing. Not until 1832, as part of the Bourgeois Monarchy's policy of "recuperating" the legacy of empire, was Napoleon restored to the top of his column, but Seurre's new bronze statue had him dressed in a frock coat and sporting a small, nonmilitary hat; this, after all, was a *Bourgeois Monarchy*, which reduced everything about it to its own utterly unheroic dimensions, and the pusillanimity of its compromise citizen-emperor excited widespread derision from critics at all points on the political spectrum.

In 1840, at the urging of his prime minister, Adolphe Thiers, Louis-Philippe agreed, rather against his better judgment, to request permission from the British government to have Napoleon's remains brought back from Saint Helena for reburial in France. The British, somewhat surprisingly, were quick to agree, the necessary funds were enthusiastically voted by the Chamber of Deputies, and on 7 July 1840 the *Belle Poule* duly set sail from Toulon for the South Atlantic with the king's youngest son, the prince de Joinville, on board to superintend the transfer. It was a somewhat dangerous ploy that risked reigniting old conflicts in France and adding fuel to some newer ones, but by 1840 the Bourgeois Monarchy had weathered and repressed the rioting of 1830–34, and doubtless the cabinet felt that it had nothing to lose, and perhaps something to gain, by legitimating—and by the same stroke neutralizing—the memory of empire by itself sponsoring the return of the emperor's remains to France.

The strength of the myth of Napoleon—perhaps at its height in the 1830s, both in France and abroad—lay in the fact that almost all sections of society, from peasantry to bourgeoisie, from the urban working classes and students to all but the most diehard legitimists, could find something to identify with in the Napoleonic legacy, and by making that legacy its own the Bourgeois Monarchy could, it believed, strengthen its cross-class support and simultaneously defuse Bonapartism's disruptive potential. It sought to foreground Napoleon the military hero at the expense of Napoleon the absolute dictator, and to that end decided that the emperor's remains should be reinterred not at the foot of the Colonne Vendôme (as Hugo had urged in another poem "A la Colonne" of October 1830) or in the Panthéon, both being deemed too controversial and central for comfort, but in the relatively remote and politically uncontentious Hôtel des Invalides, the military hospital, asylum, and church on the Left Bank that Henri IV had founded in 1604. If Napoleon had sought to "vaccinate" the French against religion in the Concordat, the Bourgeois Monarchy sought forty years later to vaccinate them against the memory of the emperor himself.[17]

On 8 October 1840 the *Belle Poule* reached Saint Helena, and on the night of 14–15 October, beginning at midnight as though in some ghoulish Gothic romance, the emperor's body was exhumed. All were amazed to find it almost perfectly preserved. Returning to Europe, the *Belle Poule* docked at Cherbourg on 30 November; the body was transferred to a series of smaller vessels and transported via Rouen—where huge crowds turned out to greet it—to Courbevoie, on the great loop of the Seine to the northwest of Paris, where it was unloaded on 15 December and provisionally placed in the inevitable Greek-style pine-and-plaster temple that had been hastily built to receive it. A massive funeral carriage designed by Henri Labrouste brought it into the city: a monument in itself drawn by sixteen white horses and surmounted by fourteen plaster caryatids supporting the coffin, which a vast purple covering effectively shrouded from view. Watched by possibly the largest crowds that had ever gathered in Paris, the imperial juggernaut lumbered along the Champs Elysées on the freezing morning of 15 December, crossed the Place de la Concorde, and headed toward the Invalides, where the procession was met by Louis-Philippe with his family and cabinet. The coffin was unloaded, blessed by Monseigneur Affre, the archbishop of Paris, who would be killed in the insurrection of June 1848, and provisionally installed in an enormous temporary catafalque, from which it would later be transferred to a permanent sarcophagus designed by Visconti in the dome of the Invalides. It had been one of the greatest "events" in the history of Paris, but at its heart lay a deception brilliantly pinpointed by Hugo in his diary entry that night:

> It is undeniable that this entire ceremony had the conspicuous quality of sleight-of-hand [*escamotage*]. The government seemed to be afraid of the phantom it was conjuring up. They seemed to display and hide Napoleon at the same time. Everything that would have been too grand or too moving was obscured. The real and the imposing were concealed away with a military parade; the

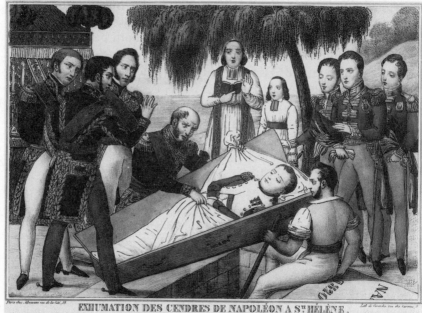

EXHUMATION DES CENDRES DE NAPOLÉON A St HÉLÈNE .

Exhumation of Napoleon's remains at Saint Helena. This popular print of 1840, by Gosselin, shows the virtual "resurrection" of Napoleon before the transfer of his allegedly unblemished remains for final entombment at the Invalides. (Musée Carnavalet, Paris, © Photothèque des Musées de la Ville de Paris.)

army was conjured away with the National Guard; the Chambers were conjured away within the church of the Invalides; the coffin was conjured away with a cenotaph.[18]

The "Saint-Denis of the Bonapartes," as Jean Tulard calls the Invalides,[19] was not formally inaugurated until well into the Second Empire, in April 1861, and the remains of Napoleon's brothers Jérôme and Joseph were transferred there in 1862 and 1863, respectively. After the fall of Napoleon III, the Bonapartist myth temporarily lost its allure, but when it revived in the mid-1880s, the Invalides naturally became a focus of the revitalized cult. A memorable chapter in Maurice Barrès's *Les Déracinés* (1897) shows a group of displaced and confused students from the Lorraine—by then severed from France and under German control—gathering around the emperor's tomb in May 1884 to commune in the memory of the Superman, whom they see as a "Professor of

Energy" and to whom they look not just for personal inspiration and re-demption but for the total transfiguration of France and for the recovery of the "lost provinces" to the east. "The emperor's tomb," writes Barrès,

> is not a place of peace for twenty-year-old French youths, not a philosophical ditch in which a much agitated body is now decom-posing; it is the crossroads of all those energies called audacity, willpower, appetite. For a century, the imagination, everywhere scattered, is concentrated on this point.... Here one does not hear the silence of the dead, but a rumor of heroism; this well beneath the dome is the epic clarion that vibrates with a breadth that causes the hair of the whole younger generation to rise.[20]

Where this cult of national energy as embodied in Napoleon might lead is revealed by a little-known incident that occurred in the dying days of another *année terrible,* 1940. For over a century Bonapartists had sought the return to France of the remains of Napoleon's only son, the duc de Reichstadt (1811–32), otherwise known as the king of Rome, Napoleon II, or, to Bonapartist romantics, L'Aiglon (the Eaglet), who had died in exile in Vienna and was buried in that city's Capuchin church. A determined attempt to negotiate the return of the body in the centenary year 1932 came to nothing, and it was left to Hitler to decree its transfer as a gauge of the "solidarity" between the Reich and its col-laborationist puppet, the Etat Français of Marshal Philippe Pétain.

The body arrived at the Gare de l'Est by night escorted by soldiers of the Wehrmacht and was taken through the snowy streets of Paris, still at night, on an artillery carriage drawn by a tractor. Reaching the Invalides, it was handed over by the German ambassador, Otto Abetz, to a galaxy of Vichyists including Admiral Jean-Louis Darlan; the neosocialist (i.e., fascist) leader Marcel Déat; the education minister, Abel Bonnard; and the pro-Vichy actor-playwright Sacha Guitry, whose father, Lucien, had appeared in the first performance of Edmund Rostand's nationalist drama *L'Aiglon* forty years earlier. That this parodic "return of the ashes" took place entirely by night obviously restricted its symbolic efficacy. One daring cabaret singer reputedly suggested that, given the cold, occupied Paris had greater need of coal than of ashes.[21]

It would be wrong, or at least simplistic, to suppose that the original return of the emperor's remains led directly to the improbable election of his nephew Louis Napoleon to the presidency of the Second Republic in December 1848, but the widespread, cross-class imperial cult that it was supposed to enlist to the advantage of the Bourgeois Monarchy undoubtedly opened the way for Louis Napoleon's electoral triumph and subsequent military putsch. Until 1848 the cult of the emperor and the person of Louis Napoleon were almost entirely disconnected, save in the minds of a hard core of Bonapartist fanatics. The recognized Bonapartist pretender since the death of L'Aiglon, Louis Napoleon was generally regarded as a semicomic peripatetic conspirator whose ludicrous attempts to launch Bonapartist coups at Strasbourg (1836) and Boulogne (1840) had led to his imprisonment, just weeks before his uncle's remains were returned with such would-be pomp and circumstance, in the fortress of Ham, in the northeast of the country. Escaping in 1846 disguised as a building worker (a disguise so effective that another worker, on seeing him, said, "Ah, there's Badinguet," whence the derisive nickname under which republicans would later excoriate him), Louis Napoleon had fled to London and remained there until he was elected in absentia to the republican Assembly in a by-election of June 1848. The fact that three of his cousins, including the famous "Plon-Plon," had already been elected in the main poll in April suggests that a Bonapartist bandwagon was well under way. Prevented from taking his seat, Louis Napoleon stood, again in absentia, in a further by-election in September and was elected by a still greater margin than before. It was only then that he returned to France and to a nationwide wave of Bonapartist fervor, carefully nurtured and orchestrated by a growing band of propagandists and agents provocateurs, many of then recruited among veterans and the *classes dangereuses,* and whom Daumier captured for his time and ours in the tatterdemalion figures of Ratapoil and Casmajou.

That this cult rested on a genuine popular base is not to be doubted: "At the present moment," declared *L'Evénement* on 25 September 1848, "the people believe vaguely that it is the emperor who is returning and not the prince, the uncle and not the nephew. Since 1815 the people have been waiting for Napoleon. Sunk in ignorance and suffering, they need an ideal, a vision, a love; that ideal, that vision, that love is the emperor."[22] Thanks in part to his pamphlet *L'Extinction du paupérisme* (1844), which he had written at Ham, Louis Napoleon could be readily projected as the savior of the oppressed, and cries of "Poléon, nous l'aurons!" and "Vive Poléon!" came to be heard more and more frequently and loudly in working-class districts in Paris and elsewhere, especially after the crushing of the June insurrection had discredited the bourgeois republic in the eyes of radical Montagnards and *démoc-socs.* The fact that Bonapartist fervor could be accompanied by cries of either "Vive la République!" or "A bas la République!" reveals the complexity of the social and political issues at stake. But popular support, both urban and rural, made Louis Napoleon's success in the presidential elections almost inevitable. One barely literate voter in the Marne scrawled the following illuminating comment on his ballot: "Vive Napoléon puisqu'il est bon. En cas de représentants, je n'en quon n'est pas. Un bon Napoléon les quonnais mieux que moi puisqu'il les choisis lui-même" (Long live Napoleon since he is good. As for representatives, I don't know any. A good Napoleon knows them better than me since he chooses them himself).[23]

Louis Napoleon received three-quarters of all votes cast, winning absolute majorities in sixty-two out of eighty-five departments and, perhaps most significant, *all* of the Paris arrondissements, middle-class west and working-class east alike. Almost overnight, yesterday's scapegoat had become today's would-be messiah; Badinguet had somehow metamorphosed into the prince-president, and his further evolution into Emperor Napoleon III after the coup of 2 December 1851 (timed to coincide, obviously, with the anniversary of his uncle's coronation) was seen by many contemporaries, including Baudelaire and the anarchist Pierre-Joseph Proudhon, as proof of his "providential" character and capacity to rule. As Daumier's great painting, already referred to, suggests, Barabbas not only had supplanted the Christ-Republic in the people's affections but was well on the way to becoming a makeshift Christ figure himself. The former exile had driven thousands of republicans into exile, not least Victor Hugo, who would spend the next twenty years in Jersey and Guernsey, publishing the savagely brilliant *Les Châtiments* (1853), in which the "crime" of "Napoléon le Petit" on 2 December is characteristically seen as history's expiation and revenge for his uncle's violent coup of 18 Brumaire. "History repeats itself," wrote Karl Marx, famously, in *The Eighteenth Brumaire of Louis Napoleon* (1852), "the first time as tragedy, the second as farce." Stunned into despair, Baudelaire confessed that the putsch had completely "depoliticized" him (*le 2 décembre m'a tout à fait dépolitiqué*).[24]

Yet twenty years on, the scapegoat-turned-savior was a scapegoat again, and the kind of animalizing images that had accompanied and accelerated the fall of Louis XVI and Marie-Antoinette were recycled to damn Napoleon III and *his* foreign consort.[25] After the crushing defeat sustained by his army at Sedan on 2 September 1870, the emperor surrendered to the Prussians in the persons of King (soon to be Kaiser) Wilhelm and Bismarck and, after a period of detention in Germany, was allowed in March 1871 to follow the path trod by Charles X and Louis-Philippe and seek sanctuary in England. By a savagely ironic historical twist, he landed at Dover just as members of the Orléans family were about to embark on their return journey to France.[26]

Meanwhile in France the Third Republic had been declared. Paris had been besieged by the Prussians from September 1870 to January 1871, at which point, to the fury of Parisians, the Bordeaux-based government of the Republic had signed an armistice with the invaders, as part of which, in a foretaste of June 1940, Prussian troops marched down the Champs Elysées on 1 March 1871. As hostility mounted in Paris to the increasingly right-wing republican government now based in Versailles, an unexpected power vacuum made it possible for radicals to declare the city an autonomous commune and, with strong working-class and significant lower-middle-class support, to embark on the most extraordinary political and social experiment ever undertaken in one city. Driven out of the center of Paris by the massive program of urban transformation undertaken by the emperor and his prefect of Paris, Baron Haussmann, working-class Parisians had—to use an image that recurs obsessively in the literature of the time—been exiled into poorly constructed and ill-equipped new developments on the northern and eastern periphery of the city, from which, with mounting resentment, they watched the prosperous, the powerful, and the pleasure-loving take over *la Ville-Lumière,* which some of them, in their fury, took to calling Napoléonville.[27] As the historian Jacques Rougerie has written, the Paris Commune was at its heart an attempted "reconquest of the city by the city," a reannexation of "true Paris" (the center) by those "true Parisians" (the working classes) who had been expelled to its margins by and during the Second Empire.[28]

This being so, it is small wonder that the Communards sought to de-Napoleonize the city when it so unexpectedly had fallen into their hands, and that any statues celebrating the Bonapartist dynasty would be immediate and irresistible targets. Already in 1866, the future Communard Jules Vallès had made "Fewer statues, more men!" his watchword, and, none too subtly, had urged his fellow Parisians to take revenge on that "population of mannikins [*peuple de bonshommes*] on whose heads birds bill and coo or flit about, which have no use but to perpetuate the feeling of idolatry, and whose marble or stone overcoats have cost just as much as would, during a terrible winter, a thousand meters of sackcloth [*bure*] to clothe a frozen population of sufferers." "Deaf and dumb, petrified in their immobile and comic solemnity,"[29] statues nonetheless embody power at its most remote and intangible (and consequently at its most indestructible), the power of the dead (and their allies) over the living, and in a truly democratic society would probably be done away with entirely. For republicans, the most offensive statue of all was the Colonne Vendôme, and in the early 1840s Heinrich Heine had predicted that, should a socialist government come to power in France, "the rage for radical equality would be capable of overturning the whole column in order for this symbol of vainglory to be entirely razed from the earth.[30] It was, then, in keeping with an ancient iconoclastic tradition that, on 12 April 1871, the Commune issued the following decree:

> *The Commune of Paris:* Considering that the imperial column in the Place Vendôme is a monument of barbarism, a symbol of brute force and of false glory, an affirmation of militarism, a negation of international law, a permanent insult by the victors to the vanquished, a perpetual threat to one of the three great principles of the French Republic, Fraternity, *decrees:* First and only article: The Column in the Place Vendôme shall be demolished.[31]

Contrary to widespread belief, Courbet (who was not a member of the Commune at the time) did not sign the decree, but it would be with his name that the so-called *déboulonnement* (dismantling) of the column would henceforth forever be associated. After several delays, the operation went ahead on 16 May 1871 under the overall control of a Citoyen Iribe, a civil engineer and member of the Positivist Club. Here is the account given in Jack Lindsay's biography of Courbet:

> At the base of the shaft on the side that faced the rue de la Paix was made a triangular cut extending through about a third of the diameter; on the opposite side at the same level the stone was sawn through and iron wedges inserted, the lowest bronze plates having first been taken off. A very strong cable was looped round the Column's top at the height of the platform and attached to a pulley that was linked, by a cable passing through it three times, to another pulley fixed in the ground. From this cable was wound round a winch placed opposite the Column near the intersection of the Place and the rue Neuve-des-Petits-Champs. This winch was firmly anchored to the ground. To deaden the fall the ground had been covered by a bed of sand, over which twigs and a thick layer of dung were strewn....
> From noon on a large crowd had gathered in the rue de la Paix near the Place, into which access was forbidden to the public.... About 3:30 the winch began to turn; the cable stretched and grew

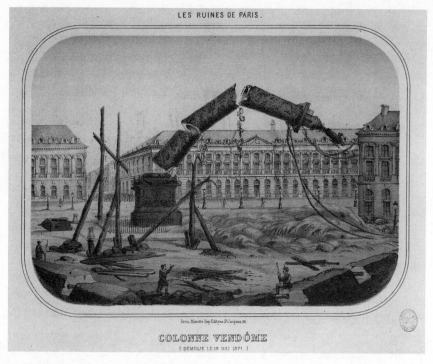

LES RUINES DE PARIS.

COLONNE VENDÔME
(DÉMOLIE LE 16 MAI 1871.)

The ruins of Paris: the Colonne Vendôme. This anonymous engraving of 1871 dramatically depicts the demolition of the Colonne Vendôme but omits the vast crowd that witnessed the event. (Musée Carnavalet, Paris, © Photothèque des Musées de la Ville de Paris.)

taught.... After the strain had been applied for several minutes, something was heard to snap; the pulley fixed to the ground ... had just broken. The contractor sent for a stronger one, which was installed....

About 5:30 several military bands, assembled in the corners of the square on the side nearest the rue Saint-Honoré, played the Marseillaise. All was ready for fresh application of tension to the cable. It had been stretched tight for only a few minutes when the Column was seen to tilt. When it had inclined very slightly from the perpendicular, it suddenly broke into segments, which crashed to the ground, making a tremendous noise and raising a thick cloud of dust. At once the spectators ... surged forwards to the immense ruin, clambering onto and examining the blocks of stone. Several members of the Commune made brief speeches; red flags were brought form headquarters and set on the Column's pedestal.[32]

How has this remarkable event, almost the last that the Commune organized in concert, been interpreted, both at the time and by subsequent commentators? For the men of the right, the writer Maxime Du Camp (1822–94) at their head, its meaning, like the meaning of everything else the Commune undertook, was utterly simple. The *déboulonnement* revealed the Commune's materialism, its hatred of each and every ideal, at its most bestial and base: "This rage to take it out on material things, this fetishism in reverse which is the height of fetishism, which was the sickness of the Commune, appeared in all its intensity at the moment of the column's fall [*lors du renversment de la colonne*]."[33] Another reactionary writer, Catulle Mendès (1841–1909), saw it not so much as a murderous attack on the father by rebellious youth as a macabre defiling of his tomb by a mob of vengeful body snatchers: "Don't think that demolishing the Vendôme Column is just toppling over a bronze column with an emperor's statue on top; it's unearthing your fathers in order to slap the faceless cheeks of their skeletons and to say to them: You were wrong to be brave, to be proud, to be grand! You were wrong to conquer cities, to win battles. You were wrong to make the world marvel at the vision of a dazzling France." The reaction of the Communard Louis Barron could not be more different:

Tuesday, May 16. I saw the Vendôme Column fall, it collapsed all in one piece like a stage set on a nice bed of trash when the machinist's whistle blew. Immediately a huge cloud of dust rose up, while a quantity of tiny fragments rolled and scattered about, white on one side, gray on the other, similar to little morsels of bronzed plaster. This colossal symbol of the Grand Army—how fragile, empty, miserable it was! It seemed to have been eaten out from the middle by a multitude of rats, like France itself, like its old tarnished glory, and we were surprised not to see any [rats] run out along the drainpipes. The music played fanfares, some old graybeard declaimed a speech on the vanity of conquests, the villainy of conquerors, and the fraternity of the people, we danced in a circle around the debris, and then went off, very happy with the little party.

On the basis of these and similar accounts, modern writers have had no difficulty in seeing the demolition as a figure of castration, as a carnavalesque reversal (corresponding to the physical upending of the column) of the repressive structures of society and the state. Kristin Ross sees it as part of the Commune's "attack on verticality" and its related desire to create open, "horizontal" social and political spaces, a project that she finds reflected in the poetry of the Communard sympathizer Arthur Rimbaud.[34]

In the present book's terms, the dismantling may be seen as yet another sacrificial killing of the father, a ludic reprise of 14 July 1789 and 21 January 1793: there is the same sense of collective communion, the same *jouissance* as the hated head falls, the same desire to take possession of the scattered remains of the body as though it contained some sacred potency that the *sacrifiants* might make their own. In his fictional account in *La Colonne* (1901), Lucien Descaves (1861–1949), clearly drawing on eyewitness evidence and possibly on his own childhood memories, describes how speaker after speaker, official and otherwise, declaimed his or her hatred of Napoleon and all that he stood for, how members of the crowd inspected the "broken vertebrae" of the column and "picked up fragments of it, entrails or skin" to take home with them. Others used their cameras to take visual possession of the scene as families and friends posed for group photographs on the ruins. One worker—he was certainly not alone—kicked the emperor's severed head as though "putting a full stop under the exclamation mark" in order to finally kill off this corpse of the past, whose humiliation would console "the thousands of corpses lying in their tomb" that Napoleon was responsible for.[35]

In an article of 1929 titled "Architecture" Georges Bataille argued that it is through monuments that state and Church "impose silence on the masses," and that it is the fear they inspire that explains, for example, the storming of the Bastille: "it is difficult to explain this movement of the crowd other than as by the animosity of the people against monuments that are its true masters."[36] So too with the Colonne Vendôme: it represented the structured superego of the past, and its upending the victory of Eutrepelia, the spirit of play, over the combined forces of Thanatos and repression, whence the overwhelming feeling of happiness that came over the crowd, less than a week before the onset of the *Semaine sanglante*.[37] It was inevitable, then, that when "moral order" was restored, the column was immediately rebuilt at a cost of 350,000 francs, charged directly to Courbet, ruining him and shortening his life.

The new statue was inaugurated on 30 May 1873, an "enormous pole," wrote the Communard historian Prosper-Olivier Lissagaray (1838–1901), symbolizing the power of the reconquering bourgeoisie and needing the "scaffolding of thirty thousand corpses": "Like the mothers of the First Emperor, how many of those of our days have not been able to look at that bronze without weeping."[38]

Perhaps the one consolation was that no effort would be made to return the remains of Napoleon III. His body remains in England. He died at Chislehurst in Kent in January 1873 and was buried in the small Gothic-style church that the former empress Eugénie had built on the manor estate at Farnborough in Hampshire, where she moved after her husband's death. Eugénie herself, who died in 1920, aged ninety-four, is buried there too, as is her son, Louis, the prince imperial, killed in South Africa in 1879, aged twenty-three, under a hail of assegais, having impetuously enlisted in the British army in its campaign against King Cetewayo of the Zulus.[39]

From Napoleon to Badinguet to Plon-Plon and Loulou, and from Austerlitz to Sedan to Ityotosi: history first as mimesis and then as bathos. Thus three generations of Bonapartes (Napoleon, L'Aiglon, Louis Napoleon, the Prince Imperial) died in exile, rejected by most of their countrymen, revered by a few, a mixture of scapegoat, saint, and potential savior of their people, a psychological and ideological inheritance that would be passed on, via the hapless General Boulanger, to their most obvious twentieth-century successors, Marshal Pétain and General de Gaulle.

5

HEART OF THE CITY
Place de Grève/Hôtel de Ville
(1789–1871)

If any one Parisian site deserves to be called the city's political epicenter, it is not the left's talismanic Place de la Bastille or Place de la République to the east, and certainly not the bastions of parliamentary democracy to the south and the west (the Palais-Bourbon and the Palais du Luxembourg, homes, respectively, of the Chamber of Deputies and the Senate), but rather the Place de l'Hôtel de Ville, traditionally known as the Place de Grève, located precisely at the city's physical center, just to the northeast of Notre-Dame, across the narrow neck of the Seine, at the interface, as it were, of the traditional and extremely approximate division of Paris into a working-class east and middle-class west. Aside from its important, if ancillary, role in the events of 14 July 1789, the Hôtel de Ville was on four separate occasions—July 1830, February 1848, September 1870, and March 1871—the scene of a major struggle between center and left over the substance and symbols of political power, a struggle that in all cases but the last ended in a notable triumph for the center, which, its victory ensured, promptly moved to the right.

During the pivotal Three Glorious Days of 27–29 July 1830, a combination of parliamentary disaffection and popular rioting unseated the reactionary Bourbon monarchy of Charles X, creating a power vacuum that might just have been filled by a republican government but for the prompt action of the representatives of the *grande bourgeoisie,* led unofficially by the eminent banker Jacques Laffitte. Some of the most serious anti-Bourbon agitation took place on and around the Place de Grève, and it was the obvious place for Eugène Delacroix to locate his iconic *La Liberté guidant le peuple,* less accurately known as *Liberty on the Barricades,* painted between September and December 1830. The new king, Louis-Philippe, purchased it in May 1831, supposedly to pla-

cate republican opinion, and then promptly consigned it to the base-
ment of the Louvre lest its presence act as a focus for the hostility that
was already gathering momentum against the new regime.[1] *La Liberté
guidant le peuple* has often been interpreted as an image of "the people"
in the broad, ecumenical sense of the term—all the classes of society,
minus the Church and the aristocracy, effectively no different from the
old Third Estate—gathered around the figure of Liberty, in whose hands
the Tricolor acts as a symbol of national unity, guiding the top-hatted,
rifle-bearing young man, the saber-wielding, smock-clad worker, the
pistol-toting Paris street urchin, and the uniformed student from the
Polytechnique to victory over monarchical tyranny. But contemporary
opinion saw it much more as an image of "the people" in the restrictive
sense of *le peuple ouvrier,* the working people of Paris, and middle-class
observers were shocked that Liberty appeared even to have hair under
her arms.[2] The dispute over the meaning of the painting—did it
represent the people as a whole, or only the lower-class section of the
people?—goes to the heart of the paradoxical event it depicted: the July
revolution was made possible only by the intervention into national politics, for the first time since the late 1790s, of working-class Parisians
from the north and east of the city, but their victory was hijacked forthwith by the politicians of the *grande bourgeoisie* in the west acting in the
name of—inevitably—"the people."

On the afternoon of 29 July, the Hôtel de Ville fell to a combination
of middle-class constitutional monarchists and a much larger number of
popular insurgents, and an uneasy dyarchy installed itself within, led by
the aging marquis de Lafayette (1757–1834) for the constitutional
monarchists and, for the lower-class rabble, a former captain in
Napoleon's navy called Dubourg, who, styling himself "General," had
bought the appropriate uniform from a secondhand clothes dealer before taking his place as the self-elected head of the popular uprising.[3]

Meanwhile, on 31 July, in the center-west of the city, the political representatives of the *grande bourgeoisie* forgathered at the Palais-Royal,
where they were joined by their preferred candidate for the throne, the
duc d'Orléans (1773–1850), son of the regicide Philippe-Egalité, guillotined under the Terror, and scion of the minor branch of the French
royal family. Mounted on a mare named almost parodically Clio, the
duke left the Palais-Royal for his rendezvous with history at the Hôtel de
Ville, followed by a cortege of ninety or so deputies with Laffitte at its
head riding in a black sedan chair and, bringing up the rear, also in a
sedan chair, the veteran liberal monarchist, philosopher, and novelist
Benjamin Constant (1767–1830).

At first the procession was greeted by Tricolor-waving, cockade-wearing crowds, but as it neared the Place de Grève it encountered open hostility as cries of "Vive la République!" and "A bas le duc d'Orléans!" began to mingle with the expected "A bas les Bourbons!" Eventually the duke and his retinue had almost to fight their way through the crowd into what the duc de Broglie called "the headquarters of the nascent republic" (le quartier général de la république en herbe), where they were received by the greatly relieved Lafayette. Amid scenes of great confusion, "General" Dubourg and his supporters were quickly sidelined, and the duke and the marquis—the sources do not reveal who preceded whom—went out onto the Hôtel de Ville balcony, where, draped in a Tricolor flag, they embraced in full view of the seething multitude below. The sight was enough to sway a majority of those present, and, in the words of the future Orléanist minister Odilon Barrot, "the revolution was terminated" to cries of "Vive Lafayette!" and "Vive le duc d'Orléans!" More cynically as well as more realistically, Lamartine would write later that "the republican kiss of Lafayette had made a king."[4] Or, as many observers, Stendhal and Balzac among them, would put it, the upper-middle-class Chaussée-d'Antin in the west of the city had joined forces with the working-class faubourg Saint-Antoine in the east to defeat the aristocratic faubourg Saint-Germain south of the river, only for the Chaussée-d'Antin forthwith to exclude the faubourg Saint-Antoine from power in the name of the people and the nation. The inside world of the politicians had triumphed over, or hoodwinked, the crowd that gathered outside,[5] and, after signing in triplicate a contract with "the people" that effectively sidelined the people who had made possible his accession to power, the duc d'Orléans was formally installed as Louis-Philippe, king of the French rather than king of France, a crucial distinction that did not escape the attention of the commentators of the time.

Eighteen years later, minus a few months, the scenes at the Hôtel de Ville in July 1830 were replayed in crescendo, with Louis-Philippe now the disgraced and humiliated carnival king and Lamartine now playing the role of Lafayette as representative and spokesman of the politicians within. Marginalized in July 1830 on the Place de Grève, the republican movement reasserted itself boldly in 1830–34, then, pursued by draconian legislation, went underground, occasionally resurfacing for some desperate bomb outrage or would-be coup de main. The republicans led a conspiratorial half-life until the social and political crisis of 1847–48 gave them a mass hearing both among the disaffected middle classes and the people, in the sense of the working people—or, as some radicals were beginning to say, the proletariat—of Paris, Lyon, and other large cities.

By now, however, the question was no longer, as the revolutionary conspirator Auguste Blanqui (1805–81) so tellingly puts it, of just changing words but of changing *things*.[6] For tens of thousands of working-class people, and for the middle-class radicals who sought to enlist them, the Republic was no longer an end in itself but a political means toward engineering fundamental social and economic transformation. Socialism—the word had been coined in the early 1830s by the radical philosopher Pierre Leroux (1797–1871)—was the new rallying cry of the radicalized working classes, and their emblem was no longer the Tricolor but the red flag, which had been flown for the first time in Lyon in 1834 by rebellious silkworkers, emblazoned with the unforgettable words "Vivre en travaillant ou mourir en combattant" (Live working or die fighting).

When, therefore, three days of rioting in February 1848 brought the Bourgeois Monarchy to its knees, the politicians of the center—which had moved to the left—found themselves in a far more critical situation than the one that had confronted their equivalents in July 1830. After invading the Palais des Tuileries and, in a carnivalesque reversal of the established order of things, installing themselves as makeshift kings and queens in the royal apartments, bedecking themselves in the deposed royal family's finery and perfumes, and making love in the abandoned royal beds, the insurgents next took over the Hôtel de Ville, proclaimed a republic, and were in due course joined by the nervous representatives of the parliamentary opposition to the former regime, men such as François Arago, Louis-Antoine Garnier-Pagès, Adolphe Crémieux, Jacques-Charles Dupont de l'Eure, and, as their unofficial leader, the poet and historian Alphonse de Lamartine (1790–1869).

Installed by popular acclaim as the provisional government of the new republic, the men of the center found themselves joined not just by left-wing (but still middle-class) republicans like Louis Blanc and Alexandre Ledru-Rollin but, with heavy and unmistakable symbolism, by a working-class revolutionary known to history as *l'ouvrier Albert,* a mechanic, real name Martin, and a veteran of the left-wing secret societies of the former regime. Immediately the division between center and left came to a head over the question of the appropriate flag for the new republic. For the left, the Tricolor stood for compromise, ideological obfuscation, and the fiction of cross-class national unity; for the center, the red flag meant, quite simply, chaos.

As tensions mounted both inside and outside the Hôtel de Ville, Lamartine made his way down to its entrance, where, in the words of

"Daniel Stern" (the nom de plume of the remarkable comtesse d'Agoult [1805–76], republican aristocrat, mistress of Franz Liszt, and mother of Cosima Wagner), he addressed the crowd, "his arms crossed over his chest, letting his confident, gentle look roam over faces contorted with anger and disarming the deepest suspicions with a smile."[7] In what was clearly a remarkable speech, he won over the crowd by contrasting "the red flag making the rounds of the Champ de Mars, trailing in the blood of the people, with the Tricolor going round the world, everywhere bearing the name and glory of the *patrie*." The red flag that had been flying from the statue of Henri IV was forthwith replaced by a Tricolor, and, as Flaubert would tartly but accurately put it in *L'Education sentimentale* (1869), "everyone united beneath its shadow, each party seeing only its own of the three colors—and vowing, as soon as it was strong enough, to tear out the two others."[8] The "inside" had won its first victory over the "outside," and, as a concession to the crowd, decreed that a red cockade should henceforth surmount the flagpole and that the red segment of the Tricolor should be placed on the left of the flag, closest to the pole, to demonstrate its primacy over the other two colors under the new order of things. The "war of the colors" would continue throughout the three and a half years of the Second Republic's duration, but as "inside" steadily got the better of "outside," especially after the official government of the Republic presided over the repression of the working-class insurrection of June 1848, red shirts, red braces and belts, red pipes, and red café awnings and shutters were driven gradually out of public view, along with those other totemic symbols of February 1848, the liberty trees, and when the crunch came and the Republic itself was destroyed by the Bonapartist putsch of December 1851, virtually no working-class Parisians stood up to fight for the Red, White, and Blue; after all, for those on the left, the Tricolor had long been the ensign of a political fudge.

So powerful is the grip of historicism on French political life that the scenario of July 1830 and February 1848 was reenacted not once but twice during the *année terrible* of 1870–71. As soon as news of Napoleon III's defeat and capture by the Prussians at Sedan reached Paris on 4 September 1870, moderate republicans and revolutionaries alike converged, mindful of earlier precedents, on the Hôtel de Ville in a bid to fill the vacuum in authority before their rivals could do so. The Goncourt diary contains an unforgettable description of the streets of Paris on that critical day, beginning with the scenes outside the Chamber of Deputies in the west of the city, south of the Seine, where just a few working-class smocks create blue and white splashes against the predominant black of middle-class outfits and where many people, apparently irrespective of class, are carrying fronds or have attached sprays of leaves to their hats like so many miniature portable liberty trees. Closer to the center of the city, working-class people greet each other with the cry "Ça y est!" One man tears the white and the blue out of a Tricolor and flourishes the red that remains, and the N's and the imperial eagles of the former regime are either concealed behind old newspapers or festooned with bunches of flowers. The whole of Paris, it seems, has come outside, and "pavements and thoroughfares, everywhere is covered, everywhere is full of men and women who have spilled out of their *chez soi* onto the street, as on one of the city's days of festivity"; some men have even dyed their beards bright red. By half past five in the afternoon, the Hôtel de Ville is covered with row upon row of frock coats and smocks sitting at the windows, legs hanging outside, like "a crowd of street urchins [*titis*] in the 'gods' of a Renaissance sculpture."[9] Once more the outside had briefly invaded the inside, though, as in 1830 and 1848, the politicians of the center would once again contrive to keep it from power, if only for a few months, while, with Paris under siege by the Prussians, the official government of the Republic fled first to Tours and then to Bordeaux, leaving the capital under the control of a military-civilian authority headed by General Trochu.

On 31 October 1870, learning of the surrender of Marshal Bazaine's army of 170,000 men at Metz and inflamed by the rumor that he had done a deal with the Prussians to keep his army intact for later use against Paris, members of the various factions of the city's ultraleft—internationalists, Jacobins, Blanquists—staged a one-day occupation of the Hôtel de Ville during which each group issued its program and announced its provisional government in competition with the others, until in the evening troops loyal to the Government of National Defense reentered the building by an underground passage and drove the invaders back out to the streets, where their power base lay.

The outside launched another botched invasion of the Hôtel de Ville on 22 January 1871, but it was the signing of an armistice on 29 January, followed by the symbolic occupation of the city on 1 March, when the whole of Paris stayed at home while the enemy marched along the deserted Champs Elysées, that opened the way for the revolutionaries to seize power. Nationwide elections brought a conservative, indeed promonarchist, Assembly to power, Adolphe Thiers (1797–1877) was named "head of the executive power," and Assembly and government duly moved from Bordeaux to Versailles. After a limited working-class uprising in Montmartre early on the morning of 18 March 1871, Thiers decided, for reasons that are still debated today, to relinquish the capital to the effective control of the far left, which, dominant in the National Guard and the citywide Committee of the Twenty Arrondissements, now had both the arms and the organization to seize it with both hands. Throughout the whole day the city hung in the balance as moderates and revolutionaries jockeyed for position, with the Hôtel de Ville the obvious prize to be captured. It was only at 10 P.M. that the moderates, in the persons of Jules Ferry and Jules Favre, both future prime ministers of the Third Republic, abandoned the building to the far-left national guardsmen, whose commander, Brunel, promptly had the red flag hoisted on its flagpole.

It was a moment of epoch-making symbolic importance. After repeated failures stretching back to July 1830, the outside had finally made the inside its own, or, in the words of the Commune's leading modern historian, "the City had reconquered the City" (*la Ville venait de reconquérir la Ville*),[10] and, in the shape of the Central Committee of the National Guard, reannexed the space from which so many working-class Parisians, and not a few middle-class ones as well, had felt physically or psychologically expelled under Napoleon III; those exiled to the north and east of the city had, through the National Guard, reclaimed possession of its center. There followed a confused period of eight or nine days, which ended when, on 26 March, citywide elections returned a clear left-wing majority to power. The next morning, in the account given by the passionately pro-Commune historian Lissagaray,

> two hundred thousand wretches [*misérables*] came to the Hôtel de Ville to install those whom they had elected. The battalions [of the National Guard], drums beating, flags surmounted by the red cap of liberty [Phrygian cap], with red fringes attached to their rifles ... , flowed down all the streets leading to the Place de Grève, like the tributaries of a gigantic river. In the middle of the Hôtel de Ville, up against the central entrance, a great platform was erected. The bust of the Republic, its red scarf aslant over its shoulder, festooned with red bundles [of sticks—the Roman fasces—symbolizing republican unity], soared protectively over everything. Huge streamers on the front of the building, on its belfry, flapped in the wind to send greetings to France.... The flags ranged in front of the platform, most of them red, some of them Tricolors, all of them with red bows and tassels, symbolized the coming of the people to power. As the battalions took up their positions, singing exploded, bands played the "Marseillaise" and

the "Chant du Départ," bugles sounded the charge, and the cannon of the Commune of 92 thundered on the quai.[11]

Amid this unprecedented bringing together of the sacred emblems and relics of left-wing republicanism, the Commune was proclaimed, and power was handed over by the Central Committee of the National Guard to the seventy or so elected members of the new municipal authority,[12] who, in a series of breaks with tradition, were officially delegates (*mandataires*) and not representatives of their electorates, were paid no more than the average wage of Parisian workers, and wore no uniform or other regalia that might set them apart from those who had elected them. An unparalleled experiment in direct democracy, the Commune would, for the two months of its existence, administer the city in the interests, as it saw them, of its working-class population, until, as we shall see, it perished in the equally unparalleled bloodbath of the all too accurately named *Semaine sanglante* (21–28 May 1871).

As the Commune retreated to its working-class heartland in the east of the city, the Hôtel de Ville went up in flames, torched by the departing Communards themselves, and by eleven on the morning of 24 May, "the old house, witness to so many treacherous oaths [*parjures*], where the people so many times installed powers that then turned their rifles upon them, cracked and collapsed along with its true master."[13] The reconstruction of the building, in almost exact imitation of the early seventeenth-century original,[14] took from 1873 to 1883, but it is to be doubted whether, even in July 1936, August 1944, or May 1968, red flags often flew in its vicinity, let alone on top of its flagpole.

For Parisians of the first half of the nineteenth century, however, the Place de Grève was not just the site par excellence of political change. In the first place, it was here that the hiring of the city's 40,000-plus building workers took place, and Martin Nadaud (1815–98), a migrant stonemason from the Auvergne who later became a Paris city councilor, left a vivid description in his *Mémoires de Léonard, ancien garçon maçon* (1895), the best of the few working-class autobiographies of the century, of how the square appeared to him when he first came to Paris as a lad during the recession of the early 1830s:

> That Place de Grève, the last vestige of the old slave market of antiquity, was crawling with gaunt, emaciated men, resigned, none too sadly, to their starvation wages. They could be seen shivering with cold beneath tattered smocks or threadbare jackets, stamping on the cobbles to warm themselves up a bit. When, around nine

o'clock, they left this place of desolation and misery, some of them would head for the gates of the barracks to pick up a few spoonfuls of soup, thanks to the generosity of our gallant soldiers. Others would hang around on the quais near the numerous itinerant saleswomen, who, in return for one or two sous, would let them have a cup of foul-tasting coffee, a bit of bread, and some reasonable potatoes. Most simply went back to their boardinghouse [*garni*].... During the sixty years that I have lived in Paris and London, I have seen building workers withstand painful crises indeed, but none but that of 1848 could possibly be compared with that of 1833 and 1834, the one I'm talking about here.[15]

Workers disgruntled about pay or conditions would walk off construction sites and head back to the square in the hope of being rehired on better terms, whence the expression *faire la grève,* which by the mid–nineteenth century had entered the national, and not just the Parisian, lexicon as the term for "to strike."

But, more still than this, until 1832 the Place de Grève was the location of public executions in Paris, and had been since Whitsunday 1310, when two alleged heretics, one of them the remarkable mystic Marguerite Porette, and an apostate Jew were burned alive at the orders of Philippe le Bel. Over the following centuries the square witnessed a multitude of executions involving victims famous and obscure, by hanging (for the poor), decapitation (aristocrats), burning at the stake (heretics and sodomites), and breaking on the wheel, quartering, and other mutilation (for parricides and for regicides actual or intended). Among the most celebrated victims were François Ravaillac, the assassin of Henri IV, hanged, drawn, and quartered in 1610; Cartouche, one of a number of French Robin Hoods, broken on the wheel in 1721; and, most notorious of all, Robert-François Damiens, author of an attempt on the life of Louis XV, who in 1757 was subjected to a series of tortures so appalling—searing with sulfur and molten lead and oil, disembowelment, severing of the right hand (the standard punishment for parricides prior to execution), followed by being torn apart by hawsers hooked into his flesh and attached to four horses—that his death has obsessed the French literary-philosophical imagination ever since, from Casanova through Baudelaire and Huysmans to Michel Foucault.[16] The ritual killing of de Launay and de Flesselles on 14 July 1789 could not have taken place on a more symbolically charged spot, and it was also on the Place de Grève that the Revolution's first judicially convicted political victim, the alleged counterrevolutionary marquis de Favras, was hanged in February 1790; "your life is a sacrifice that you owe to public security and tranquility," opined the presiding judge, and de Favras went to his death before a crowd of 50,000 people who chanted, "Jump, marquis, jump, marquis!" as he went up to the gallows, and bellowed "Again, again!" when the "action" was over.[17] That de Favras was hanged rather than beheaded (as had been the custom for aristocrats) was a result of a "democratic" law of December 1789 that prescribed the noose for all capital offenders; even death was now subject to the egalitarian principle.

That principle was pushed still further by Dr. Joseph-Ignace Guillotin's invention, following an earlier device patented by Dr. Antoine Louis (the "Louisette"), of a machine designed to extend the revolutionary concepts of *humanité, égalité, rationalité* into the domain of judicial death.[18] The guillotine was first put into action on 25 April 1792, when a common thief and assassin named Nicolas-Jacques Pelletier was executed before a predictably large crowd on the Place de Grève, the victim being clad, for reasons that are unclear, in the traditional red shirt of the parricide, and the lever being raised by none other than the ancien régime's executioner in chief, Charles-Henri Sanson, now known not as the *bourreau* (executioner) but by the title—rational, secular, sanitized—of *exécuteur des jugements criminels*. As Daniel Arasse has written, the guillotine was at once a laicization, mechanization, and banalization of death. It humanized by, paradoxically, dehumanizing, by replacing the human agency of headsman and hangman by the impersonal operation of the lever and blade. It was held to be painless, though there was, both at the time of the guillotine's introduction and throughout the century that followed, a copious medical, philosophical, and anecdotal literature asking whether the severed head remained conscious and, if so, for how long.[19]

The first political *guillotinade,* that of Louis-David Collenot d'Angremont, was carried out on the Place de Grève on 21 August 1792, whereafter political executions were transferred away from the heart of the city to the Place du Carrousel, the Place de la Révolution, the Champ de Mars, and the Barrière du Trône Renversé, the precise location at any one time depending on a complex of political factors.[20] For the rest of the revolutionary and Napoleonic periods, the Place de Grève seems to have been reserved for nonpolitical executions.

No such distinction was observed by the restored Bourbon monarchy. As early as July 1816 three members of the so-called Conspiracy of Patriots were executed on the Place de Grève, having first had their right hands amputated, the traditional mutilation for parricides, for their target had been the father of fathers, the king. On 7 June 1820, Louvel, the deranged assassin of the duc de Berry, slain outside the old Opéra on 14 February, was guillotined, but the most celebrated political execution conducted on the Place de Grève was that of the Four Sergeants of La Rochelle (Sergeants Bories, Raoulx, Pommier, and Goubin), who, as members of the nationwide clandestine network known as the Carbonari or Charbonnerie, had conspired with other veterans of the Napoleonic armies and various teachers and students in Paris to overthrow the Bourbon regime. On the evening of 21 September 1822 the four young men were executed on the Place de Grève, and their cries of "Vive la liberté!" and "French blood is about to flow!" were greeted in silence by the appalled and apparently sympathetic crowd. Later that evening Louis XVIII and his court celebrated the birthday of Mademoiselle at the Pavillon Marsan, a coincidence that lowered the king still further in the eyes of his opponents.[21]

Only the Terror was more extravagant in its use of the death penalty than the restored Bourbon monarchy, which handed down no fewer than 1,986 death sentences in France as a whole between 1816 and 1820 alone, with a further 554 between 1826 and 1830, of which 360 were carried out.[22] It is scarcely an accident, therefore, that many of the most important French texts attacking capital punishment date precisely from the last years of the Restoration Monarchy and the first of its bourgeois successor: François Guizot's *De la peine de mort en matière politique* (1822); Charles Lucas's *Du système pénal et du système répressif en général, et de la peine de mort en particulier* (1827); Hugo's *Le Dernier Jour d'un condamné,* of 1829, followed by the preface of March 1832; Jules Janin's *L'Ane mort et la femme guillotinée,* also of 1829; a typically pungent *Scène populaire dessinée à la plume,* on a public execution, by Henri Monnier in 1830; Lamartine's ode "Contre la peine de mort" of December that year; Charles Nodier's *Histoire d'Hélène Gillet* of February 1832; Hugo's *Claude Gueux* of July 1834; and so on. Nor is it any accident that the greatest fictional work of the year 1830 itself, Stendhal's *Le Rouge et le noir,* and its supreme musical masterpiece, Hector Berlioz's *Symphonie fantastique,* both climax with the guillotining, real or imaginary, of the hero. By one of the most ironic reversals of French history, the guillotine, which owed its initial notoriety to the execution of Louis XVI, was by the mid-1820s inexorably associated with the regime of his brothers.

After the fall of Charles X, there were great hopes among abolitionists that the guillotine would finally be consigned to history, at the very least for political offenses. But, despite Louis-Philippe's personal opposition to the death penalty, the guillotine was retained for both political and criminal executions, and abolitionists were forced to acknowledge, with Victor Hugo, that "the scaffold is the one structure that revolutions never demolish."[23]

If execution by guillotine was seen by the Jacobin Amar as the Revolution's "red mass," its eucharistic sacrament, the attention of the "congregation" was focused equally on the human host and its consecrating "priest," the *exécuteur des jugements criminels,* as he had been known since 1787, while remaining *le bourreau* in everyday speech. Both before, during, and after the Revolution, the figure of the executioner, principally in the person of Charles-Henri Sanson (1739–1806) and his numerous executioner agnates and affines, exercised a prodigious hold over the popular and literary imagination of France. In one sense the polar opposite of the king, the *bourreau* was in another sense his virtual double, as awesome, as set apart, in a word as sacred as the reigning monarch himself. King and executioner were as closely linked, linked in their very difference, in the imaginative world of the Old Regime, as were king and fool, their secret kinship recognized by the popular designation of the *bourreau* as "Monsieur de Paris" (or "Monsieur de Rouen" or whatever), with its simultaneous royal and ecclesiastical overtones. If the Bourbons had been kings of France since 1589, the Sansons had been executioners, from father to son, since 1688. Kings became kings when their fathers died, whatever their age, and so, amazingly, did *bourreaux* become *bourreaux:* on the death of Charles Sanson in 1726, his son Jean-Baptiste was appointed public executioner at the age of seven, and until his majority he attended executions conducted by his deputy or "regent."[24] Like kings and their offspring, executioners and their offspring married among themselves: the ramifying Bourbon dynasty had its parodic counterpart in the Sanson dynasty, which in time supplied, or was linked by marriage to, the executioners of Etampes, Meaux, Rennes, Orléans, Reims, Soissons, Tours, Blois, Melun, and many more besides.

The executioner's person was, like the king's, charged with sacred mana. Neither he nor any of the objects he used should be touched, money due him should be placed on the counter or even hurled at his feet, his glass should be smashed after he had drunk from it, and so on.[25] But just as the king traditionally possessed thaumaturgic powers, so the executioner was sought out, even as he was shunned, as a setter of broken bones or healer of epilepsy: "the executioner is a bit of a doctor," wrote Félix Pyat in 1841, "just as the doctor is a bit of an executioner."[26] If the king lived apart from his subjects, so did the executioner, often in a red-painted hovel outside the bounds of the polis, like the surviving Maison du Bourreau at Provins, near Paris. And so on and so on: in a large number of ways, king and *bourreau* were related to each other as positive to negative or, to borrow Robert Hertz's famous distinction, as *sacré de droite* to *sacré de gauche*.[27] Or, as Balzac put it in his apocryphal memoirs of Sanson, *Souvenirs d'un paria* (1830), the executioner, marked by the original taint (*souillure*) of his birth, is "the nether king" (*le roi d'en bas*), separated by an "immense interval" from the "king above" (*le roi d'en haut*), whose powers he reproduces in grotesque form: "I contaminate [*je flétris*] everything I touch; like a splash of oil, the contamination spreads, and it advances step by step, and from generation to generation."[28]

By 1830 or so, and certainly by 1850, most of these folk beliefs and practices had disappeared, though the executioner retained his sacred aura. In his chapter on the guillotine in his great compendium *Paris, ses organes, ses fonctions et sa vie* of 1872, Maxime Du Camp writes of the executioner that

> people no longer ask him for the grease from corpses to make love potions and mysterious unguents; but he remains nonetheless an obscure and much dreaded personage over whom there hangs an unjust fall from grace—for if the law is to be executed, there must be an executioner—and Monsieur de Maistre was unable to raise him in the estimation of the public by saying that he was the linchpin of the social edifice.[29]

The allusion here is to the single most notorious description of the executioner in French literature, the reference point of every subsequent discussion, the truly remarkable excursus in de Maistre's posthumous *Soirées de Saint-Pétersbourg* (1821), in which the Count, the mouthpiece of the ultraroyalist and ultra-Catholic author, invites his interlocutors and readers to, as he puts it, "meditate on the *bourreau*." Although, says the Count, the executioner is "made like us externally," everything combines to set him apart as "an extraordinary being" from the rest of humanity, sacred in the double sense of *fascinans et tremendum*:

> And yet all greatness, all power, all hierarchy [*subordination*] is based on the executioner: he is the horror and the bond of human association. Take away this incomprehensible agent from the world, and instantly order gives way to chaos, thrones are overturned, and society vanishes. God, who is the author of sover-

eignty, is also the author of punishment: he has suspended our earth on these two poles; for Jehovah is the master of the two poles, and on them he makes the earth turn.[30]

These words will reverberate throughout the nineteenth century, exciting horror, combined perhaps with an unacknowledged shudder of excitement, in opponents of capital punishment such as Hugo (whose writings on the death penalty may be read as sustained anti-Maistrian polemic) and, in the case of some of its proponents, such as Baudelaire and Huysmans, striking some deep chord with their sadomasochistic temperaments and the Sado-Catholic ideology in which they clothed them. They are present, for example, in Jules Janin's strange work *L'Ane mort et la femme guillotinée* of 1829 when the executioner proclaims that he enjoys "the one legitimate right that has not been denied one single instant during our times," and explains how

> Revolution, anarchy, Empire, Restoration, nothing made any difference; my right has always remained in its place, moving neither a step forward nor a step back. Beneath this right, royalty bowed its head, then the people, then the Empire; everything passed under the yoke; I alone have no yoke; I have been stronger than the laws, whose supreme sanction I am; the laws have changed a thousand times over, I alone have not changed once, I have been as unwavering as destiny and as strong as duty, and I have emerged from so many ordeals with a pure heart and conscious of my virtue.[31]

If, as Hugo argued in his preface of 1832 to *Le Dernier Jour d'un condamné,* "the social edifice of the past rested on three columns, the priest, the king, and the executioner,"[32] it followed that to attack the executioner was to attack king and priest, and vice versa; whence, in some considerable measure, the frequency and urgency of attacks on capital punishment under the Restoration Monarchy. The *bourreau* stood for the whole Catholic-legitimist worldview, of which, as de Maistre clearly saw, he was both foundation and linchpin: "all hierarchy is based on the executioner." But the implications of abolitionism went further. At the theological core of legitimism lay the doctrine of original sin, of some aboriginal calamity, willed by man, which could be redeemed only by Christ's atoning sacrifice and of which, in the meantime, the consequences had to be restrained by the repressive apparatus of the royalist-Catholic state, the panoply of torture and retribution, of which the death penalty was the central and indispensable component. It is here that the essential dividing line falls between supporters and opponents of the death penalty. For supporters, crime, especially violent crime, was an expression of man's primordial sinfulness, and the criminal could atone for it only by offering up his life in sacrifice, even as Christ offered up his life to redeem humanity from Adam's sin. For opponents, crime was, as Hugo said in the preface to *Le Dernier Jour,* "an illness," social or psychological in origin, "and that illness will have its doctors who will replace your judges, its hospitals that will replace your convict settlements [*bagnes*]."[33]

It did not necessarily follow that all legitimists favored capital punishment for criminal offenses or that all liberals and republicans favored its abolition, at least for so-called political crimes, but attitudes toward execution did correlate closely with acceptance or rejection of the Catholic doctrine of original sin. Paradoxically, once more, it was the legitimists, whose totemic monarch had died on the scaffold, who became the scaffold's most resolute defenders, and liberals and republicans who, seeing what the paradigmatic sacrifice-by-guillotine of 21 January 1793 had led to (the Terror, the Empire, Restoration), were most eager to abolish blood sacrifice, to limit its application, or at the very least to render it socially invisible.

The secret affinity between king and executioner has a further unexpected consequence: that every condemned prisoner becomes something of a king when confronted with the executioner. In the preface to *Le Dernier Jour,* Hugo writes that many Parisians have no distractions other than the "free spectacle of royal pageantry and executions on the Place de Grève, that other free spectacle,"[34] pointing to an initial link between king and victim, while in the narrative itself the condemned man thinks constantly of the king and of what unites him with and divides him from the monarch, who "in this very city, at this very hour, and not far from here, in another palace, ... also has guards at all his doors, a man unique as you are in the midst of the people, with this difference, that he is as lofty as you are low."[35] As he is driven by open cart to the Place de Grève, there are cries from the crowd of "Hats off! Hats off!"—"as for the king," the prisoner comments, adding wryly, "Hats for them, the head for me."[36] If the king is desacralized, or differently sacralized, when he mounts the scaffold, the common prisoner is, for a few instants, invested with the sacred aura of a king, set apart by his sacrificial role and regalia, until the descending blade makes an ignominious headless trunk of him. Tonsured, he is also something of a priest, and as he steps out onto the boards for his final performance, he becomes an entertainer or player before the crowd. In a stunning text of 1884 titled "La Guillotine," Jules Vallès writes of one prisoner who mounted "the scaffold like the stairs of a theater ... , pale as though he were already dead—the flour-covered face of a clown."[37]

Now one can understand the imaginative logic of why, at the beginning of *Les Misérables* (1862), it is an acrobat or entertainer whom Monseigneur Bienvenu accompanies to the gallows; why, once more, it is an entertainer, the clown-conspirator Fancioulle in the prose poem "Une mort héroïque" (1863), who is Baudelaire's archetypal sacrificial artist victim; and why the boy victim in "La Corde" (1864) poses not just with "a tramp's violin" but with "the Crown of Thorns and the Nails of the Passion."[38] One can understand, too, the particular resonance for Baudelaire of the horrendous pantomime scene related in *De l'essence du rire* (1855):

> For some misdeed or other, Pierrot was finally due to be guillotined. Why the guillotine rather than hanging, the scene being in England? ... I don't know; no doubt to add to what follows. The fateful instrument was thus already erected on a French stage that was greatly surprised by this romantic novelty. After having struggled and bellowed like a bullock scenting the slaughterhouse, Pierrot finally went to his end. His head was severed from the neck, a big white and red head, and rolled noisily past the prompter's nook, revealing the bleeding disk of the neck, the severed vertebra, and every detail of a piece of butcher's meat freshly cut for display. But, suddenly, the shortened torso, moved by the irresistible monomania of a thief, stood up, triumphantly filched its own head like a knuckle of ham or a bottle of wine, and, much quicker-witted than noble Saint Denis, stuffed it into its pocket![39]

Guillotined, martyred acrobat and crucified Christ are emblems not only of each other but of the supreme Baudelairean victim, the sacrificial poet, whom "the blind Angel of expiation"[40] has set apart from the rest of humanity to atone on its behalf for some unnamed and perhaps unnamable sin. In the circumstances, it is, at the very least, piquant that, spotting Baudelaire dining in the Café Riche in October 1857, not two months after the condemnation of *Les Fleurs du mal,* the Goncourt brothers should have described him as "tieless, bare-necked, his head close-cropped, in true guillotine attire [*en vraie toilette de guillotiné*]." But, they add, when he speaks, "his voice sharp as a blade," the poet "aims at and hits the tone of a Saint-Just [*vise au Saint-Just et l'attrape*]."[41]

"It would perhaps be a joy to be alternatively victim and executioner," wrote Baudelaire toward the end of his life.[42] If Baudelaire's exemplary artists are "souls destined to the altar, sacred in a manner of speaking," fated to "march to death and glory by way of a permanent sacrifice of themselves,"[43] they are also, in their way, executioners, *exécuteurs des hautes œuvres*, relentless in their pursuit of their goal, comparable, as Baudelaire says of Delacroix, to those "ancient sovereigns of Mexico, to that Moctezuma whose hand, well practiced in sacrifice, could in a single day immolate three thousand creatures on the pyramid altar of the Sun."[44] If the *bourreau* is an artist, proud of both his strength and his touch—"no one can break on the wheel like I can," boasts Maistre's executioner[45]—the bored artist-dandy for his part "dreams / Of scaffolds, as he puffs his water pipe" ("Au lecteur"),[46] or, as Baudelaire puts it in the third of his "Spleen" poems ("Je suis comme le roi d'un pays pluvieux"):

> Rien ne peut l'égayer, ni gibier, ni faucon,
> Ni son peuple mourant en face du balcon.
> Du bouffon favori la grotesque ballade
> Ne distrait plus le front de ce cruel malade....
>
> [Nothing can cheer him, game or falconry, / Not even subjects dying at his door. / The comic jingles of the court buffoon / Do not amuse this twisted invalid.][47]

The king, the executioner, the clown, the beheaded: linked together in a powerful thematic nexus, this sacrificial quartet reaches out beyond Baudelaire to the collective imagination of the nineteenth century as a whole. How telling that, in another cultural context entirely, the condemned man in "The Ballad of Reading Gaol" should be wearing something like a cricket cap on his head as he goes out to die.[48]

Although, to the disappointment of many liberals, the Bourgeois Monarchy did not abolish capital punishment, it did bring in one crucial innovation that further undermined its legitimacy in the eyes of supporters and opponents alike. As well as abolishing judicial torture, including branding (*flétrissure*) and the mutilation of parricides before their execution, the new regime quickly decreed that executions would no longer be carried out, as they had been since time immemorial, at four in the afternoon on the Place de Grève, in the center of Paris; henceforth they would be transferred to the Barrière Saint-Jacques, on the southern perimeter of the city, and there they would take place, still in public, at first light. The new location was consecrated, as it were, by the execution of one Desondrieux on 3 February 1832. This removal of the guillotine from center to periphery is clearly correlated with the "great enclosure" of the insane studied by Michel Foucault, with the relocation of cemeteries beyond the city limits that had been under way since the late eighteenth century, and such similar measures as the banning of the slaughtering of animals within the city and the construction of abattoirs outside it.[49] In a large number of ways, *le sacré de gauche* was being expelled from the city proper into the ambiguous limbo of the countryside, there to be rendered invisible, at least to the city's middle-class residents. In addition, the virtual desacralization of the monarchy in 1830 had as its corollary the effective desacralization and occultation of the executioner.

This attempted concealment and denial of the guillotine did not, of course, satisfy abolitionists such as Hugo and Lamartine. On the contrary, the abolitionist case was strengthened, for, with the effective disappearance of the guillotine from everyday life, the deterrence argument that defenders of the death penalty, then as now, made so much use of became increasingly difficult to invoke. Now that executions were carried out "on the sly" (*en tapinois*), as Hugo witheringly put it, how could people possibly be deterred by something they never saw?

> But look, are you seriously trying to create an example when you miserably slit the throat of some poor devil in the most secluded corner of the outer boulevards? On the Place de Grève, in the middle of the day, fair enough; but at the Barrière Saint-Jacques! at eight in the morning! Who is passing by at that hour? Who is out and about? Who realizes that you are killing a man there? Who suspects that you are creating an example there? An example for whom? The trees on the boulevard, apparently.[50]

With the *escamotage*, or conjuring away, of the guillotine—Hugo's expression again[51]—the whole sacrificial concept of capital punishment was seriously weakened. It became difficult to view the *bourreau* as, in Lamartine's words, "the executor of a kind of priesthood [*sacerdoce*] of humanity"[52] when he had, in effect, become a simple operator or public functionary, clad like every other official of the Bourgeois Monarchy (including the bourgeois monarch himself) in a simple black suit. The significance of what had happened was clearly perceived by Félix Pyat:

Formerly, when kings were legitimate, the executioner, people say, was legitimate as well. The executioner is dead! ... Long live the executioner! and Sanson II replaced Sanson I just as Louis XVI replaced Louis XV. Now the monarchy of the Place de Grève is no more absolute than that of Abdul I. It has its charter [*charte*], or its specifications and conditions; it does not exist by its own right, by the grace of God, but by adjudication, after sealed tender; it is constitutional.[53]

It followed that "the Place de Grève having been wrested by the people from the *bourreau* as from the king," the guillotine was also "a casualty of July [*une vaincue de juillet*]."[54] Now that executions were carried out semi-invisibly (though still in public) on the periphery of the city, "glorifiers of the executioner," if they survived, were hard put, in Lamartine's words, to attribute "an expiatory and regenerative power [*vertu*] to the blood that is shed" and to see the executioner as "the priest of flesh, the sacrificer of humanity."[55]

After 1830, capital punishment still had supporters aplenty, but few enthusiasts; arguments for retention were pragmatic rather than metaphysical or theological. No longer an altar, the scaffold became an anonymous social mechanism. Not surprisingly, the number of executions dropped sharply, averaging about thirty a year for the whole of France throughout the Bourgeois Monarchy.[56]

Few regretted the effective disappearance of the guillotine from public life. Among those who did, or who seemed to, was the young Gustave Flaubert (1821–80), who, in his *Par les champs et par les grèves* (1847), brings together in a single complex meditation many of the archetypal figures and features of "premodern" urban life on the eve of their extinction or exclusion:

In the past, when one went for a walk, there was a good chance of encountering bears, tumblers [*bateleurs*], tambourines [*tambours de basque*], red-costumed monkeys dancing on a dromedary's back, but all that has similarly disappeared, hounded out in like fashion, proscribed beyond possibility of return; the guillotine is located beyond the tollgates and functions clandestinely, convicts travel in a closed carriage, and processions are prohibited! Before long, traveling players will have disappeared as well, to give way to magnetic séances and reformist banquets, and the tightrope artiste leaping in the air, with her spangled dress and long balancing pole, will be as far removed from us as the nautch girl [*bayadère*] of the Ganges.[57]

Guillotine and entertainer form, it seems, an inseparable imaginative and social dyad, such that the exclusion or occultation of either necessarily requires the marginalization of the other. Both belong, in their different but related ways, to the ambiguous liminal realm of the sacred, which, in a whole series of ways, the dominant secularized culture of the Bourgeois Monarchy and beyond sought to exclude from the polis, while stopping short of actually abolishing it: a parallel with the attempted but wholly unsuccessful marginalization of prostitution may also suggest itself. In the connected realms of death (the cemeteries), madness (the asylums), sexuality (prostitution), popular pleasures (strolling players), and justice (prisons, the guillotine), it was a matter less of abolishing *le sacré de gauche* than of clearly separating it from *le sacré de droite* and of banishing it, like the lower classes, from center to periphery, where it could be both preserved and denied. To that extent, the removal of the guillotine beyond the city is symptomatic of the massive desacralization of life that took place in France during the first half of the nineteenth century, the demotion of the executioner from public sacrificer to barely visible functionary being as vital to the construction of the new bourgeois order as the parallel downgrading of charismatic king of France to contractually bonded king of the French in 1830.

Concomitantly, opposition to that order from the left sought the total destruction of the guillotine, not its simple removal from the public realm. The first stage of that process was achieved by the ending, in one of the first measures passed under the Second Republic, of capital punishment for political offenses. In one move the new regime distanced itself not merely from its predecessor but from the First Republic, which in other respects served as its prototype. In February 1850, Victor Schœlcher, the principal proponent of the law that abolished slavery at the same time as the death penalty for political offenses, proposed the abolition of the guillotine altogether. The proposal was rejected, but by the 1860s most factions of the French left (as well as many individuals in the liberal center) were opposed to the death penalty as such. During the Commune, some ultraleftists called for the return of the guillotine for political offenses—a *cantinière* of the 74th Regiment called for four guillotines to be operating nonstop—but more typical of Communard opinion were those men and women of the eleventh arrondissement who gathered in front of their local town hall and, by the statue of Voltaire (an early abolitionist), solemnly incinerated a specially created guillotine to cries of "Down with the death penalty!" Thus, in another notable reversal of history, did the Commune of 1871 seek to distance itself from its prototype of 1793–94.[58]

With the transfer of executions to the Barrière Saint-Jacques, after 1830 there were fewer emblematic victims to whet the curiosity, excite the compassion and solidarity, or sate the blood lust of the Parisian public, and fewer opportunities, too, for the condemned to invest themselves with the martyrological aura of their forebears. One partial exemption was Pierre-François Lacenaire (1803–36), who, born into a respectable middle-class Lyon family, lived a life divided among crime, prison, and periods of enlistment in the army followed by desertion, until, in December 1834, he and an accomplice (who was also possibly his lover) murdered a fellow criminal named Chardon and his aged mother before ransacking their wretched living quarters on the Passage du Cheval-Rouge, not far from Les Halles. What marked out Lacenaire from the generality of murderers was a combination of his origins, his utter lack of remorse, and his not inconsiderable literary talent, which, thanks to the publication in *Le Charivari* and *Le Corsaire* of a number of ballads and other poems extolling the criminal life, made him well known to the crime-obsessed literary public of the 1830s, even before the publication of his posthumous *Mémoires* in May 1836 endowed him with the mana of a real-life satanic saint à la Byron.[59]

In his *Mémoires,* of which only the final pages appear to have been ghosted, Lacenaire presents himself as foredoomed to die under the guillotine's blade. As a youth, he witnessed an execution on the Place des Terreaux in Lyon, and his devout and law-abiding father, who accompanied him, warned his wayward son, predictably, that that was how he would end up if he failed to mend his ways. "From that moment," says Lacenaire, "an invisible bond existed between me and the appalling machine.... How often have I been guillotined in my dreams!"[60] According to one of the innumerable stories circulating in Paris, many of them launched by the murderer himself, Lacenaire even had calling cards printed bearing the inscription "Pierre-François Lacenaire, fiancé of the guillotine."[61] He was probably the first killer to manipulate the media and so transform himself into a public spectacle *before* his execution, *fascinans et tremendus,* like Lucifer himself. In early manhood, according to his own account, he made a conscious decision to become the scourge of society and to draw "a line of eternal separation between myself and the world; thus did I cross the Rubicon";[62] "it was the entire social edifice that I wanted to attack in its foundations, in its rich, its hard-hearted, egotistical rich."[63] Describing himself as a "materialist" and implicitly associating himself with the Parisian and Lyonnais insurgents of the "time of riots," he decided, he says, to murder Chardon and his mother as a "bloody vindication of my life, a bloody protest against this society of egotists that had rejected me."[64] The whole of history appears to him as a war of executioners against victims: if he cannot be one of the former, he will espouse the lot of the latter, consciously, deliberately, and to the full.[65]

At his trial, wearing a stylish blue coat (conceivably an echo, as with Robespierre, of Werther's "suicide suit"), Lacenaire made no attempt to defend or excuse himself, and was executed, along with his accomplice, Avril, on 9 January 1836 at the Barrière Saint-Jacques in the presence of five or six hundred spectators. Reputedly he twisted his head upward to watch the blade fall upon him.[66] "It was only in Paris that I wanted to die," he wrote in his *Mémoires*, "I do not conceal it, it would have greatly displeased me to do business with a provincial executioner."[67] Perhaps his only regret was that, Satan and Christ rolled into one, he was deprived of the supreme stage of the Place de Grève in mid-afternoon to act out his final transfiguration.

After 1851, even the Barrière Saint-Jacques was considered too public, and executions in Paris were carried out in front of the Grande Roquette prison, in the east of the city, until 1900, when they were transferred even farther from the city center, to the forecourt of La Santé prison. It was on the Place de la Roquette that, at dawn on the morning of 19 January 1870, the second most famous French murderer of the nineteenth century, the twenty-one-year-old Jean-Baptiste Troppmann, was guillotined in the presence of a huge crowd that included Maxime Du Camp, presumably doing research for the relevant chapter of his magnum opus on Paris; the dramatist Victorien Sardou (1831–1908), author of the play on which Giacomo Puccini based *Tosca;* and Ivan Turgenev (1818–83), in whom the occasion inspired what is probably the most searching and certainly the most harrowing description of a public execution in France.

Troppmann had been convicted of killing a mother and her five (seven, according to some accounts) children on the Plaine de Pantin, in the notorious area outside the fortifications in the northeast of the city, in September 1869. Crowds had been gathering outside La Roquette for several days before the execution in the hope of seeing the guillotine (*les bois de justice*) being bolted together, and when Du Camp and Turgenev arrived around 11 P.M. on the night of the 18th, a massive throng was already in position, men, women (many of them prostitutes of varying status), even children combining to make what Turgenev calls a kind of elemental rumbling, roaring noise like an "unending Wagnerian crescendo, not rising continuously, but with huge intervals between the ebb and flow."[68] The guillotine stands out "dimly and strangely rather than terribly against the dark sky," possessed of "a sort of sinister shapeliness, the shapeliness of a long, carefully stretched-out swan's neck. The large, dark-red wicker basket, looking like a suitcase, aroused a feeling of disgust in me."

The rumbling of the crowd, interspersed with songs, jokes, and the occasional shout of protest against this or that member of the imperial family, grows louder as the hour of the execution approaches, and, inevitably, a "heavy, rank breath of alcoholic fumes" begins to impregnate the night air. Street urchins clamber up into the surrounding trees, "whistling and screeching like birds," and Turgenev refrains from watching the testing of the guillotine as "the feeling of some unknown transgression committed by me, of some secret shame," becomes increasingly difficult to repress; it is as though the horses munching their oats in their nosebags are "the only innocent creatures among us all."

Invited by prearrangement into the prison, Du Camp and Turgenev eventually find themselves in the presence of Troppmann himself, still protesting his innocence but accepting the ministrations of a priest, happy as a child being undressed when the prison guards remove the straitjacket in which he had been confined. What, Turgenev asks himself, is sustaining Troppmann in his final extremity? Innate courage, or the desire to cut a figure before his audience as he prepares his farewell performance? The group is joined by the executioner, M. Heidenreich ("Indric" to the crowd outside), who, in his white necktie and black suit, looks "for all the world like a diplomat or a Protestant pastor." The ritual *toilette du condamné* is duly performed: the coarse cloth of the prisoner's uniform is cut away from his neck, exposing his shoulder blades, and "thick strands of wiry, dark-brown hair [slide] over the shoulders and [fall] on the floor"; one lock lands on Turgenev's boot. The Russian cannot take his eyes off the murderer's hands, "once stained with innocent blood, but now lying so helplessly one on top of the other": the erstwhile executioner is now unequivocally a victim.

At five to seven, the execution party goes out to the forecourt, and an "unbroken, ear-splitting, thunderous wave" assails them as soon as they step over the threshold. Seeming to Turgenev as tiny as a child, Troppmann is seized by "two men pouncing on him from the right and the left, like spiders on a fly." At that point, with "the ground slowly rising and falling under my feet," Turgenev can take no more; he looks away, and a short while later he hears "a light knocking of wood on wood—that was the sound made by the top part of the yoke with the slit for the passage of the knife as it fell round the murderer's head and kept it immobile.... Then something suddenly descended with a hollow growl and stopped with an abrupt thud.... Just as though a huge animal had retched.... I cannot think of any better comparison. I felt dizzy. Everything swam before my eyes."

By looking away, Turgenev failed to see the incident that caused Troppmann's death to enter the annals of Parisian executions: somehow the condemned man contrived to bite one of "M. Indric's" fingers, adding a minor streamlet of blood to the gory occasion.[69] As at the execution of Louis XVI, and no doubt on countless similar occasions in the intervening period, two men managed to break through the cordon of soldiers and, "crawling under the guillotine, [began] wetting their handkerchiefs in the blood that had dripped through the chinks of the planks": even in the age of positivist rationalism, the sacrificers were still eager to commune in the blood of the victim. The crowd dispersed, their faces instinct with "an expression of boredom, fatigue, dissatisfaction, disappointment, dull, purposeless disappointment," as at the end of an orgy that had somehow gone wrong. Turgenev looked round at his fellows: "not one of us, absolutely no one looked like a man who realized that he had been present at the performance of an act of social justice: everyone tried to turn away in spirit and, as it were, shake off the responsibility for this murder." All that remained for Turgenev was "a feeling of involuntary astonishment at a murderer, a moral monster, who could show his contempt for death": like so many of the guillotined, before and since, Troppmann had managed to transform execution into self-transfiguration.

Like Lacenaire before him, he begat a significant literary offspring, most notably the "Soliloque de Troppmann" by the execution-obsessed piano-playing troubadour Maurice Rollinat (1846–1903), the godson of George Sand and a fixture at the Chat Noir in the 1880s and 1890s.[70] As late as 1935, Georges Bataille gave the name Troppmann—too-much-man or too-little-man [Trop-peu-mann]?—to the narrator of his pornographic extravaganza Le Bleu du ciel (first published 1957), having already used the murderer's name as a pseudonym when writing the scatological W.C. of 1926. "I want to be tortured and executed [supplicié]," declares his alter ego in Ma mère (1954–55), "I would like to laugh in my agony [supplice]."[71] Damiens; Louis XVI; Lacenaire; Tapner (the murderer whose hanging at Guernsey in 1854 so obsessed the exiled Victor Hugo);[72] Troppmann; the doctor-poisoner Couty de la Pommerais (executed 1883, and the principal focus for Villiers de l'Isle Adam's guillotine-inspired fantasies, to be discussed shortly); the anarchist Emile Henry, guillotined in May 1894, who, as he went to his death, appeared to Georges Clemenceau as "a vision of Munkacsy's

Christ, with his crazed look, his appallingly pale face, stubbled with sparse, tortured red hair," and whose appearance overwhelmed Barrès with "the tragic beauty of his revolt and of his white denuded breast":[73] the martyred body of the condemned man, what Baudelaire, referring to Damiens, characteristically called *l'ivresse du supplicié*, the intoxication, the ecstasy, of the victim, is one of the abiding obsessions of the nineteenth-century literary imagination.

If the left wanted to abolish the death penalty and the center to render it invisible, the right, particularly the legitimist right, sought, logically enough, to restore it to public visibility and so reinstate it as a sacrament of expiatory suffering and atonement. As a disciple of de Maistre, who had come to see virtually the whole of existence (and particularly the sexual relations of men and women) as a perpetual dialectic of executioner and victim, Baudelaire was adamant in his defense of the death penalty as a "mystical idea" designed to redeem both criminal and society, and requiring, "in order that the sacrifice may be perfect," not merely consent but joy on the part of the victim. Accordingly, "to give chloroform to a condemned man would be an act of impiety, because it would take away his consciousness of his grandeur as a victim and destroy his chances of gaining Paradise."[74] The courage displayed by Orsini, the would-be assassin of Napoleon III, at his execution on 13 March 1858 is a likely source of the remarkable prose poem "Une Mort héroïque" (1863), referred to above. In 1852 a curious work dedicated to "Sanctissimo Pio Nono," titled *De la loi du talion et de la peine de mort dans les sociétés modernes* and written by the otherwise unknown Henry Imbart and Frédéric Le Blanc, sought to reinstate the executioner as the incarnation of what they called the Not Me of society, law, and God, who, by putting to death the earthly Me of the capital offender, gives his spiritual self at least a possibility of redemption:

> At the final moment, at the foot of the scaffold, the confessor presents the crucifix to the criminal. In this final embrace of the God-Man and the sinner, there appears and is made manifest the pardon of the victim through the mouth of the priest. It is the sacred chrism, the balm that must serve as a vehicle to the patient, urging him to repair, in a worthy and heroic manner, the assault that he committed, with premeditation, on one of his brothers, like him a member of society and humanity."[75]

Not surprisingly, there were violent protests from the right when, in 1885, the moderate republic decided, while still preserving the principle of public execution, to render the prisoner's death effectively invisible by doing away with the scaffold and performing the execution at ground level. For Villiers de l'Isle Adam (1838–89), not an orthodox believer but close to the Sado-Catholic tradition initiated by de Maistre and a writer permanently obsessed with the theme of execution,[76] removal of the scaffold undermined the whole sacrificial meaning of capital punishment, which required precisely that the "expiating agony" of the victim be seen by the vast crowds that, the transfer to the outskirts notwithstanding, still gathered to witness public executions. A regular witness of executions himself (so much so that, according to Bloy, *messieurs de la guillotine* themselves considered him an "enlightened connoisseur" of their art), Villiers protested in his brutally titled *Le Réalisme dans la peine de mort* of February 1885 that the steps of the scaffold are "the *property* of every condemned man," and that to deprive him of the right of ascending them in full view of the crowd is to deny him "the illusion, the *nonetheless sacred* illusion," of dying better than he has lived and so of expiating the sin he has committed. Every public execution, Villiers avers, is a "theater of mysterious symbols," not one of which can be elided or suppressed without weakening the others and depriving the whole drama of its properly sacred gravitas. It follows that the guillotine minus its scaffold is a "farmyard guillotine" (*guillotine de basse-cour*), "fallen, underhanded, oblique," and the death it deals out is as banal and unredeeming as the death the condemned man himself inflicted, whence the "impressions of butchery caused by this guillotine lying absurdly in ambush at ground level."

Like the faithful at high mass, the crowd attends public executions in order "to commune morally and as closely as is possible with the horror of a man who, alone among his fellows, knows in advance the instant when he will die." To deny the congregation full view of the human host is to deny it full communion and to reduce the victim's death to a trivial event. The conclusion, for Villiers, is self-evident: "Let us either restore to Justice the Scaffold in all its salubrious and sacred horror, or let us consign it to the abattoir, with no more homicidal shilly-shallying; this degraded, evil guillotine, which humiliates the nation, disgusts and scandalizes every thinking person, and strikes fear in no one."[77]

Of course, no such choice was made, and the neither-public-nor-private, semivisible execution continued to be the norm in France until just before the outbreak of World War II, the last publicly executed prisoner being the serial killer Eugène Weidmann at Versailles in June 1939. Proposals by the Senate in 1885 and again in 1898 to move the guillotine within prison walls were rejected by the Chamber of Deputies, with abolitionists, mainly Radicals and Socialists, voting for the retention of public executions lest the guillotine simply be forgotten if allowed to carry out its work in private.[78]

By the mid-1850s, and certainly by the mid-1870s, the once vibrant, if squalid and intermittently dangerous, heart of Paris had been successfully domesticated, transformed into largely ceremonial space by the simple expedient of driving its human population outward to the periphery. After 1871, the Hôtel de Ville never again played a major part in national politics, and with the abolition of the post of mayor of Paris it ceased even to be the cynosure of municipal affairs. Bereft of its scaffold and no longer used for the hiring of workers, its square became just another hyposignificant space in the center of the city. In the early 1830s the Palais-Royal was purged of what Balzac called the "terrible bazaar"—terrible but, like everything terrible in the human comedy, utterly alluring—that spilled over the whole of its immense central courtyard, especially the congeries of wooden stalls and shacks known as the Galeries de Bois, whose "infamous poetry" brought together, of an afternoon and evening, all manner of buyers and sellers, buskers, acrobats, puppeteers, ventriloquists, writers, gamblers, drinkers, and prostitutes and their clients. It was "horrible and gay," says Balzac in *Illusions perdues* (1837–43), and by the mid-1830s it was already the empty, meaningless space it has remained ever since.[79]

The street stalls that lined the Pont-Neuf, the only tollfree bridge in the center of Paris, were also removed, and the highly variegated population of tradesmen who operated there—all the knife sharpeners, hawkers of stories of murders and accidents, sellers of paper windmills, boot laces and ribbons, ratcatchers and dog groomers, and so on and so on—found themselves increasingly regulated, harassed, and driven out of business by a combination of economic change and bureaucratic control; everywhere the inside world of the municipal authorities was asserting its control over the outside world of the street.[80]

Finally, and perhaps most striking of all, the extraordinary mini-city of hovels and stalls that spread across the present Place du Carrousel under the windows of the Louvre was razed to the ground in the early 1850s. The contrast between its former vitality and the empty square that replaced it prompted the greatest of all poems of urban nostalgia, Baudelaire's "Le Cygne" of 1859, with its bitter acknowledgment that, though "the old Paris is no more," "the form of a city changes more quickly, alas! than the heart of a mortal," and that, as the old city metastatizes into the new, he alone, Baudelaire, remains unchanging and unchanged in his suffering:

Paris change! mais rien dans ma mélancolie
N'a bougé! palais neufs, échafaudages, blocs,
Vieux faubourgs, tout pour moi devient allégorie
Et mes chers souvenirs sont plus lourds que des rocs.

[Paris changes! but nothing in my melancholy / Has budged! new
palaces, scaffolding, building blocks, / Old faubourgs, everything
becomes an allegory for me, / And my dear memories are heavier
than stone.][81]

Everywhere the heterogeneity of *le vieux* Paris, with its vivid
chiaroscuro of poverty and wealth, its alveolated structure of largely
self-contained, autonomous urban villages, was giving way to the mono-
chrome of the modern metropolis, spatially homogenized but no less divided sociologically. By the 1880s, the outside had been effectively colo-
nized by the inside, and both *sacré de droite* and *sacré de gauche* had,
each in its way, been fatally diminished, the first nationalized and transformed into a tourist spectacle, the second driven out of the center of the
city and rendered to all intents and purposes invisible. Confronted by a
largely desacralized city, the urban pilgrim such as Huysmans could but
turn away from the "Saharas of the Carrousel"[82] and the boulevards'
mirage of modernity and look both inward, into his most secret self, and
sideways rather than outward, into the city's most obscure recesses, in
search of those oases of spirituality he so craved.

6

THE MIRACULOUS MEDAL
Rue du Bac (1830)

Compared with the later Mariophanies of La Salette (1846) and Lourdes (1858)—to say nothing of Knock (Ireland, 1879), Fatima (Portugal, 1917), and Medjugorje (Croatia, 1980s)—the apparitions at the Rue du Bac between July and December 1830 may seem to be no more than a prelude to greater things, of little lasting moment in themselves. They inspired no mass pilgrimage of the kind that made Lourdes a Catholic mecca after 1870, nor did the nun to whom the apparitions occurred—the twenty-four-year-old novice Catherine Labouré—achieve anything like the public notoriety of Bernadette Soubirous of Lourdes or Thérèse Martin, the Little Flower of Lisieux, whose *Histoire d'une âme* would become a best-seller in the early years of the twentieth century; indeed, while her visions became known nationally and internationally, her identity remained concealed even from her fellow sisters in the order of the Sisters of Charity, in which she lived a life of self-effacing dutifulness up to her death in 1876.

There were other differences, too, between Catherine and the later visionaries. She was not especially young, unlike Bernadette (who was fourteen at the time of the apparitions at Lourdes) or the children of La Salette, Pontmain (1870), and Fatima, and, though her origins were rural, she was neither a servant, a shepherdess, nor illiterate. The Labourés are described as large landowners (*gros propriétaires*), her father had been mayor of the village of Fain-les-Moutiers in the Champagne, and she was able to read, though perhaps not proficiently, by the time she came to the Rue du Bac as a novice in 1830.[1] She probably spoke patois more readily than French, but at least the Virgin was able to address her in the national language rather than in the regional vernacular she had to use at La Salette and Lourdes. Finally, Catherine's visions occurred not on an Alpine mountainside or before a grotto in the Pyrenees but in the very heart of the national capital, and it is in the first instance as a Parisian phenomenon that they must be understood, as part and parcel of the crucial years 1830–34, which Parisians would for decades refer to as "the time of riots" (le temps des émeutes): four years of almost continuous moral panic that the cholera epidemic of the spring, summer, and autumn of 1832, merging with the working-class uprising of June that year, would transform into an urban version of the Great Fear that had swept through the French countryside in the spring and summer of 1789.

Any account of a Marian vision must combine an exploration, where possible, of the individual psychology of the visionary or visionaries concerned with an understanding of the various milieux—local, regional, national, international—in which it is propagated and received.[2] It must also examine the politics of the Church at all the appropriate levels from parish priest to pontiff, for it is ultimately the Church that authenticates or invalidates the vision in question and so channels or disowns the wave of popular piety to which it almost invariably gives birth. Of all the alleged sightings of the Virgin in nineteenth-century France, the Church finally gave its sanction to only a handful—the Rue du Bac, La Salette, Lourdes, and Pontmain—and rejected, or only partly validated, a host of others whose claims to authenticity often seem as good, or as bad, as those elevated to canonical status. It may be that no Marian vision is intrinsically more probable or improbable than another. There is no inherent reason why Catherine Labouré's visions of 1830 should be considered authentic while those of the fourteen-year-old shepherdess Marie-Jeanne Grave at Notre-Dame de Redon-Espic in the Périgord in 1814 should be dismissed by the Church as spurious;[3] no reason why the distinctly suspect Mélanie Calvat (aged fifteen) and Maximin Giraud (eleven) should be believed at La Salette in 1846, while the assorted goatherds, shepherdesses, and servant girls who claimed to have seen the Virgin at various places in the Drôme in 1848–49 should be rejected out of hand by the local bishop;[4] and no reason, finally, why the five children of Pontmain should be treated as authentic visionaries by the Church while Estelle Faguette, a thirty-one-year-old chambermaid in the service of the comte de La Rochefoucauld at Pellevoisin in the Indre who experienced a series of visions in 1876, should now be almost totally forgotten, despite having been discreetly received by Leo XIII in 1900.[5] Clearly social and political contexts play crucial parts in the transformation of an inherently nonrational event into an authenticated vision, and it is this general truth that, perhaps more clearly than any subsequent instance, the case of Catherine Labouré so abundantly demonstrates.

The eighth of ten surviving children, Catherine lost her mother at the age of nine in 1815, and spent the following three years with an aunt at Saint-Rémy, five miles or so from her father's farm at Fain-les-Moutiers. She clearly missed her mother acutely, and had been seen to climb on a chair to kiss a statue of the Virgin in the dead woman's bedroom and to ask her to take the place of the mother she had lost. She also remained strongly attached to her father, the running of whose household, along with the bringing up of her younger sister and brother, became her sole responsibility when she returned to Fain at the age of twelve. Already Catherine was showing signs of intense devotion, fasting on Fridays and Saturdays and walking some distance to attend mass on Sundays (the church at Fain had no resident priest), and in her early teens determined to follow her elder sister Marie-Louise into the order of the Sisters of Charity. Sometime in the mid-1820s she had a dream in which an elderly priest—whom she subsequently identified with Saint Vincent de Paul (1581–1660), the founder of the order—stared at her silently as though in reproach, intensifying her desire to devote her life to the care of the sick and the poor. However, her father refused her permission to join the order when she attained her majority in 1827, and sent her to Paris, where for some eighteen months she worked in a restaurant owned by her widowed brother Charles on the Rue de l'Echiquier, in the present tenth arrondissement. Still determined to follow her religious vocation, Catherine made contact with the Sisters of Charity, and in January 1830, after returning to Fain, persuaded her father to let her follow her sister into the order; Pierre Labouré refused, however, to pay the customary dowry. It was paid by another brother, Hubert, a junior lieutenant in the gendarmerie who had at one time served in Charles X's personal guard in Paris. On 21 April 1830 Catherine arrived at the order's mother house on the Rue du Bac, on the Left Bank in the present seventh arrondissement, and was immediately plunged into a series of intense religious experiences that would culminate in the first of her visions on the night of 18–19 July 1830.[6]

On Sunday, 25 April, just four days after Catherine's arrival in Paris, the last great religious ceremony of the increasingly clericalized Restoration Monarchy took place when the remains of Saint Vincent de Paul were transferred with much civic and ecclesiastical pomp from Notre-Dame to the chapel of the mother house of the Lazarist order on the Rue de Sèvres, less than three hundred yards from the seminary on the Rue du Bac. All the novices of the Sisters of Charity joined the thousand-strong procession, which, headed by the papal nuncio and the archbishop of Paris, took six hours to move from Notre-Dame to the Rue de

Sèvres, where the saint's remains were placed in a sumptuous silver reliquary surmounted by a waxen effigy of "Monsieur Vincent" himself. The procession undoubtedly had a political motive—in the words of the nuncio, it "greatly afflicted and irritated liberals, who had to concede that religion still had strength in the number of its faithful in the capital, where impiety thought it held sway"[7]—and was followed by a week of devotions at the Lazarist house, which the sisters of the Rue du Bac attended each day and at one of which Charles X himself was present, and in all likelihood seen by Catherine.

In 1856, recounting her experiences of a quarter of a century before, Catherine said that "her feet were off the ground" (*elle ne tenait plus à la terre*) throughout the octave held in honor of the founder of her order, whom, her biographer suggests, she spontaneously identified with the other figures of authority in her strongly hierarchical universe: the king, the pope, the superior of her order, and, not least, her father, whom she had certainly angered by her insistence on following her religious vocation.[8] During the octave week, Catherine had repeated visions of Saint Vincent or his heart hovering, as it were, over a reliquary containing lesser relics of the saint in the chapel at the Rue du Bac. He appeared to her first in white, symbolizing, she later said, "calm, innocence, and union," then in fiery red (*rouge de feu*), representing charity and the renewal and extension "to the farthest ends of the earth" of the order he had founded, and finally in red-black (*rouge noir*), which plunged Catherine into an overwhelming sadness related—or so she later would claim—to the "change of government" that would take place in July 1830.[9]

Deeply disturbed, Catherine told her confessor. For a month nothing happened until at mass on the Feast of the Holy Trinity (6 June) she had a vision of Christ in the Blessed Sacrament. He appeared to her, she later said, "like a king, with the cross on his breast [that seemed] to flow down [*coulait*] onto the feet of Our Lord. And it seemed to me that Our Lord was stripped of all his adornments. Everything flowed and sank down to the earth. [*Tout a coulé à terre.*] It was then that I experienced the blackest and most somber thoughts.... I cannot explain it, but I thought that the king of the earth would be destroyed [*perdu*] and stripped of his royal garb."[10] A remarkable prophecy of the Restoration Monarchy's imminent dissolution or a retrospective gloss abetted by Catherine's strongly legitimist spiritual directors? Whatever the "truth," the assimilation of Christ and king was almost certainly made at the time, and the political content of the Marian visions that began six weeks later would be even more explicit, even allowing for much ex post facto interpretive embellishment.

On the night of 18–19 July, four days after Charles X's dissolution of Parliament, which precipitated his downfall, Catherine was awakened from her sleep by a child of four or five clad in white and suffused in miraculous brightness, whom she subsequently identified as her guardian angel. It was the eve of the Feast of Saint Vincent de Paul, and, like the other novices, Catherine had been given a tiny fragment of the saint's surplice. Following common popular practice, she had swallowed it, confident that, through Monsieur Vincent's intercession, she would at long last see the Good Mother she longed for: "I had gone to bed with . . . the thought that I would see my Good Mother that same night. I had wanted to see her for so long."

The child led her into the chapel, which, to her surprise, was illuminated "as for midnight mass," and, at the child's behest, she knelt down beside the seat (*fauteuil*) assigned to the order's spiritual director. There came a rustling as of a silk dress, and a figure whom Catherine could not at first recognize materialized on the altar close to a picture of Saint Joseph and seated on a *fauteuil* "like that of Saint Anne." But it was not Mary's mother but, the child explained, the Holy Virgin herself, and Catherine experienced "the sweetest moment of [her] life" as she knelt before her, hands resting on the Virgin's knees, to receive the celestial message: Catherine would suffer but know glory and joy, times would be bad, misfortunes (*malheurs*) would fall upon France, and the throne would be overturned (*renversé*). Religious orders, including her own, would decline and then revive. As for the clergy of Paris (at this the Virgin began to weep, as she would later do at La Salette), there would be victims, and the archbishop himself would be stripped of his vestments and killed. The streets would flow with blood, the cross would be spurned and cast down to the ground, and the whole earth would be plunged into misery and woe.

Having delivered her baleful tidings, the Virgin disappeared as swiftly as she had appeared, and the child, still radiating light, led her back to her room. It was 2 A.M. The whole experience had lasted three hours from beginning to end. Not surprisingly, Catherine did not get back to sleep that night.[11]

This account conflates two accounts given by Catherine, one in 1856 and the other shortly before her death in 1876, and there is obviously no way of distinguishing what she felt and thought at the time from what she may have added subsequently, either independently or at the instigation of her superiors and spiritual advisers. In 1876 she claimed that the Virgin told her that the archbishop of Paris would die "in forty years' time"; this is almost certainly an ex post facto addition to designate the killing of Archbishop Darboy in May 1871, though the theme of the death of an archbishop could well have been present in the original vision, or added after the killing of Archbishop Affre on the barricades in June 1848. But with this probable exception, the core of Catherine's narrative was probably what she told her confessor, as the Virgin had instructed her, immediately after the vision.

According to the account he published in March 1834, Monsieur Aladel dismissed the whole business as illusion and imagination at the time, but just over a week later, between 27 and 29 July, the throne of Charles X was indeed toppled, and a wave of anticlerical violence was unleashed to accompany the collapse of his ultra-Catholic regime. Religious houses were invaded and ransacked, mission crosses were pulled down, priests were attacked on the streets, and the archbishop of Paris, Monseigneur de Quélen, was obliged to remove his ecclesiastical vestments—note the stripping of the archbishop in both of Catherine's accounts—and take refuge in disguise.

Amidst this upsurge of anticlericalism, both the Lazarist house on the Rue de Sèvres and the seminary on the Rue du Bac escaped intact, and Monseigneur Frayssinous, Charles X's minister of religion, had sought sanctuary from the crowd at the Rue de Sèvres in apparent fulfillment of the Virgin's prediction to Catherine that "a pursued bishop would seek refuge with the Lazarists."[12] For Aladel and for Monsieur Etienne, the procurator general of the Lazarist order, in whom he confided, there was clearly more to Catherine's revelations than the novice's fantasies they at first appeared to be.

For four months after the first vision and the fall of the old order, there were no further incidents, but on the evening of 27 November, Catherine had a second vision of the Virgin while at prayer in the chapel. This time, according to Aladel's 1834 account, she appeared as a picture, clad in a white dress, blue cloak, and saffron-yellow veil (*un voile aurore*) with "bunches" (*faisceaux*) of brilliant rays of light issuing from her hands and symbolizing, so she explained to Catherine, "the graces that Mary obtains for mankind." Around the picture Catherine read the following invocation inscribed in letters of gold: "O Mary, conceived without sin, pray for us who have recourse to you." Catherine, according to one of her later accounts, fell into ecstasy—"je jouissais," she says, using a word whose common sexual sense in French argot is "to come"[13]—and as the picture turned round, she saw on the reverse the letter *M* surmounted by a small cross and set above the sacred hearts of Jesus and Mary. It was at this point that the Virgin gave the order that would bring Catherine and the Rue du Bac worldwide renown: "A medal must be struck based on this model, and those who wear it with an indulgence attached and who say this short prayer will enjoy a very special protection from the Mother of God."

When Aladel was told of the vision, he again reacted with skepticism, and he warned Catherine against surrendering to her imagination. To no avail, however, for in December Catherine had a third and final vision, again in the chapel in the early evening, when the Virgin appeared once more as a speaking picture to reiterate her instructions and promises of 27 November and telling Catherine that she would see her no more, though she would hear her voice speaking to her in prayer.

On 30 January 1831 Catherine took the veil and in February left the Rue du Bac for the Hospice d'Enghien at Reuilly, on the southeastern outskirts of Paris, where, brief intervals apart, she would remain for the rest of her life and where she and her vision of the miraculous medal might well have been totally forgotten but for her determination that it be known and for a remarkable convergence of political, social, and ecclesiastical circumstances that persuaded her superiors that its disclosure and propagation were in the interests of the Church.[14]

Although there can be no satisfactory explanation of Catherine's visions—to reduce them to a displaced longing for her dead mother is clearly inadequate[15]—certain conditions did combine to create in her an emotional, mental, and spiritual propensity to some kind of paranormal experience: her excitement at being permitted at last to follow her religious vocation followed immediately by the transfer of Monsieur Vincent's remains, the turmoil of the Three Glorious Days (and particularly the sacking of the archbishopric, of which she cannot have been unaware), together with the succession of Marian feast days that punctuated her visionary period and may have kept her on a more or less permanent spiritual high, and so on.[16] The subsequent adoption of her visions by the Church and the mass production and diffusion of the miraculous medal, however, are more readily explicable in sociological and political terms. By the end of 1830, the honeymoon of the Bourgeois Monarchy had already turned sour, and riots at the trial of Charles X's ministers in December revealed the extent and intensity of popular disillusion brought on by continuing economic recession, which the new government exacerbated when in January 1831 it abolished the charity workshops that had been set up to provide emergency employment and relief.[17]

In February 1831 the archbishop's palace was again invaded and ransacked, and the first silkworkers' uprising in Lyon in December that year prompted, as we have seen, widespread fears of an imminent "barbarian" assault on the precarious citadel of civilization. In March 1832 the first deaths from cholera were reported, and in the months that followed Paris was enveloped in a full-scale moral panic in which fears of disease and fears of social and political upheaval merged into a single terrifying amalgam.[18] Cholera was popularly attributed to the deliberate poisoning of wells (a reworking of a familiar topos of antisemitism), and in April 1832 at least five alleged poisoners—variously held to be legitimists, Bonapartists, and republicans—were snatched from the police and lynched by the mob. Doctors and medical students were also attacked (and in at least one case murdered), and even the city's ragpickers (*chiffonniers*) rioted when the prefecture for the first time entrusted the collection of street rubbish to a private company.

As wealthier Parisians left the city, the entire urban economy virtually collapsed, and in June the funeral of General Maximilien Lamarque acted as the focus for a full-scale working-class uprising, in which renegade legitimists and Bonapartists also played a part. There were innumerable strikes, and the first genuinely working-class political formation, the Society of the Rights of Man, was set up to give voice to the citywide sense of anger and frustration, and in so doing added to the generalized fear of conspiracy and plot. Discourses of disease and revolution flowed into and reinforced one another. Working-class radicals saw the cholera epidemic as an attempted purge of the city's poor by the upper classes, while for established opinion disease and revolution flowed from a single source that had to be extirpated and destroyed. Legitimists, for their part, saw both disease and social unrest as divine punishment for the 1830 revolution and its anticlerical excesses: "The wrath of the God of justice is mounting and soon every day will count its thousand victims, the crime of the destruction of the archbishopric is far from having been atoned for."[19] Even after the cholera abated, toward the end of 1832, social and political unrest continued, reaching a climax with the second silkworkers' uprising in Lyon (April 1834) and the contemporaneous republican uprising in Paris, the suppression of which brought the so-called time of riots to a close.

Far from allaying the climate of anguish, the end of overt disruption promoted fears of subterranean threats to society, to which attempts on Louis-Philippe's life in 1835 and 1836, combined with the attempted Blanquist coup of May 1839, lent more than a semblance of credibility. To fears of political conspiracy was added the more generalized fear of the *classes dangereuses* fomented by the *Gazette des Tribunaux*, the memoirs of the former police chief Vidocq (1775–1857), novels such as Eugène Suë's *Les Mystères de Paris* (1842–43) and Balzac's *Splendeurs*

The miraculous medal shows the Virgin as she allegedly appeared to Catherine Labouré in 1830. On the reverse, an interlocking cross and letter *M* surmount a double image of the Sacred Heart. (Photographic and Design Unit, University of Sussex.)

et misères des courtisanes (1838–47), and would-be sociological studies such as Frégier's *Des classes dangereuses dans les grandes villes* (1840). It was into this climate of pervasive anxiety that the cult of the miraculous medal was launched in the summer of 1832.

In the absence of conclusive documentary evidence, it cannot be proved that Aladel and Etienne were prompted by the general sociopolitical situation to accede to Catherine's requests and approach Monseigneur de Quélen with a view to having the medal struck and distributed; it should be stressed, however, that the decision to do so appears to have been taken *before* the outbreak of cholera, and that the request was readily granted by the archbishop, who, having twice been expelled from his palace in the space of six months, was presumably responsive to any measure that might ease the anticlerical tenor of the times. The design for the medal was broadly based on Catherine's own specifications (though the image of the Virgin derived from Edme Bouchardon's well-known statue in the Eglise Saint-Sulpice), and its manufacture was entrusted to a jeweler named Vachette on the Quai des Orfèvres. He delivered the first 1,500 copies on 30 June 1832, at a time when, after a brief lull, the cholera epidemic was regathering momentum.

At first the medal was distributed by the Sisters of Charity in person, and almost immediately miraculous cures were reported. Alone in her class not to wear the medal, the eight-year-old Caroline Nenain of the parish of Saint-Germain-l'Auxerrois was afflicted with the disease but was instantly cured when given one by the sisters. But by the time the epidemic abated in the autumn of 1832, only 10,000 medals had been distributed, and the real explosion of the cult developed only in 1833 and 1834, in a climate of continuing moral and political trauma. Conversions were now reported, such as that of an "enraged and blaspheming" soldier in Alençon who, given a medal on his deathbed in June 1833, began to pray and lament that he had learned "to love so late and so little." Visions of the medal were reported from Spain in August 1833, and in the spring of 1834 *Le Mois de Marie* published Aladel's account of the visions. It later went into multiple editions in book form, over 50,000 being sold in 1834 alone. By 1835 over a million copies of the medal were in circulation, the figure rising to 10 million by the end of the decade, and reports of cures and conversions were received from the United States in 1836, Poland in 1837, China and Russia in 1838, and even Abyssinia in 1839.[20] The medal still flourishes today, and will make an unexpected reappearance later on in this book.

Much of the success of the cult can be attributed to the Archbrotherhood of the Most Sacred and Immaculate Heart of Mary, founded in 1836 by the abbé Dufriche-Desgenettes, the curé of Notre-Dame-des-Victoires in the present first arrondissement.[21] A returned émigré, the abbé had despaired over the lack of religious observance in his parish, and while saying mass on 3 December 1836 heard a voice urging him to consecrate the parish to the Most Sacred and Immaculate Heart of Mary. His project of founding a confraternity devoted to the Virgin was immediately welcomed by Monseigneur de Quélen, and by 1838 no fewer than 7,892 branches had been established in France, a sure sign of the revived strength of Marian fervor that the miraculous medal had partly stimulated and partly capitalized on. Total membership stood at a remarkable 709,531 in July 1839, making Notre-Dame-des-Victoires the center of the Marian cult in Paris, as it remains, located, as Huysmans nastily put it in *Les Foules de Lourdes* (1906), in "the most contaminated part of the city, close to the Bourse, in the very encampment of the Jewry [*Juiverie*] of banks and drapery."[22]

Implicitly anti-Judaical if not antisemitic, the miraculous medal achieved its most celebrated conversion when, on 20 January 1842 in the Church of Sant' Andrea della Fratte in Rome, a young Alsatian Jew named Alphonse Ratisbonne had a vision of the Virgin exactly as on

Catherine's medal, immediately converted to Catholicism, was received by Pope Gregory XVI, and, together with his brother Théodore, who followed him into the Church, founded the Community of Notre-Dame de Sion for the conversion of Jews. There were doubtless those on the outer fringes of the Church who believed that the Ratisbonnes' conversion heralded the mass conversion of Jews, which, in strict orthodoxy, is the necessary prelude to the Second Coming of Christ. The connection between Marianism and millennialism would be even more marked at La Salette.

What, then, is the significance of the revelations on the Rue du Bac and the miraculous medal to which they gave birth? In the first place, the medal's prodigious success indicates that, despite the evident decline of formal religious belief and practice, there was still a massive reservoir of popular piety, often semimagical in character, that the Church might tap (but probably not control) in times of social and political crisis. The mass-produced medal was, as it were, the urban-industrial equivalent of the scapulars, relics, and holy fountains and springs of a still thriving rural religiosity that pointed to people's need for direct access to the sacred even when they rejected the mediating role of the Church. Second, the medal continued and heightened the trend toward the feminization of religion, on which we have already remarked. Revealed to a woman and representing the blessed among women, the medal was in the first instance distributed by women and—though evidence is lacking—probably to women more readily than to men. It is as though the male God and the masculine Jesus were felt to be remote and threatening, whereas, in the words of the *Memorare,* it was "a thing unheard of" that anyone having recourse to the Virgin's protection, imploring her help or seeking her intercession, should be "left forsaken." As the doctrine of expiatory suffering, combined with such practices as deferred absolution and infrequent Communion, made not only God's love but Jesus' seem terribly conditional, so believers fell back on Mary—"our only saviour from an abstract God," in the words of the nineteenth-century English Catholic poet Coventry Patmore—as the only guaranteed source of unstinting and unconditional love.

As Claude Guillet has observed, Catherine's visions marked the beginning of a new era of Catholic piety, irrational, "feminine," and childlike, centered on the image of the Sacred Hearts of Jesus and Mary and the doctrine, formally endorsed by the Church in 1854, of the Immaculate Conception. In this reading, the Rue du Bac began a drift toward immanentism, toward the immediacy of a thaumaturgical goddess whose tangible presence in the "world-mothering air" (Gerard Manley

Hopkins) that enveloped humankind tended to eclipse all three Persons of the Holy Trinity: no one who witnessed the funeral of Diana, princess of Wales, can doubt the prodigious mobilizing force of the anima archetype. It was a sensuous, even sensual Catholicism that would culminate in Lourdes and the Sacré-Cœur and whose "ultimate political avatar," says Guillet, would be the Vichy regime.[23] The miraculous medal was certainly political, but it was not overtly politicized by the Church as La Salette, Lourdes, and Pontmain would be after 1870 and, still more blatantly, Fatima after 1917 and the various Marian apparitions in Spain and Italy during the 1940s and 1950s.[24] Yet the trend was clear by the 1840s and would become clearer still in the 1850s and 1860s; if God, in the famous witticism of the early 1870s, sat on the right, the Mother of God would, alas, be seated still farther to *his* right on the benches of the celestial chamber.

7

KILLING THE LIVING,
BURYING THE DEAD
Père-Lachaise (1804–1945)

In 1765 the Parliament of Paris issued a decree that inaugurated, though this could hardly have been foreseen at the time, one of the most remarkable cultural revolutions of modern France: it banned all future burials in churchyards and called for the removal of the two hundred or more parish graveyards within Paris out beyond the city's formal limits, where huge new municipal cemeteries would in due course be created. Accordingly, the city's principal graveyards were progressively closed— the cemetery of the Saints-Innocents in 1780, those of Saint-Roch, Sainte-Eustache, and Saint-Sulpice in 1781, Saint-Louis in 1782—and the corpses exhumed and transferred, often in the teeth of considerable public resistance, to improvised mass burial places, often abandoned quarries, at Claimart, Vaugirard, and Montmartre.

Issued primarily for reasons of public sanitation, the decree revolutionized almost overnight the ancestral relationship between the living and the dead, who since time immemorial had, so to speak, cohabited in the city's center but were henceforth to be rigidly segregated: the living within the city's formal limits, the dead without. The disaggregation of the living from the dead was accentuated by the construction between 1784 and 1790 of a customs wall (the *mur d'octroi*) that encircled the entire city, and was institutionalized by the opening of new specially constructed municipal cemeteries located beyond the wall in the first quarter of the nineteenth century. The first was the Cimetière de l'Est, always known as Père-Lachaise after Louis XVI's confessor, Père François de La Chaise d'Aix, who had lived there on Jesuit-owned land until his death in 1709; it was formally opened on 1 Prairial An XII (21 May 1804), and was followed by the Cimetière Montparnasse in 1824 and the Cimetière Montmartre in 1825.[1]

Following the pattern of public executions, other taboo activities were systematically shifted from center to periphery. The slaughter of animals, for example, was no longer carried out by individual butchers on their own premises but was transferred to abattoirs established between 1807 and 1812 on the outskirts of the city; the final concentration of all slaughtering activities at La Villette during the Second Empire completed this process of purification-by-segregation.[2] Similarly, the city's rubbish dumps and cesspools were located immediately outside the *mur d'octroi,* most notoriously at Montfaucon, to the northeast, and it was to the same no-man's-land beyond the pale that human detritus— the insane, the indigent, and the delinquent—were increasingly consigned. Such heavy industry as existed in early nineteenth-century Paris was also located as a matter of policy on the city's perimeter, notably at La Chapelle and La Villette, to the northeast, and many of the forty or so entrances (*barrières*) into the city were notorious haunts for criminals, particularly those of La Courtille, Combat, and Ménilmontant, as were, a little farther out, the abandoned quarries of Montmartre, Montrouge, and the Buttes-Chaumont.

Such, then, was the limbo landscape, part country, part city, half savage, half civilized—again, the terms are Hugo's, this time in *Les Misérables*[3]—that surrounded early nineteenth-century Paris. But if the *barrières* struck fear and repulsion in the hearts of many bourgeois in the prim west of the city, they exercised an equally powerful attraction both for the working-class east and for many middle-class dissidents—students, artists—on account of the array of pleasures they offered alongside and inseparable from the ever-present reminders of death, disease, and criminality. In the first place, there sprang up immediately outside the *barrières,* where alcohol was cheaper, a profusion of what were known as *guinguettes:* establishments large and small, luxurious and seedy, where working-class and many lower-middle-class Parisians would throng in their thousands every Sunday to eat, drink, and dance. There were important concentrations of *guinguettes* at the *barrières* of Montparnasse, Clichy, Montmartre, Rochechouart, La Chapelle, La Villette, and Ménilmontant, but the most popular center was the Barrière de Belleville and its extension, La Courtille (now the Rue de Belleville), where every Sunday in the 1830s and 1840s a "veritable tidal wave of workers, bourgeois, clerks, *grisettes,* nursemaids, and soldier boys" flooded into such establishments as the Folies-Belleville, the Grande Chaumière, and the Ile de l'Amour. *Guinguettes* were also an important focus for prostitution, particularly in the south of the city, where all the way from the Barrière de Grenelle in the west to the

Barrière d'Italie in the east low-grade prostitutes were to be found living and working in sheds, huts, and even, according to one writer, holes in the ground, drawing their miserable clientele of travelers, soldiers, and Sunday-afternoon excursionists. At each of the *barrières,* then, there grew up a kind of city in miniature—or even, as one modern writer has said, "a city in reverse" (*une ville à l'envers*)[4]—devoted to food, drink, dancing, and sex and catering to between 30,000 and 50,000 Parisians each weekend.

In a large number of ways, therefore, the *barrières* were a negation of the spiritual, moral, and political values on which the city was based, and it was as though, in a movement analogous to the "great enclosure" of the insane described by Michel Foucault,[5] the polis were seeking to banish literally beyond the pale those of its aspects that were felt to be unseemly, unsightly, or morally obnoxious. Death, detritus, drink, crime, prostitution, even labor itself were, quite simply, to be rendered invisible. In part (or at least in intention), the structure of early nineteenth-century Paris would seem to correspond closely to the opposition between a "pure" or "positive" center and an "impure" or "negative" circumference that anthropologists, notably Georges Bataille's one-time associate Roger Caillois (1913–78),[6] have discerned in the structure of primitive and premodern settlements.

There is, however, one crucial difference. Although the "sacred" buildings of pre-1850 Paris—Notre-Dame, the Louvre, the Palais des Tuileries, the Hôtel de Ville, and the Palais de Justice—were located at the center of the city in conformity with the traditional pattern and although there was certainly a growing tendency to relegate, where possible, negative aspects of the city's life to the periphery, it was precisely at the center that the most sordid, crime-ridden, and unsanitary areas of the city were to be found, notably on the Ile de la Cité and among the teeming slums and rookeries of the Right Bank opposite. Pure and impure, positive and negative were inextricably commingled in *le vieux Paris,* so that, as we have seen, one of the most squalid slum areas in the whole city—celebrated with mingled horror and affection by Baudelaire in his great poem "Le Cygne" of 1859, by which time it had been demolished—was actually located between the Louvre and the (also no longer existent) Palais des Tuileries, more or less where I. M. Pei's glass pyramid now delights or infuriates the viewer, while the criminal lairs described in Eugène Suë's serial novel *Les Mystères de Paris* (1842–43) were located in the immediate vicinity of the twin foci of moral good and social order represented by Notre-Dame and the Hôtel de Ville. In short, it was not just in the faubourgs that the modern-day

"barbarians" were to be found, as the *Journal des débats* had put it in
1831; the point was rather, as Suë, drawing heavily on James Fenimore
Cooper, declared at the opening of his massive potboiler, that the
savages of civilization are even now among us. By further concentrating
the emblems and edifices of power at the center of the city, ridding the
Ile de la Cité of its slums, and compelling its population to join the great
exodus eastward and outward, the transformation of Paris during the
Second Empire may be seen as a (largely successful) attempt to disentangle pure and impure and to restore the ideal opposition of center and circumference, to the great relief, naturally, of those in whose hands power
was increasingly concentrated, to say nothing of their supporters in the
middle-class west, for whom at last the city center became accessible.

For all this, thousands of middle-class Parisians (and, as the century
advanced, thousands of working-class ones as well) were drawn each
Sunday toward the city's periphery to celebrate a form of worship that
was rapidly displacing the orthodox Catholicism to which almost all of
them still nominally adhered. The object of this striking new cult was
the dead, its principal shrine the cemetery of Père-Lachaise, and its
greatest annual solemnity the feast of All Saints (*la Toussaint*), which by
the 1860s was drawing over 400,000 visitors—a staggering one in three
of the population—to the great cemeteries on the city's outskirts. More
and more, metropolis and necropolis became mirror images of each
other: "the people in the common grave; the middle class in temporary
concessions; the aristocracy of finance in perpetual concessions. The
population of cemeteries thus finds itself divided between the dead who
own their grave and those who don't: the proletarians and the taxpay-
ers" (Alphonse Esquiros, 1844).[7]

But there was more to the form and disposition of the city's cemeteries than simple class stratification. Dreading the anonymity of the
common grave where deceased paupers were stacked virtually on top
of one another in makeshift plywood or cardboard coffins that soon
rotted away, leaving only an undifferentiated magma of human remains,
all classes of Parisian society aspired to the closed individuality of
a properly identified family plot: individual autonomy plus family
solidarity, the epitome of the bourgeois worldview, which more and
more lower-class Parisians were making their own. In the circumstances,
it was hardly surprising that upper-class funerary architecture increasingly mirrored the extroversion and stylistic confusion of the
apartment houses in the western districts where they lived: Greek,
Roman, Etruscan, Byzantine, Gothic, Renaissance, modern, juxtaposing
obelisks with dolmens, Attic stelae with Italianate balustrades, a Babel

of architectural languages in keeping at least with the stylistic het-
eroglossia in the city below.

In the mid-1860s, as part of his root-and-branch modernization of
the city, Napoleon III's prefect of Paris, Baron Georges-Eugène
Haussmann, proposed that future burials should take place still farther
outside Paris, indeed away from the city entirely, at Méry-sur-Oise, thirteen miles to the northwest, whither the dead would be transported by
train at night and buried with maximum speed, discretion, and effi-
ciency. The outcry was immediate and vociferous, the threat of "the
banishing of the dead," as Victor Fournel (1829–94) put it in 1870,
uniting all classes against the proposal and its author, who was quickly
forced to abandon it. The idea of "a single distant necropolis, a vast and
glacial funereal Siberia, where the dead would be transported like convicts [in English in the original] in repulsive conditions to rest in solitude, exiled from both the hearts and eyes of those who loved them,"[8]
was quite simply anathema to a culture now geared to self-worship in
the guise of reverence for the dead and to the cult of the family enshrined
in the private plot in Père-Lachaise or Montmartre. No cemetery, no city
(*pas de cimetière, pas de cité*): it was right that the dead should be
placed at a distance from the living, but not that the distance should be
so great as to preclude regular, indeed weekly, communion between the
living and their loved ones. By the 1870s, no fewer than 70,000 people
per week were visiting the city's cemeteries.

Though the Church still conducted the majority of funerals, there can
be little doubt that the cult of the dead was, despite appearances, fundamentally opposed to Christian beliefs and ethics. Some churchmen, such
as Monseigneur Jean-Joseph Gaume, writing in the 1870s (and writing in
capitals lest his reader miss the point), thought that "THE CEMETERY IN THE
NINETEENTH CENTURY IS THE LAST THEATER OF THE BITTER STRUGGLE OF SA-
TANISM AGAINST CHRISTIANITY," the transfer of the dead from parish grave-
yard to effectively secularized cemetery being part of "the plan of universal destruction, conceived by the Revolution," designed to "extinguish
promptly the feeling of filial piety toward the dead."[9] But this was hardly
the case, for it was precisely the removal of the dead that had precipitated
and made possible the cult, and the policy of removal had been favored at
least as much by regimes of the right as by those of the left.

Far more perceptive was the former curator of the cemetery of Marseille, one Bertoglio, who, writing in 1889, linked the cult of the dead
directly to the *decline* in religious faith and practice, for why, he pertinently asked, should one care for the graves "of those whose fate has
been decided for all eternity"? He traces the origins of the cult of the

dead back to Paris "about two generations ago," linking it to the city's "growing theological emancipation": "As God is more and more eliminated and even forgotten, the cult of the dead spreads unceasingly and penetrates even the most modest existences."[10] Ironically, the human tide that ebbed and flowed each Sunday between city center and circumferential cemeteries was one further symptom of the "melancholy, long, withdrawing roar" of the "sea of faith" that, not too long before, had girded Paris as it had the whole kingdom of France, "elder daughter of the Church."[11]

It is entirely appropriate, therefore, that what is perhaps the single most dramatic moment in nineteenth-century French fiction—the burial of Père Goriot in Balzac's eponymous novel of 1834 and Rastignac's defiant panoramic gaze over Paris ("A nous deux maintenant!")—should be set in the cemetery of Père-Lachaise in the early months of 1820. For what is at stake here is not the death and burial of just one particularly hapless father figure but of the paternal principle itself—not for nothing did Balzac change the title of the final section of the novel from "Death of a Father" to "Death of *the* Father"[12]—and the consequent liberation of the henceforth sovereign ego to create its own destiny over and against not just the rest of society but the universe and, ultimately, God—or, rather, the now empty concept of God.

Biblical and especially Christological allusion come thick and fast in the last pages of the novel. After a gruesome parody of the Last Supper at which the lodgers of Maison Vauquer noisily tuck into one of fat Sylvie's afternoon spreads, totally indifferent to the "petit mortorama" that has just taken place upstairs, a cut-price hearse arrives around three (the traditional hour of Christ's surrendering of the spirit) to take the corpse of the tragicomic father-martyr to the church dedicated to the first Christian martyr, Saint-Etienne-du-Mont, where it is mechanically given a third-class, 70-franc funeral service lasting barely twenty minutes: no mass, naturally, just a *Libera* and a *De Profundis* perfunctorily sung by whatever ecclesiastical personnel happens to be around. Then, followed by two empty carriages emblazoned with the coats of arms of Goriot's perfidious sons-in-law (*deux voitures armoriées, mais vides*)— as telling an image as can be conceived of the divorce of signifiers from their signifieds, of the essential hollowness of post–ancien régime, postrevolutionary, post-Napoleonic Restoration society—Goriot's hearse is drawn up to Père-Lachaise, which it reaches, appropriately and ironically enough, around six in the evening, the traditional hour of Christ's entombment. In the presence only of Rastignac and the significantly named servant Christophe, "who felt obliged to pay his final respects to a man who had caused him to obtain several decent tips," Goriot is consigned to the earth with unseemly haste by two gravediggers, who, halfway through their task, badger Rastignac for a tip.[13] His pockets empty, Rastignac has to cadge 20 sous from Christophe. The organic *Gemeinschaft* of the past has gone for good, leaving only autonomous ego agents bound together solely by the cash nexus.

As a "damp twilight" descends over Paris—a wintry *Götterdämmerung* fifty years or more in advance of Wagner and Nietzsche—Rastignac is overwhelmed by a "loathsome sadness" (*une horrible tristesse*) as Christophe leaves him standing in archetypal isolation before the city that lies "tortuously coiled" (*tortueusement couché*) beneath him, like a woman at the feet of her lover. It is then that, arms crossed in a quintessential Napoleonic fashion, he issues his magnificent challenge to the city he has come to conquer. His eyes seize avidly on the space between those two Napoleonic markers, the Colonne Vendôme and the Invalides, both of them "emptied" of their imperial content, for the former emperor is far away in exile in Saint Helena, where lives the high society (*ce beau monde*) that he had longed, and still longs, to "penetrate." If Rastignac is a Nietzschean superman *avant la lettre,* he is a decidedly unheroic and conformist one, for his grandiloquent challenge to Parisian society is immediately deflated by his decision to descend from his lofty vantage point in order to dine with Delphine de Nucingen. After the crucifixion of the father, after the burial from which he surely will not rise again on the third or any other day, comes the communal meal with the daughters. If the novel, in George Lukac's celebrated definition, is the epic of a world abandoned by God, then surely there is no better or earlier example than *Le Père Goriot.*[14]

The funeral of Père Goriot, already heavily ironic, is given a further parodic twist in Flaubert's description of the funeral of Monsieur Dambreuse in *L'Education sentimentale* (1869), a ceremony that also burlesques one of nineteenth-century France's most striking political inventions: the funeral as antigovernment manifestation.[15] At times of political repression, notably under the Restoration Monarchy, during the "time of riots" in the early 1830s, and again under the Second Empire, funerals of prominent opposition figures were transformed into major expressions of political discontent, especially when, as was common, the funeral terminated at Père-Lachaise. Thus the funeral of General Maximilien Foy in 1825 drew a crowd of 100,000, who sought thereby to register their opposition to the autocratic rule of Charles X, while that of the liberal deputy Jacques-Antoine Manuel attracted a similar number in 1827. In June 1832 the funeral of the Napoleonic general

Maximilien Lamarque triggered the major working-class-cum-republican uprising so memorably evoked and analyzed in *Les Misérables,* and in 1857 the funeral of the democratic poet Pierre-Jean de Béranger brought an estimated 200,000 "mourners" to Père-Lachaise in a gesture of opposition to Second Empire repression. It was indeed another political funeral—that of the republican journalist Victor Noir, killed while acting as a second in a duel involving the emperor's second cousin, Prince Bonaparte—that in January 1870 signaled the Empire's imminent demise by drawing 200,000 hitherto dispersed and mutually ignorant opponents to the cemetery at Neuilly, in the western suburbs, and so, as Jules Vallès put it in *L'Insurgé* (1886), permitting the "republican shreds" (*des lambeaux de République*) to "stick themselves back together" (*se recoller*) in the blood of yet another emblematic victim.[16]

A mere six months after the Empire's collapse in the wake of crushing defeats by the Prussian armies, the Republic would itself be rent into two contending camps—"socialist" Paris versus "moderate" Versailles—at whose final bloody confrontation in the eastern arrondissements Père-Lachaise would cease to be just a site of memory and mourning and become one of mayhem and massacre at the culmination of the century's greatest paroxysm of violence, the all too accurately named *Semaine sanglante* of May 1871. Surpassing in intensity both the Terror of 1793–74 (but not, perhaps, the contemporaneous suppression of the Vendée uprising) and the violence of June 1848, the last week of the Commune is the supreme internal political holocaust of postrevolutionary France, equaled only, if at all, by the so-called *guerre franco-française* of 1944–45. It also produced the most "sacred" of the left's *lieux de mémoire,* the Mur des Fédérés, and requires us to discuss it in some detail, not in order to disentangle history from myth—a vain undertaking, at least in this instance—but to show how the mythologized history of both right and left draws on and reworks the sacrificial paradigm whose lineaments should by now be relatively clear.

On Sunday, 21 May 1871, the siege of Paris by the army of the "moderate" republican government based at Versailles, which had begun immediately after the declaration of the Commune two months before, on 18 March, finally paid off when several companies of troops were able to enter Paris via an unmanned section of the city ramparts at Point du Jour, in the southwest.[17] The initial inroads made, progress was rapid as Versailles troops poured en masse into the city: they took virtually the whole of its western third by the evening of the 22d, Montmartre and Montparnasse on the 23d, and the whole of the center and the Latin Quarter by the evening of the 24th. At that point battle began in earnest for the Commune's heartland in the eastern third of the city, both north and south of the Seine.

As the hours and the days went by, the remnants of the Commune's officials, troops, and supporters were pressed back into Ménilmontant, Belleville, and La Villette, with the Buttes-Chaumont and Père-Lachaise providing the principal strong points from which the Commune's remaining artillery could bombard the rest of the city. As they retreated back onto their eastern fastness, the Communards had set fire to many public buildings, notably the Palais des Tuileries and the Cour des Comptes (the government accounting office), giving rise to the persistent and almost entirely fallacious myth of the *pétroleuses,* those still more fearsome versions of the *tricoteuses* of 1793–74: disheveled, drink-crazed working-class banshees who hurled milk bottles full of flaming kerosene at buildings to which postage-stamp-sized labels bearing the letters "B.P.B." (*bon pour brûler,* fit for burning) had previously been stuck—even, in some versions of the myth, wearing wigs doused in inflammable substances, which they would suddenly snatch off, ignite, and send flying at this or that target.[18] Whatever the causes of the fires (and the Versailles troops certainly had a hand in them), by the 23d, Paris, in the words of the great Communard historian Prosper-Olivier Lissagaray, "seemed to writhe in an immense spiral of flames and smoke" as the "capricious flames threw up a flamboyant architecture of arches, cupolas, and fantastical edifices."

After fierce fighting at the Place de la Bastille and the Place du Château-d'Eau (the present Place de la République), the surviving Communards made their last stand in and around Père-Lachaise, which was taken by the Versailles troops on the 27th after hand-to-hand combat raged among the tombstones, the antagonists "rolling and dying in the same grave holes," and then in a final redoubt on the Rue Haxo and the Rue Ramponneau in Belleville. At the very last, a solitary Communard sniper held out on the Rue Ramponneau, successfully smashing the flagpole bearing the Versailles Tricolor, not once, according to Lissagaray, but three times. Around one o'clock on the afternoon of the 28th, he finally gave up and walked away, to safety it appears, and after two months' dramatic existence and a week's desperate but ineffective resistance, the red flag of the Commune succumbed to the red, white, and blue of the official Republic.

In all, 110,000 Versailles troops had confronted something like 20,000 supporters of the Commune—a far cry from the citywide uprising that romantic revolutionaries had anticipated—but it should be stressed that the actual fighting for the city caused few casualties: about

400 killed and 1,100 seriously wounded on the government side, perhaps 2,000 dead on the Communard side.[19] In other words, the massive bloodletting that gave the *Semaine sanglante* its baleful name took place after or aside from the actual or military engagement, and its raison d'être was not military but political.

Each side, of course, had its highly symbolic individual deaths. Among the leading "martyrs" on the left were the deputy Jean-Baptiste Millière (not in fact an out-and-out supporter of the Commune), whose execution was ordered "between the cheese and the fruit course" (*entre le fromage et la poire*) by the Versailles general Ernest-Louis-Octave Courtot de Cissey as he dined at the restaurant Foyot near the Luxembourg Gardens, and who was shot on the steps of the Panthéon with the appropriately ecumenical cry of "Vive l'humanité!" on his lips;[20] the Polish general Jaroslaw Dombrowski, killed early in the fighting and given a hero's burial at Père-Lachaise just before it fell;[21] Eugène Varlin, bookbinder and revolutionary theoretician and activist, shot on the Rue des Rosiers in Montmartre on 28 May; and the veteran Jacobin revolutionary Charles Delescluze, who died in what appears to have been a deliberate act of self-immolation on the Place du Château-d'Eau, marching "with no companion other than his severe conscience" toward the Versailles troops' barricade, "just as the Montagnards of old went to the scaffold," and thus continuing the republican tradition of self-martyrdom inaugurated by the republican deputy Victor Baudin in December 1851.[22]

But it was the killing of approximately sixty (and not one hundred, as is commonly said) hostages by the Commune that gave the martyrological tradition of the right its most potent holocaustal victims since the Terror, particularly as around half of the dead were priests or religious, the most celebrated casualty being the archbishop of Paris, Monseigneur Darboy, who had been arrested on 4 April on suspicion of communicating with the enemy. The hostages, who also included paramilitary police loyal to Versailles, an assortment of police spies, and a banker, a lawyer, and a government official, were killed in three batches during the *Semaine sanglante*: Archbishop Darboy, Father Duguerry of the Madeleine, three Jesuits, and the president of the Court of Appeals at the prison of La Roquette on 24 May; five friars from the Dominican house at Arcueil, arrested and then shot on 25 May on the Avenue d'Italie after having apparently been told they were free; and, on 26 May, thirty-six policemen, ten priests, and four spies were taken from La Roquette to the Rue Haxo and there shot despite vigorous efforts on the part of Varlin to save their lives.

MORT DE MONSEIGNEUR L'ARCHEVÊQUE DE PARIS.

Le 24 Mai dans l'après midi un membre de la commune fit appeler les otages; les premiers qui sortirent furent Monseigneur Darboy, l'abbé Surat, grand vicaire, Monsieur le Président Bonjean, Monsieur Deguerry Curé de la Madeleine et les Pères jésuites Ducoudray et Clerc. Ils notables personnages furent fusillés dans la cour de la Roquette par un groupe d'insurgés à qui Monseigneur adressa ces dernières et nobles paroles : « Ne profanez pas le mot de liberté il n'appartient qu'à nous car nous mourons pour elle et pour la foi. »

The execution of Archbishop Darboy and other priests and religious at the Cour de la Roquette on 24 May 1871. This anonymous engraving records the archbishop's alleged last words to his executioners: "Do not profane the word 'liberty'; it belongs only to us, for we are dying for it and for faith." (Musée Carnavalet, Paris, © Photothèque des Musées de la Ville de Paris.)

Although these killings are often scandalously glossed over by supporters of the Commune (including Lissagaray, for whom the Dominicans of Arcueil are "apostles of the Inquisition," fully deserving of their fate), it should be stressed that only those of Darboy and his fellows were sanctioned by a high-ranking official of the Commune (Charles-Théophile Ferré), and that he acted in the face of extreme pressure exerted by a highly aroused crowd that had just massacred one of the very few aristocratic supporters of the Commune, the young comte de Beaufort, on the usual grounds of espionage and treachery. Delescluze had tried to prevent this killing, just as later Varlin would try to save the hostages of the Rue Haxo. In short, there is absolutely no evidence of a concerted policy of killing hostages, whatever Versailles propaganda would later claim to the contrary.

It is not, however, such individually identifiable killings that give the *Semaine sanglante* its unmistakably "modern" character and make of it less a reprise of the nonetheless extensive and extremely violent mopping-up operation that followed the suppression of the June insurrection in 1848 than a kind of colonial raid conducted on the streets and squares of Paris rather than in Kabylia or the Rif. In 1871, unlike 1848, the government's objective was not so much to "expiate," as Adolphe Thiers put it on 22 May, the "crimes" of the Commune—its greatest crime being, of course, its very existence—or even to exterminate or otherwise eliminate those responsible, but to terrorize the entire community that made the Commune possible and so destroy the many-headed "socialist Hydra" for generations to come. Since the goal was not punishment for individual offenses but a kind of cleansing operation (Lissagaray actually uses the word *épuration,* purge),[23] anyone, man, woman, or child, of working-class origin or appearance was a suitable case for treatment, irrespective of his or her beliefs and actions under the Commune; which is how the number of those killed by the Versailles supporters—anywhere between 20,000 and 35,000, with the higher figure the more likely—came to equal or exceed the number involved in the actual defense of the city.

The killings began as soon as the Versailles troops had "liberated" a particular district: first at Montmartre, where on 23 May forty-three men, three women, and four children were shot on their knees in the highly symbolic house on the Rue des Rosiers where Varlin would die on the 28th; then at the fashionable Parc Monceau, which became, in Lissagaray's expression, the "principal abattoir" for the whole seventeenth arrondissement; and finally, as street after street, district after district fell to Versailles, at the Châtelet, the Luxembourg Gardens, the Buttes-Chaumont, the prison at La Roquette, and, most notoriously of all, Père-Lachaise. Young and old were rounded up at random for the flimsiest of reasons, or for no reason at all other than their dress or appearance; as in June 1848 dirty hands were a fatal giveaway. Many were shot on the spot, often with some gratuitous humiliation added at the whim of the killers, like the old man seized on the Rue Crozatier who, according to Lissagaray, asserted his right at least "not to die *dans la merde*" when an officer forced him into a pile of ordure to be shot,[24] or after the briefest of "trials" before improvised military courts. So obsessive was the link in the Versailles mind between red wine and red politics that the necks of wine bottles were thrust into corpses' mouths, or the label "Ivrogne" (drunkard) was pinned to their chests.[25] Many victims were denounced by so-called *brassardiers,* government supporters who emerged from their hiding places wearing red, white, and blue armbands (*brassards*) as soon as their districts were liberated and proceeded

to denounce neighbors as *communeux, partageux* (communists, shar-
ers), or whatever other term of abuse they preferred in the vast lexicon
of hatred spawned by the events of *l'année terrible*. Bands of Versailles
troops turned on isolated victims, as in the following incident recounted
in an article titled "What an American Girl Saw of the Commune" published in *Macmillan's Magazine* in 1892:

> I saw four soldiers and an officer; two of the soldiers were half-
> dragging a man who was on his knees before the officer begging
> for his life. It made my blood run cold ... to see that poor wretch
> on his knees, screaming to be spared, and the officer holding a
> pistol at his head. The soldiers kicked him to make him get up,
> and hit him on the head, so that you could hear the blows across
> the street. Someone from a window called out to the officer not to
> shoot him before so many women and children, so they pushed
> and kicked him until they came to the end of the street, and there
> they shot him. As he was being dragged past our house they
> stopped for a moment, and I saw a little boy about five years of
> age go up and kick the man while he was begging for pity.[26]

Bodies were buried pell-mell, if at all. Lissagaray describes the limbs
of victims protruding from shallow mass graves at the Parc Monceau,
and bloated bodies rising to the surface of the artificial lakes at the
Buttes-Chaumont; still more sinister, ovens (*fours crématoires*) were
used to incinerate corpses en masse.[27]

Once "order" was restored in the city, the rounding up of suspects
took on a more structured aspect. Arrests were "normalized," and
columns of prisoners were marched through the streets of Paris out to
Versailles, where crowds greeted them with volleys of abuse, ordure,
and broken glass. As Lissagaray wrote in justifiable fury, there was no
cruelty more insatiable than that of the archetypal French bourgeois
Joseph Prudhomme in 1871 ("L'inassouvissable cruel, c'est Prudhomme").[28] At Versailles, Sedan and Metz proceeded to judge Paris
("Sedan et Metz allaient juger Paris"), and those whom the defeated
army of 1870 had defeated could expect no mercy.[29] Once convicted,
prisoners were taken by the thousand to the docks of the river port of
Satory, "an immense walled parallelogram whose clay soil the slightest
rain turned into mud," which rapidly became "the favorite excursion of
respectable Versailles society," and thence to prison or to pontoons
moored off the north and east coasts of France. Thousands were
shipped out of France entirely, principally to penal colonies in New

Caledonia, from which they could not return until the passing of the amnesty in 1880.

Repression and revenge on this massive scale were prepared, made possible, and legitimated by the huge array of stereotypes produced not only by the Versailles press but by almost every writer—and they were legion, for, as Lissagaray wrote, publishers wanted books on the Commune and nothing else ("les éditeurs ne voulaient que du communard")[30]—who put pen to paper on the subject of the events of 1870–71. Aside from such accredited poets of the Commune as Eugène Pottier (1816–87), composer of "L'Internationale," only the sixteen-year-old Arthur Rimbaud (1854–91) and the sixty-nine-year-old Victor Hugo stood apart from the torrent of anti-Communard invective, and even Hugo, whose L'Année terrible (1872) remains a masterpiece of humanitarian commitment, was anything but a supporter of the Commune.

Among the antagonists, every kind of hysterical fantasy was channeled into a never-ending litany of hatred and terror, as floods of Paris brûle, Paris en flammes, Le Carnaval rouge, Barbares et bandits, and Mystères de l'Internationale poured from the nation's presses. It was not just hacks like Paul Saint-Victor and Jules Claretie or accomplished literary journeymen like Flaubert's friend Maxime Du Camp who joined the throng, or writers of known extreme right-wing views like Arthur de Gobineau or Jules Barbey d'Aurevilly; the tone, language, and obsessions of such first-rank figures as Flaubert, Edmond de Goncourt, Gautier, Leconte de Lisle, and even George Sand are of a piece with those of the lowest kind of Versailles scribe.[31] Whatever the writer's individual talent, an all-encompassing animalizing or racializing discourse reduces the Communards to the level of "apes mixed with tiger cats" (singes mâtinés de chats-tigres), "taproom Caesars" (Césarillons d'estaminet), "epileptic puppets," "pyromaniacs" (all Du Camp in Les Convulsions de Paris [1889]), "monstrous Calibans," "moustachioed Shakespearean witches," "European thugs" (Gautier), "Anabaptists of Munster" (Sand), "bulls, pigs, rams, goats" (Elémir Bourges), and so on and so on. The Commune itself was "a bloody bacchanale," "an attack of moral epilepsy," "an orgy of kerosene and brandy," "a case analogous to the St. Anthony's fire, the St. Vitus' dance, the possessions of the Middle Ages" (Du Camp again).[32] Gautier spoke for a whole class and worldview when he wrote (in his Tableaux du siège of 1872) that under every large city there lie "lion pits, thick-barred caves in which wild, evil-smelling, and venomous beasts are locked away," and that catastrophe will supervene whenever the cage door is left open to release "the hyenas of 93 and the gorillas of the Commune."

Not surprisingly, and with considerably more justification, apologists for the Commune responded with an animalizing, racializing discourse of their own. In a striking reversal of a well-worn analogy, Lissagaray likened the Versailles supporters to Tartars falling upon the modern-day Rome that was Paris, while the crowds that hissed and pelted the columns of Communard prisoners he compared to so many "Caribs," their savagery all the more fearsome for being elegantly clothed in bourgeois finery.[33] Never, perhaps, has class conflict been closer to an outright war of the "races" than it was in France in May and June 1871.

Predictably, all parties from the far right through the moderate republican center to the far left saw the *Semaine sanglante* as an appalling but necessary holocaust from which the new order of their choice might eventually be born or reborn. The belief that *l'année terrible* was punishment and expiation for the "excesses" of the Second Empire was as widespread as the later belief that the defeat of 1940 was punishment and expiation for *l'esprit de jouissance* supposedly rife under the Third Republic; it was this spirit of political and social decadence that prompted the right, with the Church in its van, to embark on the construction of Sacré-Cœur during the first years of what Lissagaray witheringly called *le MacMahonnat,* the seven-year presidency (1873–79) of the right-wing general MacMahon (1808–93), dedicated to the restoration of moral order after the turmoil of 1870–71.

Even a republican as socially moderate but politically passionate as Zola made the discourse of sacrifice his own in *La Débâcle* (1892), the penultimate novel of the Rougon-Macquart cycle, in which the fratricidal conflict of Versailles and Paris—embodied in the figures of the "good" soldier Jean Macquart and his friend, the wild revolutionary romantic Maurice Levasseur, the former inflicting a fatal wound on the latter when they accidentally meet on the barricades during the *Semaine sanglante*—is seen as the necessary precondition for national rebirth and redemption. As he dies, Maurice repents of his radicalism, seeing in his death at the hands of his "brother" and in the destruction of the Commune at the hands of Versailles a victory for "the healthy part of France, the reasonable, well-balanced [*pondérée*], peasant part, that which had remained closer to the soil," over "the mad part, exasperated, corrupted by the Empire, driven off the tracks by fantasies and pleasures [*détraquée de rêveries et de jouissances*]." But, he now recognizes, "the bloodbath was necessary, French blood too, the abominable holocaust, the living sacrifice, amidst the purifying fire. Henceforth, the corpse had risen to the most terrifying of agonies, the crucified nation was expiating its faults and was going to be reborn." With this, all is ready for the regulation Zolaesque triumph of Eros over Thanatos, "the certain rejuvenation of eternal nature, eternal humanity, the renewal vouchsafed to whoever hopes and toils, the tree that casts forth a new and powerful shoot, when the rotten branch has been cut off whose poisoned sap was causing the leaves to yellow." The novel ends with Jean Macquart, alias the Third Republic, striding off into the future to confront "the great and arduous task of remaking the whole of France anew [*la grande et rude besogne de toute une France à refaire*]."[34]

A similar but far more deeply felt use of the language of Christian sacrifice for non- or even anti-Christian ends is it be found in Eugène Pottier's superb poem "Le Pressoir" (The Wine Press), first published in 1891 after Pottier's death but instinct with all the eddying moods of apocalyptic despair and angry, insistent hope that characterize *l'après-Commune*. Fusing the crucial French socialist themes of red Christ, red blood, red wine, and red politics, the poem likens the crushing of grapes into the must from which the new wine will be fermented to "the vast hecatomb of martyrs swooning unto death," and urges those imprisoned or in exile, "squeezed dregs" though they are, not to despair but to pour forth their souls into "the cup of the future," for of a certainty "the great thirst will return." The poem concludes with one of the most remarkable images in French socialist poetry:

Quand viendra le beau vendémiaire,
On verra, des pressoirs sacrés,
Le vin, l'amour et la lumière
Couler pour tous les altérés;
Du gibet quittant les insignes,
Jésus déclouant ses bras las,
Au Calvaire planté de vignes
Mettra sa croix pour échalas.[35]

[When the beautiful month of Vendémiare [September–October in the revolutionary calendar] comes, / From the sacred presses we will see / Wine, love, and light / Flow for all those who thirst; / Leaving the marks of the gibbet, / Jesus, unnailing his weary arms, / On Calvary planted with vines / Will place his cross like a supporting stake.]

From the thousands of victims swallowed up by "the Versailles Moloch" in May to the "hecatombs of the unknown" executed, imprisoned, or transported in the months thereafter "in silence like the last combatants of Père-Lachaise in the obscurity of the night,"[36] the whole Commune experience lent itself to a holocaustal, martyrological interpretation closely patterned on the arrest, passion, and resurrection of Christ. Revolutionary Christology gave meaning to the horrors perpetrated on the "killing streets" of Belleville and Montmartre and in the "abattoirs" of the Parc Monceau and Père-Lachaise, and made it possible to view them as a necessary preparation and prelude to the grape harvest to come. Or, as Pottier put it in his most famous poem after "L'Internationale," "Elle n'est pas morte, Nicolas": The Commune is dead, long live the Commune![37]

If Montmartre was the Calvary of the right, the left's combined Gethsemane and Golgotha was Père-Lachaise, and it was here that the Commune would be celebrated and remembered. But the cemetery had a gruesome fascination for the right as well, and it is there that Elémir Bourges (1852–1925) places the opening scene of his confused would-be Wagnerian summation of recent French history, *Les Oiseaux s'envolent et les fleurs tombent* of 1893. The centerpiece of the first chapter is the arrival at Père-Lachaise of two wagonloads of corpses—those of the hostages executed by supporters of the Commune at La Roquette—and their ritual desecration against the backcloth of an urban Walpurgisnacht as Paris burns below. A mass of drink-crazed Communards, soldiers, and civilians, men and women alike, press around the wagons when suddenly "a colossal, thick-set *fédéré*" seizes a corpse clad in a purple cassock and, raising it as high as his arms permit, "proudly presents to Paris in revolt ... the corpse of its pastor": it is the body of Archbishop Darboy, which, as in some obscene parody of the Ecce Homo, the Commune is offering to his flock.

But the horrors are only beginning, for the Communards, having vented their wrath on the enemy corpses, now turn on each other. Hordes of revolutionary maenads and bacchantes, complete with the inevitable whores and—an innovation by Bourges—a *kerosene*-drenched Negro in spahi uniform, his head lolling from shoulder to shoulder, perform a wild, drunken reel among the tombstones until one woman falls and is torn apart by the others. The iron grilles of family crypts are tricked out with this or that bloody organ of her body, and the ritual *sparagmos* (evisceration) ends with another woman skewering the victim's heart on her saber and shrieking, "Two sous for the heart of Jesus!" while "beneath the fiery sky the maniacal dance continued."[38] If this farrago of sacrificial themes was meant to blacken further the memory of the Commune by associating it with some satanic parody of the blood sacrifice of Christ, it probably succeeded with the audience for which it was intended. If nothing else, it shows how deeply rooted in the nineteenth-century psyche was the obsession, dating back to the death of de Launay and the others in 1789 and strengthened by the massacres of September 1792, with the killing, dismemberment, and ritual display of sacrificial victims singled out for "treatment" virtually at random. To cap it all, these horrors are recounted partly through the eyes of a watching Jewish secondhand clothes dealer named Chus, who, siding with the Communards, nonetheless escapes their eventual fate to continue his clandestine quest for power under the restored Third Republic. The link between anti-Communard writing and the antisemitic outpourings of the 1890s and 1930s could hardly have been more clear.

If the memory of Père-Lachaise churned up a turmoil of negative images in the minds of the right, for the left its meaning, and above all the meaning of the wall against which hundreds of Communards had been shot, was positive and clear. As Pottier put it in "Le Mur voilé" (1886), the contrast between the "proudly festooned sepulchres" (*sépulcres fleuris d'orgueil*) of the bourgeoisie and the "grassless, treeless soil" where the "vanquished of May" had been mown down spoke for itself:

Ton histoire, bourgeoisie,
Est écrite sur ce mur.
Ce n'est pas un texte obscur.

. . . .

Ta féroce hypocrisie
Est écrite sur ce mur![39]

[Your history, bourgeoisie, / Is written on this wall. / It's not an obscure text. / ... / Your ferocious hypocrisy / Is written on this wall!]

In fact the cult of the *Mur des fédérés* was slow to get under way, and it was not until the 1880s that the commemoration of the *Semaine sanglante* supplanted that of 18 March among those Parisians who remained loyal to the memory of the Commune.[40] For many years, though, the authorities exercised tight control over the commemoration: militants were searched as they filed into the cemetery by batches, and while red banners—banned in the street—could be unfurled and red wreaths (provided their inscriptions were not too radical) placed in crevices in the wall or hung from hooks, speeches were forbidden and revolutionary songs proscribed, especially in the 1890s, when anarchists regularly tried to sing "La Ravachole," their incendiary reworking of "La Carmagnole," composed in honor of François Ravachol, who was executed in 1892 for various acts of "propaganda of the deed" and whom many regarded as yet another sacrificial victim, even as "a sort of violent Christ"—had he not been thirty-three years old when he died?—whose "legal murder" would inaugurate a new era for humanity.[41]

By the 1890s, however, conflicts within the ranks of the commemorators were more likely to provoke violence than their common opposition to the police: in 1888 an anarchist had fired a shot at a Blanquist at the wall, and fights broke out again in 1890. Gradually, however, both the march to the cemetery and the commemoration itself became part of the accepted political calendar, prompting the hard-line Blanquists to withdraw entirely, and, after their split at the Congrès de Tours in 1920, Socialists and Communists commemorated the *Semaine sanglante* on different dates, reuniting—and then briefly—only in 1935, during the buildup to the Popular Front of the following year. The cult of the *Mur des fédérés* reached its apogee in May 1945, when the procession to the cemetery became an expression of postliberation effervescence and unity, as well as a means for the Communists to build up popular hostility to Marshal Pétain, jailed since April that year and shortly to be brought to trial.

With the Communist presence ever more strongly felt, the wall was gradually transformed into a kind of party pantheon, with monuments or plaques commemorating Communist resistance heroes such as Colonel Fabien, party leaders (Maurice Cachin, Maurice Thorez, Jacques Duclos), and writers (Henri Barbusse, Paul Eluard), as well as sculptures in memory of Dachau, Ravensbrück, Oranienburg, and other concentration camps. There is also a monument to the resisters executed in 1941 at Châteaubriant and Mont-Valérien. Perhaps the most moving memento, though, is the black marble plaque commemorating the last surviving Communard, Adrien Lejeune, who died as late as 1942 in Novosibirsk, in the Soviet Union, where he had moved in 1926, and whose remains were transferred to the foot of the wall during the centenary of the Commune in 1971. By then, however, the *montée au mur* was barely more than a memory, and in 1983 the wall was declared to be a historical monument—"not necessarily a sign of death," comments its historian, Madeleine Rebérioux, "but not necessarily a sign of life either."[42] Another site on the once politically supercharged map of Paris was succumbing to hyposignificance, carrying with it the memory of "the martyrs of May" and their truly heroic experiment in self-governing, "socialism in one city."

8

CONVERSION?
Paul Claudel at Notre-Dame
(Christmas 1886)

Paul Claudel's "conversion" to Catholicism in 1886—the reasons for the quotation marks will become apparent in due course—was by no means the only such experience of spiritual regeneration and reorientation to occur in the French intellectual-artistic milieu between 1870 and 1914, but it was certainly the most spectacular, as well as the most talked and written about. For the literary critic Charles Du Bos (1882–1939), who himself "converted" to Catholicism in 1927, it was nothing less than the late nineteenth century's equivalent of the conversion of Paul the Apostle.[1] Poeticized and mythologized almost from the outset, Claudel's conversion presents a number of distinctive features that mark it off from the experiences of other noted literary and intellectual converts. In the first place, it took place when Claudel was only eighteen, whereas most parallel cases occurred when the subject was in his or her thirties or older (as with, in chronological order, the conversions of Chateaubriand [1798, aged 30], Verlaine [1874, 31], Charles de Foucauld [1886, 33], Huysmans [1892, 44], Francis Jammes [1905, 37], Raïssa and Jacques Maritain [1906, aged 23 and 24 respectively], Charles Péguy [1907, 34], Jacques Rivière [1913, 27], Ernest Psichari [1913, 30], Francis Poulenc [1936, 37], and Simone Weil [1938, 29]),[2] and it turned upon—or at least was made to turn upon in Claudel's repeated and highly self-conscious recensions of it—on a single life-transforming event rather than an extended process of self-discovery and eventual commitment to the Church.

Strictly speaking, almost all the above instances, including Claudel's, involved less *con*version, in the sense of a radical switch or turning to an entirely new faith and practice, than a *re*version to the religion in which the subject had been brought up. They were not shifts from one church to another, in the manner of John Henry Newman, Gerard Manley Hopkins, or Evelyn Waugh, and their meaning was often less a breach with the established order than a return to it. Some conversions did involve such a break with the past, as in the cases of Jews such as Max Jacob, Raïssa Maritain, and Simone Weil, who became Christians if not, in Weil's case, practicing Catholics, and in almost every instance the literary-intellectual convert was led to reject, nominally if not always in practice, the values—secularist, hedonistic, aestheticist—that held sway in the milieu that he or she had formerly inhabited. Conversion to Catholicism in an officially Catholic country was by no means as straightforward as it sounds, and confronted the convert with conflicts of belief and behavior that frequently required a whole lifetime to resolve, as the case of Claudel, apparently so clear-cut and total, was to demonstrate in such abundant ways.

Claudel wrote about his conversion on four principal occasions, twice in prose and twice in verse, and discussed it in the radio interviews he conducted with Jean Amrouche in the early 1950s. Each successive version adds new details and interpretations that progressively dramatize an event that at the time may obviously not have had the meanings later attached to it. The first and most neutral of the four accounts is the letter that Claudel wrote from China in January 1904 to Gabriel Frizeau, yet another recent convert to Catholicism, to whom Claudel speaks as a convinced and untroubled believer despite being in the throes of an appalling conflict between spirit and flesh involving the woman who would later appear, transfigured, as Ysé in the great drama *Partage de midi,* written in 1905. Claudel begins his letter by assuring the apparently vacillating Frizeau that he, like all Catholics, has been called to experience the "immense, insane, blessed Joy" of knowing that there exists "outside ourselves and within ourselves a distinct being called God, infinitely pure, infinitely tender, infinitely innocent, who knows us and loves us with a personal love, us ourselves, Paul Claudel and Gabriel Frizeau." He then mentions in passing his supposedly "pious childhood," spent mainly at Villeneuve-sur-Fère in the Aisne, where he was born in August 1868, followed by the "infamous lycée"— in Claudel's case Louis-le-Grand, to which he had been sent in 1882— and the "infamous doctrines of the day, the philosophy of Kant and Renan," the latter "a wretch" who, at the school's prize-giving day in 1883, had proffered the most horrible blasphemy ever to emerge from human lips: "*Peut-être* que la vérité est triste" (*Perhaps* the truth is sad). It seems to have been the "perhaps" rather than what follows that Claudel found most despicable.

Describing himself not for the last time as a prisoner in the strait-jacket of nineteenth-century scientific positivism, Claudel then states, briefly and without further elaboration, how, at vespers in Notre-Dame on Christmas Day 1886, he had the revelation while listening to the Magnificat "of a God who was stretching out his arms to me." Nothing more is said, and Claudel goes on to evoke the four years of conflict, hesitation, and confusion that elapsed before, on Christmas Day 1890, again at Notre-Dame, he was finally led to confess and take Communion (apparently for the first time since his First Communion, at the age of eleven, in May 1880), and "from that moment on, all doubts disappeared and I have not ceased to believe down to the last iota everything taught by Holy Catholic Church, unique and infallible repository of truth; I may have sinned but I have never ceased to believe in the love that my God has for me, and in the unfailing treasure that he has placed in the hands of his priests."

There follows a series of reflections on God's love for his creatures; a reminder to Frizeau, quoting Pascal, that "you would not seek me, if you had not already found me"; and a set of practical recommendations that Claudel has evidently followed since his own return to the Church: regular confession and Communion, a good spiritual director, "the most humble forms of devotion," above all the rosary, that "admirable invention," regular works of charity in the context, perhaps, of joining the local branch of the Société de Saint-Vincent de Paul.[3] Despite the writer's evident fervor and conviction, the emphasis is clearly on conversion as a process rather than a once-and-for-all event.

The second prose text, "Ma conversion," written in 1913 at the request of a Dominican friar and published in the Catholic Revue de la jeunesse, is altogether more explicit, detailed, and dramatic.[4] Claudel is now concerned to maximize the difference between his state of mind before and after 25 December 1886 and so to absolutize what happened to him at vespers in Notre-Dame that day. In what is undoubtedly the best known of the four main accounts, conversion is presented emphatically as event rather than process. As before, Claudel alludes to the good First Communion that he made as an eleven-year-old before claiming to have lost all religious faith in consequence of the secular-rationalist instruction he had received even before entering Louis-le-Grand in October 1882, at the age of fourteen, by which time he was, he says, an out-and-out nonbeliever. The usual culprits are brought out for ritual denunciation—Ernest Renan's biblical criticism; the neo-Kantianism of his philosophy teacher, Burdeau; more generally the "yoke of matter" that is held to have stifled French thought in its entirety in the 1880s—and a number of personal details complete the picture of total estrangement from the faith in which he had been nominally brought up: his "deep terror" of death born of the spectacle of his maternal grandfather's death from stomach cancer in 1881, and the "immorality" of his personal behavior at the time, by which he appears to mean masturbation, since it is likely that Claudel remained a virgin until the beginning of his liaison with "Ysé" in 1901.[5]

There was at least one "fissure," however, in the "materialistic prison-house" (*mon bagne matérialiste*) in which he was languishing: Arthur Rimbaud's *Illuminations,* read when they were first published in *La Vogue* in May–June 1886, followed by *Une saison en enfer* sometime during the autumn before his conversion, which, he says, "gave him a vivid and almost physical impression of the supernatural," without, however, lifting the state of "asphyxia and despair" that was his habitual lot.

It was, in short, a kind of Babylonian captivity—the image comes from a much later Claudelian text[6]—that the young Champenois in exile lived through in Paris in the 1880s, years spent wandering, in Claudel's highly mythologized account, through streets he expected to be called Rue de l'Enfer or Carrefour du Désespoir but that turned out to be merely the Rue Saint-Jacques or Rue du Faubourg-Poissonnière, looking out over the City of Dreadful Night from the vantage point of the Pont d'Austerlitz or the Jardin des Plantes and feeling all of Rastignac's "radical separation" at Père-Lachaise, but none of his desire to dominate and act, just a "longing for the Ocean, something in desperation that would at last be equal to my lungs!" It was from this "appalling madreporic prison" (*affreuse prison madréporique*—the submerged maternal image may be significant) that the conversion event of Christmas Day 1886 would offer at least the beginnings of deliverance.

"Such," the 1913 text resumes, "was the unhappy child who, on 25 December 1886, made his way to Notre-Dame to follow the Christmas office there." Having given so negative a picture of his preconversion condition, Claudel heightens it by claiming that it was only a "superior kind of dilettantism," a desire to obtain "material" for various "decadent [literary] exercises," that led him to the cathedral that day. After attending high mass "with but mediocre pleasure," he returned later in the day, "having nothing better to do," to find vespers now in progress. It was then, standing beside the now famous "second pillar at the entrance of the chancel to the right of the sacristy," that "the event that dominates my entire life" so unexpectedly took place. Clad all in white, the choirboys of Notre-Dame and the seminarians of Saint-Nicolas-du-Chardonnet were singing what Claudel would later learn to be the Magnificat, and as the music wafted over him, "in an instant my heart was touched and *I believed.*" The heart of the "poor desperate child" had been miraculously opened, and as the sounds of "Adeste fideles" replaced those of the Magnificat, sobs and tears racked his whole being as he surrendered to the "lacerating sense of the innocence, the eternal childhood of God" and experienced with utter certainty the simple presence and is-ness of the God of love: "God exists, he is there. He is someone, he is a being as personal as I am! He loves me, he is calling me."

At the end of the service, Claudel left the cathedral, and with it, in his 1913 account, the sum total of his former worldview: "The edifice of my opinions and knowledge remained standing, and I saw no defect in them. All that had happened was that I had emerged from it. [Il était seulement arrivé que j'en étais sorti]." He walked back "through rainy streets that now seemed to me so strange" to the family home at 31 Boulevard de Port-Royal, took a "Protestant Bible" given to his sister, the sculptor Camille Claudel, by a German girlfriend, and opened it twice at random (these details are not in "Ma conversion" but in the radio interviews with Amrouche), first at the account of the disciples' encounter with the resurrected Christ at Emmaus and then at Proverbs 8, in which "the Wisdom of God is symbolized as a woman"—the source, Claudel would later claim, of all those women in his work who represent "either the human soul, the Church, the Holy Virgin, or Sacred Wisdom."[7] By a further coincidence—no coincidence at all, of course, for the symbol-obsessed poet—the Bible's original German owner was called Laetitia (Joy).[8]

As in the letter to Frizeau, Claudel next evokes the four years that elapsed before his definitive return to the Church at Christmas 1890, four years of "resistance" in which, by his own account, he tried to fight off the implications of the "revelation" he had received at Notre-Dame. There were fears of telling his family, especially his strongly antireligious sister Camille (whom the gift of the Bible had singularly failed to convert), about what had happened, fears that becoming a practicing Catholic might prejudice his future career as a diplomat under the strongly anticlerical Third Republic, fears that Catholicism might inhibit his writing or even require him to renounce it entirely. He describes his reading (an unlikely combination of Rimbaud, Pascal, Bossuet, the stigmatic Catherine Emmerich, and the *Imitatio Christi,* the last-named proving to be "of terrible harshness"); his first botched attempt to confess at his local parish church, the Eglise Saint-Médard, spiritual home of the early eighteenth-century convulsives; his eventual discovery of the worthy abbé Villaume as spiritual director; and, finally, his Communion at Notre-Dame four years to the day after the original "miracle." Everything flows of a piece, not assuredly without conflict, from this foundational event, which marks, in the 1913 account, an absolute dividing line between before and after, a clear and indisputable sign that Jesus—mentioned by name only very late in the text—is indeed the Son of God, whatever Renan and his sister Camille might have to say on the subject, and that it was "to me, Paul, that he was speaking and to whom he was promising his love."[9]

Between the letter to Frizeau and "Ma conversion," Claudel had written (1907) and published (1910) another work inspired by Christmas 1886, the third of the *Cinq grandes odes,* appropriately titled "Magnificat." This magnificent text was composed in China two years after the collapse of the author's relationship with "Ysé" and in the year after his marriage to Reine Sainte-Marie Perrin (March 1906), which marked his full integration into the Catholic social order. The poem also gains a particular resonance from the birth of the couple's first child, Marie, in January 1907, one of its major themes being the change in the poet's relationship to God and humankind now that he himself has become a father ("Maintenant entre moi et les hommes il y a ceci de changé que je suis père de l'un d'entre eux").[10]

The ode begins, appropriately enough, with the first line of Mary's Magnificat, "Mon âme magnifie le Seigneur" (My soul magnifies the Lord [Luke 1:46]), which has the effect of partly feminizing the poet-speaker. It then reprises, in the sinewy, irregularly inflected lines that Claudel had already made his own, all the key images and motifs that would feature later in "Ma conversion," while adding others that raise still higher the metaphysical and mythical claims that are being made for what the poet has experienced: the walk along "that street that goes down toward Notre-Dame" (presumably the Rue Saint-Jacques), the comparison between the poet and an athlete or gladiator about to enter the arena, a further set of self-aggrandizing biblical analogies (Joseph in the well, Moses crossing the Red Sea, Saul/Paul on the road to Damascus), the flood of tears released at the sound of "Adeste fideles," the overwhelming sense of being "chosen among all those of my age," of being personally addressed by a being as personal as himself ("Vous m'avez appelé par mon nom.... Et voici que vous êtes quelqu'un tout à coup!"), above all the encounter, in the words of "Ma conversion," with the "eternal childhood of God," which restores the poet to a condition of spiritual childhood, as enjoined in Matthew 8:3 (not quoted by Claudel, but implicitly present throughout the poem): "Unless you change and become like little children, you will never enter the kingdom of heaven."

So tightly meshed and ambivalent is the network of family relationships evoked in the poem—God is Father and Son, Mary is Mother and daughter, the poet himself is father and son-daughter—that it is never entirely clear quite who in the poem is being "magnified": is it Jesus, Mary, Paul Claudel, or all of them inseparably? Is the child whom "Adeste fideles" urges the faithful to come and adore ("Venez, fidèles, et adorons cet enfant nouveau-né") the God-child Jesus or the newly (re)born poet whom, a shepherd or wise man to himself, he has suddenly confronted wrapped in swaddling clothes and lying in a manger in Notre-Dame? Self-glorification and the glorification of God are never far apart in Claudel's work, and there can be little doubt that he recognizes and intends such confusions of meaning, the encounter with God and the encounter with self being for him one and the same:

Qui ne croit plus en Dieu, il ne croit plus en L'Etre, et qui hait l'Etre, il hait sa propre existence. Seigneur, je vous ai trouvé.

(He who no longer believes in God no longer believes in Being, and he who hates Being hates his own existence. Lord, I have found you.)

Or, as Claudel would later put it, "I need him in order to be me [J'ai besoin de lui pour être moi]"; "it is through being You that I become more Me [c'est en étant Toi que je deviens davantage Je]."[11] Is this Saint Augustine's *Intimior intimo meo* or a theistically upgraded version of Barrès's *culte du moi* or Rimbaud's *JE est un autre*? It is a question that Claudel's early plays, especially *Tête d'or* (first version 1889, second version 1894), with its confused welter of sensationalism and symbolism, notably fail to resolve, wavering as they do between Nietzschean self-magnification and would-be Christian self-abasement before "God." Even Claudel would later acknowledge that in Tête d'or's will to power and order there was more than an adumbration of the fascism to come.[12]

Claudel returned for a last time in print to the happenings of 25 December 1886 in a poem of that title written in the darkest days of the Occupation at Brangues in the Ain, where, his diplomatic and, to a large extent, his poetic careers now over, he was devoting his retirement to a succession of works of biblical exegesis (*Le Rose et le rosaire, Emmaüs, Paul Claudel interroge le Cantique des Cantiques,* etc.), which, in the view of those few who have read them, count among the supreme masterpieces of twentieth-century French prose. "Le 25 décembre 1886" differs from all previous treatments of Claudel's conversion in that it attributes it unambiguously to the unilateral intervention of the Virgin Mary ("C'est tout de même vous, Madame, qui avez eu l'initiative"), she who has overseen the whole of his subsequent life, all his failures and sins ("Alors tout ce qui est arrivé depuis, Madame, tant pis c'est vous qui avez la responsabilité!"). Now, as death approaches, he invokes her once more in preparation for that moment when he will appear before her "blessedly intact and empty / fundamentally cleansed of all this insipid literature." "All this paper I have accumulated behind me, it's enough to make one weep and laugh" (Tout ce papier que j'ai accumulé derrière moi, il y a de quoi pleurer et il y a de quoi rire!).[13] All the usual images and motifs are present, above all the white surplices of the choirboys and white cloth on the altar, but greater prominence is given than ever before to the music that is responsible for releasing "that reservoir of powerful tears" as God says to the poet (or is it the poet says to God?), "Tu es à moi" (You are mine).[14]

What is striking is how, from 1904 to 1942, the whole experience of conversion has been progressively feminized and infantilized. In 1904 it is an adult male God speaking to an unhappy adolescent boy; in 1907 it is almost as a double of Mary and his newborn daughter, Marie, that Claudel receives the good tidings from above; and in 1913 the crucial notion of the "eternal childhood of God" first comes to the fore, and by some special grace the poet lights on the female figure of Wisdom, who *plays* in the presence of God (see Proverbs 8:30–31). Finally, in 1942, it is Mary herself and virtually alone in "Notre-Dame, la femme-Eglise," who is responsible for bringing the child-self to his Child-Father in heaven. What has happened is, in the terms of Claudel's famous "parable" of 1925, that "Animus," the conscious, willing, masculine surface-self, has progressively given way before "Anima," the spontaneous, pliant, feminine deep self who creates and regenerates through self-surrender to the not-self; or, in the equally famous terms of the *Art poétique* (1904), *connaissance* and *co-naissance* (knowledge and co-birth) are one and the same thing.[15] Claudel may have believed his "conversion" to be unique, but in its insistence on spiritual childhood and the feminine, it was all of a piece with the century of Catherine Labouré, Bernadette Soubirous, and Thérèse Martin (whose own "definitive" conversion had occurred, as Claudel would never cease to recall, after midnight mass at Christmas 1886 in the small town of Lisieux in Normandy), to say nothing of the retinue of ecclesiastically unratified female seers, hysterics, and stigmatics.

So: Conversion or "conversion"? Most of Claudel's readers and critics have taken "Magnificat" and "Ma conversion" at face value, not questioning the writer's projections of 25 December 1886 as a moment of decisive *metanoia,* a clear-cut dividing line between before and after. Claudel's transcription of what happened has, however, been challenged by Henri Guillemin, a fellow Catholic and friend of Claudel. Beginning with an article published in 1957, two years after the poet's death, Guillemin, in modern parlance, deconstructed the increasingly sharp opposition that Claudel sought to construct between his pre- and post-Christmas selves, and in doing so came to play down, almost to the point of dismissing, the significance of the "Notre-Dame experience." Guillemin's studies, brought together as Le *"Converti" Paul Claudel* in 1968, are a model of precise and sympathetic scholarship, and he has no difficulty in demonstrating the existence, sometime before December 1886, of palpable religious longings in the young Claudel (most notably in the poem "Pour la messe des hommes: Dernier sacrifice d'amour," clearly dated 30 August 1886, which brings together many of the key later motifs: tears, sobbing, water, music, an essentially feminized Christ speaking to an essentially feminized and infantilized but—here—ultimately unbelieving humanity),[16] and, correspondingly, in showing the continuation, well beyond December 1890, let alone December 1886, of beliefs and attitudes that Claudel later claimed to have set firmly behind him.

Yet, despite the brilliance of Guillemin's argument and his remorseless accumulation of evidence, few can doubt that 25 December 1886 *was* a decisive turning point in Claudel's life, even if it was not the absolute caesura between before and after into which he subsequently and progressively mythologized it. What is striking is how he interprets it or, more precisely, what he does *not* say about the origins of the "revelation" that would bring him back to the beliefs and practice that he in fact abandoned, and then probably only in part, a mere four (or at most seven) years before: hardly the kind of radical reorientation undergone by a Huysmans or a Foucauld. The conversion is consistently presented in essentially philosophical terms, the recurring target being "la sinistre Université de France"[17] and its presiding bicephalous deity, Taine-and-Renan, who, it was wittily said, were to French thought in the late nineteenth century what Tarn-and-Garonne were to its administrative geography: "the name of a collegial magistracy."[18] Thus, even in "Magnificat," the most obviously emotional of the various accounts, the poet thanks God for saving him from the fate of "the Voltaires, and the Renans, and the Michelets, and the Hugos, and all the other rogues [*infâmes*]," whose souls are with those of "dead dogs" and whose books are "in the dunghill [*fumier*]": "they are dead, and their very name after their death is a poison and a putrescence [*pourriture*]."[19]

Despite the proliferation of family imagery, especially in "Magnificat," Claudel nowhere—or not at least until the radio interviews of 1951–52, and then only tentatively—probes the possible psychological origins of his crisis and its resolution: in his relationship with his cold, physically undemonstrative, and only nominally Catholic mother; in his severe anticlerical father, who brought him to Paris to prepare him for entrance into the Ecole Normale Supérieure and who could not forgive him when he failed the *baccalauréat* in 1883 at the early age of fifteen; and, not least, in his decidedly ambivalent relationship with his exceptionally gifted and tragic elder sister, Camille, the sensual, unbelieving, and eventually deranged model and Other of all the female Wisdom figures in his work, who needs to be set beside him as his complementary equal and opposite rather than relegated to the margins of art history, as she was in the end relegated to the margins of life and society.

Thus, while Christmas 1886 was by no means the absolute dividing line Claudel later claimed it to be, it undoubtedly constituted a watershed event in his life, pointing back to family life at Villeneuve-sur-Fère in the Aisne and forward to the nearby abbey of Igny, which also played a crucial role in Huysmans's conversion, and beyond to the abbey of Ligugé near Poitiers, to Foutchéou and Tientsin in China, where Claudel lived through the greatest moral crisis of his life and produced some of his greatest work, and finally to Brangues, where even his old age was not free of conflict and controversy. "*Plus jamais Claudel!*" (Never again Claudel!) ran the celebrated student slogan in May 1968, and one can understand why: Claudel is not the most sympathetic French Catholic writer of our period, but he is undoubtedly the richest and most energetic, and whatever he may have written, most notably during the Spanish Civil War and again in 1940–44, history will, in Auden's famous backhanded compliment in "In memory of W. B. Yeats" (1939), "pardon him for writing well"[20]—if, that is, it does not first forget him along with Péguy, Bernanos, and Maritain, who bulked so large in their day but are now less and less read outside Catholic circles.

9

CHURCH PROWLING

The Back-to-Front Pilgrimage
of Joris-Karl Huysmans
(1884–1892)

On 12 July 1892, Joris-Karl Huysmans, minor civil servant and, at forty-four, renowned novelist of decadence and the occult, left Paris for the Trappist monastery of Notre-Dame d'Igny, midway between Fère-en-Tardenois and Fismes, on the northernmost fringes of Claudel's home territory.[1] It was, if not the climax, then at least the decisive stage in a conversion process that, in the space of eight years, had taken Huysmans from the desperate prayer that concludes the summa of decadence that is *A rebours* (1884), through the occultist-satanical extravaganza of *Là-bas* (1891), back into the church in which he, like Claudel, had been baptized but from which he had been estranged throughout his adult life and not just for three or four years in his mid-teens, as Claudel had been before the dramatic revelation of Christmas Day 1886.

The process that was to make of Huysmans the most celebrated literary convert of fin-de-siècle France began, in retrospect, with the publication of a work, *A rebours*, that on the surface could not have been more opposed to the spirit and values of Christianity, if not to the aesthetics of Roman Catholicism, which it extravagantly praises as a counter to the horrors of contemporary "Americanism." Reviewing the novel, the great Catholic novelist and critic Barbey d'Aurevilly (1808–89) had repeated the judgment first made more than a quarter of a century earlier with regard to Baudelaire: " 'After *Les Fleurs du mal*,' I told Baudelaire, 'it only remains for you to choose between the muzzle of a pistol and the foot of the cross.' Baudelaire chose the foot of the cross. But will the author of *A rebours* make the same choice?"[2]

Joris-Karl Huysmans (1848–1907). Jean-Louis Forain (1852–1931) painted this portrait more than twenty years after the subject's death. (Musée Carnavalet, Paris, © Photothèque des Musées de la Ville de Paris.)

Huysmans, prefacing a new edition of the novel in 1903, replied in all simplicity that "the choice is made," even though, as the preface makes clear, the choice was anything but painless and straightforward. Indeed, so complex and protracted was the conversion process that Huysmans later wrote that "it was through a glimpse of the supernatural of evil that I first obtained insight into the supernatural of good. The one derived from the other. With his hooked paw, the Devil drew me toward God."[3] He was referring to the extraordinary events and experiences recounted in *Là-bas,* in which Durtal takes over from Des Esseintes as Huysmans's alter ego and mouthpiece and continues the back-to-front pilgrimage that in *A rebours* had ground to a halt in an impasse of subjectivism. If there is no release from modern materialism in artifice and the utmost refinements of desexualized eroticism, then perhaps magic and the occult will provide the solution.

Durtal is writing a study of Gilles de Rais, "the Des Esseintes of the fifteenth century,"[4] and has cloistered himself mentally in Bluebeard's castle at Tiffauges in the Vendée, which Huysmans had visited in September 1889 in the company of Francis Poictevin, the first of Huysmans's fellow pilgrims whose lives were to end in insanity.[5] In order fully to impregnate himself with the spirit of late medieval occultism, Durtal decides to investigate its contemporary survivals, and through his friend Des Hermies makes contact with a galaxy of fin-de-siècle satanists, magicians, alchemists, and astrologers, most of whom are based at least partly on individuals whom Huysmans had consulted, and in some cases become deeply involved with, in the course of writing the novel. Through Durtal's inquiries, the reader is introduced to the renegade Chanoine Docre, supposedly based on a Belgian priest named van Haecke,[6] who, like all satanists, "believes in Christ because he hates him" and has even had an image of Christ tattooed on the soles of his feet "in order the better to crush him";[7] to Madame Hyacinthe Chantelouve, who accompanies Durtal to a black mass celebrated by Docre and thence to the back room of a wine merchant, where she seduces him, revealing as she does so a sacrilegious depravity that appears to include inserting a consecrated host in her vagina as they couple;[8] and, by report, to a certain Dr. Johannès, who, from his base in Lyon, that "refuge of mysticism and haven of preternatural ideas,"[9] is engaged in a cosmic struggle with the satanic magic of Docre and his followers.

Through these and similar figures the reader gains access to a curious and disturbing (anti)religious underworld, part real, part invented, in which spiritualism, sexual perversion, and madness intersect, populated by men and women who, thirsting for some kind of absolute gratification but despairing of or hostile to orthodox Christianity, turn to satanism as a way out of the "materialist prisonhouse" of late nineteenth-century France. "The adherents of satanism," says Des Hermies, "are mystics of an obscene kind, but nonetheless mystics," their longing for the absolute of Evil [l'au-delà du Mal] being but an inverted and perverted form of the saint's longing for the absolute of Good,[10] with, however, one crucial difference: "If the absolute of Good and the beyond of Love [le là-bas de l'Amour] are accessible to certain souls, the absolute of Evil cannot be reached."[11]

Although he does not appear in person in the novel, the crucial figure for Huysmans is clearly Dr. Johannès, the "antipode" of Chanoine

Docre, who as exorcist, prophet, and magus musters the forces of Good in their everlasting combat with Evil. Johannès is a barely fictionalized transcription of the former abbé Jean-Antoine Boullan, whom Huysmans first contacted by letter in February 1890 for information and guidance concerning the occult, and who, from then until his death in January 1893, would play an increasingly important part in the novelist's quirky and roundabout return to orthodoxy. But orthodox the former abbé most definitely was not, and though at the time Huysmans believed him to be an agent of Good, he discovered after the abbé's death that in life Boullan was at least as close to the world of Chanoine Docre as he was to that of Johannès, and that, if he was fighting ultimately for the triumph of Good (as he understood it), then the weapons he used were regularly those supplied by the enemy.

Born on 18 February 1824 in the village of Saint-Porquier in Tarn-et-Garonne, Boullan had been ordained in 1848 and had, as a member of the Congregation of the Missionaries of the Precious Blood, spent several years in Italy before returning, via Alsace, to Paris in 1856.[12] Here he collaborated with the abbé Pillon de Thury on the review *Le Rosier de Marie,* revealing a particular preoccupation, typical of Catholic fundamentalists of the time, with the Marian apparition at La Salette and repeatedly predicting the imminent arrival of the "Reign of Mary" on earth. In 1856 he went, perhaps not for the first time, to La Salette. There he encountered a young Belgian lay sister (*converse*) named Adèle Chevalier, who, after experiencing a series of visions at the convent of Saint-Thomas-de-Villeneuve at Soissons, had been released by her alarmed superiors and had taken up more or less permanent residence at La Salette, believing herself to be charged with the supernatural mission of atoning for the sins of the world by taking its sufferings willingly on herself. It was an extreme version of the doctrine of vicarious suffering or "mystical substitution," which, as we shall see, had already become the central idea—sometimes, it seems, the only idea—of nineteenth-century French Catholicism, and which would be the lodestar of Huysmans's own theology and practice.

Boullan became first Adèle's spiritual director and then, almost inevitably, her lover, and in due course the couple established, purportedly with the approval of Pius IX (with whom Boullan certainly had an audience in September 1858, as well as consulting with the celebrated curé d'Ars), the so-called Society for the Reparation of Souls (Œuvre de la Réparation des Ames), with headquarters at Sèvres, in the diocese of Versailles. If Boullan had remained notionally orthodox up to this point, he soon went beyond every kind of religious pale as he gathered about him at "Bethlehem" on the Avenue Bellevue an array of plainly disturbed or perverted men and women, eight in all, among them two gyrovagous priests, the abbés Wauters and Delétang, and their respective female disciples, Catherine van Griecke, a Belgian woman whom even Boullan judged to be hysterical, and an incurable epilectic named Zoé Le Grix.

What went on at Bethlehem remains, in the nature of things, shadowy in the extreme, but clearly involved exorcism of individuals, both inside and outside the "community," who were believed to be in the throes of demonic possession, and various kinds of ritual healing based either on the application of a mixture of consecrated hosts and human excrement or on physical and spiritual union with Jesus or one or another of the saints. Boullan regularly officiated as an *alter Christus* at these sexualized parodies of the sacrament of Communion. There are reports, which by definition can be neither discounted nor given absolute credence, that when Adèle gave birth to a child (fathered by Boullan) precisely at the moment of consecration at one so-called mass, the priest—who still had not been excommunicated—took the neonate and ritually immolated it on the altar.[13] It was presumably practices such as these that finally caused Catherine van Griecke to denounce Boullan and his disciples to the bishop of Versailles and led to the Œuvre de la Réparation's repeated changes of location in the early 1860s.

Finally the law caught up with Boullan and Adèle. Both spent time in prison for financial corruption, if not for the depraved religio-erotic practices in which they had engaged. On his release in 1864, Boullan revived the Œuvre de la Réparation. Returning to Rome in 1868, he was promptly interned by the papal authorities; it was while in detention in Rome that Boullan wrote the so-called pink notebook, in which he confesses his various crimes and which Huysmans found among his papers after his death. In 1930 the great Catholic orientalist Louis Massignon handed it over to the Vatican Library, where it reportedly remains sub rosa to this day.

Released in 1869, Boullan gained control of the *Annales de la sainteté au dix-neuvième siècle,* which served as the vehicle for his increasingly heterodox ideas until 1875, when he was at last expelled from the Church. At this point Boullan began corresponding with the aged heresiarch Pierre-Eugène-Michel Vintras (1807–85), who, after a conversion experience in 1838, had founded the so-called Œuvre de la Miséricorde, which, with its spiritual headquarters in the village of Tilly-sur-Seulle, not far from Vintras's hometown of Bayeux, eventually had branches (called *septaines,* after the seven gifts of the Holy Spirit) in Nancy,

Avignon, Lyon, Poitiers, Angers, Le Mans, Castres, Niort, Montpellier, and Cahors, as well as Paris, where the cult was centered on the home of a Dr. Godier, on the now demolished Rue Neuve-des-Mathurins.

Taking the "angelic" name of Sthrathanaël, Vintras recruited widely among people who, for whatever reason, were frustrated with Catholic orthodoxy. His teaching on the imminent arrival of the "Third Reign" of Jesus, the Reign of the Holy Spirit, had a definite appeal for the outer fringes of the legitimist cause whose millennialist expectations had been raised by the arrival from Germany of the improbable Naundorff, whose claim to be the long-lost son of Louis XVI, and hence Louis XVII of France, gained the assent of many credulous ultraroyalists. One of Vintras's most ardent adherents—Eve to his Adam in the regenerated Eden of the spirit—was the comtesse d'Amaillé, the so-called Joan of Arc of the Vendée, who, as Dhocédhoël, joined him in Paris after the cult was condemned by the Vatican in 1843 (and Vintras sentenced to five years' imprisonment for theft), and the couple set out to convert the capital to the new faith from their base at 20 Rue de la Chaussée d'Antin, in the expensive northwest of the city.

It was now that Vintras, following further attacks from the Church, adopted the inverted cross as the symbol of the new dispensation of which he was the prophet, inverted because the Reign of the Suffering Christ had been superseded by the Reign of the Holy Spirit of Love. Stigmata, bleeding hosts, glossolalia, visions: no spiritual experience, however extreme or unusual, seems to have been foreign to the Œuvre de la Miséricorde. Some of Vintras's followers went even further. The former abbé Maréchal (Ruthmaël) founded a splinter group known as the Sainte Liberté des Enfants de Dieu, whose male members were encouraged to offer a "love sacrifice" to God that took the form of mutual or group masturbation, while female cultists were required to "commune" sexually with the Paraclete's emissary on earth—the former abbé himself, of course.[14] Clearly this was the kind of church with which Boullan's Œuvre de la Réparation might profitably amalgamate.

Boullan and Vintras met twice, first in Brussels and then in Paris, before Vintras's death in December 1875, at which point Boullan declared himself his successor. In due course Boullan moved to Lyon, where his leadership was readily accepted by the Misericordist groupuscule that forgathered at number 7 Rue de la Martinière, home of the architect Pascal Misme, otherwise known as the Pontiff of the Divine Melchizedean Chrism. Here Boullan continued to teach Vintras's doctrine of the imminent arrival of the Third Reign, the Age of the Paraclete, which would succeed the Second Reign of the crucified Christ as

this had succeeded the First Reign of the Judaic Law, and regularly celebrated the so-called Sacrifice of the Glory of Melchizedek or Provictimal
Sacrifice of Mary, which, Huysmans writes in *Là-bas*, represents "the
mass of the future, the glorious Office of the Reign of the divine Paraclete on earth," a sacrifice offered in gratitude to God by "regenerated
Man, redeemed by the effusion of the Holy Spirit of Love."[15] Huysmans
does not add—indeed, at the time of writing he probably did not
know—that the Sacrifice of the Glory of Melchizedek also involved
"Unions of Life," in which adepts were almost certainly encouraged to
have sexual intercourse with each other (and, presumably, with Boullan)
as earthly embodiments of this or that celestial entity.

In his theory and practice of "erotic paracletism"[16] Boullan had an
indispensable ally in his middle-aged housekeeper, Julie Thibault
(1839–1907), who features in Huysmans's novels as the harmless religious eccentric "Madame Bavoil." In 1895, after the deaths of both
Boullan and Misme, she moved into his bachelor flat on the Rue de
Sèvres as combined lodger and housekeeper.[17] Married at seventeen,
Madame Thibault had soon abandoned her husband to pursue her
"spiritual mission," which, in the first instance, seems to have involved
her visiting all the major Marian shrines of France and then of the rest of
Europe. Traveling always by foot and carrying just a bundle of clothes
and her umbrella, she lived on a diet of milk, bread, and honey, and her
pilgrimages probably took her up to 25,000 miles on foot. She had a
particular attachment for the shrine of Mary Magdalene at Saint-
Maximin-la-Sainte-Baume in Provence, for the Saintes-Maries-de-la-
Mer in the Camargue, and, inevitably, for La Salette, which, says
Madame Bavoil, is "the Virgin for the few," as opposed to Lourdes,
which is "the Virgin for everyone."[18] In 1874 Madame Thibault met
Vintras in Paris, and by 1883 had joined the "church" on the Rue de la
Martinière in Lyon, actively participating in the Sacrifice of the Glory of
Melchizedek. She was known to fellow cultists as variously Achildaël,
"la Femme Apostolique," "l'Epouse Joséphique," "la Mère dans la Mis-
sion de la Maternité de la Lumière de l'Amour," and so on.

A tiny moon-faced woman, invariably dressed in black and forever
clutching a prayer book, Madame Thibault continued to celebrate the
Provictimal Sacrifice of Mary when she moved into Huysmans's flat, and
presumably the now wholly orthodox novelist must have seen her don her
green and white vestments and perform the ritual (which involved consecrated wafers that she seems to have stolen from churches) before what,
with a fine contempt for French genders, she called the "petite autel" (little altar) that she had brought with her from Lyon for that purpose.[19]

Huysmans made contact with the Rue de la Martinière group through another decidedly wayward woman named Berthe Courrière (1852–1916), one of the several models that he had for Madame Chantelouve in *Là-bas*. If anyone initiated the novelist into the full range of satanic practices, it was Berthe Courrière, a well-known adept of the occult, who in September 1890 was committed to a mental asylum when she was found naked outside the presbytery of the abbé van Haecke, the putative model of Huysmans's own Chanoine Docre, in Bruges. At the time Huysmans met her, in the late 1880s, she was the mistress of the writer and critic Remy de Gourmont (1858–1915).[20]

A further source for Madame Chantelouve (and conceivably the real-life perpetrator of her trick with the Communion wafer) was another dabbler in the occult named Henriette Maillat, with whom Huysmans had a brief and disappointing affair around this time and who numbered among her former lovers Léon Bloy and the self-proclaimed grand master of the Rosicrucian Order, "Sâr" Joséphin Péladan (1859–1918). Among male informants were the poet Edouard Dubus, an addict of magic and morphine, who was to die insane in 1895, and another morphine addict and Rosicrucian, the marquis Stanislas de Guiata, who died of an overdose three years later, at the age of twenty-seven.[21]

That all these individuals seem to have known each other (and, in the case of Boullan and Guiata, to have engaged in a bitter struggle for control of the occultist milieu) suggests the extent and ramifications of the fin-de-siècle religious underworld, which at one of its extremes merged with the weirder varieties of orthodox or near-orthodox Catholicism and at the other fed into every imaginable cult, fad, and religio-political movement: spiritism, astrology, Wagnerianism, Symbolism, Naundorff-ism, Theosophy, Cabala, telepathy, table turning, whatever. It was a world that drew the perverted, the deranged, and the spiritually lost in equal proportions and over which death and insanity hovered as a perpetual threat: as G. K. Chesterton said more than once, when people no longer believe in God, they believe in anything. To cap it all, Huysmans's long-term partner, Adèle Meunier (d. 1895), who was not in any way involved in the occult, was committed to the mental hospital of Sainte-Anne in Paris for the last two years of her life.

When, therefore, Huysmans made contact with the Boullanist-occultist milieu, he was venturing into something indisputably real and charged, at the very least, with dangerous potential. In the event, he seems to have experienced only the relatively benign aspects of Melchizedekism, those that most resembled orthodox Catholicism, and to that extent his encounter with the Rue de la Martinière group marked a decisive step toward, rather than away from, the recovery—or, more accurately, the discovery—of faith. Indeed, the crucial experience had probably occurred before Huysmans wrote to Boullan in February 1890.

In August 1888, in the course of a holiday in Germany divided, characteristically, between visits to museums and visits to brothels, Huysmans had been stunned by the discovery, in the tiny museum of Cassel, of a *Crucifixion* by Matthias Grünewald, an extraordinary description of which occupies the opening pages of *Là-bas*. Here the altarpiece—foreshadowing the still more remarkable Grünewald *Crucifixion* that Huysmans was to see in Colmar in 1903—is presented initially as a supreme instance of the "spiritualist naturalism" that, in opposition to Zola's materialist naturalism, Durtal is pursuing in his own writings. But the response to "this most human of Christs," "the Christ of the Poor," already goes far beyond the merely aesthetic and programmatic, and, confronted by it, Durtal readily acknowledges that religion alone "is still able to soothe, with the softest of unguents, the most impatient of wounds," and that, although he does not, or not yet, believe in all that it teaches, he nonetheless accepts the reality of the supernatural.[22] In retrospect, it is clear that Huysmans was en route toward Catholicism from that moment on.

In his preface of 1903 to *A rebours,* Huysmans confessed that he understood virtually nothing about the "subterranean workings" of his soul between the publication of that novel in 1884 and the appearance of *Là-bas* seven years later, in 1891. It was a period of "incubation," he says, in which God, unknown to him, was at work "excavating" the galleries of his inner life, laying new foundations, installing the fuses, and igniting the spark that years later would culminate in the moment when "I prayed for the first time and the explosion took place."[23]

After the revelation of Cassel, Durtal-Huysmans continues to "prowl" (*rôder*) around Catholicism, doing the rounds of the parish churches and religious houses of Paris as simultaneously he does the rounds of its brothels and restaurants. Often separated by no more than a few minutes' walk, church and brothel become analogues of each other, opposed but complementary, in which, pilgrim and pursuer of prostitutes combined, author and character seek ever more recherché satisfactions of the mind and the senses, conscious, however, that in both religious house and house of ill repute what they really crave lies beyond the superficial pleasures that, amid many disappointments, they occasionally experience in each. What is on the surface a straightforward moral conflict between spirit and flesh is, deep down, a far more complex transformative process, and Durtal-Huysmans realizes that his sexual and spiritual cravings are at some deeper level connected as he goes from brothel to church and from church to brothel, looking to the Virgin for what he has failed to find in the whore and to the whore for what the Virgin has failed to deliver. Hence the continual to-ing and fro-ing between Huysmans's favorite church, the Eglise Saint-Séverin in the Latin Quarter, and his favorite brothel, La Botte de Paille, on the nearby Rue Mazarine. If the Virgin is a tart offering herself to all and sundry, then the tart—and particularly Huysmans's favorite, Fernande, who features in his novels as Florence—is equally a surrogate Virgin, and each in her way is leading him to God. "Tu crois à la Vierge, toi, à cette gonzesse?" (You believe in the Virgin, you, that tart?), she says,[24] little knowing the part she is playing in the mysterious drama of her client's salvation.

After exchanging letters with Boullan and receiving from him copious documentation on the occult, Huysmans went to Lyon in September 1890 and returned "deeply troubled" by the "singular things" he had witnessed at the Rue de la Martinière.[25] The round of visits to churches, brothels, museums, and restaurants continued as though, failing to find the religious nourishment he craved, Huysmans were reduced to a kind of collector's mania, at once and inseparably aesthetic, erotic, and spiritual, collecting, comparing, and collating experiences, forever on the brink of the one great Experience that would put an end to his prowling. "In church," Durtal admits, "I am turned on [emballé] only by art, I go there to see and to listen, and not to pray; I am seeking not God but my own pleasure.... I am almost in heat [enflammé] in the nave, less warm on the forecourt, and absolutely frozen when I'm outside," whence the precipitate flight to the Rue Mazarine and the warmth of Fernande-Florence's flesh.[26]

On Christmas Day 1890—the same day that Claudel first took Communion at Notre-Dame—Huysmans attended vespers at the tiny Franciscan chapel on the corner of the Rue de la Glacière and the Rue de l'Ebre, located as by preternatural design between the mental asylum of Sainte-Anne and another favorite pickup place, the Bal du Château Rouge. Here in the company of the secondhand bookseller and police spy Gustave Boucher, Huysmans listened entranced to the plainsong and followed with a typical blend of erotic and religious excitement the procession of laywomen and nuns that wound around the church, impressed not only by the "majesty" and "incredible distinction" of the women but by the "extraordinary" movement of their hips as they knelt and kissed the floor of the church.[27] In En route the eroticism of the moment is explicitly dwelt on:

[Durtal] listened, moved by the childlike naturalness of the chant, and suddenly, in a flash, brutally, without his understanding anything about it, the posture of the girls kneeling on their chairs before him provoked heinous memories within him. He fought back against them, trying to repress the assault of these shameful thoughts [*ces hontes*], and they persisted. A woman whose perversions drove him wild with desire was there before him, and he saw her flesh swell beneath her silken and lace blouse; his hands shook, and feverishly they opened her delicious and abject perfume box [*cassolettes*].[28]

As the only man present, Durtal is invited to join the procession and ends up, as Huysmans and Boucher would do, kneeling at the Communion rail in front of the altar. Later, at Igny, Huysmans would be haunted by the similarity between the postures of prayer and the postures of sex, but in *En route* Durtal feels only discomfort and embarrassment as the wax—unhappy symbol!—drips from his candle and threatens to splash down on the overcoat he is wearing.[29] No doubt Huysmans and his companion continued their Christmas devotions elsewhere, in the company of Tache du Vin and Mémèche, or other such "exquisite princesses" of their acquaintance.[30]

And so it went on, with Huysmans edging closer and closer to the Church, only to draw back time after time from the final decisive commitment. Church prowling, interspersed with brothel prowling as ever, continued: high mass at the Benedictine chapel on the Rue Monsieur on the morning of Holy Thursday in March 1891, with a visit to Sainte-Anne de la Glacière later in the day; Saint-Sulpice for vigil on Good Friday; the chapels of the Poor Clares and the Carmelite Sisters on the Avenue de Saxe, then a few days later the Benedictines on the Rue Tournefort, where the chant is said to be even more "authentic" than at the Rue Monsieur, and so on and so on, collecting churches and chapels like so many antiques, while all the time the image of Fernande-Florence's body—no longer her face or even "the place of admissible pleasures" but the "obscure region where that creature transferred the seat of her senses"[31]—would interpose itself between him and the supposed object of his devotion.

On 28 May 1891, however, Huysmans took a more decisive step than ever before when, through the intervention of that inveterate priests' groupie Berthe Courrière, now released from the mental asylum, he was introduced to the abbé Arthur Mugnier (born 1853), then curate at the Eglise Saint-Thomas-d'Aquin and with an established reputation as a spiritual director. Explaining that, after his recently published "black book" on the occult, he now wished to write a "white book" on Catholicism—the *A rebours* of *Là-bas,* as he put it elsewhere[32]—and that, in order to do so, he had first to "whiten" himself, Huysmans famously asked the abbé: "Have you any chlorine for my soul?" (Avez-vous du chlore pour mon âme?).[33]

From that point on, events gathered momentum, but it was still more than a year before Huysmans became a communicating member of the Church. Significantly, his encounter with Mugnier, whom he now saw on a regular basis, did not cause him to distance himself from Boullan, and the two are fused in the figure of the abbé Gévresin, who directs Durtal's spiritual quest in *En route.*

In July 1891 Huysmans returned to Lyon, that "city of nut cases" (*ville des toqués*), for a further immersion in the world of "pythonesses, somnambulists, mystical heresiarchs, and psalm-singing silkworkers,"[34] followed by a brief pilgrimage to La Salette in the company of Boullan, "le Père" Misme, and "Maman Thibault," which was followed in its turn by a far less spiritually rewarding stay at La Grande Chartreuse, high in the Alps.

Predictably, the intensification of Huysmans-Durtal's spiritual life did not diminish his obsession with Fernande-Florence, not least because she now had an American admirer who was promising to set her up in a bar in Cincinnati. Prayers to the Virgin—"Forgive, Holy Virgin, the shit that I am" (Pardonnez, Sainte Vierge, au salaud que je suis)[35]—are intercut with visits to the whore, which the abbé Gévresin helps to justify when he explains how Virgin and whore meet in the person of Mary Magdalene, that figure of Eve who "conveys the words of the Devil to man" and then mutates from Eva to Ave when on Easter morning she brings the apostles the good news of the resurrection of their Lord.[36] Salvation is mediated through the very origin of sin, and it was, appropriately enough, thanks to another such spiritual double agent, the inevitable Berthe Courrière, that Huysmans was present, along with his dubious friend Boucher (who also later converted), at the clothing of a Benedictine sister at the Rue Monsieur in November 1891. Movingly described in *En route,* it marks a further station on his *via tortuosa* back to the Church.

Finally, in early June 1892, Huysmans told Mugnier that he felt as ready as he ever would be to confess and take Holy Communion, and asked him to recommend a religious house outside Paris where he might make a retreat and in due course actually (re)enter the Church, around which he had been prowling for so many years. The abbé knew the guestmaster at Notre-Dame d'Igny (Notre-Dame de l'Atre in *En route*), and in early July it was agreed that Huysmans would go to the monastery for a week. On the 11th Huysmans duly packed his port-manteau with spiritual and material provisions for his stay—"selections from the works of Ruysbroek, the recorded visions of Catherine Em-merich, chocolate and tobacco, matches and napkins, pencils and paper, packets of antipyrine and a phial of laudanum"[37]—and, after a farewell dinner at the restaurant Mignon on the Boulevard Saint-Germain, em-barked upon what he naively believed would be the final stage of his spiritual journey the following day.

If Huysmans-Durtal imagined that he would find inner peace at La Trappe, the first night in his cell was enough to disabuse him. Not just Fernande-Florence but a whole host of succubi people his dreams: "It was no longer the familiar, involuntary act, the vision that ceases just at the moment when the sleeping man embraces the loving form and is about to melt into her; it was that but better than in nature, long, com-plete, accompanied by every kind of prelude, detail, and sensation; and discharge [*le déclic*] took place, with an extraordinary painful sharp-ness, in an unprecedented spasm of relief."[38] At mass the next morning, he is the only person present not to take Communion, and he feels "pushed to one side, treated, as he deserved, like an outsider, separated like the goats in the Gospels, set apart far from the sheep, on the left hand of Christ."[39]

While preparing, in a state of mounting spiritual anguish, to make his confession, Durtal goes out into the monastery garden, and is con-fronted by what seems like an allegory of his whole situation. Beside a dark stagnant pond, and reflected in it, stands a huge wooden cross bearing a white marble Christ; a swan moves slowly across the water to-ward him. The swan is his soul, which must be saved from the brackish waters of the pond—his life up to now—and only Christ can save it through a new crucifixion, not on Golgotha, in the open air, in the light, but by plunging head downward, at night, into the muddy depths at his feet. Finding some solace in this image, Durtal eventually makes a "con-fession in reverse" (*une confession à rebours*)—how could it be other-wise?—beginning with what he considers to be a few minor sins and building up to his sacrilegious coupling with Hyacinthe Chantelouve. He duly receives absolution, though the monk who confesses him warns him that "the conversion of the sinner is not his healing, but only his convalescence," and that as grace accomplishes its work in him, the pa-tient should expect to be "tortured by imagination": "It caused you greatly to sin and, by a just revenge, it will cause you greatly to suffer."[40]

No warning, however, could prepare Durtal for the mental ordeal of the days that follow. When, the day after confession, he comes forward to take Holy Communion, his mind is assailed by all manner of incongruous thoughts and distractions. The wafer sticks to his palate and he has to twist his tongue around in order to free and then swallow it "like a crêpe," after which he is plunged into a "state of absolute torpor," as though "the sacrament had somehow anaesthetized his spirit."[41]

The next day is worse still. Kneeling before a statue of the Virgin, Durtal finds himself filled with the "spirit of blasphemy": "he wanted at all costs to insult the Virgin; it seemed to him that he would experience a bitter joy, a pungent pleasure, in soiling her, and he held himself back, screwing up his face so as not to emit the trooper's insults that rushed to his lips, clamoring to escape."[42] The torment continues back in his cell, especially when he kneels to pray, and "this posture brings back memories of Florence stretched across the bed. He stood up, and his old aberrations came back to him."[43] Beneath the official text of his prayers runs a continuous involuntary subtext of sacrilegious images and thoughts, most of them grossly sexual or excremental, which "crucify" him before even the most anodine of images: "He tried to focus on the statue of Saint Joseph before which he was standing and he struggled to perceive it alone, but his eyes seemed to turn inside out, and open buttocks filled them. There came a throng of blurred and confusingly colored apparitions, which took on a precise shape only at the places craved by the age-old infamy of man."[44]

And so it goes on, day after day and night after night, throughout Durtal's stay at La Trappe: "impure visions" followed by scruples and doubts, spiritual dryness leading to nondesire for the Eucharist (*l'indésir de l'Eucharistie*) that is the reason for his presence, above all the "demonic, insidious, obstinate, and almost visible action"[45] of the subconscious as it bombards his consciousness with one obscene, incongruous image or thought after another. Truly, as Durtal's confessor warns him, "no place on earth is more haunted [by the Devil] than a cell; no one is more harassed than a monk."[46]

Thus it is that by the end of his retreat, and although he has accomplished the appropriate rite of passage, Durtal feels more confused and more lost than he had felt when he set out from Paris: "Ah! he said to himself, I have lived twenty years in ten days in that monastery, and I have come out of there with my brain shattered and my heart shredded to pieces; I am screwed up for good [*je suis à jamais fichu*]. Paris and Notre-Dame de l'Atre have rejected me in turn like a wreck, and now I am condemned to live like an odd sock [*à vivre dépareillé*], because I am still too much a man of letters to make a monk, and yet I am already too much a monk to remain among men of letters."[47]

There has been no moment of illumination, no crossing of the Red Sea, no road to Damascus, only the bitter realization that, as Huysmans would put it to René Dumesnil a few months before he died, "conversion is a switching of tracks [un aiguillage], but the individual is still the same train."[48] Yet many will find the story of Huysmans's conversion more moving, precisely because it is so antiheroic, than the greatly mythologized once-and-for-all revelation of Claudel. Quite simply, it took courage as well as honesty to admit to "hearing the contrary of what one thinks grumbling on in oneself,"[49] to recognize the involuntary urge to blaspheme against one's deepest belief, to besmirch what one loves, and anyone with any experience of the spiritual life will sympathize with Huysmans-Durtal's powerlessness to stanch the flow of obscene and incongruous images and thoughts that perpetually interrupt and disrupt his faltering attempts at prayer. Huysmans's back-to-front pilgrimage reminds us, as Mauriac perceptively wrote of En route, that grace never suppresses nature even when it converts: "When its lightning strikes an aesthete, a decadent, he remains that decadent and that aesthete; but it so happens that the best of himself and the worst are equally used: the whole of Des Esseintes is necessary to give Durtal."[50]

The first action of grace is not, to use Huysmans's image, to purify the pond water of the soul but, by stirring it, to muddy it still further, as though the Spirit abhors stagnation more than impurity, not least because impurity is the precondition of growth. Huysmans was to visit Igny on three more occasions (in August 1893, during the autumn of 1894, and in July 1896), with much happier results than in July 1892, but the visits were only a prelude to yet more collecting and comparing, the length and breadth now of France rather than merely of Paris: Saint-Wandrille, Fiancey, Solesmes, Paray-le-Monial, Brou, Saint-Maur de Glanfeuil, Ligugé, Chartres, and Lourdes, to name but the principal stages of his spiritual-artistic Tour de France. Nowhere would he find lasting solace for his soul, but what matter? At least now he was en route rather than motionless in his bachelor apartment in Paris.

10

MARBLE VERSUS IRON
Sacré-Cœur and the Eiffel Tower
(1871–1914)

Sacré-Cœur is the least loved of the major Paris monuments. The left detests it because of the politics of its origins,[1] liberal Catholics are embarrassed by its mixture of nationalism and religious masochism, and its neo-Byzantine massiveness benumbs the feelings and intellect even as it overwhelms the eye of the politically and religiously neutral. And yet it remains one of the most visited buildings in Paris, less, no doubt, for itself than for the unequaled panoramic view it affords over the city, and despite its architectural heterogeneity, it has progressively become as much a naturalized part of the cityscape as its equally heterogeneous and near contemporary antithesis and complement on the Right Bank opposite, the Eiffel Tower. To understand the duel and dialogue between these two archetypal structures, it is necessary to return to the darkest days of the Franco-Prussian War and Siege of Paris, and read the text of the so-called National Vow of January 1871, which, after the consecration of Sacré-Cœur in 1919, was engraved in marble and mounted on one of the eastern walls of the basilica:

> In the presence of the misfortunes that afflict France, and of the perhaps greater misfortunes that threaten her still; in the presence of the sacrilegious attacks committed in Rome against the rights of the Church and of the Holy See and against the sacred person of the Vicar of Christ; we humble ourselves before God, and, uniting in our love the Church and our fatherland, we recognize that we have been guilty and that we are justly punished; and to make honorable amends for our sins and to obtain pardon for our faults from the infinite mercy of the Sacred Heart of Our Lord Jesus Christ, as well as the extraordinary aid that alone can deliver the

Sovereign Pontiff from his captivity and bring the misfortunes of
France to a close, we promise to contribute to the erection in Paris
of a sanctuary dedicated to the Sacred Heart of Jesus.[2]

The National Vow (of which the above is an abridged and somewhat
toned-down version)[3] was first made on behalf of the French people by
a prominent Catholic layman, Alexandre Legentil (1821–89). Once the
national crisis had receded, Legentil, together with his brother-in-law,
Hubert Rohault de Fleury (1828–1910), was quickly able to enlist the
full official backing of the Church for his ambitious project. Although
the original vow had been made before the declaration of the Paris Commune, the events of March–May 1871, added to the disasters of the
Franco-Prussian War, the loss of the Papal States in the course of the
unification of Italy, and the effective incarceration of Pius IX in the Vatican, gave an irresistible edge to its call for personal and national atonement. The cause was enthusiastically adopted by the newly appointed
archbishop of Paris, Cardinal Guibert, two of whose predecessors had
met violent deaths at the hands of "the left"—Monseigneur Affre in
June 1848 and Monseigneur Darboy in May 1871—and who, though
by no means an extremist by the Ultramontane standards of the time,
was anxious to exploit the theme of *Gallia Pœnitens* (Penitent Gaul) to
the full. In this he was strongly supported by the president of the Republic, Marshal MacMahon, and by the succession of governments,
nominally republican but in reality Catholic-legitimist to the core, that,
under the slogan of "moral order," dominated French political life from
the crushing of the Commune until the constitutional crisis of May 1877
brought a government of authentic republicans to power for the first
time. On 24 July 1873 the National Assembly gave *its* assent to the project, with the various right-wing groups from avowed and crypto-royalists
to the Bonapartist rump predictably voting strongly in favor and, equally
predictably, republicans of all hues voting massively against.

A huge fundraising operation was set in motion, and after a nationwide competition, the neo-Byzantine design submitted by the architect
Paul Abadie, a disciple of Viollet-le-Duc already renowned for his work
on the cathedrals of Angoulême and Périgueux, was selected by the so-
called Committee of the National Vow, which had overall responsibility
for the project. The first stone was laid on 16 June 1875, the ceremony
being timed to coincide with a mass in Rome at which Pius IX, in a gesture of cosmic inclusiveness, dedicated the whole universe to the Sacred
Heart of Jesus. Beginning as a personal vow by a leading Parisian
Catholic, the cause of Sacré-Cœur swiftly became the cause of the

Church Universal, and from 1875 until 1889 in particular, the eyes of the Catholic world would be focused on Montmartre as the symbol par excellence of the Church's struggle with modernity.

The rapid nationalization and internationalization of Legentil's vow can be understood only in the context of the extraordinary wave of politicized mysticism that swept through the Church during the protracted pontificate of Pius IX (1846–78) and whose impact was nowhere greater than in the traumatized, humiliated France of the early 1870s. Pius's pontificate began with a series of liberal reforms in the Papal States that led many progressive Catholics, Montalambert (1810–70) and Frédéric Ozanam at their head, to see in him a model for their own kind of socially democratic Catholicism. Yet any hope of reconciling 1789 with the teachings and traditions of the Church ended once the challenge to the temporal powers of the papacy in 1848–49 led Pius into unconditional opposition to modernity in all its guises: parliamentary democracy, liberalism, secularism, rationalism, and socialism, all of which he saw as consequences of the nineteenth century's rejection of Christ and His Church.

Increasingly identifying the fate of the Church with that of his own person—it was he who originated the notorious and much quoted dictum *La tradizione sono io* (Tradition is me)[4]—Pius IX proceeded to issue a series of bulls that solidified the Church in its opposition to "the world." In proclaiming the doctrine of the Immaculate Conception of the Blessed Virgin Mary in 1854, he gave the cult of the Virgin a new impetus that propelled it into even more emotional and antirational forms antipathetic to Protestants, secularists, and liberal Catholics alike, and the condemnation in 1861 of the abbé Godard's *Les Principes de 1789 et la doctrine catholique* prepared the way for the *Syllabus errorurum* of 1864, which anathematized modern thought in all its forms. Even moderate forms of rationalism and secularism were condemned, along with the belief that "the Roman pontiff can and must be reconciled with and compromise with progress, liberalism, and modern civilization."[5]

Even more than modernity, it was liberal Catholicism that was the real target of the pope's obloquy. In 1870, against the background of the Franco-Prussian War and the annexation of the Papal States into a new, unified Italy, came the culminating promulgation of the doctrine of papal infallibility at the First Vatican Council. The infallibilization of the pope combined with the anathematization of his opponents destroyed for the foreseeable future all possibility of dialogue between the Church and the emerging democratic, rationalist, secularist order of Western Europe,

with newly republican France at its head. Beleaguered in his Vatican fastness, Pius IX symbolized the intransigence of the Church amidst an ocean
of "errors"; Armageddon was at hand, pitting Christ, His Church, and
His people against the Antichrist of modernity, and in the circumstances
of 1870–71, it seemed that Antichrist might win.

As Rome moved to the doctrinal and ecclesiological right, so too did
the Church in France, sometimes in the wake of the Vatican, sometimes
leading it on. Liberal Catholicism hardly survived the June Days and the
killing of Monseigneur Affre (a moderate himself), as erstwhile progres-
sives, headed once more by Montalambert, rallied to the Party of Order
and, in due course, to the Second Empire, before resuming once again a
critical standpoint from the mid-1850s on. The Gallican mainstream
likewise supported the new Napoleon, but the obsequiousness with
which it did so, particularly at the time of the Italian crisis of 1859–60,
actually strengthened the hand of the emerging Ultramontane faction,
which rapidly assumed intellectual leadership of episcopacy, clergy, and
laity alike; only Archbishop Dupanloup of Orléans kept the intellectual
traditions of Gallicanism alive and intact. As early as 1849 one Ultramontane prelate, Bishop Salinis of Amiens, opined that "the most characteristic feature of the present time is the movement toward Rome.…
Rome is the center of the hopes of Catholicity; it is therefore from Rome
that the movement that will regenerate human societies must begin."[6]

Hitherto the preserve of a disaffected intellectual élite (Bonald, Ballanche, de Maistre, the early Lamennais of the *Essai sur l'indifférence*
[1817–23]), the Ultramontane idea became part of the national consciousness in the 1850s and 1860s, thanks in large part to the journalistic talents of Louis Veuillot (1813–83), a populist and Catholic intransi-
gent who, through his journal *L'Univers,* reached both bishops and
parish priests and through them a substantial lay public as well. Veuillot's Ultramontanism, said Ozanam, was geared not "to convince unbe-
lievers but to raise the passion of believers"; it was unsubtle, anti-
intellectual, and, like the later antiliberalism of a Bloy or a Bernanos,
deliberately extreme in expression. It was Veuillot's principal regret, for
example, that "they did not burn John Huss earlier, that Luther was not
burned with him, and that at the time of the Reformation there was not
one prince in Europe with enough piety and political sense to start a cru-
sade against the countries it had infected."[7] Ultramontane discourse became increasingly rabid in works such as the abbé Morel's *Incartades
libérales* (1859) and the 1,200 pages of the same writer's *Somme contre
le catholicisme libéral* (1876) and reached some kind of climax in the
defense of the *Syllabus errorum* in *L'Encyclique du 8 décembre 1864 et*

les principes de 1789 by the Ultramontane deputy Emile Keller (1828–1909), for whom the choice before France was one of disarming simplicity: either the infallibility of Revolution or the infallibility of Rome. "It is time to look Revolution in the face and to tell it: 'You shall go no further.'"[8]

But Second Empire Ultramontanism was not just a political, doctrinal, and ecclesiological idea. If it had some of the most eloquent French bishops (Gerbet of Perpignan, Pie of Poitiers) as its voice in the pulpit and a cabal of perfervid journalists promoting it in the press, it needed the spiritual and emotional backing of the Catholic laity in all regions and classes to become the truly mass phenomenon into which it would develop in the 1870s and 1880s. Much of its grassroots vitality came from the liturgical reforms initiated by Don Guéranger of Solesmes (1810–75), the restorer of the Benedictine order in France, who, beginning with his "Considérations sur la question liturgique" of 1830 and especially through the pages of *L'Année liturgique* (founded 1841), was responsible for reintroducing unified Roman liturgical practices in place of the ragbag of "Gallican" liturgies that had developed piecemeal over the centuries; between 1845 and 1860 no fewer than fifty-one dioceses adopted the full Roman liturgy.

With the improvement of transport, more and more pilgrims, both clerical and lay, were able to go *ad limina apostolorum* and, like Madame Gervaisais in the Goncourt brothers' anticlerical novel of that name (1869), experience at firsthand "the immense holy contagion" of triumphalist Romanism at its source. In Rome, with its endless succession of capitular, votive, and conventual masses, its oratories, ossuaries, and relics, "piety ferments like Nature under the Tropics."[9] It was at Rome that Veuillot had been converted in 1838, and thither that he regularly returned in order pointedly to contrast the *Parfum de Rome* (1861) to *Les Odeurs de Paris* (1867). French bishops joined with fellow prelates from all over the world to celebrate in the pope's presence the proclamation of the Immaculate Conception in 1854 and the mass canonization of Japanese martyrs in 1862 and 1867. In 1862 eighty priests from the diocese of Nîmes were taken to Rome by their Ultramontane bishop, and hundreds of young Catholics, mainly from heartlands of devotion such as the Vendée and the Gard, enlisted in the Pontifical Zouaves, many of them dying for the papal cause at the battle of Castelfidado in 1860. Emmanuel d'Alzon, the founder of the hard-line Ultramontane Assumptionist order, was a frequent pilgrim *ad limina,* as was another Assumptionist, Père Vincent de Paul Bailly, the future editor of *La Croix,* which in the 1890s would proudly proclaim itself to be "the most anti-Jewish [newspaper] in France, the one that carries Christ on its masthead, a sign of horror to Jews."[10]

For those who, for whatever reason, could not make the pilgrimage to Rome, there were hundreds of pilgrimages, great and small, within their reach: Notre-Dame-des-Victoires in Paris, Notre-Dame-de-Fourvière in Lyon, and the church of Père Jean-Baptiste-Marie Vianney in the nearby village of Ars; there were the great Marian pilgrimages, both the old (Notre-Dame-de-Rocamadour) and the new (La Salette and Lourdes), not to mention the 592 local Marian shrines officially recognized by the Church in the late 1860s. What one historian has called "affective Ultramontanism"[11] also manifested itself in the burgeoning cult of Saint Philomena, promoted in particular by Pauline Jaricot (1799–1862), founder of the Œuvre de la Propagande de la Foi in Lyon, who in 1835 had made a pilgrimage to Mugnano del Cardinale, near Nola, where the saint's supposed relics (unearthed in the catacombs of Rome in 1802) were displayed. The cult was especially strong in the Lyonnais—it appears that by the 1840s half of the girls in the parish of Ars were called Philomène—but had shrines throughout France, at Neuville-sur-Seine in the Aube, Tours-en-Vimeu in the Somme, Herly, Liettres, and Crépy in the Pas-de-Calais, and Guingamp in Britanny.

Everywhere the emphasis was on the emotional, the spectacular, the corporeal, and not infrequently the sanguinary. When it was not Mariocentric, Ultramontane piety was unambiguously, almost viscerally Christocentric, promoting the cult of the Holy Face (sponsored by Louis Dupont, the "holy man of Tours," and later transfigured in the art of Georges Rouault), the adoration of the Blessed Sacrament, the feast of Corpus Christi, and most especially the cult of the Sacred Heart of Jesus, based on the visions and writings of the Visitandine sister Marguerite-Marie Alacoque (1647–90), whose beatification in 1864 and canonization in 1920 transformed the small town of Paray-le-Monial (Saône-et-Loire) into a pilgrimage center on a par, for a time, with La Salette and Lourdes.

The cult of Sacré-Cœur focused on Jesus' unconditional love for the faithful (especially for the faithful in France), urging them to seek solace and healing for their wounds in Christ's own wounded heart, displayed, strawberry-like, often dripping with blood, entwined in thorns or transfixed by swords, on an endless succession of images, statuettes, ex-votos, and medals, many of them emanating from the so-called Sainterie at Vandreuve in Champagne—in reality little more than a Christian art factory—which by the 1870s were, according to Viollet-le-Duc, "spreading through country parishes with the speed of phylloxera."[12]

Here was affective, antirational, antimodern devotion with a vengeance, foregrounding at once the need for penitence and expiation, the spiritual benefits of suffering, and as a reward the certainty of Christ's love and forgiveness; if anything reinforced the idea of Christianity as "a sanctification of suffering and pain," as Gide was to put it in *Les Nouvelles Nourritures* (1935), it was the cult of the Sacred Heart in the 1860s and 1870s.[13]

With the successive defeats and disasters of 1870–71, the cult finally came into its own, most graphically, perhaps, in the Sacred Heart flag, inscribed with the motto "Heart of Jesus, save France" embroidered by the nuns of Paray-le-Monial, under which the Pontifical Zouaves, returning from Rome to defend their Catholic motherland against the Protestant invader, fought at the battles of Patay and Loigny led by General de Charette, a direct descendant of the great leader of the Vendée. Legentil was in Poitiers when he made his vow, at the heart of the war-stricken catchment area that also produced the Mariophany at Pontmain (17 January 1871), and the sight of the Zouaves returning from battle with their blood-splattered banner must have added one further touch to the apocalyptic mood of the times.

The final touch, though, was supplied by simultaneous happenings in Rome. First, the bull *Pater æternus* (18 July 1870) declared the pope's ex cathedra utterances infallible, with the support of the overwhelming majority of the now thoroughly Ultramontanized French episcopacy. Dupanloup voted against, having protested in vain against Cardinal Barnabo, prefect of the College of Propaganda, for "driving the bishops like pigs," and when Monseigneur de Marguerye, another dissenter, returned to his see at Autun, his diocesan clergy drowned out his explanation of how he had voted by stamping on the wooden floor of the chapter house, forcing him into resigning the see.[14] But almost immediately afterward the Papal States were invaded by Italian nationalist forces and Pius IX became, in effect, a voluntary prisoner in the Vatican. All-powerful and all-weak, he appeared to many believers as *alter Christus,* a figure of Christ, a far more poignant victim of the realpolitik of the century than even his predecessors and namesakes Pius VI and VII, both exiled and imprisoned by Napoleon, the former dying in misery at Valence in 1799, the latter, more fortunate, drawing massive crowds in Limoges, Toulouse, Montpellier, and Aix as he returned to Rome from captivity in 1814. In Pius IX the Ultramontanes had the archetypal martyr they needed, and an explicitly Christological cult swiftly developed around him. For the bishop of Tulle, the pope was "the continuing Word incarnate"; for Monseigneur Lagrée of Rennes he was "the actor and beacon [*l'acteur phare*], the suffering servant ... , sated with outrages beyond number, flagellated by revolutions, stripped by his executioners. ..."[15] The language of the Passion was transferred in toto from Christ to His vicar, and the theme of the suffering pope would endure for half a century and more, producing a supreme literary masterpiece in Claudel's trilogy of historical plays, *L'Otage* (written 1909–10), *Le Pain dur* (1913–14), and *Le Père humilié* (1916).

The decision to construct a sanctuary to the Sacred Heart having been taken with the enthusiastic backing of a reactionary church and a reactionary state acting in concert, the question next to preoccupy the Committee of the National Vow was the site. Legentil's original idea was that the new Opéra of Charles Garnier—the archetypal Second Empire construction, still far from completion—should be demolished and the site and the materials used for a basilica, to "make honorable amends for the scandal and extravagance" of the temple of pleasure it would duly replace.[16] When this plan was rejected, the committee next turned to the site of the recent massacre of priests on the Rue Haxo in Belleville, but this was found to be too remote from the center and too low-lying to provide a cynosure of piety and penitence for the whole of the city; eventually a Chapel of Hostages was built on the site, complete with a reconstruction of the cells in La Roquette prison, where Archbishop Darboy and his fellow martyrs met their end.[17] Only then did the committee turn to what in retrospect seems the only possible site: Montmartre, doubly appropriate as the place of the martyrdom of Saint Denis—the decapitated patron of a decapitated (and decapitating) city—and more recently as the site (specifically 8 Rue des Rosiers) where, on 18 March 1871, two generals, Claude Lecomte and Clément-Thomas, had been executed by a firing squad on the very day that the Commune was declared, and where—though only the left mentioned this—Eugène Varlin had been taken and shot in revenge at the end of the *Semaine sanglante*. As the supposed heartland of the Revolution, Montmartre was, as the committee's official bulletin put it in 1875, "the place chosen by Satan for the first act of the horrible saturnalia that was to cause such ruins and give the Church—at the very heart of Christianity, in France!—such glorious martyrs."[18] In addition, of course, it was by long tradition a place of sinful singing and dancing, prostitution and crime, and as such "a mountain of shame and mud, of murder and blood"—in short, Paris's very own Sodom and Golgotha rolled into one, "holy and guilty, pure and besmirched," the divinely appointed place for the offering up of an atoning sacrifice in marble and gold.[19]

So blatant was the symbolism of the basilica's location and so unambiguous its ideological message that it inevitably excited the antagonism of even the moderate left, let alone that of surviving supporters of the Commune. Democratic Christians such as Anthime Corbon were also disgusted by the display of antirevolutionary triumphalism, and even a right-wing Catholic such as Huysmans was repelled by the *viscérolâtrie* to which the basilica was dedicated.[20] A "mastodon of stone," a "heterogeneous megastructure" without links to the other buildings on the Butte, the basilica represents, in the words of one modern critic, an "architecture of imposition" rather than of integration[21]—in short, the spirit of moral order made stone. A pen-and-ink wash by the great Swiss artist-anarchist Alexandre Steinlen (1859–1923) explicitly likens it to a "new Bastille,"[22] while an anonymous drawing in the anticlerical *La Lanterne* shows it in the grips of a batlike priestly Nosferatu complete with the slogan—should any reader be so crass as to miss the point—"Voilà l'ennemi."[23] Gambetta's famous watchword was given a further twist in the widely read *Les Cordicoles* (1902), by the anticlerical zealot Gustave Téry, for whom the basilica was

> the masterpiece of the Catholic machine; it really is here, on this joyful eminence [*cette butte joyeuse*], between the Chat Noir and the Moulin de la Galette, that the heart of moribund Christendom is beating.... Everything converges on Sacré-Cœur or radiates from it. In the ecclesiastical body, it plays the part of that pulsating pump to which physiologists compare the heart.

Whence the double conclusion: "Le cordicolisme [cult of the Sacred Heart], voilà l'ennemi!"; "*Cordicole* or socialist: that is the choice."[24]

Throughout the 1870s and 1880s, Sacré-Cœur and its anticlerical enemies engaged in what can be described only as an incessant battle of symbols, as each side sought to face down the other by deploying its semiological battalions to its greatest advantage. Iconographically, Sacré-Cœur opposed Marianne with an alternative set of archetypal feminine figures—Mary, Mary Magdalene, Joan of Arc, *la France chrétienne*[25]—and its murals and statues offered a reading of French history wholly at variance with that put forward in the official school texts of the Republic: not Alésia or Bibracte but Tolbiac and Reims were the matrix of the nation; Clovis, not Vercingetorix, was its foundational hero;[26] and to the republican apostolic succession of Du Guesclin and Bayard, Turenne, Mirabeau, Lafayette, and Desmoulins, the basilica opposed Charlemagne, Saint Louis, and Louis XIII, XIV, and XVI, with Joan of Arc remaining contested ideological and historiographical territory.

On 14 July 1892 a luminous cross was mounted on the basilica's scaffolding, "an insult to the feelings of the population of Paris," according to L'Autorité, a symbol of "cretinization [abêtissement] and hypocrisy" at odds with the values of Liberté, Egalité, Fraternité being celebrated on the streets of the city down below.[27] Republicans, for their part, proposed unsuccessfully in 1873 that "a colossal Statue of Liberty" be erected directly in front of this "last expression of Catholic fetishism,"[28] and in 1884 achieved a minor onomastic victory when the Rue de la Fontenelle, running to the rear of the basilica, was renamed the Rue du Chevalier de La Barre, after the nineteen-year-old aristocrat who had been tortured and executed at Abbeville in 1766 for having sung "impious songs" and refused to take off his hat as a procession of Capuchin monks passed by. A statue of the chevalier was erected on the square in front of the basilica in 1905, showing him clad in rags, his limbs twisted in torture, with Voltaire's Dictionnaire philosophique and the executioner's ax at the foot of the stake to where he is tethered. The statue remained there until 1927, when it was removed to a less controversial location, slightly to the west on the Rue Azaïs, where the Communards had positioned their cannon. The Germans melted it down in 1941, and only its plinth now survives, though various freethinking groups have pressed for the statue's restoration; indeed, a group calling themselves "Friends of the Chevalier de La Barre" threatened in 1989 to decapitate the statues on the Via Crucis at Rocamadour if it were not replaced.[29]

In 1911 the Jewish Catholic convert Max Jacob—one of the very few avant-garde artists in Montmartre for whom Sacré-Cœur was not a symbol of artistic and ideological regression—published a satirical poem in Saint Matorel poking fun at the use made by anticlerical politicians of La Barre's death, a touch prematurely, perhaps, since it would be latter-day versions of the chevalier's tormentors who would be responsible for his own arrest and transportation to the concentration camp at Drancy, in the northern suburbs of Paris, where he died of pneumonia in March 1944.

The most tragic of the Church's Second World War martyrs (though it was, of course, as a Jew and not as a Catholic that he was arrested), Jacob might be said to have been an indirect victim of the very Catholicism into which he converted, for antisemitism was without question an integral rather than coincidental part of the Ultramontane creed. As the struggle between Church and Republic intensified in the late 1870s and early 1880s, particularly over the issue of control over schools, both parties had recourse to a set of stereotypes and myths, invariably involving the notion of conspiracy, with which to justify their positions and denigrate those of their adversaries. For the Church, the enemies, either as distinct forces or, more often, imagined as acting in concert, were Protestantism, Jewry, and Freemasonry, with Gallicanism and "philosophy" not far behind, accused severally or en bloc of having fomented the Revolution of 1789 and of having since then infiltrated every branch of society and the state, with the possible exceptions—but could anyone be *totally* sure?—of the Church and the army. For Père Emmanuel d'Alzon, the hugely influential founder of the Assumptionist order whom we have already encountered as a frequent pilgrim to Rome, Freemasonry was "the daughter of Satan," "the clericalism of the devil," whose one aim was the destruction of the Church and which in a myriad secret ways was engaged in subverting Catholic France, most notably in her pedagogical mission:

> The secret societies are invading everything: the freedom of educa-
> tion, the honor of the clergy, the rights of charity, freedom to
> pray, everything is ravaged by them. Their adepts, seated on their
> parliamentary or ministerial chairs, declare to our Mother
> Church: Thou shalt not teach! We must have the children of the
> people to form socialists, and the children of the bourgeoisie to
> prepare freethinkers.[30]

The legitimist and Ultramontane Jacques Crétineau-Joly (1803–75) revived for a new generation the myth of the philosophical-Gallican-Masonic origins of the Revolution, originally formulated in the 1790s by the abbé Barruel, and saw in Rome, Italy, and the Jesuits France's one bulwark against its multiple enemies within; in Italy, he said, "everything is Catholic, even the sun."[31] From Masonic conspiracy to Jewish plot was but the shortest of steps, and in 1880 the curé of the village of Mirebeau-en-Poitou, the abbé Chabauty, duly published *Les Francs-maçons et les Juifs,* purporting to demonstrate the links, indeed the effective identity, between the two groups; he received letters of congratulation from no fewer than twenty French bishops.[32] From then until well after the Dreyfus affair, a torrent of antisemitic materials sprang from church sources, almost always with the formal or informal support of one or more bishops: *La Prépondérance juive* (1899) and *L'Antéchrist* (1905) by the Jewish convert Abbé Joseph Lemann; *Le Mystère du sang chez les Juifs* (1890) by the abbé Desportes, who, like many another antisemite of the time, used the disappearance of a Christian girl in the Hungarian village of Tiszla-Eszlar in 1882 to revive the age-old theme of

Jewish ritual child murder; and the abbé Demnise's scabrous *Poésies patriotiques* (1896), of which the lines "Here comes a dirty Jew.... He comes straight from Hell, and rivals his own boss, the Devil" appear to be a representative sample.[33]

Needless to say, the Church was not the only source of fin-de-siècle antisemitism—its combined publications reached only a fraction of the public commanded by Edouard Drumont's 1,200-page diatribe *La France juive* of 1886 and its associated journal, *La Libre Parole*—but modern historical research has endorsed the testimony of the abbé Brugerette, one of the very few pro-Dreyfus priests, that at the time of the affair "a Catholic could only be anti-Dreyfus.... The prisoner on Devil's Island encountered in the ranks of the Catholic orthodoxy a nearly unanimous opposition. ... In the course of this unfortunate Dreyfus affair, the passions aroused by antisemitic hatred have led the Christian conscience in the most deplorable derelictions."[34] The presence of antisemitism was felt both in the Church's intellectual heights and in its lowliest pews. For the ordinary faithful, the Good Friday prayer "Pro perfidis Judaeis" (after which, unlike the other prayers, the congregation did *not* kneel) would confirm the Jews' collective guilt as "Christ-killers," and, with the exception of Péguy, Mauriac, and Jacques Maritain (whose wife, Raïssa, was a Russian Jewish convert), almost all the leading Catholic writers from 1870 to Pius XI's condemnation of Action Française in 1926 were open antisemites, like Léon Bloy (*Le Salut par les Juifs,* 1892) and Georges Bernanos (*La Grande Peur des Bien-Pensants,* 1931),[35] or equivocal in their attitudes, like Claudel in the trilogy of plays referred to earlier.

The principal source of Catholic antisemitism was without doubt the Assumptionist newspaper *La Croix,* published from 1883 on and edited by Père Vincent de Paul Bailly, the former almoner to the Pontifical Zouaves in Rome. *La Croix* relayed all the usual antisemitic clichés from child murder to international plot (which it believed to be organized by a sect called Sons of the Widow, the widow in question being Jerusalem deprived of its temple),[36] but gave a particular salience to the traditional theme of Jewish deicide and to the enigmatic Gospel text "Salvation is of the Jews" (John 14:22), which also greatly preoccupied Bloy. Interpretations of this text brought together three paradoxical and perhaps contradictory ideas: first, that the Saviour of the Christians was himself a Jew (and not a Celt, as some of the racial, as opposed to biblical, antisemites believed); second, that the Jews, as alleged killers of Christ, were also, by the same token, the unwitting agents of the redemption of the world; and finally, in Bloy's words, that "Jews will be converted only when Jesus comes down from his cross, and Jesus will come down from it when the Jews have been converted."[37] By thus making Christ's Second Coming conditional on the conversion of the Jews, Catholic antisemitism implied that Jews had to be both preserved and reviled, humiliated and at the same time protected, so that Christians could define themselves and their faith over and against them; and because Christianity's greatest enemies were necessary to Christians' salvation, Catholic antisemitism could never countenance a "final solution," for to do so would flout God's inscrutable soteriological project.[38] Not that this ambiguous need for the Jews implied any desire to bring them in from exclusion or to treat them as anything other than accursed creatures of Satan, whatever their personal virtues and merits:

> Yes, they are accursed if we are Christians. Hence must they not at least share in the horror that the accursed snake causes in nature? Poets sing of the dove, but never of a nest of reptiles, be they ever so innocent. Not all serpents that crawl on the face of the earth are venomous, however, but malediction applies invincibly to all.[39]

For Bloy the very squalor and ugliness with which he associates Jews were proof of their place in the scheme of salvation, their "imperturbable identity," whether on the banks of the Danube, in Poland, Russia, Germany, Holland, France, or North Africa, marking them off as damned *and* elect, sacrificial victims that ended up as uncannily similar to the Christ they have killed.[40] This, perhaps, is the meaning of the myth of the Wandering Jew, so widely diffused in nineteenth-century France through Eugene Suë's mammoth potboiler, *Le Juif errant* (1844–45), Edgar Quinet's philosophical epic *Ahasvérus* (1833), and the rudimentary woodcuts that, according to Champfleury, hung in every miserable hovel alongside images of that other blessed and cursed wanderer, Napoleon:[41] "The Wandering Jew takes upon himself one sin only, that of being the Executioner, but this is the greatest of all possible sins, the murder of God. By his suffering he atones for this sin and relieves other people of all responsibility. He is, in fact, a kind of Christ figure himself."[42]

Another theme highlighted by *La Croix* is the Jews' responsibility for capitalism, which, following the Church's principal social thinkers, Albert de Mun, René de La Tour Du Pin, and Frédéric Le Play, it held accountable for the disintegration of the corporate communities of old, for the substitution of the cash nexus for the reciprocities of feudal society, and for the replacement of the ancien régime's hierarchy of orders with the class conflict of postrevolutionary France. This notion led to some curious convergences with the thought of the far left, for by the end of the century, as Michel Winock has written, antisemitism was "the socialism of Catholics."[43] Taking Gambetta's watchword and turning it on its head. the abbé Féret published a work called *Le Capitalisme, voilà l'ennemi,* which *La Croix* reviewed with approval; and at the time of the collapse of the Catholic bank, the Union Générale, in 1882, and of the Panama scandal in 1892 (when the Jewish financier. Jacques Reinach, anticipating Stavisky, committed suicide upon being accused of corruption), the newspaper carried denunciations of capitalism as violent as anything to be found in the pages of the anarchists' *Le Père Peinard* or the Guesdists' *Le Parti ouvrier.* Remarkably, when troops fired on May Day demonstrators at Fourmies, near the Belgian border, in 1891, adding nine further exemplary victims to the left's martyrology, *La Croix* blamed the Jewish, not the Socialist, international: "Who does the killing? The Jew. At Fourmies, prefect and subprefect are Jews.... At Fourmies, it was to uphold the modern economic system, so profitable to Jews, that young Isaac [the subprefect] brought the soldiers and the riot together and caused guns to go off."[44] The tradition of Catholic anticapitalism would be revived, minus the antisemitism, by the intellectuals of *Esprit* in the 1930s, whence it would feed into the program of the Vichy regime's Ecole des Cadres at Uriage, in the Alps. The Charte du Travail of 1941 was the culmination of over a century of anticapitalist corporatist thinking that had begun with the vicomte de Villeneuve-Bargemont's *Traité d'économie politique chrétienne* of 1834 and reached its fullest formulation in the work of La Tour Du Pin and Le Play; the convergence between "social Catholicism" and Vichyist thinking on work and the family was virtually complete.

Faced with the Church's obsession with Jewish and Masonic plots, the left replied with a plot mania all its own, which, like its rivals, built on known or invented "facts" and worked them up into an all-encompassing and all-explaining grand theory of the world. What the Jew and the Freemason were for the right the Jesuit was for the left. "Imagine a gigantic telegraph network encompassing the universe and converging on a single center," wrote Bouis in *Calottes et soutanes: Jésuites et Jésuitesses* of 1870, "each member of the Society of Jesus is a wire; the General is the center."[45] Jesuits were likened to wolves, foxes, snakes, chameleons, spiders. and octopi. "Ignatian reptiles" (*ces reptiles d'Ignace*), wrote Madier de Montjou in 1880, were to be found "everywhere, like the hideous octopus, stretching out and positioning their ominous arms to entwine and stifle the *patrie,* drawing in with their suckers its wealth, its intelligence, and its conscience."[46] Varying the metaphor, the republican educationist Paul Bert called in 1880 for "a more energetic insecticide" to eliminate clerical pests, a task he would pursue with a vengeance when he became minister of public instruction the following year. There was nothing that the Jesuit myth, like its Jewish and Masonic counterparts, could not explain; even the Commune, claimed *Le Jésuite rouge* of 1879, was a Jesuit plot designed to create Jesuit martyrs, a foretaste of the later antisemitic theory that Jews organized Auschwitz and Treblinka to win world sympathy for the Zionist cause.[47] The hub of the Jesuit conspiracy was located at the order's Parisian house on the Rue des Postes, whence, via the adjoining Ecole Sainte-Geneviève, it was believed to be flooding the *grandes écoles* with its candidates (known as *postards*) who would in due course emerge to dominate the whole state apparatus. In 1876 it was claimed that Jesuit-trained candidates for the Polytechnique entrance examinations had prior knowledge of the questions, just one rumor among many that would lead to the complete ban on teaching by members of religious orders in 1882. Even the Société de Saint Vincent de Paul was said to be a front for Jesuit activities and, like the Jesuits themselves, to form a "state within the state," engaged in infiltrating and subverting the *patrie* from within.[48]

In order to combat the alliance of *le sabre et le goupillon* (the saber and the aspergillum—in other words, the army and the Church), the left embarked on a massive propaganda campaign, conscious as it did so that by focusing its own and the public's attention on the clerical-military complex it could close and obscure the differences within its own ranks; the clerical scapegoat was as necessary to republican unity as the Jewish or Masonic scapegoat was to that of the right. The myth of Jewish child sacrifice was countered by the ghoulish misdeeds of *l'Eglise sanglante* recounted in such works as *Les Crimes de cléricalisme* of 1900, and an actual kidnapping in Italy in 1858, with the apparent connivance of Rome, of a Jewish child whom a Christian servant had secretly baptized during a serious illness (the so-called Mortara affair) was used for half a century or more to corroborate every fear of a ramifying worldwide Jesuit conspiracy.[49] Anticlerical zealots drafted a *Contre-catéchisme élémentaire* that negated or inverted point for point the Church's own catechism, and the scurrilous priest-baiter and hoaxer Léo Taxil—author of, among other works, *Les Amours secrètes de Pie IX* (1881), *La Confession et les confesseurs: Les Livres secrets des confesseurs, dévoilés aux pères de famille* (1883), and *L'Empoisonneur Léon XIII et les cinq millions de chanoine* (1883)—composed an "anti-

L'Araignée. This brilliant image, published in the left-wing satirical weekly *L'Assiette au beurre* on 16 February 1902, typifies the "plotomania" of the period. The artist, the Swiss Socialist Alexandre Steinlen, has transformed Sacré-Cœur into an image of the pope seated at the center of an all-embracing spider's web of prostrate priests and monks. (Reproduced by permission of the Bibliothèque Nationale de France.)

clerical Marseillaise" in which "Aux urnes" and "Votons, votons" stand duty for the "Aux armes" and "Marchons, marchons" of the original.[50] Finally, if the Church had its martyrs in the victims of the Rue Haxo and other massacres, the anticlericals had theirs in Dreyfus and—since a dead martyr is better than a live one—in the Spanish republican Francisco Ferrer, who, executed for his political activities in Barcelona in 1909, was promptly transformed into the freethinkers' Christ, complete with his agnostic Calvary and rationalist stations of the cross: "Along the way stained with blood of the Crucified Victims of Free Thought [*les Crucifiés de la Pensée Libre*], Ferrer fell, he too, assassinated by a gutless, fearful king who obeyed the peremptory orders of the Spanish congregations."[51]

When Sacré-Cœur was constructed, all of these fears, myths, and obsessions found their inevitable focus, not least because Saint Ignatius himself had for a time been trained at a monastery located at the Butte. Graphic artists such as Steinlen seized on the basilica's unmistakable form to give shape to their and their age's conspiratorial fantasies. His cartoon *L'Araignée* (1902) brilliantly conflates basilica, papal miter, and spider's head and depicts thousands of kneeling clerics and monks doing obeisance to the arachnidan idol on the hill, whose spindly legs reach out over them and whose web seems to stretch to the farthest ends of the earth.[52]

The ideological conflict between Church and Republic came to a head in 1889, the centennial of the fall of the Bastille and the Declaration of the Rights of Man, which was also, by happy or unhappy coincidence, the bicentennial of the most important of Saint Marguerite-Marie Alacoque's visions, the so-called Demands of the Sacred Heart to Louis XIV of 1689, in which Louis is urged to dedicate himself, his kingdom, and his subjects to the Sacred Heart. He never did so, thus, in the view of the more febrile "Cordicolists," preparing the way for the deposition and execution of his grandson just over a century later. The years 1689, 1789, 1889—it was too much for any Ultramontane to resist, whence the flood of hysterical theodicies published under Church auspices in the late 1880s, of which the abbé Emile Bougaud's *Histoire de la bienheureuse Marguerite-Marie* of 1874 offered a foretaste:

> 1689! We stop unwillingly at that which immediately evokes another: 1789! Just a century elapses between the moment when a humble virgin, hidden in the depths of a cloister, points out to Louis XIV the ark of salvation prepared by the goodness of God, and the moment when the storm arises that will sweep away the monarchy and all monarchies with it. And that was only the beginning of our woes! Move on from 1789 to 1889: a new century scarcely less sad than the previous one, in which darkness reigns in the minds of men, and coldness in their hearts. It is for times such as these that Providence prepared devotion to that Heart which is gentle and humble, which was so fitting to the century of Louis XIV, and which will painfully but surely find its way in the midst of these catastrophes.[53]

Hoping to explode once and for all the "myth" of 1789 and so undermine the Republic's celebration of its foundational events, the Church mobilized its ideological heavyweights in a succession of publications, conferences, and other events that reveal the utter refusal on the part of the overwhelming majority of Catholic cadres—bishops, clergy, and influential laity alike—to countenance any compromise with the spirit and values of even the most moderate phase of the Revolution, let alone with the radical developments of 1792–94. Catholic students whistled and jeered during the course on the Revolution given at the Sorbonne by the great left-wing historian Alphonse Aulard, and a succession of Church or Church-sponsored "historians" put forward their own counterhistories of the period and its consequences, with Monseigneur Freppel of Angers setting the tone of interpretation and discussion in his *La Révolution française à propos du centenaire de 1789*, published on the very first day of the centenary year:

> It was in 1789 that there was accomplished in the social order a veritable deicide, analogous to that perpetrated seventeen centuries earlier on the person of the Man-God [*l'Homme-Dieu*] by the Jewish people, whose historical mission offers more than one point of similarity with that of the French people.[54]

Not to be outdone by his ecclesiastical superior, Père Félix republished his *Qu'est-ce que la Révolution?* of 1879 and laid out a typically stark opposition: "Between Christianity and Revolution any union is illusory, any peace impossible, any truce artificial; the triumph of the one entails the ruin of the other," especially when the Revolution is made in the name of socialism, "that which is most antichristian in antichristianism," "the consummation and plenitude of antichristianism."[55] Never was the Church more thickly "wrapt in the old miasmal mist" (T. S. Eliot, "The Hippopotamus") than in the summer of 1889 in France, as, forgetting entirely the Sermon on the Mount, it vainly sought, in the terms of its principal "social" thinker, Frédéric Le Play, to set the Decalogue against the Declaration of the Rights of Man and of the Citizen and all that it implied. Marble-like, its collective mind set in stone; it glowered, threatening and threatened, from its beleaguered fortress in Montmartre out across a city now thoroughly given over to worshiping the golden calf of *Liberté, Egalité, Fraternité* for all it was worth.

As it happened, the idol of the Republic, the totemic structure with which it challenged the Church's marmoreal fixity on the Right Bank opposite, was made not of gold but of the archetypally modern substance, iron, and the values it embodied were everything the Church most abhorred: openness, rationality, science, progress, humanity.[56] The Eiffel Tower was the centerpiece of the Exposition Universelle, which the centrist government of Charles de Freycinet had initiated in 1886 to mark the centenary of the events of 1789, and from the moment work began on its construction in early 1887 it had inevitably provoked controversy, most notably the so-called Artists' Protest of February 1887, in which a disparate group of writers, painters, sculptors, architects, and "amateurs"—most but by no means all of them representative of the most regressive branch of their calling—condemned the "gigantic black chimney stack" that hence-

The 300-meter Eiffel Tower in 300 lines of poetry. An anonymous "concrete poem" (1889), dedicated to Alexandre-Gustave Eiffel, assigns a line of poetry to each of the tower's 300 meters. An "ode to Paris and to France," the poem celebrates the French revolutionary and republican tradition and explicitly opposes the tower to Notre-Dame: "My height is without equal. The ancient and lofty cathedral of Notre-Dame only reaches my knees." (Musée Carnavalet, Paris, © Photothèque des Musées de la Ville de Paris.)

forth, they claimed, would dominate the Parisian cityscape, "crushing with its barbarous mass Notre-Dame, the Sainte-Chapelle, the Tour Saint-Jacques, the Louvre, the Dome of the Invalides, the Arc de Triomphe, all our humiliated monuments, our diminished architecture, which will disappear in this stupefying dream."[57] Most commentators, however, and certainly the bulk of the population of Paris, were enthralled as the metallic structure rose with extraordinary speed, as though impelled by some autonomous energy, above the Paris skyline. As the Eiffel Tower took shape, many observers explicitly contrasted its dynamism and modernity to the ancient buildings of Paris. The novelist and critic Eugène-Melchior de Vogüé (1850–1910) imagined a dialogue between it and the rival towers of Notre-Dame, very much to the disadvantage of the latter:

> Old abandoned towers, you are no longer listened to. Do you not see that the world has changed its pole, and that it is spinning on my iron axis? I represent universal force, disciplined by reason. Human thought courses through my limbs. My brow is ringed with lightning stolen from the source of light. You were ignorance, I am Science.[58]

Throughout the two years of the Eiffel Tower's construction, the Republic in fact underwent sustained threat to its survival in the form of General Georges Boulanger (1837–91), who, in and out of government, attracted a heterogeneous coalition of disaffected royalists, Bonapartists, ex-Communards, and new-style secular nationalists, backed by substantial numbers of alienated workers, especially in Paris, and who, after a spectacular by-election victory in Paris on 27 January 1889, might have emulated his model and hero, Louis-Napoleon, and seized political power by force.[59] On the night of his electoral triumph, however, he demurred, opting (or so it is said) to celebrate with his mistress in private rather than launch a putsch on the streets, and his support vanished even more swiftly than it had cohered. On 1 April, a political April fool rather than an exemplary victim, a pastiche of the pastiche that was Louis-Napoleon, Boulanger fled to Belgium, where in 1891 he committed suicide on the grave of his deceased mistress. By perfect symmetry, work on the Eiffel Tower was completed on the very eve of his flight, and the right-wing *Correspondant* was entirely correct when it remarked the following October that "the conqueror of Boulangisme, the great electoral agent, was the Exposition Universelle."[60]

Officially opened on 6 May 1889 and occupying the whole of the Champ de Mars, where the Fête de la Fédération had been celebrated ninety-nine years before, the Exposition with its metallic palaces and galleries resembled, in the words of its modern historian, "a Versailles in reverse, democratized and modernist."[61] Its highlight, apart from the opening of the Eiffel Tower itself, was the great "republican banquet" held in the Palais de l'Industrie on 18 August, when, in part imitation of the great collective meal of 14 July 1790, 11,250 mayors from all over France and the colonies, together with over 2,000 other guests, communed eucharistically in the name of the republican trinity. To celebrate the centenary of the night of 4 August 1789, when the feudal regime was effectively abolished, three heroes of the First Republic (La Tour d'Auvergne, François Marceau, and Lazare Carnot) and one of the Second (Victor Baudin, the republican deputy who had offered up his life resisting the Bonapartist coup of 1851) were formally "Pantheonized," and on 11 September 20,000 people packed into the Palais de l'Industrie to hear the inaugural performance—by a 1,200-strong orchestra and choir—of the *Ode Triomphale* by the centenary's official composer, the remarkable Augusta Holmès (1847–1903), the Anglo-Irish goddaughter (and perhaps daughter) of Alfred de Vigny and inspiration of César Franck's overheated Piano Quintet. Finally, on 21 September, the anniversary of the declaration of the First Republic in 1792, Jules Dalou's monumental statue *Le Triomphe de la République* was unveiled on the Place de la Nation, a counterpart to the same sculptor's *La République* (1883) on the renamed square of that name and to Bartholdi's *Liberté,* which had been offered to France's transatlantic sister republic in 1886. Almost twenty years after its formal declaration, the moderate Republic had won the battle of symbols and could at last—though still, as it turned out, prematurely—consider itself secure from challenges on the right and the left.

Not all Church dignitaries had boycotted the centenary celebrations—the presence of the bishop of Versailles was noted at the inaugural ceremony of 6 May, timed to coincide with the opening of the Estates General at Versailles a hundred years earlier—and the appearance around this time of flags on which the Sacred Heart was superimposed on the Tricolor indicates a willingness, even among some Cordicoles, to compromise with the Republic. The following year, on 12 November 1890, the so-called Toast of Algiers (when Cardinal Lavigerie of that city publicly proposed a toast to the Republic) pointed the way to the rallying of moderate Catholics to the Republic, a movement not merely encouraged but made binding by Leo XIII's encyclical *Inter sollicitudines* of February 1892.[62] But ultra-Catholics still held back, among them the two most gifted Catholic writers of the period, Joris-Karl Huysmans and Léon Bloy, who both saw the Exposition, and above all the Eiffel Tower, as proof of the "deicidal" character of contemporary secular culture.

For Huysmans, the Age of Iron was necessarily a negation of the Age of Faith. Already Zola had celebrated the poetry of iron in *Le Ventre de Paris* (1873), implicitly contrasting Victor Baltard's iron pavilions in the reconstructed Halles with the stone of the nearby Eglise Sainte-Eustache, to the evident advantage of the former. Huysmans reversed the antithesis: iron was anti-art, anti-poetry, anti-God, and Eiffel's "infundibuliform grille" an "empty obelisk," as inherently meaningless as the obelisk of Luxor on the Place de la Concorde.[63] If the Palais de l'Industrie was a "church consecrated to the cult of gold," in which "the richest man in the world, the American pope Jay Gould," celebrated not a black but a yellow mass by consecrating that sacrament of modernity, a blank check, then the Eiffel Tower was the steeple of a new church, Notre-Dame de la Brocante (Our Lady of Barter), summoning the faithful by means of cannon, not bells, to celebrate "the mass of finance, the vespers of speculation [*les vêpres de l'agio*], and the liturgical feast days of Capital."

Bloy, needless to say, went still further. Taking the contemporary cliché of the Tower of Babel, he brilliantly turned it inside out, so that the new "Babel of iron" becomes the antithesis of the biblical Babel of brick, a Babel in reverse at which the scattered, linguistically divided millions reconvene to applaud and congratulate one another, "to lick each other, reciprocally, people to people, from the tips of the toes to the top of the skull," even to "enter one into another, fraternally and conjugally." But this hybrid cosmopolitanism will not herald the coming of world peace, for at a given signal the peoples will part company again, this time withdrawing just a short distance from each other in order to engage in what a later age would call "mutually assured destruction": "It will be the oft announced Pentecost of massacres and exterminations, the washing in fire of fragmented, excessive societies that are to be reamalgamated with one another in the crucible of a superhuman conflagration, after their scum has been removed in the cauldron of a Mediterranean of blood!" A "vertical bridge" between earth and heaven, the Eiffel Tower is a Promethean challenge to "that old abandoned cathedral to be glimpsed in the pale distance"; a "piece of vainglorious ironwork" (*une quincaillerie superbe*), it soars like "a beacon of shipwreck and despair" over the city's poor, who will, in the future as in the present and the past, be "crushed, pounded, kneaded, devoured, vomited, swallowed again, and revomited three score and ten times [*jusqu'à septante fois*]," but should they look toward "that sterile Babel of iron, which will seem to mock their death throes," they will find no "crucified image of the adorable Child" to console them, only "the most arrogant building that men have ever constructed" in, alas, "the most Christian of all the lands of the earth."[64]

A quarter of a century after the inauguration of the Eiffel Tower, Bloy's vision of Armageddon would come true, but by that time the tower—photographed, painted, and reproduced ad infinitum—had become a familiar, integral part of the Parisian cityscape, as "natural" as the rival towers of Notre-Dame, which it would henceforth complement rather than oppose.[65] In his great poem-manifesto of modernism, "Zone" (1913), Guillaume Apollinaire sees the Eiffel Tower as a shepherdess watching over the bleating flock of the city's bridges ("Bergère ô tour Eiffel le troupeau des ponts bêle ce matin"),[66] and though for Apollinaire religion alone remains wholly new and alive in a city in which even the motor car now seems ancient, this was not a view widely shared.

Certainly it was not shared by Zola, whose *Paris* (1898) is from beginning to end a denunciation of Christianity in general and of Sacré-Cœur in particular. The novel confronts the brothers Pierre and Guillaume Froment, the first a priest attached to Sacré-Cœur who has sought in vain to recover his lost faith through pilgrimages to Lourdes and to Rome, the second an anarchist activist who, in his despair, wants to destroy himself and some major Parisian monument—the Opéra, the Bourse, the Arc de Triomphe, Sacré-Cœur, no matter—and is largely indifferent to how many others perish along with him. He decides on Sacré-Cœur as the site and object of his personal holocaust not just because it is the most accessible target but because he is "importuned" and "exasperated" by its simple existence:

> It's impossible to imagine a piece of more imbecilic nonsense, Paris, our great Paris, crowned, dominated by this temple built to the glorification of the absurd. Is it not unacceptable, after centuries of science, this slap in the face to simple common sense, this insolent triumphalism, up there, in the full light of day? They want Paris to repent, to do penance for being the liberating city of truth and justice.... Let the temple collapse with its god of falsehood and serfdom! and let it crush under its ruins the mass of the faithful, so that the catastrophe, like the geological revolutions of old, might re-echo in the bowels of humanity, might renew it and change it.[67]

Pierre finally confronts his brother deep beneath the basilica just as Guillaume is about to blow himself, the sanctuary, and ten thousand pilgrims into fragments, and talks him out of his suicidal and murderous act. The irony, however, is that Pierre feels no differently about Sacré-Cœur and the religion it embodies than his anarchist brother: Christian charity is "illusory, useless," the Gospel is collapsing, the end of the Book is at hand, and the whole idea of redemption through Christ has run aground.[68] Christianity—by which Pierre, like Zola, means Catholicism—is a "religion of torture and nothingness," a bloodthirsty cult in which an executioner-God (*un Dieu bourreau*) is locked in sadomasochistic love-hatred with a "castrated, threatened, scourged humanity," in which nature has become an enemy and life a curse and "death alone is gentle and liberating"[69]—a not inaccurate summary of what fin-de-siècle French Catholicism had become under the influence of Ultramontanism and its interconnected doctrines of expiatory suffering and the reversibility of grace.

In *Travail* (1901), Zola himself turns terrorist and fictively demolishes the dilapidated sixteenth-century church that adjoins the utopian community of La Crêcherie. As cracks and crevices appear in its superstructure, the abbé Marie prepares to say a last mass in solitude, in the presence of only "a great Christ made of painted and gilded wood" whose "pale, pained, martyred body" is stretched out above the altar, "spattered with black blood whose drops streamed down like tears." Bits of masonry and plaster start to rain down on the altar, and in desperate prayer the abbé entreats God to spare his "august home" and restore it to its former stability and strength. To no avail, for at the moment that the priest raises the chalice, "it was not the miracle sought that occurred, it was annihilation." Steeple and vault collapse simultaneously, and no trace of either the abbé's body or the painted wooden Christ can be found: "Another religion was dead, the last priest saying his last mass, in the last church."[70]

Like all of Zola's later novels, both *Paris* and *Travail* end with a vision of forthcoming rebirth and fecundity, of "life" triumphing over the "religion of misery and death" that is Ultramontane Catholicism, and of France being restored to its historical mission of propagating the values of liberty, equality, and fraternity to the world. Notre-Dame and Sacré-Cœur are razed from the Parisian skyline—and so, for that matter, is the Eiffel Tower—as, reconciled, Pierre and Guillaume, with Guillaume's wife and their three children, look confidently into the future, unaware (or conveniently forgetting) that the life and fecundity that later novels extol are inseparable, by the novels' own admission, from the forces of death and destruction, that there is no life without struggle and violence and certainly no rebirth without death, and that Eros and Thanatos are not so much adversaries as bedfellows, locked together in an embrace that is at once destructive and creative.

But in the end it was Bloy's vision of generalized conflict rather than Zola's of universal rebirth that proved the more percipient. Far from disappearing from the landscape, the cathedrals continued to haunt the French imagination as symbols of lost wholeness and community, especially when the Age of Iron, in the form of shrapnel and shells, was unleashed against the most revered national shrine, the royal cathedral of Reims. But before that happened, on the very last day of peace (31 July 1914), the conflict between "the two Frances," the France of Sacré-Cœur and the France of the Eiffel Tower, came to a head in a café on the Rue Montmartre, the Fleet Street of Paris, in the second arrondissement, and produced a sacrificial victim whose mana is exceeded only, if at all, by that of Louis XVI, although, needless to say, with very different political meanings and effects.

"Ils ont tué Jaurès!" (They have killed Jaurès!). As deputy for the southwestern mining town of Carmaux between 1893 and 1898 and again since 1902, as founder of L'Humanité (1904), and as joint leader and premier spokesman of the Section Française de l'Internationale Ouvrière (SFIO) since its formation in 1905, Jean Jaurès (1859–1914) had so often championed the victims of "them" in the course of his journalistic and political career that it was hardly surprising his followers believed that he had himself finally fallen victim of "their" diabolical machinations. In fact, his assassin, the twenty-nine-year-old Raoul Villain (1885–1936), a fanatical and probably deranged ultra-Catholic and nationalist, was almost certainly acting alone, although, as a member of the Jeunes Amis de l'Alsace-Lorraine (and former member, surprisingly, of the "left-wing" Catholic organization Le Sillon, which had been condemned by the Vatican in 1910), he was obviously responsive to the massive hate campaign that the right had unleashed against Jaurès since 1910; no connection, however, has ever been proved with Action Française, the most likely perpetrators of a concerted assassination attempt.[71]

By his own later testimony, Villain first thought of assassinating Kaiser Wilhelm II, but changed his mind because the kaiser was, he said, "perhaps the only European sovereign who was a connoisseur of art" (Villain had enrolled as a student at the Ecole du Louvre in June 1914). His next target was the former prime minister Joseph Caillaux (1863–1944), whose advocacy of an income tax had pushed the right-wing press to such extremes of vituperation that on 17 March 1914, his wife, Henriette, fearing still more damaging revelations, had shot and killed the editor of *Le Figaro,* Gaston Calmette, in his office at the paper's headquarters on the Rue Montmartre.

Villain had clearly been stalking Jaurès for some time, and on 30 July had gone to the Socialist leader's home at Passy, in the west of Paris, in furtherance of his murderous designs. Jaurès was in Brussels, attending a meeting of the Socialist International in the hope of averting the impending Europe-wide conflict, but when he returned to *L'Humanité*'s premises the following day, Villain appears to have been ready and waiting. Around 9 P.M. on the evening of the 31st, Jaurès and eleven colleagues and friends (later joined by a twelfth, making up the canonical Last Supper complement) went to dine at the nearby Café du Croissant, on the corner of Rue Montmartre and the street of that name. It was a sweltering evening and the cafe's windows were open, veiled only by a half curtain. Jaurès was just digging into his strawberry tart when a revolver poked through the curtain and fired two shots, one of which hit Jaurès in the neck, killing him virtually instantly.

The assassin was captured within minutes and stated at the local police station that he had acted as he had "because M. Jaurès betrayed his country by campaigning against the Three Years" (the law of 1913 extending to three years the period of compulsory military service) and because he believed that "one can punish traitors and lay down one's life for such a cause."[72]

When Germany declared war on France on 3 August, after France's general mobilization on the 1st, the French authorities, fearing public disorder, decided not to bring Villain to trial until the end of hostilities. Jaurès was buried on 4 August 1914 in the last and greatest of the political funerals of the "long nineteenth century," and when Villain was eventually tried, in March 1919, he was, to the outrage of Jaurès's supporters, acquitted by a predominantly right-wing jury on the grounds of mental instability. He later moved to Ibiza, where, at the start of the Spanish Civil War (13 March 1936), he was killed by an anarchist commando; apparently he died after lying on a beach for many hours, tormented by ants in his death agony. It is unlikely that his killer knew his identity, which did not, of course, prevent Jaurès supporters in France from seeing his death as a condign historical nemesis.[73]

Though the act of a probably deranged individual, the assassination of Jaurès can be understood only in the general ideological context of the last years of the so-called Belle Epoque, when a still more virulent brand of nationalism, centered on but not limited to Action Française, succeeded the already violent strand of the time of the Dreyfus affair. In 1913, writing under the pseudonym Agathon, Alfred de Tarde and

Henri Massis, both ultranationalists, published *Les Jeunes Gens d'aujourd'hui,* their celebrated inquiry into the moral and political attitudes of contemporary youth, limited, in effect, to male students at the *grandes écoles* and the Sorbonne. The study revealed—hardly surprisingly, given the right-wing climate of the Latin Quarter at the time—a belief not just in the inevitability of war but in its moral value, a commitment to action at all costs, accompanied by a contempt for liberal-humanist (and moderate Catholic) values of tolerance, justice, and rational debate. These were the years when the nationalist cult of Joan of Arc reached its near-hysterical apogee, and on 22 January 1914 Jaurès had himself used the occasion of the funeral of his Protestant comrade Francis de Pressensé to warn the students of the Ecole Normale Supérieure, of which he was an alumnus, against the cult of action and instinct, which he implicitly associated with the teaching of Henri Bergson. "Today the affirmation of peace is the greatest of all combats," he declared to his audience, only to be answered a fortnight later by a display of chauvinist fervor at the massively attended funeral of the veteran jingoist Paul Déroulède (1846–1914).[74]

In November 1912, Jaurès had attended, and enthralled, the extraordinary congress of the Socialist International held in the cathedral of Basel in Switzerland, in the course of which, invoking Schiller's inscription on the great cathedral bell, he made his celebrated plea for international peace: *Vivos voco,* I call on the living; *Mortuos plango,* I pity the dead; *Fulgura frango,* I break the thunderbolts of war. Inspired by the display of international working-class opposition to war enshrined in the cries of "Guerre à la guerre!" and "Krieg gegen Kriegen!" (War against war) that broke out in the cathedral, Jaurès went on to challenge the extension of military service in France from two to three years, first proposed in March 1913. It was this campaign that led to the scurrilous attacks on Jaurès's person and politics, not just from the usual suspects in the right-wing gutter press but from former comrades in the Dreyfus cause, such as Charles Péguy, who saw in Jaurès's pacifism an apparent surrender to and complicity with the "Pan-German cause." For Maurice Barrès, recycling his earlier animadversions against Dreyfus, Jaurès was a "citizen of Europe" who had already "half-abandoned France." The Socialist leader's knowledge of German and familiarity with German philosophy were bitterly criticized ("Frankreich spricht, still Herr Jaurès! [France speaks, be quiet, Mr. Jaurès!]," bellowed *L'Echo de Paris* in March 1913), and, not to be outdone, *La Croix* published on its cover portraits of Jaurès and the kaiser with the legend "Deux Amis [Two friends]" underneath.

Some right-wing "commentators" saw Jaurès as an agent, inevitably, of "the Rothschilds," but the most incendiary attack came, to the regret of all his admirers, from Péguy. "As soon as war is declared, the first thing we will do is shoot Jaurès. We will not leave this traitor behind us to stab us in the back." If even Péguy could resort to the already suspect image of the stab in the back or, specifically invoking the execution of Louis XVI, call for a revolutionary tumbril to convey Jaurès to the guillotine and for a roll of drums to drown out his voice, then it is hardly surprising that a half-crazed extremist such as Raoul Villain should, in keeping with the activist cult of the times, and blinded by the language of sacrifice, move from propaganda of the word to the lethal deed.[76]

With Jaurès's death, the faint hope that cross-national working-class solidarity might avert the impending continental conflict collapsed literally overnight, and on 3 August, Miguel Almereyda, a former ultra-royalist turned anarchist-pacifist, characteristically announced in *Le Bonnet rouge* that henceforth the "Marseillaise" and the Tricolor would replace the "Internationale" and the red flag as the anthem and banner of the left.[77] (Three years later, on 20 August 1917, charged with inciting the massive mutinies in the French army during the spring of that year, Almereyda was found dead in his cell at Fresnes, in circumstances that suggested suicide to some and judicial murder to others.)[78] The collapse of his internationalist dream did not, however, impede—rather it aided—the almost instantaneous "Christologization" of Jaurès. Not content to liken Jaurès to "Plato, Newton, Danton, Voltaire, Rousseau, Marx, Musset, Hugo" (*L'Humanité,* 1 August 1915), Jaurès's hagiologists did not shrink from comparing the blood he had shed in the cause of international peace with the blood Christ had shed for humanity; "Worker," declared an election poster of 1919, "think of Jaurès, who died for you." Most famous of all is the song "Jésus ... Jaurès ... ," published in 1916 by the veteran Socialist troubadour Gaston Montéhus:

Tous ceux qui ont voulu sur terre
Faire le bien, la charité,
Ont dû monter le dur calvaire
Où Jésus fut persécuté.
Ils sont nombreux, les grands apôtres,
Les âmes pures aux nobles cœurs
Qui ont succombé pour les autres
Dans les larmes et les douleurs.

. . . .
Il en est un, ô prolétaire

Qui était digne d'être Dieu,
Le plus doux des humanitaires,
Le plus savant, le plus précieux.
Amis, mettez sur ce socle de pierre
A la place où Jésus-Christ reposait,
La première victime de la guerre,
Le grand Jaurès! l'Apôtre de la paix!

[All those who wanted on earth / To do good, to act charitably, / Have had to climb the harsh Calvary / Where Jesus was persecuted. / There are many of them, the great apostles, / Pure souls with noble hearts, / Who have perished for others in pain and tears. / ... / There is one of them, O proletarian, who was worthy of God, / The gentlest of humanitarians, / The wisest, the most precious. / Friends, place upon this pedestal of stone, / In the place where Jesus Christ once lay, / The first victim of the war, / The great Jaurès! Apostle of peace!]

A text of 1933 went even further and elevated Jaurès into a eucharistic offering in which his peace-loving disciples might commune:

Que sous ton nom, Jaurès, on communie
Dans l'appel des jours meilleurs![79]

[In your name, Jaurès, may we commune, / In the expectation of better days!]

Pipes, penknives, hairpins, hand mirrors, even nutcrackers were produced bearing the Socialist leader's image or effigy,[80] and a famous image of 1917 by A. Domins showed the dead Jaurès resting like Christ in the arms of Mary-Marianne, her fist clenched and a Phrygian cap on her head, under the title "The Republic weeps for Jean Jaurès and will avenge him."[81]

It was not long, however, before Jaurès's image and memory were being claimed by the centrist politicians and parties he detested little less than those of the out-and-out right. His image enshrined in dozens of statues, especially in the south, his memory was itself petrified and emptied of ideological content, and when his remains were duly interred in the Pantheon in November 1924, the procession was led by the Radical prime minister Emile Herriot and his colleagues, followed by a delegation of miners from Carmaux, with an unofficial cortege of Commu-

"The republic weeps for Jean Jaurès and will avenge him." This drawing of 1917 by A. Domins shows Jaurès in the traditional pose of the dead Christ, watched over by a notably belligerent Mary-Marianne. (Collection du Centre National et Musée Jean Jaurès, Castres.)

nists—for the French left had by now split at the Congrès de Tours (1920)—bringing up the rear. "That second cortege was necessary," says one of the left-wing students in Paul Nizan's novel *La Conspiration* (1938), to prevent the complete reincorporation of Jaurès's memory into the consensualist politics of the left coalition.[82]

When, in 1981, the newly elected Socialist president, François Mitterrand, a man whose Florentine duplicity and cynicism placed him at the moral-political antipodes of the SFIO's founder, laid a red rose before Jaurès's memorial plaque in the Panthéon, the act was tantamount to a negation of everything Jaurès had stood for. As so often before, commemoration in France has meant, in effect, neutralization and obfuscation by official encomium.

The shot that killed Jaurès was, as the English poet Geoffrey Hill puts it in the opening line of his remarkable poem "The Mystery of the Charity of Charles Péguy" (1984), the "crack of the starting-pistol" that triggered the Gadarene rush to slaughter across the continent of Europe.[83] Tens of thousands of men died on the French side alone in the first weeks of the war, among them Péguy himself, killed at Villeroy, fifteen miles to the east of Paris, on 5 September, possibly—there is no definite evidence one way or the other—after settling his

differences with the Church by taking Communion (preceded, perhaps, by asking forgiveness for his part in the murder of Jaurès) and
certainly in fulfillment of his famous prophecy in the mammoth poem
Eve (1913):

Heureux ceux qui sont morts pour la terre charnelle,
Mais pourvu que ce fût dans une juste guerre.
Heureux ceux qui sont morts pour quartre coins de terre.
Heureux ceux qui sont morts d'une mort solonnelle.
Heureux ceux qui sont morts dans les grandes batalles,
Couchés dessus le sol à la face de Dieu.

. . . .

Heureux ceux qui sont morts dans cet embrassement,
Dans l'étreinte d'honneur et le terrestre aveu.[84]

[Happy are those who have died for the carnal earth, / Provided
that it was in a just war. / Happy are those who have died for four
corners of earth, / Happy are those who have died a solemn death.
/ Happy are those who have died in mighty battle, / Laid out on
the soil in the presence of God. / ... / Happy are those who have
died in such an embrace, / In union with honor and in acceptance
of the earth.]

In his panoramic account of the summer of 1914 in the penultimate
part of *Les Thibault* (1922–40), Roger Martin Du Gard (1881–1958)
evokes both the murder of Jaurès, the reaction of Parisians—"the whole
of Paris seemed outside," as on the eve of a revolution that never takes
place[85]—and the general mobilization that followed on 2 August. On
the afternoon of 1 August, Jacques Thibault asks his fiancée, Jenny, to
play Chopin's Third Etude to remind them of happier times they have
spent together, and they look out over the "luminous panorama" of the
city, from which scarcely a cry of "A bas la guerre!" has been heard
since the death of Jaurès. The next day the couple crisscross the city in
the hope of finding some sign of opposition to war. On the Place des
Pyramides, Emmanuel Frémiet's equestrian statue of Joan of Arc, the
cynosure of chauvinist demonstrations since its unveiling in 1874, is festooned in bunting and flowers, as is the statue of Strasbourg on the
Place de la Concorde, where the traffic sweeps by as on any ordinary
day: there is not a sign of the antiwar demonstration scheduled to take
place there. They continue their quest along the *grands boulevards,* then
down the Rue Caumartin to join the Rue Saint-Lazare:

Suddenly, as they arrived in front of Saint-Louis d'Antin, a deafening racket filled the space: the great bell of the church was
loudly tolling a single note one after another, distinct, resonant,
solemn. People, rooted to the spot, stared at each other for a moment, stupefied. Then they began to run off in all directions.... In
the distance, other bells swung into action. In an instant, the Paris
sky had become like a bronze cupola, everywhere resounding to
the same insistent rhythm, sinister as a death knell.[86]

It is a suitably ominous response to the jubilant bells of Notre-Dame
de Paris with which we began. "Ça y est," people say to themselves and
to each other, that's it, the general mobilization is declared, and a citywide movement to the main-line stations begins, taking Jacques
Thibault to Switzerland in a final desperate effort to reconvene the Socialist International and his brother Antoine to the battle front.

Over the next four years, the nineteenth-century discourse of sacrifice, of Gethsemanes, Golgothas, and Passions, of Precious Blood and
expiatory suffering, took on a direct physical immediacy that most of its
proponents had longed for as a release from the penal colony of secular
inauthenticity and that not a few would still welcome even when Mort-
Homme, Hill 304, and the Chemin des Dames had revealed the reality
beneath the language of redemption through suffering.

11

OPERATION SPRING BREEZE
Rue des Rosiers, Vel' d'Hiv', Drancy
(July–August 1942)

Annette Muller's parents arrived in Paris from their native Galicia, in Poland, in 1929. Her father was aged twenty, her mother twenty-one, and the reason for their departure, unlike that of the thousands of Eastern European Jews who converged on Paris between 1881 and 1939, was not the threat of antisemitic persecution but, more mundanely, their families' disapproval of their relationship. A few months after their arrival in Paris, their first child, Henri, was born, followed by Jean in 1931, Annette in 1933, and Michel in 1935. All the children, but not their parents, were duly declared to be French citizens, and the fact that all were called by French forenames at home, despite having received formal Jewish first names, may be taken as evidence of their parents' desire, if not to "assimilate" into French society to the point of losing their Jewishness, then at least to identify fully with the country they saw, the Dreyfus affair notwithstanding, as some kind of haven for Jews. France owed its philosemitic reputation to a decree of 27 September 1791 that had extended full civil rights to French Jews on condition only that they renounce their status as a separate community; as Clermont-Tonnerre had famously put it as early as December 1789, defining in advance the whole tradition of republican assimilationism: "Everything must be refused to Jews as a nation, but everything granted to Jews as individuals. They must make up neither a political body nor an order within the State. They must be citizens as individuals [il faut qu'ils soient individuellement citoyens]."[1]

In common with thousands of other Jewish immigrants, the Muller family found accommodation in the Belleville-Ménilmontant area, first in the Rue des Envierges, then in the promisingly named Rue de l'Avenir nearby, and Annette's childhood was spent amid the constant whir of sewing machines and the acrid heat of steam irons, for, again in common with thousands of others in their situation, her parents worked in the garment industry, employed at home by a garment manufacturer, almost certainly Jewish himself, from whom they received orders, materials, and payment per garment they produced. The family was not markedly religious—Annette's father was even something of a socialist, and his prayer shawl and tefilin only occasionally left the drawer in which they were kept—and, though mother and father addressed each other in Yiddish, they did their best to speak French to their children; Annette was continually being told "Manche! Manche!" as she fiddled with her food,[2] and she cringed when, out in the street, her mother called out, "Hori, Joa, Michal" to her sons in an accent that, in the increasingly antisemitic atmosphere of the late 1930s, was heavily stigmatized as the telltale sign not just of Jewishness but, still worse, of *foreign* Jewishness. But, in other respects, the Mullers were as "integrated" as it was possible for a Polish-Jewish family to be; they went to the cinema on the Sabbath, had both Jewish and Gentile friends, and celebrated Christmas. The children attended a Catholic school without attracting any hostility, and early in the war Madame Muller was even briefly drawn toward Catholicism. Even so, Annette once called her parents *sales étrangers* (dirty foreigners) to their faces when they spanked her, and told them to "go back where they came from."[3] If nothing else, their accents still marked them out as Other, and even as a six- or seven-year-old Annette was clearly aspiring to integral Frenchness.

The Mullers' evident willingness to engage constructively with Gentile society and culture and their desire to privatize, but not to renounce or suppress, their Jewishness brought them into line with the traditional assimilationist orientation of French, and particularly Parisian, Jewry since 1791, though it was a tradition that by the 1930s was being increasingly challenged by precisely the most recent influx of Eastern European Jews, to which the Mullers belonged. In 1789 there were probably no more than 500 or 600 Jews in the whole of Paris,[4] certainly nothing amounting to a Parisian Jewish "community," but with the passing of the decree of September 1791, significant numbers of Sephardic Jews from Bordeaux and the former papal territories of Avignon and the Comtat Venaissin (Carpentras, the Isle-sur-la-Sorgue, and Cavaillon), followed almost immediately by even larger numbers of Ashkenazim from Alsace and Lorraine, began to move to the capital. In common with the vastly greater number of Gentile migrants, they identified Paris with economic opportunity, social promotion, and liberation from customary ties and restraints.

With the further recognition of Judaism, along with Catholicism and Protestantism, as an official state religion under Napoleon, the Jewish population of Paris rose to about 3,000 in 1808 and to almost 9,000 in 1831. It continued to increase exponentially throughout the Bourgeois Monarchy, the Second Republic, and the Second Empire, which, with the Pereires and the Foulds at the forefront of the imperial elite, has often been seen as the golden age of Parisian Jewry. More and more, Paris was becoming the center of French Jewish life as a whole; by 1852 its Jewish population was already the twelfth largest in the world, and the proportion of French Jews living in the capital rose from 5.83 percent in 1811 to 11.38 percent in 1841, 20.38 percent in 1853, and 26.20 percent in 1861.

Until 1871, most Parisian Jews, Sephardim and Ashkenazim alike, were eager not to display their Jewishness and sought in general to merge with the population as a whole, but the surrender of Alsace and Lorraine to Prussia in 1871 precipitated an immediate and substantial influx of Jews from the East, whose language and more obviously public practice of their religion gave them, in comparison with their self-effacing predecessors, a distinct identity as a group. Just a year after the French defeat, 48 percent of Jewish males in the capital and 36 percent of females were natives of Alsace-Lorraine, exciting comment, and sometimes alarm, both in the existing Jewish community and among scaremongers in the wider society, still traumatized by, and desperate to explain, the events of *l'année terrible*. Nonetheless, it would be as much a mistake to overstress the otherness of this newer Jewish population as it would be to exaggerate the degree of assimilation of the core community with which it in fact rapidly agglutinated. Both old and new Parisian Jews were eager to be both French and Jewish, indeed to be French before, but not to the exclusion of, being Jewish. In keeping with Clermont-Tonnerre's injunction, they practiced their religion more as individuals than as a collectivity, carefully demarcating their private religious beliefs and practices from their increasingly prominent roles in the public life of the city.

As a whole, Parisian Jews notably prospered between 1830 and the early 1880s, not just in the banking and business elite of the Eichtals, the Rodrigueses, the Foulds, Pereires, Furtados, Sterns, Goudchaux, and, above all, Rothschilds, but in the middle range of economic and professional activities as well. Notwithstanding a high proportion (20 percent) of Jews living in extreme poverty in the early 1850s, Parisian Jews were better off than the city's population as a whole; a large proportion of the less prosperous worked as self-employed artisans or in commerce, and no part of the city could be described as forming anything like a "Jewish quarter." Even so, despite the dissemination of Jews throughout the city and their high degree of at least outward integration in its culture, their prominence in the world of finance was equated with dominance as early as 1845, when the utopian socialist Alphonse Toussenel published *Les Juifs, rois de l'époque,* now widely recognized as the founding work of modern antisemitism, as opposed to the traditional anti-Judaism of the Church.

Linking with all the other conspiracy theories of the 1840s—Jesuits, criminals, socialists—the myth of the Jewish conspiracy against French society found, for the moment, few people prepared to give it much credence, but it established itself in the political and social unconscious of the times, requiring only a series of changed circumstances and a new set of political crises and scandals for it to be taken over by tens of thousands of otherwise levelheaded Frenchmen and Frenchwomen as *the* key, peremptory and all-embracing as the revealed religion whose loss it often supplanted, to the complexities and anxieties of the society and era they lived in.

The successive waves of antisemitism that eventually engulfed almost the whole of French society in the last two decades of the nineteenth century derived much of its power to persuade and explain from two developments, the one objective and statistically verifiable, the other probable but susceptible of no actual proof, that occurred in what was fast becoming not one Jewish community in Paris (assuming that such a unified community had ever actually existed) but a set of increasingly distinct and only loosely interlocking communities. The pogroms that followed the assassination of Tsar Alexander II in 1881 propelled, for the first time, large numbers of non-French Jews toward Paris, Jews who spoke Yiddish, were open and even demonstrative in their religious practice, and were notably poorer than even the Alsatian immigrants of the previous decade. After 1881 it became possible to speak not only of a Jewish working class in the city but also of a genuinely Jewish quarter, for while the better-off French Jews now lived scattered in the bourgeois west of Paris, new arrivals gravitated to what soon became known as the Pletzl, or *petite place*: the warren of streets in the fourth arrondissement around the present Métro Saint-Paul, the Rue Pavée, Rue du Roi de Sicile, and, best known of all, the Rue des Rosiers, which to this day is the most visibly Jewish street in the city, with its synagogues, schools, cafés, kosher butchers, delicatessens, and restaurants, among them the famous restaurant Goldenberg, the target in 1982 of an antisemitic bomb outrage that left six people dead and twenty-two injured. Into this knot of streets crowded hundreds of the poorest and least assimilable immigrant families, most of which would, in due course, move out to the ninth, tenth, eleventh, and twelfth arrondissements, where they found cheap accommodations and employment in trades that were becoming increasingly stereotyped as Jewish: leather goods, furs, clocks and watches, jewelry, millinery, the garment industry as a whole, and street vendors of every hue and description. As one cohort of immigrants moved out of the Pletzl, another moved in.

The pogroms of 1881 were followed by those of Kishiner and Jitamir in 1903, which were followed in their turn by a mass exodus of more radical Jews from Russia and Poland after the failure of the Revolution of 1905. Having doubled, thanks to the post-1871 Alsatian migration, from 24,000 to 40,000 between 1872 and 1881, the Jewish population of Paris now doubled again between 1881 and 1914, principally as a result of the influx from Russia, Poland, and Romania. It was an increasingly segmented population, however, divided between French and foreign Jews, a division that correlated largely with that between relatively well off and relatively poor, with the most recent Alsatian arrivals sandwiched uneasily between. The three subcommunities viewed one another with mutual mistrust and sometimes antipathy. Each had its own community organizations, publications, schools, and places of worship, and intercommunity marriages were rare in the extreme.

The major conflict was about what it meant to be Jewish. The older French community and the more upwardly mobile Alsatians called themselves *Français israélites*, not *Israélites français*, setting their Frenchness decisively before and above their Jewishness, which they defined almost exclusively in terms of religion. In contrast, Eastern European Jews, victims almost without exception of antisemitic hostility, defined their Jewishness primarily in terms of ethnicity and were unwilling to follow the core community in its traditional quest for social invisibility and for "de-Judaization" in public if not in private. The opposition between "French" and "foreign" Jews that would prove so baleful under Vichy was already clearly in place by 1914.

But it was less demographic changes, significant though they were, that prompted the upsurge of antisemitism in the 1880s and 1890s than the increased prominence, real or alleged, of French Jews in the political, intellectual, and artistic life of the capital, which led in due course to the identification of Jews with the detested Republic—*la gueuse*, the bitch—and to the poisonous interlude of the Dreyfus affair. Egged on by Edouard Drumont's turgid polemic *La France juive* of 1886 and the antisemitic rag that it spawned six years later, *La Libre Parole*, opponents of the liberal Republic—not all of them, by any means, on the reactionary right[5]—seized on the undoubted salience of Jews in certain areas of French life to explain what they saw as an all-encompassing disease of national decline, political corruption, financial chicanery, and moral and artistic decadence. Whether it was in music (Jacques Offenbach, Giacomo Meyerbeer, Valentin Alkan, Fromental Halévy), the theater (Rachel, Sarah Bernhardt), publishing (Michel and Calmann Lévy), journalism (Joseph Reinach, Bernard Lazare), philosophy (Henri Bergson), linguistics (Michel Bréal), or the nascent social sciences (Emile Durkheim, Marcel Mauss, Lucien Lévy-Brühl), "the Jew" seemed to be playing a disproportionate part in the intellectual and artistic life of the nation, and threatened to extend his—or, more rarely, her—hegemony still further in the century to come. By now there was no need to demonstrate the alleged Jewish stranglehold on banking and finance, particularly after the collapse in 1882 of the Catholic Union Générale, widely attributed to that increasingly mythical entity, "the Rothschilds," and the protracted Panama scandal, which provided grist for many an antisemitic mill between 1888 and 1893, until the providential discovery of an alleged Jewish traitor at the heart of French military intelligence conveniently superseded it.

What was new under the Third Republic was the unprecedented prominence of Jews in French political life, not just notable individuals such as Adolphe Crémieux (1796–1880), instigator of the decree bearing his name that extended full French citizenship to the Jews of Algeria in 1870, or Alfred Naquet (1834–1916), mover of the bill of 1884 that, to the outrage of Catholic opinion, legalized divorce, but the scores of otherwise obscure Jewish deputies, senators, *conseillers généraux*, and other republican officials whose advance, particularly after 1880, seemed to justify all the antisemites' fantasies about a Jewish takeover of the State. For obvious reasons, all these so-called *Juifs d'Etat* were passionate supporters of the Republic,[6] whence the inevitable syllogism: If all Jewish politicians are republicans, the Republic is Jewish. By the early 1890s, the theme of the Jewish Republic enjoyed as much currency among reactionaries as the earlier topos of the Jewish bank continued to enjoy on both antirepublican right and anticapitalist left. For enemies of the liberal Republic, the revelation of the supposed treachery of Captain Alfred Dreyfus corroborated everything they had been saying for ten years and more: the Jews *were* conspiring against the French state, they *were* in league with the archenemy across the Rhine, they *had* infiltrated the Republic with a view to turning it to their own nefarious purposes. Perhaps the most terrible thing about the Dreyfus affair is that the supposed crime of the eponymous villain surprised and scandalized almost no one: Dreyfus was a Jew, and it was simply in the nature of Jews to betray and suborn.

Despite the twelve-year crisis (1894–1906) to which the affair, in its multiple ramifications, subjected the French state, it is too often forgotten that in the end the anti-Dreyfus coalition of Catholics, monarchists, ultranationalists, former Bonapartists and Boulangists, militarists, and antisemites suffered a notable defeat at the hands of their republican-democratic adversaries. Many Jews believed that the eventual exoneration and reinstatement of Dreyfus gave decisive validation to the Yiddish saying *lebn vi Got in Frankraykh,* to live like God in France,[7] and indeed the years from the resolution of the affair to the onset of the next crisis in the early 1930s appear, in retrospect, as an interlude of tranquility and security compared to the turbulence that went before and the fears, and eventually the horrors, that succeeded it.

The election of Henri Bergson—the first Jew so to be honored—to the Académie Française in February 1914 was seen by many of his co-religionists as proof that the synthesis of Frenchness and Jewishness of which they had dreamed had at last been achieved.[8] The war that broke out a few months later gave French and foreign Jews alike the chance to prove their loyalty to nation and Republic in the most concrete of ways. Out of a total Jewish population, French, foreign, and North African, of 190,000, 40,000 fought in the war (including 8,500 foreign volunteers), with 7,500 killed, 1,600 of them foreign. The story of Rabbi Abraham Bloch, killed while taking a crucifix to a wounded Catholic soldier in August 1914 and himself dying in the arms of a Catholic chaplain, was cited as proof of the *Union Sacrée* of Catholics and Jews and prompted even the archnationalist and antisemite Maurice Barrès to include Jews among *les diverses familles spirituelles de la France* in his 1917 work of that name.[9]

After the war, immigration, be it Jewish or Gentile, was actively encouraged by the French state to remedy the chronic labor shortage, and while the much larger numbers of Catholic Poles and equally Catholic Italians and Spaniards settled, respectively, in the North and the Midi, their Jewish counterparts headed in their overwhelming majority along the by now traditional road to the capital. Between 1920 and 1930, 70,000 Jews from Eastern Europe settled in Paris, joining the 20,000 still "unassimilated" prewar foreign immigrants, not to mention 15,000 "other" Jews from the Maghreb and the Levant, with the result that by 1930 foreign Jews constituted a decisive majority in the city's total Jewish population of 150,000. But this unprecedented influx of migrants did not, in itself, lead to any upsurge of antisemitism. The publication of the bogus *Protocols of the Elders of Zion* in 1919 had, at the time, little impact in France, and in 1924, seven years after Drumont's death in obscurity and penury, *La Libre Parole* suspended publication for lack of readers and advertisers. In 1931, in *La Grande Peur des Bien-Pensants,* his would-be *défense et illustration* of Drumont's career, the old-style Action Française militant Georges Bernanos was even reduced to deploring the demise of the vigorous antisemitism of his street-fighting years, before the outbreak of war.

Even as Bernanos was writing, however, the conditions that would lead to the eruption of an antisemitism even more virulent than what went before were taking shape both inside and outside of France. In 1931 the Wall Street crash made its delayed impact on the national economy, casting tens of thousands out of work, and two years later Hitler's rise to power in Germany brought the first wave of between 17,000 and 20,000 Jewish refugees across the Franco-German frontier, bound principally, as ever, for Paris. Concomitantly, the small ultraright groups that emerged in the 1920s developed into full-fledged leagues that clashed with the police on the Place de la Concorde on the night of 6 February 1934, it being, of course, no coincidence at all that it was the alleged financial chicanery of an immigrant Jew, the Ukrainian Alexandre Stavisky, that served as the focus for the rioters' confused hatreds and fears. Between 1933 and 1939, perhaps as many as 100,000 Jews of all nationalities fled to France, as first the return of the Saar to the *Vaterland,* then *Kristallnacht,* and finally the *Anschluss* and the annexation of Czechoslovakia brought home the danger of Nazism to Jewish life and limb.

Not all of these refugees remained in Paris, or indeed in France, but by the outbreak of war the city's Jewish population was exceeded only by those of New York and Warsaw;[10] as early as 1933 one journalist was writing of "Canaan-on-the-Seine" in the antisemitic *Candide.*[11] As had happened in the 1880s and again after 1905, the new arrivals were markedly different—in language, religious practice, and concept of Jewishness—from the old assimilated nucleus of Parisian Jewry, congregating in certain parts of the city and its environs (the Pletzl, Belleville-Ménilmontant, Clignancourt, and Saint-Ouen, close to the Marché aux Puces), organizing themselves in region-based mutual aid societies known as *Landsmanschaften,* and endeavoring, with their synagogues and schools, cafés, restaurants, and newspapers (no fewer than 133 Yiddish-language periodicals were established in France between 1918 and 1939),[12] to reproduce the conditions of life in the shtetl in the interstices of their city of refuge.

According to Israel Jefroykin, writing in 1935, "the immigrant Jew sees himself as the bearer of authentic Jewish culture and sees the native Jews as neither here nor there."[13] For their part, the elite of Parisian Jewry regarded the newcomers with a mixture of concern and contempt, fearing that their blatant *Yiddishkeit* would fan the flames of recrudescent Jew hatred. Even Annette Muller, who has little to say about Jewish politics in Paris, speaks harshly of the assimilated "aristocrats," for whom there was nothing more shaming than the Yiddish or the "Manche! Manche!" of their outlandish co-religionists, especially those from Galicia. Even Jews from other parts of Poland, she claims, held them to be the lowest of the low.[14]

Nothing better illustrates the upsurge of antisemitism after 1933 than the circulation figures of the two leading antisemitic dailies: *Candide,* up from 265,000 in 1935 to 465,000 the following year, and *Gringoire,* up from 325,000 in 1934 to 650,000 in 1936. In addition, the openly fascist *Je suis partout,* edited by Robert Brasillach and Lucien Rebatet, had sales of between 40,000 and 80,000 per week, to which must be added a host of smaller Jew-baiting canards: *Le Défi, Le Pays libre, Le Porcepic,* and *La France enchaînée,* this last being the house journal of the Anti-Jewish Assembly of France, founded by Louis Darquier, alias Darquier de Pellepoix, a member since May 1935 of the Paris city council (where he publicly addressed one fellow councilor as "a dirty little Jew" and later punched him in the face during a meeting) and future head of the General Commissariat on Jewish Questions under Vichy.[15]

The election in May 1936 of the Popular Front, headed by the "Jewish rabbi" Léon Blum, brought antisemitic fury to its odious climax. On 6 June 1936, Xavier Vallat, also destined for higher things under Vichy, openly deplored in the Chamber of Deputies that the "ancient Gallo-Roman nation" of France, as he put it, was henceforth to be governed "by a Jew," "a subtle Talmudist,"[16] aided and abetted, according to the hacks of the antisemitic press, by a veritable tribe of Jewish advisers and experts. *Le Franciste* claimed that Blum's closest adviser was a Mlle Swarrrtzzsann, herself assisted by "MM. Bloch, Moïse, Cahen, and Lévy," while *Je suis partout* published a cartoon by Hermann-Paul showing a caller at one or another ministry asking for a "Monsieur Lévy" and being asked by the porter, "Which one?"[17]

Nor was antisemitism the preserve of the Parisian gutter press, or even of openly pro-fascist writers such as Pierre Drieu La Rochelle and Louis-Ferdinand Céline (1894–1961), whose prewar pamphlets *Bagatelles pour un massacre* (1937) and *L'Ecole des cadavres* (1938), followed by *Les Beaux Draps* in 1941, are grotesque masterpieces of antisemitic diatribe. "Respectable" authors such as Marcel Jouhandeau (one of several possible inventors of the well-worn topos of "Rather Hitler than Blum"),[18] Paul Morand, Thierry Maulnier, Henri Massis, and Claude Roy added their voices to the throng, and at the Quai d'Orsay, the diplomat-dramatist Jean Giraudoux (1882–1944), author of the pacifist *La Guerre de Troie n'aura pas lieu* (1935), openly called in 1939 for the setting up of a "Ministry of Race." The torrent of antisemitic innuendo and obloquy became so strong that in April 1939 a decree named after Paul Marchandeau, the minister of justice at the time, outlawed incitement to racial hatred in the press. From then until the defeat of June 1940 open antisemitism did indeed disappear from even the ultraright press, but the measure needed to have been taken, at the very least, two or three years before. Significantly, one of Vichy's earliest acts, taken on 27 August 1940, was to repeal the decree in question.

When, in September 1939, *l'Histoire avec sa grande hache* ("History with a capital H," or, alternatively, "History with its great ax")[19] finally fell, the total Jewish population of France is generally estimated at between 300,000 and 330,000; twelve months later, after the defeat, that figure had grown by a further 10 percent as a result of the influx of Jewish refugees from Holland and Belgium and of the German policy of expelling Jews from the *Vaterland* to the unoccupied zone, whither the Jewish population of Alsace-Lorraine, reannexed by the Reich in July 1940, were also directed.[20] If these figures are assumed to be roughly correct, 8 persons in every 1,000 (0.7 percent) out of a total population of 43 million present on French soil at the time of the defeat were Jewish by the pre-Vichy definition of the term. From this point on, all statistics must be viewed with caution. Probably something like 90,000 of the total Jewish population belonged to the traditional kernel of "French" Jewry, though by 1939 thousands of later immigrants had become naturalized French citizens, and one of Vichy's first tasks would be to weed out "genuine" French nationals from "bogus" interlopers. Given the considerable movement of population at the time and further moves both ways across the dividing line after the signing of the armistice, the Jewish population of Paris is especially difficult to quantify. Between 140,000 and 150,000 is a reasonable estimate for the start of the Occupation, split by a ratio of approximately 2 to 1 between "French" ("traditional" plus "naturalized") and "foreign"; perhaps 35,000 of these were children under the age of fifteen, a high proportion of them French citizens, like the four Muller children, simply by dint of having been born on French soil.

Jews, both "French" and "foreign," had enlisted in large numbers in the French army at the outbreak of war, their 60,000 conscripts and volunteers making up 20 percent of the total Jewish population, as against 15 percent of the population as a whole. Of these 60,000 fully 16,000 were foreign Jewish volunteers, many of whom probably hoped to obtain full French citizenship by this route. Many more were rejected for active military service, among them Annette Muller's father, who, disappointed, rejoined his wife and children in the village of Saint-Bié-en-Belin in the Sarthe, where they had been evacuated as a "large family" at the start of the war. When German soldiers entered the village in June 1940, he had the unwelcome task, as the one local tailor, of sewing the campaign decorations on their uniforms.[21]

There is no need to retrace here in detail the successive antisemitic measures enacted by Vichy, most of which automatically applied to both unoccupied and occupied zones.[22] It is necessary, however, to repeat the consensus view of all the best modern histories, led by Michael R. Marrus and Robert O. Paxton's pioneering *Vichy France and the Jews* (1981), that these measures, beginning with the infamous *Statut des Juifs* of 3 October 1940, were by no means forced on a reluctant Vichy by an overbearing occupying power but constituted a series of independent decisions and actions on the part of a viscerally antisemitic pseudo government eager to prove and enhance its autonomy of action. Furthermore, while the German decrees of the time still defined Jewishness essentially in terms of religion, the *Statut des Juifs* spoke explicitly of people "of Jewish race" and accordingly gave a much broader definition of who was a Jew—someone with two Jewish grandparents rather than three if the individual in question was married to a Jew—than the regulations currently in force in the *Vaterland* itself. Not surprisingly, the German occupying force would in due course be happy to take over Vichy's far more ecumenical concept of who was and was not a Jew.[23]

None of the initial anti-Jewish measures—notably the imposition of a quota in a range of professions and the expropriation of a number of "Jewish businesses"—had much impact on a family as poor as the Mullers, though the compulsory stamping of the word *Juif* or *Juive* on identity documents in red letters 1.5 centimeters (over half an inch) high, imposed in the occupied zone in October 1940, cannot, to say the least, have been of any reassurance to Annette's mother and father. Returning to Paris with their parents, the children were placed in a Catholic school on the Rue Olivier-Métra, in the twentieth arrondissement, where, as before, they seem to have experienced no prejudicial treatment at all, but the frequent absences of their father, constrained from the beginning of 1941 to work as a logger in woods belonging to the Rothschilds at Creil, to the north of Paris, brought to the household "an ambience of insecurity and temporariness. We felt a threat hanging over us."[24]

It was not long before the Mullers learned of the first roundups in Paris. On 14 May 1941, 3,750 Polish, Czech, and Austrian Jews were rounded up by the French police and dispatched to the concentration camps of Pithiviers and Beaune-la-Rolande, in the Loiret. Between 20 and 23 August a cordon was thrown around the eleventh arrondissement by French and German police acting in tandem, and 4,000 Jews, most but not all of them "foreign," were interned in the transit camp of Drancy, on the northeastern outskirts of Paris, not far from the airport at Le Bourget.

On 12 December the Germans, for the one time during the Occupation, acted largely independently of the French police, arresting 743 Jews, all of them successful professionals and all of them French, in reprisal for the first killings of German soldiers by the emerging resistance. Ninety-five hostages, fifty-three of them Jews, were executed at the fortress of Mont-Valérien, on the western periphery of the city, and the first convoy of 1,112 Jews, both French and foreign, left Drancy bound "for the East" on 27 March 1942. Only nineteen of them would return at the end of the war.[25]

Meanwhile torrents of Judeophobia were pouring not only from the specialist antisemitic press but from once "respectable" dailies such as *Le Matin, France-Soir,* and *Le Petit Parisien,* and antisemitism in France plumbed new depths with the German-inspired but French-staffed exhibition "Le Juif et la France," which opened at the Palais Berlitz, close to the Opéra, in September 1941. Announced by a massive poster depicting a "classic" hook-nosed Jew coiled avariciously around the globe, his rapacious talons reaching out toward France, the exhibition featured large-scale models of "the Jewish eye," "the Jewish ear," and, inevitably, "the Jewish nose" to facilitate identification of the nation's racial enemies. The exhibition attracted 200,000 paying visitors before it closed in January 1942, a considerable figure but one apparently well below that anticipated by its organizers.[26] Yet neither the outpourings of the professional Jew-baiters in the press nor the relative success of "Le Juif et la France" should lead one to conclude that Parisians as a whole subscribed to the image of "the Jew" as an active threat to their lives with which they were confronted on a day-to-day basis. The evidence points rather to the widespread existence, before July 1942, of a form of "soft" or "ordinary" antisemitism that routinely equated Jews with the black market but did not otherwise differentiate them from other official targets of German and Vichy propaganda: Freemasons, Communists, Gaullists, "foreigners." Indifference rather than support, and certainly rather than hostility, was the most common reaction to the *Statut des Juifs* and the antisemitic measures that followed it in the course of 1940 and 1941, and it was only in the summer of 1942 that public opinion would swing decisively in favor of the Jewish victims of combined German-Vichy persecution and break with the forms of normalized antisemitism that had hitherto held sway.[27]

Away from the center of Paris, the Mullers may have been screened from the worst kinds of media antisemitism, but there was no way they could escape the legislative vise now tightening around the city's Jewish population. A letter from their relatives in Poland, followed by a total unmisinterpretable silence, left them in no doubt as to what was going on "in the East," and their anxiety increased when Monsieur Muller was arrested (by a French gendarme), interned at the Chancelade, and then released. More and more discriminating measures were enacted on Vichy's own initiative, and Jews were successively forbidden to own bicycles, radios, and telephones (and also to use public phone booths), banned from libraries, theaters, swimming pools, restaurants, and public gardens (including both the Bois de Boulogne and the Bois de Vincennes), and permitted to shop only between three and four in the afternoon, by which time many shops had exhausted their day's stock and had closed. As a final humiliation, Jews were forced to travel in the rear carriage of the Metro, and Annette Muller recalls the letters DUBO, DUBON, DUBONNET moving past on the stations and forming a "haunting refrain" that, mingling with the clattering of the carriages, already evokes the long-distance trains that would shortly be leaving Paris with their human cargoes bound for the East. Returning one Sunday from Bobigny, the children see the watchtowers of Drancy loom up in the distance, so notorious now that people were already speaking of *Drancy-les-tours* and *Drancy-le-trou-aux-Juifs,* and the very name Drancy sends shudders down the little girl's spine.[28]

By now the children were being made to feel their Jewishness even at the otherwise welcoming Catholic youth club they continued to attend, but the crucial turning point came with the order, issued by the Germans on 29 May 1942 but never imposed by Vichy so long as it remained in control of its zone, that all Jews aged over six would be henceforth obliged to wear a yellow six-pointed star "having the dimensions of the palm of the hand" and bearing the word JUIF in black letters on the left breast of whatever upper garment they were wearing. Like thousands of Jewish mothers, Madame Muller duly sewed regulation stars on her boys' tweed jackets and on Annette's navy-blue pullover and flower-patterned dress and then gritted her teeth in pride and defiance whenever she and the children walked along the Rue de Pixérécourt or the Rue des Pyrénées in Belleville-Ménilmontant. But Annette herself felt shamed, not so much by the occasional antisemitic comment directed at the family as by people turning away and refusing to acknowledge her and their presence. But many Jews shared Madame Muller's bitterness and pride and, to the Germans' discomfiture, hundreds of star-wearing Parisians—not all of them Jewish—gathered on the *grands boulevards* between the Opéra and the Place de la République on the afternoon of Sunday, 10 June 1942, to register silent defiance. Some non-Jewish Parisians were actually interned at Drancy for wearing yellow stars marked "Auvergnat," "Gay," "Danny," and, in one case, even "Swing," while some students wore badges marked JUIF, standing, they said, for "Jeunesse universitaire intellectuelle française" (French Intellectual University Youth),[29] though there was no French equivalent, then or later, of the concerted wearing of Stars of David by non-Jews that is credited with having saved the bulk of the Jewish population of Denmark from transportation and death.

Despite such signs of defiance, and signs, too, of a shift of public opinion in their favor, few Jews in Paris in the summer of 1942 could have been in much doubt that their situation was destined to deteriorate still further, but the suddenness and character of the crunch when it came left most in utter bewilderment. Unknown to anyone in France, a decision had been made in January 1942 at the so-called Wannsee Conference in Berlin to transform the already massive but so far uncoordinated killing of Jews into a systematic program of racial extermination, and an initial quota of 100,000 Jews, to be dispatched to the East in thrice-weekly convoys, was allocated to France. Knowing that he had neither the personnel nor the trains to handle such a large contingent, Theodore Dannecker, head of the Gestapo Jewish Affairs Service in France, settled on an initial installment of 39,000 Jews, aged between sixteen and sixty, to be delivered to the East over three months at the rate of three trainloads per week: 22,000 of these were to come from the departments of the Seine and the Seine-et-Oise, 6,000 from the rest of the occupied zone, and 11,000 from the unoccupied zone. The Germans' plan made no distinction between French Jews and foreign, and 9,000 of the former were initially included in the overall total.[30]

With their revised figures in hand, the Germans then approached Vichy for assistance in France's contribution to their Operation

Reinhardt, named in memory of the recently assassinated Reinhardt Heydrich, which they now, with macabre mock-poetry, dubbed Operation Spring Breeze—*Vent printanier* in French. Dannecker knew that without French participation, he could not arrest, intern, and transport so large a number of Jews, especially if a quarter of them were French, without risking the possibility of serious public dissent. Approached, Vichy initially stalled and then acquiesced in the person of Pierre Laval, restored to power after a break of some sixteen months in April 1942, on condition that no French Jews were included in the target figure of 39,000 for France as a whole. As a quid pro quo, Laval on his own initiative proposed that foreign Jews under the age of sixteen, whom the Germans had ruled out at least for the time being, be included in the total, thus establishing the holocaustal logic of Vichy's Jewish policy almost in passing: sacrifice "foreign" Jews, men, women, and children alike, in order to save "French" Jews, disregarding in the process the inconvenient fact that many of the children earmarked as foreign were, like the young Mullers, actually French by virtue of having been born on French soil.

The principal agent of Vichy's this-for-that policy was the regime's chief of police, the high-flying civil servant René Bousquet (1909–93), who, based in Vichy, had responsibility for the French police in both unoccupied and occupied zones, including no fewer than 30,000 in Paris under the immediate authority of his deputy, Jean Leguay (1909–79). A special "Jewish section" had already been set up at the Prefecture of Police under a career policeman named François, who worked in close cooperation both with Dannecker and with Vichy's own Commissariat on Jewish Questions, whose original chief, Xavier Vallat, had been replaced in April 1942 by the even more rabidly antisemitic Darquier de Pellepoix. Leguay and François had in their possession a card file containing the names of 150,000 Jews in Paris and the department of the Seine, indexed not only alphabetically but by occupation and street, with cards of different colors distinguishing French Jews from foreign. The file, a considerable feat of administrative exhaustiveness, had been created in September–October 1940 by a civil servant attached to the Prefecture of Police named André Tulard (1899–1967), acting under the direction of General de La Laurencie, the representative at the time of the Vichy government in Paris. Without that file, whose supposed rediscovery in 1991 precipitated a further round in postwar France's seemingly never-ending "Vichy syndrome,"[31] there can be little doubt that the roundup of 16–17 July 1942 and its successors could not have been conducted with even the limited effectiveness that it was. Though of German instigation,

Operation Spring Breeze was from the outset planned, organized, and carried out by officials and police whose ultimate loyalty and responsibility were to the Vichy regime.

In the second week of July 1942, files containing the details of 27,388 foreign Jews, men, women, and children, were picked out by officials reinforced by women assistants recruited for the purpose and passed on to the police.[32] Some of the names were leaked to the Rue des Rosiers, and many Jewish men, including Annette's father, went into hiding in the naive belief that only they, and not their wives and families, would be targeted in the roundup that none doubted would shortly occur. The night of 13–14 July having been rejected as politically incendiary, the operation, planned in meticulous detail, swung into action at four o'clock in the morning of Thursday, 16 July: *jeudi noir,* Black Thursday, as it would inevitably be known ever after by those who survived it. In all something like 9,000 men, all of them French, took part in the carefully synchronized operation, the majority of them policemen, divided into 880 teams for the purpose of making the initial arrests, plus 400 members of Jacques Doriot's fascist Parti Populaire Français and, perhaps most disturbing, the drivers of the fifty or so buses—regular employees of the Compagnie des Transports/Région Parisienne (TCRP), or so it appears—responsible for ferrying the detainees to their immediate and ultimate Parisian destinations.

The scenes at the Rue de l'Avenir were replicated in apartment after apartment across Paris: loud bangs on the door at four in the morning, two or three policemen making their entrance, their beige French uniforms at once alarming and reassuring, shouts of "Get up, get dressed, quick, quick!" frightening, certainly, but less so than the dreaded *"Raus! Raus!"* of the occupier, Madame Muller on her knees sobbing and begging the intruders to take her but not the children, frantic scrambling around for clothes and the two days' supply of food they were instructed to take with them. Curiously, Annette was allowed out to "buy a comb," almost certainly a sign, widely attested elsewhere in the city,[33] that the police were giving her a chance to escape—a chance that, despite the urging of the old woman who sold her the comb to run away, Annette was too bewildered and frightened to seize.

Mother and children were then marched, carrying their bundles like hundreds of other detainees, through the streets to what Annette calls just "a room," presumably one of the so-called primary centers, such as the gymnasium Japy in the eleventh arrondissement, to which those arrested were initially taken pending their eventual "concentration" elsewhere in the city. Wherever the room was located, Madame Muller was able to persuade a sympathetic, or morally troubled, French policeman to turn a blind eye as her two eldest boys, Henri and Jean, slipped away in the chaos. Finally, one of the legendary buses—just ordinary single-deck Parisian buses, in no way adapted for their new and nefarious purpose—took Annette, Michel, and her mother across Paris to a building that reminded her of the Cirque d'Hiver, where she had seen *Snow White and the Seven Dwarfs* the previous year. It was not, however, the Cirque but an equally familiar landmark in Parisian popular culture, the Vélodrome d'Hiver, always known as the Vel' d'Hiv', the indoor bicycle track that, until its demolition in 1959, stood on the Rue Nélaton in the fifteenth arrondissement, on the Left Bank, close to the present Pont de Bir Hakeim.

Thus far, the Mullers' experience of the roundup had been rather less traumatizing than that of many of the detainees who, busload by busload, now arrived at the Vel' d'Hiv'. Many were injured or sick; some had been betrayed by neighbors or by that bugaboo of the Parisian imagination, the concierge (others had been saved by exactly the same persons); all were in a state of extreme shock. Among those scheduled for detention who did not arrive at the Vel' d'Hiv' were the mothers who had flung first their children and then themselves out of the windows of their apartments. Still more tragic were those who had attempted suicide and failed, such as the mother and child on the Rue Trousseau in the eleventh arrondissement who landed in a police safety net, and still others whom police, with supreme irony, prevented from gassing themselves. In all, there were at least a hundred suicides on the early morning of 16 July.[34]

Into the Vel' d'Hiv' were eventually crammed 7,000 detainees, over 4,000 of them children under the age of sixteen. Single adults and couples without children were ferried directly to Drancy, giving a grand total of 12,884 persons arrested during the two-day operation (11,363 on 16 July, 1,521 the day after), 3,031 men, 5,802 women, and 4,051 children—considerably less than half of the 28,000-plus foreign Jews who had been targeted, thanks to a combination of advance warnings permitting flight or concealment, police inefficiency, much of it intentional, and the willingness of non-Jews to hide Jewish neighbors or provide false information. For every case of French complicity with Operation Spring Breeze there is at least one case of active or passive opposition. The decisive swing of French public opinion against Vichy and in favor of Charles de Gaulle is widely, and with some plausibility, dated from the impact that the spectacle—which the Vichy authorities made little attempt to conceal—of 16–17 July had on previously indifferent or even casually antisemitic Parisians.[35]

The Vel' d'Hiv' had seats for 15,000 spectators, as well as the open space inside the track, and had already served as a reception center for foreign refugees, many of them Jewish, before the defeat. It was also well known for its prewar political meetings, and, by macabre coincidence, the *fine fleur* of Parisian antisemitism—Vallat, Darquier, Léon Daudet, Philippe Henriot—had gathered there in July 1937 along with thousands of other ultrarightists to congratulate the Ur-fascist Charles Maurras (1868–1952) on his release after serving a prison sentence for his violent attacks on Léon Blum, who himself was brought to trial by Vichy in February 1942 and interned by the Germans in Buchenwald for the duration of the war.[36] Now, however, the prospect was not to seat 15,000 cycling enthusiasts (or, for that matter, 15,000 French fascists) but to accommodate 7,000 anxious detainees who had to eat, sleep, wash, and, most difficult and humiliating of all, find somewhere to urinate and excrete, watched over by French guards from whom the more sympathetic elements had now been weeded out and with never more than two doctors, and for long periods none at all, to attend to their needs.

"There was piss and shit everywhere," Annette Muller would write more than twenty years after the event, and every account attempts to evoke the appalling stench that soon enveloped the whole stadium as huge queues formed outside the handful of toilets and people began to relieve themselves wherever they could. Hunger and thirst were succeeded by dysentery and enteritis, epileptic fits and seizures of violence and madness, all made more horrendous by the laughter and squeals of the smaller children as they played among the folding seats around the cycle track. When Annette saw a naked man racked with convulsions, his eyes staring out of their sockets and his "hideous sex" clearly visible between his emaciated thighs, it was as though "all my childhood lurched [*basculait*] at the sight of this naked, tormented body. I had a revelation of the world of adults, dirty, sick, pitiable. I pitied them but at the same time I despised them, just like the morning of 16 July when I saw my mother begging on her knees in front of the policemen in beige."[37]

Soon people began to die, of disease, in childbirth, by suicide as mothers, a child or children in their arms, flung themselves off the upper tiers of seats onto the mass of detainees below; others begged visiting doctors and nurses to put them out of their misery by administering an injection.[38] On Sunday, 19 July, the detainees began to be moved out, and the Mullers were taken by truck 100 kilometers to the south, to the camp of Beaune-la-Rolande, in the Loiret, not far from Orléans. Others were taken in the buses in which they had arrived to the Gare d'Austerlitz, where they were transferred to trains bound for either Beaune or the nearby camp of Pithiviers. Again little attempt seems to have been made to conceal their departure, which was observed by, among others, the wife of François Mauriac, who happened to be at the station at the time.[39]

At Beaune the men were separatêd from the women and children, and Annette again felt a mixture of pity, hatred, and contempt as she watched crowds of naked women jostling for position at the camp's meager washing facilities. Sometimes people from the village of Beaune stared at the internees through the barbed-wire perimeter fence before being driven away by the guards, all of them, as before, French. When it became known that mothers and children were to be separated, Madame Muller desperately sought out Madame La Rochelle, the commander of the women's section of the camp, in the hope of keeping Annette and Michel with her, either at Beaune or on the train that everyone now knew would shortly take the adults "to the East." To no avail: mother and children made their pitiful farewells, never to see each other again, and several days later Annette and Michel, their heads shaved and with yellow stars both stitched and crudely painted on their clothes, were marched past the onlooking villagers to Beaune station, three kilometers away, whence they were taken by cattle truck to the camp whose very name had already caused Annette to shudder.

Drancy had been constructed in the late 1930s to provide a base and lodgings for the Parisian gendarmerie and, as such, was completely unlike the barbed wire and huts of Pithiviers and Beaune. It consisted essentially of a single U-shaped block of buildings, four stories high, with a cinder-covered courtyard at its center, surmounted by the sinister watchtowers that Annette and her brothers had already seen in the distance a few months before. From September 1939 to June 1940 it had served as an internment center for French and foreign Communists whom the French government had rounded up after the signing of the Nazi-Soviet pact. Under ultimate German control, but manned almost exclusively by French personnel up until the summer of 1943, Drancy received its first intake of Jewish internees in August 1941. Thereafter it would function as the fulcrum of the whole system of deportation from France, from the first convoy of 27 March 1942 to the last of 17 August 1944, just two days before the liberation of Paris. In all, no fewer than 67,000 out of 76,000 Jewish deportees would depart from Drancy for what the camp children, innocently or cynically, called Pitchipoi, the name of a far-off imaginary land in a Yiddish folktale.[40]

Drancy, 1944. In sharp contrast to the received image of the concentration camp, Drancy consisted of a U-shaped block of buildings originally constructed in the late 1930s to provide accommodations for Parisian gendarmes. The photograph shows the central courtyard and one of the towers mythologized in the image of "Drancy-les-tours" and "Drancy-le-trou-aux-Juifs." (Reproduced by permission of the Centre de Documentation Juive Contemporaine, Paris.)

Before we follow Annette and Michel Muller's path to and from this "antechamber of Auschwitz" on the outskirts of Paris,[41] the question of responsibility for the roundup of 16–17 July 1942 requires consideration, in the absence, however, of clinching evidence as to whether, at the time, even Laval was aware of what was really happening in the East.[42] Regarding the issue of *ultimate* responsibility, and in opposition to what has, since the reopening of the whole history of Vichy in the late 1960s, become as tenacious a myth as the earlier myth of French noninvolvement in the Final Solution, it should be stressed that Operation Spring Breeze was not initiated by Vichy, and that Vichy's collaboration, though certainly willingly given, in the roundup of foreign Jews in both occupied and unoccupied zones was motivated by political rather than ideological considerations. Neither Laval nor his chief of police, René Bousquet, was an antisemite of the Vallat or Darquier type. It was reasons of state, certainly not the desire to have Jews exterminated en masse, that led them to comply with the Germans' request for

Jewish children arrive at Drancy pending their dispatch to "Pitchipoi" in "the East." This etching by the deportee Georges Horan was published in 1945 as one of a series titled "At the Threshold of the Jewish Hell." The image makes clear the central role played by French gendarmes in the whole process of arrest, internment, and deportation: not a single German uniform is to be seen. (Reproduced by permission of the Centre de Documentation Juive Contemporaine, Paris.)

assistance: in its French application, the Final Solution was a German invention.[43] That said, there can be no doubt that Operation Spring Breeze was, from beginning to end, organized and manned by French officials and personnel responsible in the first instance to Leguay at the Prefecture of Police and to his superior, Bousquet, in Vichy. Compilers of the card file, arresting policemen, bus drivers, guards at the Vel' d'Hiv', Beaune-la-Rolande, Pithiviers, and Drancy, all were without question French, as were most of the guards and all of the trainmen on the eastbound convoys, at least up to the frontier, now at Neuberg (Novéant) in the Moselle, where German personnel relieved them.[44] Finally, there can be no doubt that the inclusion of children in the target figure of 28,000 for the occupied zone occurred as a result of Laval's intervention alone; the policy, derived from this original decision, of using foreign Jews as a shield behind which to protect French Jews was of his personal devising, and rested ultimately on a total indifference to what might happen to the "foreign" children, many, perhaps most of them, French citizens, so long as the "French" went comparatively untouched.

The indisputable, and indisputably voluntary, involvement of at least 10,000, and probably many more, French nationals in the events of 16–17 July and their aftermath has inevitably led many observers to see the roundup as a French crime, responsibility for which reaches well beyond its perpetrators and the government on whose orders they were acting to embrace the French nation, and even the French people as a whole.

Largely repressed or elided for twenty-five years while the Gaullist "resistentialist" myth was in the ideological ascendent,[45] the tragedy and scandal of the Vel' d'Hiv' returned to public consciousness with the publication in 1967 of Claude Lévy and Paul Tillard's painstaking and passionate *La Grande Rafle du Vel' d'Hiv*, whose findings were diffused to a still wider audience by Marcel Ophüls's banned television film *Le Chagrin et la pitié* (released in the United States and Britain as *The Sorrow and the Pity*) of 1971. Until then any French involvement in the Holocaust had been denied more or less as a matter of policy. In his 1956 film about the camps, *Nuit et brouillard* (*Night and Fog*), Alain Resnais had been obliged to airbrush the French kepis from the newsreel film of Pithiviers he had used, and even so, the film was not accepted for showing at the official film festival at Cannes.[46]

By the fiftieth anniversary of the roundup, in 1992, the countermyth of French complicity—not just of the complicity of Vichy and its supporters—in the Final Solution had gained such a hold on a section of French public opinion that the commemoration of the event caused a major political controversy that culminated in the president of the Republic, François Mitterrand, being whistled and booed at the official ceremony, which he attended without speaking.[47] Truly, as has been said, "what is remembered in sadness cannot be easily commemorated" (ce qui est tristement mémorable n'est pas aisément commémorable).[48] A petition published in *Le Monde* on 17 June 1992 under the auspices of a Comité Vel' d'Hiv '42 and signed by over two hundred "artists, writers, and academics" (but not, conspicuously, any leading historians of Vichy) called for a public acknowledgment by the president of the active involvement of what it termed the *Etat français de Vichy* in the "persecutions and crimes [committed against] the Jews of France."[49] On 14 July, two days before the scheduled commemoration, Mitterrand refused to make any such acknowledgmuet, on the grounds that it did not behoove him, as president of the Fifth Republic, to speak in the name of a pseudo regime that had abolished the Third Republic and held the very principle of republicanism in opprobrium.

Meanwhile, the situation was exacerbated by the disclosure, on 10 July, that for several years the president had been having a wreath placed on the tomb of Marshal Pétain on the Ile d'Yeu, off the Vendée coast, in commemoration of 11 November 1918. The revelation prompted many petitioners to suspect that Mitterrand was covertly sympathetic to Vichy; such suspicions were further inflamed by the publication in 1994 of Pierre Péan's *Une Jeunesse française: François Mitterrand, 1934–1947*, which detailed the future president's involvement in right-wing student politics in the 1930s and the period he spent as a Vichy official before he joined the Resistance as "Morland." By 16 July 1992, what had begun as a desire for an official acknowledgment of Vichy's responsibility for—and not just its voluntary involvement in— the roundup and similar outrages had mutated, in effect, into a campaign against Mitterrand himself, to which the far right, as well as elements of the left, lent their enthusiastic support. On the morning of the 16th, huge crowds spilled across the Boulevard de Grenelle close to the former site of the stadium, and the president's appearance was greeted with jeers and cries of "Mitterrand à Vichy!"[50] Even when, two years later, on 17 July 1994, the official monument to the roundup was unveiled by the president on the banks of the Seine close to the original site, its commemorative plaque was found to refer merely to "crimes against humanity committed under the de facto authority known as the 'Government of the French State' (1940–1944)"—"under," not "by," which for many observers was a further whitewashing of French responsibility for the crimes.[51]

By the time the monument was inaugurated, the Vel' d'Hiv' had received its last victim in the person of its chief executor, René Bousquet himself, shot in his apartment on the Avenue Raphaël just off the Bois de Boulogne in June 1993 by a deranged publicity seeker named Christian Didier.[52] Imprisoned in 1945, Bousquet had been convicted four years later and sentenced to five years' loss of civil rights, the sentence being immediately commuted for "acts of resistance" in which the defendant had supposedly engaged. Released, Bousquet embarked on a highly successful career as director of, inter alia, the Bank of Indochina, the Indo-Suez Bank, and the French-Asian Bank, as well as, extraordinarily, running Jaurès's old newspaper, *La Dépêche du Midi,* in the 1960s. His role in the events of 16–17 July 1942 was revealed to the public in an article in *L'Express* in October 1978 grotesquely titled "A Auschwitz, on n'a gazé que les poux" (At Auschwitz, they only gassed lice) and written by none other than Darquier de Pellepoix, who, from the safety of Franco's Spain, where he had fled at the end of the war, was now sedulously engaged in the emerging pseudoscience of *négationnisme,* or Holocaust denial.

It was not until September 1989, however, that the charge of crimes against humanity was finally brought against Bousquet, by the Jewish lawyer-investigator Serge Klarsfeld on behalf of the Association of the Sons and Daughters of Deported Jews. There then began four years of legal-political chicanery remarkable even for the French courts, giving rise to the suspicion that Bousquet had friends (or enemies) in high places who were determined at all costs that his trial not begin, as indeed it had not done by the time he was killed, whence further speculation that his assassin had been engaged by persons or parties unknown to carry out the deed. But Didier (who has yet to be tried) was almost certainly acting on his own personal account: "I had the impression I was crushing a snake," declared the former chauffeur of Alain Delon, Catherine Deneuve, and Salvador Dalí at the impromptu press conference he called after committing his crime.[53]

In all, 75,721 Jews were deported from France to the East, the vast majority of them passing, as we have seen, through Drancy. Of these, some 24,000 were French Jews, as opposed to 26,300 from Poland, 7,000 from Germany, 4,500 from Russia, 3,300 from Romania, and 2,500 from Austria. The proportions gave specious corroboration to Vichy's claim, at the post-Liberation trials, that it had "shielded" French Jews from the Holocaust by handing over foreign sacrificial victims at a ratio of 2 to 1.[54]

One French Jewish victim whom the policy—if policy it was—did not save was the Christian convert Max Jacob, who died at Drancy of pneumonia on 5 March 1944, a victim of the biological definition of Jewishness that was Vichy's principal contribution to the Shoah in France. Of those deported, 6,012 were aged under twelve, 13,104 between thirteen and thirty, and 8,687 over sixty. Only 2,500 of those who left France ever returned.[55]

By a combination of miracle and manipulation, Annette and Michel Muller escaped deportation. Shortly after arriving at Drancy from

These Jewish internees at Drancy in 1942 are almost certainly victims of the roundup of 16–17 July. (Reproduced by permission of the Centre de Documentation Juive Contemporaine, Paris.)

Beaune-la-Rolande, they were moved on again by police car—Annette says that their four guards were weeping—to the Asile Lamarck, in the heart of Montmartre, where, along with hundreds of other children, they were interned pending deportation to the East. Suddenly, in mid-November 1942, the Muller children were taken out of their "home" and enrolled at an elementary school on the Rue Muller—"the same name as mine"—which leads up to the Basilica of Sacré-Cœur, that monument to Catholic intransigence that had played so important a part in the diffusion of France's homegrown variety of antisemitism, of which they were now victims. At the school, with their hair still cropped and still wearing their regulation yellow stars, the children did their lessons despite their classmates' taunts of "dirty Jews," which once made Annette wet herself in the middle of the playground.

Then, with no explanation, a nun in a white-winged coif appeared, accompanied by a Madame Fossier, the concierge of the house on the Rue de Guignier where Annette's father had taken refuge on the eve of the roundup. The two women took Annette and Michel away, first to the Rue de Guignier and then to a convent in the center of Paris—no ordinary convent, either, but the mother house of Catherine Labouré's order of the Sisters of Charity, on the Rue du Bac.

What had happened was this: Monsieur Muller had been joined in his refuge by his two elder sons, and he knew now, if ever he had not known, that the situation was desperate: "*Seife* [soap]," replied a German soldier when Muller asked him what would become of an elderly Jewish couple being arrested. In the following weeks, Muller went everywhere in quest of news of the rest of his family: to the Red Cross, back to the Rue de l'Avenir—where the concierge, having ransacked the apartment, tried to hand him over to the police who were still combing the streets—and finally to La-Roche-sur-Yon in the Vendée, where the family had once stayed. Returning in desperation to Paris, Muller impulsively approached a nun on the platform at the Gare Saint-Lazare and begged for her help. It was Sister Clotilde, the nun who would eventually come to collect Annette and her brother. She took their father back to the convent on the Rue du Bac, where—conceivably mindful of the conversion of another Jew, Alphonse Ratisbonne, in 1842—she had him kiss the chair where the Virgin had first appeared to Catherine Labouré in July 1830.

With Sister Clotilde's help, the two elder boys were sent to an orphanage run by her order at L'Hay-les-Roses on the southern outskirts of Paris, and Muller then contacted a fellow Galician Jew named Israëlovitch, who, in Annette's words, "was collaborating with the Germans and Vichy police." For old times' sake and Muller's entire savings, Israëlovitch agreed to intervene with the authorities on the family's behalf. Israëlovitch was himself deported the next year, and did not return. Thus it was that in November 1942 two Jewish children found themselves kneeling beside a Catholic sister in front of "the sacred chair where the Immaculate Conception had sat," she in whose name so many of the excesses of Ultramontanism had been committed and who now— or so Sister Clotilde, at least, would have firmly believed—had intervened with a still higher authority on the children's behalf.

Jean, Henri, Annette, and Michel were reunited and spent the rest of the Occupation in an orphanage run by the order at Neuilly-sur-Seine, on the western outskirts of Paris, where, on Sister Clotilde's instructions, they suppressed their identity and all they had been through: "We were no longer Jews. Nothing had existed."[56] Shortly before they left the Rue du Bac, Sister Clotilde gave them each a miraculous medal and Annette wore hers on a thick chain around her neck. She, her father and brothers, but not her mother, had survived: there are some miracles that not even a miraculous medal can procure, even helped by a proverbially mercenary Jew named, with almost preternatural irony, Israëlovitch.

12

PURGING THE CITY
Paris Libre
(August 1944–October 1945)

Destined, in the space of little over a week, to turn the world of occupation and collaboration upside down, the Paris insurrection of August 1944 began, appropriately enough, with an act of inversion that was both dramatic and, given the protagonists' earlier record, ironic in the extreme: the city's police force went on strike.[1] Already on 14 July—which, curiously, continued to be commemorated, if not celebrated, under the Vichy regime—the police had done little to prevent or disperse the many demonstrations and meetings, reportedly involving over 100,000 participants, that had been held at various points in the city, including the Champs Elysées and the Place de la République, and in the Communist-dominated suburbs—Puteaux, Nanterre, Aubervilliers, Ivry, Villeneuve-Saint-Georges. After a further month of waiting as the Allied invading force moved steadily but, for Parisians, far too slowly eastward, the city's preponderantly Communist railway workers began an indefinite strike on 10 August, and on 15 August the three resistance movements within the Parisian police—the Communist Front National de la Police (the prime mover both now and later), the Socialist Police et Patrie, and the Gaullist Honneur de la Police[2]—decided, with the backing of the Comité Parisien de Libération (CPL), to call an all-out strike beginning the next day.

The CPL was the Parisian expression of the most representative and inclusive national resistance movement, the Conseil National de Résistance (CNR), which brought together the three leading factions within the Resistance: Communist, Socialist, Gaullist. Headed by the veteran Communist militant André Tollet, the CPL controlled, often more in name than in reality, the various factions that made up the local Forces Françaises de l'Intérieur (FFI), led by another Communist, Rol-Tanguy, a Breton-born metalworker and former member of the International Brigade in Spain, whose power base lay in the Parisian section of the Communist resistance movement, the Francs-Tireurs et Partisans (FTP).

The situation was complicated still further by the appointment, also on 14 August, of Alexandre Parodi as Parisian representative of de Gaulle's Gouvernement Provisioire de la République Française (GPRF), with clear instructions from the general that any insurrectional movement in Paris must remain subject to his overall control lest an autonomous and, by definition, Communist-dominated body take de facto command of the city: "I urge you always to speak out loudly and clearly in the name of the State," de Gaulle told his delegate-general in no uncertain terms. "The various forms of the Resistance are means. The State is above those forms."[3] Thus even before the outbreak of insurrection, tensions were present that would surface during and after the event.

The Communists wanted an autonomous, popular uprising, led by the FFI, with the FTP in their van, but involving the whole population organized in district-based local liberation committees, with the aim of liberating the city, if possible, before the arrival of the Allies. The concept owed much to the French revolutionary tradition of sections and clubs capped by a guiding vanguard of militants, though the later claim by their rivals that the Communists sought to establish a Commune-style authority in the city and so pass instantly, as the party's rallying cry had it, "from Resistance to Revolution" is unlikely in view of the opposition of both the party leader, Maurice Thorez (still in the Soviet Union, whither he had fled in 1939), and of Stalin to any such move. For their part, the noncommunists on the CPL were certainly not opposed to a unilateral uprising, but they saw it as operating in tandem with, and remaining ultimately subordinate to, the Allied advance, while the GPRF, in the person of Parodi, was determined that any insurrection should remain under its aegis and was anxious that no autonomous authority should constitute itself in Paris before Allied troops—and de Gaulle was determined that his own Forces Françaises Libres (FFL) should be first on the scene—were able to enter the city.

Over seventy years later, 1871 was on everyone's mind, either as extravagant dream or, as it turned out, equally extravagant fear, and, as we shall see, what gives August 1944 and its sequelae their particular feel is the conviction of all French parties to the event, resisters, collaborators, and liberators alike, that they were engaged in a reenactment of the revolutionary scenarios of the past, not just of *l'année terrible* but of 1848, 1830, and especially 1789–93. Never was Paris so steeped in historicism as during the Seven Glorious Days of August 1944, and never were historical precedents and parallels so frequently invoked as during the notably less glorious weeks and months that ensued.

On 16 August, 15,000 Parisian policemen went out on strike and, wearing civilian clothes, mixed with the population without initiating any insurrectional activity. Many, no doubt, were committed long-term resisters with no stain on their records, but many, too, must have taken part in the roundup of July 1942 and its successors and were anxious now, in a much-used expression of the time, to *se dédouaner,* to clear their names before the customs inspectors of the coming new order, by ostentatiously engaging in overthrowing the failing old order they had so cravenly served.

The police were quickly joined on strike by postal workers, nurses, and undertakers, the Metro ceased to operate, and in an atmosphere of impending upheaval, many agents, servants, and puppets of the Reich decided that the time had now come to head "to the East," meaning in their case first Alsace-Lorraine and then Germany itself. Laval, in Paris since 9 August, left on the 17th after presiding over the final meeting of his cabinet, his flight prompting droves of collaborators to follow in his wake. Collaborationist journalists were notably quick off the mark, and over the following days the wits and wags of the city made great play of asking at newspaper kiosks for the latest number of *Je suis parti* (loosely, "I'm outta here").[4]

Much against his will, Pétain was taken by the Germans from Vichy to Belfort on 20 August, and thence across the frontier to the spa town of Sigmaringen, just north of Lake Constance, where he would in due course be joined by the upper crust of the French ultraright—Jacques Doriot, Marcel Déat, Joseph Darnand, Fernand de Brinon, Jean Luchaire, Louis-Ferdinand Céline, Lucien Rebatet, as well as Laval—together with some 1,500 lesser collaborationist fry.[5]

For the moment, some 17,000 German soldiers remained stationed in Paris, under the command of the newly appointed general Dieter von Choltitz. His task, and theirs, was to confront a combined force of 20,000 Fifis, as members of the FFI were affectionately known, who between them possessed a paltry arsenal of 83 Bren guns, 86 submachine guns, 562 rifles, 825 pistols, 192 hand grenades, and a woefully limited ammunition supply.[6] Some FFI units were well trained and experienced, such as that in the southeast of the city led by the Communist Pierre Georges, famous throughout the Resistance movement as the Colonel Fabien who, in August 1941, had inflicted the first actual casualty on the occupying force when he gunned down a junior naval officer named Moser in the Metro station of Barbès-Rochechouart. Other units consisted of poorly armed amateur enthusiasts with little idea of what urban guerrilla warfare involved beyond the inevitable images of the barricaders, street urchins, and *pétroleuses* of *la Semaine sanglante,* all of whom would beget a numerous mid-twentieth-century progeny. Beyond these lay countless thousands of Parisians, unarmed, undisciplined, unpredictable, who, after four years of occupation, were awaiting only a sign to embark upon an urban equivalent of the mass uprising that in September 1792 had crushed a Prussian army at Valmy. Needless to say, this too was a parallel that was widely drawn at the time.[7]

The sign, and the start of the insurrection proper, came on the morning of Saturday, 19 August, when, with the backing of the CPL, 3,000 striking policemen stormed the Prefecture of Police—instantly and inevitably likened to the Bastille—where they confined Vichy's prefect of police, Bussières, to his quarters and installed the GPRF nominee, Luizet, in his place. The prefecture's central courtyard, named after Jean Chiappe, the right-wing prefect of police at the time of the Stavisky affair, was immediately rebaptized the Court of 19 August to signal, in the traditional manner, the break with the former order of things. A police band began to play the "Marseillaise" and a Tricolor bearing the Cross of Lorraine was hoisted on the flagpole, visible proof that some fundamental transformation, indeed a total inversion, of the status quo was at last under way.

As German tanks took up position on and around the Ile de la Cité, bands of Fifis, their nickname endowing them with "the lightness of birds,"[8] sped to take over as many mini-Bastilles as they could: the central Halles, the central post office on the Rue du Louvre, the central telephone exchange on the Rue de Grenelle, the gasworks at La Villette, as well as an assortment of ministries and *mairies* over which, in an essential gesture of symbolic reappropriation, the Tricolor was instantly flown. Bestowing of new names and restoration of Tricolor and "Marseillaise" to their former salience and meaning: already, by the end of day one of the uprising, the obvious but effective semiotics of liberation had been clearly established.[9]

Thanks to the mediation of the Swedish ambassador, a partial truce was concluded between the police in the prefecture and their German assailants, a move condemned by the Communists, who saw in it a check and a threat to the citywide uprising they longed for. Suspicion of the Communists' intentions led the historically minded Parodi to order the capture of the Hôtel de Ville by noncommunist members of the CPL first thing on the morning of 20 August, lest its balconies be used, as they had been in 1830, 1848, 1870, and 1871, to proclaim a new and inevitably radical regime that would already be in place when the Allies arrived. But the Gaullists were not opposed to popular insurrection in principle, only to a popular insurrection initiated and directed by Communist cadres, and it was a Gaullist official, Colonel de Marguerittes, Resistance name Lizé, who on 21 August gave the order for a general uprising, and specifically for the raising of barricades, the expression par excellence of the Parisian insurrectionary tradition.

By the 21st, the police had been off the streets for close to a week, and, in one of her remarkable memoirs of the time, Marguerite Duras describes driving a captured *milicien* (French member of the fascist *milice*) named Ter to the Chaussée d'Antin, where he was to be held pending almost certain execution at the hands of the Fifis, whose hardness of outlook comprehensively belied their feather-light acronym:

> The weather is beautiful, very bright. There are no police. The police fought alongside the people of Paris, and they have not yet resumed their functions since the Liberation of Paris. For three days, the streets have been without police. Cars full of FFI travel in all directions, along one-way streets as well, at breakneck speed, making generous use of the pavements when passing. A frenzy of disobedience, an intoxicating freedom, has taken hold of the people. Ter is fascinated by the speed of the cars, the number of cars, the guns protruding from their doors, glinting in the sun. "Let's make all we can of it," D. suddenly says, "there are still no police, that kind of thing happens only once in a century...." Ter turned toward D., who kept the revolver trained on him. And he laughed. "True enough, that."[10]

After Lizé's call to revolt, over 600 barricades almost instantly appeared in and around the center of the city, conjured up, as always in the past, as if by some anonymous collective magic, with particularly notable concentrations in the streets at the foot of the Boulevard Saint-Michel and in Huysmans's beloved Quartier Saint-Séverin, proof positive that, in the seventy or so years since the Commune, Parisians had lost none of their skills when it came to fashioning barricades out of the random raw materials offered by the streets of their city. In his novel *Au bon beurre* (1952), Jean Dutourd describes with typical irony one such barricade as a "pure objet d'art," utterly irrelevant in military terms, which its creators lovingly elaborate and extend, adjusting a chair or two here, adding some extra cobblestones there, making sure that the totemlike Tricolor is planted at a suitably evocative angle, taking every conceivable step to ensure that their masterpiece is a complete "commemorative reconstitution of the Revolution of 1848."[11]

Men, women, and children—likened automatically to so many Gavroches and Baras—commune with one another in erecting these extemporized monuments to the Parisian revolutionary tradition, affirming their common humanity, their shared Frenchness, above all their Parisianness, over and above divisions of age, sex, class, and political affiliation as, quite often in full consciousness of what they are doing, they set about emulating their forebears of 1789, 1830, 1848, and 1870–71. Like the dismantling of the Colonne Vendôme in May 1871, the barricades of August 1944 marked an apotheosis of *homo ludens parisianus*. The spirit of carnival and charivari were abroad as, for the first time in four years, the pleasure principle was free to express itself in the teeth of the self-denying Lenten discourse of Pétainism. Not for nothing did Sartre, in the series of reports he wrote for *Combat* at the time, speak of the barricades as constituting so many "little open-air popular clubs" in which, for perhaps the last time in Parisian history, the microcommunity of the *quartier* attained its maximum intensity.[12]

All the time that the inversion of the old order gained irresistible momentum in Paris, Allied forces, freed at last from major German resistance, were accelerating eastward. It was no part of Eisenhower's overall plan to capture Paris at this stage, lest it delay his advance and, furthermore, confront him with the invidious task of provisioning an increasingly malnourished population of millions. However, the outbreak of fighting and the fear, once again, that it might lead to the installation of a Communist-dominated paragovernment caused him to rethink his strategy and, with no little reluctance, to permit de Gaulle and the FFL to take possession of the city in advance of the main Allied thrust.

At 7:15 on the evening of 22 August, General Omar Bradley ordered the FFL's General Leclerc (Jacques-Philippe de Hautecloque) to move forward with his Second Armored Division, consisting of 15,000 men and 200 tanks, and, unaided, to take the French capital in the name of the GPRF. Advancing at great speed, on the afternoon of 23 August Leclerc reached Rambouillet, where he conferred with de Gaulle and arranged to rendezvous with him two days later at the Gare Montparnasse, so confident were both men now that the liberation of Paris was a fait accompli.

By the evening of the 24th, Leclerc was on the southern outskirts of the city and decided to send a small detachment of armored cars under Captain Raymond Dronne to test out the terrain in preparation for a full-scale advance the next day. Avoiding the main boulevards and so skirting the few remaining German strong points in the south of the city, around 8:45 P.M. Dronne reached the Hôtel de Ville, where he was greeted by Georges Bidault on behalf of the CNR and by Parodi for the GPRF. Even as Dronne made his way toward the Ile de la Cité, news of the impending liberation spread by a combination of word of mouth, bicycle couriers, and radio broadcast, the last transmitting an appeal to the capital's priests to ring the bells of their churches. At 9:10 P.M. the bells began to sound an enthralling citywide carillon, which shortly afterward the great bell of Notre-Dame brought to its height. For Parisians, deprived of the sound of church bells since the start of the war, it was the *In hoc signo vinces* for which they had been waiting. A witness wrote:

> It's over. Paris is freed.... On the evening of the 24th, at nightfall, the bells, all the bells of Paris, began to ring out. With an almost sacred emotion and with tears, genuine tears, I went out onto the balcony with my family; what resonance, what grandeur, what gravity, what joy to hear this formidable concert of more than a hundred steeples and bell towers in the mild shade of the immense capital city.... Robert comes home. We share our joy with each other. And then, suddenly, we hear a bell. A grave, splendid sound: the great bell of Notre-Dame. The sound swells and spreads in a beneficent wave over the suffering, still burning city. From our balcony we hear this voice that was silent for so long and that is reborn in liberated Paris. People talk to each other from window to window. General Leclerc is there; that is why the voice of our basilica is leaping across to us, above the fires of the capital below.[13]

As in Hugo's great campanological symphony in *Notre-Dame de Paris*, the bells bind the city's *quartiers* together as one, and the great bell of the cathedral consecrates the insurrection to God or to History, according to ideological taste, and calls all Parisians, whatever their faith, to commune with each other through the resurrected body of their city.

By presenting himself at the Hôtel de Ville, Dronne both confirmed the Gaullists in the CPL as the liberated city's accredited spokesmen and, at least for the time being, sidelined Rol-Tanguy and the FTP, even though they had without question been the insurrection's principal strike force. Leaving the Hôtel de Ville, Dronne then went over to the Prefecture of Police, which, despite the installation of a Gaullist (Luizet) as prefect, was still the unofficial headquarters of the more radical and romantic participants in the uprising.

One such romantic, though scarcely a radical, was the twenty-four-year-old Jean Dutourd, alias Commandant Arthur (after Rimbaud?), who, as it happened, was in the prefecture awaiting, like everyone else, the imminent arrival of the Second Armored Division. To Dutourd's surprise, the deus ex machina, when he eventually appears, is a short, thickset man with an intimidating air, clad in a khaki-green American uniform but sporting a French artillery kepi, swarthy, unshaven, with hands and face stained by the grease and grime of his tank. When it becomes clear that Dronne really is Leclerc's personal emissary, someone orders the police band to strike up the "Marseillaise," and everybody in the prefecture rushes over not so much to greet him as to touch him, so replete with significance is his mere presence among them:

> He was the first French soldier belonging to our little army from over the seas. He was welcomed like a prince, like Napoleon arriving from the island of Elba. He was more than a soldier; he was a symbol. In his person, *la France combattante* joined hands with *la France résistante,* free France with slave France. From that moment on, there were no longer two Frances but a single nation that was in the process of being reborn, that once again was going to be indivisible.[14]

Amidst all the brouhaha, Dutourd is struck by the fact that Dronne never once smiles. Despite his unprepossessing appearance, it is clear that he belongs to a different order of reality from that of the insurrectionary bandits who jostle to greet him, their bandoliers slung *zapatista*-style over their shoulders, their short red scarves and shirts open to the waist giving them an air of unruly boy scouts against the disciplined men of the FFL who are about to succeed them. By the evening of 24 August, the tank had taken over from the barricade and the Molotov cocktail, and though it took Dutourd and others several more days to realize it, the Fifis had already been consigned to the dustbin of revolutionary mythology.

Les voilà! On the morning of 25 August, columns of the Second Armored Division entered Paris from the south and west of the city, and by two in the afternoon all German resistance had ended. As the last swastikas were hauled down from the Palais du Luxembourg, the Hôtel Meurice, and the Hôtel Majestic, a huge Tricolor flew from the Arc de Triomphe, another from the Eiffel Tower, and at 3:30 P.M. Choltitz formally capitulated at the Prefecture of Police.

When Leclerc and de Gaulle made their prearranged meeting at the Gare Montparnasse, de Gaulle was furious and dismayed to discover not only that Rol-Tanguy's signature was featured on the act of capitulation but that, by oversight or sleight of hand, it actually appeared above Leclerc's. What de Gaulle then did testifies both to his clarity of purpose and to his remarkable sensitivity to the political meanings of place. Rather than heading directly, as everyone expected, for the Hôtel de Ville, de Gaulle went first to the Ministry of War, on the Rue Saint-Dominique in the seventh arrondissement, as befitted the last and—since Vichy was in his view both illegitimate and illegal—also the present minister of war of the French Third Republic. Apart from a band of occupying Fifis who were swiftly ejected, "nothing," de Gaulle would write in his *Mémoires de guerre,* "had changed in the interior of these venerable premises. All that was missing was the State, and it was my responsibility to restore it there to its place."

At the ministry de Gaulle received not the CNR or the CPL, and certainly not the leaders of the FFI or the FTP, but only his own nominees on the GPRF, Luizet and Parodi; it was, to reintroduce an earlier distinction, the beginning of the triumph of inside over outside. At his subordinates' insistence, de Gaulle reluctantly agreed to go to the Hôtel de Ville, pausing en route at the Prefecture of Police, which he thereby secured for the GPRF against any possibility of an FFI-FTP takeover; the dyarchy within *la France résistante* was decisively resolved in favor of its Gaullist component.

Arriving at the Hôtel de Ville, de Gaulle adamantly refused to heed Bidault's exhortation to "proclaim the Republic" in the traditional manner, from the balcony, for the very good reason, as he tersely explained, that "the Republic never ceased to exist." Then, raising his arms in the form of a V, de Gaulle addressed the vast crowd from the balcony, delivering, apparently off the cuff, one of the very greatest of his speeches, and in the process sidelining all the intermediary bodies, Gaullist, Communist, or whatever, that stood between him and the nation. In short, de Gaulle used the balcony of the Hôtel de Ville to proclaim not the Republic but the state, identified in the early-evening sunlight with his own massive person.[15]

The apotheosis of de Gaulle and the covert reinstallation of the state continued the following day with a triumphant procession along the Champs Elysées to Notre-Dame, with de Gaulle offering himself to the assembled multitude like some kind of sacrament of national unity, France made flesh, and reputedly growling "Back a little, sir, back a little" at any errant general or resistance leader who got even a step in front of him. Although many accounts, such as Simone de Beauvoir's in *La Force de l'âge* (1960), refer to that event not as "a military parade, but a popular carnival, disordered and magnificent,"[16] it is clear in retrospect that 26 August marked the end of the insurrectionary gala and that, even as Parisians reveled in what the autobiographer and anthropologist Michel Leiris (1901–90) characteristically called "the hurly-burly of a fiesta,"[17] the lineaments of a Lenten return to order and restraint were all the time being relaid about them. Interestingly, the phrase Leiris uses, *le tohu-bohu d'une fête,* takes over the Hebrew word for the waters of chaos from which, in Genesis 1:1, God draws forth the ordered cosmos of the heavens and earth. On 26 August 1944 Yahweh–de Gaulle created order about him even as he appeared to surrender to chaos, and no doubt, as he did so, he saw that it was good.

Outside and exposed, the general was actually preparing the return of power to the inside, and it was this that Dutourd had dimly glimpsed the previous day when, after observing the final stages of the victory on the streets, he had returned to a prefecture of police now very different from what it had been on the evening of the 24th:

> The prefect's salons were even more crowded than they had been the previous day. I noted that the number of elegant strangers had increased. Truly, peace was supplanting war, and it was impossible for me not to be saddened by that. Where had these young whippersnappers [*freluquets*] come from? I observed them without sympathy. They belonged to a world situated at the antipodes of mine. What had they done during the years of resistance? Nothing dangerous, certainly. They had hobnobbed [*coqueté*] with Vichy ministers, or prospered in the beneficent shadow of organizing committees. They were well bred and contemptuous; they wore fine blue pin-striped suits, silk ties, brilliantly polished shoes. It was for them that we had suffered so much, for them that our mates [*copains*] had died.[18]

As the men in suits take over from the man-boys in sweaty shirts and shorts, Dutourd has a sudden foretaste of the postwar world: "I understood how the combatants were going to be sidelined, how they were going to become impotent, moaning old veterans, full of memories and regrets. Our time was well and truly over."

De Gaulle's appearance at the prefecture shortly afterward on the way to his personal transfiguration at the Hôtel de Ville only strengthened this sense of a return to order. "I was struck by his size," writes the future Gaullist Dutourd, now seeing his hero-to-be for the first time, "by the height of his kepi, by his thinness, by the whiteness of his complexion, by the severity of his expression." The general showed little or no emotion, dispensed no words of congratulation or triumph. In everything he did, says Dutourd, he displayed a "horror of this *chienlit*" about him, an untranslatable but singularly well chosen word, derived from *chie-en-lit*, shitting in bed, and meaning, among other things, carnival revelry and masquerade. In the midsummer battle between Carnival and Lent, it was Lent, in the forbidding person of the thin, pale-faced Charles de Gaulle, that was already in charge even before the great city-wide carnival of 26 August.

All this makes it necessary to qualify Alain Brossat's seminal rereading of the Liberation as a carnivalesque ritual of reversal. No doubt, as Brossat brilliantly shows, August 1944 displays many of the features of the classic ritual of carnival, as analyzed by Mikhail Bakhtin, Emmanuel Le Roy Ladurie, and others:[19] the temporary displacement of the powerful by the powerless, the systematic squandering of accumulated riches and resources (buried bottles of vintage champagne and concealed hocks of ham in the case of the Seven Glorious Days), the release of pent-up frustrations taking now benign, now malignant expression, the triumph of Eros, Porneia, and Mimesis, sex, scatology, and masquerade, over the forces of Thanatos, the victory of youth over age, and so on and so on. At once archaic and modern, the Liberation was, as Brossat puts it so well, "a great ethnographic event," a "reactualization of the inexhaustible anthropological capital [*fonds*] of the feasts of youth of the past, carnivals and charivaris, kermesses and village fairs [*frairies*]."[20]

It was all these things, certainly, but, like the classic carnival itself, it was all the time unwittingly preparing its own eventual recuperation by a higher order than the discredited one it contested. Even as it challenged the castrating grandfather figure of Pétain,[21] it was preparing his replacement by the forbidding father figure de Gaulle, soon to be joined, after his return from the Soviet Union in November 1944, by the Communist leader Maurice Thorez, whose discourse, beneath the obvious ideological differences, was no less inimical to the spirit of carnival than that of Marshal Pénitence and General Carême themselves.[22]

So too with the constant, indeed obsessive, reference to the revolutionary past. "I was scarcely in 1944," wrote Dutourd twenty years after the event, "I was in '48 or in '71"[23]—and he was hardly a radical. On both right and left, and in the political center as well, everyone, it seemed, was reenacting some revolutionary scenario or another: the Hoche and Bara companies of the FTP, the Vendée as they hurled Molotov cocktails in the narrow streets on the Left Bank, collaborators terrified of Communists on the impromptu Committees of Public Safety that sprang up to judge them, even the GPRF's own delegate in Paris acclaiming a new Fête de la Fédération not confined to the Champ de Mars but spreading across the whole city.[24] No doubt this cult of the past, already well attested in 1848–51 and 1870–71,[25] spurred many Parisians to action, and is not to be decried in principle as mere revolutionary pageantry, an imitation of an imitation of an imitation. Nonetheless, it did render itself vulnerable to outflanking by another reading of French history, cold-headed, conservative, even cynical, such as that proposed—and acted upon—by de Gaulle.

"De Gaulle does not speak of the Commune," Marguerite Duras complains in *La Douleur*, written in April 1945 but not published until forty years later. "He says that the defeat of 1870 consecrated the existence of Germany-Prussia [*l'Allemagne prussienne*]. The Commune, for de Gaulle, enshrines that vicious tendency of the people to believe in its own existence, in its own strength." So be it, but de Gaulle's reading of history was both superior to and ahead of that of his critics. While romantics and radicals were still celebrating their version of the Fête de la Fédération, de Gaulle was already thinking of Thermidor, and as they went around Paris in search of Vichyist Colonnes Vendôme to demolish, he was working to avoid any possible reprise of the *Semaine sanglante*. Finally, Notre-Dame, the sound of whose great bell ringing out on the evening of 24 August had conferred a properly sacred quality on the task of liberating the city, had, by the 26th, been co-opted into the Gaullist project, and by April 1945 Duras is to be found bitterly citing a sermon given from its pulpit: "Popular uprisings, general strikes, barricades, etc. It would make a very fine film. But is that anything but a theatrical revolution? A true, profound, durable change? Look at 1789, 1830, 1848. After a period of violence and a few revolutionary tremors, the people get weary and have to go back to work and earn their living." Whence the conclusion: "When it comes to containing [*quand il s'agit de ce qui cadre*], the Church does not hesitate, it approves."[26] Whether as tragedy or as farce, history really does repeat itself, but always to the advantage of the powerful. As in 1830–34, 1848–51, 1870–71, so in 1944–45: the bright tomorrow was being closed off and silenced by the very forces that popular insurrection had brought to power.

Thanks in large measure to Choltitz's evident reluctance to make a fight of it, the Liberation of Paris was probably as uncostly in terms of lives lost as it could have been: 2,887 Germans killed as opposed to 1,482 French, 582 of these being civilians.[27] Nor, contrary to widespread myth, was there any massive bloodletting in the wake of the Liberation, either in Paris or in France as a whole. All the best calculations[28] give a total figure for the whole of France of some 9,000 killed during the so-called *épuration sauvage* (savage purge: summary judgments and executions, improvised courts-martial, and individual score settling and reprisals) of 1944–45. A quarter of these deaths took place before the Allied landing on 6 June 1944, a further half between then and the Liberation, and only the remaining quarter afterward. The purge was more of a southern than a northern phenomenon, more rural than urban, and was restricted in scale and severity in Paris first by the flight of large numbers of collaborators and irregulars soon after the police strike began and then by the briefness of the hiatus between the end of German control and the installation of the GPRF, which moved quickly to round up potential victims of wildcat justice and, somewhat more slowly, to set up the appropriate judicial machinery for dealing with suspected collaborators.

The remnants of the German occupying force were, in the main, subject more to derision and humiliation (being forced, for example, to parade, charivari-style, with toilet brushes for guns over their shoulders)[29] than to outright violence. Dutourd recalls seeing a file of German soldiers on the Rue de Rivoli, hands above their heads in what wags called "a double Nazi salute," literally trembling with fear as the crowd spat and punched at them, despite the efforts of their Fifi escort, and of Dutourd himself, to protect them.[30] *Miliciens,* most of them young like Duras's Ter, were in a far more vulnerable position, and there are reports—no doubt exaggerated but almost certainly based on fact—of improvised prisons on the Boulevard de Courcelles, the Boulevard Haussmann, and the dental school on the Avenue de Choisy in the thirteenth arrondissement, where collaborators were held, possibly tortured (there are ominous allusions to dentistry), and some of them almost certainly executed.[31] Perhaps the *miliciens* whom Sartre saw on the Rue de Buci with their trousers down and being treated to an energetic spanking by passers-by were fortunate that they were taken away, trousers still around their ankles, in a police van rather than in a truckload of Fifis.[32]

The most infamous example of instant revenge concerned women accused of having practiced "horizontal collaboration" with the enemy. The phenomenon of *la tonte*, the shearing—the ritual cropping of the hair of the women so accused, usually accompanied by partial or total stripping, inscribing of swastikas in black paint on heads or breasts, and similar disfigurements—is a national rather than merely a Parisian scandal. Rather than remaking, after so many others, the obvious points concerning the frequent injustice of the charges and the invariable obscenity of the punishment, we should perhaps, again following Alain Brossat, stress the *limits* to the popular vindictiveness involved.[33] With

its improvised scaffold, the *toilette* of the victim, and other accompany-
ing rituals, *la tonte* resembled a guillotining, minus actual decapitation.
It is as though the people doing the shearing and the crowd egging them
on and vilifying the shorn woman nonetheless recognize their kinship
with her and, seeing that her horizontal collaboration is only a variant
on their own forms of complicity with the occupier, do not push their
desire for vengeance to its logical conclusion. For the women who underwent it, *la tonte* was without doubt "a fate worse than death," yet its
effect, paradoxically, was to preserve them from death at the hands of
the mob they might otherwise have fallen prey to.

More justified and scarcely less publicized was the widespread detes-
tation of what we might call chic collaboration: the open "cosying up,"
as Isaiah Berlin, a frequent visitor to post-Liberation Paris, once put it,[34]
to the Germans on the part of large portions of *le tout Paris*— actors
(Sacha Guitry, Arletty, Danielle Darrieux), singers (Tino Rossi), night-
club owners (Suzy Solidor), fashion designers (Coco Chanel), restaura-
teurs (the owner and headwaiter of Maxim's), and dancers (Serge
Lifar)—all of whom found themselves at odds with the public or the authorities (or both) after the Liberation. Guitry and Rossi were imprisoned at Fresnes, which resisters came to regard as some kind of extension
of Le Bœuf sur le Toit, before being released. Others who with much less
justification found themselves being harassed were Mistinguett, Edith
Piaf, Maurice Chevalier, Fernandel, and the filmmaker Henri-Georges
Clouzot. It did no good for society women who had enjoyed dubious
sleeping arrangements under the occupier to protest, in a famous joke of
the time, that their "asses might be international, but their hearts were
French."[35] In the late summer and autumn of 1944, while the public in
general remained remarkably lenient toward Pétain himself,[36] there was
a widespread desire for emblematic victims of note, and anyone in the
public eye guilty of even a hint of complicity with the enemy was likely to
be singled out as a target for the resentments, frustrations, and, not least,
the suppressed sense of guilt abroad in society at large.

In the wake of the Liberation, the new authorities arrested up to
10,000 suspected collaborators, most of whom, in a macabre inversion
of the old order, found themselves interned at some point in the Vel'
d'Hiv' or at Drancy. Those with a sense of history took sardonic pleasure in being incarcerated in the prison on the Quai de l'Horloge close
to the Conciergerie, where royalist victims of the Terror had spent their
last days. Pierre Taittinger, owner of the Grands Magasins du Louvre
and Vichyite president of the Paris Municipal Council, found himself in
the cell occupied by Archbishop Darboy before his execution in May

1871.[37] Everywhere historically minded collaborators lived in fear of latter-day September massacres. The problem was that most of those arrested were relative small fry—*lampistes,* in the expression of the time, subalterns who might be strung up from a lamppost while their far guiltier superiors escaped scot-free. Most of the leading figures at Vichy and almost all of the prominent Paris-based French fascists had fled to Germany, where they continued to live out their fantasy role as a government-in-exile in Sigmaringen castle.

One substantially represented category of internee was well known to the authorities, the Resistance, and the public at large: writers, journalists, and broadcasters who, unlike many other suspected collaborators, particularly industrialists and civil servants, had incriminated themselves in their writings or public statements. In some cases, there was no doubt at all as to the accuseds' record under the Occupation. Drieu La Rochelle and Brasillach had collaborated quite openly, and both were in Paris (Brasillach in Fresnes, Drieu still at large after two botched suicide attempts). In the absence of bigger names, such as Céline, Lucien Rebatet, and Alphonse de Chateaubriant (all in Germany), lesser figures were the first to be judged.

More dubious, and far more extensive in number than the open collaborators, were the writers who were held to have cautioned Vichy or the Occupation with what they had written, who had published in the "wrong" journals (notably the *Nouvelle Revue Française,* which Drieu had edited with German support) or with the "wrong" publishing house—and here the list was a long and important one, since both Gaston Gallimard and Bernard Grasset stood accused of collaboration—or whose themes, ideas, and views were held to be broadly congruent with this or that aspect of Vichy ideology. At one or another time, and with more or less justice, all of the following were victims of either open accusation or sustained whispering campaigns from which they emerged legally innocent but with their personal and artistic reputations besmirched: Jean Giono, Colette, Henry de Montherlant, Claudel (whose "Homage au Maréchal Pétain" of 1941, followed three years later by a similar verse paean to de Gaulle, stuck in many a throat), Jouhandeau, Paul Léautaud, and Paul Morand. Morand was exculpated as a writer but found guilty for his record as a diplomat, and would spend the next thirty years just across the Swiss frontier at Vevey.

No doubt the ardor with which these and other writers were pursued, most avidly by fellow authors, owed much to the fact that so many writers and intellectuals in the opposed political camp had died at the hands of the Germans or Vichy, either as Jews, such as Max Jacob, or as members of the Resistance: the medieval historian Marc Bloch (1886–1944), the Marxist philosopher Georges Politzer (1903–42), the critic and novelist Jean Prévost (killed at the Vercors in 1944), Jacques Decour (academic and founder of *Les Lettres Françaises,* the leading journal of the literary resistance), and, perhaps most tragic of all, the poet and former Surrealist Robert Desnos (1900–1945), news of whose death at the concentration camp of Terezin in Czechoslovakia in June 1945 reached Paris just as the final round of "media trials" got under way. In the age of "committed literature," when so many writers had suffered or died for what they had written, writers who had, or could be seen to have, committed themselves to the wrong side, or who had not committed themselves openly at all, could expect little mercy in an atmosphere that wanted culprits—any culprits—to be called to account.

The first writer to be tried (23 October 1944) and executed (9 November) was the otherwise little known Georges Suarez (54), who, on the basis of articles written for the periodical *Aujourd'hui,* of which he was editor, was found guilty, in the words of his prosecutor, of being *embauché* (in the hire of) and *emboché* (Germanized by) the Reich.[38] He was followed by, among others, the naval historian Paul Chack, a member of the Antibolshevik Action Committee and other fascist or fascistic organizations, executed in January 1945 after de Gaulle refused to commute his sentence; and by the journalist Henri Béraud, who before the war had been responsible, in the pages of *Gringoire,* for so hounding the Popular Front's interior minister, Roger Salengro, on account of his alleged desertion from the army in 1915, that Salengro had committed suicide in November 1936.[39] Béraud continued his pro-German, antisemitic outpourings during the Occupation, but de Gaulle commuted his sentence from death to hard labor for life on the grounds that, unlike Suarez and Chack, he had not actively colluded with the enemy.

The first major figure to come before the courts was the thirty-five-year-old Robert Brasillach, whose trial began on 19 January 1945. Brasillach's record, both before and during the Occupation, on *Je suis partout, Révolution nationale, La Gerbe,* and other fascist publications was known to all, and he made no real attempt to defend himself. He won the respect of no less an observer than Simone de Beauvoir for the way in which, through his bearing, he was able to transform himself from *bourreau* into victim. "We desired the death of the editor of *Je suis partout,*" she wrote in February 1946, "not that of this man ready to die well. The more the trial took on the appearance of a ceremony, the more it seemed scandalous that it could lead to an actual spilling of blood."[40] After an appeal for clemency signed by, among others, Paul Valéry,

François Mauriac, Paul Claudel, Georges Duhamel, Jean Anouilh, Jean Paulhan, Jean Cocteau, and Albert Camus (the last on the grounds of his hostility in principle to capital punishment) was turned down by de Gaulle, Brasillach won further respect for his courageous and dignified bearing at the Fort of Montrouge, where he was shot on 6 February 1945, eleven years to the day after the riots on the Place de la Concorde had first brought him to fame. He was not the first, nor would he be the last, collaborator able to turn trial and execution to his own martyrological advantage, casting himself, notably in his final prison writings from Fresnes, as some kind of holocaustal offering to History.

With considerably less dignity, the seventy-six-year-old Charles Maurras was sentenced at Lyon in January 1945 to solitary confinement for life, plus the newly devised punishment of *indignité nationale,* for repeated pro-German stances and utterances during the Occupation. "C'est la revanche de Dreyfus [It's Dreyfus's revenge]!" he shouted out on learning the verdict, as blind to the changed political circumstances as he was physically deaf to the trial he had just sat through.[41]

On 16 March 1945, just as the first political trials were about to begin before the newly created High Court of Justice in Paris, came the news of the death the previous day of the most famous writer-collaborator of all. As early as the Allied landing in North Africa in November 1942, Drieu had realized that the Axis cause was lost, and his actions and writings over the next two and a half years reveal him to be obsessed with realizing, in his words, "a death worthy of the revolutionary and reactionary that I am."[42] A "neither right nor left" fascist of the classic kind, his ideological purity untainted by the real world of political choices, Drieu accused the Nazis, to say nothing of their French imitators, of never having been "true" fascists, of being "bourgeois" reformers who were ultimately afraid and unwilling to challenge, in the name of socialist-fascist internationalism, the twin enemies of capitalism and nationalism. "I long for the triumph of totalitarian man over the world," he wrote as the Allies advanced toward Paris, claiming, in all seriousness, that he was a "communist" at heart and that he wanted to fight "with the Russians" to prevent an American takeover of Europe. Above all Drieu wanted to die, and to die well. He had, as he recognized, always wanted to die, and the *Récit secret* that he wrote in the last months of his life explores his lifelong obsession with suicide and death, the mystic-erotic allure of self-annihilation, the desire to offer himself up, as Brasillach had done, as a sacrificial hostage to History.

In mid-1943 Drieu began seriously to plan his own death. In November that year he went to Switzerland and ostentatiously returned in order to prove, to himself and to others, that he could, if he wished, escape the impending disaster: his death was to be wholly voluntary, a willed holocaustal sacrifice and transfiguration of the self into the Self as the mystical texts that Drieu was reading—Meister Eckhardt, the Upanishads, the *Sophar,* the Tao—enjoined. On 11 August 1944, when most collaborators were already preparing their flight, Drieu told a friend whom he met on the Place des Invalides near his home that he was going to leave *proprement*—properly, cleanly—by which he plainly did not mean joining the exodus to Germany. After a final walk through the neighborhood—one wonders whether he crossed the Seine to the Place de la Concorde, that Saint Peter's Square of French fascism—he returned to his ninth-floor flat on the Avenue de Breteuil, where, after apparently making love to an unnamed woman and spending two hours reading mystical texts in which, he said in one of several farewell letters, he found "a joy beyond joy," he took what should have been a lethal dose of luminal, possibly given to him by his first wife, a doctor, at the beginning of the Occupation. But, just as Drieu had botched his whole life, so he was fated to botch the act of final self-annihilation that was supposed to metamorphose his existence into destiny.

What followed was anything but the "proper" departure he had planned. On the morning of 12 August, his cook returned to the flat to collect the handbag she had left the previous day and, finding Drieu unconscious but still alive, arranged for him to be taken to the Hôpital Necker, close by. There his life was saved, and on 15 August, the day the police strike began, he was being transferred, still unconscious, to another hospital by ambulance when it ran out of gas on the Boulevard Delessert, in the seventeenth arrondissement. By coincidence or design, the driver of the ambulance was his first wife, Colette Jeramec; still more remarkably, his second wife, Alexandra Sienkiewicz, happened to be driving past at the time and was able to provide enough gas for the ambulance to take its comatose passenger—who had titled one of his novels *L'Homme couvert de femmes*—on to the hospital. As soon as he recovered consciousness, Drieu tried to commit suicide again, this time by slashing his wrists. This effort too he botched. Staggering to a washbasin to make the blood flow faster with cold water from the tap, he swooned, lost his balance, and, grabbing at his bed as he fell, accidentally pressed the call button. A nurse arrived, and the second suicide attempt, like the first, was aborted.

On recovering, Drieu went into hiding in an apartment on the Rue de Grenelle owned by a Professor René Lagroux. In October 1944, as the purge gathered momentum about him, he secretly left Paris for a country villa at Orgeval, to the northwest of the city, belonging to an American woman, Noël Murphy, whom, thanks to his German contacts, he had been able to save from internment in 1942. Here he worked on his final, uncompleted novel, *Mémoires de Dirk Raspe,* based on the life and death of that other *suicidé de la société,* Vincent van Gogh. When his presence became known, he moved to his first wife's country house at Chartrettes, near Melun, to the southeast of Paris.

At the beginning of March 1945, Drieu was back in Paris, staying at Colette Jeramec's laboratory on the Rue Staint-Ferdinand in the seventeenth arrondissement. By now the purge was closing in on Drieu, in the person of the redoubtable Communist journalist Madeleine Jacob (Céline, another of her prime targets, called her the muse of the charnel house), who told the American reporter Janet Flanner day after day, "I'll have your boyfriend's head."[43] But Drieu was bent, in effect, on purging himself. In a projected speech in his defense—a speech he must have realized he would never deliver—he declared himself to be "an internationalist and revolutionary" and urged his accusers to

> be true to the pride of the Resistance as I am true to the pride of the Collaborators. Do not cheat me any more than I am cheating you. Sentence me to death. Yes, I am a traitor. Yes, I worked with the enemy. I offered the enemy French intelligence. It is no fault of mine if this enemy was not intelligent. Yes, I am no ordinary patriot, no limited nationalist: I am an internationalist. I am not only a Frenchman, I am a European. You are European too, whether you know it or not. But we played and I lost. I demand the death penalty.[44]

On 15 March 1945 Drieu finally became the Baudelairean *héautontimorouménos,* the self-executioner that temperament and history had fated him to be, and, to make doubly sure this time he would not fail, swallowed three tubes of gardenal in his first wife's laboratory and turned on the gas, having already famously specified that there should be "no men except Malraux" at his funeral.[45] Even so, he was still only in a coma when Dr. Jeramec discovered him, but he died an hour later. Paradoxically, Drieu's death, the grotesque Grand Guignol character of which few can have known, would transform him, the archfascist, the traitor, into a model of existential authenticity, the emblematic committed-writer-who-dies-for-his-cause: "He made a mistake, but he was sincere, he proved it," Sartre would write with unfeigned admiration in *Qu'est'ce que la littérature?* three years after Drieu's death.[46]

The media trials continued after Drieu, notably with the convictions of the broadcasters Paul Ferdonnet (executed 4 August 1945) and Jean Hérold-Paquis (executed 13 October 1945). In what seems a gratuitous act of vindictiveness, Hérold-Paquis's secretary, Simone Delb, was sentenced to hard labor for life.[47] But as the Allies advanced into Germany, bigger fish were becoming available, though some leading collaborators would escape retribution completely, either through death like "Grand Jacques" Doriot (shot in his car on the open road by two planes, Allied in one account, German in another, leading to claims by fellow fascists that he had "offered himself as a sacrifice" on the altar of Franco-German solidarity)[48] or through flight: Marcel Déat to Italy, where he died in 1955; Darquier de Pellepoix to Spain; Céline, another unreconstructed Holocaust denier, to Denmark, whence he returned with a pardon in 1951, dying ten years later; and Alphonse de Chateaubriant, who died in a Swiss monastery later in 1945. Darnand and Laval managed briefly to escape, Darnand to Italy, where he was captured disguised as a monk, Laval to Barcelona, whence he was extradited by Franco.

Pétain, alone and self-deluded to the last, made no attempt to avoid apprehension, and despite offers of asylum in Switzerland, where he had reluctantly allowed himself to be taken, freely crossed the Franco-Swiss frontier at Verrières-sur-Joignes on 26 April 1945 and surrendered to General Koenig, the Free French victor of Bir-Hakeim, in person. Stones were thrown at the train in which Pétain and his wife were then conveyed to Paris, and at Pontarlier 2,000 demonstrators gathered to chant "Shoot the old traitor!" and "Pétain-Bazaine to the stake!" The reference, now almost automatic in the Communist press, was to the French marshal who had infamously surrendered to the Prussians at Metz in October 1870, allegedly after doing a deal with Bismarck to use his army against the Socialists in Paris: one can see why the analogy appealed to L'Humanité. The 1945 May Day parades were duly transformed into a mass demonstration against the bicephalous bogeyman Pétain-Bazaine (or Bazaine-Pétain), as was the annual march to the Mur des Fédérés on 28 May.[49] L'Humanité demanded that "a sacred hatred, a living hatred, an efficacious hatred" be visited upon the eighty-nine-year-old ex-head of the Etat Français,[50] who, for the time being, remained interned, reputedly in deluxe conditions, with two nuns to look after him, at the Fort of Montrouge, to the south of the city.

As the first deportees began to return from the East in the first weeks of May, leaving all who saw them distraught by their appearance,[51] anti-Pétain feeling began inexorably to mount. In September 1944, only 32 percent of those polled had wanted Pétain even to be tried, and a mere 3 percent wanted him executed. But by May 1945 public hostility, which at the Liberation had been directed almost entirely against the "dauphin," Laval (for whom 65 percent favored the death penalty in October 1944), now gathered around King Pétain as well: close to 40 percent wanted him sentenced to death, with only 20 percent favoring acquittal.[52] It was like a speeded-up rerun of 1789–93. The "people," whose anger had initially been targeted at the king's ministers (and, in the earlier instance, his wife), now wanted the monarch himself—and, as we shall see, in the history-obsessed climate of 1944–45 there were plenty of people, at least on the right, who saw explicit analogies between what was happening to Pétain and the fate of Louis the Last in 1792–93.

The principle of bringing Vichy leaders to trial had already been established and acted upon before the Liberation of France. In March 1944, the former Vichy interior minister Pierre Pucheu had been put on trial in Algiers, accused of, among other things, having personally selected the hundred or so hostages—mainly Communists, but including the Catholic naval officer and resister Honoré d'Estienne d'Orves—whom the Germans had shot in Châteaubriant (Loire-Atlantique), Mont-Valérien, and elsewhere in October 1941 in retaliation for Fabien's killing of the junior naval officer Moser; he was also widely believed to have been present at the interrogation of Georges Politzer before his death. Pucheu was executed on 20 March 1944, but his courageous demeanor—he shook the hand of each member of his firing squad and personally gave the order to fire—showed how readily humiliation might be transformed into martyrdom.[53]

Martyrdom and expiatory self-sacrifice had, of course, defined the whole of Pétain's political and moral project ever since the far-off days of June 1940, when he had made France "the gift of his person." Suffering vicariously for France, he asked the French to suffer with him in order to atone for and remedy the individual and collective sins that had brought disaster on the nation. No regime since the Restoration, not even General MacMahon's "moral order" of the 1870s, also born of the experience of defeat and social dislocation, had made such openly political use of the figure of Christ as Vichy did or had so valorized the themes of crucifixion and redemptive suffering. Vichy ideology explicitly cast Pétain as, in the words of one encomiast, a "new Christ" who had "sacrificed himself in order to make possible ... the redemption of defeated France."[54] Even Charles Spinasse, a former minister of the Popular Front and a Freemason to boot, opined that the "crucifixion" of democratic institutions was "necessary to prevent the country from succumbing to violence and anarchy."[55] For four years Pétain had addressed the French as a composite father or grandfather figure—a mixture, in Gérard Miller's scathing terms, of Père Fouettard, Père Gâteau, and a "sad Père Noël"—who offered his "children" succor and protection provided only that they suffer and submit: "No, it is not in vain that we labor; no, it is not in vain that we weep; no, it is not in vain that we suffer.... Happy the suffering that will win us salvation."[56] Having refused to abandon his children in 1940, this aging man of sorrows had now voluntarily returned to them for judgment. It was not just monarchy reincarnate that was to be tried in the person of "Philippe VII," it was, in the view of his supporters, someone not far below Christ himself who was to be hauled before the assorted high priests and Pontius Pilates of the Resistance.

On 22 July 1945, Pétain was brought by police van from Montrouge to the Ile de la Cité, where he would be interned throughout the trial at 34 Quai d'Orfèvres, directly adjoining the Palais de Justice.[57] The Communist press had campaigned loudly for Pétain to be tried "in the presence of the people" at a spacious venue like the Palais Bourbon or the Palais du Luxembourg, but de Gaulle, in a variation on the inside-outside theme, had ordered that the trial take place in semiprivate in a court of the Palais de Justice so small that journalists had literally to sit on each other's lap in order to report it. At 2 P.M. on the afternoon of the 23d, Pétain made his entrance, wearing a khaki uniform set off by a single decoration, France's highest, the *médaille militaire,* and holding his triple-oak-leaf kepi in one hand and in the other a white paper scroll, his prepared statement; to Jules Roy (1907–2000), who was present throughout the trial, it looked like a substitute for the marshal's baton he was now, of course, forbidden to bear. Standing, aged but visibly in good health, to be charged under the name of Henri-Philippe-Bénoni-Omer Pétain, he reminded Roy of "King Lear hounded from his own palace";[58] although Roy was no Pétainist, the comparison recurs at intervals throughout his account.

The High Court of Justice, set up by decree in November 1944 with the specific purpose of trying major collaborators, was presided over by Judge Paul Mongibeaux, who, like most of his colleagues, had taken the oath of loyalty to Pétain in 1941 and applied Vichy legislation apparently without qualm or question. The prosecution was in the hands of Maître André Mornet, well known as the prosecutor of spies (including Mata Hari), deserters, and mutineers in World War I, who had not taken the oath of loyalty but had requested—fortunately for him without success—to be included in the team prosecuting Edouard Daladier and Léon Blum

The trial of Philippe Pétain at the Palais de Justice, July–August 1945. In this, the only known photograph of the proceedings, Pétain is seated at the center-right of the courtroom, with his marshal's kepi on the table before him. (Reproduced by permission of the Centre de Documentation Juive Contemporaine, Paris.)

at Vichy's show trial of Third Republic politicians, held, with disastrous consequences for Vichy's image, at Riom in 1942. The special jury consisted of twenty-four "good men and true" (at least as far as the prosecution was concerned), twelve of them chosen from among the members of Parliament who in June 1940 had not voted for the abolition of the Third Republic, and twelve others selected from a panel of accredited resisters. A packed jury, a judge and prosecutor eager to deny or expunge their ambiguous record under Vichy, inadequate defense access to crucial documentation, hasty and biased pretrial investigation: it is not difficult to see why, in 1945 and ever since, Pétainists have disputed the validity of their hero's trial. On the other hand, the marshal's supporters bombarded the jurors with hate mail and worse, making it necessary to check their food each day for possible poisoning and even, at one stage, to issue them guns for their own protection.

It is not necessary to follow here Pétain's trial in any great detail. After delivering his prepared opening statement, in which he cast himself as France's shield acting in conjunction with de Gaulle's sword for the nation's ultimate deliverance, Pétain refused to take further part in the proceedings, thus earning the nickname Motusalem in *Le Canard enchaîné*, an untranslatable pun based on *motus* ("mum's the word") and Mathusalem (Methusaleh).[59] A procession of Third Republic politicians—Blum, Daladier, Paul Reynaud, Albert Lebrun—appeared like ghosts from an age gone by to testify before the court to Pétain's treachery. *L'Humanité*'s anti-Pétain rhetoric became more and more inflammatory, deploying the same sacrificial logic that Robespierre and Saint-Just had used against Louis XVI: "We demand the death sentence for Bazaine-Pétain. Justice requires it. Morality requires it. The Nation requires it. Death to the sinister old man so that the youth of France can live. Death to Pétain so that France can live."[60] Correspondingly, and inversely, Pétain's supporters worked to promote the Christ-king analogy. A secretly circulated prayer implicitly compared the marshal with Christ, to whom it addressed the following petition, to be accompanied by a decade of beads on the rosary:

> Lord Jesus, if, in thy infinite wisdom, thou permittest that thy servant be misunderstood [*méconnu*] and condemned as thou wert thyself by official justice and by the justice of the people who preferred Barabbas to thee, thy will be done! We know that when thou demandest of one of thy servants that he mount the Cross, it is not because thou abandonest him, but because thou lovest him. Receive then this sacrifice for the world and for France![61]

References to Pétain's self-elected and self-imposed "crown of thorns" became almost routine,[62] and Jacques Isorni, Pétain's youthful defense counsel, deployed the full range of historical-sacrificial analogies when he addressed the marshal—to whom he had, inevitably, promised "the gift of his person"—privately in the following terms:

> Remain the same. You are still marshal of France and chief of state. You must become so once more. Have you forgotten the trial of Joan of Arc, the captivity of the emperor on Saint Helena, the trial of Louis XVI? Millions of French people think unceasingly of you. For them you remain a symbol, an ideal.[63]

But Pétain had no more chance before the High Court of Justice, or so his supporters would claim, than Joan before her judges at Rouen, Louis before Robespierre and Saint-Just, or—pushing the Christological image to its near-sacrilegious extreme—Jesus before Annas, Caiaphas, and the Sanhedrin. On 15 August 1945—the same day the war ended with news of the capitulation of Japan—Pétain was duly found guilty and condemned to death, all the Resistance jurors voting in favor and all but three of the parliamentarians voting against. The jury also recommended, however, that in view of Pétain's great age, the death penalty not be carried out, a rider that "Charles XI"—de Gaulle, who would have preferred Pétain not to be tried—was happy to accept.

By coincidence, 15 August was also the Feast of the Assumption and the anniversary of Louis XIII's consecration of France to the Virgin in 1638, as well as, unofficially, la Saint-Napoléon, the anniversary of Napoleon's birth. At midnight on the 14th/15th, Pétain, close now to the Church after a freethinking past, attended a private mass in his cell, and Roy—who was, to repeat, no Pétain cultist—imagined the occasion as the marshal's own personal assumption into History.[64] Having heard the verdict, he was taken by ambulance in the late afternoon of the 15th—a decoy of police vehicles having left the Quai d'Orfèvres in advance—to the airport of Villacoublay and flown in de Gaulle's own Cross of Lorraine–bearing Dakota to Pau, where he was interned at the Fort du Portalet in the same cell—number 5—in which the former Popular Front minister Georges Mandel had been imprisoned on his orders in July 1940.[65] From there he was in due course transferred to the Ile d'Yeu, off the coast of the Vendée. (True to its obsession with "Pétain-Bazaine," the Communist press would have preferred the island of Sainte-Marguerite, off Cannes, where Bazaine had earlier expiated his "treachery.") Pétain was interned at the Fort de la Pierre-Levée, so called because it was built on the site of a menhir, and Madame Pétain took up lodgings at the island's only hotel and visited him each day at the permitted hour.[66]

Disavowed by his home village of Cauchy-à-la-Tour in the Artois, refused permission to be buried in the remains of the fort of Douaumont at Verdun, Pétain remained on this mock–Saint Helena of an island until, Motusalem to the end, he died at the age of ninety-five in July 1951. Despite a long campaign—and at least one attempt (in 1973) by a far-right commando to steal and "repatriate" his remains[67]—he has not been reburied at Verdun, since this move would undoubtedly be interpreted as a rehabilitation by the state. As we have seen, however, his ostracizing by most of the nation he claimed to protect did not prevent an annual wreath being placed on his grave on the orders of a president of the Republic whose record under Vichy is as clouded and contradictory, if not as his, then at least as that of the president and prosecuting counsel of the court that condemned him.

After King Philippe came the turn of the dauphin. Extradited from Spain, Laval had already testified at his superior's trial, prompting Madeleine Jacob to fresh heights of vindictive glee: "Pierre Laval! Philippe Pétain! Under our eyes at one and the same time and both of them captive! There they are reunited, uniformed shame and shame in a gray suit...."[68] Fiddling continually with his famous white tie— "What is Laval?" General Maxime Weygand once asked "A tie."[69]— Laval refused to be cast as the evil genius of Pétain, the scapegoat's scapegoat, as it were, and did his utmost to make Pétain responsible for the crucial policy decisions. Pétain, for his part, claimed to have experienced "a very violent reaction" when he heard Laval proclaim, in his infamous radio broadcast of June 1942, "I desire victory for Germany, for without it communism will soon have established itself everywhere in Europe."[70]

Laval's own trial, opening on 5 October 1945, appeared at the time, and appears still more so in retrospect, as a total antithesis of Pétain's. Whereas Pétain had maintained almost without interruption a dignified silence, Laval, a lawyer, spoke in his own defense, and spoke interminably, garrulously, colloquially, even addressing as *tu* the parliamentary jurors he knew, until abruptly absenting himself in mid-trial. Unlike Pétain, who had his defense team and substantial support both inside and outside the courtroom, Laval was completely alone, rejected by everyone except his own family. "There is this fellow [*type*] alone in the middle of a large room," wrote Claude Roy, another former rightist who had moved to the left, "a life-size character no longer on a par with the hatred that weighs on him." What was being conducted was not a trial but a "sacrilegious Punch and Judy show [*guignol*] performed by bad actors," in which accusers and accused belonged to the same world and were, indeed, one as guilty as the other:

We expected a trial, it's a settling of accounts that's beginning. It's not France that's putting Laval on trial, but his brothers, one wants to say his accomplices. What with his ermine robe and his tuft of hair on his lower lip like Napoleon III [*son impériale*], the first president of the court looks like a bearded woman [*femme à barbe*] in a fur coat. For his part, the public prosecutor [*procureur*] in his red robe reminds one of those characters whom department stores get to dress up as Father Christmas.... What France cannot forgive Laval is the fact that he never said no. And before him, to judge and interrogate him, are two men who have spent their whole lives saying yes.[71]

With the Resistance jurors almost entirely Communists, there was never any doubt that Laval would be convicted and condemned to death, with, needless to say, no recommendation for mercy. At Fresnes, where he was placed in irons on arrival, Laval spent his last days drafting a final letter of self-justification in which he announced his determination to die by his own hand, "by poison, like the Romans." On the morning of 15 October 1945, the day scheduled for his execution, as the court officials entered his cell, Laval swallowed a phial of cyanide, in all likelihood given to him by Dr. Destouches, alias Louis-Ferdinand Céline. Unfortunately, he failed to shake the phial in advance in order fully to activate the poison, and as his body began to tremble and convulse, desperate prison doctors thrust a tube down his throat and, over the next two or three hours, pumped out his stomach, amidst an appalling stench, no fewer than seventeen times, before declaring him able to go before the firing squad—not, however, at Montrouge, as was originally intended, but behind the prison at Fresnes, where the Germans had carried out their executions.

Half-carried, without shoes, but having had the strength, pride, and presence of mind to don the inevitable white tie and tricolor scarf, he was taken outside. "C'est fini, Pierrot, mais toi, finis beau [It's finished, Pierrot, but you, finish well]," his wife had said when they made their farewells. "Assassins, assassins, courage, Pierrot," chanted his fellow collaborator-prisoners as he was carried away. Pierrot-Laval was shot strapped to a chair, apparently in the face as well as in the body, despite having asked his executioners to aim at his heart and not kill him *salement*. None of the standard histories of the purge says where he was buried.[72] So great was the hatred of everything he had done, been, and touched that even his chauffeur was condemned to hard labor.[73]

Although the details of Laval's death were not known at the time, even the Communist press, Madeleine Jacob at its head, had to admit that his trial had been so biased as to have had "the prodigious effect of making Laval look like a victim of justice."[74] There was more satisfaction in the outcome of the more straightforwardly criminal trials: in the sentencing of Joseph Darnand, commander of the Milice, executed in October 1945; of the *miliciens* responsible for murdering Georges Mandel and Jean Zay in June–July 1944; and of the notorious Bony-Lafont gang, which, from its "headquarters" on the Rue Lauriston in the sixteenth arrondissement, acted as hired killers for the Gestapo, eight of whose members were shot at Montrouge in December 1944.[75]

But by the spring of 1945, there were signs of disquiet across the political spectrum about the general direction in which the purge was heading. On the right, the reservations were obviously self-interested. For Paul Léautaud, using the inevitable historical parallel, the whole thing was "a veritable repetition of 1793 in the name of so-called justice,"[76] while from the pulpit of Notre-Dame, the Reverend Father Panici warned against the possibility that the desire for revenge would lead to "new tortures, new massacres."[77] Among Catholics untainted by any complicity with Vichy—and they were few on the ground—François Mauriac deplored the way the purge had degenerated into a "switching of positions of executioners and victims" (un chassé-croisé de bourreaux et de victimes)[78] and, putting the virtue of charity above the principle of justice, devoted his column in Le Figaro to the cause of forgiveness and reconciliation with such passion that Le Canard enchaîné dubbed him "Saint-François-des-assises."[79] He was challenged by Camus in the pages of Combat—"Every time I speak of justice concerning the purge, M. Mauriac talks about charity," he famously wrote in January 1945[80]—but even he, like others on the noncommunist left, was becoming repelled by the spectacle of what Esprit called an "inglorious sans-culotterie" in pursuit of its prey.[81] "The very word épuration is already painful enough in itself," Camus wrote in August 1945, "the thing has become odious."[82] The time had come, wrote Raymond Aron in Les Temps modernes in October 1945, for a purge of the purgers.[83]

In France as a whole, approximately 160,000 cases of alleged collaboration were considered by the courts, almost half of them being dropped or ending in acquittal.[84] Of the remaining accused, 40,249 (25 percent) were sentenced to dégradation nationale (essentially suspension of all civil rights), 26,289 (16 percent) to imprisonment, 13,211 (8 percent) to temporary or permanent hard labor, and 7,037 (4 percent) to death, 4,397 of these in absentia, with 767 actual executions; to these must be added the estimated 800 military personnel who were executed after trial by a separate military tribunal.[85] In Paris, 372 death sentences were pronounced, of which 110 were actually implemented.[86] The distress felt by many at the time, and vindicated by recent historians, stemmed from the fact that the purge fell with particular severity on certain groups while sparing others almost entirely. Economic collaboration by industrialists and businessmen was conspicuously underpunished, and the profits many made with impunity from work on the Germans' Atlantic Wall were often adduced as proof of the purge's underlying class character.[87] Similarly, the Catholic Church, whose role in the legitimation of Vichy was preponderant, notwithstanding numerous if usually tardy counterexamples, from bishops to ordinary communicants, underwent no public purge, and Pétainist clergy either became

Gaullists overnight or kept their allegiance to Vichy to themselves; the part played by certain prelates, priests, and monks in protecting, concealing, and obtaining a secret presidential pardon for the *milicien* Paul Touvier is notorious.[88] On the other hand, there is general agreement among recent historians that writers, journalists, and broadcasters suffered disproportionately on account of their visibility and the ease with which the positions they took under the Occupation could be documented. They were present in Paris at a time when the leading Vichyites and fascists were in Germany, and they were tried, condemned, and, in a disproportionate number of cases, executed as substitutes for the far guiltier fugitives. In particular, their public disgrace shielded many economic collaborators from judicial pursuit, and the scorn expressed by the literary critic Jean Paulhan (1884–1968) in *De la paille et du grain* (1948) seems, in retrospect, only too well justified:

> The purge bears hard on writers. Engineers, contractors, and
> stonemasons who built the Atlantic Wall are strolling around
> quite peacefully among us. They are busy building new walls.
> They are building the walls of new prisons, in which are interned
> journalists who made the mistake of writing that the Atlantic Wall
> was well built.[89]

In addition, attitudes, and consequently verdicts and sentences, varied from region to region, and also shifted significantly by the month. Regarded with remarkable lenience in September 1944, Pétain had become a hate figure for many by the time he was tried, partly because of the Communist press's vituperative campaign against him, partly because of the horror generated by the return of the deportees in May 1945, and partly, Jean-Pierre Rioux suggests, because by June 1945 the public wanted a suitably emblematic victim—and who was more emblematic than Pétain?—to bring the whole purge process to a close.[90] Finally, many were troubled by the ease with which sentences were commuted or quashed when the accused—René Bousquet is a typical instance—produced even the flimsiest evidence of "resistance." The amnesties of 1951 and 1953—supported by the right and condemned, inevitably, by the left—only reinforced the feeling that collaborators were being let off virtually unpunished. By 1954 fewer than 1,000 were still in detention; by 1956, 62; by 1958, when de Gaulle returned to power, 19; and by 1964, none at all.[91]

A good deal is known about the modus operandi of the various courts involved in the purge, and the reactions of the accused, when not documented, can be readily surmised. There is little concrete information, however, about their accusers and pursuers; little, in any case, to take us beneath the surface of their vituperative discourse into the complexity of motive that may be lurking beneath. On this question, it is striking, for example, how many of the judges and prosecutors of the High Court of Justice—and the same was almost certainly true of the lesser criminal and civil courts—themselves had, at best, ambiguous records under Vichy. Almost all judges had, by definition, taken the oath of loyalty to Pétain, and, as we have seen, the prosecutor at Pétain's trial, André Mornet, had even volunteered to act in the show trials at Riom. Moreover, some of the most zealous pursuers of collaborators in the press may have had motives less pure, or certainly less straightforward, than the undeviating ideological rigor their public statements expressed. Communists as a whole had every interest in diverting attention from their own smudgy record between the signing of the Nazi-Soviet pact and the German invasion of the Soviet Union in July 1941, and their increasingly hysterical campaign against "Pétain-Bazaine" was surely directed as much at camouflaging their own recent past as it was at punishing the marshal. Among individual Communists, Claude Morgan of *Les Lettres françaises* vied with *Franc-Tireur*'s Madeleine Jacob in the intensity of his persecutory zeal, losing, quite rightly, no opportunity to denounce Vichy's "crimes against man" and hounding individual Vichyites, particularly writers close to or not explicitly opposed to the regime, with vituperative fury. It is, therefore, at the very least interesting to learn that Morgan's father, the Academician Georges Lecomte, was a Pétainist of note.[92] Was Morgan attacking his father in attacking Pétain and his followers? expunging his own sense of guilt at being the son of a well-known *maréchaliste?* or even unconsciously protecting his father by diverting attention from the small fry to the big fish of the regime? In the absence of any full-scale study, the suspicion remains that the most relentless scourges of Vichy were precisely those men and women whose oppositional credentials were slightest, all the eleventh- or thirteenth-hour resisters who, literally and metaphorically, came out at last in August 1944, all the so-called *naphtalinés,* civilian and military, who enlisted in the Resistance when it was sweeping everything before it, their "uniforms" reeking of the mothballs in which they had packed them away in June 1940.[93]

One of the few works to probe the psychology of the accuser is Jean Dutourd's *Le Demi-Solde* of 1966. Here the accuser, or judge, is the author himself, co-opted in the autumn of 1944 by the so-called Professional Journalists' Identity Card Commission, a subcommittee of the passionately anti-Vichy National Writers' Committee. As its name indicates, the commission's task was to vet applications for official journalist status and to reject any applicants suspected of complicity with Vichy, and so, in effect, deny them the possibility of making a living in their chosen profession. Dutourd accepted his nomination with alacrity—"I saw it as a great honor, I was going to be Saint-Just"—and, once a week over the next few months, sat with three other "commissioners" at a cloth-covered table on a podium as a succession of "postulants" come to submit their requests:

> The unfortunate applicant appeared before us and answered our questions. This situation, which ought to have horrified me, which horrifies me today, greatly amused me. It gave me an utterly disgusting feeling of power. Behind my green cloth, my face impassive and with a solemn demeanor, I had the illusion of belonging to the Committee of Public Health. I would have liked my colleagues to have an attitude as majestic as mine; but it was not Robespierre or Dubois-Crancé who sat at my side: just a few petits bourgeois of the journalistic world, truly surprised at being transformed into agents of retributive justice [*justiciers*] and surmounting their unease with difficulty.

Dutourd has no qualms about having denied cards to the obviously compromised:

> What I blame myself for is the satisfaction I felt in seeing, standing humiliated before me, men who were twenty years older than I was, men whose names I had in some cases known while I was still in short pants, and whose principal crime, after all, had been to exercise the only trade that they knew.... I also blame myself for the lessons in civic morality that I delivered from time to time to these poor bastards [*bougres*], who sometimes listened to them with a hangdog look, sometimes with a hint of insolence in their eyes. The heart of the matter was that here again, stiff-backed and frowning behind the commission's cloth-topped table, I was greedily wreaking vengeance on my childhood. I had been given the power to condemn interwar France [*la France de l'entre-deux-guerres*], and I was condemning it in the name of the child who had detested it. I was enjoying the intoxicating victory of the dunce [*cancre*] whom events have justified against the high fliers and even the teachers. Through these unfortunate, discredited

journalists, I was lashing out at my family, my schoolteachers, at the whole odious France of just a short time ago. In short, what I experienced there, in miniature, and without fully realizing it, were the appalling feelings that must have filled the souls of the Marats, the Collot d'Herbois, and the Fabre d'Eglantines as they sent to the guillotine a society that had committed the unforgivable sin of not having recognized in them a great doctor, a great actor, and a great poet.

"One is happily Manichean when one is twenty-four," Dutourd concludes.[94]

It was some kind of primary Manicheanism to which large sections of the French public, particularly its professional formers of opinion, succumbed in 1944–45, in response to a historical conjuncture whose main characteristic was to blur all but the most clear-cut opposition between innocence and guilt and, with the exception of out-and-out fiends (Darquier, Darnand, the three *miliciens* who plucked out the eyes of captured *maquisards,* placed live cockchafers in the sockets, and sewed up the lids,[95] and many more like them), to dissolve black and white into an infinite gradation of overlapping moral grays. By targeting obvious collaborators and by projecting their failures, cowardices, and guilts onto others whose records were, in some cases, only somewhat more compromised than their own, the grays were able to whiten their souls and to put themselves forward as resisters when, in their heart of hearts, they must have known they were anything but.

Yet to view the purge as a straightforward case of individual and collective scapegoating would be to miss the complexity of motive that underpinned the whole process. Jean Plumyène, in one of the earliest and best studies of Pétain, was certainly right when he said that the marshal's image in 1944–45 was a mirror in which France reluctantly perceived a reflection of itself: "In the person of Pétain, it is itself that France is preparing to burn in effigy; it is itself that France *punishes* for not having succeeded in resisting Hitler's armies in 1940, and for having played only the role of an accessory in the victory over Nazism."[96]

But, as we have seen, French public opinion was remarkably forgiving toward Pétain in September 1944, and if it subsequently hardened against him, the jury that reflected that hardening and condemned him accordingly also recommended that the death sentence not be carried out, ostensibly on the grounds of the marshal's great age, backed up by the recognition of his role in the Great War, but also, and more profoundly, because it recognized in him an image of itself and the nation he embodied, and, while refusing to condone, nonetheless forbore to exact full revenge. Similarly, as we have also seen, it is the limits, as well as the horror, of *la tonte* that need to be stressed: the men and women who wield the scissors hurt and humiliate, but, recognizing their moral consanguinity with the women they sheer, draw back from the lethal vengeance they might otherwise have wrought. Symbolically, the pursuers both punish and forgive themselves on and through the person of the pursued. The victim is not so much cast out of the polis in the manner of the classic scapegoat as consigned to a moral in-between land, humiliated but at least partly reintegrated, as though to remind the citizens that they, like their victims, are, in the manner of Racine's heroes and heroines, neither wholly innocent nor wholly guilty.

Pétain's actions and choices during the Occupation placed him, wrote Mauriac the day after the verdict, "midway between treason and sacrifice."[97] How appropriate, therefore, that he should have spent his last days not on some far-off New Caledonia, like the exiled Communards, but on an island just off the coast of the Vendée, separate from but a part of the country he had both betrayed and, according to his own lights, protected, and which, in simultaneously condemning and forgiving him, had recognized him at the last as one of its own.

13

CONCLUSION
Blood in the City,
1789–1945

What general patterns or structures of meaning emerge from this now completed journey from station to station along the Via Dolorosa of a century and a half of Parisian history? Or, to play on the meaning of "stations," what thematic correspondences link the nodal points of this study into an interconnecting Metro-like system, binding them both horizontally and vertically into what Baudelaire in his great sonnet "Correspondances" called *une ténébreuse et profonde unité,* a deep, dark unity? Less intricate than the Paris Metro with its thirteen inter-knitted lines, the present work has been organized around five principal thematic arteries—secularization, conspiracy, scapegoating, sacrifice, and blood—which here will first be explored severally before being brought together in a coda on the greatest of all the "affairs" in the affair-ridden history of postrevolutionary France, an affair that up to now has been lurking in the wings of this study but that must now come to center stage: the condemnation of Dreyfus in 1894 and the twelve-year crisis it gave rise to.

SECULARIZATION

The first and clearest pattern to emerge from this study is the seemingly irresistible spread of a secular worldview, of which the triumph of republicanism over its ideological rivals, finally secured in 1877 and reversed only by foreign invasion in 1940, was the clinching political expression. Frequently but never decisively challenged, and never as complete as its partisans hoped or its enemies feared, the spread of secularization is to be observed most tangibly in the decline of religious practice among all classes of the Parisian population (through markedly more among men than among women), somewhat less clearly in their actual beliefs, and concretely in the physical structure of their city.

Measured by all the usual criteria (baptisms, funerals, and the crucial "Easter barometer"), active membership of the Church was in decline even before the Revolution, with, for example, only 6,000 out of the 75,000 parishioners of Saint-Eustache taking Communion on Easter Day 1767.[1] Prerevolutionary indifference was accentuated and given an ideological rationale by the dechristianizing drive of the mid-1790s, and neither the Concordat nor any subsequent evangelization campaign was able to arrest, though the latter did somewhat palliate, the massive drift away from the Church. This development affected all classes in the capital—the Church was, if anything, more condemnatory of the "irreligion of the black hats" than it was of the indifference or hostility of their smock- and cap-wearing inferiors, for which most bishops and priests accepted part responsibility—and by the middle of the century a huge gulf had opened up between the Church and what Sainte-Beuve tellingly called the "immense diocese of freethinkers."[2] This gulf was partially bridged by the continuing allegiance of at least middle-class women to the teachings and sacraments of the Church. Writing in 1883, the archsecularist Ernest Renan was only slightly exaggerating what any Parisian priest could have confirmed from weekly observation of his congregation's sexual composition when he declared that "religion is maintained in the [modern] world only thanks to women [la religion n'est plus maintenue dans le monde que par la femme]."[3]

The much-heralded "return" of upper-middle-class men to active religious practice after the upheavals of 1848–51 and 1870–71 was always more of a hope than a reality, and the post-1885 wave of "conversions" among artists and intellectuals, of which Claudel's was the most spectacular and Huysmans's the best known, was confined to a limited, through admittedly highly visible, section of the city's population. As one recent historian of the Church has written, what the Concordat actually produced was a citywide "discordat" between the bulk of the male population and the Church.[4] The separation of Church and state in 1905 did no more than formalize the separation that had taken place over the last century and more between men's actual lives and the rites and sacraments of the Church. When Renan maintained in 1883 that "religion has become irrevocably a matter of personal taste,"[5] he was doing no more than stating the obvious, at least where the male population of Paris, upper, middle, and lower class alike, was concerned.

Religious belief cannot, of course, be quantified in the manner of religious practice, but here too the evidence suggests a significant, though less profound or extensive, penetration of a secularist *mentalité*. The properly Christian content of Christianity seems to have undergone an unmistakable dilution. Belief in Christ as the Man-God, *totus homo totus Deus*, of orthodoxy gave way to one or another form of Arianism, with the stress being placed more and more on Christ's teaching rather than on the mystery of the incarnation of His divinity in man. The *Deus absconditus* of Pascal evolved almost imperceptibly into the *Deus otiosus* of Voltaire, and as he did so, belief in divine Providence slipped into an effective Pelagianism, the natural theology of the self-made man of all ages. As theism lapsed into deism, the way was open for a further shift into agnosticism, even out-and-out unbelief, particularly for men who had attended those "seminaries of atheism" (Lamennais, 1823),[6] the *collèges royaux*, ancestors of the lycées, and the *grandes écoles* they furnished with students. "A very large part of the population no longer admits the existence of the supernatural," wrote Ernest Renan,[7] whose *Vie de Jésus* (1863) had done so much to "desupernaturalize" the Man-God Christ and transform him into the "incomparable man" Jesus.

There was, to be sure, a massive Christological revolution in the wake of the disasters, in both France and Italy, of 1870–71, as the loving, suffering Christ of an earlier age returned in the cult of the Sacred Heart, sustained in his agony and aided in his love by the alternately weeping and smiling lady of the Mariophanies. But for the bulk of the male population of Paris, Ultramontane emphasis on suffering and its increasingly reactionary political subtext can only have accentuated their distaste, even their disdain, not just for the Church but for Christianity itself. Faced with an eruption of often hysterical pietism, much of the male population (and no doubt a significant part of the female as well) became still further set in what Bernanos, writing in 1931, called their "hatred of the spiritual"; "they simply took their precautions against the divine" and looked forward to their ultimate objective, "a society without God," of which *L'école sans Dieu* (the school without God), achieved by stages between 1882 and 1904, was both the inevitable forerunner and the indispensable means.[8]

"The world today is without mystery," proclaimed, without the slightest regret, indeed with unmistakable braggadocio, Marcellin Berthelot (1827–1907), professor of organic chemistry at the Collège de France, in 1885, "and the rational concept [of reality] is extending its fatal determinism even into the realm of morality."[9] But not everyone applauded such scientistic triumphalism or welcomed the radical disenchantment of the world it proclaimed, and the nineteenth century is just as much the age of the creation of unorthodox substitute religions as it is of the decline of orthodox belief and practice per se. Many educated Parisian men who lost their faith (or never possessed any) moved, like Renan himself, from spirituality to one or another form of idealism:[10] rationalism, humanism, scientism, progressivism, all of which were amply catered to and encouraged in their local Masonic lodge. Others, suffering from what the Republic's accredited historian and director of the Ecole Normale Supérieure, Ernest Labisse (1842–1922), diagnosed in 1890 as a "nostalgia for the divine," turned to one or, usually, more than one of the countless pseudoreligions that the nineteenth century either inherited from the past or devised for itself and that we have seen in action, often to baleful effect, in the milieu frequented by Huysmans: Theosophy, Rosicrucianism, the spiritism of "Allan Kardec" (the "astral" name of Denisard Rivail [1804–69]), Swedenborgianism, table-turning, even, in a handful of extreme instances, full-blooded satanism.

For others, socialism (more closely related in its earliest forms to occultism than is commonly realized)[11] and, later, communism took on all the characteristics of an ersatz religion, as did fascism at the opposite extreme of the political spectrum. In the case of a nihilistic minority—the early Malraux, Montherlant, Artaud, Bataille—death became the only transcendent reality in a desacralized universe, to be courted with all the terror and longing with which a Teresa of Avila or Angela of Foligno had once approached God. For many, of course, there was only the longing and the waiting. "J'attends Dieu avec gourmandise" (I am waiting greedily for God), wrote Rimbaud in *Une saison en enfer* (1873),[12] foreshadowing Simone Weil's lifelong wait for God (which in her case involved virtual self-starvation to death),[13] not to mention Samuel Beckett's sardonic, despairing *Waiting for Godot* (1952).

For Bernanos and those of his ideological persuasion, the "God of a universe without God," "the future master of a standardized planet," could only be Man himself, "half Saxon, half Jewish," the *homo mechanicus neo-barbarus,* rational, scientific, calculating, of "American" capitalism.[14] But, in the wake of the devastation of world war, many writers went further, calling in question the very humanist-rationalist values that an earlier generation had sought to install in the place of the religious values of the past. "So many horrors could not have been possible without as many virtues," wrote Paul Valéry in his great essay "La Crise de l'esprit" (1919). "Knowledge and Duty, could it be you are suspect?"[15] The next logical step was taken by Malraux in his hugely influential *La Tentation de l'Occident* of 1926, in which his supposedly representative Chinese intellectual Ling W.-Y. tells his French counterpart, A. D., that "the absolute reality for you was God, and then man; but

man has died, after him God, and you are looking in anguish for someone to whom to confide his curious heritage."[16] Whoever or whatever
that was, it could no longer be "science," which in *L'Avenir de la science* (published in 1890 but written some forty years earlier) Renan had
declared to be a religion charged with the task of "organizing humanity
scientifically" in the confident knowledge that "there is no supernatural."[17] To which Malraux, speaking for an entire postwar generation,
retorted that "our civilization, since it has lost all hope of finding in science the meaning of the world, is devoid of any spiritual objective."[18]
After the death of God, the death of "Man," or at least of the individu-
alist rational man of a hundred prewar ideologues; after the eclipse of
the supernatural, the demise of "Nature." Truly, as Valéry said, the postwar European Hamlet was haunted by millions of ghosts.[19]

The secularization of the city's public spaces proceeded pari passu
with that of the private mental space of the bulk of its male citizenry.
The logic that commanded Haussmann's transformation of Paris in the
1850s and 1860s, and which continued to inform subsequent urban
policy, was based on a rational, scientific conception of space, and his
long rectilinear boulevards transecting the living substance of the city
with little regard to *quartier* or community applied the model of the
Panopticon to the problems of urban function and form. Haussmannization was less an experiment in city planning than an epistemological
revolution translated into buildings and streets.[20] It supplanted one
conceptual model, the organic, the prerational, the feudal, with another,
the organized, the rational, the modern, and it was this colonization of
one *episteme* by another that led a whole succession of writers on -
Paris—above all Victor Fournel in prose[21] and Hugo and Baudelaire in
poetry—to stigmatize the changes taking place all about them as a
comprehensive homogeneization-cum-militarization of the "old Hydra-
headed Lutetia" of the past:

> ... plus de rues
> Anarchiques, courant en liberté, bourrues,
> Où la façade au choc du pignon se cabrant,
> Le soir, dans un coin faisait rêver Rembrandt;
>
> . . . .
>
> Alignement! Tel est le mot d'ordre actuel.
>
> . . . .
>
> Ce vieux Paris n'est plus qu'une rue éternelle
> Qui s'étire, élégante et belle comme l'I,
> En disant: Rivoli! Rivoli! Rivoli![22]

[No more anarchical streets, / Freely running, shaggy-haired, / Where the sight of a façade rearing up / Of an evening against a gable made one dream of Rembrandt / ... / Alignment! Such is the directive of the present time. / ... / The Paris of old is no more than a single eternal street, / Stretching forth, elegant and beautiful as the letter *I,* / proclaiming: Rivoli! Rivoli! Rivoli!]

As baroque profusion succumbed to scientific rationality masquerading in a pseudoclassical veneer, so every aspect of Parisian life felt the effects of standardization. Street numbering was rationalized, immensely facilitating the mechanisms of institutional control, and the introduction of a standardized "street furniture"—billboards, drinking fountains, and the ubiquitous wrought-iron urinals—made one Parisian boulevard virtually interchangeable with another. The ideological warfare between the "two Frances"—monarchist versus republican, authoritarian versus democratic, Catholic versus secularist—was translated, very much to the ultimate advantage of the second terms of the three pairs, into the naming of streets and the erection of monuments.

The first revolution's policy of substituting "egalitarian" for "feudal" street names (pursued with such root-and-branch rigor that the Rue Honoré Chevalier actually became the Rue Honoré-Egalité) was continued, in a modified and much edulcorated form, by subsequent regimes eager to expunge, according to case, provocative royalist, imperial, or socialist allusions in the street plan of the city.[23] The gradual triumph of the Republic was enshrined in the naming of streets after, first, the heroes of the Enlightenment and the Revolution (Voltaire, Rousseau, Lavoisier, Lafayette, Mirabeau, Danton, but not, self-evidently, Robespierre and Saint-Just, who still have no Parisian street to commemorate them), then a batch of notable Forty-eighters (Lamartine, Raspail, Ledru-Rollin, Louis Blanc), followed by a clutch of Third Republic worthies (Gambetta, Jules Ferry, Jules Simon) supported by partisans of the scientific secularist worldview (Louis Pasteur, Claude Bernard, Marcellin Berthelot, Pierre and Marie Curie) and set off by a host of republican writers and intellectuals (Zola, Hugo, Renan, Anatole France). Only a handful of Catholic-monarchical street names survived the comprehensive republicanization-cum-secularization of the city's main thoroughfares (Henri IV and Jeanne d'Arc were acceptable, but not Louis XIV, and certainly not Louis XV or Louis XVI).

A similar policy was pursued with regard to public statuary. Of the 150 statues erected in Paris between 1870 and 1914, 67 have been classified as commemorating men of letters, 65 men of "progress" (women of progress being apparently as sparse as women of letters), 65 politicians, and 45 painters and other artists, the discrepancy between the grand total and the combined individual categories being explained by the inclusion of more than one man of progress or politician under the rubric of men of letters as well; military men are notable for their total exclusion.[24] Statues of notable secularists or victims of religious persecution were erected to counter any hint of Catholic resurgence, such as the statue of the humanist Etienne Dolet (burned at the stake in 1546 and commemorated in the crucial year 1889 with the inscription "Victim of religious intolerance and royalty") and that of the chevalier de La Barre, provocatively unveiled before Sacré-Cœur at another critical juncture, 1906, in the ongoing conflict between the "two Frances." Ironically, it was on this very street that the most ultra of all ultra-Catholics, Léon Bloy, took up residence in 1905 and here that, a few months later, he received the visit of Jacques and Raïssa Maritain that set in motion the most notable joint conversion of the Belle Epoque.[25]

Finally, churches, including Notre-Dame, were disaggregated from the buildings that surrounded them, an eloquent transposition into the text of the city of the separating out of the sacred and the profane, of the divorce of religious signifiers from their signifieds, and of the breach between the Church and the overwhelming majority of the city's male population. The definitive republicanization of the Panthéon in 1885 could be, and was, interpreted as a triumph of the secularist principle, and even the building erected explicitly to challenge that principle—Sacré-Cœur—was rapidly "naturalized" as part of the Parisian landscape and transformed, like Notre-Dame before it, into a tourist spectacle.

The combined result of these changes was that Parisians of the 1880s and beyond lived out their lives in an effectively desacralized urban environment, one bereft of its earlier spiritual density and increasingly limited to a monosemantic dimension of being. Accordingly, those in quest of the sacred—either, like Huysmans, of the traditional Catholic sacred or, like the Surrealists, of some immanent, modern expression of *das ganz Andere* (wholly other)[26]—had to go farther afield, into the outer arrondissements or even beyond, or, alternatively, into the hidden recesses that survived in the city center, to locate it: the Eglise Saint-Séverin or Notre-Dame-des-Victoires in Huysmans's case, the Passage de l'Opéra and the Buttes-Chaumont for Aragon's *Paysan de Paris* (1926), or, for André Breton, either the Place Dauphine—that triangular "sex of Paris," with its narrow vagina-like entrance and pubic foliage of trees located at the very center of Paris, on the Ile de la Cité—or the incongruously isolated Tour Saint-Jacques, celebrated in *Nadja* (1928), "alternating zones of well-being and unease" marked with the double seal of interdict and attraction that is forever the sign of the sacred.[27]

Only in the gaps and fissures in the city's otherwise homogeneous and hyposignificant surface was the marvelous to be found, whence, in large part, the prodigious attractions of brothels and cabarets to seekers after the sacred like Bataille and his close associate Michel Leiris, the latter drawn to the Sphinx or the Tabarin as though to "the Porch of the Stoics or to caves, which history and ethnography show us to have been chosen so often as sites of initiation":[28] what fissure could be more dangerous and alluring (and ultimately more accessible) than the sex of a whore? For men for whom the official *sacré de droite*, whether of Church or Republic, was without meaning or attraction, there remained only the pursuit of the far more ambivalent *sacré de gauche*:[29] not the blood of Christ but the blood of the corrida (Bataille, Masson, Montherlant, Leiris); not Mary or Marianne but their degraded sister, the whore; or those other taboo locations—the fairground, the slaughterhouse, the sewers, the shantytowns of vagrants and scavengers in the *zone* (the wasteland beyond the city walls)—that writers and artists scoured for revelation and excitement during the Belle Epoque and the years between the wars. Of the writers considered in this study, only Claudel had his moment of revelation on duly consecrated ground, and even he (if we trust his account) happened to be there only by chance.

Chance, indeed, was the post-Christian Parisian's substitute for grace. What is longed for and pursued—to the extent that such an encounter can, without contradiction, be consciously sought—is what Leiris calls the experience of "tangency" between self and not-self, when each opens up to the other and, as at the instant of orgasm, meet in intense but, by definition, momentary fusion.[30] Such moments of "communication"—the term now is Bataille's[31]—between self and city are the urban neophyte's sole Eucharist, a foretaste of the total initiation or revelation that will come, if at all, only at the instant of death. They are commonly mediated by some female intercessor, such as Breton's Nadja or Desnos's Louise Lame,[32] whose miraculous materialization out of the very heart of the city is its equivalent of the Mariophanies in the grotto of Massabielle or on the mountainside at La Salette. But such moments vanish as suddenly and gratuitously as they came, so that, even illuminated by the grace of the surreal encounter or even, in the case of Claudel, by grace *tout court*, the life of the urban mystic, orthodox or not, must be lived in the one-dimensional space of a city in which, as in Claudel's early play *La Ville* (1897), man, self-regarding, self-creating, rational Third Republican man, has usurped the place once occupied by the pagan or Christian divine:

> Il n'est plus de dieux et le vent leur traverse la bouche;
> Nul prêtre, l'autel au ventre, n'honore plus la Nuit étoilée et la double porte du Soleil.
> Au lieu de l'idole qui sur le parfum du vin et sur la fumée de l'holocauste
> Ouvrait un nez de bois et des yeux de porcelaine,
> L'homme lui-même est monté sur le piédestal.
> Et le monde lui a été livré dans l'immensité de son herbe, et nous y avons établi des chemins de fer.
> Et chacun, au repos, s'assoit à son propre autel.[33]

[There are no gods any more, and the wind blows through their mouths; / No priest, his belly pressed to the altar, honors any longer the Night studded with stars and the double door of the Sun. / Instead of the idol that on the perfume of wine and on the smoke of the holocaust / Opened up its wooden nose and its porcelain eyes, / Man himself has mounted the pedestal. / And the world has been handed over to him in the immensity of its grass, and we have built railways across it. / And everyone, at rest, sits at an altar to himself.]

CONSPIRACY

The distance from secularization to conspiracy theories of history is not great, the belief that history is governed by this or that "hidden hand" or by this or that confraternity, religious order, race, or class acting in concert and in secret being, as Karl Popper once wrote, "just a version of ... theism, of a belief in gods whose whims and wills rule everything. It comes from abandoning God and then asking: 'Who is in his place?'"[34] This is not, of course, to claim that conspiracy theories emerge only in periods of declining religious belief. Clearly neither the massacre of Saint Bartholomew's Eve (24 August 1572), for example, nor the Revocation of the Edict of Nantes (October 1685) would have occurred had not those responsible believed that French Protestants were engaged in a seditious plot against Catholic society. But the frequency of conspiracy theories, the intricacy of their structures, and their power to persuade are enormously enhanced when they are able to fill the epistemological void left by the eclipse of orthodox religion as an explanatory system. In the eighteenth century, as theism frayed into deism among the elite and religious practice waned among the mass of the Parisian population, the conspiracy, particularly in the form of the famine plot, emerged first as a supplement to, then as a substitute for, the all-embracing certainties of faith, supplanting earlier notions of a beneficent cosmic order with that, both alarming and reassuring at the same time, of a maleficent social order controlled, as by some *deus absconditus,* by a cabal of diabolically motivated persons known or unknown. Every five or ten years, eighteenth-century Paris was seized by the belief that the king's ministers and intendants, his family, and possibly even the king himself were conspiring with grain merchants (the infamous "hoarders") and perhaps with foreign governments and powers to drive up the price of bread for their own economic and political advantage, even if it meant pushing "the people" to the very brink of starvation. Needless to say, belief in the existence of a famine plot often caused the very shortage of food it claimed to explain and, with remarkable self-reinforcing logic, imposed a coherence of human intentionality on a crisis typically brought about by vagaries of climate combined with the capricious workings of the market.[35] The famine plot persisted into the Revolution and beyond, and still surfaced at intervals in the later nineteenth and even early twentieth centuries.[36] It lay behind the lynching of Foulon and Bertier de Sauvigny in July 1789, and such was public revulsion at the figure of the hoarder that in 1794 one former royal minister was executed for his alleged part in the alleged famine plot of 1763–64, all of thirty years earlier.[37]

A variant of the famine plot was the myth of child abduction and murder. In this version of the nutritional theme, "the authorities" were not so much depriving "the people" of food as seizing their children in order to satisfy their own appetites, both alimentary and (possibly) sexual. In May 1750, as rumors spread that "innocent" blood was being sought to cure the leprosy of an unnamed member of the king's immediate family, collective passions rose to such a pitch that an officer of the watch named Labbé was seized on the Pont Marie and accused of accosting a child with a view to abducting him. The hapless officer was hauled to the Rue Saint-Roch and there lynched, his corpse being then ritually carried through the streets and displayed before the residence of the minister in charge of law enforcement in Paris. The next night a cat was slaughtered outside the home of Labbé's mother and given an elaborate parody funeral, complete with intonation of the "De profundis" and the "Libera me"; for their part, the authorities condemned the "company of brigands"—one of the most common and loaded terms, as we shall see, in the lexicon of conspiracy—who had thus attempted to "stir up the people," as though "the people" were not capable of stirring themselves up by the power of mutual suggestion.[38]

The myth of child abduction was destined for a long life. Widely recycled in the 1880s and 1890s in the form of "Jewish ritual child murder," it resurfaced in the 1950s and 1960s in the belief, reported in Toulouse, Arras, Lille, Valenciennes, Strasbourg, Chalon-sur-Saône, Dinan, Laval, Châtelleraut, Amiens, and Orléans, where a full-scale moral panic resulted, that adolescent girls and young women were disappearing (or, rather, being disappeared) from the cubicles of (usually Jewish-owned) clothing shops, whence, bound and drugged, they were conveyed along subterranean passages to the Loire, the Somme, or some other local river, destined for eventual shipment to the brothels of Latin America or the harems of the Orient.[39] In the 1980s, children were said to have been bitten by snakes, scorpions, and bird-eating spiders deliberately concealed in yucca plants and bunches of bananas: sales of potted plants at Monoprix and Unimag reportedly plummeted, and Taiwanese-made teddy bears were also suspected.[40] Significantly, supposed child abductors were routinely compared to Herod or Barbe-Bleue (Bluebeard), the mythical murderer and devourer of children based on the figure of Gilles de Rais (1404–40), who was so to preoccupy the French literary imagination from Huysmans to Bataille and Michel Tournier.[41] Perhaps the revulsion felt at Klaus Barbie's abduction of the forty-four Jewish children hidden at Izieu (Ain) in April 1944 owes something to the horror and terror associated with his near-homonym, Barbe-Bleue.[42]

With the coming of revolution, conspiracies, real or imagined, or more commonly half-real, half-imagined, proliferated as never before, and, for the first time, what François Furet has called the "dialectic of people and plot"[43] became one of the great structuring themes of French history, a heuristic status it has never since lost. The Revolution was born amid plot mania, reproduced and replicated itself by accusation and counteraccusation of conspiracy, and finally consumed itself in a welter of plot-inspired collective paranoia. Simply to list, let alone to describe or explain, all the plots and the counterplots that took place in fact or in fantasy (or, more normally, in the infinitely suggestible border zone between one and the other) is a near-impossible task, made only superficially easier by separating the revolutionary versions of the theme from their royalist/counterrevolutionary rivals.

From the moment Louis XVI dismissed Necker on 11 July 1789, the king, his family, and his ministers were held to be in league with his Austrian brother-in-law Emperor Joseph II in a conspiracy of royalist

Europe aimed at stifling the revolutionary Hercules at birth. The flight of the king's brother, the comte d'Artois (the future Louis XVIII), to Turin soon after the fall of the Bastille and the debacle of Varennes—that "coronation in reverse," as Furet calls it[44]—gave the belief an all too solid grounding in reality.

Beginning in the immediate aftermath of 14 July, one "aristocratic" or "foreign" plot was spun out of or alongside another, many of them real, like the royalist fanatic François Froment's never-ending machinations in the south, with their quaintly named affiliates—*cébets* (onions eaters) and *poufs rouges* (red pompons)—and the rather less quaint massacres and countermassacres they provoked.[45] Others were invented or substantially elaborated by revolutionaries eager to discredit each other as much as their supposed common enemy, like the so-called Batz Conspiracy, alias the Foreign Conspiracy, largely dreamed up by the Jacobins in late 1793 to bring Jacques Hébert and his followers to the death by guillotine they so enthusiastically advocated for others.[46] To a greater or lesser extent, the principal plots concocted or alleged by the revolutionaries were variations on the motif of complicity with foreigners. After the Girondins (October 1793) and the Hébert faction (March 1794), Danton's supporters were in due course accused in April 1794 of doing what they had condemned their enemies of doing and were executed as agents of the nefarious designs of Turin, London, and Coblenz; for good measure, they received the traditional demonological tag of *affameurs* (famine plotters) as well.

Other plot accusations were even more farfetched or took genuine expressions of popular discontent to be the work of politically motivated agents provocateurs, thus exonerating the revolutionary authorities of any responsibility for the economic and social collapse over which they presided. The food riots of February 1793, at least partly fomented by the so-called *enragés* under the former priest Jacques Roux, one of Louis XVI's chief tormentors on the day of his death,[47] were interpreted as the result of a full-scale conspiracy, which they certainly were not. The accusation drove Roux—a *furieux*, in Michelet's damning description—to eventual suicide on 10 February 1794.

In May that year, the former *fermiers-généraux* (tax farmers), among them the great chemist Antoine-Laurent Lavoisier, were accused of plotting against the Republic, resulting in a further freight-load of probably innocent victims for the revolutionary tumbrils. When Lavoisier asked for a stay of execution in order to complete a vital experiment, he was bluntly told that the Revolution had "no further use for chemists" and went forthwith to the scaffold.[48] By this stage all semblance of rationality had long gone, and the Jacobin Couthon declared almost proudly, and certainly without any hint of criticism of himself and his fellow accusers, that "a revolution like ours is no more than a rapid succession of conspiracies, since it is the war of tyranny against liberty, of crime against virtue." It followed that the enemies of the *patrie* should be "less punished than annihilated."[49]

As the Jacobins accused all and sundry of plotting against the Republic, so their enemies responded with ever more outlandish counteraccusations. A harmless, if crazed, mystic named Catherine Théot (from *theos,* god), the self-styled "Mother of God" and harbinger of the Messiah, was said to be part of a Robespierrist plot aimed at securing absolute power for *l'Incorruptible,*[50] and it was outrageous fantasies such as this, deliberately fostered by Robespierre's opponents, that finally precipitated the spate of legalized bloodletting that history disguises and dignifies under the name of Thermidor. The principal agents of the obsession with conspiracy finally fell victim, as they were fated to do, of their own murderous brainchild, which had sent so many rivals to the scaffold.

Conspiracies, real and imagined, continued after Thermidor, most notably François-Noël "Gracchus" Babeuf's seminal Conjuration des Egaux of 1796, the model and inspiration of many a nineteenth-century revolutionary coup de main, which ended, inevitably, in the death of its leader on the guillotine in May 1797.[51] The popular insurrections of 12 Germinal and 1–2 Prairial Year III (1 April and 20–21 May 1795) and the royalist one of 13 Vendémiaire Year IV (13 October 1795) were attributed, with varying degrees of justification, to the conspiratorial machinations of this or that party, and produced their due quota of emblematic victims. A notable casualty of the last fling of revolutionary sans-culottism was Gilbert Romme, the chief proponent of the revolutionary calendar in the already far-off days of 1793 (and an early advocate of votes for women), who committed suicide along with two other Jacobin diehards on 17 June 1795.[52]

Despite all the differences in scale, characters, and intention from one alleged conspiracy to the next, what stands out is the remarkable sameness of the demonizing terminology used to describe the conspirators: cannibals, bloodsuckers, Hydras, monsters, serpents, Vandals, Visigoths (Barère once even spoke of "a Vandal or Visigoth League," lest anyone miss his intent),[53] and especially the accursed triumvirate, the foreigner, the aristocrat, and the brigand. The foreigner is invariably referred to as "on" or as "il" or "ils," in opposition to "nous." He is the polymorphously perverse Other, merging in Protean style with any number of other enemies of the people, so that the lexical combinations "foreigners and nobles," "foreigners and moderates," "nobles, foreigners, the idle, mercenary mouthpieces," and so on issue spontaneously from the mouth of speaker after speaker.[54]

The word "aristocrat" underwent an even more remarkable semantic dilation, ceasing early on in the Revolution to designate just the former nobility and coming rapidly to include those whom Mirabeau, even before the fall of the Bastille, called "the aristocrats, both noble and common [*tant nobles que roturiers*], who treat the people like scum [*canaille*]." Thereafter its compass of obloquy broadened so much that in 1792 Boissy d'Anglas could say that "it designates with the utmost clarity anyone who does not want equality, in other words, an enemy of the public." When some bright soul stumbled on the fact that *aristocrate,* give or take an *r* and a *t,* was an approximate anagram of "Iscariote," the way was open for still more elaborate demonizations;[55] "IT IS THE ARISTOCRACY THAT CRUCIFIED THE SON OF GOD," thundered the Girondin Abbé Fauchet, while for one Benoist Lamothe it was self-evident that Jesus was the victim of a Pharisaical plot and of the machinations of the "Judaical aristocracy." Truly, as *La Quotidienne* declared in 1797, when the Terror was over,

> the word "aristocrat" has, by itself, caused more than three hundred thousand French people to perish. Analyzed correctly, our revolution is a revolution of grammarians who battle and cut each other's throats in order to dethrone words, and our liberty resembles to a T those magicians in fairy stories who would overthrow nature by pronouncing a few quaint expressions.[56]

But the most loaded term in the lexicon of conspiracy (and, by quasi-automatic extension, in that of scapegoating as well) was the word "brigand," its traditional associations of violence and outlawry now reinforced, unetymologically, by the verb *briguer,* to scheme, to conspire. The word first came to the fore during the Great Fear of the summer of 1789, and it derived much of its power to alarm and explain from the still vivid memory of the bands of vagabonds that had roamed the French countryside since time immemorial, as well as of the more organized gangs of bandits and highwaymen led by such folk-devils-cum-heroes as Cartouche (1693–1721) and Mandrin (1725–55); the depredations, actual and invented, of the Nivet gang (1728–29) and the Rafiat gang (1731–33) still haunted the rural and urban imaginations alike, and as recently as 1783 a notorious bandit named Robillard had been broken on the wheel at Montargis.[57]

"Brigands" were known, or believed, to constitute a "separate society modeled on civil society," with their own hierarchies, rituals, and language,[58] and it was this image of a criminal antisociety that proved so potent in the summer of 1789 and would be endlessly recycled during and after the Revolution, preserving its power to terrify and excite throughout the nineteenth century and beyond. "Fear was universal," wrote Georges Lefebvre in his pioneering study of the Great Fear, "the currents moved with great speed: hence the impression that the Great Fear broke out everywhere simultaneously 'almost at the same time.' "[59] In fact, as Lefebvre showed, things were much more piecemeal and conjunctural, but in both city and countryside the conviction rapidly took hold that France as a whole was in the grip of an epidemic of brigandage, that brigands were "hand in glove with the aristocracy" (and hence with foreigners), so that "one way or another, fear of brigands and fear of aristocrats always managed to occur simultaneously in the mind of the people."[60]

It goes without saying that "the aristocrat-brigand" was a "phantom figure,"[61] born of an unprecedented experience of political turmoil, social dislocation, and impending economic disaster. In the circumstances, it is remarkable that only three suspects appear to have been killed in the course of what French peasants would long refer to as l'anno de la paor, the year of the fear.[62] A detailed study of the Great Fear in the Soissonais has shown that the noun "brigand" was invariably linked in public discourse with verbs such as "force," "smash," "crush," "steal," "burn," "threaten," and, perhaps most evocatively, "walk" and "spread," with their combined connotations of nomadism and contagion. "Brigand" was a portmanteau word that bore "the vast common meaning of 'outside': outside old-regime legality, outside the rigid, faltering home-parish organization of society, outside the physical and social limits of cultivation." It stood to the word "people" in its new revolutionary sense as negative to positive; indeed, it was "the term peuple turned inside out,"[63] just as the supposed councils and oaths of the criminal band parodied and inverted the procedures of the emerging democratic order.

When recycled, as it soon was, in a thousand revolutionary speeches, "brigand" took on still more radical connotations of outsideness: outside the patrie, outside society, outside civilization itself. But, of course, the brigand was not physically outside the patrie, even if he was morally and politically. Mobile and invisible, he was perhaps even more thoroughly inside than the most regular citizen, just as the foreigner had succeeded in infiltrating the very substance of civil society. It was the condition of being an insider-outsider (just as the foreigner was an outsider-insider) that made the brigand so dangerous and that would in due course mark him out for extermination in the Terror in Paris, Ville Affranchie (Lyon), and Ville-Sans-Nom (Marseille) and, in far greater numbers, in the appropriately "savage" and "nocturnal" *bocage* (woodland and pasture land) of the Vendée.

It was not long before the counterrevolutionaries in London, Turin, and Coblence, compulsive fomenters of conspiracy, developed a full-fledged conspiracy theory of their own, thus demonstrating the truth of Richard Hofstadter's observation that "a fundamental paradox of the paranoid style [in politics] is the imitation of the enemy,"[64] though in the case of the French Revolution there is no easy distinction, and perhaps no distinction at all, between the model and the imitator, or between conspired against and conspirator. Hardly had the Bastille been taken than *Les Conspirateurs démasqués* (1789) by the comte Ferrand attributed the whole crisis to the combined machinations of the duc d'Orléans, Lafayette, and Necker, the last being not merely a foreigner and a banker but a Protestant heretic to boot. Once launched, the search for the "hidden hand" behind the revolutionary rupture produced a predictable sequence of culprits, most of them destined to make regular reappearances in the political crises of the next century and a half: philosophes, Voltaire and d'Alembert at their head (the favorite bugaboos of Joseph de Maistre), Jansenists (as in Antraigues's portentously titled *Dénonciation aux Français catholiques des moyens employés par l'Assemblée nationale pour détruire en France la religion catholique,* published in London in 1791), Protestants in general (for de Maistre, using the capital letters he and his kind were so inordinately fond of, the Revolution was "INCONTESTABLY THE DAUGHTER OF THAT OF THE SIXTEENTH CENTURY," like everything else he disapproved of),[65] though only rarely and episodically Jews, despite the fact that later reactionaries would see the Emancipation decree of 27 September 1791 as one of the Revolution's most sinister and symptomatic enactments. But it was the abbé Barruel (1741–1820) who, in a succession of works of which the five-volume *Mémoires pour servir à l'histoire du Jacobinisme* (1797) was the most widely read, produced the most cogent explanatory thesis: it was all the doing of the Bavarian Illuminati, founded in 1776 by Adam Weishaupt, professor of law at the University of Ingolstadt, who, with remarkable speed, had managed to infiltrate the body politic of France and bring down Church and monarchy together. The prototype of every subsequent theory of the Masonic takeover of France, Barruel's *Mémoires* depict the Illuminist countersociety as the inverted double—secret, hierarchical, and pyramidal in structure—of the king-and-pope-centered order it set out to subvert:

> In this French revolution, everything, even its most terrifying crimes, has been foreseen, reflected upon, concerted (*combiné*), resolved, and decreed (*statué*):everything has been the effect of the deepest villainy (*scélératesse*), because everything has been pre-pared and brought to pass by men who alone possessed the thread of conspiracies that had long since been woven in secret so-cieties, and who had been able to choose and hasten the moments favorable to plots.[66]

Barruel's "solution" to the enigma of Revolution was taken up by counterrevolutionaries the length and breadth of Europe and beyond, producing such masterpieces of the paranoid imagination as John Robison's *Proofs of a Conspiracy against All the Religions and Govern-ments of Europe, Carried On in the Secret Meetings of Free Masons, Illu-minati, and Reading Societies,* published in Edinburgh in 1797, immedi-ately translated into French, and destined to have a huge influence across the Atlantic, where the "Illuminist thesis" has been revamped for contem-porary usage by none other than the televangelist and one-time candidate for the Republican presidential nomination, the Reverend Pat Robertson, in his 300-page disquisition *The New World Order* of 1995.[67]

The coming to power of Napoleon brought a halt neither to con-spiracies nor to conspiracy theories. A succession of plots—the Opéra plot, the Chevalier plot, the so-called Rue Nicaise affair (all 1800)—marked Napoleon's consulate, leading, under the Empire, to the more se-rious conspiracies of the counterrevolutionaries Pichegru and Cadoudal (1804), and, in October 1812, to the botched coup d'état led by General Charles-François Malet; needless to say, the ringleaders of these and sim-ilar plots ended their lives on the scaffold. The Restoration Monarchy marked some kind of golden age for the conspiratorially minded, being shot through from beginning to end by what Stendhal—the most secre-tive and conspiratorial of all French novelists—memorably called *le génie du soupçon,* the genius or, better, the genie of suspicion.[68] Liberals such as Stendhal widely, and not without some justification, regarded the Restoration as a whole, and particularly the reign of the out-and-out re-actionary Charles X (1824–30), as the working out of a Catholic-royalist conspiracy that originated in a shadowy organization that undoubtedly existed, the Chevaliers de la Foi, founded in 1809 by Ferdinand de Bertier, son of the Bertier de Sauvigny lynched in July 1789.

The Chevaliers have been well described as a product of "a reviving sense of medieval chivalry and the flourishing anti-Freemasonry of royalist circles" that characteristically imitated the structure and mentality of the very secret societies held responsible for fomenting the Revolution in the first place; it is no accident that the abbé Barruel was the society's organizational consultant. Consisting of a typically pyramidal organization of autonomous cells known as *bannières,* each headed by a *sénéschal* after the manner of a chivalric order like the Knights of St. John or of Malta, the Chevaliers made use of the customary "heady array of secret handshakes, signs, and menacing oaths as candidates were inducted from one organizational ring and one level of knowledge to the next."[69]

At the opposite ideological pole from the Chevaliers, but again mirroring their structure and mentality as the Chevaliers mirrored theirs, were the Carbonari (often referred to in France as the Charbonnerie), whose members, organized in the usual self-contained cells known as *ventes* or units of twenty conspirators, were recruited among students, serving soldiers, and veterans of Napoleon's armies. A succession of coups de main in 1821–23 centered on military towns such as Saumur and Belfort added to the general paranoia of the times and produced the usual batches of victims for the guillotine, most notably, of course, the Four Sergeants of La Rochelle, executed in 1822.

More significant in the long term were the working-class mutual aid societies that were beginning to emerge in such cities as Paris and Lyon. With all "coalitions," "associations," and "corporations" still legally prohibited, the mutual aid societies operated clandestinely and could, when the circumstances required it, become nuclei for more organized popular protest. It was one such occasion, the Parisians riots of November 1827, that first brought to the fore a young provincial who, present and absent, in person and in legend, was to influence the course of revolutionary politics in Paris for almost half a century: the conspirator par excellence, Auguste Blanqui (1805–81), known not for nothing as *l'Enfermé* (the prisoner).

After the Revolution of 1830, both conspiracies and conspiracy theories underwent a significant mutation. The "classical" political conspiracy, of both right and left, continued, if not to flourish, then at least to occur with some regularity, with almost comical results in the case of the former (the duchesse de Berry's farcical attempt to revive counter-revolutionary activity in 1832, Louis Napoleon's even more bathetic coups de main at Strasbourg in 1836 and again at Boulogne in 1840) and with only marginally more seriousness in that of the latter. The time of riots of 1830–34 saw the formation of the first genuinely working-class political organization in France, the semiclandestine Society of the Rights of Man, as well as of a profusion of mutual aid societies and pro-duction societies, which, added to the traditional guilds, gave some basis in fact to the belief, now widely held in government circles, in the existence of a Hydra-headed "federation" of republican-socialist "cor-porations" or "cells" encompassing, if not the whole nation, then at least Paris and Lyon. Such organizations were in reality usually apoliti-cal or even antipolitical in character, aiming as they did to bring about social and economic change from below rather than, as they saw it, merely a change of political regime from above. The tradition of the Carbonari-style political conspiracy was maintained by the desperadoes that planned the assassination attempts on Louis-Philippe in 1835 and 1836 and by secret societies such as the Société des Familles and the So-ciété des Saisons, which, coordinated by Blanqui, launched a full-fledged putsch in May 1839, in which a force of 700 to 800 manual workers and small shopkeepers briefly occupied the Hôtel de Ville.

As we have seen, the cholera epidemic of 1832 resurrected many of the atavistic fears associated with the Great Fear, including rumors of well poisoning, traditionally blamed on "the Jews," which would re-crudesce at intervals so long as Parisians drew their drinking water from wells. New, or nearly new, bogeymen appeared alongside traditional folk devils, most notably the Jesuits, whose evil designs on the whole of French society, its government, its army, its hospitals, and especially its universities and schools, were asserted and "proved" in a multitude of publications, from Michelet and Quinet's Des Jésuites (1843) to Eugène Suë's massive potboiler Le Juif errant (1844–45). The Jesuit panic played on deep-seated fears of child abduction and torture ("C'est nous qui fessons / Et qui refessons / Les jolis petits, les jolis garçons" (It's we who flog / and flog again / the pretty little ones, the pretty boys), sing the Jesuits in Béranger's "Les Révérends Pères"),[70] and recycled the classic theme of semimagical control-from-afar through the agency of zombi-fied converts, to which Aigrigny gives blood-curdling expression in Le Juif errant:

> Then, into these soulless bodies, mute, sullen, cold as corpses, we
> breathe the spirit of our order; instantly the corpses walk, act,
> carry out orders, but without leaving the circle in which they are
> forever enclosed; it is thus that they become members of this gi-
> gantic body whose will they mechanically perform, but of whose

plans they are ignorant, just as the hand performs the hardest
tasks, without knowing, without understanding, the thought that
directs it.[71]

What anti-Masonism and, eventually, antisemitism would be for the
right, anti-Jesuitism would, especially at the time of Dreyfus, be for the
left, it having been Jules Michelet and Edgar Quinet's great contribution
to conspiracy theory to postulate the Revolution as "the enduring antithesis of Jesuitism, and vice versa."[72] The later myth of the *postard,* the
alumnus of the Jesuit school on the Rue des Postes, bent on infiltrating
this or that institution for the benefit of his masters, derives intellectu-
ally from the work of France's greatest historian and takes his sinister
coloration from the fiction of Suë.

By the early 1840s, with political opposition apparently in abeyance,
it was less the political conspiracy that haunted the collective imagination, popular, bourgeois, and official alike, than the belief in the existence of vast criminal networks dedicated to the infiltration and under-
mining of established society. Building on the traditional image of the
Hun and the Visigoth, and adding for good measure the new and suitably exotic figures, derived from James Fenimore Cooper, of the Mohi-
can and Iroquois, writers and journalists invented a full-scale invasion-
by-stealth by "barbarians" who, thanks to their mastery of disguise,
were frequently indistinguishable from those whose power, position,
and wealth they so mercilessly coveted. "The barbarians we speak of are
living in our midst," wrote Suë in the opening chapter of his massively
popular serial novel *Les Mystères de Paris* (June 1842–October 1843),[73]
spreading out from their headquarters in the squalid drinking dens on
the Ile de la Cité or around the Place de Grève, speaking an
impenetrable argot and using a sign language known only to themselves,
and in general working their way into every nook and cranny of the city
in pursuit of their nefarious designs. The mythical criminal of Bourgeois
Monarchy Paris is a combination of Argus, Proteus, and Briareus: all-
seeing, able to assume any appearance or identity he wills, and with
multiple arms extending spider- or octopus-like to encompass the whole
city. Hidden at the heart of a vast web of associates, invisible but omniscient, the master criminal, typified by Balzac's sphinxlike Vautrin, with
his innumerable aliases, controls everything from afar like some *deus
absconditus,* projecting himself into minions like Lucien de Rubempré,
whose will he transforms into his own.

Arrayed against the chameleon-like criminal is a being who, characteristically, is once again his almost exact mirror image: the detective,

police inspector, or chief of the Sûreté, often an ex-criminal himself, with a criminal's Protean ability to assume many guises, yet another unseen seen like the real, if greatly self-dramatized, François-Eugène Vidocq (1775–1857) or Hugo's Inspector Javert stalking Jean Valjean from afar, delighting sadistically in the godlike power he exerts over the unwitting object of his gaze, postponing the moment of capture as a lover defers the moment of orgasm:

> Even when Jean Valjean thought that he was most secure, the eye of Javert was upon him.... Then [Javert] began to play. He had one ravishing, infernal moment; he let his man go before him, knowing that he held him, but wanting to postpone as long as possible the moment of arrest, happy to feel that he was taken, and seeing him free, gloating over him with that voluptuousness of the spider who lets the fly flutter away or the cat who plays with the mouse.... Javert was in ecstasy [*Javert jouissait,* the common French term for "to come"]. His net was solidly meshed, he was sure of success; all he had to do now was to close his hand.[74]

The almost interchangeable images of criminal and policeman are linked to the cognate figure of the all-seeing, all-knowing moneylender, typified by Balzac's Shylockian Gobseck, who gradually mutates into the more modern and more rational, but still deeply demonic, figure of the financier or "capitalist," who, in the city of Eichthal, Pereire, or "the Rothschilds," is almost invariably imagined as a Protestant or a Jew. It is this humus of social and economic obsession that in 1845 produced Alphonse Toussenel's *Les Juifs, rois de l'époque,* the work that is widely seen as marking the transition from old-style religious anti-Judaism to modern, socially, economically, and politically motivated antisemitism. It was typical of the times that Toussenel was a man of the left. The importance of the 1830s and 1840s for conspiracy theories of society and politics cannot be insisted on too much: the modern myths of the Mafia godfather, the omniscient but corrupt detective or police chief, the sinister Catholic confraternity O(cto)pus Dei, the ubiquitous, omnipotent elder of Zion, all have their distant roots in the Paris of the Bourgeois Monarchy.[75]

By the late 1840s, all the signifying units of the discourse of conspiracy were in place, and it is unnecessary to take this chronological account any further. Subsequent decades would work endless variations on the corpus of images and themes bequeathed by the great Revolution and elaborated and supplemented by the regimes that succeeded it, amplifying here, modifying there, but always preserving the same underlying structure of meaning. As economic, social, and political circumstances changed, so the dramatis personae of conspiracy theory evolved with them, without losing their basic identity. Thus that ancestral bogeyman the "hoarder" is recognizable in *les gros* (the "big ones," the rich and powerful) and *les deux cent familles* (the two hundred families that supposedly enjoyed the riches and the power), which so haunted both left and right in the interwar period.[76] After the defeat of 1940, he resurfaced in the form of the black-marketeer. Similarly, the Argus-eyed moneylender—"my eye is like God's; I see into men's hearts; nothing is hidden from me"[77]—metastatizes first into the financier and capitalist, then into the international currency speculator, and finally, abandoning human identity entirely but not the power to see and control, into the multinational company.

The theme of the Masonic conspiracy has been endlessly recycled, from *La Croix* in the 1890s to the Front National's *Présent* and *Identités* in the 1980s and 1990s,[78] and reached the statute book in the form of Vichy's laws against "secret societies" of 13 August 1940 and 11 July 1941. The names of 14,600 Masonic officers were published in the *Journal officiel,* and the newly appointed director of the Bibliothèque Nationale, Bernard Faÿ, a noted specialist on the "Masonic origins" of the French Revolution, superintended the publication of a mass of "Masonic documents." They notably failed, however, to prove the lodges' responsibility for the Popular Front, the defeat of 1940, and whatever other political crimes of which they had been accused.[79]

The myth of the "Jewish international" has run on and on, now dormant, now virulently public (as in the 1890s and 1930s), but never disappearing, cunningly disguising itself as anti-Zionism when open expression is impossible, as variable as the chameleon-like Semite it denounces. Only the most recent additions to the stock of folk devils seem immune to accusations of conspiracy, immigrants from black Africa presumably because they lack the necessary intelligence, Algerians and their offspring because they have *les lobbies cosmopolites et droit-de-l'hommistes* of the left and the *socialo-positifs* (after *séro-positifs,* HIV-positive) of the moderate right to do their conspiring for them.[80] From the famine plots of the 1720s and 1730s to the Jewish-Masonic plots of the 1890s and beyond, the structure of the conspiracy myth has been remarkably persistent, as though there lies at its heart a single quasi-metaphysical obsession that recruits first this out-group, then that, in order to body forth and explain a scarcely changing array of fantasies and phobias, irrespective of whether the myth in question belongs to the left or the right.

In fact, there have been changes over time and, despite their obvious similarities, the conspiracy theories of left and right are not interchangeable. As Geoffrey Cubitt, one of the best writers on the theme, has pointed out, most conspiracy theories up to and including those advanced by revolutionaries of this or that hue between 1789 and 1794 "typically offered insight not into the activities of secret political actors," as did the competing counterrevolutionary theories of the time and most later conspiracy myths, but rather "into the hidden sense of visible politics."[81] In other words, the question was not who was controlling Mirabeau, Danton, or Robespierre, with or without their knowledge, but what Mirabeau, Danton, and Robespierre were knowingly doing behind their and other people's backs. The conspiracy as envisaged by revolutionary denunciators such as Marat and Saint-Just is always a form of what in Italy is known as *dietrologia,* or "behindology," conscious, deliberate, and delusive.[82] To that extent, as François Furet has argued, conspiracy theories of this kind are an "imaginary discourse" or "delirium" on power, the "antiprinciple" of the revolutionaries' belief in democracy as an expression of the conscious collective will of "the People."[83] If democracy enacts the general will of the nation, the plot is the product of the will of an individual or faction and is thus, by definition, antinational. Bitterly opposed though they are, democracy and the first kind of plot or plot myth embody a voluntarist conception of politics. Counterrevolutionary conspiracy theories like that of Barruel are significantly different, for here the emphasis is on the involuntary nature of politicians' actions and decisions, controlled as they are, almost invariably without their knowledge, by this or that conspiratorial cabal: Illuminati, Protestants, *philosophes,* either separately or, more often, acting secretly in concert. The idea of the voluntary conspiracy theories seems to express the worldview and political position of men who believe (almost certainly wrongly) that they are in charge of events, while the counterview that politicians' actions are involuntary and controlled from afar reflects the terrified consciousness of men who have lost control not just of public events but of their own personal lives and are desperately looking for explanations for this unwanted condition of powerlessness: in a word, proactive revolutionaries versus reactive reactionaries.

In the nineteenth century, as we have seen, the first type of conspiracy theory was largely replaced or absorbed by the second. Whether the conspiracy concerned is the doing of Jesuits, Jews, Freemasons, criminals, or capitalists, the emphasis is now always on the omniscience of the conspirators operating behind the scenes and, by necessary corollary, on the nescience of the actors performing at center stage: the latter are but puppets manipulated by an invisible puppeteer, pawns pushed this way and that by an unseen international Grand Master or, to take an image from another culture entirely, zombies whom an all-powerful magician has emptied of their own personalities and wills and filled, or possessed, them with his own.

It is not difficult to see that the shift from the voluntarist to the ant-ivoluntarist version of conspiracy is congruent with the shift from a traditional, or personalized, to a modern, or depersonalized, model of society, from one in which individuals feel, and are felt to be, able to initiate actions voluntarily to one in which they feel acted upon by a host of faceless abstractions—the market, capital, bureaucracy, democracy (in the sense of rule by the mass), all acting in inscrutable concert—that control them invisibly from afar like the Yahweh of the Old Testament. In short, in the new conspiratorial universe of the nineteenth century, no one, revolutionary or reactionary, republican or royalist, secularist or believer, feels in control of anything much any more. All the interlocking conventicles, camarillas, conclaves, consistories, and covens that proliferate in conspiracy theories figure the anonymous mechanisms and structures of the modern capitalist-bureaucratic state while endowing them with a conscious intentionality they do not in reality possess. More generally, the theme of the all-seeing but unseen eye that recurs in myth after myth embodies the panoptic imperative that Michel Foucault has shown to be present in the theory, if not always the practice, of the nineteenth-century prison, hospital, and mental asylum and, by extension, in the *episteme* of modern society as a whole. The world of the conspiracy is one in which signs are divorced from their signifieds, in which nothing refers and in which "the system" has taken the place of the God of tradition and assumed all his traditional attributes—all, that is, except the love that he supposedly has for his creatures. When God's love no longer moves the sun and other stars, when the cash nexus seems to override and determine every other human bond, all that is left is Power, anonymous, subjectless, invisible Power, and it is this that the conspiracy theorist cannot abide but that he must at all costs explain.

If, as Karl Popper suggests, the conspiracy theory is a substitute for theism, it has theism's capacity both to alarm and to assuage. At first the unseen, all-seeing eye of "the system" is as terrifying as God's, but the whole point of conspiracy theory is that it permits the "believer" to overcome that terror and to substitute the conscious will of person or persons initially unknown but in principle knowable for the blind interaction of anonymous forces. Conspiracy theory inverts but preserves the hierarchical structure of the theistic universe. Reality is controlled not from Olympus but from the Plutonian depths, whence the conspiracy theorist's obsession with catacombs, labyrinths, and underground passages, even with the Metro, which antisemitic fantasists of the Belle Epoque believed to be part of a Jewish plot literally to undermine Paris.[84] What the historian Raoul Girardet calls "the bestiary of the Plot"[85]—all its serpents, rats, leeches, octopi, and spiders, the last often replaced by the telegraph in the fantasies of the technologically minded—expresses the same terror of the unknown, but also explains and allays it. The very illogicality, to nonbelievers, of the conspiracy myth conceals, for the believer, a transcendent logic, for as Richard Hofstadter wrote in the essay to which one returns again and again, conspiracy theory "is nothing if not coherent." "In fact," he continues,

> the paranoid mentality is far more coherent than the real world, since it leaves no room for mistakes, failures, or ambiguities. It is, if not wholly rational, at least intensely rationalistic; it believes that it is up against an enemy who is as infallibly rational as he is totally evil, and it seeks to match his imputed total competence with its own, leaving nothing unexplained and comprehending all of reality in one overarching, consistent theory.[86]

Conspiracy theorists are natural Manichees: they simplify the complexity of social and political conflict into a straightforward dualism of Ormuz and Ariman, lightness and darkness. They are also inveterate structuralists: they look beneath the surface of circumstance and conjuncture to discern the invariant structure beneath. Like Oedipus, they confront the sphinx of modernity and, after a moment's reflection, come up with the answer to the riddle: not Man, but "the Jesuit," "the Jew," "the Mason," "the Communist," or whatever. It is this, to quote Hofstadter again, that explains the "apocalypticism of the paranoid style," that makes of it "a secular and demonic version of adventism."[87]

But, as Hofstadter further points out, conspiracy theorists almost always draw back from the pessimistic implications of their theory. They almost always believe that if they expose the conspiracy's mechanisms and motives and if they name the individuals and organizations behind it, then the conspiracy can be defeated and order restored to the established society it threatens. To that extent, what is most dangerous about conspiracy theories is their optimism. They do not merely explain, they promise redemption, even if, like the "redemptive antisemitism" (Saul Friedländer)[88] of the Third Reich, aided and abetted by half-knowing puppet regimes like Vichy, it requires the extinction of an entire race to reach the promised millennium.

SCAPEGOATS

Between 1789 and 1945 there were twelve formal changes of regime in France (thirteen in Paris, if one counts the Commune as an actual regime),[89] to which may be added major shifts in the balance of power within certain regimes, most notably during the First and Second Republics, which were scarcely less critical than actual constitutional changes. Almost all of these de jure or de facto transitions were marked by the killing, expulsion, or internal exclusion of individuals and groups associated with the previous regimes, often so blatantly that, viewed from a vantage point above the fray, the history of France since July 1789 appears as an alternating sequence of killings and counterkillings, expulsions and counterexpulsions, with "White" Terror (1795, 1814, 1848, 1871) succeeding the "Blue" or the "Red," and with one set of scapegoats following another to the scaffold, the stake, or simply the wall in an unending to- and fro-ing of violence.

From the lynching of de Launay and de Flesselles to the judicial murder of Laval and the ritual exclusion of Pétain, each incoming regime or new order has felt the need to establish its legitimacy by slaying or excluding one or more representatives of its predecessor. It as though only blood (or, failing that, exile or imprisonment) can sacralize the passage from one regime to another, as though either the crowd or the new government, or both, feels it necessary to purify the polis through the ritual extermination or exclusion of some polluting embodiment of the former order of things, not just its figurehead or leader (which would be comprehensible) but others held to be tainted by or inseparable from it: "hoarders" (1789), "brigands" of this camp or that (1793–94), "Jacobins" (1795, 1814), "ultras" (driven into so-called internal exile in 1830), "Reds," *démoc-socs*, and other partisans (1848, 1851, 1871), Jews and Freemasons (1940), collaborators (1944–45). Probably no other European nation has so incorporated the figure of the scapegoat into its political rituals; at every critical conjuncture, it seems, there is always an individual or group being brought to trial, executed, hounded into exile, or, all too often, driven to the wall by a crowd baying for his, her, or their blood. Any explanation for the frequency of such ritual bloodletting must delve beneath politics and ideology, beneath sociology and individual psychology, into anthropology—particularly the anthropology of religion—and it is to the work of René Girard, from *Le Sacré et la violence* (1972) to *A Theatre of Envy* (1991), his study of Shake-spearean drama, that, in the first instance, the present inquiry looks for some pattern or logic beneath what might otherwise appear as a random cortege of victims.[90]

On the basis of an extensive study of literature (particularly Greek tragedy and the nineteenth-century novel) and myth, Girard maintains that all human societies have their origins in violence, that the passage from primal horde to human community is brought about by what he calls an act of foundational violence (*violence fondatrice*) directed by the horde against one of its members. That person thus becomes a target and focus for rivalries and aggressions that, if allowed to develop, would necessarily submerge the horde in a chaos of competing and mutually destructive desires, a kind of Hobbesian war of all against all that Girard calls "undifferentiated violence." Girard's hypothesis goes beyond conventional accounts of scapegoating, because, for him, the violence of scapegoating lies at the very origin of society and is not to be counted as one among others of its by-products. Societies, he claims, are born when the war of all against all is transformed into the war of all against one—one who, for whatever reason, is singled out to become the object whereon the undifferentiated violence of the mass can be focused, projected, and temporarily neutralized. The ensuing killing of the singularized victim by the mass marks an attempt to drive out "bad" violence by "good," and for a time the originary murder does indeed install a simulacrum of peace among those who have engaged in it. It is not long, however, before the competing desires and aggressions that occasioned the initial killing return, threatening as they do so to plunge the group once more into the chaos of undifferentiated violence from which the differentiated—and differentiating—violence of scapegoating had temporarily delivered it.

Faced with the return of generalized violence, the community reacts either by killing one or more of its members, who ideally should be both part of and apart from the group as a whole (prisoners, for example, or invalids or slaves), or, more commonly, by reenacting the generative act of violence in the symbolic or surrogate form of sacrifice: all sacrificial rites are, according to Girard, repetitions in disguised or sublimated form of the originary murder. This new act of "good" violence, be it real or symbolic, directed against some differentiated victim seemingly delivers the group from the threat of "bad," undifferentiated violence, but, as with the originary act of violence itself, its efficacy is strictly limited. Sooner or later the threat of inner-directed violence returns, necessitating further acts of other-directed, surrogate or sublimated violence, and so on and so on, in an indefinitely repeated cycle of violence, counter-violence, and counter-counterviolence.

Founded in and through violence, human societies, according to Girard, can sustain or renew themselves only in and through violence, extruding from their midst now this scapegoat, now that, channeling internal violence now against this out-group, now against that, forever deluding themselves that a fresh act of "good" violence can deliver them from the reality of the "bad" violence that lies within them, rooted, perhaps, in the nature of human desire itself.[91]

While Girard's hypothesis concerning the origins and trajectory of human societies does not offer any straightforward key to the course of French history since July 1789, it does make it possible to read that history, and particularly its repeated acts of individual and collective violence, in a new and suggestive light. From a Girardian perspective, the killing of de Launay and de Flesselles on 14 July 1789 marks the act of foundational violence that draws a new order, or the possibility of a new order, out of the sclerosed disorder of the ancien régime. The Fête de la Fédération, held precisely a year later, is a communion feast celebrating the originating sacrifice and, all too briefly, renewing its unitive force. But the potential for intestine violence sublimated or disguised by the communal rite erupts shortly afterward in a chaos of competing desires and ambitions, necessitating further recourse to the violence of sacrifice, with the king himself now constituting the new emissary victim. Yet even the sacrifice of the symbolic father does not long prevent fratricidal violence from breaking out among his now liberated "sons," whence the need for further acts of ritual extermination and exclusion (Girondists, Hébertists, Dantonists, Jacobins), until a new kind of father figure, a deus ex machina from the nation's wildest and least integrated outpost (Corsica), seizes power by force and, after several years of constitutional ambiguity, creates a new kind of authoritarian order (the Empire), its proclamation coinciding almost exactly with the ritual murder of a prominent member (the duc d'Enghien) of the one collectivity, the old royal family, that can still challenge his power. But, once unleashed, the spiral of violence cannot be contained, and the whole of subsequent French history constitutes, again in Girardian perspective, a working out and repetition of those paradigmatic killings in the afternoon and early evening of the first 14 July.

Since that inaugural act, violence has been a repeated (and, in the Girardian context, inevitable) leitmotiv of French history, with accumulated aggression being directed either against this or that foreign power or nation (particularly England and Germany, and often in justified response to those countries' own violence) or, more characteristically and scarcely less destructively, by the right, but with the left far from innocent, against a range of sociopolitical groups that, though differently defined, share the quality of being both part of and apart from the main body of French society. Colonial violence, which the raids of working-class Paris in 1848 and 1871 so closely resemble, constitutes a further category, often an amalgam of internal and external forms of aggression. It cannot be discussed here, but it is at the very least deeply significant that on the very day that Nazi Germany surrendered (8 May 1945), the French army in the Sétif region of Algeria embarked on a series of massacres. In response to the killing of 103 French victims (soldiers plus *colons*), the army's attacks produced many thousands of Algerian casualties, exactly how many is not known, but certainly many times more than the number of French men, women, and children killed by the Germans and their allies in the massacres of Ascq, near Lille (2 April 1944), and, most notoriously, of Oradour-sur-Glanes, near Limoges (10 June 1944).[92]

"The designation of a scapegoat has always paid off," Guy Birenbaum has written in connection with what another commentator has called the "heterophobia" of "that immense exclusionary machine that is the [Front National]."[93] Yet, as the present study surely shows, perhaps with a repetitiveness that mirrors the repetitiveness of political violence in postrevolutionary France, the contemporary Front National is only continuing a tradition that goes back to the origins of the modern French state, something that has happened so regularly, and in accordance with such a fixed pattern, that the bicentennial of 1989 might more truthfully have commemorated two hundred years of scapegoating than two hundred years of *Liberté, Egalité,* and *Fraternité.*

Distinguishing, for the moment, the emblematic victims of the right from those of the left, the former would include, in roughly chronological order, Freemasons, Protestants, Jacobins, Blues, liberals, *démocsocs,* Reds, Communards, Jews, Freemasons again, anarchists, Protestants again, *métèques* (Mediterraneans), Communists, Jews again, immigrants and Jews and Freemasons again, again, and again. A select list of the scapegoats of the left would feature, again in approximate sequence, *aristos,* "hoarders," *fédérés,* Whites, Jesuits, Jews, "speculators," landlords, bourgeois, clericals, capitalists, *les gros, les deux cent familles,* collaborators, and so on. Sometimes, of course, the scapegoat-victims are individualized: Marat, Robespierre, Dreyfus, and Jaurès for the right, Louis XVI, Napoleon, and Pétain for the left.

The scapegoating of women, from the princesse de Lamballe, the supposed lover of Marie-Antoinette, killed in the massacres of September

1792, and Marie-Antoinette herself, through the collective fantasy of the *pétroleuses* in 1871 and the execution of Mata Hari (Margaretha Zelle) by firing squad at the Château de Vincennes in October 1917, to the ritual humiliation of "horizontal collaborators" in the summer of 1944, is a specific instance of the broader phenomenon of sexual stereotyping and will be examined in detail in a later volume.[94]

Almost all scapegoats are believed to be in league with foreigners, be they *aristos,* capitalists, Socialists, Jesuits, Jews, or the "cosmopolitan human-rightsists" so abominated by the contemporary Front National. They are the internalized outsider, the "enemy within," and it is precisely this ambiguity that requires that they be outed openly and completely and then expelled from the polis. All scapegoats, whether individuals or groups, are both part of the nation and, given the circumstances, readily separable from it, and it is precisely this duality that permits their constitution as others or, more precisely, as others-who-are-also-the-same. It is, indeed, their sameness as much as their otherness that makes them such perfect targets for collective violence.

In the right context of collective angst and suspicion, almost anyone can become a target, an outlet for the fears and fantasies of the crowd or of the state. A single word, a simple misunderstanding, can sometimes mean death, as the unfortunate Germaine Quetier discovered when, on 7 July 1794, at the height of Jacobin-inspired paranoia, she was heard to say "in the presence of several citizens" that she (or they) needed a king (*il fallait un roi*). Accused, she replied that she meant she wanted not a king "like Capet or whoever" but *un rouet,* a spinning wheel, *roi* being pronounced *rwè* in the language of the court, whereas the popular pronunciation was, as in modern French, *rwa*. Her explanation did not prevent her from being guillotined as a royalist and foreign agent.[95]

Many victims, like Germaine Quetier, are entirely innocent, but the situation of most is morally equivocal: the privileged and the powerful now brought down for ritual humiliation and sacrifice. Many are victimizers turned victims, executioner-martyrs now terrorized by those they had formerly terrorized. All are monsters, not just in being (in the eyes of their tormentors) morally repugnant, but more in their doubleness, their hybridity, that quality they have of being at once "us" and "not-us," of being French and not French at one and the same time. All, finally, are believed to be engaged in some plot or conspiracy against the French nation and people, be it famine plot or foreign plot, Jesuit conspiracy or Jewish, Socialist, or Communist "International." Indeed, from the "flour war" of 1775 through the killings of July 1789, the September massacres and the Terror to the June Days and the *Semaine sanglante,* there is probably no major instance of political violence in France in which fear of conspiracy is not in some way involved. Conspiracy, scapegoating, and violence form a single complex or nexus, and, though each is in theory conceivable without the other, in practice they are only rarely encountered in isolation.

The French Revolution obviously did not invent scapegoating per se—"witches" had, from the fifteenth to the early eighteenth century, provided precisely the focus for collective phobias and fantasies that subsequent political scapegoats would afford,[96] and Damiens was explicitly designated as a scapegoat when he met his horrific end in 1757[97]—but it did transform scapegoating into a more or less integral component of national politics. Although revolutionary idealists defined the French Republic as "universal"—"the designation French and *universal* will become synonymous," declared the Prussian-born Anacharsis Cloots (1755–94), the self-styled "Orator of the Human Race," in 1793[98]—in practice its "universalism" depended on the prior exclusion of all otherness. In his seminal *Qu'est-ce que le Tiers Etat?* (January 1789), the abbé Siéyès had declared "aristocrats" to be "foreign to the nation" on account of their "idleness," the very existence of a privileged caste constituting "a social crime, a veritable act of war," "an act of treason to the commonwealth," whose membership is to be restricted, both in theory and in practice, to the Third Estate; even before the Estates General had convened, the First Estate had been explicitly excluded from "the nation."[99]

Based on a primary act of exclusion, the Revolution proceeded to exclude first one "faction" or "corporation," then another from the so-called universal Republic, its exclusionary zeal reaching its peak in 1793–94, when linguistic unity, among other things, was declared to be essential to national unity, whence the need, in the words of the abbé Grégoire, both to "universalize" and "revolutionize" (*révolutionner*) French by suppressing all local and particularist "idioms." Or as Barère put it in his great speech of 8 Pluviôse An II, "Federalism and superstition speak Low Breton; emigration and hatred of the Republic speak German; counterrevolution speaks Italian, and fanaticism speaks Basque. Let us crush [*cassons*] these instruments of harm and error."[100]

Just as Jews could become full French citizens on condition that they renounce the corporate expression of their Jewishness, so acceptance as "French" entailed abnegation of any national, ethnic, linguistic, or cultural difference, a requirement that would shortly have sweeping consequences in colonial theory and practice as well as in the construction of a unitary national identity. In practice, the much-vaunted "assimilationism" or "universalism" of the French republican tradition is based on a deep-seated heterophobia, which expresses itself with particular intensity in the Republic's educational ideology, whence the systematic efforts to root out patois under the Third Republic and more recent controversies concerning the wearing of "Islamic scarves" in French schools.[101]

The fate of Anacharsis Cloots himself—guillotined as an Hébertist and foreign agent in March 1794—stands as a tragic and ironic prologue to the history of republican pseudo-universalism. Even this "citizen of the human race," a native of Prussia, "future department of the French nation," was, at the last, considered more foreign than French, more particular than universal. "Yes," declared Robespierre as he denounced him, "foreign powers have in our very midst their spies, their ministers, their treasurers and police. Cloots is a Prussian. I have told you the history of his political life. Deliver your verdict."[102]

For the French republican tradition, therefore, each and every expression of otherness is a further fortress to be stormed; truly, "it is not with impunity that one adopts the model of a united people capturing an almost empty Bastille."[103] But the heterophobia inherent in the nationalism of the counterrevolutionary right is even more dangerous, since the right's conception of national unity is based not on ideology, language, or culture (until recently the French right has been notably more sympathetic to patois and regional identities than the left) but on religion and "race." The Catholicization and racialization of French national identity was a cumulative process that began in the immediate aftermath of the Revolution, incubated between 1830 and 1870, and then exploded with virulent force in the 1880s and 1890s. Characteristically, its architects were thinkers associated as much with the left (Michelet, Renan) as with the right (Drumont, Barrès, Maurras), with Péguy, the only authentic Catholic among them, occupying, as ever, an ambiguous intermediate zone. The inevitable consequence of this redefinition of national identity in religious-racial terms was what Pierre Birnbaum has called "the diabolization of the adversary";[104] in other words, the explicit denial of full Frenchness to all who were not "racially" French, adhered to a religion other than Catholicism, or had no religion at all: specifically, Jews, Protestants, Freemasons, and *métèques,* the "four confederated Estates," in Maurras's words, with which "real power" in France was identified.[105] In theory, therefore, both the "open nationalism" of the Republic and the "closed nationalism" of the reaction were based on a refusal in principle of otherness.[106] If the consequences of the reaction's racially and religiously motivated exclusion of *l'Etranger de l'intérieur,* the internal Foreigner (Maurras),[107] were more baleful than the Republic's ideologically motivated exclusion, both necessarily implied the othering of potential scapegoats as the sine qua non of national identity. A theory of identity based on such an inaugural act of exclusion was almost bound to produce a theory—a procession, a cortege—of actual suffering victims.

If the ideological function of scapegoating is clear, its psychopolitical and emotional functions are even more so. The year 1940 offers an exemplary instance of its role in the collective psychology of a nation. What Claude Bourdet calls "a bout of self-punishing madness" (*une folie d'autopunition*) combined with "a wave of almost sexual admiration for the potency [*puissance*] of the victor" initially caused the entire population, including the government elite, to blame themselves for the catastrophe that had befallen the nation.[108] It is this feeling of collective masochism and guilt that Camus captures so perfectly in Paneloux's homily in *La Peste* (1947) and Sartre in the almoner's address to the prisoners of war in *La Mort dans l'âme* (1949), with its typical exhortation to those "who are neither completely innocent nor certainly the most guilty" that "if there is fault and if there is atonement [*expiation*], there is also redemption [*rachat*]."[109] This collective wallowing in guilt was not, Bourdet admits, without its pleasurable dimension, but, he continues,

> guilt [*la culpabilité*] is even more agreeable if the best part of it can be transferred to others. The new governing élite [*les nouveaux dirigeants*, i.e., Vichy] considered themselves guilty, in this perspective, only to the extent that they had not succeeded in taking power sooner. The real culprits were the workers, left-wing ideologues, Freemasons, Jews, Communists, and in general the whole republican system. It was thus possible there and then to cease proclaiming one's guilt [*battre sa coulpe*]; one proclaimed others to be guilty, self-punishment gave way to punishment, and one could rush headlong into this with a violence that was all the greater in that it was based on a colossal lie; at Vichy, it was precisely the principal culprits who were in power: all those who, clearly or confusedly, had for years considered fascists and Nazis as their allies, and the people as their enemy.[110]

In this perspective, 1940 repeated the well-established precedent of 1793–94, 1814–15, and 1870–71: blame anyone other than oneself. But the pleasure of scapegoating is not just negative, but positive. It consists, in the Girardian formula, in the union of all against one, in "unanimity minus one,"[111] and the emotional satisfactions it affords are enormous: the satisfaction of not being alone, of being absorbed in community; of knowing Good and Evil to be absolutely distinguished one from the other and of knowing oneself to belong to the Good, to be good beyond any possibility of equivocation or taint; of having any internal psychological or moral conflicts or doubts transformed into a straightforward Manichean opposition of (collective) self versus other. "Us" versus "Them," all those "good people who love themselves hating together" (*braves gens qui s'aiment de détester ensemble*), as Anne Tristan, quoting Albert Cohen, puts it in her remarkable memoir of six months spent in the Front National.[112]

No one has better expressed the sheer pleasure of scapegoating than Sartre in *Réflexions sur la question juive* (1954). The scapegoating community is a community held together by something far more powerful than love, the ecstasy of collective anger directed outward against a powerless victim or victims. It is egalitarian in a way that no actual society has been or is likely ever to be: rich and powerless, old and young, male and female merge together as one in pursuit and punishment of their prey; the scapegoating crowd is a pack.[113] Above all, says Sartre, "it is *amusing* to be antisemitic"[114]—amusing to announce a visit to the lavatory as "going to write to the Jews" (polite euphemism in certain circles at the time of the Dreyfus affair),[115] amusing to claim that "only lice were gassed at Auschwitz" (Darquier de Pellepoix, 1979), amusing to describe the Holocaust as a "point of detail" in the history of the Second World War (Jean-Marie Le Pen, September 1987) and to dub a political opponent "Monsieur Durafour-crématoire" (Le Pen, September 1988).[116] And it is the sheer fun of being part of a crowd united against a terrified Other that makes it likely, as Anna Tristan tells the various followers of Le Pen she has known, that "this logic of the scapegoat" will continue as long as humanity itself, or at least until "it [has crushed] all of you, and all of us" (*elle vous, elle nous broiera tous*).[117]

SACRIFICE

Although there is no necessary connection between scapegoating and actual physical violence—the scapegoat can be expelled, marginalized, or simply imprisoned—the act of killing tends to follow so rapidly on the act of "othering" that they constitute the two sides of a single lethal exclusionary project. This book has brought together an extraordinary sequence of politically motivated killings, extending over more than a century and a half, involving individual victims, groups, and sometimes whole communities, and ranging from spontaneous lynchings by "the people" to carefully choreographed show trials and executions sponsored by the state. In order to impose some conceptual order on this historical bloodbath, I propose, following Brian Singer,[118] to divide the killings into two broad categories: those in which, in Singer's terms, the victim is "ingested" by a given collectivity, and those in which he or she is expelled from the polis.

Singer uses this opposition to distinguish between the character of revolutionary violence in France before and after the massacres of September 1792, which, in his typology, marked the transition from the ingestive to the exclusionary model of killing. My own use of the opposition is somewhat different, and ranges over a considerably longer time span. By exclusionary or eliminationist violence I designate all those acts whereby the sacrificing group seeks to purify itself and the polis by simply removing the polluting presence from its midst, putting it to death, and, commonly, rending and dispersing its remains until, finally, nothing, or next to nothing, is left either of its physical being or, ideally, of what it represented morally or spiritually to its supporters or allies. The paradigmatic acts of eliminationist violence were, on the spontaneous level, the lynching of de Launay and de Flesselles and, on the organized state level, the trial and execution of Louis XVI. Contrasted to such acts is the ingestive or incorporative model of sacrifice. Here it is not the sacrificing group that plays the primary role, but the group from whose midst the victim has been taken and slain, which then reabsorbs him or her, duly enhanced morally and spiritually as a result of the violence undergone, into its corporate self in the form of the martyr. The exemplary instances of ingestive sacrifice are the killings of Marat (slain by a royalist and reincorporated by republicans) and, once again, although, of course, from an antithetical standpoint, Louis XVI (slain by republicans and reincorporated by royalists). What is an exclusionary sacrifice for one group is, almost by definition, an ingestive sacrifice for the group from which the victim has come; or, to put it more simply, one group's scapegoat is the other group's martyr. Most of the examples that follow are taken, inevitably, from the years 1789–94, before an attempt is made to generalize the model to cover all the acts of politically inspired violence of the following century and a half.

The pattern of spontaneous eliminationist violence almost never varies. The sacrificing group seizes on one or more individuals whom it instantly defines as "other" (characteristically using a rapidly conventionalized lexicon of exclusion: "monsters," "brigands," "cannibals," and the like), subjects them to various forms of ritual humiliation (taunting, jostling, pelting with stones, excrement, or other putrescent materials), and kills them in messy and summary fashion (often using penknives, jimmies, meat choppers, and other improvised weapons) before parading the victims' dismembered remains around the vicinity and finally consigning them beyond the limits of the community, in a river or quarry or other disaffected, out-of-the-way spot. In the state-sponsored version of the exclusionary sacrifice, ritual humiliation is usually expressed in discursive form (the language of monsters and brigands), the display of the victims' remains is normally reduced to a momentary but nonetheless supercharged minimum, and the authorities take care to destroy the bodies completely, in the (usually forlorn) hope that no cult will grow up around the memory of the victims if no gravestones or other monuments exist to give them a focus. The killings of de Launay, de Flesselles, Bertier, and Foulon clearly fall into the spontaneous version of the exclusionary sacrifice; the execution of the marquis de Favras in February 1790 provides the first instance of the state-sponsored variety; and the massacres of September 1792 are positioned midway between the two. In this latter case, the death squads were clearly incited by duly elected revolutionary politicians, with, for example, the Jacobin Collot d'Herbois describing 2 September, the first day of the massacres, as "the great article of the Credo of our liberty," adding that "without that day our revolution would never be consummated [*accomplie*]."[119]

Septembriseurs characteristically subjected their victims to impromptu trials, which it would be wrong to dismiss as window dressing or parody; the objective of the massacres was to cleanse the polis of imaginary foreign agents and, as such, it required more than just a veneer of revolutionary justice. On the other hand, the killers went about their business armed with cutlasses, cudgels, axes, or the tools of whatever day job they followed, and they also, notoriously, engaged in ritualized torture, humiliation, and mutilation of their victims, especially, it seems, when the latter were women: the aristocratic Mlle. de Sombreuil was reputedly forced to drink a glassful of blood to save the life of her father;[120] a flower seller, one Marie Gredelier, who had murdered and mutilated her lover, had her breasts cut off and a lighted torch introduced into her vagina before she was killed;[121] and, as we have seen, the princesse de Lamballe's head and possibly her genitalia were promenaded through the streets, the princesse having previously undergone a four-hour interrogation at the hands of her tormentors.[122]

It was doubtless the spectacle of barely controlled semi-official violence that prompted the revolutionary politicians to take the Terror firmly under their wing and give it a structured and fully institutionalized form.

"Let us be terrible to prevent the people from being so," Danton famously declared after the massacres,[123] a remark capped for sheer blood-curdling horror by the little-known Jean-Baptiste Drouet a year later when he declared, "Let us be brigands for the happiness of the people."[124] The institutionalized terror that resulted is best viewed as the most extreme instance of heterophobia in French history. The revolutionaries justified their "purification" of the nation with reference to the purification to which they had subjected themselves. "If we purge ourselves," declared Garnier, the Jacobin deputy of Saintes (the hometown of Joseph-Ignace Guillotin), "it is in order to have the right to purge France; we shall leave no heterogeneous body [*aucun corps hétérogène*] in the Republic."[125] To be other, even to be individual, was to be guilty. "France, you will be happy when you are finally cured of individuals," declared "Orator" Cloots in his *Appel au genre humain* of 1793, little realizing, presumably, where his geometrical logic would lead him the following year.[126]

"The minority is always guilty, even if it is morally in the right," wrote Restif de La Bretonne in *Les Nuits révolutionnaires* (1790),[127] and between the winter of 1792 and the summer of 1794 one minority after another was sent to the scaffold in furtherance of "the triumph of innocence" (Saint-Just):[128] first a minority of one (Louis XVI), a "monster" (Grégoire),[129] a "stranger in our midst" (Saint-Just again),[130] slain "in order that the *Patrie* might live"; then minority parties in the Assemblée (Girondists, Hébertists, Dantonists), followed by the surviving minorities of a class (the aristocracy) and a calling (priests and nuns). Having founded their power on the judicial murder of the former father of the nation, the revolutionaries construed any attack on the Revolution or themselves as a parricidal act. When Cécile Renault, who had tried to kill Robespierre with a penknife on 24 May 1794, went to the guillotine on 2 June, she wore the red shirt of the convicted father-killer, just as Charlotte Corday had done the previous year.[131] Finally, the logic of eliminationist terror turned against that "hermaphroditic race of new Cromwells," Robespierre and his followers themselves,[132] and it was their turn to be flung from the Tarpeian rock of revolutionary justice into what no one had yet thought of calling the dustbin of history. "In the inextricable and sanguinary condition in which the Republic found itself before 9 Thermidor," wrote the anti-Robespierrist Marc-Antoine Baudot after the event, "it was possible to get out of this horrible situation only by the death or ostracizing of Robespierre. Therefore, in the struggle of 9 Thermidor, the question was not of principles but of killing."[133] The logic of extrusive sacrifice could not be expressed more clearly, or more cruelly.

The structure of "ingestive" sacrifice inverts almost point for point that of its exclusionary counterpart. Dismemberment is replaced by the will to re-member, both literally and metaphorically, as the bereaved group from which the victim was taken strives to preserve his or her body from decay as long as possible and to use it as the focus around which its shattered unity might be reconstituted and in whose real, and then remembered, presence its members may commune with one another. The first such martyred body to be officially sanctified was that of Louis Simonneau, mayor of Etampes, killed on 3 March 1792 by a crowd of rioting peasants—instantly dubbed "bandits," "cannibals," and "brigands" by Simonneau's thurifers—when he attempted to enforce regulations on food rationing.[134] As it happened, it was the "moderate" wing of the revolutionary movement, backed by some constitutional monarchists, who organized the Fête de la Loi held on Sunday, 3 June 1792, to honor Simonneau's sacrifice—for the radicals, Marat condemned him as "an artisan of famine, of the race of hoarders [*un ouvrier de famine ... de race accapareuse*]"[135]—and they did so in conscious retaliation for the left's Fête de la Liberté, held on 15 April to celebrate the springing from prison at Châteauvieux (Nancy) of Swiss guards incarcerated there for mutinying against their "loyalist" officers in August 1790.[136]

Thereafter, it was the radicals, Jacobins in the van, who spearheaded the cult of the revolutionary martyr with a succession of mass demonstrations, processions, and civic festivities honoring, among others, the "boy martyrs" Bara and Viala; the Jacobin Lepeletier de Saint-Fargeau, killed on the eve of the king's execution by a royalist assassin named Philippe Pâris, who later committed suicide when captured in Normandy; Joseph Chalier, the virtually certifiable leader of the Jacobin Terror in Lyon, guillotined by his federalist enemies on 17 July 1793, his execution apparently timed to coincide with that of Charlotte Corday; and Corday's own sacrificial victim, Jean-Paul Marat.

Marat's beatification has been extensively studied,[137] and the inhumation of his heart at the Club des Cordeliers, the headquarters of his political faction, on 28 July 1793 to the strains of the chant "O cor Jesus, ô cor Marat" was the first of a whole litany of comparisons between the Nazarene and *L'Ami du Peuple*. "Both wanted equality," declared one such idolater. "Jesus put down the pride of the scribes and the Pharisees, and Marat that of the nobles and priests; both detested hoarders and speculators: Jesus overthrew the tables of the money changers in the temple, and Marat did not cease to protest against the bankers of the Rue Vivienne."[138] Only one Cordelier, Brochet, had the nerve and integrity to

protest against this rampant messianism: "Marat is not made to be compared with Jesus. That man gave birth to superstition, he defended kings,
and Marat had the courage to crush them."[139]

The structure of one ingestive sacrifice much resembled another. First
the body of the revolutionary martyr—exclusively male except for the
nineteen-year-old republican Perrine Dugué, killed by counterrevolutionaries at Thorigné in the Mayenne on 22 March 1796[140]—was displayed in public for as long as was hygienically possible: Lepeletier de
Saint-Fargeau at the Place des Piques (the former Place de Vendôme), on
the plinth where Louis XIV's statue had stood before its removal in August 1792; Marat at the secularized Eglise des Cordeliers, and in a position that exposed the martyr's wounds like the stigmata of Christ. Burial
followed, and then immortalization by icon, in the form, ideally, of an
altarpiece by David, whose dramatic painting of the assassinated Marat,
still with Corday's treacherous letter of introduction in his hand, has
been well described as a "sans-culotte Pietà,"[141] and whose uncompleted commemorations of Lepeletier and Bara are likewise conceived as
"slogan paintings for the masses,"[142] sometimes in deliberately provocative imitation of the mass (as at Chalier's funeral in Lyon, where the
radical déchristianizer Grandmaison drank from a chalice and proclaimed, "Verily I say unto you, my brothers, this is the blood of kings,
the true substance of republican communion, take and drink this precious substance"),[143] but more commonly in the form of an open-air
meal, more reminiscent of the feeding of the five thousand than of the
Eucharist. Thus at the *fête révolutionnaire* honoring Bara's martyrdom
held at Arles on 7 July 1794, people arrived carrying bottles of wine and
staffs from which hung "bunches of turnips, onions, garlic, leeks, arti-
chokes, a slice of cheese, bacon, sausage, an anchovy, a herring, a small
piece of game," which, having sat down, they proceeded to eat.[144] As
they did so, a guillotine was trundled from one town square to the next,
a macabre reminder that, in the words of one modern historian, "it was
in the name of its own wounds that the Republic sought and obtained
the Great Terror."[145]

Royalists and counterrevolutionaries obviously had few, if any, opportunities to stage commemorative feasts in honor of *their* martyrs, although,
as we have seen, from the moment Louis XVI stepped onto the scaffold on
21 January 1793, royalist propagandists set out systematically to liken his
sacrifice to Christ's, even casting Marie-Antoinette as an improbable
Magdalene. Presumably the individuals who dipped their handkerchiefs in
his blood (as spectators did in Troppmann's almost eighty years later) were
ghoulish pranksters rather than crypto-royalist "communicants," but their

action testifies to the power of the idea of ingestive sacrifice over people whose First Communion had in all likelihood been their last. In the Vendée, scores, perhaps hundreds of altars, chapels, and oratories were erected during the Restoration and afterward to commemorate the region's counterrevolutionary martyrs, establishing a cult that still has its votaries today among local people and, less honorably, among the politicians and ideologues of the far right.[146] The later cult of Joan of Arc has many of the characteristics of an ingestive sacrifice, to be set beside the much less successful attempts to promote the duc d'Enghien and the assassinated duc de Berry as royalist martyrs. Bonapartists had their martyrs in Napoleon himself and, in much muted form, in the duc de Reichstadt and the prince imperial. In general, however, the cult of the political martyr is more a phenomenon of the left than of the right, if only because, the first revolution apart, the left has so many more martyrs to venerate.

Since 1815 the exclusionary sacrifice has been practiced intermittently by the left, with the killings of Archbishops Affre (June 1848) and Darboy (May 1871), like those of Generals Lecomte and Clément-Thomas at the start of the Commune, clearly falling into that category, as do the far more justifiable killings, both legal and extralegal, of 1944–45: Henriot, Brasillach, Darnand, Laval. The right has probably engaged in fewer acts of individual elimination (Jaurès, Georges Mandel, Jean Zay), preferring mass hecatombs of exclusionary victims (June 1848, May 1871, July 1942) to picking off this or that exemplary scapegoat. A possibly unique instance of one right-winger killing another is provided by the assassination of Darlan by the royalist (but anti-Vichyist) Fernand Bonnier de La Chapelle in North Africa on 24 December 1942. Bonnier was executed two days later—even Vichy kept Christmas Day sacred. The inclusionary sacrifice was regularly celebrated throughout the period covered by this book, and with far greater intensity by the left than the right, not least because forms of constitutional or legal opposition were so often denied it. The outstanding instances are the following:

1. The Massacre of the Rue Transnonain (April 1834), immortalized by Daumier's extraordinary lithograph.
2. The fusillade of the Boulevard des Capucines (February 1848), the inaugural act of the February revolution, when the victims' bodies were conveyed through the streets like so many votary offerings.
3. The self-immolation of Victor Baudin (December 1851).
4. The victims of the *Semaine sanglante,* especially those shot at Père-Lachaise, commemorated ever since by the left's ingestive sacrifice par excellence, the annual procession to the Mur des Fédérés.

5. The assassination of Jaurès (July 1914).

6. The exemplary deaths of a succession of resistance heroes and heroines: the Communists shot at Châteaubriant and elsewhere (October 1941), the execution of Gabriel Péri (December 1941) and Georges Politzer (May 1942), the deaths of Bertie Albrecht (thought to have killed herself rather than undergo further torture at Fresnes in May 1943) and Danièle Casanova (killed by typhus at Auschwitz, also in May 1943, and systematically cast as a resistance Joan of Arc by Communist propaganda).

The great political funerals of nineteenth- and early twentieth-century Paris—from Manuel (1827), Lamarque (1832), Béranger (1857), Victor Noir (1870), and Victor Hugo (1885) to Jaurès (1914)—are all clearly variants on the ingestive paradigm, their Communion-like character being explicitly dwelt on in many writings of the time. Finally, Pantheonization—from Marat (1793) to Jean Moulin (died in July 1943 on his way to a concentration camp in Germany, after having been interrogated and tortured by Klaus Barbie in Lyon, Pantheonized 1964) via Zola (whose accidental death in October 1902 by carbon monoxide poisoning caused by a blocked chimney in his Paris apartment raised suspicions of anti-Dreyfus foul play and completed his consecration by the left)[147] and Jaurès (Pantheonized 1924)—represents the ultimate apotheosis as the martyred body of the Hero is received into the corporate body of the Nation, though as the example of Marat ("depantheonized" after Thermidor) makes clear, such incorporation does not exclude the possibility of subsequent expulsion.

Even when their sacrificial character was long since forgotten, the left marked its festivals and anniversaries with quasi-eucharistic rituals of eating and drinking. From the first Fête de la Fédération of 1790 through the republican agapes of 1848–51 to the huge open-air blow-outs in the working-class districts of Paris every 14 July, from the first modern *fête nationale* of 1880 until the outbreak of war, when French men and women have wanted to celebrate the *res publica,* they have sat down at table in public and eaten and drunk to their fill. In the songs of the working-class troubadour Pierre Dupont (1821–70), Lyon-born and, for a time, a close friend of Baudelaire, the eating of bread—preferably white—and the drinking of wine—almost obligatorily red—become republican-socialist sacraments, harbingers of the communistic millennium to come:

La terre va briser ses chaînes;
La misère a fini son bail;

Les monts, les vallons et les plaines
Vont engendrer par le travail.
Affamés, venez en foule
Comme les mouches sur le thym.
Les blés sont mûrs, le pressoir coule:
Voilà du pain, voilà du vin.
   ("Le Chant des paysans," 1849)[148]

[The earth will break its chain; / Misery has ended its lease; / Hills, vales, and plains will give birth thanks to [human] work. / All you who are hungry, gather in your crowds, / Like flies on flowers of thyme. / The cornfields are ripe, the wine press is flowing: / Here is bread, here is wine.]

The message of Eugène Pottier's "La Bouteille inépuisable" (no date) is even more clear-cut. From the bottle of revolution will flow endlessly the deep-red wine of *Liberté, Fraternité, Egalité* that ignorance and poverty and the social and political forces that sustain them have kept hidden away under lock and key from those whom, in the one song for which he is now remembered, Pottier strikingly called *les damnés de la terre,* the wretched of the earth.[149] What the Church and its Communion rail were for the Ultramontane right, so the bars of the cabaret and the café were for the republican-socialist left. A sump of drunken rebelliousness in the eyes of reactionaries, the cabaret was for someone like Zola—no radical but a republican to the bone—a republic in miniature in which Marianne carouses with her republican brothers and sisters: "*Eh bien!* let the people go to the cabaret and, linking arms, raise their glasses high with the Republic [*qu'il y aille boire chopine, bras dessus bras dessous avec la République*]!"[150]
   Even today the link between the Republic and food and wine has not altogether been lost, as anyone who has walked through the table-crowded streets of Paris on the evening of 13 July—the 14th itself is for military parades and official speeches—can readily testify. Whether anyone recalls that the great blow out commemorates the killing of de Launay and de Flesselles as well as the taking of the Bastille itself is, of course, another matter entirely.
   The eucharistic character of the republican fête links up with the continuing, if displaced, vitality of the figure of Christ, stripped of many of his doctrinal attributes, among a supposedly dechristianized populace. That the right should have likened its principal martyrs, from Louis XVI to Pope Pius IX, to Christ is hardly surprising, and when, in June 1848,

Archbishop Affre prepared to mount the barricades in the cause of peace and reconciliation, there to be felled by a bullet coming from one side or the other, it was with complete moral and doctrinal consistency that he put himself forward as an *alter Christus:* "My God, I offer you my life, accept it in expiation of my sins, and in order to halt the shedding of the blood that is flowing.... I would die content if I could hope for the end of this horrendous civil war, if my sacrifice put an end to so many woes."[151] But, as we have seen, between 1830 and 1870 in particular the legitimists' Christ was challenged by the figure of Christ-the-first-republican and Christ-the-first-socialist, advanced both by radical (and increasingly heterodox) theologians like Lamennais and his followers and by a host of working-class publications and images: tracts, poems, songs, woodcuts, and lithographs. Entering a tailor's workshop in the late 1840s, one working-class journalist was shown a lithograph representing "Jesus crowned with thorns and leaning on two allegorical figures: Liberty and Equality. In this moving image, the Son of God holds under his naked feet the demon of pride, which spews forth gold, and the word 'Hope' is inscribed in the beaming disk that shines over his head, full of tenderness and mildness." The lesson for workers is obvious: "Jesus is the finest model that has been offered to man.... He was born poor, like all of us; he worked, he suffered persecution. He died for the sake of justice, nailed to a hideous gibbet, and he has never ceased to be gentle, humane, chaste, compassionate."[152]

If Jesus was the first socialist martyr, it was only logical to compare subsequent martyrs to the cause to their illustrious prototype, and, while the figure of the republican-socialist Christ went into abeyance, without disappearing completely, after the Commune, the tradition of the Christlike socialist martyr that appears to begin with the cult of Marat in 1793 continued to thrive, reaching its apogee with the "crucifixion" and instant beatification of Jaurès in 1914. It is still clearly present in Paul Eluard's moving and widely circulated homage to Gabriel Péri, the Communist official executed at Mont-Valérien in December 1941 in reprisal for the killing of German soldiers by the Resistance:

Un homme est mort qui n'avait pour défense
Que ses bras ouverts à la vie.
Un homme est mort qui n'avait d'autre route
Que celle où l'on hait les fusils.
Un homme est mort qui continue la lutte
Contre la mort, contre l'oubli,
Car tout ce qu'il voulait

Nous le voulions aussi.
Nous le voulons aujourd'hui
Que le bonheur soit la lumière
Au fond des yeux au fond du coeur
Et la justice sur la terre
Il y a des mots qui font vivre
Et ce sont des mots innocents
Le mot chaleur le mot confiance
Amour justice et le mot liberté
Le mot enfant et le mot gentillesse
Et certains noms de fleurs et certains noms de fruits
Le mot courage et le mot découvrir
Et le mot frère et le mot camarade
Et certains noms de pays de villages
Et certains noms de femmes et d'amis
Ajoutons-y Péri
Péri est mort pour ce qui nous fait vivre
Tutoyons-le sa poitrine est trouée
Mais grâce à lui nous nous connaissons mieux
Tutoyons-nous son espoir est vivant.[153]

[A man has died whose one defense / Was his arms open to life / A man has died who had no other way / Than that of hatred of guns / A man has died who continues the fight / Against death against oblivion / For what he wanted / We wanted too / We want it today / Let happiness be the light / In the depth of eyes in the depth of the heart / And justice upon earth / There are words that give life / And they are innocent words / The word warmth and the word confidence / Love justice and the word freedom / The word child and the word kindness / And certain names of flowers and certain names of fruits / The word courage and the word discover / And the word brother and the word comrade / And certain names of places and of villages / And certain names of women and of friends / Let us add Péri to them / Péri died for that which makes us live / Let us embrace each other his breast is holed / But thanks to him we know each other better / Let us embrace his hope is living still]

From the execution of Lepeletier in January 1793 to the execution of Péri a century and a half later, the sacrificial paradigm hardly varies. "It is all of us that have been wounded," it was proclaimed at one memorial ceremony in honor of Lepeletier, "his martyred body is our own as well,"[154] but it is in and through the martyr's wounds that the survivors will renew their solidarity and find new strength and courage for the fight. A non-Christian writing about a non-Christian for an audience made up of Christians and others, Eluard unobtrusively draws on the image of Christ's Passion and of the mass to bring home his message. Péri's arms were open to life as Christ's were to all and sundry during *his* life and as they were on the cross where he died; Péri bears good news for mankind like his namesake Gabriel before him; the simple words he uttered give life like Jesus' parables. He has not perished (*péri*), for the very bullet wounds that tore open his chest became, like Christ's wounds, the healing ground in which those who follow him can communicate with each other and reaffirm their hope in the future. Though dead, Péri is really present in the minds and memories of those faithful to his example, and "Let us embrace" echoes the sign of peace exchanged before the taking of Communion. Secularized, blood had not lost its power to heal and redeem; indeed, it flows with an abundance scarcely matched even during the Age of Faith, as we shall see.

BLOOD

Il me semble parfois que mon sang coule à flots,
Ainsi qu'une fontaine aux rhythmiques sanglots.
Je l'entends bien qui coule avec un long murmure,
Mais je me tâte en vain pour trouver la blessure.
A travers la cité, comme dans un champ clos,
Il s'en va, transformant les pavés en îlots,
Désaltérant la soif de chaque créature,
Et partout colorant en rouge la nature.
  (Baudelaire, "La Fontaine de Sang")

[Sometimes it seems my blood spurts out in gobs / As if it were a fountain's pulsing sobs; / I clearly hear it mutter as it goes, / Yet cannot find the wound from which it flows. / Then through the city, coursing in the lists, / It travels, forming islands in its midst, / Seeing that every creature will be fed / And staining nature its flamboyant red.][155]

Blood obsessed the nineteenth- and early twentieth-century French imagination as did no other substance, and it would be possible to stock a modest bookshelf with works bearing the word *sang* in their title, among them *Sueur de sang* (the title both of a book of short stories by Léon Bloy [1893] and of a collection of poems [1935] by the unclassifiable Freudian-Catholic-Surrealist poet Pierre-Jean Jouve [1887–1976]); *Le Sang du pauvre* (1909), also by Bloy; an early novel by Mauriac, *La Chair et le sang* (1920); Louis Guilloux's *Le Sang noir* (1935), and, at the end of our period, Simone de Beauvoir's *Le Sang des autres* (1945) and, the work with the most eloquent and symptomatic title of all, Maurice Barrès's *Du sang, de la volupté et de la mort* of 1894. If the lynching of de Launay and de Flesselles and the execution of Louis XVI inaugurate the history of modern France, at its literary and ideological portal stand the figures of the marquis de Sade (1740–1814) and Joseph de Maistre (1755–1821), the radical atheist and the militant theocrat, opposed in everything save their shared belief (from which they drew very different consequences and conclusions) in the natural viciousness of man and in their common obsession with the violent shedding of blood. Set in labyrinthine châteaux or catacomb-like prisons, the Sadean universe with its obsession with plots, betrayals, denunciations, and vicious torture and murder appears as a fantasmagorical image of both the oppressive patriarchy of the old regime and the generalized terror of the new. Sade's minutely choreographed orgies parody and subvert the rituals of the *fête révolutionnaire,* whose life-giving fountains and springs are inverted in the deathly gushing of blood and other bodily fluids—sweat, tears, urine, excrement, sperm—that irrigates the *fête de la perversion* and acts as the founding sacrament of the blasphemous anticommunion of libertines.[156]

In the Sadean orgy, the participants rend each other open, penetrate and are penetrated, in an attempt to transcend the limits of individual identity less in fusing with the Other than in negating his or her autonomy entirely. Bodily substances have a demonically lustral quality in Sade's rituals as they jet and squirt over the participants, blurring their separate identities: "Fuck [*le foutre,* semen], the ejaculate from the dildoes, and blood flooded us from every side; we were swimming in the waves of it all."[157] One libertine, Clairwil, "rubs her clitoris over the bloody wounds she has inflicted on one unfortunate man; blood pours forth when the hymen is broken, when flesh is bitten, more rarely from male organs, or when the heart is torn out; blood is especially enjoyed when it pours out from buttocks and anus."[158] Sadean blood is copious and active, flowing inexhaustibly forth in "floods" and "great gushes." It is not merely shed, it is swallowed and ingested, leading, by the perverted logic of libertinage, to the ultimate sacrilege of cannibalism, even of "incestuous anthropophagy" when Noirceuil in *Histoire de Juliette*

(1797) somehow contrives simultaneously to sodomize one son, feed on his heart, and murder another son, all the while being sodomized by another roué:

> With these words, he throws himself upon his son Phaon, thrust into his ass, has himself fucked, and orders me [Juliette], while I am being frigged by Théodore, to tear the living heart out of the child he is fucking, and give it to him that he may devour it. The villain swallows it, while at the same moment plunging a dagger into the breast of his other son.[159]

The Sadean universe is animated, like the Revolution itself, by a primordial parricidal urge that reaches its climax in Juliette's torture and killing of her long-lost father, Bernole, whose name (from *berner,* to dupe) reduces him to a parody of the patriarchal principle. Driven to distraction by his daughter's perverse cruelty, Bernole "throws himself headfirst to the ground, cracks open his skull, and floods of blood gush forth" over the room, whereupon Juliette, declaring that "this blood is mine, and it is with rapture that I see it spilled," proceeds to masturbate her father to orgasm and receives into "her incestuous entrails the germ of a fruit like unto the one he left one day in her mother's womb." Having absorbed the blood and seed of "this first mover of her existence"— her father, his phallus, and the patriarchal principle rolled (as it were) into one—Juliette completes her negation of the Other, who also stands for the Wholly Other, for God, by killing and burying her father the next day;[160] an *ens causa sui,* she has, like the Revolution, supplanted both father and God in a carnival of violence, in which, by committing the supreme crime, she has attained to the summit of physical and spiritual *jouissance.*

It is precisely for the crime of substituting himself for God and the father as center and ground of the universe that, in Joseph de Maistre's patrocentric Ultramontane vision, man must atone, if need be by offering up his own body and blood as Jesus offered up his life to the Father as a ransom for the sins committed by his earthly sons and daughters. For de Maistre, as for the whole legitimist-Ultramontane tradition he largely founded, the execution of Louis XVI mirrors and repeats the primordial revolt against God, and is itself reflected in every subsequent act of revolt against the patriarchal principle in society; all sin is both parricidal and regicidal in intent and effect. In his remarkable essay *Eclaircissement sur les sacrifices* (1810?), one of the founding masterpieces of the comparative study of religion, de Maistre establishes the universality of blood sacrifice as a ritual practice, showing how in every culture known to him and his times, an "expiatory virtue" attaches to the "effusion of blood," not just to blood per se (and still less to flesh) but to its violent emission, to the actual deed of causing it to be shed, in the form of either animal sacrifice or human self-offering "even unto death."[161] Quoting Hebrews 9:22, *Sine sanguine non fit remissio* (if there is no shedding of blood, there is no remission; Jerusalem Bible), de Maistre explains how primitive and pre-Christian man, dimly conscious of having committed the primordial sin of substituting himself for God, sought to atone by offering up an animal or, in extreme circumstances, a human victim, a foreigner, an enemy ("Host," says de Maistre, comes from *hostis,* enemy), in substitution for himself, so that the slaying of the victim takes the place of actual self-sacrifice.[162]

The Christian, however, *is* required to sacrifice himself, physically if necessary, and not a substitute victim, by accepting and indeed actively seeking occasions for suffering and, by virtue of the principle of the reversibility of merits, atone for the sins of others (as well as his own) by willingly transforming himself into an expiatory offering. The voluntary assumption of suffering, if need be even unto death, repairs the cosmic equilibrium ruptured by man's original sin. By suffering, the Christian participates in and completes Christ's suffering on the cross and so brings to perfection the "universal idea of *communion through blood.*" In so doing, he becomes a co-author, even as he becomes a co-sufferer, of his own redemption and mankind's, actively collaborating in God's salvific purpose as embodied in the mass, in which the Word made flesh is communicated under the species of bread and wine to the faithful and "radiating from the center of the All-Powerful [*de la toute puissance*] who is everywhere, enters complete and intact [*toute entière*] into each mouth, and is multiplied infinitely without ever being divided."[163] Thus it is that "more rapid than lightning, more active than a thunderbolt, theandric blood penetrates the guilty entrails in order to consume their impurities." The Christian's willingness to suffer with and for Christ, of which the willingness to shed blood with and for that of his Saviour is the ultimate expression, combines or cooperates with the real presence of Christ's body and blood in the mass to bring to its sublime apotheosis the universal principle—and here, as so often, de Maistre has recourse to capital letters to underline his capital argument—of "LE SALUT PAR LE SANG,"[164] salvation in and through blood: the blood of the innocent redeems, in the strict etymological sense of pays for, ransoms, buys back, the sins of the guilty, thanks to the mysterious operation of the cosmic principle of reversibility or vicarious suffering.

Mario Praz's epoch-making *Romantic Agony* (1933) established beyond doubt the extent and intensity of the "divine marquis's" impact on the nineteenth-century French (and indeed European) imagination. Scarcely less important is the influence of de Maistre on the theological imagination of the next century and a half and thus on the bulk of French Catholic and Catholic-inspired literature produced between the first and second Vatican councils. Either directly or through the work of his epigone Blanc de Saint-Bonnet (1815–80), whose *La Douleur* (1849) was one of the most widely read Catholic works of the century,[165] de Maistre's ideas, particularly his revalorization of the traditional doctrine of redemptive suffering, influenced several generations of Catholic or Catholic-influenced writers: Ballanche and Bonald (1754–1840) early on in the century, then Barbey d'Aurevilly and Baudelaire ("Maistre and Edgar Poe taught me to reason"),[166] followed by Huysmans, Bloy, Claudel, and Bernanos, as well as writers of dubious orthodoxy such as Vintras and Boullan.

The theology of reversibility and vicarious suffering will be taken up in later volumes along with the question of male and female sanctity.[167] For our purposes here, we need only retain the two critical ideas: the Christian's obligation to suffer along with his Redeemer and the belief that, by willingly assuming such suffering, be he or she never so innocent, the Christian can literally purchase the salvation of others. Extreme adherents of the idea like (inevitably) Léon Bloy believed, or appear to have believed, that the proportion of happiness to pain in the world remained constant and that, accordingly, any happiness was bought at the expense of suffering by others; by corollary, willingly to take suffering upon oneself (as Christ, preeminently, had done on the cross) was automatically to relieve the suffering of someone somewhere and to contribute to the general salvation of humankind. This reasoning led Bloy and extremists like him to the perversely logical conclusion of actually willing disasters on some—preferably innocent but, failing that, on the guilty—in order that the sufferings of the many might thereby be "paid for" and alleviated.

On 4 May 1897 an annual Catholic-sponsored charity sale was held on the Rue Jean-Goujon, off the Champs-Elysées, where, on a vacant plot of land, a wooden mock-up of a medieval *quartier* of Paris had been erected to house the various stalls. The so-called Bazar de la Charité was, as usual, well supported, not least by many grandes dames of Catholic high society, but catastrophe ensued when the flimsy construction suddenly caught fire, causing a frantic rush for the exit in which 121 people, at least 110 of them women, were burned or trampled to

death. So great was the holocaust that wives who had told their husbands they would be attending the Bazar that afternoon and spent it
with their lovers instead reportedly had a hard time explaining how they
had survived. While *le tout-Paris* mourned the hecatomb of this "feminine Agincourt," as one newspaper described it, *La Croix,* quoting,
after de Maistre, the *sine sanguine* of Hebrews 9:22, saw the blaze in
which "lilies of purity" had perished alongside "roses of charity" as an
act of divine Providence, inflicting suffering on the nation's innocent for
the redemption of its guilty. Bloy went even further, writing to a friend
that "the small number of victims, it is true, limited my joy": if the innocent have to be massacred (and for Bloy it is axiomatic that they do),
let them be so in thousands rather than hundreds, especially when the
agent of their destruction is fire, "the roaring, darting dwelling place"
(*l'habitacle rugissant et vagabond*) of the Holy Spirit himself.[168]

Blood is the supreme expression of suffering and hence, by the same
token, the sign par excellence of divine election. The nineteenth century
as a whole showed an abiding obsession with the phenomenon of
stigmatization, as evinced in the remarkable cases of the so-called Living
Crucifix, Anne Catharine Emmerich (1774–1824) of Westphalia, whose
forehead, hands, and feet bled continually from 1794 to her death, and
of the Belgian-born Louise Lateau (1850–83), whose hands and feet
bled on a reputed 800 occasions with clockwork regularity on Fridays,
who was said to have been able, while in ecstasy, to converse in languages she had never learned, such as English and Latin, and who, seal-
ing her likeness to Christ, died at the age of thirty-three years.[169] Such
cases inspired both neurological and mystical interpretations. Henri
Legrand Du Saulle argued in *Les Hystériques* (1891) that "many
women *Saints* and *Blesseds*," including Catherine of Siena, Joan of Arc,
Teresa of Avila, and Marguerite-Marie Alacoque, the visionary of Paray-
le-Monial, were "nothing other than simple hysterics." Antoine Imbert
Courbeyre, in his *La Stigmatisation, l'extase divine et les miracles de
Lourdes: Réponse aux libres penseurs* (1894), countered that their issue
of blood had no known physiological or psychological etiology and
could be interpreted only as a sign of supernatural intervention.[170] Writers divided on similar lines, with the Belgian naturalist novelist Camille
Lemonnier (1844–1913) arguing in *L'Hystérique* (1885), his fictionalized account of the Lateau case, that Sister Humilité's "appalling crucified beauty" (*effroyable beauté de crucifiée*) had psychosomatic origins
and that the "fetid pool of blood" that regularly bathed her feet "as in a
slaughterhouse" was linked to the delayed onset of menstruation[171]—
"the wound of her sex appeared to her moreover as proof of an expia-

tion she was undergoing"[172]—which in turn was a manifestation of her underlying hysterical character.

This view of the stigmatic as "mysterical" (Luce Irigaray's term)[173] was rejected in Barbey d'Aurevilly's remarkable novel *Un Prêtre marié* (1865), in which the young woman Calixte, *la sainte Expiante*,[174] bleeds continually from her forehead, which she girds with a scarlet headband like a crown of thorns to atone for the sin of her father, Sombreval, who during the Revolution had (like, be it noted, Baudelaire's own father) renounced holy orders, married, and fathered a child. Barbey defined this heinous sin as "deicidal and parricidal at one and the same time"—"he had KILLED GOD."[175] For this sin of sins, his wholly innocent daughter willingly accepts all the sublime tortures that God, in his mysterious love for both the saint and the sinner, asks her to assume, as he does all those "Christian Medusas whose open foreheads pour forth the true blood beneath the thorns of a mystical coronation" and who thereby achieve true "Christian beauty, the double poetry, the double virtue of Innocence and Expiation."[176]

By the end of the century French Catholic writing was awash with the redemptive blood—almost all of it issuing from the feet, palms, foreheads, flanks, and wombs of women—of what Huysmans, in his wholly typical work of 1901 on the appalling sufferings of Saint Lydwine de Schiedam (1380–1433), called "those atoning souls who renew the agonies [*les affres*], who nail themselves to the place left empty on the cross by Jesus [and who are] thus, in some way, doubles [*sosies*] of the Son."[177]

As usual, Léon Bloy went farther along this Via Dolorosa than any of his co-religionists and contemporaries. Where they, for instance, contemplated Mary in her glory from afar, Bloy identified with her ignominy as she stood in agony at the foot of the cross, her dress bespattered with "the blood of the Flagellation, the blood of the Crown of Thorns, the blood of the nails, the blood of the [centurion's] Lance, of all the scarlet gush of blood [*jaillissement écarlate*] that she received full in the face when the high mass of Redemption was celebrated."[178] Pushing his thought to and perhaps beyond the brink of blasphemy, Bloy sees Mary not just as a bloodstained witness to the Crucifixion but as an actual agent of it. It is she who, from his childhood, prepares and offers up her Son to God, and who, in one of the most audacious of all Bloy's exegetical speculations, becomes Judith to his Holophernes: "prophetically she sees herself standing on Calvary before the sacred face of the true Holophernes slaughtered [*égorgé*] by herself."[179] "Mary is the True Cross," he says, citing the Spanish mystic María of Agreda (1602–65), the implication of the Mary/Judith parallel being that she is at once the mother, lover, and killer of her Son. Never one to draw back before the associative logic of his imagination, Bloy elsewhere figures copulation as crucifixion, with the man as Christ "nailed" to the cross that is his partner. The idea is so scandalous that even Bloy, though writing in his private diary, feels obliged to put it into Latin:

> Membrum virile symbolice Crucis effigies ab antiquitate videtur. Christus moriens in patibulo, emisit Spiritum. Vir Coïtans et hoc modo cruciatus in muliere anhelans, emittit semen.[180]

> (Since antiquity the male member has been seen symbolically as an effigy of the Cross. Christ, dying on the gallows, emitted the Spirit. Man as he copulates, crucified and panting on the woman, emits the seed.)

Bloy's own cross was the extraordinary Anne-Marie Roulé (1846–1907), whom he had met in 1877 and who, like so many of the women in Huysmans's circle, combined eroticism, mysticism, and madness in an irresistible—to decadent French Catholics—amalgam, being certified insane in 1882 while her relationship with Bloy still continued and spending the rest of her life as a patient in the Maison du Bon Sauveur in Caen.[181] Anne-Marie provided the model for Véronique Cheminot, the mistress-mystagogue of Caïn Marchenoir—Bloy himself in all his ranting glory—in *Le Désespéré* (1887), where the logic of expiatory suffering is pushed a further step along the road that leads, presumably, to the ultimate *imitatio Christi*, actual self-crucifixion. Véronique is in the habit of entering this or that Parisian church at random, going into the confessional, and, "thirsting after contempt, desperate to be trampled underfoot," announcing to the bewildered priest, "Father, I am a dirty prostitute."[182] Even when the priest agrees to hear her confession, the penance he imposes is never hard enough, so Véronique decides to take the business of expiation into her own hands. First—the reference to the repentant Magdalene is obvious and explicit—she hacks off her magnificent blond hair and then, a self-shorn foreglimpse of the *tondues* of 1944, goes to a back-street fence-cum-pimp-cum-abortionist—it being 1887, his name is, inevitably, Judas Nathan—whom she asks, at a price, to pull out all her teeth without any anaesthetic. There follows one of the most appalling scenes in the whole of French literature as Véronique settles into a leather armchair, tilts back her head to expose a "double row of luminous teeth" to the attentions of her chosen "torturer." Sade and de Maistre meet as "streams of foaming blood" froth from her mouth onto the canvas apron Nathan has tied round her neck. After the top row of teeth has been completely removed, the "executioner" wants to stop, but the "astounding martyr" signals to him to press on. When the ordeal (*supplice*) is over, Véronique looks at her "mutilated martyr's head" and, "with that frenzy for humiliation which is one of the features of mystical love, picked up the hand of the filthy bandit [*l'immonde bandit*] through which every kind of foulness had passed, and kissed it—as the instrument of her martyrdom!—with her bloody and misshapen lips."[183] It seems impossible to go beyond this "astounding holocaustal prank" (*étonnante fredaine d'holocauste*),[184] but of course Bloy can, elsewhere attributing an expiatory virtue to excrement as well as to blood. If the Word became flesh, it also presumably became shit, and, resourceful as ever, Bloy finds the word *merde* anagrammatically hidden in the first five letters of "*re-demption*."[185] Eschatology and scatalogy meet: truly, as Marchenoir-Bloy says, "I shall enter Paradise wearing a crown of turds [*j'entrerai dans le Paradis avec une couronne d'étrons*]."[186]

But Catholics had no imaginative monopoly on the shedding of blood, and it sluices in torrents through the literature of the nineteenth century, particularly in the wake of the *Semaine sanglante,* and as a secular equivalent of the revived cult of the Sacred Heart. It positively inundates Octave Mirbeau's sadomasochistic farrago *Le Jardin des supplices* of 1899 ("Blood everywhere, and wherever there is more life, everywhere horrendous torturers delving into the flesh, sawing bones, gouging the skin, a sinister joy on their faces"),[187] gushes without surcease through the *littérature maudite* of the 1880s and 1890s, abates when real, historical blood is being shed in unprecedented quantities between 1914 and 1918, reappears, scarcely diminished, in Surrealist and related texts between the wars, flows through highbrow pornography from *Histoire de l'oeil* (1928) to *Histoire d'O* (1962), before being stanched—at least in French metropolitan literature[188]—sometime in the early 1960s. Much, but not all, of the blood shed is female. Sometimes that blood is life-enhancing and -sustaining, like the menstrual blood that belatedly issues from Pauline Quenu in Zola's antiphrastically titled *La Joie de vivre* (1884), a "triumphant song of health," the sacrament of "life accepted, life loved in its functions, without disgust or fear,"[189] or in the "beautiful, warm, red blood" of the sea—that "feminine" element par excellence—so rapturously celebrated in Michelet's extraordinary *La Mer* (1861).[190] Normally, however, the blood that flows naturally out of women—be it the blood of menstruation, defloration, or childbirth—is experienced by men as either disgusting or threatening, or both, and it yields none of the thrill that accrues to the equally threatening blood that issues from—in most cases literally— manmade wounds to the woman's throat or breasts.

The motif of the severed female head—Marie-Antoinette and Char- lotte Corday in recent French history, Anne Boleyn and Mary Queen of Scots from over the Channel, Saint Dorothy in Christian hagiology, the Gorgon Medusa in Greek myth[191]—obsesses the nineteenth-century French (male) imagination almost as much as that of the severed male head. In Baudelaire's lurid poem "Une martyre" (1857), the "red, living blood" that oozes from a headless female trunk is swallowed up by the sheets on which it lies "with the avidity of a meadow," while the head it- self sits on the bedside table "like a buttercup," the role of its sightless eyes devolving on the "diamond-like gaze" of the "flaming secret eye" of the garter that still adorns the truncated corpse.[192]

But the voluptuous terror associated with the wounded or martyred woman is as nothing beside that inspired by *la belle dame sans merci*, who beheads, has beheaded, or delights in the severed head of the man she love-hates and desires: Judith and Salome, Mathilde de La Mole in Stendhal's *Le Rouge et le noir* (1830), or—decapitation replaced metonymically by the cutting of the hair—Delilah. To discuss this theme and all the French writers, painters, and musicians who have engaged with it (Gustave Moreau, Flaubert, Huysmans, Jules Laforgue, Camille Saint-Saëns, Leiris, whose *L'Age d'homme* [1939] is a veritable anthol- ogy of archetypal wounded and devouring women)[193] would take us out of cultural history and into psychoanalysis. Suffice it to say that the de- capitation motif, male and female, though present in the literature, music, and poetry of other European cultures, is markedly more insis- tent in France than anywhere else, and that its salience can scarcely be unrelated to the "red mass" of the Terror and the continuing looming presence of the guillotine.[194]

Sometimes the sacrificial victim is not human but animal, and Bloy believed that the whole animal kingdom was suffering vicariously on man's behalf: "The enormous mass of their sufferings forms part of our ransom, and all along the chain of animals, from man to the lowest of brutes, universal Pain forms a single identical propitiation."[195] The theme of the suffering animal pervades the whole of Baudelaire's poetry, from "L'Albatros" of his youth to his very last text, the prose poem "Les Bons Chiens" (1867), inspired by the spectacle of the pariah street dogs of Brussels.[196] Though it does not bleed, the eponymous swan of "Le Cygne" (1860) constitutes one of the supreme sacrificial victims of the whole of his and nineteenth-century France's poetic output. At a time when violence to animals was becoming a rarer sight in cities, if not in the country (the first law against cruelty to domestic animals dates from 1850, bearbaiting and dog- and cockfighting had been effectively proscribed, and the slaughtering of animals, an everyday street event, horses included, in eighteenth-century Paris, had long been confined to municipal abattoirs on the outskirts),[197] any suffering inflicted on animals was likely to be interpreted in a sacrificial sense. The militant Communarde Louise Michel (1830–1905) traced her horror of the guillotine to the childhood spectacle of "a headless goose walking with its bloody neck still upstanding, stiff with the red wound where the head was missing."[198] The experience, during the siege of Paris in 1870–71, of eating not only horsemeat but dogs, cats, rats, and an assortment of kangaroos, antelopes, giraffes, and the elephants Castor and Pollux from the zoo may have made some Parisians, at least, reflect on what underlay their peacetime carnivorous pleasures.

Edmond Goncourt, still mourning the recent death of his younger brother, Jules, has left remarkable descriptions in his diary of starving horses on the aptly named Boulevard d'Enfer being traded, branded, and receiving their "passport for the abattoir,"[199] of sampling camel kidneys and elephant blood sausage,[200] and of the sight of a flayed donkey (un écorché qui est un âne) displayed, festooned with roses and foliage, at one particular hippophagie (horsemeat butcher shop) on the Rue Neuve-des-Petits-Champs.[201] Nothing, though, can equal the horror of eating a blackbird he has killed with a potshot in his garden at Passy, having previously, as any connoisseur of japonaiserie would do, decapitated one of the last of his pullets with a scimitar. As he sits down to consume his miserable trophy, he suddenly feels, nonmetempsychosist though he is, that "something of my brother had passed into this tiny winged creature, into this mourning bird of the air; and I had an undefined fear of having destroyed, with the bullet I had fired, something other-worldly and friendly that was watching over and protecting my person and the house. It's stupid, it's absurd, it's crazy; but it was an obsession that lasted the whole evening!"[202]

There were others, of course, who enjoyed watching animals being slaughtered or, rather, who derived an ambivalent thrill, at once existential, aesthetic, and erotic, from the sight of their blood spurting forth into the sunlight. If, for successive generations of French writers and artists, Spain was the land of authenticity and passion, it was in some large measure because it was the home of the bullfight, of real bullfighting, that in which the bull is ritually immolated, not the species of taunting and dodging typically practiced in the southwest of France.[203] For

Montherlant, writing in *Les Bestiaires* (1926), the bullfight—of which he had direct personal experience—was an emblematic encounter between self, death, and destiny, an encounter charged with erotico-mystical mana, in which the matador, by risking his all, puts death to death and so attains to the one kind of eternity that remains in a de-sacralized age: the eternity of danger willingly assumed and overcome with style and panache, with the final thrust of the sword being likened, all very predictably, to the moment of orgasm when the matador makes the feminized bull this total possession.[204] Following his mentor, Bataille, for whom, as we have seen, the spectacle of the death by goring of the matador Manuel Granero had been one of his (perhaps literally) seminal experiences, and using concepts drawn from Hubert and Mauss's classic *Essai sur la nature et la fonction du sacrifice* of 1899, the anthopologist and autobiographer Michel Leiris interpreted the corrida in his brilliant essay *Mirroir de la tauromachie* (1939) as a modern sacrificial ritual, more dynamic and also more "authentic" than the traditional kind, because here the sacrificer, the matador, is every bit as threatened with violent death as the victim. Mingling the metaphysical and the erotic, Leiris casts the bullfight as an archetypal duel-embrace between self and not-self in which, weaving his cape with the utmost dexterity and daring, the matador approaches as closely as he possibly can to that point of absolute tangency with the Other—here the bull's horns—that, for Leiris, means death, before deflecting the Other from his path with a deft turn of his wrist until, with pass following pass in a mounting crescendo of tension, he finally puts death to the bull amidst the quasi-orgasmic ovation of the crowd.

The analogy between the wound made by the sword and the wound—*la plaie*—of the vulva is made explicit by Leiris, as it is in the drawings by André Masson that illustrate his text. For Leiris, the goal of the bullfight, as of eroticism and poetry, is "to incorporate death into life, to render it in some manner voluptuous."[205] In writing, he says in his preface to *L'Age d'homme,* later expanded into the great essay of 1946 "De la littérature considérée comme une tauromachie," he seeks to "introduce if only the shadow of a bull's horns into a work of literature," to expose himself before the public as the matador risks his all in the path of the bull and so "write a book that would be an act" (*faire un livre qui soit un acte*),[206] as decisive and stylish as the climactic *mise à mort* of the bullfight. Literature becomes in theory if not—as Leiris is too intelligent and self-critical not to realize—in fact a sacrificial ritual in which the writer-*matador*, both sacrificer and victim, achieves his apotheosis in miniature as he cuts off his (strictly metaphorical) bull's ears and testicles and flings them into the crowd. Blood alone gives authenticity to the ritual (whence Leiris's obsession with wounded and wounding females from Lucrezia to Judith), and a bullfight without death is like sex without orgasm: "The moment when, the bull well positioned, the torero prepares for the final kill constitutes without doubt the culminating point of the bullfight: a second of anticipation during which it seems that, like an imminent orgasm, the shattering conclusion to the tragedy is brewing. Experienced at that moment as more of an animal than ever, the bull seems to have come to maturity as a fountain of blood."[207]

The Spanish Catholic philosopher Miguel de Unamuno once compared the stricken bull to Christ crucified,[208] and it is, of course, Christ's blood that, more than any other, flows through the Catholic and Catholic-related literature of nineteenth-century France. Indeed, as Frank Paul Bowman has demonstrated in a superbly documented study, it, and religious blood in general, does more than merely flow, it "bursts forth, streams, jets, pushes through the skin of the stigmatics, pulsates through the ventricles of the Sacred Heart," suffusing the religious sensibility of the age with its "vertiginous and synesthetic viscosity."[209] Some Catholics—principally priests and religious, but doubtless some of the laity as well—did more than meditate upon the Precious Blood of Christ and caused their own blood to flow in sympathetic imitation of his; the great Dominican preacher Jean-Baptiste Lacordaire (1802–61) is said by his official biographer to have paid "a Savoyard boy" (*un petit Savoyard,* a term that usually designates a chimney sweep's assistant, a "climbing boy") to whip him before his fellow priests in expiation of his sins, while the bedsheets of Jean-Marie Vianney (1786–1859), the saintly curé of the village of Ars, near Lyon, are reported to have been regularly stained with blood as a result of his self-flagellation.[210]

Of all nineteenth-century meditations on the body of the crucified Christ, none dwells more searingly or more complicitously on its bloody humiliation than Huysmans's evocation, at the beginning of *Là-bas,* of the Matthias Grünewald crucifixion he saw at Cassel in Germany in July 1888, a prelude to his later encounter with the same artist's Isenheim altarpiece at Colmar in September 1903. Of the Colmar masterpiece Huysmans writes that it is "the hosanna of gangrene, the triumphal song of putrescent flesh [*caries*]," the whole painting sounding with the echo of a "death mystique," as though Christ is a beast of prey that has been hunted and hounded to death, and now his pursuers are sounding the kill over his carrion.[211] The description in *Là-bas* is more developed and far more extreme. "Smeared with blood and bespattered with tears," this Christ is no "Galilean Adonis" but "a corpse in eruption," a "Christ with tetanus," splayed on the cross like a corpse on a morgue slab, abandoned by man and by God, having accepted for man's sake "that his divinity be as it were interrupted from the time of the slaps in the face [*soufflets*], the scourges, the insults, and the spitting up to the appalling suffering of an agony without end." Behold then the Man:

> Disconnected, almost wrenched out of the shoulders, Christ's arms seemed garroted throughout their entire length by the coiled thongs of the muscles. The broken armpit was cracked open [*l'aisselle éclamée craquait*]; the fully open hands brandished haggard fingers that nonetheless bestowed their blessing, in a confused gesture mixing prayer and reproach; the pectorals trembled, smeared with sweat like butter; the torso was grooved with circular trenches formed by the exposed rib cage; the flesh was swollen, blue-colored and as though rubbed with saltpeter, stippled with flea bites and pinpricked by the tips of the scourges, which, snapped off under the skin, still torture it, here and there, as with slivers of broken glass.[212]

Christ's blood contaminates before it saves, saves *because* it contaminates, spilling over the holy women present at the cross, who, as with Bloy, are more than just witnesses of the Passion but co-actors, protagonists, in Christ's agony; Huysmans even describes Mary as a "salutary Eumenide," an "amorous maenad," a "sad, holy ghoul."[213] The result of this obsession with blood and with suffering, for Huysmans as for Bloy, is that their Catholicism ends, as it were, on Good Friday. As Durtal-Huysmans admits in *L'Oblat* (1903), it was Holy Week, not Easter (and certainly not Christmas), that "best suited his aspirations and his tastes; he could clearly see Our Lord only on the cross and the Virgin in tears. The Pietà rose up in his sight well before the crib."[214] Absurdly, Good Friday becomes a day of rejoicing and Easter Sunday an occasion of appalling suffering and guilt, as Bloy confessed to his diary in April 1895:

> Easter. I am cold to the depths of my soul and I am as close as possible to despair. Such is the effect of this great feast day upon me. Easter Sunday is habitually painful to me, sometimes terrible. Impossible to conceal my distress, which comes down, more or less, to this: I am unable to feel the joy of the Resurrection, because, for me, the Resurrection never comes to pass. I always see

Jesus in agony, Jesus on the cross, and I cannot see him otherwise.
... This perpetual beginning over again of the ecclesiastical year,
always the same, without the Lord ever bursting forth in glory
[*sans que jamais le Seigneur éclate*]![215]

"La Résurrection, pour moi, n'arrive jamais": Bloy's desolate words
might stand as an epigraph to the whole of nineteenth-century French
Catholicism. Perhaps it would take the unparalleled bloodletting of two
world wars for the Church to reinscribe Easter at the center of its faith
and to find artists—musicians rather than writers or painters—to proclaim what is truly the Good News of Christianity: "Je suis ressuscité, je
suis ressuscité.... De mort à vie je passe," as Olivier Messiaen's risen
Christ rapturously sings in *Chants de terre et de ciel* (1938): I have risen,
I have risen, from death to life I pass. But by that time, the mass of
French people, repelled by a century and half of right-wing Sado-
Catholicism, had long since ceased to listen to the Church and turned
definitively away.

It is, therefore, the figure of a martyred, often decapitated human
body, male and female, that dominates French history, literature, and
painting from the Terror to the Liberation. In history it recurs almost
without significant interruption from the first killing of July 1789, from
the grass, straw, and other ordure stuffed into the mouth of Bertier de
Sauvigny, to the ninety-nine hostages hanged from trees, lampposts, and
balconies by drunken French and German *gestapistes* around the main
square of Tulle in the Corrèze in June 1944. To the numerous writers
and intellectuals who met violent deaths as a result of war, Resistance
activity, or bigotry (Charles Péguy, Ernest Psichari, Alain-Fournier, Paul
Nizan, Georges Politzer, Jean Prévost, Marc Bloch, Max Jacob, Robert
Desnos) or as suicides (Montherlant [1971] and Drieu, who shared the
conviction of his doppelgänger, Gilles, that "nothing is done save
through blood" [*rien ne se fait que dans le sang*][216] but who was unable
nonetheless to kill himself "properly") may be added two others whose
deaths have acquired an archetypal significance: the poet André Chénier
(1762–94), guillotined as a moderate two days before the fall of
Robespierre and, with the English poet-suicide Thomas Chatterton
(1752–70), the supreme emblem of the writer martyr for the romantic
generation,[217] and Gérard de Nerval (1808–55), found hanged on the
Rue de la Vieille-Lanterne on 26 January 1855, both date and place sug-
gesting to some a mysterious cabbalistic significance.[218]

As for violent deaths in nineteenth- and twentieth-century French literature, their number is so great and their meaning, underneath changes

of situation and form, is so unvarying that only a few of particular pertinence to the themes of this book can be mentioned. First there is Stendhal's Julien Sorel in *Le Rouge et le noir,* whom we first encounter "all bloody" after he has been beaten by his father, and whose death on the guillotine is prefigured in the rising and falling blade of his father's sawmill, in the lopped chestnut trees of his hometown, Verrières (Julien has "dark chestnut-brown hair" into the bargain), and in the crimson curtains and blood-red reflections in the local church, in which he commits the crime for which he is executed, not to mention the fact that he shares his first name with a martyred apostate and that, like another nonconformist slain by the powers that be, he is the son of a carpenter. To give a final and perhaps fantastical twist to these many strands of meaning, Stendhal's real surname, Beyle, means "ax" or "blade" in German (a guillotine is a *Fallbeil*), and when the novelist chose the German city of Stendal as one of the more than a hundred pseudonyms that he used at one time or another, he added an *h—une hache—*to make it "Stendhal."[219]

The theme of parricide that is so pronounced in *Le Rouge et le noir*— Stendhal once wrote that learning of Louis XVI's death when he was a nine-year-old in Grenoble gave him "one of the greatest movements of joy" in his life, not least because his detested father had been following the king's trial "as though it had been that of an intimate friend or a relative"[220]—is also present in Flaubert's *La Légende de Saint Julien l'hospitalier* (1877), which catalogues the victims of this archetypal *homo necans* from the mouse he kills as a child, wiping its blood away with the sleeve of his coat, through a veritable holocaust of badgers, wolves, and stags, until finally he kills his mother and father "by accident," leaving the bodies bleeding into their bedsheets beneath an ivory carving of Christ, and in a room stained scarlet by light streaming through a stained-glass window similar to the one that will eventually commemorate the redeemed and beatified ex-psychopath in the village church in Normandy that gave Flaubert the idea for his story.[221] As Julien's self-imposed program of penance, culminating in his voluntary embrace of the Christ-Leper, reveals, the thematics of expiation by suffering and, if necessary, by self-immolation went well beyond the reactionary Catholic milieu of Huysmans or Bloy.

No nineteenth-century French writer was more preoccupied with violence than Victor Hugo, who believed that the *H* of his surname replicated the frame of the guillotine and marked him out as the one to lead the struggle against it. Hugo's great novel of the Revolution, *Quatrevingt-treize* (1874), written with the experience of the *Semaine sanglante* still seething within him, concludes with his hero, Gauvain—the French form of Gawain, as befits one in search of the Holy Grail of nonviolence and justice—condemned to the guillotine for betraying, for humane reasons, the Revolution in its war against the Vendée insurrection. On a sunlit Britanny morning, as peaceful as the scene about to be enacted is savage, Gauvain goes out to confront the red-painted "monster of wood" with its triangular blade standing out black against the blue of the sky, "a silhouette of hard, straight lines" rising up like a "hieroglyph" of cruelty and shame opposite the oppressive stone tower of the past that has given birth to this new instrument of torture as surely as the last syllable of its name—*la Tourgue*—contains the first letters of the word "guillotine": "And the guillotine was right to say to the great tower: I am your daughter." Gauvain bares his white, girllike neck, more beautiful than ever, and at the very instant that the blade begins its descent, his political rival and spiritual father figure, the Jacobin fanatic Cimourdain (the name amalgamates *cimetière,* cemetery; Cimmeria, the land of perpetual darkness; *mourir,* to die; and *cime,* meaning the Mountain, the Jacobins) shoots himself in the heart, and the two "tragic sister souls" die together in a homoerotic *Liebestod,* "the shadow of the one commingled with the light of the other."[222]

All this, remarkable enough in itself, becomes even more so when one learns of the impact *Quatrevingt-treize* had on someone who really did shoot himself in the heart: Vincent van Gogh, on 27 July 1890, somewhere in the fields around the village of Auvers-sur-Oise, to the northeast of Paris, where he died of his wounds in his squalid attic room at the Café Ravoux on the early morning of 29 July. One of the minor characters of *Quatrevingt-treize* is a republican soldier named Radoub, who, in the course of the Vendée campaign, has his ear half cut off by an enemy bullet. Hugo, possibly thinking of Peter's severing of the ear of the high priest's servant on the eve of the Passion (Luke 22:51), dwells in some detail on Radoub's mutilated ear and how he binds his head with a handkerchief, almost exactly like the one van Gogh gloomily sports in his celebrated self-portrait *L'Homme à la pipe* (January 1889), painted, as it is hardly necessary to recall, barely a month after the painter had cut off the lobe of his ear and offered it to a prostitute in a brothel in Arles that he and Paul Gauguin regularly frequented. Van Gogh had earlier written of finding in *Quatrevingt-treize* a portrait of himself "in reverse,"[223] and his self-mutilation links up with other themes developed in the present study in several remarkable ways. Van Gogh is known to have attended bullfights at Arles, one of the few towns in France where actual killing was permitted,[224] and the offering of the self-severed ear echoes the tossing of the bull's ear into the crowd, where, ideally, the most beautiful *aficionada* present catches it in lieu of the whore. Torero and *toro* at one and the same time, van Gogh came close on the night of 23 December 1888 to achieving that state of total tangency between self and not-self that the Leirisian bullfighter approaches and then narrowly avoids.

It was van Gogh's self-mutilation that first prompted Leiris's intellectual guide, Bataille, in an article of 1930 published in *Documents,* to develop a coherent theory of sacrifice, involving what he called a "rupture in personal homogeneity, the projection out of oneself [*hors de soi*] of a part of oneself," the shedding of blood corresponding to the ejaculation of semen or the eructation of spittle, another of Bataille's obsessions at the time.[225] Finally, before rejecting as fanciful any connection between Radoub's mutilated and bandaged ear and the painter's self-administered injury, we should note, first, the similarity between the names Gauguin and Gauvain[226] and then the far more remarkable fact that "Gauvain" is more or less exactly "van Gogh" in reverse. Could the man whom Antonin Artaud famously called "societ's suicide"[227] have seen in *Quatrevingt-treize* some kind of template for his life, modeled his self-mutilation on Radoub's war wound, and taken Gauvain's execution or, more likely, Cimourdain's shooting of himself in the heart ("A stream of blood came from his mouth, he fell down dead")[228] as both a premonition and a pattern of his own self-extinction? Still more, did the simultaneous death of the two "tragic sister souls" suggest Theo and himself, so wedded to each other that they were virtually one person, each so dependent on the other for his sense of existence that Theo, disturbed in mind and broken in body, was to die less than a year after Vincent in Utrecht (25 January 1891), his body being reburied alongside and finally commingling with that of his brother in the cemetery of Auvers in 1914?[229]

Two final examples, each as appalling as Véronique Cheminot's dental appointment in *Le Désespéré*. The first is the conclusion of Flaubert's "Carthaginian" novel *Salammbô* of 1862, an almost indescribably bloodthirsty account of the war of the "Barbarians" against the Punic Republic of Hamilcar Barca, father of the eponymous heroine. The Barbarians are aided by rebellious mercenaries formerly in the service of Carthage and led by Mâtho, thief of the sacred veil of the Carthaginian goddess Tanit and, for one night, the lover of Salammbô, who sacrifices her virginity to him in order to retrieve it. The novel culminates in a holocaust of killings without parallel in French literature, and possibly any other. First the besieged and thirst-ravaged Carthaginians make sacrifices to their god Moloch-the-Devourer to obtain rain, knowing full well that, "any profit having to be purchased by some kind of loss, and every transaction being determined by the need of the weaker party and the exaction of the stronger, there was no suffering too considerable for the god, for he took delight in the most horrible and they were now at his mercy. It was necessary, therefore, to satisfy him completely."[230] Moloch-Baal, as opposed to the goddess Tanit, represents the "tyranny of the male principle," and it is this that "dominates every consciousness" on the day of the sacrifice.[231] What is required is an "individual sacrifice, a wholly voluntary oblation" on the part of the rich and the powerful, but, none being willing to offer up his or her own life, their children are singled out as substitute victims, though Hamilcar substitutes a substitute for the substitute when he replaces his son Hannibal with a slave boy of the same age, an ancient-world version of the Second Empire practice of paying a lower-class replacement to stand in for an upper- or middle-class conscript.

In preparation for the sacrifice, the priests systematically mutilate themselves with daggers and other such weapons, slashing their cheeks, piercing their nipples with skewers, donning crowns of thorns, and dancing wildly around the children who have been herded together as provender for the god. As befits the sanguinary occasion, both Hamilcar and the priests are dressed all in red. Parents throw their valuables into the sacrificial pyre before the statue of Moloch in the hope that the Devourer will spare their offspring, but he will not be bought off at so low a price, and, one by one, the children are fed into the flames, the priests all the while intoning a chant "celebrating the joys of death and the rebirths of eternity." "But still the appetite of the God was not sated, he still wanted more," and more and more children are consigned to the huge pyramidal pyre, which rises up "completely red like a giant covered in blood," its "head flung back, staggering under the weight of its drunkenness."[232]

At last the offering is accepted; rain falls and is collected by the Carthaginians, who then feel—and here Flaubert displays an intuitive sense of the logic of sacrifice[233]—"the need to cast onto others the furious excesses that they had not been able to deploy against themselves. A sacrifice of this kind was not to be useless; although they felt no remorse, they found themselves carried away by that frenzy caused by complicity in irreparable crimes."[234] The sacrificers now look for scapegoats on whom to vent their guilt at having sacrificed their children rather than themselves, and so fall with fresh fury on the Barbarians and their rebel mercenary allies. More frenzied bloodletting ensues, with

Hamilcar dispatching herds of heavily armored elephants into the enemy ranks, each elephant's trunk being fitted with a razor-sharp blade— Flaubert uses the crucial word *hache*—which they swish this way and that, wreaking unspeakable carnage.[235]

Eventually the Barbarians and their allies are trapped in a mountain gorge. Hemmed in on all sides, they begin to cannibalize their dead for want of other food, and when this supply is exhausted, they set about killing their prisoners and wounded, sometimes to eat them, but sometimes, too, "out of ferocity, without need, to satiate their fury."[236] In desperation, friends who had developed "strange loves" in the absence of women and formed "obscene unions as serious as marriages" engage in gladiatorial love combats in which both are destroyed,[237] leaving their bodies as food for lions and jackals.

And so it goes on in an unimaginable crescendo of violence, counterviolence, and counter-counterviolence, as though to demonstrate in advance the Girardian principle of the uncontrollable contagiousness of violence. Hamilcar takes ten Barbarians hostage and crucifies them; the Barbarians retaliate exponentially by crucifying thirty Carthaginian elders, including the senior statesman Hannon, who is nailed to a cross "writhing like a sea monster being slit open on the shore," his body eventually so shredded by the nails that "all that remained on the cross was formless debris, like those bits of animals hunters hang on their doors."[238]

Still worse is to come. Vultures descend to feed on the crucified Barbarians, recalling another nightmarish sacrificial scenario, Baudelaire's shocking "Un voyage à Cythère" (1851–52), where flocks of Hitchcockian birds perch about a "singular object" seen hanging from a "symbolic gibbet" on the Island of Love in expiation for some unspeakable sexual sin:

De féroces oiseaux perchés sur leur pâture
Détruisaient avec rage un pendu déjà mûr,
Chacun plantant, comme un outil, son bec impur
Dans tous les coins saignants de cette pourriture;
Les yeux étaient deux trous, et du ventre effondré
Les intestins pesants lui coulaient sur les cuisses,
Et ses bourreaux, gorgés de hideuses délices,
L'avaient à coups de bec absolument châtré.

[Ferocious birds were gathered, snatching at their food, / Raging around a hanging shape already ripe; / Each creature worked his tool, his dripping filthy beak, / Into the bleeding corners of this rottenness. / The eyes were two blank gaps, and from the hollow paunch / Its tangled guts let loose, spilling over the thighs, / And those tormentors, gorged with hideous delights, / Had castrated the corpse with snapping of their beaks.][239]

Flaubert, at least, does not describe the results of the vultures' attentions, but he has further horrors in store. The Barbarians are defeated and the rebel mercenary leader, Mâtho, is captured and singled out for a death befitting the violator and thief of the veil of Tanit. Now it is the "female principle," even more violent than the male, that dominates proceedings, and a "mystical lasciviousness" swirls through Carthage as it is decreed that Mâtho will die "the kind of death in which the entire city might participate, with all hands, all arms, every Carthaginian thing, including the flagstones of the streets and the waves of the gulf, being able to tear, crush, and annihilate him."[240] On the day of his ritual immolation, "bent double and with the terrified look of a wild beast suddenly let loose," Mâtho is brought out before the assembled populace of the city, his "victim's body ... invested with an almost religious splendor," which the crowd, especially the women, lean forward to see. His ordeal begins, as terrible and protracted as the death of a hundred cuts inflicted on Bataille's ecstatic martyr, Fou-Tchou-Li, for his Via Dolorosa is to take in virtually every street of the city, his every step being marked by blows, insults, and other humiliations, none of them, however, serious enough to kill or even to fell him, for his agony is to be drawn out as long as possible and he is never to lose consciousness. As he advances, he is "palped, prodded, scratched" by a thousand sharp fingers. "A boy tore off his ear, a girl ... slit open his cheek, people tore out handfuls of hair and slices [*lambeaux*] of flesh; others wetted his face with sponges oozing with filth suspended from sticks. From the right side of this throat a jet of blood gushed forth; immediately delirium set in." Mâtho, a classic insider-outsider, an employee who has betrayed his employer, becomes the ultimate scapegoat:

This last of the Barbarians represented all the Barbarians, the whole of the army; they took vengeance on him for their disasters, their terrors, their humiliations. The rage of the people grew even as it was sated ... ; every opening in the walls was filled with heads; and the evil that they could not do to him, they howled it in his face.

By now the whole of Carthage has become "a vast din of barking" as its human quarry is hounded to death. Mâtho is branded, sprayed with scalding oil, like the miserable Damiens, forced to walk over glass shards, and lashed with whips made of hippopotamus hide. At last, somehow still alive, he arrives in the presence of Salammbô, who that day is to be married to the Numidian prince Narr'Havas but is still drawn erotically to the man who took her virginity, even though—or perhaps precisely because—the man in question "no longer has anything human about him other than his eyes":

> He was a long, completely red shape; his broken bonds hung
> along his thighs, but they could no longer be distinguished from
> the tendons of his wrists, which had been completely ripped bare;
> his mouth was gaping wide open; from the sockets of his eyes
> there rose a pair of flames that seemed to shoot up into his hair;
> and still the wretch was walking![241]

Not for much longer, though. No sooner does he set eyes on Salammbô than, in a final convulsion, he dies, whereupon his breast is cut open—Damiens again—by one of Moloch's "red priests" and his "bright-red heart" is offered up to the setting sun, whose rays transfix it like so many arrows: the Sacred Heart—in the double sense of the word "sacred," pointed out by de Maistre long before Durkheim, of "holy" and "accursed"[242]—of the barbarian Mâtho offered up two centuries and a half before that of the reprobate Galilean. It is the climax, in every sense of the word, of the entire bloodthirsty orgy: "Carthage was as though convulsed in the titanic spasm of joy and of hope without bounds."[243] Just as Gauvain and Cimourdain must die simultaneously in a moment of complete tangency, so Salammbô succumbs, presumably self-poisoned, as the frenzy of sacrifice explodes all about her. With her lips wide open like those of a woman in orgasm, her unfastened hair sweeping down to the ground, she is like a sacrificial victim herself.

What inner psychological demons drove Flaubert to devise this extraordinary bloodbath can only be guessed at. As a re-creation of the ambience of sacrifice, it most certainly out-Batailles Bataille and shows a de Maistrian insight into the logic of expiatory violence; as literary pornography, it almost, but not quite, out-Sades Sade. As fictionalized anthropology, it brings out starkly the nature of the sacrificial community—the unity of all versus one—and clearly demonstrates the self-multiplying quality of violence, which, in Girardian terms, only the violent death of an exemplary victim—in this case Mâtho—can bring to a (temporary) halt. But it is as an image, admittedly luridly overdramatized, of contemporary history that *Salammbô,* though no historical allegory, has particular claims on our attention, for it is as though

Flaubert had fed into it all the recent or relatively recent violence of French history, from the Terror to the suppression of the working-class uprising of June 1848, to produce both an analeptic image of antiquity and a proleptic vision of the *Semaine sanglante* and still greater horrors to come. How, when reading of the sacrifice of the children of Carthage to the "tyranny of the male principle" of Moloch, not to think forward to Père Roques, that rock-hard emblem of patriarchy, firing at random into the mass of starving insurgents penned into the Tuileries cellars?[244] And how not to connect Mâtho's death throes with the killing of the Christlike republican idealist Dussardier—"he fell on his back, his arms spread as on a cross"[245]—on the evening of 2 December 1851, another victim of repressive authority, though wielded this time by the totalitarian socialist turned totalitarian Bonapartist Sénéchal, whose curious name ("seneschal, " from Latin *senex,* old + Germanic *skalkaz,* servant) suggests a combination of authoritarianism and obsequiousness, *sénéchal* being also the title of cell leaders in the ultraroyalist Chevaliers de la Foi?[246]

If *Salammbô* points forward to the *Semaine sanglante,* our final example comes from a novel—Zola's *Germinal* (1885)—written well after that event but whose every page is instinct with the memory of the Commune and the massacre that ended it. The incident in question is one of the most famous and disturbing of Zola's many crowd scenes: the death and mutilation of that modern "hoarder," the shopkeeper Maigrat, whose name—evocative of *maigre,* skinny—designates not his own generous proportions but the fact that he has grown fat on the emaciation of others. As the miners' strike threatens them with poverty and impending starvation, the women of Montsou embark on a hunger march, a march reminiscent historically of that of the women of Paris on Versailles in October 1789 but shot through, at a deeper level, with lingering fantasies of the *pétroleuses* and with the mythical archetype of the Bacchae.

After crisscrossing the countryside from coal mine to coal mine chanting "Bread! Bread! Bread!" the women finally return to their village, where they are about to take out their frustrations on Cécile Grégoire, the teenage daughter of a well-meaning but ingenuous local middle-class family whose home they have already invaded. Fearing the worst, Etienne Lantier, the unofficial strike leader, diverts the women's fury from Cécile toward Maigrat's nearby shop, the door of which he begins to attack with the now inevitable *hache.* Terrified by the din of the "brigands"—Maigrat's historically supercharged term—battering on his door, the shopkeeper attempts to escape from an upstairs window and clamber over the roofs to safety. However, such activity is beyond both his strength and agility, and he falls off a shed roof, gashing his head open and spilling his brains on the ground (*la cervelle avait jailli*).

As soon as the "band" of women—Zola's word—see the "thin red thread" of blood trickling down the wall, they stop clamoring at the door and, "seized [*prises*] by the intoxication of blood," surround and insult the "still warm corpse" with their laughter, "howling into the face of death the long drawn-out rancor of their breadless existence." Then la Maheude, their de facto leader, commits an act that has a historical pedigree of more than a century: she stuffs dirt into the dead shopkeeper's mouth, shrieking, "Come on, eat up, eat up, you who used to eat us!"

But, as ever, there are greater horrors to come, and a woman known as la Brûlé proposes, to general approval, that they "cut him like a tomcat [*un matou*]," whereupon Mouquette, a miner's daughter of distinctly easy virtue who specializes in mooning and flashing at the strikers' adversaries—another traditional rebellious gesture, much favored by prostitutes, and observed and brilliantly described by Hugo on the barricades in June 1848, with fatal results for the woman who exposes herself to enemy fire[247]—debags the shopkeeper while another woman lifts up his legs to assist her. Then la Brûlé grabs hold of what Zola calls his "dead virility" and, with a huge heave of her whole body, tears it loose and brandishes "the rag" (*le lambeau*), a "packet of hairy, bloody flesh" (*un paquet de chair velue et sanglante*), laughing in triumph, "I've got it! I've got it!"

While Etienne and the other men look on in paralyzed horror (to say nothing of Madame Maigrat, transfixed at her window), the women move off with their "abominable trophy," passing it from hand to hand "like an evil beast, from which each of them had once had to suffer [a reference to Maigrat's willingness to take payment "in kind"], and which they had at last crushed, which they saw there, inert, lying in their power." Inevitably, la Brûlé sticks "the rag" on the end of her stick and waves it around "like a flag"—a very red flag—as the "howling stampede" (*débandade hurlante*) of women falls in behind her. The gesture reproduces, even as it turns literally upside down, the traditional hoisting and flaunting of the scapegoat's severed head, a bloody carnivalesque inversion of an already theatrical occasion that replaces the *testa* with the testes. "Drops of blood rain down [as] from a hunk of meat on a butcher's stall," exactly like the "impure blood" that drips from Villeneuve's famous image of Louis XVI's severed head, only now more tainted than ever.

Other elements in the account take on a new salience when read in the appropriate historical and anthropological contexts. The women, for example, address Maigrat's dead body as a *cochon* (pig), and Madame Hennebeau, the wife of the principal mine owner, thinks that they must have raided the local butcher shop and are flaunting "a piece of pork" (*un débris de porc*) before she realizes what is really up aloft there. This suggests not only the revolutionary image of the *roi-cochon*, as opposed to the *roi-boulanger* (discussed in chapter 3), but reminds us of the annual Easter ritual of pig killing in countless farmyards of France so brilliantly studied by Claudine Fabre-Vassas, in which, as she tells us, the pig was systematically likened to Judas, the color red being traditionally the color of Jews long before it was the color of revolution.[248] Thus it is that Maigrat's miserable "rag" becomes the focus of multiple historical and cultural meanings, which vary from the women themselves to those—working-class men and the middle classes in general— who look on aghast and, of course, to Zola himself: fear and hatred of the "hoarder" on the part of the women, especially as this one has exacted his own petit bourgeois version of the droit de seigneur, mixed up confusedly with fear and hatred of Jews, fear of social revolution and public disorder on the part of middle-class onlookers, summed up in the image of the brigand, and, on the part of Etienne and of his creator, fear of the banshee, the maenad, the revolutionary Bacchante associated with the figure of the *pétroleuse;* fear, in the last instance, of untrammeled womanhood itself, all this concentrated and projected onto the "evil beast, the crushed beast" dangling from the end of a stick. With this red vision of horror, standing out against the encircling gloom, we move on to our final and most famous avatar of the scapegoat.[249]

"THE GREATEST MARTYR OF ALL TIME"

Secularization, conspiracy, scapegoating, sacrifice, blood: if there truly is a paradigm that repeats itself at regular intervals throughout French postrevolutionary history, all of these elements should be clearly present in the Dreyfus affair, that archetypal crisis of the French body politic, so pure and clear in its outlines despite the overwhelming complexity of its detail that it was, and still is, commonly referred to simply as *l'Affaire.*

Concerning secularization, the presence of the vast majority of France's active Catholic population, clergy and laity alike, in the anti-Dreyfus camp does not mean that the affair was primarily, or even to a significant extent, a religious crisis. As the leading Dreyfus supporter,

Bernard-Lazare, saw as early as 1894, the passions that caused, accompanied, and were unleashed by the trial, degradation, and expulsion of Captain Dreyfus were of a distinctly new kind in French history. Since the early 1880s, he wrote in *L'Antisémitisme, son histoire et ses causes* (1894), "anti-Judaism [had] changed into antisemitism."[250] "Antisemitism" was a new word, coined in 1879 by Wilhelm Marr, to denote a new phenomenon, a hatred of Jews whose rationale was no longer pseudo-theological but political, economic, "scientific," biological, in keeping with the secular temper of the age. Yet both the pursuit and the defense of Dreyfus rapidly assumed the intensity of a religious cause for those engaged in them, especially among Dreyfus's supporters, for whom the vindication of the captain's innocence became far more than a political campaign, rather an act of faith, often born of a quasi-religious conversion experience, that mobilized the whole of the believer's thoughts and actions. Dreyfusism, Péguy famously wrote in *Notre jeunesse* (1910), had been first and foremost a "mystique," which had subsequently degenerated into "politics." In the mystique three mystical strands, the Jewish, the Christian, and the republican, had converged and culminated before petering out in the merely political compacts, conflicts, and compromises that followed the granting of the presidential pardon in September 1899.[251] On both sides, the Dreyfus affair mobilized religious emotions and mentalities in an essentially secular cause, but if the Dreyfus supporters eventually triumphed, it was because their mystique, unlike their adversaries', was ultimately founded on reason and empirical truth. As Anatole France so memorably (if untranslatably) put it, "Nous aurons raison parce que nous avons raison" (We will win because we are right).[252]

The second element—the belief in the existence of a plot—pervaded the entire affair, with good reason as far as Dreyfus's defenders were concerned, for the military establishment had indeed plotted or connived in Dreyfus's original conviction, and then devised or accepted one piece of bogus evidence after another to uphold that conviction and cover up its own sordid role in the whole business. Although some Dreyfus defenders' claims regarding the "Jesuit network" centered on the order's school on the Rue des Postes were typical products of nineteenth-century plotomania, the various sections of the French ultraright, the military high command, the majority of the prelacy, the Bonapartist and legitimist rumps, the survivors of Boulangism, and the antisemitic press *were* engaged in a concerted campaign to overthrow the democratic Republic, or at least to push it in a decidedly authoritarian direction, and to this end they were prepared to use any kind of "evidence" to prove the existence of a Jewish-backed "syndicate of treason" bent on releasing Dreyfus and handing over France to the control of "international" and "cosmopolitan" agencies, be they "German," "Protestant," "Jewish," or, typically, all three acting synergistically. The conspiracy obsessions prompting or released by *l'Affaire* conformed to the prototypical pattern of the 1790s, the plot being, now as then, the fantasmagorical shadow side of political democracy: a "superpower" had infiltrated and was controlling the machinery of state, politicians were "nothing but" puppets being manipulated by this or that international operator, the whole of political life was a gigantic charade, into which, however, the conspiracy theory permitted preternatural insight.[253] Amidst all the ignorance, chicanery, disguise, and mendacity of institutional democracy, only the conspiracy theorist *knew* what was truly afoot, his obsession bestowing upon him the gift of total, all-encompassing vision in an age increasingly riven with relativism and doubt. When God is dead, only belief in a hidden puppeteer can confer order and pattern on the *mysterium magnum* of politics, economics, and international diplomacy interacting in concert.

The Dreyfus affair did not *produce* a scapegoat, or scapegoats, in the manner of earlier political crises. It was, from beginning to end, *about* a scapegoat surpassing all other scapegoats, though, as it evolved, it extruded further exemplary victims on both sides, until it became difficult to tell scapegoaters from scapegoated, so venomous was the climate, so encouraging of reciprocal accusation and aspersion.

Dreyfus himself was the insider-outsider par excellence: Jewish, Alsatian, intelligent, distant in manner, his timidity easily taken as arrogance; in short, the least clubbable or collegiate of men in an army that, since the defeat of 1870–71 and the triumph of the Republic in 1877, had become a refuge for disaffected Catholic aristocrats and sons of the *grande bourgeoisie*. Of the 365 names in the 1878 promotion at Saint-Cyr, the French West Point, 102 were preceded by "de," and in 1886 140 out of 410 "passing out" had received private Catholic schooling.[254] It was not a place for a Jew, even an archetypally assimilated Jew like Alfred Dreyfus, to be at a time of institutional crisis.

No one on the General Staff had the slightest doubt as to Dreyfus's responsibility for the so-called memorandum containing the offer of French military secrets that was "discovered" through "la voie ordinaire" (the usual way), the code term for a French cleaning woman named Madame Bastian, employed by the German embassy, who allegedly found it in the wastebasket of the German military attaché in October 1894. He was Jewish, his handwriting supposedly bore a resemblance to that of the memorandum, and that was enough: "That Dreyfus is capable of treachery I deduce from his race," wrote Maurice Barrès in 1902, three years after Dreyfus's innocence had been definitively established.[255]

Dreyfus's "degradation," following his conviction, at the Ecole Militaire on the Place de Fontenoy, close to the newly completed Eiffel Tower—the symbol of everything his accusers detested—had all the characteristics of a public execution minus actual death. On the early morning of 5 January 1895, crowds gathered as at the Place de la Roquette, some of those present hurling stones—and many more cries of "Dirty Jew!" and "Death to the Jews!"—at the black horse-drawn prison wagon in which Dreyfus arrived from the military prison on the Rue du Cherche-Midi. His epaulettes, brass buttons, gold officer's braid, and red trouser stripes had previously been loosened and his ceremonial sword scored through so that it would break swiftly and cleanly: plainly the military was leaving nothing to chance.[256] Standing in the middle of the central courtyard of the Ecole, Dreyfus was duly stripped of his regalia, leaving him, in the words of the ultraright journalist Léon Daudet, looking like "a rigid puppet, pale and weasel-faced, with a body stripped piece by piece of all the things that had given him social value and rank." As Zola, not present at the event, would imagine it at the time of his own later trial, it united "all against one, who proclaims his innocence, the ferocity of the crowd."[257] It was like the *toilette du guillotiné* conducted in public, leaving Dreyfus symbolically naked and castrated in the "black rag" (his word) of his uniform, loose threads hanging from it, with broken sword and desecrated regalia lying in a heap on the ground in front of him, the whole ritual being performed in the presence of several hundred troops, two detachments from each regiment garrisoned in Paris, and a delegation of dignitaries, diplomats, and journalists, including Sarah Bernhardt in the first category and Theodor Herzl, correspondent of the Viennese *Neue Freie Presse,* in the second, his espousal of Zionism being commonly dated from his revulsion at seeing Dreyfus's humiliation that day. For the far right, that humiliation was the direct, inevitable, and thoroughly justified consequence of his race. "This wretch is not French," declared Daudet, "he is the color of treason" (*il est couleur traître*), as only befits a "ghetto wreck," an *épave de ghetto.* Even his dignified bearing told against him. "Judas walks too well," wrote Barrès, for whom the whole spectacle was "more exciting than the guillotine."

After the degradation, Dreyfus was taken by train, in irons and handcuffs, and after waiting all night at the Gare d'Orléans without food and

drink to La Rochelle, where again stones were thrown at him, to temporary confinement on the Ile de Ré and thence to the "dry guillotine" of the
penitentiary on the Iles du Salut, off the coast of French Guiana, where he
was detained on the Ile du Diable, the infamous Devil's Island, previously
and with heavy symbolism reserved for convicts with leprosy.[258]

There he was to remain from April 1895 to June 1899, when he was
brought back to France for retrial at Rennes, spending his time reading,
writing letters to his wife, and filling notebook after notebook with curious almost identical drawings, prevented by a double palisade from
seeing anything but the sky, and spending at least some of his sentence in
irons at night. "I speak to you as though from the tomb," he wrote to
Lucie Dreyfus, likening himself, Jew though he was, to a Trappist monk
in his cell, of undergoing his "Calvary" and "martyrdom" on his "lost
rock," the most tragic and innocent of a succession of French generals,
leaders, and writers to be condemned to island-bound exclusion:
Napoleon; Victor Hugo; Bazaine; the Communard journalist Henri de
Rochefort (1831–1913), who, exiled to New Caledonia, escaped and
was amnestied, and, shifting his position like so many ex-Communards,
become a supporter of Boulanger and later a vociferous accuser of Dreyfus; Pétain brought the tradition to an ignominious close. Zola described Dreyfus in so many words as an "expiatory victim."[259] Even his
first accuser, General Du Paty de Clam, told him that "if you are innocent, you are the greatest martyr of all time."[260]

From this prototypical scapegoat many lesser scapegoats were
cloned, all of them, guilty and innocent, fulfilling much the same expiatory function. Foremost, and quite justifiably, among the bugaboos of
the Dreyfus camp was Marie-Charles-Ferdinand Walsin-Esterhazy
(1847–1923), the actual author of the memorandum, who, but for the
fact that he was not a Jew, fulfilled all the conditions of insider-
outsiderdom at least as well as did Dreyfus: an illegitimate scion of the
great Hungarian noble family that employed Haydn, an antisemite who
sponged off Jews and even acted as the second for one Jewish officer in a
duel against Drumont, a womanizer, gambler, and swindler for whom
selling military secrets to the Germans was just the next logical career
move. Carried in triumph by the crowd when he was acquitted of writing the memorandum in January 1898—"Hats off to the martyr to the
Jews!" cried one decidedly overenthusiastic fellow officer[261]—Esterhazy
was finally unmasked. He fled via Belgium to England in September that
year, admitted his authorship of the memorandum in the press, and,
never having returned to France, died in 1923 under the name of
"Count Jean de Voilemont."

Dreyfus's accusers had any number of scapegoats to choose from, including another army officer: Colonel Georges Picquart (1854–1914), like Dreyfus an Alsatian but a Catholic, who first established Esterhazy's responsibility for the memorandum and was posted to Tunisia for his pains in late 1896, the hope being, according to Blum, that an Arab bullet would quickly finish him off.[262]

Other Dreyfus defenders of less than impeccable Frenchness—that is, Catholic and "Aryan," to use a term then being made current by pseudoscientific racists such as Georges Vacher de Lapouge[263]—were stereotyped in the now familiar fashion. The Protestant president of the Senate, Auguste Scheurer-Kestner (1833–99), an early and influential supporter of Dreyfus and another Alsatian, was attacked as a *boche,* a "Prussian," and a "servant of the Germans" on account of his religion and Teutonic-sounding surname, and was so frequently and abusively attacked in the Senate that, rising to speak, he seemed to Romain Rolland like a "sixteenth-century Huguenot" going to the scaffold for his beliefs.[264] No doubt many Dreyfus accusers rejoiced when this "lipomatous gorilla"[265] died accidentally on the very day that Dreyfus was finally released (19 September 1899).

The Jews Joseph and Théodore Reinach, nephews of the baron de Reinach who had committed suicide during the Panama scandal of 1892, were likened by Léon Daudet to "Orang leading Ourang" as they entered a room,[266] in keeping with the tendency to animalize opponents made explicit in Lenepveu's series of fifty-one political posters published under the title of *Musée des horreurs* in 1899–1900.

Finally, Zola—that "Genoan" (Daudet), that "rootless Venetian" (*Vénétien déraciné,* Barrès)—was subject to a campaign of vilification rivaled only by that of Dreyfus himself after the publication of *J'Accuse* in *L'Aurore* on 13 January 1898 led him, successively, to trial, conviction, temporary reprieve, reconviction, and eventual self-exile in England in July of that year. Stones were thrown at him and his wife at their home at Médan. Lenepveu depicted him—predictably and, we now know, symptomatically—as a pig squatting on a pile of his own obscene novels, holding a brush in one of his trotters, with which he smears a map of France from a potful of *caca international* held in the other.[267] It was only one of a veritable latrine-load of excremental images lavished on the author of *Le Ventre de Paris* and *Germinal;* one illustration, titled "Zola-Mouquette. Le fondement de l'affaire Dreyfus" has him contemptuously baring his rump (inscribed "Mon coeur à Dreyfus") like la Mouquette in the novel,[268] while throughout Catholic France babies' potties were known as their "Zolas."[269]

One party's bogeyman was the other party's martyr, and even before the affair itself, a vast crowd of supporters and sympathizers had attended the funeral of a Jewish officer, Captain Armand Mayer, who, in the summer of 1892, had been killed in a duel with the notoriously antisemitic marquis de Morès.[270] The Dreyfus supporters' principal martyr—apart, of course, from Dreyfus himself—was Bernard-Lazare, the pseudonym of Lazare Bernard (1865–1903), author of the seminal *Une Erreur judiciaire: La Vérité sur l'Affaire Dreyfus* (1896) and, in Péguy's memorable description, an "atheist streaming with the word of God" (*cet athée ruisselant de la parole de Dieu*),[271] whose early death at the age of thirty-eight was widely attributed to his unremitting exertions in the Dreyfus cause. Rejected by most fellow Jews as a socialist troublemaker and shunned as a Zionist fanatic by non-Jewish Dreyfus defenders, Bernard-Lazare died in virtual isolation, without having witnessed the total vindication of the cause, and his sparsely attended funeral on 4 September 1903 belongs, numbers apart, to the great martyrological tradition of the long nineteenth century. Determined, as he put it, that "the first man to stand up for the Jewish martyr should be a Jew,"[272] he is presented in Péguy's great threnody as nothing less than a secular saint and by Léon Blum as something perhaps even greater: *un juste* (a righteous man).[273]

The Dreyfus affair witnessed the last flurry of duels in French political history;[274] a derisory attempt at a coup d'état staged by the nationalist diehard Paul Deroulède (1846–1914) on the occasion of the state funeral of President Félix Faure (23 February 1899); an attack on his successor, Emile Loubet, at the racecourse of Auteuil by another half-crazed antisemitic aristocratic, the baron de Christiani, admittedly armed with nothing more lethal than his cane (4 June 1899); a forty-day siege of "Fort Chabrol," the headquarters of Jules Guérin's Antisemitic League near the Gare du Nord, terminated by the stench inside rather than by any paramilitary action (August 1899); the attempted assassination of Dreyfus's lawyer, Fernand Labori, at the retrial at Rennes (14 August 1899); and, most serious of all, a wave of antisemitic riots in January–February 1898, especially violent in Algiers, but attested in no fewer than fifty-five places in France. In Paris, "individuals with Jewish features were grabbed, surrounded, and roughed up by delirious youths who danced round them, brandishing flaming torches, made from rolled-up copies of *L'Aurore*."[275] The Dreyfus family home on the Boulevard Sébastopol was attacked and stoned on 11 February, and there were several attacks on Jewish-owned department stores by disgruntled small shopkeepers, whose resentment is described by one modern historian as "a resurgence of the age-old hatred of the hoarder."[276] Finally, an attempt was made on Dreyfus's own life on the occasion of Zola's Pantheonization in June 1908, the culprit, yet another antisemitic fanatic named Grégori, being acquitted on all charges in September.

The violent act that eclipsed all others in its resonance was, however, self-inflicted, though there were those who doubted at the time—and some who doubt to this day—that the death of Colonel Hubert-Joseph Henry at the fortress of Mont-Valérien on the night of 30–31 August 1898 was really a suicide. It was Henry who, in October 1896, had fabricated the supposed letter from the Italian military attaché to his German equivalent that explicitly named Dreyfus as the spy and so put a temporary halt to calls for a retrial. Further forgeries followed, but it was not until mid-August 1898 that Henry was finally exposed and, admitting his guilt, interned on 30 August at Mont-Valérien. There his body, the throat cut and the cell spattered with blood, was discovered the following morning; religious burial was refused by the Church. Whether, in Péguy's words, it was a "death or simulation of death, assassination, murder, suicide, or simulation of suicide,"[277] Henry's "disappearance" (*disparition*) effectively proved Dreyfus's complete innocence, and his supporters well knew it. But for the most extreme of Dreyfus's enemies, Henry's death, whatever its cause, was that of a martyr and hero; against all logic, they believed it validated their cause. On 7 September 1898 Charles Maurras published in *La Gazette de France* an article that almost overnight established him as the leader of the French ultraright. Titled "Le Premier Sang de l'affaire Dreyfus," it celebrated Henry as a martyr, beyond all considerations of right and wrong, to the nationalist cause and hymned his blood as the "precious blood" of an authentic Christ of reaction:

> Colonel, your blood, which streamed to the middle of the cell from the camp bed on which you were stretched out, has, according to newspaper reports, been carefully sponged away on the orders of the commandant of Mont-Valérien. But that is a great error. Be sure that, of this precious blood, the first French blood shed in the Dreyfus affair, there is not a single drop that is not still steaming, wherever the heart of the nation is throbbing. This blood is steaming and will cry out until its effusion is expiated, not by you who succumbed to a magnificent despair, not even by Cavaignac's irksome ministerial clique [a reference to the minister of war, who finally exposed Henry], but by your original executioners, whom I designate here, the members of the syndicate of treason.[278]

As a statement of the sacrificial paradigm, this could hardly be bettered. All the crucial elements are present—blood, communion in and through the blood of the martyr, expiation, conspiracy—and events shortly afterward would lift them to a still higher level of political potency. In a series of articles published in *Le Siècle*, Joseph Reinach, the Dreyfus accusers' chief hate figure after Zola, claimed that Henry had been not merely a forger but Esterhazy's accomplice from beginning to end. Henry's widow threatened to sue, and Drumont, never one to miss an opportunity for mischief, opened a public subscription through the pages of *La Libre Parole* to meet her legal expenses. The result was the so-called *monument Henry*, a study of which offers the most chilling of insights into the political and psychological netherworld of the turn of the century.

Between 14 December 1898 and 15 January 1899, 25,000 people contributed to the *monument Henry*, donating a grand total of 131,000 francs.[279] The subscribers came from every class and calling of French society; only peasants were notably underrepresented in the overall profile.[280] Many working-class contributors had personal grudges against Jewish employers, signing themselves variously as "a Yid's valet," "Jeanne, ex-maid of some Yids," "a waiter, victim of the suppression of tipping by the Jews at Le Mans."[281] Shopkeepers regularly described themselves as victims of "unfair" Jewish competition, and students (who made up a remarkable 8.6 percent of the subscribers, although they constituted well below 1 percent of the French population) expressed disgust at the alleged domination of university faculties by Jews.[282] Some (mainly female) had had unhappy love affairs with Jews, and one subscriber described herself simply but revealingly as a "victim of a cruel and unjust world."[283] A certain Paul Valéry, known to have been a disciple of Vacher de Lapouge at the time, donated the princely sum of 3 francs, "not without reflection": one would not expect the author of *Monsieur Teste* (1896) to do anything spontaneously.[284] Probably every subscriber found in the mythical figure of "the Jew" or "the Yid" (*le youpin*) a means of explaining and excusing his or her confusion or suffering at a time of rapid socioeconomic change, and a way of projecting outward any feelings of guilt, inadequacy, aggression, or sexuality that could not be handled within.

By the classic mechanism of scapegoating, the complex and solitary conflict of "I versus Me" was transformed into the heartwarming collective struggle of "Us versus Them." But what still surprises and shocks is the sheer violence of so many of the comments. One subscriber wanted to "circumcise [the Jews] up to the neck";[285] the abbé Cros, a former lieutenant, chillingly requested "a bedside rug made with Yid skins, so that he could tread on it night and morning"; and another man anonymously longed "to eat some Jew, so that he could defecate it." All over France, men and women were communing through the shed blood of a proven forger and possible traitor, and expelling their fears, hatreds, and frustrations in the form of Jewish flesh, cooked, burned, or excreted. Some subscribers displayed a sense of historical tradition, calling for a new Saint Bartholomew's Eve massacre or, in one remarkable case, a "return of the *noyades* of Nantes," the reference being to the drowning of hundreds of supporters of the Vendée insurrection in that city in 1793–94, grotesquely known to its republican perpetrators as "vertical deportation" or "national baptism." But with most, the impulse was crudely cannibalistic or holocaustal: "Berthe, a cook, to roast the Jews," "to make a dog's meal by boiling up certain noses," "an inhabitant of Baccarat who would like to see all the Yids, Yiddesses, and their brats in town burned in the glass furnaces here."[286]

As we have seen, Maurras's original article explicitly spoke of Henry's "precious blood" being shed for the salvation of the authentic French nation.[287] In general, however, the Christological referent was, in keeping with a long and paradoxical tradition, more prevalent on the free-thinking left than on the conventionally religious right, even though comparisons of Dreyfus with Christ were probably inhibited by the captain's Jewishness; writers in both ideological camps rarely bethought themselves of the Jewishness of Jesus. One writer, however, who did not hesitate to use—and, arguably, misuse—Christian imagery at the time of the affair was the arch-anti-Christian, Emile Zola himself. In an open letter to Lucie Dreyfus, published in *L'Aurore* on the occasion of her husband's pardon and release (29 September 1899), Zola spoke of him as "the crucified," who had at last been not merely taken down from his cross but resurrected "living and free" from the "tomb" in which he had been interred for so long. Not only this, but he had been transfigured by his sufferings: "Unjust pain has sanctified him, and he has entered, august, purified for all time, the temple of the future." Zola's secularized Christology preserves the de Maistrian model while transferring its soteriological benefits from the beyond to the future: Dreyfus has suffered vicariously for France, and his merits will revert to posterity.

The paradoxical consequence of this systematic likening of Dreyfus to Christ is that his tormentors come to occupy the place traditionally reserved for "the Jews": "Before this martyr taken down [*décloué*] from his cross, exhausted, sustained by moral force alone, they marched past in their savagery, covering him in spittle, stabbing him with their knives, pouring into his wounds vinegar and gall." The responsibility for Dreyfus's "crucifixion" will fall on the heads of his persecutors, and they will have to expiate it for all time, as the Jews the first crucifixion; as Bernard-Lazare had tellingly written, "antisemitism was born on Calvary hill."[288] Thus, even as Zola excoriated antisemitism, he unwittingly reproduced part, at least, of the mind-set that had incriminated Dreyfus in the first place. Christ and Judas, Judas and Christ, the crown of thorns and the pieces of silver: in the end, neither Dreyfus's defenders nor his attackers were able to escape the sacrificial paradigm.

No one who studies the Dreyfus affair can doubt the extent and intensity but also—and crucially—the limits of French antisemitism at the turn of the century. On the one hand, the dissemination of ideas and attitudes such as those revealed with ignominious clarity by the *monument Henry* led ultranationalists like Maurras to believe that in antisemitism they held an infallible key to success: "Everything seems impossible, or appallingly difficult, without the providential emergence of antisemitism [*sans cette providence de l'antisémitisme*]," he wrote in 1911; "through it, everything takes on order, becomes leveled out, and is simplified [*par elle, tout s'arrange, s'aplanit, et se simplifie*]."[289] The virtual omnipresence of what Blum called exclusionary antisemitism readily led into the persecutory variety ("l'exclusion a la persécution pour limite": exclusion ends in persecution)[290] and provided the reservoir of hatred and fear from which street thugs like Guérin and Morès recruited their gangs of butcher boys, small shopkeepers, and other disaffected "elements" spawned by social and economic transformation of unprecedented intensity and speed. On the other hand, the fact that a dozen proto-fascist formations such as Guérin's Antisemitic League and Dubuc's Antisemite Youth were unable to topple the Republic was due, in the first instance, to their leaders' mediocrity and incompetence, and still more to the concerted response of committed republicans of all hues, from the Socialist Jaurès to the conservative Clemenceau, with the much vilified *intellectuels*—the use of the word as a noun dates precisely from the Dreyfus affair—in their van.[291] Among these was Zola, who, as the equally courageous Blum later declared, "did not simply expose himself in the metaphorical sense, he genuinely exposed his person; he called down assassination, prison, and exile on his head. The more I reflect and the more I assess, the more I admire the Zola of 'the Affair.'"[292] In a book concerned so insistently with the violence of Frenchman on Frenchman (and, intermittently, of the violence of Frenchman on Frenchwoman), it is appropriate to conclude by saluting a triumph of nonviolence. "We were heroes," Péguy wrote with justified pride in

Notre jeunesse, "it must be said simply, because no one, I think, will say it for us."[293]

CODA: QU'UN SANG IMPUR ...

Has the history of postrevolutionary France been notably more violent than that, say, of its principal neighbors, Spain, Germany, and Italy, during the same period? In terms of sheer numbers of lives lost, probably not, though the combined casualties of the Vendée insurrection of 1793–94—possibly 300,000 in all, perhaps higher[294]—are at least comparable to the total number of deaths in the Spanish Civil War, put by Hugh Thomas at 400,000.[295] What is so striking in the French instance is less the volume of violence than the remorseless repetition of essentially the same basic scenario, often involving no more than one or two victims, from July 1789 to October 1945; from the lynching, in other words, of de Launay and de Flesselles to the execution of Laval. Virtually every change of regime for over a century and a half was marked by the putting to death of one or more—usually many more—exemplary victims; the shedding of blood sealed almost every political *rite de passage,* in a succession of politically inspired acts of violence that was all the more remarkable given the decline in the level of social violence—measured crudely by the marked nationwide drop in the number of murders—that occurred during the same period.[296]

No less remarkable than the repetition of acts of political violence was the self-repeating character of the discourse that accompanied them and which, in its turn, is refracted in the imaginative literature of the period. The victim is cast as a scapegoat to be extruded from the polis by his or her killers, and as a martyr whose memory and mana are to be ingested by the group from which he or she has been taken. The language of sacrifice is present everywhere on both right and left, and the Crucifixion—renewed, for the right, by the martyrdom of Louis XVI and, for the left, in that of every militant who ever died for "the cause"—becomes for all parties the paradigm of the expiatory or redemptive death. Each of the two Frances was obsessed by historical precedent and fitted each new death that occurred into the familiar paradigm, thus creating a kind of apostolic succession of victims and validating the prophecy made by de Maistre and others that the blood of Louis XVI would be on the head of the French nation forever.

Of course, Spain, Italy, and Germany had their exemplary victims. Without thinking too hard, one comes up with Federico García Lorca, Giacomo Matteotti, Dietrich Bonhoeffer, Claus von Stauffenberg, and

Walter Benjamin, the last committing suicide in desperation at Port-Bou on the Franco-Spanish frontier in September 1940. On a number of occasions, France itself was the stage on which foreign political conflicts were violently acted out: the assassination of King Alexander of Yugoslavia by Croat nationalists at Marseille in October 1934, the French foreign minister Louis Barthou being killed at the same time; the gunning down, at the Normandy spa town of Bagnoles de l'Orne in June 1937, of the Italian socialists Carlo and Nello Rosselli by French *Cagoulards* (fascist gunmen) acting on Mussolini's instructions; and the assassination, in Paris on 7 November 1938, of the German diplomat Ernst von Rath by the seventeen-year-old Polish-Jewish student Herschel Grynszpan, for which the so-called *Kristallnacht* of 9 November exacted terrible and wholly disproportionate revenge. Likewise, politically inspired violence in France did not begin in July 1789 nor did it by any means end in October 1945, though its principal victims since then have been French citizens of North African origin—outsider-insiders with a vengeance—with intermittent recrudescences of antisemitism to preserve continuity with the past: the bombing of the synagogue on the Rue Copernic on 3 October 1980 (when Raymont Barre, the prime minister at the time, lamented that "this odious outrage, designed to hit Jews going to the synagogue ... struck down innocent French people crossing the Rue Copernic," as though the Jews in question were neither innocent nor French);[297] the bombing of the Goldenberg Restaurant on the Rue des Rosiers in 1982, already referred to, and the desecration of the ancient Jewish cemetery in Carpentras in May 1990.

Overwhelmingly, though, the paradigmatic scapegoats of the years since 1945 have been North Africans or *Beurs* (their French-born children), either victims of police violence, like the hundred or more Algerian political protesters killed in Paris on the night of 17 October 1961, presumably on the orders or with the connivance of the prefect of Police, Maurice Papon, of whose record under Vichy much would later be heard,[298] or more recently of civilian racism, much of it committed, inspired, or, at the very least, condoned by the man and the party that wants France "to take the first right, along the Rue Charles-Maurras, then right again at the Rue Philippe-Henriot, over the Place Brasillach and past the Square Drumont, and into the Avenue du Maréchal-Pétain."[299] Thus, in the summer of 1983 alone, Toufik Ouannès, aged nine, murdered at La Courneuve; Kamel Lettad, aged seventeen, stabbed in the stomach with a pruning knife by a "commando"; Salim Grisse, killed in a racist attack in Aix-en-Provence, aged eighteen; Lhachmi Bouned, bludgeoned to death with an iron bar in Bastia, aged fifty-five;

and—a final macabre link with tradition—Zineb Sadi, aged thirty, shot three times as she crossed the footbridge at the station at Drancy.[300]

Not that "Anglo-Saxons" should be in any way complacent, particularly not the author who finished his book about violence in postrevolutionary France during the week when, in England, an official report was published, condemning police racism, on the murder in April 1993 of Stephen Lawrence, a high school student of Jamaican parentage, by a gang of white youths who attacked him with cries of "Nigger!" as he waited for a bus to take him home (and of the immediate desecration of the makeshift memorial in south London where he died); and when, from Jasper, Texas, came news of the conviction of the first of the three white men accused of chaining James Byrd (forty-nine, black) to the back of their pickup truck, dragging him for three miles, and causing him, literally, to be torn limb from limb, in an instance of deliberate, ritualized violence far more chilling than anything described in this book. For all this, the place of violence, of repeated, almost choreographed violence, in French, and particularly Parisian, history from Revolution to Liberation does seem unique, and it may be that the reader of this book will end it thinking, like its author, that no city ever had a more fitting patron saint than the headless Saint Denis, and no country a more apposite, or more unfortunate, national anthem than the "Marseillaise":

> Aux armes, citoyens!
> Formez vos bataillons!
> Marchons! Marchons!
> Qu'un sang impur
> Abreuve nos sillons!

> [To arms, citizens! / Form your battalions / Let's march! Let's march! May an impure blood / Drench our fields!]

SACRIFICIAL VICTIMS
A *Chronology*

The following chronology brings together all the individual cases of violent death mentioned in the text. I have, where possible, given the exact location.

1750	23 May	Lynching of Labbé (Rue St. Roch)
1757	28 March	Execution of Damiens (Place de Grève)
1766	1 July	Execution of chevalier de La Barre (Abbeville)
1789	14 July	Lynching of de Launay and de Flesselles (Place de Grève)
	22 July	Lynching of Foulon and Bertier de Sauvigny
1790	19 February	Execution of marquis de Favras (Place de Grève)
1791	17 July	Massacre of Champ-de-Mars
1792	3 March	Lynching of Louis Simonneau (Etampes)
	2–6 September	September massacres: lynching of archbishop of Arles, bishops of Saintes and Beauvais (Carmélites), and princesse de Lamballe (La Force)
1793	20 January	Assassination of Le Peletier de Saint-Fargeau (Palais-Royal)
	21 January	Execution of Louis XVI (Place de la Révolution)
	8 July	Death of Viala (Bonpas, near Avignon)
	13 July	Assassination of Marat (Rue des Cordeliers)
	17 July	Execution of Charlotte Corday (Place de la Révolution)
	17 July	Execution of Joseph Chalier (Lyon)
	16 October	Execution of Marie-Antoinette (Place de la Révolution)

	31 October	Execution of Girondins (Place de la Révolution)
	3 November	Execution of Olympe de Gouges (Place de la Révolution)
	8 November	Execution of Madame Roland (Place de la Révolution)
	7 December	Death of Bara (Jallais, near Cholet)
1794	10 February	Suicide of Jacques Roux
	24 March	Execution of Hébert and Hébertists (including Anarchis Cloots)
	5 April	Execution of Danton, Desmoulins, Hérault de Séchelles, and other Dantonists
	10–13 April	Execution of widows of Hébert and Desmoulins
	8 May	Execution of Lavoisier
	2 June	Execution of Cécile Renault
	16 July	Execution of 16 Carmelite nuns (Place du Trône Renversé)
	25 July	Execution of André Chénier
	28 July	Execution of Robespierre and Saint-Just (Place de la Révolution)
1795	17 June	Suicide of Gilbert Romme
1796	22 March	Death of Perrine Dugué (Thorigné, Mayenne)
1797	27 May	Execution of Babeuf
1804	21 March	Execution of duc d'Enghien (Vincennes)
	5 April	Suicide(?) of Pichegru
	25 June	Execution of Cadoudal
1812	29 October	Execution of General Malet
1820	14 February	Assassination of duc de Berry (Rue Le Peletier)
	7 June	Execution of Louvel (Place de Grève)
1822	21 September	Execution of four sergeants of La Rochelle (Place de Grève)
1825	30(?) November	Funeral of General Foy (Père-Lachaise)
1827	29(?) August	Funeral of Jacques-Antoine Manuel (Père-Lachaise)
1832	5 June	Funeral of General Lamarque
1834	13 April	Massacre of Rue Transnonain
1836	9 January	Execution of Lacenaire (Barrière Saint-Jacques)
	19 February	Execution of Fieschi
	12 July	Execution of Louis Alibaud

1848	23 February	Massacre of Boulevard des Capucines
	5 June	Death of Monseigneur Affre (Place de la Bastille) and General Bréa (Barrière de Fontainebleau)
1851	3 December	Death of Victor Baudin (Place de la Bastille)
1854	10 February	Execution of Tapner (Guernsey)
1855	26 January	Suicide of Nerval (Rue de la Vieille-Lanterne)
1857	17 July	Funeral of Béranger (Père-Lachaise)
1858	13 March	Execution of Orsini
1864	9 June	Execution of La Pommerais
1870	10/12 January	Death and funeral of Victor Noir (Neuilly)
	19 January	Execution of Troppmann (Place de la Roquette)
1871	18 March	Lynching of Generals Lecomte and Clément-Thomas (Rue des Rosiers)
	24 May	Execution of Archbishop Darboy (La Roquette)
	25 May	Death of Delescluze (Place du Château-d'Eau)
	25 May	Massacre of five Dominican friars from Arcueil (Avenue d'Italie)
	26 May	Execution of Millière (Panthéon)
	28 May	Execution of Varlin (Rue des Rosiers)
1879	1 June	Death of prince imperial (Ityotosi, South Africa)
1885	31 May	Funeral of Victor Hugo
1890	27–29 July	Suicide of Van Gogh (Auvers-sur-Oise)
1891	1 May	Massacre of strikers at Fourmies
	30 September	Suicide of Boulanger (Ixelles, Belgium)
1892	11 July	Execution of Ravachol
	20 November	Suicide of Jacques Reinach
1894	21 May	Execution of Emile Henry
	24 June	Assassination of Sadi Carnot
1895	5 January	"Degradation" of Dreyfus (Ecole Militaire)
1897	4 May	Fire at the Bazar de la Charité (Rue Jean-Goujon)
1898	31 August	Suicide of Colonel Henry (Mont-Valérien)
1899	14 August	Attempted assassination of Fernand Labori (Rennes)
1902	29 September	Death of Emile Zola (Rue de Bruxelles)
1903	4 September	Funeral of Bernard-Lazare
1908	4 June	Attempted assassination of Dreyfus (Panthéon)

1909	12 October	Execution of Francisco Ferrer (Barcelona)
1914	17 March	Murder of Gaston Calmette (Rue Montmartre)
	31 July	Assassination of Jaurès (Rue Montmartre)
	22 August	Death of Ernest Psichari (Rossignol, Belgium)
	5 September	Death of Charles Péguy (Villeroi)
	22 September	Death of Alain-Fournier (Hauts-de-Meuse)
1917	20 August	Suicide(?) of Almeyreda (Fresnes)
1932	6 May	Assassination of President Paul Doumer
1934	8 January	Suicide(?) of Alexandre Stavisky (Chamonix)
	6 February	Riots at Place de la Concorde (14 civilian casualties, 1 military)
	9 October	Assassination of Louis Barthou and King Alexander I of Yugoslavia (Marseille)
1937	9 June	Assassination of Rosselli brothers (Bagnoles de l'Orne)
	17 November	Suicide of Roger Salengro (Lille)
1938	7 November	Assassination of Ernst von Rath
1940	23 May	Death of Paul Nizan (Recques-sur-Hem, near Dunkirk)
	27 September	Suicide of Walter Benjamin (Port-Bou)
1941	21 August	Assassination of Moser (Métro Barbès)
	August	Execution of Honoré d'Estiennes d'Orves (Mont-Valérien)
	22 October	Fusillade of Châteaubriant
	15 December	Execution of Gabriel Péri (Mont-Valérien)
1942	23 May	Execution of Georges Politzer (Mont-Valérien)
	16–17 July	Roundup of Vel' d'Hiv'
	24 December	Assassination of Darlan
	26 December	Execution of Bonnier de La Chapelle
1943	28 May	Death of Bertie Albrecht (Fresnes)
	May	Death of Danièle Casanova (Auschwitz)
	8 July	Death of Jean Moulin
1944	10 January	Deaths of Victor and Hélène Basch (Neyran, Ain)
	5 March	Death of Max Jacob
	20 March	Execution of Pucheu (Algiers)
	2 April	Massacre of Ascq (near Lille)
	6 April	Arrest of 44 Jewish children at Izieu (Ain)
	8 June	Execution of 99 hostages at Tulle (Corrèze)
	10 June	Massacre of Oradour-sur-Glanes

	16 June	Death of Marc Bloch (Saint-Didier-de-Formans, Ain)
	20 June	Assassination of Jean Zay
	28 June	Assassination of Philippe Henriot
	29 June	Massacre of seven Jews at Rillieux-la-Pape (Touvier)
	7 July	Assassination of Georges Mandel
	23 July	Execution of Gilbert Dru (Lyon)
	1 August	Death of Jean Prévost (Pont Charvet, Vercors)
	9 November	Execution of Georges Suarez
1945	6 February	Execution of Brasillach (Fresnes)
	22 February	Death of Doriot (Messkirch, Germany)
	15 March	Suicide of Drieu La Rochelle (Rue Saint-Ferdinand)
	8 June	Death of Robert Desnos (Tereczin, Czechoslovakia)
	10 October	Execution of Darnand
	13 October	Execution of Hérold-Paquis (Fort de Chatillon)
	15 October	Execution of Laval (Fresnes)

NOTES

Unless otherwise stated, all works in French are published in Paris and those in English in London; where there is more than one place of publication, only the first is given.

1. PARIS À VOL D'OISEAU

1. Théophile Gautier, *Poésies complètes,* ed. René Jasinski (Nizet, 1970), 2:150–51.
2. Ibid., 210–11.
3. Alfred de Vigny, *Poèmes antiques et modernes/Les Destinées* (Gallimard, 1973), 138–39.
4. Victor Considerant, *Description du Phalanstère et considérations sociales sur l'architectonique* (1848), quoted in Françoise Choay, *L'Urbanisme: Utopies et réalités* (Seuil, 1965), 107.
5. Quoted in Louis Chevalier, *Labouring Classes and Dangerous Classes in Paris during the First Half of the Nineteenth Century,* trans. Frank Jellinek (Routledge & Kegan Paul, 1973), 155.
6. All quotations from Victor Hugo, *Notre-Dame de Paris* (Folio, 1996), 165–92.
7. For a highly perceptive discussion of nineteenth-century panoramas of Paris, see chap. 3, "The High View: Three Cityscapes," in Christopher Prendergast, *Paris and the Nineteenth Century* (Oxford: Blackwell, 1992), 46–73.
8. Emile Zola, *Paris* (Lausanne: Rencontre, n.d.), 41.
9. Hugo, *Notre-Dame de Paris,* 191–92.
10. Philippe Joutard, ed., *Histoire de la France religieuse,* vol. 3, *Du roi Très Chrétien à la laïcité républicaine, XVIIIᵉ–XIXᵉ siècle* (Seuil, 1991), 246.
11. Claude Langlois, "A l'épreuve de la Révolution (1770–1830)" in *Histoire des catholiques en France du XVᵉ siècle à nos jours,* ed. François Lebrun (Privat, 1980), 357.
12. François Mauriac, *Le Nœud de vipères* (Livre de poche, 1996), 43.
13. See Guillaume de Bertier de Sauvigny, *Nouvelle histoire de Paris: La Restauration, 1815–1830* (Association pour la publication d'une histoire de Paris, 1977), 417.
14. See Jeffrey Kaplan, "Concubinage and the Working Class in Early Nineteenth-Century Paris," in *De l'ancien régime à la révolution française,* ed. Albert Cremer (Göttingen: Vandenhock & Ruprecht, 1978), 351–52.
15. See Claude Langlois, "Pratique pascale et délais de baptême" in Joutard, *Histoire de la France religieuse,* 3:246.
16. Saint-Marc Girardin in *Journal des débats,* 8 Dec. 1831, quoted in Pierre Michel, *Un Mythe romantique: Les Barbares, 1789–1848* (Lyon: Presses universitaires de Lyon, 1981), 210.
17. See Michel Lagrée, "Exilés dans leur patrie (1880–1920)" in Lebrun, *Histoire des catholiques en France,* 421.
18. Quoted in Pierre Sorlin, *La Sociéte française,* vol. 1, *1840–1914* (Arthaud, 1969), 217.
19. Louis-Sébastien Mercier, *Le Tableau de Paris* (Maspéro, 1982), 258–62.
20. Lebrun, *Histoire des catholiques en France,* 272. Most of the details concerning the Revolution are taken from Claude Langlois and Timothy Tackett, "A l'épreuve de la

Révolution (1770–1830)," chap. 4, supplemented by Michel Vovelle, "C'est la faute à la Révolution," in Joutard, *Histoire de la France religieuse,* 3:262–70. See also Pierre Pierrard, *L'Eglise et la Révolution, 1789–1889* (Nouvelle Cité, 1988).

21. Fabre d'Eglantine, quoted in Frédéric Bluche, *Septembre 1792: Logiques d'un massacre* (Robert Laffont, 1986), 47.

22. On the revolutionary calendar, see Bronislaw Baczko, "Le Calendrier républicain: Décréter l'éternité," in *Les Lieux de la mémoire,* ed. Philippe Nora (Gallimard, 1983), 1:37–38.

23. On the cult of Marat, see Jean-Claude Bonnet, ed., *La Mort de Marat* (Flammarion, 1986), and Marie-Hélène Huet, *Rehearsing the Revolution: The Staging of Marat's Death, 1793–1797,* trans. Robert Hurley (Berkeley: University of California Press, 1982).

24. For the anti-Christian campaign, see Michel Vovelle, *La Révolution contre l'Eglise: De la raison à l'Etre Suprême* (Brussels: Complexe, 1988). Not all of the outrages described necessarily took place in Paris: I know of no Paris church steeple that was toppled by revolutionaries.

25. Mona Ozouf, *La Fête révolutionnaire, 1789–1799* (Folio, 1988), 441–74.

26. Joseph de Maistre, *Ecrits sur la Révolution,* ed. Jean-Louis Darcel (Presses universitaires de France, 1989), 132 (italics in original).

27. Louis XVI's son—whom French royalists regarded as Louis XVII even though he never ascended the throne—died in mysterious circumstances in 1795. The refusal of many ultraroyalists to accept his death gave rise to a succession of almost certainly bogus pretenders to the French throne, most notably a Prussian clockmaker named Naundorff, who arrived in France in 1833 claiming to be Louis XVII and succeeded in gaining a following among the lunatic fringe of French legitimists. See Claude Guillet, *La Rumeur de Dieu: Apparitions, prophéties at miracles sous la Restauration* (Imago, 1994), 69–76, 109–12.

28. See the classic study by Marc Bloch, *Les Rois thaumaturges* (Armand Colin, 1961), in which Charles X's coronation is discussed on 402–5.

29. On the theme of revolutionary martyrology, see Antoine de Baecque, "Le Corps meurtri de la Révolution: Le discours politique et les blessures des martyrs (1792–1794)," *Annales historiques de la Révolution française* 267 (1987): 17–41.

30. Joseph Bara (1779–93) was killed fighting for the Republic near Cholet, in the Vendée, and immediately became the focus of an organized revolutionary cult, of which Jacques-Louis David's unfinished painting *La Mort de Bara* was to be the official altarpiece. Agricol Viala (1780–93) was killed fighting for the Republic at Bonpas, near Avignon, and became the object of a similar, if lesser, republican cult. See Raymond Monnier, "Le Culte de Bara en l'an II," *Annales de l'Histoire de la Révolution Française* 241 (1980): 321–37, and Michel Vovelle, "Agricol Viala, ou Le Héros malheureux," ibid., 345–64.

31. For a discussion of the political significance of wine in the 1840s, see Richard D. E. Burton, *Baudelaire and the Second Republic: Writing and Revolution* (Oxford: Clarendon, 1991), 184–219.

32. Quoted in Pierre Pierrard, *Les Pauvres, l'Evangile et la Révolution* (1848) (Desclée de Brouwer, 1977), 181. For the whole question of Christian republican socialism in the 1840s, see Edward Berenson, *Populist Religion and Left-Wing Politics in France, 1830–1852* (Princeton: Princeton University Press, 1984).

33. For a discussion of the political significance of this poem, see Burton, *Baudelaire and the Second Republic,* 176–82.

34. Abbé Jean-Hippolyte Michon (1806–81), quoted in Pierrard, *L'Eglise et la Révolution,* 215.

35. Alistair Horne, *The Fall of Paris: The Siege and the Commune, 1870–1871* (Macmillan, 1989), 337.

36. Quoted in Jacques Rougerie, *Procès des Communards* (Gallimard/Julliard, 1978), 201.

37. Quoted in Mona Ozouf, *L'Ecole, l'Eglise et la République, 1871–1914* (Cana/Jean Affredo, 1982), 45.

38. Quoted and discussed in Jean-Marie Mayeur, *Les Débuts de la IIIe République, 1871–1898* (Seuil, 1973), 38.

39. See Rosamonde Sanson, *Les Quatorze-juillet (1789–1975): Fête et conscience nationale* (Flammarion, 1976), 80–106.

40. Quoted in Mayeur, *Les Débuts de la IIIe République*, 112.

41. Quoted in Gérard Cholvy and Yves-Marie Hilaire, *Histoire religieuse de la France contemporaine*, vol. 1, *1800–1880* (Toulouse: Privat, 1985), 73, 205.

42. Adrien Dansette, *Destin du Catholicisme français* (Flammarion, 1957), 64.

43. Quoted in Sorlin, *La Société française*, 1:217.

44. See Yvan Daniel, ed., *La Religion est perdue à Paris: Lettres d'un vicaire parisien à son archévêque en date de 1849 suivies d'un mémoire adressé au même* (Cana, 1978), 40–54 passim.

45. See Anne Martin-Fugier, "Les Rites de la vie privée bourgeoise," in *Histoire de la vie privée*, ed. Michèle Perrot (Seuil, 1987), 216.

46. The archbishop of Cambrai, quoted in Lebrun, *Histoire des Catholiques en France*, 386.

47. Ibid., 352.

48. Quoted in Cholvy and Hilaire, *Histoire religieuse de la France contemporaine*, 1:62–63.

49. See Burton, *Baudelaire and the Second Republic*, 214–19.

50. Quoted in Joutard, *Histoire de la France religieuse*, 3:273.

51. Georges Bernanos, *Journal d'un curé de campagne* (Livre de poche, 1971), 7.

52. Quoted in Lebrun, *Histoire des Catholiques en France*, 386.

53. See Jean Bastaire, *Péguy tel qu'on l'ignore* (Folio, 1995), 388–89.

54. See Cholvy and Hilaire, *Histoire religieuse de la France contemporaine*, 1:162; Joutard, *Histoire de la France religieuse*, 3:437–39.

55. See Cholvy and Hilaire, *Histoire religieuse de la France contemporaine*, 1:180.

56. M. A. Bazin (Anaïs de Raucon), *L'Epoque sans nom: Esquisses de Paris, 1830–1833* (Alexandre Mesnier, 1833), 54.

57. Letter of 10 Feb. 1848, quoted in Pierrard, *L'Eglise et la Révolution*, 153.

58. On this subject, see the wide-ranging study by Frank Paul Bowman, *French Romanticism: Intertextual and Interdisciplinary Readings* (Baltimore: John Hopkins University Press, 1990), 81–105.

59. On the general theme of conspiracy in French politics, see the essay "La Conspiration" in Raoul Girardet, *Mythes et mythologies politiques* (Seuil, 1986), 25–62. On the theme of the Jesuit conspiracy, see Geoffrey Cubitt, *The Jesuit Myth, Conspiracy Theory, and Politics in Nineteenth-Century France* (Oxford: Clarendon, 1993). See also Richard D. E. Burton, "The Unseen Seer, or Proteus in the City: Aspects of a Nineteenth-Century Parisian Myth," *French Studies* 42, no. 1 (1988): 50–68.

2. VIOLENT ORIGINS

1. The following account of the "myth" of the Bastille is based essentially on Monique Cottret, *La Bastille à prendre: Histoire et mythe de la fortresse royale* (Presses universitaires de France, 1986), reinforced by Hans-Jürgen Lüsebrink and Rolf Reichardt, *The Bastille: A History of a Symbol of Despotism and Freedom*, trans. Norbert Schürer (Durham, N.C.: Duke University Press, 1997). The account of the actual events of July 1789 is based on the standard works by Jacques Godechot, *La Prise de la*

Bastille, 14 juillet 1789 (Folio, 1989), and Guy Chaussinand-Nogaret, *La Bastille est prise: La Révolution française commence* (Brussels: Complexe, 1988). References are kept to a minimum.

2. See, among other sources, Arlette Farge and Jacques Revel, *Logiques de la foule: L'affaire des enlèvements d'enfants, Paris, 1750* (Hachette, 1988).

3. See Steven L. Kaplan, *Le Complot de famine: Histoire d'une rumeur au 18ᵉ siècle,* trans. Michèle and Jacques Revel, Cahier des Annales 39 (Armand Colin, 1982), esp. 49–56.

4. On the lettres de cachet, see Arlette Farge and Michel Foucault, *Le Désordre des familles: Lettres de cachet des Archives de la Bastille* (Gallimard/Julliard, 1982), esp. 15, 348.

5. Quoted in Jacques André, *La Révolution fratricide: Essai de psychanalyse du lien social* (Presses universitaires de France, 1993), 73.

6. Quoted from Michel Vovelle, *La Chute de la monarchie, 1787–1792* (Seuil, 1972), 110.

7. See the classic study by Georges Lefebvre, *The Great Fear of 1789: Rural Panic in Revolutionary France* (1932), trans. Joan White (New York: Schocken, 1973).

8. Details and quotations in Godechot, *La Prise de la Bastille,* 222–39.

9. All details ibid., 293–354.

10. The two texts are to be found in the *Collection des mémoires relatifs à la Révolution: Mémoires de Linguet et de Dusaulx,* ed. Berville and Barrière (Baudouin, 1821). *L'Œuvre des sept jours* is reproduced as an appendix to Chaussinand-Nougaret, *La Bastille est prise,* 139–62.

11. For this distinction, see the important article by Brian Singer, "Violence in the French Revolution: Forms of Ingestion/Forms of Expulsion," in *The French Revolution and the Birth of Modernity,* ed. Ferenc Fehér (Berkeley: University of California Press, 1990), 150–73, esp. 162–63.

12. Quoted in Godechot, *La Prise de la Bastille,* 497.

13. Simon Schama, *Citizens: A Chronicle of the French Revolution* (New York: Viking, 1989), 404.

14. Ibid., 405. All other quotations are taken from Godechot, *La Prise de la Bastille,* 374–75.

15. Jules Michelet, *Histoire de la Révolution française* (Robert Laffont, 1979), 1:152.

16. See Barry M. Shapiro, *Revolutionary Justice in Paris, 1789–1790* (Cambridge: Cambridge University Press, 1993), 47.

17. See Singer, "Violence in the French Revolution," 163. See also the interesting comments in Colin Lucas, "The Crowd and Politics," in *The French Revolution and the Creation of Modern Political Culture,* vol. 2, *The Political Culture of the French Revolution,* ed. Colin Lucas (Oxford: Pergamon, 1988), esp. 274–75.

18. Henri Hubert and Marcel Mauss, "Essai sur la nature et la fonction du sacrifice" (1899), in Marcel Mauss, *Œuvres,* vol. 1, *Les Fonctions sociales du sacré* (Minuit, 1968), 193–307, esp. 212–21.

19. François-Auguste-René de Chateaubriand, *Mémoires d'outre-tombe* (Livres de Poche, 1973), 1:221–22.

20. Quoted in Schama, *Citizens,* 446. The whole of this paragraph leans heavily on Schama's account and analysis.

21. For a detailed discussion, see Lüsebrink and Reichardt, *The Bastille,* 118–47.

22. All details in Mona Ozouf, *La Fête révolutionnaire, 1789–1799* (Folio, 1988), 59–101.

23. Michelet, *Histoire de la Révolution française,* 1:337.

24. On the Revolution's replacement of patriarchal by matriarchal imagery, see the searching analysis in Lynn Hunt, *Politics, Culture, and Class in the French Revolution* (Methuen, 1986), 52–86.

25. Victor Hugo, *Les Misérables* (Lausanne: Rencontre, 1966), 3:298–99.

26. The remains of the mummies (which were rotting away in the cellars of the Louvre) were buried in the same common grave close to the palace-museum where the bodies of the victims of July would later be interred before their transfer to the Place de la Bastille. There is thus a strong likelihood that the Colonne de Juillet is the final resting place of certain contemporaries of Ramses II as well as of the victors of July.

27. Hugo, *Les Misérables,* 3:300.

3. KILLING THE KING

1. The full account is published in Albert Soboul, *Le Procès de Louis XVI* (Gallimard/Juillard, 1973), 231–33.

2. Jules Michelet, *Histoire de la Révolution française* (Robert Laffont, 1979), 1:501–7.

3. Sébastien Mercier, *Paris pendant la Révolution, 1789–1798* (Poulet–Malassis, 1862), 1:317.

4. On caricatures of the king, see Annie Duprat, *Le Roi décapité: Essai sur les imaginaires politiques* (Editions du Cerf, 1992), esp. 170–87, where the image of the *roi-cochon* is discussed.

5. Michelet, *Histoire de la Révolution française,* 1:727.

6. See the brilliant analysis of this caricature in Neil Hertz, "Medusa's Head: Male Hysteria under Political Pressure," in *The End of the Line: Essays on Psychoanalysis and the Sublime* (New York: Columbia University Press, 1985), 179–91.

7. The quotations in this paragraph are assembled from three sources: Jacques André, *La Révolution fratricide: Essai de psychanalyse du lien social* (Presses universitaires de France, 1993), 94–105; Daniel Arasse, *La Guillotine et l'imaginaire de la Terreur* (Flammarion, 1987), 67–71; and Susan Dunn, *The Deaths of Louis XVI: Regicide and the French Political Imagination* (Princeton: Princeton University Press, 1994), 16–18. The argument advanced here is heavily dependent on all three of these remarkable studies, esp. to André, 104–5.

8. On the Sanson dynasty, see Barbara Levy, *Une dynastie de bourreaux: Les Sanson,* trans. Henri Robillot (Mercure de France, 1989). See also Richard D. E. Burton, "Le Sacrifice du Bourreau: Capital Punishment and the Nineteenth-Century French Imagination (1815–1848)," in *Repression and Expression in Nineteenth-Century France,* ed. Carrol F. Coates (New York: Peter Lang, 1996), 7–21.

9. Abbé Edgeworth de Firmant, *Dernières heures de Louis XVI, roi de France* (Baudouin, 1825), 178–79.

10. Mercier, *Paris pendant la Révolution,* 1:304.

11. Quoted in Arasse, *La Guillotine,* 82.

12. Ibid., 83.

13. Ibid. In some notes of the 1840s, Hugo describes how, after the king's death, Sanson cast the royal frock coat into the crowd, "and in an instant it disappeared, torn by a thousand hands. *Scinderunt vestimenta sua*" (Victor Hugo, *Ecrits sur la peine de mort* [Hubert Nyssen, 1979], 60).

14. See Claude Langlois, *La Caricature contre-révoultionnaire* (Presses du C.N.R.S., 1988), 194. The engraving appears to have served as frontispiece to a pamphlet titled *La Passion et la mort de Louis XVI, roi des Juifs et des Chrétiens,* which bears the motto "Crucifixerunt eum inter duos Latrones" (ibid., 248).

15. Quoted in Soboul, *Le Procès du Roi,* 195.

16. For further discussion, see Burton, "Le Sacrifice du bourreau," 10–12, and esp. Dunn, *Deaths of Louis XVI,* 38–66 (on Louis and Joan) and 67–92 (on Michelet, Lamartine, and Louis XVI).

17. All quotations from de Maistre, *Ecrits sur la révolution*, 98–113. This passage is based on Burton, "Le Sacrifice du bourreau," 8–9, where full references may be found.

18. Joseph de Maistre, "Eclaircissements sur les sacrifices," in *Les Soirées de Saint-Pétersbourg* (Pélagaud, 1862), 405.

19. All quotations from Pierre-Simon Ballanche, *Œuvres* (Geneva: Barbezat, 1830), 1:317–403. This paragraph repeats Burton, "Le Sacrifice du bourreau," 9–10, where full references may be found.

20. See, for example, Amédée Burion, *Louis XVI: Martyr dans sa royauté, dans sa famille, dans sa foi* (1854), as quoted in Richard D. E. Burton, "From Scapegoat to Martyr: The Image of Marie-Antoinette in Nineteenth-Century Catholic-Monarchist Thought," *Australian Journal of French Studies* 34, no. 2 (1997): 196–201.

21. Edgar Quinet, *La Révolution* (Brussels: Lacroix, Verboeckhoven, 1869), 1:434.

22. Quoted in André, *La Révolution fratricide*, 14.

23. Maistre, *Ecrits sur la révolution*, 168.

24. Alphonse de Lamartine, *Histoire des Girondins* (Brussels: Wouters, 1849), 1:434.

25. See Daniel Gerould, *Guillotine: Its Legend and Lore* (New York: Blast Books, 1992), 163–65.

26. All details and quotations are taken from Yannick Essertel, "La Sainte Guillotine," in *Révolution contre Révolution*, ed. Bernard Dermotz and Jean Haudry (Porte-Glaive, 1990), 73–86.

27. See Schama, *Citizens*, 842.

28. Ibid., 837.

29. Ibid., 859.

30. Ibid., 850–51.

31. Carol Blum, *Rousseau and the Republic of Virtue: The Language of Politics in the French Revolution* (Ithaca: Cornell University Press, 1986), 252–53.

32. On the language of Robespierre's arrest and sentencing, see Françoise Brunel, *Thermidor: La Chute de Robespierre* (Brussels: Complexe, 1989), 97–98, 107–8.

33. Albert Laponneraye in his preface of 1840 to Robespierre's *Œuvres*, quoted in Blum, *Rousseau and the Republic of Virtue*, 278.

34. *Chronique de Paris*, quoted in Jacques Guilhaumou, *La Mort de Marat* (Brussels: Complexe, 1989), 72–73.

35. This discussion of Marie-Antoinette is closely based on Burton, "From Scapegoat to Martyr" (see note 20 above).

36. The literature on this subject is now fairly substantial. See esp. Chantal Thomas, *La Reine scélérate: Marie-Antoinette dans les pamphlets* (Seuil, 1989), and chap. 4, "The Bad Mother," of Lynn Hunt, *The Family Romance of the French Revolution* (Berkeley: University of California Press, 1992). I have also drawn on Elizabeth Colwill, "Just Another *Citoyenne*? Marie-Antoinette on Trial, 1790–1793," *History Workshop* 28 (1989): 63–87; and Jacques Revel, "Marie-Antoinette in Her Fictions: The Staging of Hatred," in *Fictions of the Revolution*, ed. Bernadette Fort (Evanston: Northwestern University Press, 1991), 111–29.

37. This subject has been extensively treated in writing on women and the Revolution. See as a representative example Paule-Marie Duhet, *Les Femmes et la Révolution, 1789–1794* (Gallimard/Julliard, 1971), esp. 143–60.

38. Henri Monier de la Sizeranne, *Marie-Antoinette: Poème historique* (Librairie d'Amyot, 1860), 253.

39. Abbé V. Mourot, *Marie-Antoinette, ou Les Sourires et les tristesses d'une reine* (Sarlat: Bricon, 1889), xvii.

40. Louis Massignon, *Un Vœu et un destin: Marie-Antoinette, reine de France* (Chantenay, 1955), 3.

41. Léon Bloy, "Le Fils de Louis XVI" (1900), in *Œuvres de Léon Bloy*, ed. Joseph Bollery and Jacques Petit (Mercure de France, 1966), 5:154.

42. Léon Bloy, "L'Ame de Napoléon" (1912), in his *Œuvres*, 292.

43. Bloy, "Le Fils de Louis XVI," 155, 88, 71, 91. On the question of Naundorff and the survival of the dauphin, and indeed on the whole structure of feeling from which the cult of Marie-Antoinette emerges, see Claude Guillet, *La Rumeur de Dieu: Apparitions, prophéties at miracles sous la Restauration* (Imago, 1994).

44. All references are to the edition of *La Chevalière de la Mort* published by Fata Morgana, the printing of which "was completed on 21 January 1989, anniversary of the martyrdom of Louis XVI." For page references, see Burton, "From Scapegoat to Martyr."

45. Quoted in Daniel Arasse, *La Guillotine et l'imaginaire de la Terreur* (Flammarion, 1987), 128–29. On the analogy frequently made in peasant cultures between the annual killing of the pig and the Passion of Christ, see the remarkable study by Claudine Fabre-Vassas, *La Bête singulière: Les Juifs, les Chrétiens et le cochon* (Gallimard, 1994).

46. Michelet, *Histoire de la Révolution française*, 2:754.

47. See Gerould, *Guillotine*, 38, 51.

48. See Arasse, *La Guillotine*, 49–58.

49. See Linda Nochlin, *The Body in Pieces: The Fragment as a Metaphor of Modernity* (Thames & Hudson, 1994), 19. See also Nina Athanassouglou-Kallmyer, "Géricault. Severed Heads and Limbs: The Politics and Aesthetics of the Scaffold," *Art Bulletin* 74, no. 4 (1992): 601–18.

50. See Hertz, "Medusa's Head."

51. See Bram Dijkstra, *Idol of Peversity: Fantasies of Feminine Evil in Fin de Siècle Culture* (Oxford: Oxford University Press, 1986), 352–401.

52. Alain Brossat, *Les Tondues: Un carnaval moche* (Manya, 1992), 212–13.

53. Victor Hugo, *Les Rayons et les ombres*, in his *Œuvres complètes* (Lausanne: Re-contre, 1968), 18:367–68. I owe this reference to Denis Hollier's introductory essay, "Bloody Sundays," in the English translation of his *La Prise de la Concorde* (1973), which has generally influenced the present discussion. See Denis Hollier, *Against Archi-tecture: The Writings of Georges Bataille*, trans. Betsy Wing (Cambridge: MIT Press, 1989), ix–xiii.

54. François-Auguste-René de Chateaubriand, *Mémoires d'outre-tombe* (Livres de Poche, 1973), 1:501.

55. A *chapelle expiatoire* was eventually constructed on the Place Louis XVI in the present eighth arrondissement, close to the Gare Saint-Lazare, where it remains, cur-rently locked and unvisitable.

56. See Gérard de Nerval, "Embellissements de Paris" (1838), in *Œuvres complémen-taires de Gérard de Nerval*, ed. Jean Richer (Minard, 1964), 8:97–105.

57. Pierre-Joseph Proudhon, *Du principe de l'art et de sa destination sociale* (1865), quoted in Françoise Choay, *L'Urbanisme: Utopies et réalités* (Seuil, 1965), 132–33.

58. Albert Boime, *Art and the French Commune: Imagining Paris after War and Revo-lution* (Princeton: Princeton University Press, 1995), 104–7.

59. The bibliography on this subject is vast. See as an introduction Zeev Sternhell, *La Droite révolutionnaire, 1885–1914: Les Origines françaises du fascisme* (Seuil, 1983) and *Ni droite ni gauche: L'Idéologie fasciste en France* (Seuil, 1983); and Pierre Milza, *Fascisme français: Passé et présent* (Flammarion, 1987).

60. All details from Serge Berstein, *Le 6 février 1934* (Gallimard/Julliard, 1975).

61. See Michel Winock, *"Esprit": Des intellectuels dans la cité, 1930–1950* (Seuil, 1996), 107–10.

62. Robert Brasillach, *Notre avant-guerre* (Livre de poche, 1973), 198. For a similar "sacrificial" interpretation of 6 Feb., see Jean-Pierre Maxence, *Histoire de dix ans, 1927–1937* (Gallimard, 1939), 280–81.

63. Pierre Drieu La Rochelle, *Gilles* (Livre de poche, 1967), 433–36.

64. Jean-Paul Sartre, *Qu'est-ce que la littérature?* (1947) (Gallimard, 1967), 81.

65. Account based on Pascal Ory, *Les Collaborateurs, 1940–1945* (Seuil, 1980), 81–83.

66. The photograph is reproduced in Bataille's *Les Larmes d'Eros* (Pauvert, 1961). For a full discussion, see Michel Surya, *Georges Bataille, la mort à l'œuvre* (Garamont/Frédéric Birr, 1987), 103. Unless otherwise stated, all details and quotations in the present section are taken from this work.

67. Surya, *Georges Bataille*, 253–56.

68. Georges Bataille, *Madame Edwarda*, in his *Œuvres complètes* (Gallimard, 1970), 3:21.

69. Quoted in Surya, *Georges Bataille*, 246.

70. See Bataille, "La Conjuration sacrée" (*Acéphale*, June 1936), in his *Œuvres complètes*, 1:444.

71. Like virtually every other French writer on this theme, Bataille seems unaware of the earlier (1649) execution of Charles I of England.

72. All quotations from Bataille, *Œuvres complètes*, 1:500–513.

73. Georges Bataille, "Propositions" (*Acéphale*, June 1936), in his *Œuvres complètes*, 1:471.

74. The term *surfascisme* was never used by Bataille himself; it appears to have been invented by another member of *Acéphale*, Pierre Dugas (see Surya, *Georges Bataille*, 249).

75. Of those closely associated with *Acéphale* or the parallel but distinct Collège de Sociologie, only Anatole Lewitzky, a member of the pioneering Musée de l'Homme resistance group (shot at Mont-Valérien in February 1942), seems to have been an active resister. See Surya, *Georges Bataille*, 271.

4. VENDÔME/INVALIDES

1. Quoted in Jean Tulard, *Napoléon* (Fayard, 1994), 365.

2. Ibid., 142.

3. Account based on José Cabanis, *Le Sacre de Napoléon* (Gallimard, 1994), 92–101.

4. Quoted in Tulard, *Napoléon*, 397.

5. See Jean Tulard, *L'Anti-Napoléon: La Légende noire de l'Empereur* (Julliard, 1965), 46–48.

6. See Tulard, *Napoléon*, 136.

7. François-Auguste-René de Chateaubriand, *Mémoires d'outre-tombe* (Livres de Poche, 1973), 1:611–34.

8. See Tulard, *L'Anti-Napoléon*, 70.

9. For a full and incisive discussion of Gros's depiction of Napoleon, see Christopher Prendergast, *Napoleon and History Painting: Antoine-Jean Gros's 'La Bataille d'Eylau'* (Oxford: Oxford University Press, 1997), esp. 159–82.

10. Quoted in Cabanis, *Le Sacre de Napoléon*, 101. This topos is also found in popular discourse on Napoleon, as evidenced in the veteran Goguelat's great speech in Balzac's *Le Médecin de campagne* (1833): "The fact is he was ordered to do duty in Egypt. That's his resemblance to the son of God" (quoted in Jean Tulard, *Le Mythe de Napoléon* [Armand Colin, 1971], 178).

11. Quoted in Tulard, *Le Mythe de Napoléon*, 128.

12. Léon Bloy, *L'Ame de Napoléon* (Gallimard, 1983), 13–15. The quotation from Napoléon is taken from Jean Tulard, "Le Retour des Cendres," in *Les Lieux de la mémoire*, ed. Philippe Nora (Gallimard, 1983), 2:3, 88.

13. See Prendergast, *Napoleon and History Painting*, 35–44.

14. All details from Cabanis, *Le Sacre de Napoléon*, 169–77. On Beethoven's tearing off the dedication to Napoleon of his Third Symphony (later retitled the *Eroica*), see Maynard Soloman, *Beethoven* (Cassell, 1977), 132–33.

15. Quoted in Louis Hautecœur, *Histoire de l'architecture classique en France* (Picard, 1953), 5:148.

16. Quoted in Tulard, *L'Anti-Napoléon*, 31.

17. The whole of this account of the "return of the ashes" is based on Jean Tulard, "Le Retour des cendres," and the very full discussion in Michael Marrinan, *Painting Politics for Louis-Philippe: Art and Ideology in Orléanist France, 1830–1848* (New Haven: Yale University Press, 1988), 184–200.

18. Quoted from Marrinan, *Painting Politics*, 195.

19. Tulard, "Le Retour des cendres," 107.

20. Maurice Barrès, *Les Déracinés* (Union Générale d'Editions, 1986), 165.

21. All details from Tulard, "Le Retour des cendres," 107–8.

22. Quoted in André-Jean Tudesq, *L'Election présidentielle de Louis-Napoléon Bonaparte: 10 décembre 1848* (Armand Colin, 1965), 93.

23. Quoted in Bernard Ménager, *Les Napoléon du peuple* (Aubier, 1988), 107.

24. Letter to Narcisse Ancelle of 5 Mar. 1852, in Charles Baudelaire, *Correspondance* (Gallimard, 1973), 1:188.

25. For a brilliant study of anti-Bonapartist propaganda of the late 1860s and its links with Rimbaud's poetry of 1870–71, see Steve Murphy, *Rimbaud et la ménagerie impériale* (Lyon: Presses Universitaires de Lyon, 1991).

26. John Bierman, *Napoleon III and His Carnival Empire* (John Murray, 1989), 377.

27. The literature on this subject is immense. For a convenient summary, see Richard D. E. Burton, *The Context of Baudelaire's "Le Cygne,"* (Durham, U.K.: University of Durham, 1980), 35–47. The reference to Napoléonville is to be found in Alain Dalotel, Alain Faure, and Jean-Claude Freiermuth, *Aux origines de la Commune: Le mouvement des réunions publiques à Paris, 1868–1870* (Maspéro, 1980), 75.

28. Jacques Rougerie, *Paris libre, 1871* (Seuil, 1971), 19.

29. Jules Vallès, "Les Statues," in *Vallès, Littérature et révolution,* ed. Roger Bellet (Editeurs Français Réunis, 1969), 280–83 (first published in *Courrier Français,* 1 July 1866).

30. Quoted in Prosper-Olivier Lissagaray, *Histoire de la Commune de 1871* (Maspéro, 1983), 290.

31. Quoted in Jack Lindsay, *Gustave Courbet: His Life and Work* (New York: Icon, 1973), 259.

32. Quoted ibid., 261.

33. Quoted in Neil Hertz, "Medusa's Head: Male Hysteria under Political Pressure," in *The End of the Line: Essays on Psychoanalysis and the Sublime* (New York: Columbia University Press, 1985), 169–70.

34. Kristin Ross, *The Emergence of Social Space: Rimbaud and the Paris Commune* (Macmillan, 1988), 5–8. The passages from Mendès and Barron are quoted from this study.

35. Lucien Descaves, *La Colonne* (Stock, 1901), 428–29.

36. Georges Bataille, *Œuvres complètes* (Gallimard, 1970), 171. The article was first published in *Documents,* no. 2, May 1929.

37. On Eutrepelia, see the wonderful study by Hugo Rahner, S.J., *Man at Play, or Did You Ever Practise Eutrepelia?,* trans. Brian Battershaw and Edward Quinn (Burns & Oates, 1965).

38. Lissagaray, *Histoire de la Commune,* 291.

39. See Bierman, *Napoleon III,* 396–400.

5. HEART OF THE CITY

1. For an excellent discussion of the social and political meanings of the painting, see Nicos Hadjinicolaou, " 'La Liberté guidant le peuple' de Delacroix devant son premier public," *Actes de la recherche en sciences sociales,* June 1979, 3–26.

2. See Marcia Pointon, "Liberty on the Barricades: Woman, Politics and Sexuality in Delacroix," in *Naked Authority: The Body in Western Painting, 1830–1908* (Cambridge: Cambridge University Press, 1990), 66.

3. The following account is based essentially on David H. Pinkney, *The French Revolution of 1830* (Princeton: Princeton University Press, 1972), supported by Guillaume de Bertier de Sauvigny, *La Révolution de 1830 en France* (Armand Colin, 1970).

4. Quoted in Pinkney, *French Revolution of 1830*, 162.

5. On the dialectic of "inside" and "outside" in nineteenth-century Paris, see Richard D. E. Burton, *The Flâneur and His City: Patterns of Daily Life in Paris, 1815–1851* (Durham, U.K.: University of Durham, 1994), 61–69.

6. Quoted in Jean Bruhat, "Le Socialisme français de 1848 à 1871," in *Histoire générale du socialisme,* ed. Jacques Droz (Presses universitaires de France, 1972), 1:501.

7. Daniel Stern (comtesse d'Agoult), *Histoire de la Révolution de 1848* (Charpentier, 1862), 361. For a modern historian's treatment, see Maurice Agulhon, *1848, ou L'Apprentissage de la république, 1848–1852* (Seuil, 1973), 41–43.

8. Gustave Flaubert, *L'Education sentimentale* (Folio, 1990), 322.

9. Edmond et Jules de Goncourt, *Journal,* ed. Robert Ricatte (Robert Laffont, 1989), 2:274–76.

10. Jacques Rougerie, *Paris libre, 1871* (Seuil, 1971), 108.

11. Prosper-Olivier Lissagaray, *Histoire de la Commune de 1871* (Maspéro, 1983), 151.

12. In many instances, the transfer in power was a change in name only, as many members of the Central Committee had been elected to the new municipal authority.

13. Lissagaray, *Histoire de la Commune,* 337.

14. It had been extended in 1803 and again between 1837 and 1841.

15. Martin Nadaud, *Mémoires de Léonard, ancien garçon maçon* (Hachette, 1976), 131–32.

16. On Damiens, see, inter alia, Joris-Karl Huysmans, "Damiens," in *Croquis parisiens* (Plon, 1913), 109–12; Michel Foucault, *Surveiller et punir: Naissance de la prison* (Gallimard, 1975), 9–11; and Giovanni Giacomo Casanova, *Histoire de ma vie* (Plon, 1960), 3:55–56. Casanova is unable to watch the later stages of Damiens's agony, but the spectacle excites his companion Tireta to further sexual action with the two women in their company. The erotic appeal of public executions is one of the topoi of the literature on the subject.

17. See Barry M. Shapiro, *Revolutionary Justice in Paris, 1789–1790* (Cambridge: Cambridge University Press, 1993), 178–79.

18. This paragraph leans heavily on Daniel Arasse, *La Guillotine et l'imaginaire de la Terreur* (Flammarion, 1987), 19–42.

19. See ibid., 47–64. A late example of this literature is Auguste de Villiers de L'Isle Adam's *conte cruel* of 1883 titled *Le Secret de l'échafaud.*

20. See Arasse, *La Guillotine,* 135–39.

21. See Alan B. Spitzer, *Old Hatreds and Young Hopes: The French Carbonari against the Bourbon Restoration* (Cambridge: Harvard University Press, 1971), 175.

22. Maxime Du Camp, "La Guillotine," in his *Paris, ses organes, ses fonctions et sa vie* (Hachette, 1872), 3:394. The paragraphs that follow repeat much of the material and many of the ideas of Richard D. E. Burton, "Le Sacrifice du Bourreau: Capital Punishment and the Nineteenth-Century French Imagination (1815–1848)," in *Repression and Expression in Nineteenth-Century France,* ed. Carrol F. Coates (New York: Peter Lang, 1996), 13–20.

23. Victor Hugo, *Le Dernier Jour d'un condamné* (Livre de Poche, 1989), 17 (preface of 1832).

24. See Barbara Levy, *Une Dynastie de bourreaux: Les Sanson,* trans. Henri Robillot (Mercure de France, 1989), 48.

25. See Pieter Spierenburg, *The Spectacle of Suffering: Execution and the Evolution of Repression from a Preindustrial Metropolis to the European Experience* (Cambridge: Cambridge University Press, 1984), 14–28.

26. Félix Pyat, "Le Bourreau," in *Les Français peints par eux-mêmes* (Curmer, 1841), 3:117.

27. See Robert Hertz, "La prééminence de la main droite: Etude sur la polarité religieuse," *Revue philosophique* 67 (1909): 553–80. The present analysis also draws on Roger Caillois's pioneering article of 1943, "Sociologie du bourreau," reproduced in his *Instincts et société* (Gonthier, 1964), 11–34.

28. Honoré de Balzac, *Souvenirs d'un paria*, in his *Œuvres diverses* (Conard, 1956), 4.

29. Du Camp, *Paris*, 1:355.

30. Joseph de Maistre, *Les Soirées de Saint-Pétersbourg* (J. B. Pélagaud, 1821), 1:39–41.

31. Jules Janin, *L'Ane mort et la femme guillotinée* (Flammarion, 1973), 140.

32. Hugo, *Le Dernier Jour d'un condamné*, 43.

33. Ibid., 44.

34. Ibid., 23.

35. Ibid., 140.

36. Ibid., 156.

37. Jules Vallès, "La Guillotine," in his *Œuvres complètes*, ed. Roger Bellet (Gallimard, 1990), 2:1354; originally published in *Le Cri du peuple*, 30 Apr. 1884.

38. Charles Baudelaire, *Œuvres complètes*, ed. Claude Pichois (Gallimard, 1975), 1:329.

39. Ibid., 2:539. On the whole theme of the entertainer, see the classic study by Jean Starobinski, *Portrait de l'artiste en saltimbanque* (Geneva: Skira, 1970).

40. Charles Baudelaire, "Edgar Allan Poe, sa vie et ses ouvrages" (1852), in his *Œuvres complètes*, 2:249.

41. Goncourt, *Journal*, 1:301.

42. Charles Baudelaire, *Mon cœur mis à nu*, in his *Œuvres complètes*, 1:676.

43. Baudelaire, "Edgar Allan Poe," 250.

44. Baudelaire, "L'Œuvre et la vie de Delacroix" (1863), in his *Œuvres complètes*, 2:760.

45. De Maistre, *Les Soirées de Saint-Pétersbourg*, 40.

46. "L'œil chargé d'un pleur involontaire / Il rêve d'échafauds en fumant son houka."

47. Translation by James McGowan in Baudelaire, *The Flowers of Evil* (Oxford: Oxford University Press, 1993), 149.

48. Oscar Wilde, "The Ballad of Reading Gaol," in *The Works of Oscar Wilde* (Wordsworth, 1994), 136.

49. See Maurice Agulhon, "Le Sang des bêtes: Le Problème de la protection des animaux en France au 19ᵉ siècle," *Romantisme* 31 (1981): 81–109.

50. Hugo, *Le Dernier Jour d'un condamné*, 34–35 (preface of 1832).

51. Ibid., 31.

52. Alphonse de Lamartine, *Discours sur l'abolition de la peine de mort* (Charles Gosselin, 1836), 3.

53. Pyat, "Le Bourreau," 115.

54. Ibid., 119.

55. Lamartine, *Discours*, 8–9.

56. Du Camp, *Paris*, 394–95.

57. Gustave Flaubert, *Par les champs et par les grèves* (Lausanne: Rencontre, 1964), 332–33.

58. See Rougerie, *Paris libre*, 218–19, and Stewart Edwards, *The Paris Commune, 1871* (Eyre & Spottiswoode, 1971), 300.

59. Lacenaire's literary and artistic progeny is considerable: Gautier, Stendhal, and Hugo, as well as, later, Flaubert and Dostoyevsky were all greatly preoccupied by his case, and he may well be one of the inspirations of Lautréamont's *Chants de Maldoror* (1874). A selection of his poems is included in André Breton's *Anthologie de l'humour noir* (1940), and he appears in Marcel Carné's classic film *Les Enfants du paradis* of 1944 as well as in François Girod's *Lacenaire* of 1990.

60. Pierre-François Lacenaire, *Mémoires et autres écrits,* ed. Jacques Simonelli (José Corti, 1991), 82.

61. See Daniel Gerould, *Guillotine: Its Legend and Lore* (New York: Blast Books, 1992), 96.

62. Lacenaire, *Mémoires,* 104.

63. Ibid., 108–9.

64. Ibid., 147.

65. Ibid., 61.

66. See Gerould, *Guillotine,* 98.

67. Lacenaire, *Mémoires,* 153.

68. All quotations that follow are taken from "The Execution of Troppmann" in Turgenev's *Literary Reminiscences,* trans. David Magarshack (Faber & Faber, 1958), 210–31.

69. See Charles Virmaître, *Mémoires secrets de Troppmann* (Alfred Duquesne, 1870), 173.

70. See Gerould, *Guillotine,* 179–82.

71. See Michel Surya, *Georges Bataille, la mort à l'œuvre* (Garamont/Frédéric Birr, 1987), 104.

72. See Victor Hugo, "Aux habitants de Guernesey" (January 1854), and other related texts in *Le Dernier Jour d'un condamné,* 205–61.

73. Quoted in Jean Maitron, *Ravachol et les anarchistes* (Folio, 1992), 115.

74. Baudelaire, *Mon Cœur mis à nu,* 683. The earlier reference to Damiens occurs on 693.

75. Henry Imbart and Frédéric Le Blanc, *De la loi du talion et de la peine de mort dans les sociétés modernes* (Victor Lecou, 1852), 68–69.

76. See, inter alia, the short stories "Le Convive des dernières fêtes" (1874), "Le Secret de l'échafaud" (1883), "Le Réalisme dans la peine des morts" (1885), "L'Instant de Dieu" (1885), "Les Phantasmes de M. Redoux" (1886), and "Ce Mahoin!" (1887). On the theme of Villiers and capital punishment, see Pierre Reboul, "Autour d'un conte de Villiers de L'Isle Adam: *Le Secret de l'échafaud,*" *Revue d'histoire littéraire de la France* 49 (1949): 235–45.

77. All quotations from *Le Réalisme dans la peine de mort,* in Villiers de L'Isle Adam, *Œuvres complètes,* ed. Alan Raitt and Pierre-Georges Castex (Gallimard, 1986), 2:450–57.

78. See Gordon Wright, *Between the Guillotine and Liberty: Two Centuries of the Crime Problem in France* (Oxford: Oxford University Press, 1983), 170.

79. See Honoré de Balzac, *Illusions perdues* (Livre de poche, 1966), 246–52.

80. For these and similar matters, see Burton, *Flâneur and His City,* 33–34, 61–69.

81. On the old carrousel and "Le Cygne," see Burton, *The Context of Baudelaire's "Le Cygne"* (Durham, U.K.: University of Durham), esp. 32–35.

82. Joris Karl Huysmans, *La Bièvre et Saint-Séverin* (Stock, 1898), 37.

6. THE MIRACULOUS MEDAL

1. All details on Catherine's life are taken from René Laurentin, *Vie de Catherine Labouré* (Desclée de Brouwer, 1980).

2. For an exemplary discussion of the problems of interpreting Marian visions, see David Blackbourn, *The Marpingen Visions: Rationalism, Religion, and the Rise of Mod-*

ern Germany (Fontana, 1995), 1–57. See also Thomas A. Kselman, *Miracles and Prophecies in Nineteenth-Century France* (New Brunswick, N.J.: Rutgers University Press, 1983), and Michael P. Carroll, *The Cult of the Virgin Mary: Psychological Origins* (Princeton: Princeton University Press, 1986). On the cult of the Virgin Mary in general, see Marina Warner, *Alone of All Her Sex: The Myth and the Cult of the Virgin Mary* (New York: Vintage, 1976).

3. See Ralph Gibson, *A Social History of French Catholicism, 1789–1914* (Routledge, 1989), 146.

4. See Philippe Joutard, ed., *Histoire de la France religieuse,* vol. 3, *Du roi Très Chrétien à la laïcité républicaine, XVIIIe–XIXe siècle* (Seuil, 1991), 498.

5. See Blackbourn, *Marpingen Visions,* 22–23.

6. All details from Laurentin, *Vie de Catherine Labouré,* 7–36.

7. Quoted in Claude Guillet, *La Rumeur de Dieu: Apparitions, prophéties at miracles sous la Restauration* (Imago, 1994), 98.

8. See Laurentin, *Vie de Catherine Labouré,* 46.

9. "Je ne savais ni pourquoi, ni comment, cette tristesse se portait sur le changement de gouvernement." Quoted ibid., 42–44.

10. Quoted ibid., 48–49.

11. All details and quotations ibid., 50–59.

12. Ibid., 59.

13. Her actual words are even more striking: "A ce moment, or j'étais, or je n'étais pas, je jouissais, je ne sais" (ibid., 62).

14. All details and quotations ibid., 60–66.

15. See Carroll, *Cult of the Virgin Mary,* 165–69.

16. See Eugen Weber, "Religion and Superstition in Nineteenth-Century France," *Historical Journal* 31, no. 2 (1988): 406.

17. The following account is based on Alain Faure, "Mouvements populaires et mouvement ouvrier à Paris (1830–1834)," *Mouvement social* 88 (1974): 51–92.

18. See Patrice Bourdelais and Jean-Yves Raulot, *Une peur bleue: Histoire du choléra en France, 1832–1854* (Payot, 1987), and François Delaporte, *Le Savoir de la maladie: Essai sur le choléra de 1832 à Paris* (Presses universitaires de France, 1990).

19. Quoted in Bourdelais and Raulot, *Une peur bleue,* 224.

20. All details from Laurentin, *Vie de Catherine Labouré,* 69–80. Stéphane Michaud (*Muse et Madone: Visages de la femme de la Révolution française aux apparitions de Lourdes* [Seuil, 1985], 39) gives much higher figures: 150,000 medals distributed by April 1834, 20 million in 1837 alone, 100 million in all during the first decade of the cult.

21. On Notre-Dame-des-Victoires, see Guillet, *La Rumeur de Dieu,* 146–49.

22. Joris-Karl Huysmans, *Les Foules de Lourdes* (Grenoble: Millon, 1993), 68.

23. Guillet, *La Rumeur de Dieu,* 100.

24. See William Christian, "Religious Apparitions and the Cold War in Southern Europe," in *Religion, Power, and Protest in Local Communities: The Northern Shore of the Mediterranean,* ed. Eric R. Wolf (New York: Mouton, 1984), 239–66.

7. KILLING THE LIVING, BURYING THE DEAD

1. All details are taken from Philippe Ariès, *L'Homme devant la mort* (Seuil, 1977); Richard A. Etlin, *The Architecture of Death: The Transformation of the Cemetery in Eighteenth-Century Paris* (Cambridge: MIT Press, 1984); and Thomas A. Kselman, *Death and the Afterlife in Modern France* (Princeton: Princeton University Press, 1993).

2. See Maurice Agulhon, "Le Sang des bêtes: Le Problème de la protection des animaux en France au 19e siècle,' *Romantisme* 31 (1981): 81–109.

3. Victor Hugo, *Les Misérables* (Lausanne: Rencontre, 1966), 2:297–98.

4. Alain Faure, from whose superb *Paris Carême-Prenant: Du carnaval à Paris au 19ᵉ siècle, 1800–1914* (Hachette, 1978) most of these details are taken. The reference to "une ville à l'envers" is to be found on p. 16.

5. See Michel Foucault, *Histoire de la folie à l'âge classique* (Plon, 1961).

6. See Roger Caillois, *L'Homme et le sacré* (Gallimard, 1970), 62–63.

7. Quoted in Kselman, *Death and the Afterlife,* 184.

8. Victor Fournel, *La Déportation des morts: Le Préfet de la Seine et les cimetières de Paris* (Armand Le Chevalier, 1870), 90.

9. Jean-Joseph Gaume, *Le Cimetière au dix-neuvième siècle, ou Le Dernier mot des solidaires* (Gaumie, c.1873), v–vii, 23.

10. Quoted in Ariès, *L'Homme devant la mort,* 536–37.

11. The reference is to Matthew Arnold's "Dover Beach" of 1867 (*The Works of Matthew Arnold* [Wordsworth Poetry Library, 1995], 401–2).

12. See David Bellos, *Honoré de Balzac: Old Goriot* (Cambridge: Cambridge University Press, 1987), 25.

13. On the notorious mercenariness of gravediggers and other undertakers' employees, see Maxime Du Camp's entry "Les Cimetières" in his *Paris, ses organes, ses fonctions et sa vie* (Hachette, 1872), 6:152–55.

14. All quotations from *Le Père Goriot* are from the 1991 Folio edition, 361–67. The argument advanced here repeats that of Richard D. E. Burton, "The Death of Politics: The Significance of Dambreuse's Funeral in *L'Education sentimentale*," *French Studies* 50, no. 2 (1996): 157–69.

15. For full references, see Burton, "Death of Politics," 164–65.

16. Julles Vallès, *L'Insurgé* (Livre de Poche, 1972), 135. As late as 1923, the ultraright Action Française attempted, without success, to transform the funeral of its militant Marius Plateau (assassinated by a twenty-year-old anarchist named Germaine Berton) into a political demonstration. See Eugen Weber, *Action Française* (Stanford: Stanford University Press, 1962), 138–39.

17. The following account is based on a combination of the fullest nineteenth-century study, Pierre-Olivier Lissagaray's *Histoire de la Commune de 1871* (1876), and the best of the more recent accounts in English, Robert Tombs, *The War against Paris, 1871* (Cambridge: Cambridge University Press, 1981). Unless otherwise stated, all quotations come from Lissagaray, *Histoire de la Commune de 1871* (Maspéro, 1983).

18. Lissagaray, *Histoire de la Commune,* 389–90. For a good modern study of the myth of the *pétroleuse,* see Gay L. Gullickson, "*La Pétroleuse:* Representing Revolution," *Feminist Studies* 17, no. 2 (1991): 240–65.

19. See Tombs, *War against Paris,* 162.

20. See Lissagaray, *Histoire de la Commune,* 360–61, and Tombs, *War against Paris,* 184–85.

21. See Lissagaray, *Histoire de la Commune,* 333, 338.

22. On Delescluze's death, see ibid., 354–55.

23. Ibid., 384.

24. Ibid., 359.

25. Jean-Pierre Azéma and Michel Winock, *Les Communards* (Seuil, 1970), 162.

26. Quoted in Tombs, *War against Paris,* 170.

27. Lissagaray, *Histoire de la Commune,* 379–81.

28. Ibid., 379.

29. Ibid., 399.

30. Ibid., 422.

31. For a full discussion of this subject, see Paul Lidsky, *Les Ecrivains contre la Commune* (Maspéro, 1970). Unless otherwise stated, all quotations that follow are taken from this work.

32. See Lissagaray, *Histoire de la Commune,* 456–57.

33. Ibid., 384–85.

34. Emile Zola, *La Débâcle* (Livre de poche, 1973), 496–501.

35. Eugène Pottier, *Œuvres complètes,* ed. Pierre Brochon (Maspéro, 1966), 108.

36. Lissagaray, *Histoire de la Commune,* 410.

37. Pottier, *Œuvres complètes,* 165–66.

38. Elémir Bourges, *Les Oiseaux s'envolent et les fleurs tombent,* ed. Gisèle Marie (Mercure de France, 1964), 36–37.

39. Pottier, *Œuvres complètes,* 167.

40. All the details that follow are taken from Madeleine Rebérioux, "Le Mur des fédérés: Rouge, 'sang craché,'" in *Les Lieux de la mémoire,* ed. Pierre Nora, vol. 1, *La Republique* (Gallimard, 1984), 619–49.

41. See Jean Maitron, *Ravachol et les anarchistes* (Gallimard, 1992), 74. The words of "La Ravachole" are on 75–76.

42. Rebérioux, "Le Mur des fédérés," 649.

8. CONVERSION?

1. See Henri Guillemin, *Le "Converti" Paul Claudel* (Gallimard, 1968), 18. This classic study has been much utilized in the present chapter, which was written before the publication of François Angelier's *Claudel, ou La Conversion sauvage* (Salvator, 1998); despite the considerable interest of this study, I have decided not to make any changes or additions to my original text.

2. In some cases the dates given here are only approximate and indicate the first known communions after the "conversion experience."

3. All quotations from François Varillon, *Claudel* (Desclée de Brouwer, 1967), 122–26.

4. For Claudel's reservations about "Ma conversion" and the prominence that has been given to it, see Gérald Antoine, *Paul Claudel, ou L'Enfer du génie* (Robert Laffont, 1988), 64.

5. See Guillemin, *Le "Converti,"* 142.

6. Paul Claudel, *Interroge l'Apocalypse* (1940–43), quoted in Varillon, *Claudel,* 33.

7. Claudel, *Mémoires improvisés* (Gallimard, 1969), 62–63.

8 Antoine, *Paul Claudel,* 68.

9 All quotations, unless otherwise stated, from Varillon, *Claudel,* 128–34.

10. All quotations from "Magnificat" are from Paul Claudel, *Cinq Grandes Odes* (Poésie/Gallimard, 1975), 53–72.

11. Quoted in Guillemin, *Le "Converti,"* 138.

12. See Claudel, *Mémoires improvisés,* 68.

13. All quotations from Paul Claudel, *Poésies* (Poésie/Gallimard, 1993), 172–75.

14. Claudel had stressed the role of music in his conversion in a letter-article titled "Le Chant religieux," written in 1938 and published in 1940. See Varillon, *Claudel,* 134–35.

15. For the "Parabole d'Animus et d'Anima," see *Positions et propositions* I, in Paul Claudel, *Œuvres complètes.* See also Paul Claudel, *Art poétique* (Poésie/Gallimard, 1984), 66 and 84, for a discussion of *connaissance* and *co-naissance.*

16. See Claudel, *Œuvres complètes,* 1:14–16.

17. "Le Chant religieux," quoted in Varillon, *Claudel,* 134.

18. Albert Thibaudet, quoted in Paul-André Lesort, *Claudel* (Seuil, 1963), 21.

19. Claudel, *Cinq Grandes Odes,* 70.

20. "Time that with this strange excuse / Pardoned Kipling and his views / And will pardon Paul Claudel / Pardons him for writing well": W. H. Auden, *Selected Poems,* ed. Edward Mendelson (Faber & Faber, 1979), 82.

9. CHURCH PROWLING

1. Igny provides the setting for the first two parts (*L'Otage* and *Le Pain dur*) of Claudel's historical trilogy, but the monastery does not seem otherwise to have played any part in his life.

2. Quoted in Robert Baldick, *The Life of J.-K. Huysmans* (Oxford: Oxford University Press, 1955), 91.

3. Letter (undated) to Baron Firmin Van den Bosch, quoted ibid., 180.

4. Joris-Karl Huysmans, *Là-bas* (Folio, 1995), 74.

5. On Poictevin, see Baldick, *Life of Huysmans*, 238–39.

6. For a full discussion of the models for the various characters in *Là-bas*, see Baldick, *Life of Huysmans*, 136–53.

7. Huysmans, *Là-bas*, 267–68.

8. In *Là-bas*, 299, Durtal merely notices "fragments of a host" in the bed, but the confession he makes in *En route* (Folio, 1996), 343, goes considerably further: "Stammering, he related how, out of curiosity, he had attended a Black Mass and how afterward, without willing to do so, he had profaned [*souillé*] a host that that woman [Mme Chantelouve], saturated with satanism, had hidden inside her."

9. Huysmans, *Là-bas*, 319.

10. Ibid., 284.

11. Ibid., 199.

12. The account given here is based on a conflation of the following sources: Baldick, *Life of Huysmans*, 154–71; Marcel Thomas, "L'Abbé Boullan et l'Œuvre de la Réparation," in *La Tour Saint-Jacques*, no. 10, May–June 1957, 72–90; and Maurice Belval, *Des ténèbres à la lumière: Etapes de la pensée mystique de J.-K. Huysmans* (Maisonneuve & Larose, 1968), 73–124.

13. See Baldick, *Life of Huysmans*, 155; and Thomas, "L'Abbé Boullan," 86–87.

14. See Maurice Garçon, *Vintras hérésiarque et prophète* (Emile Nourry, 1928), 110. All other details are taken from this study.

15. Huysmans, *Là-bas*, 308.

16. Belval, *Des ténèbres*, 91.

17. See Pierre Lambert, "Un culte hérétique à Paris, 11, rue de Sèvres," *La Tour Saint-Jacques*, no. 10, May–June 1957, 100–113.

18. Quoted in the preface to Joris-Karl Huysmans, *Là-haut*, ed. Artine Artinian and Pierre Cogny (Casterman, 1965), 33.

19. See the photographs in Lambert, "Un culte hérétique," between 104 and 105.

20. See Baldick, *Life of Huysmans*, 137–41.

21. Ibid., 210–11.

22. Huysmans, *Là-bas*, 33–38.

23. Huysmans, *A rebours*, 74–75.

24. Huysmans, *Là-haut*, 146. *Là-haut* is the first version, uncompleted and unpublished, of what would become *En route* (1895), the novel of Huysmans's conversion.

25. See "Le Journal d'*En route*," compiled by Pierre Lambert from Huysmans's letters and notebooks, and published in *Là-haut*. The present quotation is on 222.

26. Huysmans, *En route* (Folio, 1996), 97.

27. Huysmans, "Le Journal d'*En route*," 224.

28. Huysmans, *En route*, 126.

29. Ibid., 129–30.

30. See Huysmans's letter to Boucher of 2 Jan. 1891, reproduced in "Le Journal d'*En route*," 225.

31. Huysmans, *En route*, 176.

32. Letter to Arij Prins, 26 Apr. 1891, quoted in *Là-haut*, 15.

33. The incident is recounted by the abbé Mugnier in *Joris-Karl Huysmans à la Trappe* (1927), quoted in "Le Journal d'*En route*," 237.

34. Letter to Lucien Descaves, 30 Aug. 1891, in "Le Journal d'*En route*," 246–47.

35. Huysmans, *En route*, 137.

36. Huysmans, *Là-haut*, 103.

37. Baldick, *Life of Huysmans*, 194.

38. Huysmans, *En route*, 308.

39. Ibid.

40. Ibid., 340–45.

41. Ibid., 372–73.

42. Ibid., 406.

43. Ibid., 422.

44. Ibid., 428–29.

45. Ibid., 439, 442.

46. Ibid., 432.

47. Ibid., 524.

48. Quoted in Huysmans, *Là-haut*, 42.

49. Huysmans, *En route*, 407.

50. Preface (1947) to *En route*, quoted in Pie Duployé, *Huysmans* (Desclée de Brouwer, 1968), 41.

10. MARBLE VERSUS IRON

1. Asked by *L'Express* in 1985 which Paris monument he would most like to be demolished, the future socialist prime minister Lionel Jospin replied without hesitation, "The Basilica of Sacré-Cœur! It's in my consituency, but all the same it's ugly and the circumstances of its construction symbolize the crushing of the left" (quoted in Jacques Benoist, *Le Sacré Cœur de Montmartre de 1870 à nos jours* [Editions Ouvrières, 1992], 2:855). The present section relies heavily on Benoist's massive work, and also draws on chap. 7, "Monument and Myth: The Building of the Basilica of the Sacred Heart," of David Harvey, *The Urban Experience* (Baltimore: John Hopkins University Press, 1989), 2–28, and François Loyer, "Le Sacré-Cœur de Montmartre," in *Les Lieux de la mémoire*, ed. Pierre Nora (Gallimard, 1984), 3:451–73.

2. Quoted in Benoist, *Sacré-Cœur*, 1:209–10.

3. For the original text of Legentil's vow, see ibid., 232–33. The full published version (236) notably tones down the language of the original and eliminates the attribution of France's (and Rome's) woes to "the true leader of the Protestant heresy in the world," King Wilhelm of Prussia, shortly to become emperor of all Germany.

4. Quoted in Paul Johnson, *A History of Christianity* (Penguin, 1980), 394.

5. Pierre Pierrard, *L'Eglise et la Révolution, 1789–1889* (Nouvelle Cité, 1988), 203.

6. Quoted in Philippe Joutard, ed., *Histoire de la France religieuse* (Seuil, 1991), 111, 429.

7. Quoted in Johnson, *History of Christianity*, 390–91.

8. On Morel and Keller, see Pierrard, *L'Eglise et la Révolution*, 193–205.

9. Edmond and Jules de Goncourt, *Madame Gervaisais*, ed. Marc Fumaroli (Folio, 1982), 183–85.

10. Details from Joutard, *Histoire religieuse de la France*, 3:440–43, and Pierre Pierrard, "La Renaissance des pèlerinages au XIXᵉ siècle," in *Les Chemins de Dieu: Histoire des pèlerinages chrétiens des origines à nos jours*, ed. Jean Chélini and Henry Branthomme (Hachette, 1982), 313–14. The quotation from *La Croix* is taken from Michel Winock, *La Fièvre hexagonale: Les Grands Crises politiques, 1871–1968* (Seuil, 1987), 153.

11. Claude Langlois, in Joutard, *Histoire de la France religieuse,* 3:435. Other details in this paragraph are taken from this source.

12. Quoted in Claude Langlois, "Permanence, renouveau et affrontements (1830–1880)" in *Histoire des Catholiques en France du XVe siècle à nos jours,* ed. François Lebrun (Privat, 1980), 400.

13. Andé Gide, *Les Nouvelles Nourritures,* in *Les Nourritures terrestres* (Livre de poche, 1966), 200.

14. See Johnson, *History of Christianity,* 394.

15. Quoted in Lebrun, *Histoire des Catholiques en France,* 394.

16. See Benoist, *Sacré Cœur,* 1:228.

17. Ibid., 252–53.

18. Ibid., 2:835.

19. Père Auguste Hamall in 1907, quoted ibid., 851.

20. Quoted ibid., 884.

21. Loyer, "Sacré-Cœur de Montmartre," 1:454.

22. Reproduced in Francis Jourdain, *Alexandre Steinlen* (Cercle d'Art, 1954), 87.

23. Reproduced in Harvey, *Urban Experience,* 223.

24. Quoted in Benoist, *Sacré Cœur,* 2:802.

25. Ibid., 1:637.

26. See Pierre Bergé, *L'Affaire Clovis* (Plon, 1996), 99–100.

27. Quoted in Benoist, *Sacré Cœur,* 2:789.

28. Ibid., 772.

29. Ibid., 785–86, 807–8.

30. Max Jacob, *Saint Matorel* (Gallimard, 1936), 223–24. It should be stressed that when he wrote the poem in question, Jacob had not been baptized, but had undergone his conversion experience (on 22 Sept. 1909). On Jacob, see René Plantier, *Max Jacob* (Desclée de Brouwer, 1972).

31. Quoted in Pierre Sorlin, *"La Croix" et les Juifs (1880–1899): Contribution à l'histoire de l'antisémitisme contemporain* (Grasset, 1967), 191–92. This quotation comes from an article in *La Croix* (1883) by Père Picard but reflects the thinking of the Assumptionists' founder.

32. See Pierrard, *L'Eglise et la Révolution,* 207–8.

33. See Stephen Wilson, *Ideology and Experience: Antisemitism in France at the Time of the Dreyfus Affair* (East Brunswick, N.J.: Associated University Presses, 1982), 521. Most of the details that follow are taken from chap. 14, "Religious Antisemitism among French Catholics," 509–83 of this superbly documented study.

34. Quoted ibid., 511.

35. On Bernanos's antisemitism, see Michel Winock, "Le Cas Bernanos," in his *Nationalisme, antisémitisme et antifascisme en France* (Seuil, 1982), 397–415.

36. See Sorlin, *"La Croix,"* 138.

37. Léon Bloy, *Le Salut par les Juifs,* in his *Œuvres,* ed. Jacques Petit (Mercure de France, 1969), 9:51.

38. On this question, see Hyam Maccoby, "The Wandering Jew as Sacred Executioner," in *The Wandering Jew: Essays in the Interpretation of a Christian Legend,* ed. Galit Hasan-Rokem and Alan Dundes (Bloomington: Indiana University Press, 1986), 238–39.

39. Bailly, quoted in Sorlin, *"La Croix,"* 137.

40. Bloy, *Le Salut par les Juifs,* 28–29.

41. Champfleury, *Histoire de l'imagerie populaire* (1869), quoted in Hasan-Rokem and Dundes, *Wandering Jew,* 69.

42. Hyam Maccoby, "Wandering Jew," 246.

43. Winock, *Nationalisme,* 408.

44. Quoted in Sorlin, *"La Croix,"* 100–101.

45. Quoted in Geoffrey Cubitt, *The Jesuit Myth, Conspiracy Theory, and Politics in Nineteenth-Century France* (Oxford: Clarendon, 1993), 211. All subsequent quotations and details are taken from this well-documented source.

46. Ibid., 171.

47. Ibid., 156.

48. Ibid., 220–21.

49. See René Rémond, *L'Anticléricalisme en France de 1815 à nos jours* (Brussels: Complexe, 1992), 156–57.

50. Ibid., 208–9. On Taxil's remarkable career, see Eugen Weber, *Satan Franc-Maçon: La Mystification de Léo Taxil* (Julliard, 1964).

51. *La Raison,* 25 September 1913, quoted ibid., 218.

52. Reproduced in Jourdain, *Alexandre Steinlen,* 88–89.

53. See Benoist, *Sacré Cœur,* 1:187–200.

54. Quoted ibid., 713.

55. The following account is based on Pierrard, *L'Eglise et la Révolution,* 235–46, from which all quotations are taken.

56. The present section is based principally on Henri Loyrette, "La Tour Eiffel," in Nora, *Les Lieux de la mémoire,* vol. 3, *Les France* (Gallimard, 1992), 475–503.

57. Quoted in Pascal Ory, *L'Expo Universelle* (Complexe, 1989), 40.

58. Quoted in Loyrette, "La Tour Eiffel," 482.

59. On Boulanger and Boulangism, see Jean-Marie Mayeur, *Les Débuts de la III République, 1871–1898* (Seuil, 1973), 165–80.

60. Quoted in Ory, *L'Expo Universelle,* 70.

61. Ibid., 65.

62. See Lebrun, *Histoire des Catholiques en France,* 412.

63. Joris-Karl Huysmans, "Le Fer" (1889), in *L'Art Moderne/Certains* (Union Générale d'Editions, 1975), 401–10.

64. All quotations from Léon Bloy, "Le Babel de fer" (1889), in his *Œuvres,* ed. Joseph Bolley and Jacques Petit (Mercure de France, 1964), 197–201.

65. For a brilliant discussion of the "naturalization" of the Eiffel Tower and of the way it in turn "naturalizes" Paris, see Roland Barthes, *La Tour Eiffel* (Delpire, 1964), esp. 38.

66. Guillaume Apollinaire, *Alcools* (Gallimard, 1966), 7.

67. Emile Zola, *Paris* (Lausanne: Rencontre, n.d.), 542.

68. Ibid., 135.

69. Ibid., 570.

70. Emile Zola, *Travail,* in his *Œuvres completes,* ed. Henri Mitterrand (Cercle du Livre Précieux, 1968), 7:906–8.

71. These and the following details are taken from Jean Rabaut, *Jaurès assassiné* (Brussels: Complexe, 1984), 5–10 (for the assassination) and 106–9 (for Villain).

72. Quoted ibid., 9.

73. Ibid., 157.

74. Ibid., 45–46.

75. Quoted in Madeleine Rebérioux, *Jaurès, la parole et l'acte* (Gallimard, 1994), 93.

76. All details and quotations from Rabaut, *Jaurès assassiné,* 37–41. On Péguy and Jaurès, see Richard Griffiths, *The Use of Abuse: The Polemics of the Dreyfus Affair and Its Aftermath* (Oxford: Berg, 1991), 154–70.

77. Rabaut, *Jaurès assassiné,* 82.

78. See Jean-Marie Mayeur, *La Vie politique sous la Troisième République, 1870–1940* (Seuil, 1984), 242–45.

79. All quotations in Rabaut, *Jaurès assassiné,* 155–56.

80. See Maurice Agulhon et al., *Jaurès et ses images* (Société de Bibliologie et de Schématisation, 1985), 66 (illustrations 49 and 50).

81. Ibid., 53 (illustration 38).

82. Paul Nizan, *La Conspiration* (Gallimard, 1938), 49. A Communist disgusted by the signing of the Nazi-Soviet pact, Nizan was later killed near Dunkirk in May 1940 in circumstances that have suggested to some that he exposed himself, Baudin-style, to enemy fire.

83. Geoffrey Hill, *Collected Poems* (Penguin, 1985), 183.

84. Péguy, *Œuvres poétiques complètes* (Gallimard, 1975), 1028.

85. Roger Martin Du Gard, *Les Thibault* (Livre de Poche, 1964), 4:276.

86. Ibid., 305–6.

11. OPERATION SPRING BREEZE

1. Quoted in Robert Badinter, *Libres et égaux: L'Emancipation des Juifs, 1789–1791* (Livre de poche, 1990), 137.

2. Annette Muller, *La Petite Fille du Vel' d'Hiv'* (Denoël, 1991), 33.

3. Ibid., 57.

4. All details and figures that follow are taken from Esther Benbassa, *Histoire des Juifs de France* (Seuil, 1997), 155–70.

5. See the important and controversial studies by Zeev Sternhell, *La Droite révolutionnaire, 1880–1914: Les origines françaises du fascisme* (Seuil, 1978) and *Ni droite ni gauche: L'Idéologie fasciste en France* (Seuil, 1983).

6. See Pierre Birnbaum, *Les Fous de la République: Histoire politique des Juifs d'Etat, de Gambetta à Vichy* (Fayard, 1992).

7. Quoted in Benbassa, *Histoire des Juifs*, 204.

8. See Paula Hyman, *From Dreyfus to Vichy: The Remaking of French Jewry, 1906–1939* (New York: Columbia University Press, 1979), 40.

9. See Annette Becker, *La Guerre et la foi: De la mort à la mémoire, 1914–1930* (Armand Colin, 1994), 45. A memorable painting of Rabbi Bloch and the soldier by Lucien Lévy-Dhurmer (1917) is reproduced opposite p. 34.

10. David H. Weinberg, *Les Juifs à Paris de 1933 à 1939,* trans. Micheline Pouteau (Calmann-Lévy, 1974), 8.

11. Quoted in Michael R. Marrus and Robert O. Paxton, *Vichy et les Juifs,* trans. Marguerite Delmotte (Livre de poche, 1990), 61.

12. Hyman, *From Dreyfus to Vichy,* 83.

13. Quoted ibid., 120.

14. Muller, *La Petite Fille,* 13.

15. See Ralph Schor, *L'Antisémitisme en France pendant les années trente* (Brussels: Complexe, 1992), 31–32. On Darquier, see André Kaspi, *Les Juifs pendant l'Occupation* (Seuil, 1997), 59.

16. Quoted in Schor, *L'Antisémitisme,* 173.

17. Ibid., 170.

18. Ibid., 158.

19. Georges Perec, *W, ou Le Souvenir d'enfance* (1975) (Gallimard, 1997), 17. Both of Perec's Polish-born Jewish parents were killed during the war, his father in the fighting of 1940, his mother in Auschwitz after one of the Parisian roundups of 1942–43.

20. These figures, and those that follow, are based on Kaspi, *Les Juifs pendant l'Occupation,* 20–21, 88–90.

21. Muller, *La Petite Fille,* 51.

22. For a convenient summary, see Benbassa, *Histoire des Juifs,* 253–58.

23. On this whole subject, see the authoritative analysis in Marrus and Paxton, *Vichy et les Juifs,* 17–43.

24. Muller, *La Petite Fille,* 63.

25. All details from Marrus and Paxton, *Vichy et les Juifs,* 317–19.

26. See Kaspi, *Les Juifs pendant l'Occupation,* 104–10.

27. On this whole question, see Pierre Laborie, *L'Opinion française sous Vichy* (Seuil, 1990), 270–81.

28. Muller, *La Petite Fille,* 69–72.

29. See Kaspi, *Les Juifs sous l'Occupation,* 110–11, and Marrus and Paxton, *Vichy et les Juifs,* 336.

30. See Kaspi, *Les Juifs sous l'Occupation,* 221.

31. On the memorandum affair, see Eric Conan and Henry Rousso, *Vichy, un passé qui ne passe pas* (Folio, 1996), 91–121. The term "Vichy syndrome" comes from Rousso's earlier study, *Le Syndrome de Vichy, 1944–198 ...* (Seuil, 1987).

32. All details in the present account are taken from the pioneering study, first published in 1967, by Claude Lévy and Paul Tillard, *La Grande Rafle du Vel d'Hiv' (16 juillet 1942)* (Robert Laffont, 1992).

33. See ibid., 54.

34. Ibid., 49–50.

35. See Kaspi, *Les Juifs sous l'Occupation,* 232–34.

36. See Marrus and Paxton, *Vichy et les Juifs,* 351.

37. Muller, *La Petite Fille,* 93–94.

38. Lévy and Tillard, *La Grande Rafle,* 66.

39. Ibid., 149.

40. Ibid., 163. All other details taken from Kaspi, *Les Juifs sous l'Occupation,* 264–68.

41. Kaspi, *Les Juifs sous l'Occupation,* 274.

42. For a full discussion of this question, see Marrus and Paxton, *Vichy et les Juifs,* 477–91.

43. On this subject, see the categorical assertion in Conan and Rousso, *Vichy,* 55.

44. See Lévy and Tillard, *La Grande Rafle,* 170.

45. For the term *résistentialisme,* see Rousso, *Le Syndrome de Vichy,* 100–104.

46. Ibid., 240.

47. The following account is based on the chapter titled "La Commémoration introuvable," in Conan and Rousso, *Vichy,* 47–96.

48. Robert Frank, quoted in Rousso, *Le Syndrome de Vichy,* 240.

49. See the complete petition in Conan and Rousso, *Vichy,* 51–52.

50. Ibid., 65.

51. Ibid., 91.

52. On Bousquet, see Richard J. Golsan, ed., *Memory, the Holocaust, and French Justice: The Bousquet and Touvier Affairs* (Hanover, N.H.: University Press of New England, 1996), on which the following account is based.

53. Ibid., xxxii.

54. On the whole question of the "effectiveness" of Vichy's policy, see the conclusion to Marrus and Paxton, *Vichy et les Juifs,* 491–515.

55. All figures from Kaspi, *Les Juifs sous l'Occupation,* 283.

56. All quotations from Muller, *La Petite Fille,* 111–16.

12. PURGING THE CITY

1. The following account is based principally on Henri Michel, *La Libération de Paris* (Brussels: Complexe, 1980), supported by the excellent summary in Jean-Pierre Azéma, *De Munich à la Libération, 1938–1944* (Seuil, 1979), 342–52. I have also used the lively account in pt. I of Antony Beevor and Artemis Cooper, *Paris after the Liberation, 1944–1949* (Hamish Hamilton, 1994).

2. For a full discussion of the police's role in the insurrection, see Simon Kitson, "The Police in the Liberation of Paris," in *The Liberation of France: Image and Event,* ed. H. R. Kedward and Nancy Woods (Oxford: Berg, 1995), 43–56.

3. Quoted in Michel, *La Libération de Paris*, 28-29.

4. See Pierre Assouline, *L'Epuration des intellectuels* (Brussels: Complexe, 1996), 20.

5. On Sigmaringen, see the lively account in Henry Rousso, *Pétain et la fin de la collaboration: Sigmaringen, 1944-1945* (Brussels: Complexe, 1984).

6. Michel, *La Libération de Paris*, 32.

7. See Alain Brossat, *Libération, fête folle, 6 juin 44-8 mai 45: Mythes et rites, ou Le Grand Théâtre des passions populaires*, Série Mémoires no. 30 (Autrement, 1994), 88. The whole of the present chapter is indebted to this remarkable essay, to which specific references are made at the appropriate points.

8. Jean Dutourd, *Au bon beurre* (Folio, 1972), 338.

9. Neither the "Marseillaise" nor the Tricolor had actually been banned under Vichy, but the former had been sidelined by "Maréchal, nous voilà" throughout the period.

10. Marguerite Duras, "Ter le milicien," in *La Douleur* (Folio, 1995), 188-89. "D." is Dionys Mascolo, Duras's lover and future second husband.

11. Dutourd, *Au bon beurre*, 345.

12. Jean-Paul Sartre. "Un Promeneur dans Paris insurgé," quoted in Brossat, *Libération*, 118, to which the whole of this paragraph is indebted.

13. C. de Saint-Pierre, *Des ténèbres à l'aube: Journal d'une Française* (1945), quoted in Brossat, *Libération*, 107.

14. Jean Dutourd, *Le Demi-Solde* (Gallimard, 1965), 31.

15. All details and quotations from Michel, *La Libération de Paris*, 86-92.

16. Simone de Beauvoir, *La Force de l'âge* (Gallimard,1960), 612.

17. Michel Leiris, *Fourbis* (Gallimard, 1955), 151.

18. All quotations from Dutourd, *Le Demi-Solde*, 43-45.

19. The literature on carnival is immense. For a valuable summary and critique, see Peter Stallybrass and Allan White, *The Politics and Poetics of Transgression* (Ithaca: Cornell University Press, 1986), 1-26.

20. Brossat, *Libération*, 37-38.

21. On Pétainism and castration, see the introduction by Roland Barthes to Gérard Miller, *Les Pousse-au-jouir du Maréchal Pétain* (Livre de Poche, 1988), 9-13.

22. On Thorez as a quasi-double of Pétain, see Fred Kupferman, *Le Procès de Vichy: Pucheu, Pétain, Laval* (Brussels: Complexe, 1980), 63-66.

23. Dutourd, *Le Demi-Solde*, 14.

24. Alexandre Parodi, quoted in Michel, *La Libération de Paris*, 110.

25. See the three loci classici of the Second Republic and its fall, Alexis de Tocqueville's *Souvenirs* (1850), Karl Marx's *Eighteenth Brumaire of Louis Napoleon* (1852), and Gustave Flaubert's *L'Education sentimentale* (1869).

26. Duras, *La Douleur*, 45-46.

27. Michel, *La Libération de Paris*, 99. These are the figures given by the FFI themselves after the Liberation; "civilians" presumably refers to casualties in neither the FFI nor the police.

28. See the exemplary summary in Jean-Pierre Rioux, *La France de la Quatrième République: L'Ardeur et la nécessité (1944-1952)* (Seuil, 1980), 1:49-67. The best study of the purge in all its forms is still Peter Novick, *The Resistance versus Vichy: The Purge of Collaborators in Liberated France* (Chatto & Windus, 1968), which is greatly to be preferred to Robert Aron's multivolume *Histoire de l'épuration* (Fayard, 1967-74), whose figure of 40,000 deaths is a huge exaggeration. I have also used Herbert R. Lottman, *The Purge: The Purification of French Collaborators after World War II* (New York: William Morrow, 1986).

29. See the photograph in Brossat, *La Libération*, 129.

30. Dutourd, *Le Demi-Solde*, 39.

31. Full revelations are promised by Philippe Bourdrel in the second volume of his *L'Epuration sauvage, 1944-1945;* see vol. 1 (Librairie Académique Perrin, 1988), 83.

32. See Lottman, *Purge,* 76.

33. Brossat, *Les Tondues,* 212–13.

34. See Beevor and Cooper, *Paris after the Liberation,* 90.

35. See Lottman, *Purge,* 66, where the remark is attributed to the boulevardier Jean Galtier-Boissière.

36. In September 1944, an IFOP poll reported that 58% of those canvassed did not want Pétain to be punished in any way and that of the 32% who did want retribution, only 3% thought he should be punished by death. See ibid., 92.

37. Ibid., 79.

38. Assouline, *L'Epuration,* 35.

39. On Salengro's suicide, see Louis Bodin and Jean Touchard, *Front populaire: 1936* (Armand Colin, 1972), 195–201.

40. Simone de Beauvoir, "Œil pour œil," *Les Temps modernes,* February 1946, quoted in Lottman, *Purge,* 139.

41. On Maurras's trial, see Assouline, *L'Epuration,* 56–60.

42. The following account is based on Frédéric J. Grover, *Drieu La Rochelle (1893–1945): Vie, œuvres, témoignages* (Gallimard, 1979), 49–59, from which all quotations are taken. I have also used Alistair Hamilton's introduction to his translation of Drieu's *Secret Journal and Other Writings* (River Press, 1973).

43. See Assouline, *L'Epuration,* 115.

44. Drieu La Rochelle, *Secret Journal,* 72–73.

45. Even here Drieu was to be foiled. Malraux, alias Colonel Berger, was commanding his Brigade Alsace-Lorraine in Germany, and his funeral at Neuilly was anything but "man-free," the mourners including Jean Paulhan, Paul Léautaud, the poet Jacques Audiberti, the philosopher Brice Parain, and the Gallimards, father and son.

46. Jean-Paul Sartre, *Qu'est-ce que la littérature?* (Gallimard, 1967), 81.

47. Kupferman, *Le Procès de Vichy,* 18.

48. Jean Luchaire, quoted in Rousso, *Pétain et la fin de la collaboration,* 401. See ibid., 283–87, for the circumstances of Doriot's death and the competing interpretations given of it.

49. All details from Kupferman, *Le Procès de Vichy,* 70–74.

50. Ibid., 111.

51. For an unforgettably harrowing account of the return of the deported, see Marguerite Duras, *La Douleur,* 12–85. Duras's first husband, Robert Antelme, was one of the deported who returned.

52. See Rioux, *La France de la Quatrième République,* 1:64–65, and Lottman, *Purge,* 92.

53. See Kupferman, *Le Procès de Vichy,* 30–41.

54. Pierre Taittinger, quoted in Miller, *Les Pousse-au-jouir,* 54.

55. Quoted in Yves Durand, *La France dans la deuxième guerre mondiale, 1939–1945* (Armand Colin, 1989), 23.

56. Miller, *Les Pousse-au-jouir,* 53–56.

57. The following account is based on Kupferman, *Le Procès de Vichy,* 84–127, supported by Jules Roy's eyewitness account in *Le Grand Naufrage* (Julliard, 1966). References are kept to a minimum.

58. Roy, *Le Grand Naufrage,* 27. See also 103–4 for an extended development of the theme.

59. Ibid., 103.

60. Florimond Bonte in *L'Humanité,* 3 Aug. 1945, quoted in Kupferman, *Le Procès de Vichy,* 111.

61. Quoted ibid., 93–94.

62. See ibid., 107 and 112.

63. Quoted ibid., 79.

64. Roy, *Le Grand Naufrage,* 297–300.

65. Ibid., 316.

66. See Jean Plumyène, *Pétain* (Seuil, 1964), 179–81.

67. The attempt was led by one Hubert Massol and was almost successful, the marshal's remains being recovered on the outskirts of Paris. See Conan and Rousso, *Vichy*, 58.

68. Quoted in Roy, *Le Grand Naufrage*, 145.

69. Ibid., 149.

70. Quoted in Kupferman, *Le Procès de Vichy*, 111. The account of Laval's trial and execution that follows is based essentially on pp. 128–54 of this work.

71. Claude Roy in *Les Lettres françaises*, 13 Oct. 1945, quoted in Kupferman, *Le Procès de Vichy*, 139–40.

72. All details and quotations in Kupferman, *Le Procès de Vichy*, 144–54.

73. See Assouline, *L'Epuration*, 134.

74. Quoted in Kupferman, *Le Procès de Vichy*, 137.

75. See ibid., 18.

76. Quoted in Assouline, *L'Epuration*, 92.

77. Ibid., 64.

78. Ibid., 28.

79. Ibid., 117.

80. Ibid., 46.

81. Roger Secrétain in *Esprit*, 1 June 1945, quoted ibid., 67.

82. Assouline, *L'Epuration*, 71.

83. Ibid., 148.

84. The figures that follow are from Rioux, *La France de la Quatrième République*, 1:56.

85. For this last point, see Henry Rousso, "Did the Purge Achieve Its Goals?' in *Memory, the Holocaust, and French Justice: The Bousquet and Touvier Affairs*, ed. Richard J. Golsan (Hanover, N.H.: University Press of New England, 1996), 102.

86. Lottman, *Purge*, 148.

87. See Assouline, *L'Epuration*, 122–23.

88. For a full discussion of this case, see Conan and Rousso, "Touvier: Le Dernier Procès de l'épuration?" in *Vichy*, 157–255. Touvier is widely believed to have taken part in the killing of Victor Basch (79), president of the prewar Ligue des Droits Humains, and his wife, Hélène (80), in January 1944, and to have been directly responsible for the execution of seven Jewish hostages in the cemetery of Rillieux-la-Pape on the outskirts of Lyon on 29 June 1944.

89. Jean Paulhan, *De la paille et du grain* (Gallimard, 1948), 98.

90. Rioux, *La France de la Quatrième République*, 1:64.

91. See Novick, *The Resistance versus Vichy*, 188.

92. See Kupferman, *Le Procès de Vichy*, 67.

93. On *naphtalinés*, see Beevor and Cooper, *Paris after the Liberation*, 108.

94. Dutourd, *Le Demi-Solde*, 97–103.

95. This authenticated incident is recounted in Marcel Ophüls's film *Le Chagrin et la pitié*. See the English translation of the script, *The Sorrow and the Pity*, trans. Mireille Johnston (Paladin, 1975), 166.

96. Plumyène, *Pétain*, 176.

97. Quoted in Kupferman, *Le Procès de Vichy*, 126.

13. CONCLUSION

1. Gérard Cholvy, *Etre chrétien en France au XIXᵉ siècle, 1790–1914* (Seuil, 1997), 15.

2. Quoted ibid., 31.

3. Ernest Renan, *Souvenirs d'enfance et de jeunesse* (Folio, 1983), 4.

4. Cholvy, *Etre chrétien*, 31.

5. Renan, *Souvenirs*, 7.

6. Quoted in Cholvy, *Etre chrétien*, 93.

7. Renan, *Souvenirs*, 7.

8. Georges Bernanos, *La Grande Peur des bien-pensants* (Livre de poche, 1969), 385–86, 409.

9. Quoted in Cholvy, *Etre chrétien*, 161.

10. Renan, *Souvenirs*, 204.

11. For a devastating attack on what he calls the *occulto-socialisme* (*oc-soc* for short) of the 1840s, see Philippe Muray, *Le 19ᵉ siècle à travers les âges* (Denoël, 1984), esp. 135–42.

12. Arthur Rimbaud, "Mauvais Sang," in his *Oeuvres*, ed. Suzanne Bernard (Garnier, 1960), 215.

13. See Judith Van Herik, "Simone Weil's Religious Imagery: How Looking Becomes Eating," in *Immaculate and Powerful: The Female in Sacred Image and Social Reality*, ed. Clarissa W. Atkinson et al. (Crucible, 1987), 260–82.

14. Bernanos, *La Grande Peur*, 406.

15. Paul Valéry, "La Crise de l'Esprit," *Variétés I* (Gallimard, 1924), 12–13.

16. André Malraux, *La Tentation de l'Occident* (Livre de Poche, 1972), 128.

17. Ernest Renan, *Oeuvres complètes*, ed. Henriette Psichari (Calmann-Lévy, 1948) 3:757, 765.

18. André Malraux, "D'une jeunesse européenne," in Malraux et al., *Ecrits* (Grasset, 1927), 145.

19. Valéry, "La Crise de l'Esprit," 19.

20. For a summary of the main elements of Haussmannization, see Richard D. E. Burton, *The Context of Baudelaire's "Le Cygne"* (Durham, U.K.: University of Durham, 1980), 35–50.

21. See Victor Fournel's remarkable *Paris nouveau et Paris futur* (Lecoffre, 1868), copiously drawn upon in the above.

22. Victor Hugo, "Les Années funestes," in his *Oeuvres complètes* (Lausanne: Rencontre, 1968), 23:286–87.

23. These and the following details are taken from Daniel Milo, "Le Nom des rues," in *Les Lieux de la memoire*, ed. Pierre Nora, vol. 2, pt. 3 (Gallimard, 1986), 283–315.

24. All details from June Hargrove, "Les Statues de Paris," ibid., 243–82.

25. A number of major republican statues were removed and melted down during the Occupation: those of Gambetta (Place de Carrousel), Hugo (Place Victor Hugo), Marat (Buttes Chaumont), Béranger (Square du Temple), and the Chevalier de La Barre, among others. The official reason was to obtain raw material for the German armaments industry, but ideological considerations were presumably present in deciding which statues should be taken.

26. The expression *ganz andere* comes from Rudolf Otto's classic work *The Idea of the Holy*, trans. John W. Harvey (Oxford: Oxford University Press, 1950), 25–30.

27. On the Place Dauphine, see the brilliant article "Pont-Neuf" (1950), in André Breton, *La Clé des champs* (Union Générale d'Editions, 1973), 355–65. On the whole question of the Surrealists' experience and image of Paris, see Marie-Claire Bancquart, *Paris des surréalistes* (Segher, 1972).

28. Michel Leiris, *Biffures* (Gallimard, 1948), 239.

29. On these terms, derived ultimately from the work of Robert Hertz, see Roger Caillois, *L'Homme et le sacré* (Gallimard, 1970), 48–56.

30. See Michel Leiris, *Miroir de la tauromachie* (Guy Lévis-Mano, 1964), 38–39, 57. See also his important article "Le Sacré dans la vie quotidienne," *Nouvelle Revue française* 298 (1938): 26–38.

31. See, inter alia, the section "La 'Communication,'" in Georges Bataille, *L'Expérience intérieure* (Gallimard, 1983), 110–15.

32. See Robert Desnos, *La Liberté ou l'amour!* (Kra, 1927).

33. Paul Claudel, *La Ville* (Folio, 1982), 25.

34. Karl Popper, *Conjectures and Refutations: The Growth of Scientific Knowledge* (Routledge, 1995), 123.

35. See the authoritative study by Steven L. Kaplan, *Le Complot de famine: Histoire d'une rumeur au 18ᵉ siècle,* trans. Michèle and Jacques Revel, Cahier des Annales 39 (Armand Colin, 1982).

36. On this subject, see Charles Tilly, *The Contentious French* (Cambridge: Harvard University Press, 1986).

37. See Marcel Gauchet, "Le Démon du soupçon," *Histoire* 84 (1985): 52.

38. On the events of May 1750, see Arlette Farge and Jacques Revel, *Logiques de la foule: L'affaire des enlèvements d'enfants, Paris, 1750* (Hachette, 1988), esp. 19–22, 111–16.

39. See the classic study by Edgar Morin, *La Rumeur d'Orléans* (Seuil, 1969).

40. See Véronique Campion-Vincent, "Complots et avertissements: Légendes urbaines dans la ville," *Revue française sociologique* 30 (1989): 103. See also the excellent general study by Jean-Noël Kapferer, *Rumeurs: Le Plus Vieux Média du monde* (Seuil, 1990), 132–45.

41. See Joris-Karl Huysmans, *Là-bas* (Folio, 1995); Georges Bataille, *Le Procès de Gilles de Rais* (Pauvert, 1965); and Michel Tournier, *Gilles & Jeanne* (Gallimard, 1983). The hero of Tournier's *Le Roi des aulnes* (1970) takes his name from Tiffauges, Gilles de Rais's castle in the Vendée, which Huysmans visited while researching *Là-bas.*

42. See Serge Klarsfeld, *Les Enfants d'Izieu: Une tragédie juive* (AZ Repro-Pari, 1984).

43. François Furet, *Penser la Révolution française* (Folio, 1988), 96.

44. Ibid., 107.

45. For a convenient account of the *bagarre de Nîmes* of June 1790 and the not dissimilar massacre of La Glacière (Avignon) of October 1791, see D. M. G. Sutherland, *France, 1789–1815: Revolution and Counterrevolution* (Fontana, 1985), 107–14.

46. See Norman Hampson, "François Chabot and His Plot," *Transactions of the Royal Historical Society* 25 (1976): 1–14.

47. On Roux's behavior on the morning of 21 Jan. 1793, see Jules Michelet, *Histoire de la Révolution française* (Robert Laffont, 1979), 2:261.

48. On Lavoisier and the *complot vandale* in which he was supposedly involved, see Bronislaw Baczko's article of that title in *Le Temps de la réflexion* 4 (1983): 212. The "chemists" remark is variously attributed to Fouquier-Tinville and Lavoisier's accuser, Dumas, among others, and, like all such jests, may never actually have been uttered.

49. Quoted in Françoise Brunel, *Thermidor: La Chute de Robespierre* (Brussels: Complexe, 1989), 67.

50. On Catherine Théot, see ibid., 84–85.

51. For a convenient summary, see Sutherland, *France, 1789–1815,* 295–98.

52. On these successive insurrections see ibid., 262–64, 275–77.

53. Quoted in Baczko, "Le Complot vandale," 212.

54. See the valuable lexical analysis given in Sophie Wahnich, "*L'Etranger* dans la lutte des factions: Usage d'un mot dans une crise politique (5 nivôse an II–9 thermidor an II)," *Mots* 16 (1988): 111–30.

55. See Antoine de Baecque, *Le Corps de l'Histoire: Métaphores et politique, 1770–1800* (Calmann-Lévy, 1993), 195–97.

56. All quotations in Patrice Higonnet, "*Aristocrate, Aristocratie*: Language and Politics in the French Revolution," in *The French Revolution, 1789–1989: Two Hundred Years of Rethinking,* ed. Sandy Petrey (Lubbock: Texas Tech University Press, 1989), 47–64.

57. On rural bands, see the classic study by Yves-Marie Bercé, *Croquants et nu-pieds* (Folio, 1991), and Farge and Revel, *Logiques de la foule,* 49.

58. See Michel Vovelle, "From Beggary to Brigandage: The Wanderers in the Beauce during the French Revolution," in *New Perspectives on the French Revolution: Readings in Historical Sociology,* ed. Jeffry Kaplow (New York: Wiley 1965), 287–304.

59. Georges Lefebvre, *The Great Fear of 1789: Rural Panic in Revolutionary France* (1932), trans. Joan White (New York: Schocken, 1973), 130.

60. Ibid., 122, 133.

61. Ibid., 210.

62. See ibid., 207.

63. All information and quotations from Clay Ramsay, *The Ideology of the Great Fear: The Soissonnais in 1789* (Baltimore: Johns Hopkins University Press, 1992), 146–55.

64. Richard Hofstadter, "The Paranoid Style in American Politics," in *The Paranoid Style in American Politics and Other Essays* (Jonathan Cape, 1966), 32.

65. Quoted in Gérard Gengembre, *La Contre-révolution, ou L'Histoire désespérante* (Imago, 1989), 64. This excellent study has supplied many of the ideas and details contained in the present paragraph.

66. Quoted in Raoul Girardet, "La Conspiration," in *Mythes et mythologies politiques* (Seuil, 1986), 32–33. This pioneering essay, like that of Hofstadter cited in note 64, has greatly influenced the present argument.

67. On Robinson, see Hofstadter, "Paranoid Style," 10–11. On *The New World Order,* see the review by Michael Lind ("Rev. Robertson's Grand International Conspiracy Theory"), in *New York Review of Books,* 2 Feb. 1995, 21–25.

68. Stendhal, *Souvenirs d'égotisme,* in *Œuvres intimes,* ed. Henri Martineau (Gallimard, 1955), 1394.

69. All information and quotations from Sutherland, *France, 1789–1915,* 393.

70. Quoted in Geoffrey Cubitt, *The Jesuit Myth, Conspiracy Theory, and Politics in Nineteenth-Century France* (Oxford: Clarendon, 1993), 246.

71. Quoted ibid., 290.

72. Ibid., 139.

73. Eugène Suë, *Les Mystères de Paris* (Pauvert, 1963), 1.

74. Victor Hugo, *Les Misérables* (Lausanne: Rencontre, 1966), 2:157.

75. This paragraph reworks the argument of Richard D. E. Burton, "The Unseen Seer, or Proteus in the City: Aspects of a Nineteent-Century Parisian Myth," *French Studies* 42, no. 1 (1988): 50–68, where further details and full references may be found.

76. See the excellent discussion in Pierre Birnbaum, "Des 'gros' aux 'Deux cent familles,'" in *Le Peuple et les gros: Histoire d'un mythe* (Hachette/Pluriel, 1984), 13–53.

77. Honoré de Balzac, *Gobseck, La Comédie humaine,* ed. Pierre Citron (Seuil, 1965), 2:132.

78. On anti-Masonism in the Front National, see Pascal Perrineau, "Le Front national, 1972–1994," in *Histoire de l'extrême droite en France,* ed. Michel Winock (Seuil, 1994), 286.

79. On Vichy and Freemasonry, see Robert O. Paxton, *Vichy France: Old Guard and New Order, 1940–1944* (New York: Columbia University Press, 1972), 172–73.

80. See Perrineau, "Le Front national," 290 and 276, for these expressions.

81. Geoffrey Cubitt, "Denouncing Conspiracy in the French Revolution," *Renaissance and Modern Studies* 33 (1989): 152.

82. I owe this suggestive expression to a review by Ian Thomson of Umberto Eco's *Serendipities: Language and Lunacy* (1999), in *Observer Review,* 7 Feb. 1999, 13.

83. Furet, *Penser la Révolution française,* 92.

84. See Girardet, "La Conspiration," 42.

85. Ibid., 43.

86. Hofstadter, "Paranoid Style," 36–37.

87. Ibid., 30.

88. On this concept, see Ron Rosenbaum, *Explaining Hitler: The Search for the Origins of His Evil* (Macmillan, 1998), 352.

89. No doubt my figure of twelve is open to discussion. For the purpose of the present discussion, I am counting the following as "regimes": monarchy (1789-92), First Republic (1792-95), Directorate (1795-99), Consulate (1799-1804), First Empire (1804-14/15), Restoration Monarchy (1814/15-30), Bourgeois Monarchy (1830-48), Second Republic (1848-51/52), Second Empire (1851/52-70), Third Republic (1870-1940), Etat Français (1940-44), and Fourth Republic (1945-58).

90. Girard's own bibliography is substantial, and that of books about him and his thought even more so. For a useful study of his key ideas, see Jean-Baptiste Fages, *Comprendre René Girard* (Toulouse: Privat, 1982).

91. This summary of Girard's theory of scapegoating collates a number of texts, with chaps. 2 ("La Crise sacrificielle") and 4 ("La Genèse des mythes et des rituels") of *La Violence et le sacré* (Grasset, 1985) providing the principal source.

92. Figures of between 1,500 (the French government "estimate") and 40,000 (the future Front de Libération Nationale's total) have been advanced for the number of Muslims killed in the 1945 massacre. See Bernard Droz and Evelyne Lever, *Histoire de la guerre d'Algérie, 1954-1962* (Seuil, 1982), 32.

93. Guy Birenbaum, *Le Front national en politique* (Balland, 1992), 308. On "heterophobia," see Perrineau, "Le Front national," 266, 291.

94. On Mata Hari, see Julie Wheelwright, *The Fatal Lover: Mata Hari and the Myth of Women in Espionage* (Collins & Brown, 1992). Although capital punishment for women was abolished in France in 1893, a number of other women were executed for spying during the First World War (see ibid., 104-5), as were five back-street abortionists under Vichy, their fate obviously sealed by Vichy's pro-natalist policy (see Daniel Gerould, *Guillotine: Its Legend and Lore* [New York: Blast Books, 1992], 241). On the other hand, homosexuality or accusations of homosexuality do not seem to have played any significant part in the singling out of scapegoats, except in the cases of Marie-Antoinette and the princesse de Lamballe; the only known homosexual among the male victims discussed in this book was Robert Brasillach, a notorious member of the so-called Gestapette (Gestapo + *tapette*, a queer), whose collaborationist actions and writings were enough in themselves to ensure his condemnation.

95. See Henriette Walter, *Des mots sans-culottes* (Robert Laffont, 1989), 133. Louis XVIII was widely ridiculed when, on his return from exile in 1814, he spoke of himself as *moué le roué*.

96. See Robert Muchembled, *La Sorcière au village (XVᵉ-XVIIIᵉ siècle)* (Julliard/Gallimard, 1979).

97. See the statement made by Auguste-Martin Lottin in his *Péroraison d'un discours sur la conduite de Dieu envers les hommes* (February 1757), in which Damiens's execution is explicitly likened to the Jewish ritual of the scapegoat (quoted in Pierre Rétat, *L'Attentat de Damiens: Discours sur l'événement au 18ᵉ siècle* [Lyon: Presses universitaires de Lyon/CNRS, 1979], 237). In addition to the hideous suffering inflicted on Damiens himself, his family was exiled and the house in which he was born razed to the ground, with the stipulation that no other building be constructed on the site. "Does so stupid a monster have anything in common with the nation?" asked Voltaire in a letter of 17 Jan. 1757 (quoted ibid., 216).

98. Quoted in Suzanne Citron, *Le Mythe national: L'Histoire de France en question* (Editions Ouvrières, 1987), 153.

99. For a full analysis of this point, see William H. Sewell, *A Rhetoric of Bourgeois Revolution: The Abbé Siéyès and "What Is the Third Estate?"* (Durham, N.C.: Duke University Press, 1994), esp. 58-59, from which these quotations are taken.

100. Quoted from Michel de Certeau et al., *Une Politique de la langue: La Révolution française et les patois* (Gallimard, 1975), 295.

101. See Perrineau, "Le Front national," 286–88. On the policy toward patois, see the classic study by Eugen Weber, *Peasants into Frenchmen: The Modernization of Rural France, 1870–1914* (Chatto & Windus, 1976), 66–94.

102. Quoted in Julia Kristeva, *Etrangers à nous-mêmes* (Gallimard, 1988), 242.

103. Alain Bergounioux and Bernard Manin, "L'Exclu de la Nation: La Gauche française et son mythe de l'adversaire," *Le Débat* 5 (1980): 50.

104. Pierre Birnbaum, *"La France aux Français": Histoire des haines nationalistes* (Seuil, 1993), 31.

105. Quoted ibid., 51.

106. The terms "open" and "closed" nationalism are taken from Michel Winock, *Nationalisme, antisémitisme et fascisme en France* (Seuil, 1990), 11–40.

107. Quoted in Birnbaum, *"La France aux Français,"* 66.

108. Claude Bourdet, *L'Aventure incertaine: De la Résistance à la Restauration* (Stock, 1975), 55.

109. Jean-Paul Sartre, *La Mort dans l'âme* (Folio, 1972), 305.

110. Bourdet, *L'Aventure incertaine,* 55.

111. See Fages, *Comprendre René Girard,* 74.

112. Anne Tristan, *Au Front* (Folio, 1988), 214.

113. See the classic study by Elias Canetti, *Crowds and Power,* trans. Carol Stewart (Penguin, 1992), esp. 110–13.

114. Jean-Paul Sartre, *Réflexions sur la question juive* (Gallimard, 1954), 57.

115. See Stephen Wilson, *Ideology and Experience: Antisemitism in France at the Time of the Dreyfus Affair* (Toronto: Associated University Press, 1982), 486.

116. For these two notorious incidents, see Birenbaum, *Le Front National,* 120–30 and 144–53.

117. Tristan, *Au Front,* 212.

118. See Brian Singer, "Violence in the French Revolution: Forms of Ingestion/Forms of Expulsion," in *The French Revolution and the Birth of Modernity,* ed. Ferenc Fehér (Berkeley: University of California Press, 1990), esp. 159–62.

119. Quoted in Frédéric Bluche, *Septembre 1792: Logiques d'un massacre* (Robert Laffont, 1986), 166.

120. See Pierre Caron, *Les Massacres de Septembre* (Maison du Livre Français, 1935), 57. Caron, who is generally anxious to minimize the horror of the massacres, disputes the veracity of this story.

121. See Bluche, *Septembre 1792,* 261.

122. See Caron, *Les Massacres de Septembre,* 47, 61. Caron denies that any genital mutilation took place, but see Bluche, *Septembre 1792,* 260.

123. Quoted in Daniel Arasse, *La Guillotine et l'imaginaire de la Terreur* (Flammarion, 1987), 97.

124. Quoted in Carol Blum, *Rousseau and the Republic of Virtue: The Language of Politics in the French Revolution* (Ithaca: Cornell University Press, 1986), 218.

125. Quoted in Mona Ozouf, *La Fête révolutionnaire, 1789–1799* (Folio, 1988), 191n2.

126. Quoted in Blum, *Rousseau and the Republic of Virtue,* 264.

127. Quoted ibid., 171.

128. Quoted in Marc Bouloiseau, *La République jacobine, 10 août 1792–9 thermidor an II* (Seuil, 1972), 227.

129. See Arasse, *La Guillotine,* 67.

130. Quoted in Blum, *Rousseau and the Republic of Virtue,* 175.

131. See ibid., 267. She was accompanied by no fewer than 56 other "assassins of Robespierre," all similarly clad.

132. This remarkable description of the Jacobins is attributed to the Panthéon *section* in Paris. See Bronislaw Baczko, *Comment sortir de la Terreur: Thermidor et Révolution* (Gallimard, 1989), 64.

133. Quoted ibid., 50–51.

134. See Jean-Claude Bonnet, "La Mort de Simonneau," in *Mouvements populaires et conscience sociale*, Colloque de l'Université Paris VII–C.N.R.S., 24–26 May 1984 (Maloine, 1985), 671–76.

135. Ibid., 672.

136. On the two rival fêtes, see Ozouf, *La Fête révolutionnaire*, 110–29.

137. See Marie-Hélène Huet, *Rehearsing the Revolution: The Staging of Marat's Death, 1793–1797*, trans. Robert Hurley (Berkeley: University of California Press, 1982); Jacques Guilhaumou, *La Mort de Marat* (Brussels: Complexe, 1989); and the essays collected in Jean-Claude Bonnet, ed., *La Mort de Marat* (Flammarion, 1986).

138. Sauvageot at Dijon, 25 brumaire an II, quoted in Frank Paul Bowman, "Le 'Sacré-Cœur' de Marat (1793)," in *Les Fêtes de la Révolution*, ed. Jean Ehrard and Paul Viallaneix (Societé des Etudes Robespierristes, 1977), 163.

139. Quoted in Guilhaumou, *La Mort de Marat*, 87.

140. See Albert Soboul, "Sentiment religieux et cultes populaires pendant la Révolution: Saintes Patriotes et martyrs de la liberté," *Annales d'histoire de la Révolution française*, 1957, 197–98.

141. Régis Michel, "Bara: Du martyr à l'éphèbe," in Marie-Pierre Foissy-Aufrère, *La Mort de Bara* (Avignon: Muséum Calvet, 1989), 56. See also the detailed analysis in Thomas Crowe, *Emulation: Making Artists for Revolutionary France* (New Haven: Yale University Press, 1995), 167–69.

142. Michel, "Bara," 67.

143. Quoted in Simon Schama, *Citizens: A Chronicle of the French Revolution* (New York: Viking, 1989), 779.

144. See Michel Vovelle, "Agricol Viala, ou Le Héros malheureux," *Annales de l'Histoire de la Révolution Française* 241 (1980): 354.

145. Antoine de Baecque, "Le Corps meurtri de la Révolution: Le Discours politique et les blessures des martyrs (1792–1794)," *Annales historiques de la Révolution française*, 1987, 40. The whole of the present discussion is indebted to this excellent study.

146. See Jean-Clément Martin, *La Vendée de la mémoire (1800–1980)* (Seuil, 1989), and Michel Lagrée and Jehanne Roche, *Tombes de mémoire: La Dévotion populaire aux victimes de la Révolution dans l'Ouest* (Rennes: Apogée, 1993).

147. Zola was Pantheonized on 5 June 1908, but such was the controversy still surrounding him that his coffin was taken from the Montmartre cemetery to the Panthéon the night before. Even so, an attempt was made on the life of Dreyfus, who was present at the Panthéon, by an ultraright fanatic, who succeeded only in wounding him slightly. See Joanna Richardson, *Zola* (Weidenfeld & Nicolson, 1978), 222–23.

148. Quoted in Pierre Brochon, *Le Pamphlet du pauvre: Du socialisme utopique à la Révolution de 1848* (Editions Sociales, 1957), 76–77.

149. For the words of "La Bouteille inépuisable," see Richard D. E. Burton, *Baudelaire and the Second Republic: Writing and Revolution* (Oxford: Clarendon, 1991), 212–13. The present paragraph repeats the argument (and some of the wording) laid out in greater detail, and with full references, on 200–219 of that work.

150. Emile Zola, "Causerie du dimanche" (1872), in his *Oeuvres complètes*, ed. Henri Mitterrand (Cercle du livre précieux, 1970), 14:199–201.

151. Quoted in Frank Paul Bowman, *Le Christ des barricades, 1789–1848* (Editions du Cerf, 1987), 22.

152. Jérome Pierre Gilland, *Revue anecdotique des associations ouvrières* (1850), quoted ibid., 262.

153. Paul Eluard, *Choix de poèmes* (Livre de Poche, 1963), 297–98.

154. Quoted in Baecque, "Le Corps meurtri," 23.

155. Charles Baudelaire, *The Flowers of Evil*, trans. James McGowan (Oxford: Oxford University Press, 1993), 249.

156. See Lucienne Frappier-Mazur, *Writing the Orgy: Power and Parody in Sade*, trans. Gillian C. Gill (Philadelphia: University of Pennsylvania Press, 1996), 125. The present paragraph leans heavily on this excellent study.

157. Marquis de Sade, *Histoire de Juliette* (1797), quoted ibid., 14.

158. Ibid., 15.

159. Ibid., 57.

160. All quotations ibid., 171–72.

161. Joseph de Maistre, *Eclaircissement sur les sacrifices: Les Soirées de Saint-Pétersbourg* (J.-B. Pélagaud, 1862), 2:372.

162. Ibid., 392.

163. Ibid., 402–4.

164. Ibid., 405.

165. On Blanc de Saint-Bonnet, see Richard D. E. Burton, " 'La douleur est donc un bien ...': Baudelaire et Blanc de Saint-Bonnet. Contribution à l'étude du politique et du religieux chez Baudelaire," *Lettres romanes* 47, no. 4 (1993): 243–55.

166. Charles Baudelaire, *Journaux intimes*, in his *Oeuvres complètes*, ed. Claude Pichois (Gallimard, 1975), 1:669.

167. See Richard Griffiths, *The Reactionary Revolution: The Catholic Revival in French Literature, 1870–1914* (Constable, 1966), chap. 8; and Joyce O. Lowrie, *The Violent Mystique: Thematics of Retribution and Expiation in Balzac, Barbey d'Aurevilly, Bloy, and Huysmans* (Droz, 1974).

168. See Michel Winock, "L'Incendie du Bazar de la Charité," in his *Nationalisme, antisémitisme et fascisme en France*, 83–102, from which all details and quotations are taken. Huysmans took a more charitable view of the Bazar de la Charité fire, but still stressed its expiatory character. See Griffiths, *Reactionary Revolution*, 187.

169. Details from Ian Wilson, *The Bleeding Mind: An Investigation into the Mysterious Phenomenon of Stigmata* (Paladin, 1991), 140–43.

170. On this conflict of interpretations, see Cristina Mazzoni, *Saint Hysteria: Neurosis, Mysticism, and Gender in European Culture* (Ithaca: Cornell University Press, 1996), 3–5.

171. Camille Lemonnier, *L'Hystérique* (Séguier, 1996), 157–58.

172. Ibid., 73.

173. Luce Irigaray, *Speculum de l'autre femme* (1974), trans. Gillian C. Gill (Ithaca: Cornell University Press, 1985), quoted in Mazzoni, *Saint Hysteria*, 150.

174. Barbey d'Aurevilly, *Un prêtre marié* (Folio, 1980), 163.

175. Ibid., 43, 38. On Baudelaire's father, see Richard D. E. Burton, "François Baudelaire: Un Prêtre marié," *French Studies Bulletin* 42 (1992): 19–20.

176. Ibid., 77–78.

177. Joris-Karl Huysmans, *Sainte Lydwine de Schiedam* (Stock, 1901), 101.

178. Léon Bloy, *Quatre Ans de captivité à Cochons-sur-Marne* (1905), quoted in Lowrie, *Violent Mystique*, 99. Bloy is discussing a painting of the Virgin by Félix Jennewein.

179. Léon Bloy, *Le Symbolisme de l'apparition* (1880), quoted in Bernard Sarrazin, "Sang, feu ou quoi? La Crise de l'idée sacrificielle dans l'oeuvre de Léon Bloy," *Romantisme* 31 (1981): 44.

180. Léon Bloy, *Le Mendiant ingrat* (Mercure de France, 1963), 1:125 (entry for 20 Sept. 1894).

181. On Anne-Marie Roulé, see Albert Béguin, *Léon Bloy: A Study in Impatience*, trans. Edith M. Riley (Sheed & Ward, 1947), 16–17.

182. Léon Bloy, *Le Désespéré* (Union générale d'éditions, 1983), 252–53.

183. Ibid., 219–21.

184. Ibid., 257.

185. See Sarrazin, "Sang, feu ou quoi?" 45.

186. Léon Bloy, *La Femme pauvre* (1897), quoted in Lowrie, *Violent Mystique*, 96.

187. Octave Mirbeau, *Le Jardin des supplices* (Livre de poche, 1970), 232.

188. The blood theme continues with a vengeance in francophone African literature, most notably in the novels of Rachid Boudjedra (*La Répudiation* [1969]) and Tahar ben Jelloun (*Harrouda* [1973]), and in the poetry of Tchicaya U' Tamsi (*Le Mauvais Sang* [1970]).

189. Emile Zola, *La Joie de vivre* (Lausanne: Rencontre, n.d.), 92.

190. Jules Michelet, *La Mer* (Folio, 1983), 284–85. On the whole theme of blood in Michelet, see Roland Barthes, *Michelet par lui-même* (Seuil, 1954), 107–29.

191. On this whole theme, see Jean de Palacio, "Motif privilégié au jardin des supplices: Le Mythe de la décollation et le décadentisme," *Revue des sciences humaines* 39, no. 153 (1974): 39–62.

192. Baudelaire, *Oeuvres complètes,* 1:112.

193. For a fully documented and perceptive discussion of this theme, see Bram Dijkstra, *Idols of Perversity: Fantasies of Feminine Evil in Fin-de-Siècle Culture* (Oxford: Oxford University Press, 1986), 375–401.

194. For a wide-ranging discussion, see Patrick Wald Lasowski, *Les Echafauds du romanesque* (Lille: Presses universitaires de Lille, 1991).

195. Bloy, *La Femme pauvre,* quoted in Lowrie, *Violent Mystique,* 122.

196. On this text, see Richard D. E. Burton, "Baudelaire's Indian summer: A Reading of 'Les Bons Chiens,'" *Nineteenth-Century French Studies* 22, no. 3/4 (1994): 466–86.

197. See Maurice Agulhon, "Le Sang des bêtes: Le Problème de la protection des animaux en France au 19ᵉ siècle,' *Romantisme* 31 (1981): 81–109.

198. Louise Michel, *Mémoires* (1886), quoted in Frédéric Chauvaud, *De Pierre Rivière à Landru: La Violence apprivoisée au XIXᵉ siècle* (Brepols, 1991), 239.

199. Edmond et Jules de Goncourt, *Journal,* ed. Robert Ricatte (Robert Laffont, 1989), 2:346–47 (28 Nov. 1870).

200. Ibid., 366 (31 Dec. 1870).

201. Ibid., 333 (7 Nov. 1870).

202. Ibid., 374 (14 Jan. 1871).

203. "Real" bullfighting was legally permitted in a small number of cities in France (notably Nîmes, Arles, and Bayonne), which could prove an "uninterrupted local tradition" in the matter. See Agulhon, "Le Sang des bêtes," 102–9.

204. See Henri de Montherlant, *Les Bestiaires* (Folio, 1972), 245, 253, 270, etc.

205. Leiris, *Miroir de la tauromachie,* 57.

206. Michel Leiris, "De la littérature considérée comme une tauromachie," in his *L'Age d'homme* (Gallimard, 1964), 15.

207. Note to the poem "Cadré" in the original edition of *Haut mal* (Gallimard, 1943).

208. Quoted in Sarrazin, "Sang, feu ou quoi?" 39, without full reference.

209. Frank Paul Bowman, "'Precious Blood' in Religion, Literature, Eroticism, and Politics," in Bowman, *French Romanticism: Intertextual and Interdisciplinary Readings* (Baltimore: Johns Hopkins University Press, 1990), 81–105. The quotations occur on 81 and 83.

210. Ibid., 87–89.

211. Joris-Karl Huysmans, "Les Grünewald du Musée de Colmar" (1905), in his *Trois Primitifs* (Flammarion, 1967), 25, 16.

212. Huysmans, *Là-bas,* 33.

213. Huysmans, *L'Oblat,* ed. Denise Cogny (Christian Pirot, 1992), 340–41; italics added.

214. Ibid., 283.

215. Bloy, *Le Mendiant ingrat,* 1:159 (entry of 14 Apr. 1895).

216. Pierre Drieu La Rochelle, *Gilles* (Livre de poche, 1967), 501.

217. See esp. Vigny's play *Chatterton* (1835).

218. The Rue de la Vieille-Lanterne (now demolished) was in the parish of Saint-Merri, close to the half-ruined Tour Saint-Jacques (cf. "Le prince d'Aquitaine à la tour abolie" in "El Desdichado"), where Nerval had been born on 22 May 1808, $2 + 2 + 5 + 1 + 8 + 8 = 26 \div 2 = 13$, arcane 13 being the sign of death (cf. "La Treizième revient ... C'est encore la première" in "Artémis"), and Nerval killed himself on 26 Jan. (2×13) 1855. See Frank Paul Bowman, *Gérard de Nerval: La Conquête de soi par l'écriture* (Orléans: Paradigme, 1997), 242.

219. On Stendhal's pseudonyms, see Jean Starobinski, *The Living Eye*, trans. Arthur Goldhammer (Cambridge: Harvard University Press, 1989), 78–111. For the interpretations of "Beyle" and "Stendhal," see Nicholas Rand, "*The Red and the Black*, Author of Stendhal Pseudonyms and Cryptonyms of Beyle," *Romanic Review* 80 (1989): 391–403.

220. Stendhal, *Vie de Henri Brulard*, in his *Œuvres intimes*, 93–94.

221. See Gustave Flaubert, *Trois Contes* (Folio, 1994), 85, for the description of the killing.

222. All quotations from Victor Hugo, *Quatrevingt-treize* (Folio, 1990), 474–82.

223. See Viviane Forrester, *Van Gogh, ou L'Enterrement dans les blés* (Seuil, 1984), 277, where the date of the letter in question is not given. The whole of the present discussion is based on pp. 276–80 of this exceptional study, apart from the key point concerning "van Gogh" as an inversion of "Gauvain."

224. See ibid., 276, and note 203 below.

225. See Georges Bataille, "La Mutilation sacrificielle et l'oreille coupée de Vincent van Gogh," in his *Œuvres complètes* (Gallimard, 1970), 1:258–70. The present quotation occurs on 266. On the theme of spittle, see Leiris's poem "L'Amoureux des crachats," dedicated to Bataille, in *Haut Mal* (Gallimard, 1969), 58–60.

226. See Forrester, *Van Gogh*, 279.

227. Antonin Artaud, "Van Gogh, le suicidé de la société" (K Editions, 1947).

228. Hugo, *Quatrevingt-treize*, 482.

229. On the "identity" of Vincent and Théo, see Pascal Bonafoux's introduction to van Gogh, *Lettres à son frère Théo* (Gallimard, 1988), 8.

230. Gustave Flaubert, *Salammbô*, in his *Œuvres*, ed. Albert Thibaudet and René Dumesnil (Gallimard, 1951), 1:971.

231. Ibid., 979.

232. Ibid., 981–83.

233. On the guilt felt by the *sacrifiants* (which they commonly project onto the *sacrificateur*), see the important work by Hyam Maccoby, *The Sacred Executioner: Human Sacrifice and the Legacy of Guilt* (Thames & Hudson, 1982).

234. Flaubert, *Salammbô*, 985.

235. Ibid., 1000.

236. Ibid., 993.

237. Ibid., 1001–2.

238. Ibid., 1008–9.

239. Baudelaire, *Œuvres complètes*, 1:118; *Flowers of Evil*, trans. McGowan, 257.

240. Flaubert, *Salammbô*, 1020.

241. Ibid., 1024–27.

242. De Maistre, *Eclaircissement sur les sacrifices*, 2:348.

243. Flaubert, *Salammbô*, 1027.

244. See Flaubert, *L'Education sentimentale* (Folio, 1990), 368.

245. Ibid., 450.

246. See Sutherland, *France, 1789–1815*, 393.

247. Victor Hugo, *Choses vues, 1847–1848* (Folio, 1972), 346.

248. See Claudine Fabre-Vassas, *La Bête singulière: Les Juifs, les Chrétiens et le cochon* (Gallimard, 1994), esp. chap. 4, "La Truie des Juifs," 113–47.

249. All quotations from Emile Zola, *Germinal* (Folio, 1998), 427–32.

250. Quoted in Jean-Denis Bredin, *L'Affaire* (Juillard, 1983), 32. This first-rate study is the primary source for everything that follows.

251. Charles Péguy, *Notre jeunesse* (1910) (Folio, 1993), 151.

252. Quoted in Léon Blum, *Souvenir sur l'Affaire* (1935) (Folio, 1993), 78.

253. For further elucidation of these points, see the excellent chapter "Plot Myths and Assertions of Certainty" in Richard Griffiths, *The Use of Abuse: The Polemics of the Dreyfus Affair and Its Aftermath* (Oxford: Berg, 1991), 41–52, and, more generally, Pierre Nora, "1898: Le Thème du complot et la définition de l'identité juive," in *Le Racisme: Mythes et sciences,* ed. Maurice Olender (Brussels: Complexe, 1981), 157–66.

254. See Bredin, *L'Affaire,* 24.

255. Quoted ibid., 35.

256. The present account is based on Bredin, *L'Affaire,* 11–15, supported by Michael Burns, *Dreyfus: A Family Affair, 1789–1945* (Chatto & Windus, 1992), 149–53. All quotations are taken, unless otherwise stated, from one or the other of these sources.

257. Emile Zola, "Impressions d'audiences" (1898), reproduced as appendix to *La Vérité* (Livre de poche, 1996), 668–77. The quotation is on 669.

258. Account based on Bredin, *L'Affaire,* 124–32, and Burns, *Dreyfus,* 157–69.

259. Zola, "Impressions d'audience," 676.

260. Quoted in Burns, *Dreyfus,* 147.

261. Quoted in Bredin, *L'Affaire,* 228.

262. Blum, *Souvenirs,* 58.

263. Vacher de Lapouge was the author of works such as *Race et milieu social* (1909), *L'Aryen* (1899), and *Les Sélections sociales* (1896). See Zeev Sternhell, *La Droite révolutionnaire, 1885–1914: Les Origines françaises du fascisme* (Seuil, 1978), 164–71.

264. Bredin, *L'Affaire,* 215.

265. Quoted ibid., 192. See also Burns, *Dreyfus,* 192.

266. Quoted in Burns, *Dreyfus,* 189.

267. See Norman L. Kleebatt, ed., *The Dreyfus Affair: Art, Truth, and Justice* (Berkeley: University of California Press, 1987), 244.

268. See ibid., 189.

269. This was the case in the Mauriac household, and seems to have been common elsewhere. See H. R. Kedward, *The Dreyfus Affair: Catalyst for Tensions in French Society* (Longman, 1965), 41.

270. See Michael R. Marrus, *The Politics of Assimilation: A Study of the French Jewish Community at the Time of the Dreyfus Affair* (Oxford: Oxford University Press, 1971), 196–200.

271. Péguy, *Notre jeunesse,* 193.

272. Quoted in Bredin, *L'Affaire,* 137.

273. Blum, *Souvenirs,* 39.

274. The most famous being Clemenceau vs. Drumont (February 1798), Picquart vs. Henry (March 1898), and Max Régis, antisemitic mayor of Algiers and editor of *L'Antijuif,* vs. Capt. Lévy Oger (also March 1898); only Oger was seriously hurt. See Jean Garrigues, "Des duels pour Dreyfus," in *L'Affaire Dreyfus,* ed. Michel Winock (Seuil, 1998), 133–37.

275. Roger Martin Du Gard, quoted in Wilson, *Ideology and Experience,* 111.

276. Ibid., 118.

277. Péguy, *Notre jeunesse,* 207.

278. Quoted from Kedward, *Dreyfus Affair,* 41.

279. The following account is based almost entirely on the exemplary chapter in Wilson, *Ideology and Experience,* 125–59.

280. See ibid., 127–29 and 135, for a full geographical and socio-professional breakdown.

281. Ibid., 136.

282. Ibid., 140.

283. Ibid., 143.

284. Valéry's contribution is mentioned in Hannah Arendt, *The Origins of Totalitarianism* (Allen & Unwin, 1951), 107. On Valéry and Vacher de La Pouge, see Bernard-Henri Lévy, *Les Aventures de la liberté* (Grasset, 1991), 22–26.

285. See Arendt, *Origins of Totalitarianism*, 107.

286. All quotations from Wilson, *Ideology and Experience*, 156–57.

287. The present paragraph leans very heavily on chap. 6, "Religious Imagery: The Power of Catholic Discourse," in Griffiths, *Use of Abuse*, 96–101. Unless otherwise stated, all quotations are taken from this source.

288. Quoted in Bredin, *L'Affaire*, 137.

289. Quoted ibid., 35.

290. Blum, *Souvenirs*, 69.

291. The first use of *intellectuel* as a noun is usually said to be in the title "Manifeste des intellectuels," given to a manifesto in support of Dreyfus published in *L'Aurore* the day after *J'Accuse* (14 Jan. 1898), signed by hundreds of writers, academics, and lawyers, the most prominent being Anatole France, Daniel Halévy, Lucien Herr, Léon Blum, and Marcel Proust.

292. Blum, *Souvenirs*, 120.

293. Péguy, *Notre jeunesse*, 250.

294. Some right-wing historians of this "Franco-French genocide" have claimed that the total number of deaths was closer to 500,000. For a dispassionate analysis, see François Lebrun, "La Guerre de Vendée: Massacre ou génocide?" *L'Histoire* 78 (1985): 93–99.

295. Hugh Thomas, *The Spanish Civil War* (Penguin, 1974), 790.

296. On this point, see Chauvaud, *De Pierre Rivière à Landru,* esp. 235–52.

297. See Esther Benbassa, *Histoire des Juifs de France* (Seuil, 1997), 283.

298. See Droz and Lever, *Histoire de la guerre d'Algérie,* 325.

299. François Brigneau, ex-*milicien,* to vigorous applause at a meeting of the Front National attended by Jean-Marie Le Pen, 4 Nov. 1984, quoted in Birenbaum, *Le Front national en politique,* 248.

300. See Françoise Gaspard and Claude Servan-Schreiber, *La Fin des immigrés* (Seuil, 1985), 133.

INDEX